ECONOMICS OF DEVELOPMENT

ECONOMICS OF DEVELOPMENT

Fourth Edition

Malcolm Gillis
RICE UNIVERSITY

Dwight H. Perkins
HARVARD UNIVERSITY

Michael Roemer
HARVARD UNIVERSITY

Donald R. Snodgrass
HARVARD UNIVERSITY

W. W. NORTON & COMPANY
New York London

PRINTED IN THE UNITED STATES OF AMERICA

The text of this book is composed in Times Roman
with the display set in Optima
Composition by New England Typographic Service, Inc.
Manufacturing by Maple-Vail

Cover illustration: Kuala Lumpur, Malaysia Image Bank/ James Carmichael Jr.

Library of Congress Cataloging-in-Publication Data
Economics of development / Malcolm Gillis . . . [et al.]. —4th ed.
p. cm.
Includes bibliographical references and index.
1. Developing countries—Economic policy. 2. Economic development. I. Gillis, Malcolm
HC59.7.E314 1996
338.9—dc20 95-22358

ISBN 0-393-96851-0

W. W. Norton & Company, Inc., 500 Fifth Avenue, New York, N.Y. 10110

W. W. Norton & Company, Ltd., 10 Coptic Street, London WC1A 1PU

For Elizabeth, Julie, Linda, and Anne

Contents

PREFACE xiii

Part 1: THEORY AND PATTERNS

1. INTRODUCTION 3
Terminology: The Developing World 6 *Rich and Poor Countries • Growth and Development* A Development Continuum 9 Focus of the Book 15 *Approaches to Development • Organization*

2. STARTING MODERN ECONOMIC GROWTH 18
The Developing Countries: A Glance at History 19 Colonialism and Independence 20 The Developing Countries: A Brief Taxonomy 21 The Concept of Substitutes 22 Political Obstacles to Development 24 *Political Stability • Political Independence • The Politics of Development Policy* International Obstacles to Development 28 *Gains from Trade: A Preliminary View Drawing on Experience • Imperialism* Marxian Approaches to Development 30 Modern Theories of Imperialism 31 Income Inequality and the Demand for Luxury Products 32

3. GROWTH AND STRUCTURAL CHANGE 35
Estimating Gross National Product 36 *What is Included in GNP? • Exchange-Rate Conversion Problems • Other Index-Number Problems* One-Sector Growth Models 41 *The Harrod-Domar Model • Production Functions • Sources of Growth* The Changing Structure of Output 47 Two-Sector Models 51 *The Production Function • The*

Neoclassical Two-Sector Model • **Labor Surplus in China** • **Labor Surplus in Africa** Industrial Patterns of Growth 61 *Empirical Approaches* • *Theoretical Approaches* • *Backward and Forward Linkages* Appendix: Deriving the Sources of Growth Equation 65

4. DEVELOPMENT AND HUMAN WELFARE 68
Concepts and Measures 70 *Income Distribution* • *Inequality Measures* • *Poverty Measures* • *Equality and Equity* • *Basic Human Needs and Social Indicators* • *Overall Indicators of Development* Patterns of Inequality and Poverty 80 *Kuznets' Inverted U* • *Other Influences on Inequality* • *How Growth Reduces Poverty* • *Income Distribution Models* • **South Korea** • **Brazil** • **Sri Lanka** • **India** Theories of Inequality and Poverty 87 *Ricardo's Two-Sector Model* • *Marx's View* • *Neoclassical Theory* • *Labor-Surplus Model* Strategies for Growth with Equity 90 *Redistribute First, Then Grow* • *Redistribution with Growth* • *Basic Human Needs* • *Structural Adjustment and the Poor* • *Growth and Equity: Key Policy Issues*

Part 2: GUIDING DEVELOPMENT

5. GUIDING DEVELOPMENT: MARKETS VERSUS CONTROLS 99
Managing Development 99 *Market Economies* • *Socialist Economies* The March toward Markets 106 *The Appeal of Controls* • *Resurgence of the Market* Implementing Market Reforms 111 *1. Stabilization of the Macro Economy* • **Stabilization That Worked: Bolivia, 1985–1986** • *2. Dismantling Controls* • *3. Ensuring Competition* • *4. Moving toward Scarcity Prices* • *5. Responding to Market Signals* The Transition to a Market System 125 **Stabilization and Deregulation, Indonesia, 1986–1990**

6. PLANNING MODELS 131
Consistency and Optimality 132 Keynesian Models 134 Interindustry Models 137 *Input-Output Analysis* • *Social Accounting Matrix* • *Linear Programming* • *Computable General Equilibrium Models* Project Appraisal 146 *Present Value* • *Opportunity Costs* • *Shadow Prices* • *Project Appraisal and National Goals* • *Transforming Market Prices into Shadow Prices*

7. SUSTAINABLE DEVELOPMENT 155
Market Failures 156 *The Commons* • *Externalities: A Closer Look* • **Soil Erosion in Java, Indonesia** • *Sustainable Harvests* • *The Value of Time* Policy Solutions 165 *Property Rights* • **Communal Forest Management in India** • *Government Regulation* • *Taxation* • **Reducing Water Pollution from Palm Oil Mills in Malaysia** • *Marketable Permits* Policy Failures 173 **Subsidized Deforestation of the Amazon** • **Kerosene Subsidy**

in Indonesia • **Valuing a Recreational Facility in Bangkok, Thailand** Measuring Sustainability 177 *Natural Capital* • *A Concept of Sustainability* • *Resources and National Income* • **Sustainable Development in Malaysia** Global Sustainability 182 *Malthusian Views* • *Neoclassical Views* • *Poverty and the Environment* • *Rich Nations and Poor Nations*

Part 3: HUMAN RESOURCES

8. POPULATION 191
Demographic Measures 192 A Brief History of Human Population 193 The Present Demographic Situation 196 The Demographic Future 201 The Causes of Population Growth 202 *Malthus and His World* • *Mechanisms for Reducing Birth Rates* • *Modern Theories of Fertility* Analyzing the Effects of Rapid Population Growth 207 *Optimum Population* • *Dynamic Models of Population Growth* • *Concern about the Effects of Population Growth on Development* • *Doubters and Dissenters* • *Conclusion: A New Consensus?* Population Policy 212 **Population and Family Planning in Kenya** • **Population and Family Planning in China** • *Policy Alternatives* • **Population and Family Planning in Indonesia** • *Family Planning versus Development?*

9. LABOR'S ROLE 220
Analyzing Employment Issues 221 *Growth of Labor Supply* • *Patterns of Employment* • *The Structure of Labor Markets* • **The Urban Informal Sector in Indonesia** • *Measuring Labor Supply and Utilization* Labor Reallocation 230 *Costs and Benefits of Reallocating Labor* • *Internal Migration* • *International Migration* Employment Policy 236 *Labor Absorption through Industrialization* • *Elements of a Solution* • *Factor Price Distortions* • *Correcting Factor Price Distortion* • *The Role of Technology* • *Technology Policies* • *Other Employment Policies* Employment Creation Strategies 248

10. EDUCATION 250
Trends and Patterns 251 **Education in Indonesia** • *Types of Learning* • *Characteristics of Developing-Country Education* Education's Role in Development 259 *Manpower Planning* • *Cost-Benefit Analysis* • *Cost-Benefit Analysis in Educational Planning* • **Educational Policy in Kenya and Tanzania and Its Results** • *Alternative Viewpoints*

11. HEALTH AND NUTRITION 272
Health in the Developing Countries 273 *Patterns and Trends* • *Causes of Sickness and Death* • **Health in Sri Lanka** • Effects of Health on Development 279 Environmental Health 281 Malnutrition 282 *Food Consumption* • *Nutritional Interventions* Medical Services 289 **Health in Cuba** • Health Services and the Market 293

Part 4: CAPITAL RESOURCES

12. CAPITAL AND SAVING 299
Investment Requirements for Growth 300 *Effective Use of Capital • Capital-Intensive or Labor-Intensive Investment: A Hypothetical Case • Investment Ratios in Developing Countries* Sources of Savings 304 *Taxonomy of Savings • Domestic Savings • Government Savings • Private Domestic Savings* Determinants of Private Savings 311 *Household Saving Behavior • Corporate Saving Behavior* International Mobility of Capital and Domestic Saving Mobilization 317 *Short- and Long-Run Mobility • Evidence of International Capital Mobility*

13. FISCAL POLICY 320
The Government Budget: General Considerations 321 Government Expenditures 322 *Expenditure Policies and Public Saving • Wages and Salaries • Purchases of Goods and Services • Interest Payments • Subsidies • State-Owned Enterprises • Intergovernmental Transfers* Tax Policy and Public Saving 330 *Taxes on International Trade* • **Tax Rates and Smuggling: Colombia** • *Personal and Corporate Income Taxes • Sales and Excise Taxes • New Sources of Tax Revenues • Changes in Tax Administration* • **Tax Administration in India and Bolivia in the 1980s** • *Fundamental Tax Reform* • **Lessons from Comprehensive Tax Reform: Colombia** Taxes and Private Investment 343 *Taxes and Private Saving • Taxes and Capital Mobility* Income Distribution 346 *Taxation and Equity • Personal Income Taxes • Taxes on Luxury Consumption • Corporate Income and Property Taxes: The Incidence Problem • Limited Effects of Redistribution Policy • Expenditures and Equity* • **Irrigation and Equity** Economic Efficiency and the Budget 354 *Sources of Inefficiency • Neutrality and Efficiency: Lessons from Experience*

14. FINANCIAL POLICY 358
The Functions of a Financial System 359 *Money and the Money Supply • Financial Intermediation • Transformation and Distribution of Risk • Stabilization* Inflation and Savings Mobilization 363 *Inflation Episodes* • **Hyperinflation in Peru: 1988–1990** • *Forced Mobilization of Savings • Inflation as a Stimulus to Investment • Inflation and Interest Rates* Interest Rates and Saving Decisions 373 *Interest Rates and Liquid Assets* Financial Development 376 *Shallow Finance and Deep Finance • Shallow Financial Strategy • Deep Financial Strategies • Informal Credit Markets* • **Small-scale Savings and Credit Institutions: Bangladesh and Indonesia** Monetary Policy and Price Stability 384 *Monetary Policy and Exchange-Rate Regimes • Sources of Inflation • Controlling Inflation through Monetary Policy • Reserve Requirements • Credit Ceilings • Interest Rate Regulation and Moral Suasion*

Part 5: PRODUCTION AND TRADE

15. FOREIGN CAPITAL AND DEBT 391

Foreign Aid 394 *Historical Role • Aid Institutions and Instruments • Aid and Development* Foreign Investment and the Multinationals 402 *Multinationals' Investment Patterns • Characteristics of Multinationals • Benefits of Foreign Investment • Policies toward Foreign Investment* Foreign Debt 411 *Commercial Borrowing • The Repayment Crisis • Sustainable Debt • Causes of the Crisis • Escape from the Crisis* • **The Mexican Debt Crisis**

16. AGRICULTURE 423

Agriculture's Role in Economic Development 424 *Self-Sufficiency and Dwindling World Food Supplies* Land Tenure and Reform 427 *Patterns of Land Tenure • Tenure and Incentive • Land Reform • The Politics of Land Reform • Land Reform and Productivity • Land Reform and Income Distribution* Technology of Agricultural Production 434 *Traditional Agriculture • Slash-and-Burn Cultivation • The Shortening of Fallow • Farming within a Fixed Technology • Modernizing Agricultural Technology • The Mechanical Package • The Biological Package and the Green Revolution* Mobilization of Agricultural Inputs 444 *Rural Public Works Projects* • **Labor Mobilization in Chinese Communes** • *Rural Banks and Credit Cooperatives • Extension Services • The Development of Rural Markets* Agricultural Price Policy 450 *The Multiple Role of Prices • The Impact of Subsidies • Overvalued Exchange Rates*

17. PRIMARY EXPORTS 456

Comparative Advantage 456 Export Characteristics of Developing Countries 459 Primary Exports as an Engine of Growth 462 *Improved Factor Utilization • Expanded Factor Endowments • Linkage Effects* Barriers to Primary-Export-Led Growth 466 *Sluggish Demand Growth* • **Primary-Export-Led Growth in Malaysia** • *Declining Terms of Trade* • **Ghana—A Case of Arrested Development** • *Fluctuating Export Earnings • Commodity Agreements • Ineffective Linkages • Dutch Disease* • **Nigeria: A Bad Case of Dutch Disease** • **Indonesia: Finding a Cure**

18. INDUSTRY 481

Industry as a Leading Sector 481 *Linkages • Urbanization* Investment Choices in Industry 488 *Choice of Technique • Economies of Scale • Small-Scale Industry* • **Township and Village Enterprises in China** • *Industry and Development Goals*

19. TRADE AND INDUSTRIALIZATION 501

Two Industrial Strategies 502 *Import Substitution • Infant Industries • Outward-Looking Industrialization • The Asian Tigers* Trade Policies 506 *Protective Tariffs* •

Import Quotas • Subsidies and Export Protection • Exchange-Rate Management Outcomes 519 *Import Substitution in General Equilibrium* • **Import Substitution in Kenya** • *Rents and Other Adverse Incentives • Exports, Growth, and Productivity • Factor Markets and Government Intervention • Reconciling Import Substitution and Export Growth* • **Trade Reform in Mexico, 1985–1989** World Trading Arrangements 528 *Protection in the North • Multilateral Trade Reform • Integration in the South • Static Gains from Integration • Dynamic Gains and Risks of Integration • Trading Blocs*

20. MANAGING AN OPEN ECONOMY 536
Equilibrium in a Small, Open Economy 537 *Internal and External Balance • The Phase Diagram • Equilibrium and Disequilibrium • Stabilization Policies* Tales of Stabilization 549 *Dutch Disease • Debt Repayment Crisis* • **Pioneering Stabilization: Chile, 1973–1984** • *Stabilization Package: Inflation and a Deficit* • **Recovering from Mismanagement: Ghana, 1983–1991** • *Drought* • **Accumulating Reserves: Taiwan, 1980–1987**

BIBLIOGRAPHY AND ADDITIONAL READINGS 561

INDEX 589

Preface

Economic development continues to make headlines. Long-established political and economic systems in Central and Eastern Europe, as well as Central Asia, teeter and fall, and their falls inaugurate difficult transitions to more market-oriented economies and democratic societies. Majority rule arrives in South Africa and its arrival offers hope of faster and more equitable growth in that country and transmits positive repercussions to other parts of Southern Africa. China brings population growth under control, liberalizes its economic policies, and goes on to become the world's fastest-growing economy. Mexico enters into a free-trade agreement with the United States and Canada, but stumbles when it is hit with massive capital flight. New and frightening diseases appear in some poor and misgoverned African countries. The rapid rise of the "miracle economies" of East Asia dazzles the world, as had that of Japan earlier. Policy makers in other regions grope for the "secrets" of East Asian success, hoping to apply them in their own countries. The United States Congress threatens to cut foreign aid funding and eliminate the Agency for International Development, yet market-driven intercountry flows of private capital and workers accelerate. Production of manufactures becomes increasingly "globalized" as improvements in communication and transportation reduce the relative cost of these services and allow production to take place wherever it can be carried out most cheaply. Even services of many types are increasingly traded internationally.

Television and the other news media bombard our senses daily with stories about development. The developing countries no longer seem exotic or remote to North Americans and Europeans; few now doubt that their struggle for development will have profound implications for the way people live in the high-income countries. Enhanced awareness about development creates an opportunity for those of us who write textbooks, but it also presents two challenges.

The first challenge is to keep up with the news. Development texts deal with recent history as well as tools of analysis and must be revised frequently to reflect current events. The Fourth Edition of *Economics of Development* utilizes data for years as recent as 1993, published by the World Bank, the United Nations, and other sources. It also pays more attention to matters of greatest current interest.

As in the Third Edition, we recognize one of the most far reaching trends of our time, the march away from government intervention toward greater dependence on markets as a tool of development. In addition, in this edition the growing interest in the sustainability of development is recognized in a new Chapter 7. Chapters 8 and 11 reflect the continuing debates on world population, nutrition, and health. They highlight the significant and widespread improvements in nutrition and life expectancy that have been achieved in recent years, even in the face of persistent problems such as famine and high fertility in Africa. The discussion of population points toward the probable stabilization of world population in the early part of the twenty-first century. Reflecting significant changes in the structure of production in developing countries, the discussion of international trade focuses increasingly on manufactures and less on primary commodities than in previous editions. Yet industrialization is usually based on success in exporting primary commodities, a topic discussed in Chapter 17. A new Chapter 19 provides a more-integrated treatment of trade and industrialization issues that arise in outward-looking development, now the preferred strategy in most developing countries. The discussion of stabilization problems in an open economy that appeared as an appendix in the Third Edition has been expanded into a new Chapter 20, "Managing an Open Economy."

Throughout this new edition, the reader will notice that we have adopted gross domestic product per capita at international prices (purchasing power parity) as our primary measure of development, replacing traditional figures converted from local currency to U.S. dollars via prevailing exchange rates. This is consistent with increasing interest in the purchasing power parity measure and its general acceptance as a more accurate measure of living standards.

The second challenge is more difficult. News stories about developing countries make development seem an exciting but ephemeral subject: it would appear necessary only to keep up with the latest events to capture the essence of the topic. But the reality is deeper. A textbook should distinguish between the merely evanescent and the truly enduring aspects of development. The forces underlying economic change may be barely perceptible, but they can be powerful and can radically alter a country's standard of living in two or three generations.

To meet these challenges, *Economics of Development* continues to rely on five distinguishing features: (1) It makes extensive use of the theoretical tools of classical and neoclassical economics, in the belief that these tools contribute substantially to our understanding of development. (2) It draws heavily on decades of empirical studies by economists and economic historians, studies that have uncovered and explained the structure of development, or at least narrowed our zones of ignorance. (3) It deals explicitly with the political and institutional framework in which economic development takes place. (4) It presents many real-country examples to illustrate major points, drawing on the authors' collective experience of—hard as it is for us to believe—more than a century of work on development issues. (5) It recognizes the diversity of development experience reflected in these country examples and acknowledges that the lessons of theory and history can only be applied within certain institutional and national contexts.

Organization

The basic structure of the book is similar to that of earlier editions. Part 1 introduces the concept and measurement of development, some theories developed to explain it, and the body of data that has been amassed to recognize and define development when it takes place.

Part 2 considers alternative approaches to guiding development, particularly planning and controls versus the market. It also discusses the issue of whether, in what sense, and by what means development can be made sustainable.

People make development happen and people benefit from it. Part 3 of the text deals with the contributions of human resources to development and with the transformation of human lives as a consequence of development. It includes chapters on population, labor, education, and health.

Capital, the other major physical input in the growth process, is the subject of Part 4. Topics include domestic saving and investment, fiscal policy, financial policy, and foreign capital and investment.

Part 5, on production and trade, recognizes that developing countries remain known for their heavy reliance on primary production and trade.

It also deals with the problems that arise when a country begins to industrialize and export manufactured goods. Since problems of macroeconomics stabilization frequently persist at this high stage of development, the book concludes with a discussion of the principles involved in managing an open developing economy.

Supplements

To help meet the needs of students and instructors, two supplements accompany the text. A *Study Guide and Workbook* by Bruce Bolnick of Northeastern University provides review material, self-tests, and problem sets that will help students grasp the major points more firmly. An *Instructor's Manual,* also by Bolnick, provides lecture and discussion topics along with answers to the problem sets in the workbook. Both of these supplements have been revised to match the Fourth Edition of the text.

Acknowledgments

In the course of writing four editions, we have accumulated many debts to generous colleagues who have read chapters, reviewed the entire book, tested the manuscript in their classes, or otherwise encouraged us: Paul Albenese (Middlebury College), Ralph Beals (Amherst College), Richard Bird (University of Toronto), Bruce Bolnick (Northeastern University), Paul Clark (Williams College), David Dapice (Tufts University), Shantayanan Devarajan (Harvard University), James Duesenberry (Harvard University), Sebastian Edwards (University of Southern California), Alfred J. Field (University of North Carolina), Ira N. Gang (Rutgers University), Lester Gordon (Harvard University), Arnold Harberger (University of Chicago), Sue Horton (University of Toronto), John Isbister (University of California, Santa Cruz), Alan Kelley (Duke University), Anne Krueger (Stanford University), David Lindauer (Wellesley College), Charles McLure (Stanford University), Malcolm McPherson (Harvard University), Stephen Radelet (Harvard University), Vijayendra Rao (University of Michigan), Caroline Schwartz (Emory University), David Singer (University of Connecticut), Joseph Stern (Harvard University), Thomas Tushingham (Ryerson Polytechnic Institute), Yana van de Meulen (Harvard University), Jeffrey Vincent (Harvard University) and Louis Wells (Harvard University). Although we cannot list their names, we would also like to thank the numerous teachers who responded to questionnaires circulated by the publisher. We are grateful to Adam Hirsch, who assembled much of the information used in Chapter 7.

Dedicated work on bibliography and data assembly for the Fourth Edition was carried out by Anandi Mani, Sharun Mukand, and Larry Rosenberg. Ann Grover, Faith Montgomery, Gretchen O'Connor, and Ken Repp helped to produce the revised manuscript. At W. W. Norton and Company, Ed Parsons and Carol Loomis transformed the manuscript into the book you are reading now.

We have worked toward a book that meets the expectations of all these people, and we thank them for helping us.

Houston	M.G.
Cambridge	D.H.P.
Cambridge	M.R.
Cambridge	D.R.S.

May 1995

PART 1

THEORY AND PATTERNS

1

Introduction

In 1975, when she was 17 years old, Rachmina Abdullah did something no girl from her village had ever done before.[1] She left her home in a beautiful but poor part of the state of Kedah in Malaysia, where people grow rice in the valleys and tap rubber trees in the nearby hills, and went to work in an electronics plant in the busy city of Penang, 75 miles away. Rachmina's family was poor even by the modest standards of her village, and her parents welcomed the opportunity for their daughter to earn her own keep, and possibly even send money back to help them feed and clothe the family, deal with recurrent emergencies, and raise their five younger children. With these benefits in mind, they set aside their reservations about their unmarried daughter's unheard-of plan to go off by herself to work in the city.

Rachmina got a job assembling integrated circuits (ICs) along with 500 other young women in a factory owned by a Japanese company. Every day, she patiently soldered hundreds of tiny wires onto tiny chips of silicon. It was tedious, repetitive work which had to be performed at high speed and, the management expected, with flawless accuracy. Each working day, Rachmina and her new colleagues rose very early and bicycled, walked, or bused to the factory. Being careful to arrive before the assigned hour of 7 A.M. to avoid being fined, the workers removed their shoes at the factory door, punched the time clock, and went to a

1. This narrative is loosely based on Fatimah Daud, *"Minah Karan." The Truth about Malaysian Factory Girls* (Kuala Lumpur: Berita Publishing, 1985), and Kamal Salih and Mei Ling Young, "Changing Conditions of Labour in the Semiconductor Industry in Malaysia," *Labour and Society,* 14 (1989), 59–80.

room where they changed into spotless white uniforms and slippers. Then they hurried to an assembly hall, where they heard a speech from the foreman about the day's production goals and sang the company song.

Except for one 5-minute break, which most of the young women used to fill in forms showing how much they had produced, they worked without stopping until noon, when it was time for a 45-minute lunch break. Rachmina spent this period eating and chatting with her friends in the lunch hall, where the Malay, Chinese, and Indian workers clustered in separate areas. After lunch, the women resumed the morning's routine, stopping only when the quitting bell rang at 4 P.M. Then they reversed the morning's procedure, returning to the assembly hall, singing the company anthem again, hearing another speech from the foreman, lining up to clock out, changing to street clothes, and leaving for home. By the end of her long day of steady activity, Rachmina had earned the equivalent of $2.50.

Since their hourly wages were low, the workers welcomed frequent opportunities to work overtime. Often they put in two or three extra hours in a day, for up to seven days a week. They particularly liked working Sundays and holidays, when double wages were paid. With overtime work and occasional bonuses, Rachmina was able to earn an average of $80 a month. She shared a small house in a squatter area with seven other factory workers. There was only one bedroom, so some of them slept in the lounge. By living simply and inexpensively, most of the young women managed to set aside $5 to $20 a month to send to their families in the villages. A few spent freely on clothes and cosmetics, and were criticized for it, but most led frugal lives. The young women enjoyed the unfamiliar freedom of living apart from their families.

In 1982 the electronics industry was hit by a recession. By this time Rachmina had become a line leader, responsible for supervising the work of a team of newer workers. Her factory reduced its work force, cut back on shift work, and virtually eliminated overtime. Rachmina, who was now 22 and had accumulated $400 in savings, decided it was time to return to her village, where she soon married a local man and settled down.

Rachmina's chance to work in an electronics factory came about because in the 1970s American and Japanese electronics manufacturers were moving into export processing zones (EPZs) established by the Malaysian government in several parts of the country. The government used the EPZs to tempt foreign investors to establish plants in Malaysia. The national unemployment rate was high and the government was particularly anxious to find more urban, nonagricultural jobs for the indigenous Malay population, to which Rachmina and her family belonged. The Malays had long followed a rural lifestyle and were generally much poorer than the immigrants of Chinese and Indian stock. Now the government, which relied on Malay votes and had experienced terrifying race riots in 1969, was anxious to help Malays better their economic position.

Investors were drawn to Penang as a good place to set up semiconductor assembly plants. The electronics industry had originated in high-tech locations like Silicon Valley, California. By the mid-1970s, however, demand for ICs and other electronic devices was growing by leaps and bounds and the firms were looking for overseas locations where they could carry out parts of their operations at lower cost. ICs are made in a four-step process. First, mask making, the process of designing the circuit and reducing the artwork to an overlay through high-resolution photography, is a high-skill operation. Second, wafer fabrication, the conversion of silicon into chips, is a capital-intensive process. Third, assembly, including mounting the chip on a frame, welding appropriate wires to it, and enclosing the completed chip in a resin, plastic, or ceramic covering, is very labor-intensive. Finally, testing, though also done by hand, requires some skill.

It was becoming too costly for electronic firms to meet the booming demand while carrying out all four operations in California, Japan, and similar locations. The firms decided to move their assembly and testing operations to countries where labor was cheap, compliant, and capable of learning the relatively simple skills involved. The first beneficiaries of this migration in electronics and other industries were the newly industrializing nations of East Asia, South Korea, Taiwan, Hong Kong, and Singapore. In Malaysia, the city of Penang, with its good infrastructure and English-speaking work force, also attracted foreign investors, even though the electronics industry was forced to recruit thousands of farm women like Rachmina and introduce them to the disciplines of factory labor.

Factories making 64K chips and other electronic components flourished in Penang and other Malaysian cities in the 1970s and early 1980s. Malaysia, a middle-income country previously known mainly for the export of rubber, tin, and palm oil, became the second largest exporter of electronic components, preceded only by Japan. The plants were almost all foreign-owned. They bought and sold few goods and services in Malaysia itself, and only the simpler parts of the manufacturing process were carried out in Malaysia. Drawn by generous tax exemptions and wages that averaged as little as $30 a month in 1971, the companies experienced cost increases as wages rose to $120 a month by 1980, an increase only partly offset by rising productivity. Meanwhile, advances in technology in the 1980s made ICs both more complex and smaller, and so reduced the amount of work that could be done by hand. These changes contributed to the industry shakeout that Rachmina experienced in 1982. Employment of unskilled workers dropped sharply for a while in Malaysia and other developing countries involved in electronic component assembly.

In time, however, technological advances and continuing cost pressures in the developed countries dictated that even some of the more complex parts of the manufacturing process be shifted to lower-wage countries. As wages rose in South Korea, Taiwan, Hong Kong, and Singapore, firms moved their labor-intensive operations from these NICs to the less-industrialized economies of Asia, such as Malaysia and Thailand. In this second wave of foreign investment, some of the migrating operations were owned by companies from Korea, Taiwan, Hong Kong, and Singapore. The Penang electronics industry revived. It now uses less unskilled labor and more skilled workers than before, and it produces a wider range of products for both domestic and international markets. But it revived without Rachmina, happily engaged in raising a family in her Kedah village.

Rachmina Abdullah is a personification of the nearly four billion people of the developing countries whose lives have been profoundly affected, in many different ways, by economic changes in recent years. Her story raises many issues of development that are addressed in this book. How does industrialization affect the lives of the majority of people in developing countries who are still rural and still poor? Who benefits from foreign investment and who loses, in both the developing and the industrial countries? How do governments promote investment, industrialization, and exports? How do countries educate their people to become productive workers in more advanced industries? How do countries and their people cope with the disparities between urban industrial workers and the vast majority of still-poor farmers and marginal urbanites and between the advances of some ethnic groups and the slow progress of others? This book explores the economics of these and other issues in an attempt to understand why some countries develop rapidly while others seem not to develop at all. We are concerned with both the characteristics of development and the policies that can be employed to improve development performance.

TERMINOLOGY: THE DEVELOPING WORLD

Before embarking on this complex task, we need to sort out some terms commonly used to describe developed and less-developed countries, and to suggest some possible ways to measure where a country stands along the continuum from industrial to developing countries.

Rich and Poor Countries

The countries with which this book is concerned have been labeled with many different terms. All these terms are intended to contrast their state or rate of change with those of the more modern, advanced, developed countries, so that terms tend to be found in pairs. The starkest distinction is between **backward** and **advanced** economies, or between **traditional** and **modern** ones. The "backward" economy is traditional in its economic relationships, in ways that will be described in the next chapter. However precisely and neutrally the term can be defined, it retains pejorative connotations, a touch of condescension, and is therefore not much used today. In any case, the implication of stagnation is inappropriate for in most countries economic and social relationships are changing in important ways.

The more popular classifications implicitly put all countries on a continuum based on their **degree of development**. Thus we speak of the distinctions between **developed** and **underdeveloped** countries, **more-** and **less-developed** ones, or, to recognize continuing change, **developed** and **developing** countries. The degree of optimism implicit in "developing countries" and the handy acronym LDCs for "less-developed countries," make these the two most widely used terms.[2] Developed countries are also frequently called **industrial countries**, in recognition of the close association between development and industrialization.

A dichotomy based simply on income levels, the **poor** versus the **rich countries**, has been refined by the World Bank to yield a four-part classification that is useful for many analytical purposes.[3] The developing countries are divided by income into **low-income economies** (less than \$675 per capita in 1992, converted into dollars at the current exchange rate) and **middle-income economies** (between

2. The initials have also been used, especially by the United Nations, to designate the "least-developed countries," those with lowest incomes per capita (among other characteristics).

3. World Bank, *World Development Report 1994* (New York: Oxford University Press, 1994), pp. 178–79. The World Bank, formally titled the International Bank for Reconstruction and Development (IBRD), borrows funds on private capital markets in the developed countries and lends to the developing countries; and, through its affiliate, the International Development Association (IDA), receives contributions from the governments of developed countries and lends to the low-income countries at very low interest rates with long repayment periods. The Bank is perhaps the world's most important and influential development agency. See Chapter 15 for a more complete discussion.

$675 and $8000 in 1992). The latter group is further divided into those with incomes below $2700 per capita, the **lower-middle-income economies**, and from $2700 to $8000 per capita, the **upper-middle-income economies**. (A subset of upper-middle-income countries, mostly Asian and occasionally Latin American economies whose industrial output has been growing rapidly, is sometimes called the **newly industrializing countries or economies**.) The World Bank's classification is completed by the **high-income economies** (also called the **industrial countries**), mostly members of the Organization for Economic Cooperation and Development (OECD), with incomes over $8000 per capita.

Three anomalous groups fit uneasily into this taxonomy. Five Middle Eastern petroleum exporters—Oman, Libya, Saudi Arabia, Kuwait, and the United Arab Emirates—whose incomes ranged from $6,000 to $22,000 per capita in 1992, have economies that are more traditional than the typical upper-middle income or industrialized country. Three other economies—Israel, Singapore, and Hong Kong—are considered by the United Nations (and many others) to be developing countries despite per capita incomes of over $13,000 in 1992. And the economies of Eastern Europe, including Russia, have incomes that qualify them as middle income, though some of them may better be described as industrial economies in decline or as **transitional economies** moving from controlled to market-oriented development.

A term in vogue during the 1980s, especially in international forums, was the **third world**. Perhaps the best way to define it is by elimination. Take the industrialized (OECD) economies of Western Europe, North America, and the Pacific (the "first" world, though it was never called that) and the industrialized, formerly centrally planned economies of Eastern Europe (the "second" world); the rest of the countries constitute the third world. All third-world countries are developing countries and these include all of Latin America and the Caribbean, Africa, the Middle East, and Asia except Japan. The geographic configuration of this group has led to a parallel distinction of **North** (first and second worlds) versus **South**, which still has some currency. But the South or third world encompasses a wide variety of countries, from wealthy oil exporters to very low income, poorly endowed countries.

It is necessary to be aware of these various terminologies and classifications and to recognize their exceptions and inconsistencies. But it is not wise to dwell too long over them. No system can capture all the important dimensions of development and provide a perfectly consistent, manageable framework. We generally refer to the less-developed, poorer countries as "developing countries," though other terms are used where appropriate.

Growth and Development

While the labels used to distinguish one set of countries from another can vary, one must be more careful with the terms used to describe the development process itself. The terms **economic growth** and **economic development** are sometimes used interchangeably, but there is a fundamental distinction between them. "Economic growth" refers to a rise in national or per capita income and product.[4]

4. Income per capita is measured as the gross national product (the value of all goods and services produced by a country's economy in a year) divided by the population.

If the production of goods and services in a country rises, by whatever means, one can speak of that rise as "economic growth." "Economic development" implies more. What has been happening in South Korea since 1960, for example, is fundamentally different from what has been happening in Libya as a result of the discovery of petroleum. Both countries experienced a large rise in per capita income, but in Libya this rise was achieved by foreign corporations staffed largely by foreign technicians who produced a single product consumed mainly in the United States and Western Europe. Although the government and people of Libya have received large amounts of income from their oil, they have had little to do with producing that income. The effect of petroleum development has been much as if a rich country had decided to give Libya large amounts of grant aid.

Libya's experience is not usually described as economic development. Economic development, in addition to a rise in per capita income, implies fundamental changes in the structure of the economy, of the kind observed in South Korea since 1960. Two of the most important of these structural changes are the rising share of industry, along with the falling share of agriculture in national product, and the increasing percentage of people who live in cities rather than the countryside. In addition, countries that enter into economic development usually pass through periods of accelerating, then decelerating, population growth during which the country's age structure changes dramatically. Consumption patterns also change as people no longer have to spend all their income on necessities, but instead move on to consumer durables and eventually to leisure-time products and services.

A key element in economic development is that the people of the country must be major participants in the process that brought about these changes in structure. Foreigners can be and inevitably are involved as well, but they cannot be the whole story. Participation in the process of development implies participation in the enjoyment of the benefits of development as well as the production of those benefits. If growth only benefits a tiny, wealthy minority, whether domestic or foreign, it is not development.

Modern economic growth, the term used by Nobel laureate Simon Kuznets, refers to the current economic epoch as contrasted to, say, the epoch of merchant capitalism or the epoch of feudalism. The epoch of modern economic growth is still going on so all its features are not yet clear, but the key element has been the application of science to problems of economic production, which in turn has led to industrialization, urbanization, and even explosive growth in population.

The widely used term **modernization** refers to much more than the economy. One can speak of the "modernization" of a society or of a political system, for example. But it is difficult to give the term a precise meaning. Too often there is a tendency to equate modernization with becoming more like the United States or Western Europe. Is it reasonable to say that the former Soviet Union was not modern because it was not democratic or that Japan is not modern because it still maintains certain ways of organizing business based more on its own traditions than on practices in the West? Because of the vague and misleading nature of the term, we will not use it further here.

Finally, it should always be kept in mind that while economic development and modern economic growth involve much more than a rise in per capita income or product, there can be no development without economic growth.

Much can be learned from a ten-minute perusal of Table 1–1 and Figures 1–1 to 1–4 about the nature of structural change during development and the many differences within the developing world. These data are from the World Bank's *World Development Report*, an annual publication that should become familiar to every student of development. The Bank, and most sources, classify countries by their income per capita, using the four-part division already discussed.

Although income per capita remains the most useful single indicator of development, it has many shortcomings, which we discuss in Chapter 3. One of these is

TABLE 1–1 Development Characteristics of Groups and Selected Countries, 1992

Country	GNP per capita (PPP dollars)	GNP per capita (U.S. dollars)	Energy consumption per capita (kg oil equivalent)	Rural population share (%)	Life expectancy at birth (years)	Adult literacy (%)
Low-income countries	*1,523*	*380*	*370*	*73*	*63*	*40*
Excluding China	*(1,224)*	*(311)*	*(192)*	*(73)*	*(58)*	*(52)*
Ethiopia	340	110	21	87	49	–
Mali	500	310	22	75	48	68
Tanzania	630	110	30	78	51	–
India	1,210	310	235	74	61	52
Bangladesh	1,230	220	59	82	55	65
Kenya	1,360	310	92	75	59	31
Nigeria	1,440	320	128	63	52	49
Senegal	1,750	780	111	59	49	62
Ghana	1,890	450	96	65	56	40
China	1,910	470	600	73	69	27
Honduras	1,930	580	175	55	66	27
Lower-middle-income countries	*3,001*	*807*	*622*	*61*	*63*	*35*
Pakistan	2,130	420	223	67	59	65
Bolivia	2,270	680	255	48	60	23
Cameroon	2,300	820	77	58	56	46
Philippines	2,480	770	302	56	65	10
Sri Lanka	2,810	540	101	78	72	12
Indonesia	2,970	670	303	68	60	23
Peru	3,080	950	330	29	65	15
Egypt, Arab Rep.	3,670	640	586	56	62	52
Upper-middle-income countries	*6,188*	*2,859*	*2,185*	*33*	*69*	*18*
Brazil	5,250	2,770	681	23	66	19
Hungary	5,740	2,970	2,392	34	69	–
Colombia	5,760	1,330	670	29	69	13
Argentina	6,080	6,050	1,351	13	71	5
Mexico	7,490	3,470	1,525	26	70	13
Malaysia	8,050	2,790	1,445	55	71	22
Korea, Rep. of	8,950	3,790	2,569	26	77	7
High-income countries	*19,675*	*21,990*	*5,054*	*22*	*77*	*<5*
Saudi Arabia	11,170	7,510	4,463	22	69	38
United Kingdom	16,730	17,790	3,743	11	76	<5
Japan	20,160	28,190	3,586	23	79	<5
Germany	20,610	23,030	4,358	14	76	<5
United States	23,120	23,240	7,662	24	77	<5

Source: World Development Report 1994, pp. 162, 170, 220, 222.

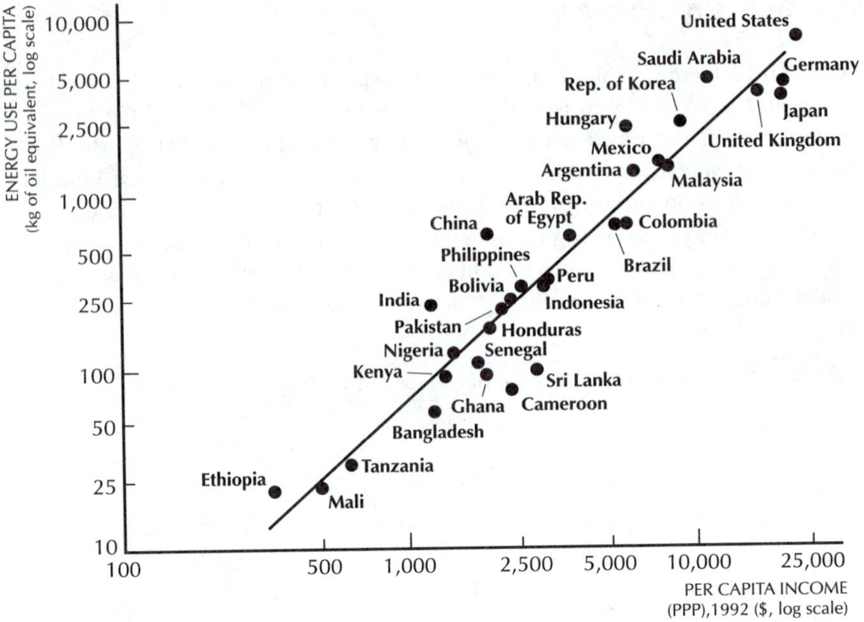

FIGURE 1–1 Energy Consumption per Capita. There is a strong tendency for energy consumption to rise with average income, though some countries use much less energy than others at the same average income.

that, in order to compare incomes among countries, all have to be converted into a common currency, typically into U.S. dollars. However, the fluctuation of exchange rates over time means that dollar incomes, and country rankings, change frequently even though the underlying situation—peoples' real welfare—has changed very little. One way to deal with this is to use a common set of prices, usually those of the United States, to measure the output of every country. Thus a haircut in India is priced the same as one in the United States, as is a ton of wheat, a telephone, or a car.

This measure of average income is called the **purchasing power parity** or PPP method. It gives a more accurate comparison of incomes among countries and will be used throughout this book. In Table 1–1, countries are ranked in order of ascending PPP income per capita (column 1). The conventional measure of income, converted at the dollar exchange rate, is shown in the second column for comparison. The countries have been classified according to their PPP incomes: low-income countries have incomes below $2,000 per capita; lower-middle-income countries, $2,000 to $5,000; upper-middle-income countries, $5,000 to $10,000; and upper-income countries, above $10,000.

A major effect of using PPP incomes is to compress the differences between rich and poor countries. Table 1–1 shows that India, for example, has an income, converted at the dollar exchange rate, just over 1 percent that of the United States. But in PPP terms, India's income is 5 percent that of the United States. For a middle-income country, say Colombia, the dollar exchange rate gives an income 6 percent that of the United States, while the PPP ratio is 25 percent, a very different picture. The PPP estimates also change the rankings of countries. Bangladesh and Pakistan, for example, move up in the rankings, while Mali and Senegal move down. At the upper end of the income scale, the United States remains the richest country in the world under the PPP standard, though not under the conventional measure.

One way to avoid the problems of comparing incomes is to use physical measures of economic modernization or industrialization. A common measure is a country's per capita consumption of energy. Figure 1–1 shows how closely energy use per capita is correlated with GNP per capita.[5]

A predominant structural characteristic of development is the growing share of both income produced and labor employed in industry. Table 1–1 and Figure 1–2 reflect this trend, inversely, in the share of the population living in rural areas. This share declines from an average of 73 percent for low-income countries to only 22 percent for high-income countries.

Rising income is not the only goal of development. People aspire to stay healthier and become better educated. Indicators for each of these aspects of well-being are included in Table 1–1, and they are also correlated with per capita income (Figures 1–3 and 1–4). Life expectancy, averaging less than 60 years in low-income countries (excluding China), rises to 77 years on average for high-income countries. But the most dramatic contrast is in adult illiteracy. In the poorest group of countries, excluding China, more than 50 percent of the adult population are unable to read. Upper-middle-income countries have reduced their illiteracy to below 20 percent on average, while in the high-income countries less than 5 percent of all adults are illiterate.

In each category there is considerable variance and hence there are some interesting exceptions. India and China consume substantially more energy per capita than other countries with similar incomes, while the Philippines consumes substantially less (Figure 1–1). The rural population share in Sri Lanka is more than twice that of Peru, a country with nearly the same income; the contrast between Malaysia, where 55 percent of the population is rural, and Argentina, where 13

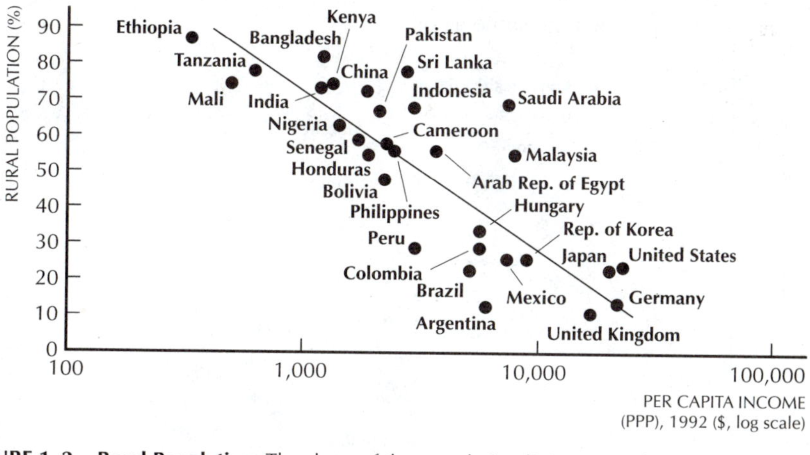

FIGURE 1–2 Rural Population. The share of the population living in rural areas declines as income grows.

5. The regression lines shown in the graphs have been calculated for the countries in our sample only. These countries have been chosen for their general interest rather than because they are a statistically representative sample.

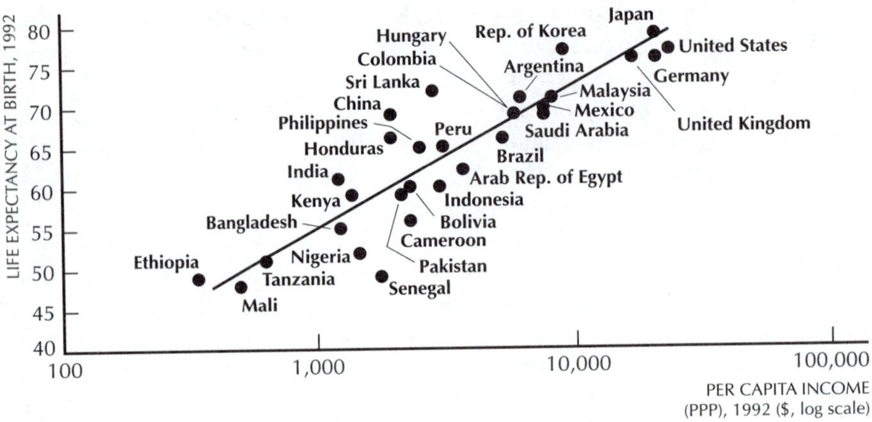

FIGURE 1–3 Life Expectancy. Although life expectancy rises with average income, there are large differences among countries with similar incomes.

percent is rural, is even sharper (Figure 1–2). Chinese and Sri Lankans live as long as Hungarians and Argentines, even though incomes in the latter countries are two to three times those in the former countries (Figure 1–3). The Philippines and Sri Lanka have adult illiteracy rates of 12 percent or less, little different from those of Colombia and Mexico, which have twice the income; in Pakistan and Egypt, with similar incomes to those in the Philippines and Sri Lanka, over half the adults are illiterate (Figure 1–4). Behind these and other variations in development lie many factors: different resource endowments, governments' varying ideologies and policies, cultural differences, colonial experience, war, and historical accident. In many cases variations suggest new theories of development and we will explore some of these in later chapters.

Development is inherently a dynamic process that cannot be completely cap-

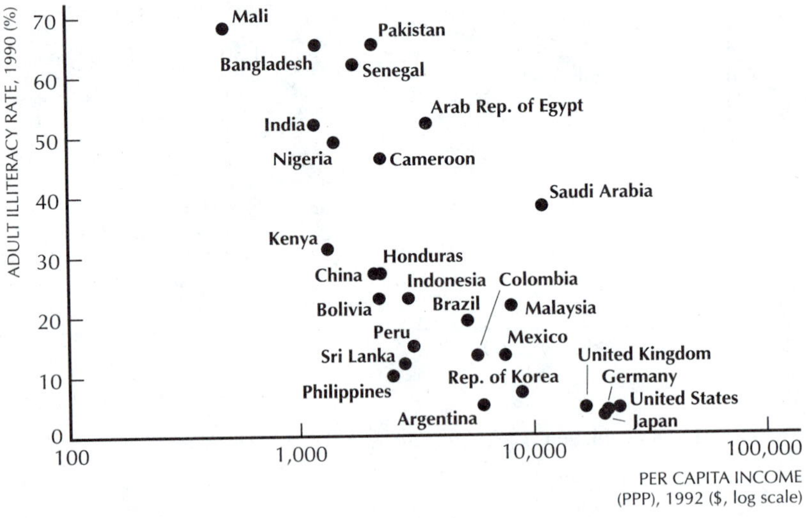

FIGURE 1–4 Adult Literacy. The rate of illiteracy among adults tends to fall as incomes rise, but some low-income countries have remarkably low rates of illiteracy.

tured by Table 1–1. Most less-developed countries have experienced growth in incomes since 1965 and many have enjoyed substantial growth, as Table 1–2 shows. The most rapidly growing countries, with incomes per capita expanding by 4 percent a year or more, have all been in Asia: China, Indonesia, Malaysia, Korea, and Japan in the table, plus Thailand, Taiwan, Hong Kong, and Singapore. There are many examples of countries with income growth over 2 percent a year. At 2 percent annual growth, average incomes double in 35 years; at 4 percent, they double in less than a generation. Most of the countries with declining average incomes since 1965 have been in Africa, though income also fell in Peru over the period. In most developing countries, manufacturing grew more rapidly than gross national product, and thus moved these economies through the inevitable struc-

TABLE 1–2 Growth of Population and Output of Groups and Selected Countries, 1965–1992 (percent per year)

Country	Population*	GNP per capita	Manufacturing value-added per capita
Low-income countries	*1.7*	*3.6*	*2.1*
Excluding China	*(2.2)*	*(1.7)*	*(–)*
Tanzania	3.0	−0.20	2.10
Mali	2.7	1.70	–
Ethiopia	3.3	−0.20	1.60
Kenya	2.7	1.90	7.20
Bangladesh	2.0	0.70	4.10
India	1.9	1.90	5.60
Nigeria	2.9	0.10	–
Senegal	2.6	−0.60	3.81
Ghana	2.9	−1.40	1.90
China	1.1	5.80	
Honduras	3.0	0.50	5.23
Lower-middle-income countries	*1.9*	*2.6*	
Pakistan	3.0	2.50	6.40
Bolivia	2.6	−0.70	2.80
Cameroon	3.0	3.00	8.88
Philippines	2.5	1.30	3.28
Sri Lanka	1.6	2.90	4.30
Indonesia	1.5	4.50	12.90
Peru	2.0	−0.20	1.12
Egypt, Arab Rep.	1.9	4.10	–
Upper-middle-income countries	*1.4*	*3.1*	
Brazil	1.6	3.30	4.83
Hungary	−0.2	–	0.00
Colombia	1.8	2.30	4.60
Argentina	1.1	−0.30	0.83
Mexico	2.3	2.80	4.44
Malaysia	2.3	4.00	–
Korea, Rep. of	1.0	7.10	14.00
High-income countries	*0.5*	*2.7*	
Saudi Arabia	3.0	2.60	7.29
United Kingdom	3.0	2.00	–
Japan	0.4	4.10	5.27
Germany	−0.1	2.40	1.79
United States	0.7	1.70	–

*Instantaneous rate of natural increase in 1992, i.e., the rate of births less the rate of deaths per hundred.
Sources: World Development Report 1992 (GNP growth rates) and *1994* (population and manufacturing growth rates).

tural change that reduces the share of income produced and labor employed in agriculture.

Perhaps the most remarkable changes in the third world since 1965 have been the virtually universal improvement in health conditions and the availability of education. From 1965 to 1992 there was a dramatic reduction in the infant death rate in every country listed in Table 1–3: declines from 177 per 1000 births to 84 in Nigeria and from 130 to 52 in Peru were typical. Primary school enrollment became universal in China, India, Kenya, and Sri Lanka and rose dramatically in most other low-income countries. With few exceptions, more than three-quarters of the eligible children attend primary school in poor countries. That healthier

TABLE 1–3 Progress in Social Well-being of Groups and Selected Countries, 1965–1992

	Infant mortality rate per 1000		Percentage of age enrolled in primary school	
Country	1965	1992	1965	1991
Low-income countries	*122*	*60*	*76*	*104*
Excluding China	*(153)*	*(85)*	*(63)*	*(88)*
Tanzania	138	92	32	69
Mali	207	130	24	25
Ethiopia	149	122	49	25
Kenya	112	66	54	95
Bangladesh	144	91	49	77
India	150	79	74	98
Nigeria	177	84	32	71
Senegal	126	68	40	59
Ghana	120	81	69	77
China	90	31	89	123
Honduras	128	49	80	105
Lower-middle-income countries	*123*	*63*	*74*	*94*
Pakistan	149	95	40	46
Bolivia	160	82	73	85
Cameroon	143	61	94	101
Philippines	72	40	113	110
Sri Lanka	63	18	93	108
Indonesia	128	66	72	116
Peru	130	52	99	126
Egypt, Arab Rep.	172	57	75	101
Upper-middle-income countries	*97*	*40*	*95*	*108*
Brazil	104	57	108	106
Hungary	39	15	101	89
Colombia	86	21	84	111
Argentina	58	29	101	107
Mexico	82	35	92	114
Malaysia	55	14	90	93
Korea, Rep. of	62	13	101	107
High-income countries	*26*	*8*	*103*	*103*
Saudi Arabia	148	28	24	77
United Kingdom	20	7	92	104
Japan	18	5	100	102
Germany	25	6	–	107
United States	25	9	100	104

Source: World Development Report 1994, pp. 214–17.

populations have also meant higher population growth (Table 1–2) is an important consideration, as discussed in Chapter 8.

It is sometimes easy to become pessimistic about further progress in developing nations, especially when confronted by gloomy predictions about their future economic growth and by the myriad problems afflicting LDCs, many of which will be cataloged in this book. As an antidote to discouragement, one needs to keep in mind the considerable economic development that has already taken place, the strong growth momentum of several countries in Asia, and the gratifying improvements in health and education that mark even the poorest countries. The question of how these benefits have been distributed among the populace will be taken up in Chapter 4 and in Part 3.

Focus of the Book

Approaches to Development

This book is not for readers who are looking for a simple explanation of why some countries are still poor or of how poverty can be overcome. Library shelves are full of studies explaining how development will occur if only a country will increase the amount it saves and invests or intensify its efforts to export. For two decades in the mid-twentieth century, industrialization through import substitution—the replacement of imports with home-produced goods—was considered by many to be the shortest path to development. In the 1970s, labor-intensive techniques, income redistribution, and provision of basic human needs to the poor gained popularity as keys to development. Most economists now counsel governments to depend substantially on markets to set prices and allocate resources. Another school of thought suggests that development is only possible if preceded by a revolution that eliminates existing elites and replaces the market with central planning. A different theme is that development will only be possible if there is a massive shift of resources, in the form of foreign aid and investment, from the richest countries to the poorest.

No single factor is responsible for underdevelopment, and no single policy or strategy can set in motion the complex process of economic development. A wide variety of explanations and solutions to the development problem make sense if placed in the proper context and make no sense at all outside that set of circumstances. Mobilization of saving is essential for accelerated growth in most cases, but sometimes may come second to a redistribution of income if extreme poverty threatens political stability or forestalls the mobilization of human resources. Import substitution has carried some countries quite far toward economic development, but export promotion has helped others when import substitution bogged down. Prices that are badly distorted from their free-market values can stifle initiative and hence growth, but removing those distortions leads to development only when other conditions are met as well. Moreover, some, but certainly not all, centrally planned economies achieved sustained periods of development with prices that bore little relation to those determined by market forces. Finally, where countries are ruled by leaders backed by interests hostile to development, those leaders and their constituents must be removed from power before growth can occur. But most developing countries have governments that genuinely want to promote development.

This book is not neutral toward all issues of development. Where controversy exists we shall point it out. Indeed, the authors of this book differ among ourselves over some questions of development policy. But we do share a common point of view on certain basic points.

First of all, this text makes extensive use of the theoretical tools of classical and neoclassical economics in the belief that these tools contribute substantially to our understanding of development problems and their solution. The text does not rely solely or even primarily on theory, however. For four decades and more, development economists and economic historians have been building up an empirical record against which these theories can be tested, and this book draws heavily on many of these empirical studies. We try to give real-country examples for virtually all the major points made in this book. In part these examples come from the individual country and cross-country comparative studies of others, but they also are drawn extensively from our own personal experiences working on development issues around the world. Among the four of us, we have been fortunate enough to study and work over long periods of time in Bolivia, Chile, China, Colombia, Ghana, Indonesia, Kenya, Korea, Malaysia, Peru, Sri Lanka, and Tanzania. At one time or another, at least one from this group of nations has exemplified virtually all approaches to development now extant.

While this book draws on classical and neoclassical economic theory, development involves major issues for which these economic theories do not provide answers, or at best provide only partial answers. Economic theory tends to take the **institutional context** (the existence of markets, of a banking system, of international trade, etc.) as given. But development is concerned with how one creates institutions that facilitate development in the first place. How, for example, does a country acquire a government interested in and capable of promoting economic growth? Can efficiently functioning markets be created in countries that currently lack them, or should the state take over the functions normally left to the market elsewhere? Is a fully developed financial system a precondition for growth, or can a country do without at least some parts of such a system? Is land reform necessary for development, and, if so, what kind of land reform? These institutional issues and many others like them are at the heart of the development process and will reappear in different guises in the following chapters.

Organization

This book is divided into five parts. Part 1 examines the main factors that prevent development from taking place and the kinds of structural change—including changes in income distribution—that occur once growth is underway. Structural change is often the result of deliberate choices by governments and Part 2 provides an introduction to issues of market-based *versus* command systems of development and to economic planning models. It also raises issues of sustainability: how far or fast can development proceed without exhausting natural resources or irreversibly degrading the environment?

Economic development is first and foremost a process involving people, who are both the prime movers of development and its beneficiaries. Part 3 deals with how human resources are transformed in the process of economic development and how that transformation contributes to the development process itself. There are chapters on population, labor, education, and health.

The other major physical input in the growth process is capital, and Part 4 is concerned with how capital is mobilized and allocated for development purposes. Where, for example, do the savings come from and how are they transformed into investment? How does government mobilize resources to finance development? What kind of financial system is consistent with rapid capital accumulation? Will inflation enhance or hinder the process and what role is played by foreign aid and investment?

Especially in the early stages of development, countries depend heavily on agriculture and on the export of foods, fuels, and raw materials. Part 5 discusses strategies to enhance the productivity of such primary industries as a first, and often a continuing, task in stimulating economic development. Ultimately, however, development depends on industrialization. Part 5 also extends our discussion of industrial development, explores trade policies to promote manufactured exports, and analyzes the macroeconomic management of a developing economy open to world markets.

2

Starting Modern Economic Growth

The era of modern economic growth is only two centuries old. Before the late eighteenth century there were individuals and families who became rich, but nations as a whole and most of the people in them were poor. An economy was seen as a pie of fixed size. One could cut oneself a bigger piece of the pie, but only by taking away a portion that originally belonged to someone else. Few saw the possibility of increasing the size of the pie so that all could have larger slices.

But the essence of modern economic growth is that, on average, the per capita income of all people in a country rises, not just the income of a select few. And as per capita income rises, other fundamental changes occur that affect the way people live. The household as a production unit declines and is replaced by larger enterprises that find it economical to locate near each other. The result is that more people live in cities and work in factories rather than on farms. As incomes rise and urbanization takes place, behavior within the household also changes. Families no longer want large numbers of children, and so the birth rate begins to fall. Modern economic growth, therefore, involves fundamental structural changes in the way both production and society are organized.

In the late eighteenth century England began to transform its economy, a process that would later be called the Industrial Revolution. By the middle of the nineteenth century other countries in Europe and North America had begun similar transformations, and toward the end of the century the first non-European population, the Japanese, had begun to industrialize. Two world wars and the Great Depression interrupted industrialization in the already-advanced countries and slowed the spread of economic advance to other parts of the globe. The Second

World War, however, also undermined the strength of European colonialism and set the stage for a widespread effort to industrialize the large numbers of newly independent countries.

One of the key characteristics of modern economic growth, therefore, is that it did not begin everywhere in the world at the same time. Instead it spread slowly across Europe and North America, but except for Japan, it did not break out of areas dominated by European culture until the 1950s and 1960s. In parts of the world the process has yet to begin.

Between those parts of the world that have achieved sustained growth and those that have not, a gap has inevitably opened up in the standard of living. The average European, American, or Japanese enjoys a material way of life that is many times richer than all but the richest individuals in Asia and Africa. But there is nothing inevitable or permanent about this gap. In the nineteenth century England was far ahead of the rest of the world, whereas today England is not even in the top ten of the richest countries in terms of per capita income. In the early 1950s Japan was poorer than such centers of European poverty as Spain or Greece, but by the mid-1980s Japanese income per capita was comparable to or above those of richer Western European countries such as France.

This chapter focuses on why these gaps in income between countries open up. Why is it that some countries began developing earlier than others? What has prevented some countries from entering into modern economic growth even today? Are the barriers that have inhibited development the result of conditions internal to the country affected, or is the lack of development in some countries today the result of externally imposed forces? A related question is whether the barriers to growth in countries are the same everywhere or whether particular conditions in one country act to inhibit growth while similar conditions elsewhere do little harm because the context is different. In much the same spirit, are there prerequisites that must be in place, such as a modern banking system, before growth can occur, or are there often substitutes available for particular prerequisites?

THE DEVELOPING COUNTRIES: A GLANCE AT HISTORY

The two features common to all traditional societies are a low per capita income and an absence of modern economic growth. Beyond these simple common features is a great diversity of national experiences about which valid generalizations are difficult to make. The use of terms such as "third world," "less-developed countries," or "developing countries" tends to obscure this diversity by implying that all countries, except those already rich, have a common experience that transcends any differences in their backgrounds and current conditions. In fact the differences between developing countries are so great that one cannot really understand their development problems without taking these differences into account.

Even within Europe on the eve of industrialization there were great differences between societies, and these differences had much to do with why development began first in Western Europe and spread only gradually to the East. In England, for example, laborers were free to change jobs and migrate to distant places, and commerce and banking had reached a high level of sophistication in the centuries preceding the Industrial Revolution. But Russia in the mid-nineteenth century was still feudal: Most peasants were tied to their lord's estate for life, and finance, industry, and transport were still in a primitive state.

In Asia, Latin America, and Africa the range of political and cultural experience is more diverse than that which existed within Europe. Great empires, such as those of China and Japan, had over a thousand years of self-governing experience, and they thought of themselves as a single unified people, rather than as a collection of ethnically distinct tribes or regions. By premodern standards China and Japan also had high levels of urbanization and commerce, and they shared Confucian values, which emphasize the importance of education. Long years of comparative stability contributed to a population increase that resulted in the great shortage of arable land relative to population that still exists in the region today. Because of the comparative sophistication of premodern commerce in East Asia, European and American merchants were never able to play a significant role in the management of domestic commerce in the region. As Chinese and Japanese merchants gradually acquired an understanding of foreign markets, they were able to compete successfully with representatives of the industrialized world in that sphere as well.

Colonialism and Independence

At the other end of this spectrum of self-government and commercial sophistication are several Southeast Asian and most African nations. Indonesia and Nigeria, for example, were really the arbitrary creations of Dutch and British colonialism, which brought together diverse groups of people who shared little in common and had no desire to maintain these externally imposed boundaries. Both Indonesia in the late 1950s and Nigeria in the late 1960s had to fight wars to keep their new countries together.

Experience with commerce in many parts of Southeast Asia and Africa was also quite limited and illiteracy was often nearly universal. Throughout the colonial era in Indonesia and many parts of sub-Saharan Africa, foreign trade and large-scale domestic commerce were almost entirely in the hands of Europeans. Small-scale commerce, particularly in the countryside, was sometimes controlled by local people, but usually it was in the hands of minorities who had immigrated from other poor but commercially more advanced countries. Thus local commerce in much of Southeast Asia was in the hands of Chinese, that in East Africa was mainly managed by Indians, while in West Africa Lebanese often played a central role. Because of inexperience the local people could not effectively compete with either these immigrant groups or the Europeans, and because they could not compete, they did not gain much experience with trade or finance. This was one of the many vicious circles so common to the plight of poor countries.

Not all experiences with colonialism were the same. In India a tiny number of British ruled a vastly populated subcontinent. By necessity the British had to train large numbers of Indians to handle all but the very top jobs in the bureaucracy and army. At the time of independence in 1948, Indians were already running most of their own affairs because there were enough trained and experienced personnel to do so. But in Indonesia there were fewer than a thousand university or other post-secondary school graduates at the time of independence, and in Zaire there were hardly any. Prior to independence even the lower levels of the central bureaucracy in Indonesia had been manned by the Dutch and those in Zaire by Belgians. In comparison, India and China in the 1940s had hundreds of thousands of university graduates.

Latin America's historical heritage is different from that of either Asia or Africa. Independence in most of the region was achieved in the early nineteenth century, not after World War II as in Asia and Africa. Although there were local populations in the region when the Europeans first arrived, the indigenous populations were killed, suppressed, or enslaved. So to meet growing labor requirements, the elites turned to voluntary and forced immigration of Europeans and Africans. Spanish and Portuguese immigrants ruled; the Africans were enslaved until late in the nineteenth century. Ignored or pushed aside, some of the original population continued to exist, but in varying numbers: Peru and Bolivia maintained large indigenous populations, whereas in Argentina native peoples nearly disappeared.

North America above the Rio Grande was also peopled by immigrants who suppressed the local population. In both North and South America slavery existed in some regions and not in others, but there were important differences between the types of colonial rule. In the north the indigenous population was more thoroughly suppressed; hence, it was small and isolated and not a factor when economic development began. European immigrants were from the economically most advanced parts of Europe, where feudal values and structures had already been partially dismantled. But Spanish and Portuguese immigrants came from an area that by the nineteenth century was one of the more backward parts of Europe. The feudal values and structures that still dominated this region accompanied these colonists to the New World. Likewise, there were also great differences within Latin America. Argentina, for example, is largely a nation of European immigrants; Mexico, Peru, and Bolivia have large indigenous populations; a large minority of Brazilians and virtually all Haitians are descended from former African slaves.

The Developing Countries: A Brief Taxonomy

It is impossible to summarize all the important differences between countries in the developing world, but those with the greatest bearing on the potential for modern economic growth in the region would include differences between:

Countries with a long tradition of emphasis on education and an elite that was highly educated, as contrasted with countries where illiteracy was nearly universal

Countries with fairly highly developed systems of commerce, finance, and transport mainly run by local people versus countries where these activities were monopolized by European or Asian immigrant minorities

Countries peopled by those who shared a common language, culture, and sense of national identity versus countries where there was a great diversity of language and culture, and no common sense of national identity or shared common goals

Countries with long traditions of self-government versus those with no experience with even limited self-government until the 1950s or 1960s

This list could be extended but the point is made. Economic development requires both a government capable of directing or supporting a major growth effort and a people who can work effectively in and manage the enterprises and other organizations that arise in the course of development. Countries that have people with at least some relevant education and experience in economic affairs and governments able to support those people are better positioned for development than countries that have people with little relevant experience and diverse groups within the country that are still arguing over their shares in what they believe, wrongly for the most part, to be a pie of fixed size.

The Concept of Substitutes

Given the great diversity in developing-country experience, it would be a counsel of despair to suggest that the way to begin development is first to recreate the kinds of political, social, and economic conditions that existed in Western Europe or North America when those regions entered into modern economic growth. England prior to the Industrial Revolution had centuries of experience with merchant capitalism, but does it follow that Ghana or Indonesia must also acquire long experience with merchant capitalism before economic development is feasible? If the answer were yes, these countries would be doomed to another century or more of poverty.

Fortunately there is no standard list of barriers that must be overcome or prerequisites that must be in place before development is possible. Instead, as the economic historian Alexander Gerschenkron pointed out, for most presumed prerequisites there are usually substitutes. The main point of this concept is best illustrated with an example from Gerschenkron's own work.[1]

Capital, like labor, is of course necessary for development, and much more will be said about both in later chapters. But Marx and others went a step further and argued that there must be an original or prior accumulation of capital before growth can take place. The basic idea came from looking at the experience of England where, Marx argued, trade, exploitation of colonies, piracy, and other related measures led to the accumulation of great wealth that in the late eighteenth century could be converted into investment in industry. Is such an accumulation a prerequisite for development everywhere or at least for a large number of countries? In the absence of a prior accumulation of capital, does economic development become impossible?

In Europe the answer was clearly no. One did have to find funds that could be invested in industry, but they did not have to come out of the accumulated wealth of the past. Germany, for example, had little in the way of an original accumulation of capital when modern economic growth began there. But Germany did have a banking system that could create funds, which were then lent to industrialists. How banks create funds is not our concern here; the point is that banks can create accounts that investors can draw on, and the creation of those accounts depends in no significant way on long years of prior savings and accumulation by merchants or other wealthy individuals.

1. Alexander Gerschenkron, *Economic Backwardness in Historical Perspective* (Cambridge, Mass.: Harvard University Press, 1962), Chap. 2.

Russia in the nineteenth century had neither an original accumulation of wealth nor a banking system capable of creating large enough levels of credit. Instead Russia turned to the taxing power of the state. The government could and did tax funds away from people and use this tax revenue for investment in industry. Russia also imported capital from abroad. Thus in Russia the government's use of taxation was a substitute for a well-developed banking system, and elsewhere a modern banking system was a substitute for an original accumulation of capital.

Similar examples of substitutes abound in today's world. Latin American countries, for example, rely heavily on financial institutions to mobilize and allocate savings. Sub-Saharan African countries, in contrast, rely more on fiscal institutions (the government budget). Factories in advanced countries with well-developed commercial networks rely on central distributors to supply them with spare parts. Rural industries in China, where commerce is less developed, make spare parts in their own foundries. As already pointed out, a number of countries in the developing world today have substantial numbers of people with training and experience in areas relevant to economic development, while the number of such people in other countries is minuscule. The most common substitute for this lack of relevant experience is to import foreigners or to rely on nonindigenous residents who have the required experience. For reasons that will become apparent in later chapters, foreigners are frequently not very good substitutes for experienced local talent, but where the latter is missing, they can fill the gap until local talent is trained.

Therefore, in the following discussion of political and social barriers to development and of what is required to initiate development, we shall not be looking for three or four universal causes of poverty or a similar number of prerequisites that must always be in place before growth is possible. Instead we shall attempt to identify some of the more common political and social barriers to development and recognize that the presence of these barriers or the absence of some "prerequisites" does not condemn a country to stagnation and poverty. There are usually ways around, or substitutes for, any single barrier or "prerequisite," but the existence of many of these barriers or the absence of a wide variety of desirable preconditions will make economic development more difficult and in some cases impossible.

The closest one can come to a single prerequisite without which economic development would be impossible is not politics or social structure but whether or not a country has access to the discoveries of modern science and innovators to adapt these discoveries for the marketplace. The industrial economy of the twentieth century would be inconceivable in the absence of the knowledge arising from such fields as chemistry, physics, and biology. A high percentage of the products in common use today, from electric power to antibiotics, did not even exist prior to the advent of modern science.

While science is crucial to economic development, it is also clear that no country today is really cut off from the main fruits of that science. Some of the great civilizations of the past probably were unable to expand beyond a certain level primarily from a lack of scientific discovery and technological advancement. It is also the case today that countries with educational and research capabilities of their own, such as South Korea and Mexico, can often make more and better use of many scientific discoveries. But even the most poorly endowed countries have access to much of what modern science has contributed since the fruits of scientific discovery are often embodied in products that are domestically manufactured by comparatively simple processes or imported as finished goods from more-advanced countries. Developing countries do not have to rediscover the basic laws of thermodynamics. For many purposes they only need to understand those laws and how they can be usefully applied or imitate others' applications of those laws or simply import the machines that embody such knowledge—all much easier than making the discovery in the first place. The issue of why some countries gained access to modern science earlier than others, therefore, is mainly of historical interest and will not be pursued further here.

In the eyes of some economists a failure to enter into modern economic growth is mainly the result of economic forces within the developing country. Since the remainder of this book is concerned with these economic forces, we shall put them aside in this chapter. As the following chapters will make clear, however, there is no single economic barrier to development that accounts for why so few countries were able to initiate growth prior to the middle of the twentieth century. Savings rates in many of these countries were too low to pay for the investment needed to achieve development, but the crucial question is why were savings rates so low. Poverty alone is not a cause of low savings rates. Even very poor countries, such as Japan in the late nineteenth century, were able to mobilize large amounts of savings. Japan could mobilize large amounts of savings in part because it had a strong governmental structure with a tradition of extracting large tax payments from the population.

Therefore, while there are economic causes for the prevalence of poverty in large parts of the world, economic explanations alone cannot account for why particular economic barriers exist. Economists are uncomfortable when they leave the realm of economic explanations, in part because the tools of economic analysis are of only limited help outside the sphere for which they were designed. But if one is seriously interested in understanding why some countries have had so much trouble initiating growth, there is little choice but to explore the relationship between economic development on the one hand, and political and social obstacles to development on the other.

Political Obstacles to Development

Economic development in England in the eighteenth century began with little direct assistance from the government, but since that time government's role in development has risen steadily to a point where successful growth is not really possible without the active support of a government. In subsequent chapters the role of many kinds of specific governmental policies in promoting economic development will be explained in detail. For our purposes here one mainly needs to know that an active, positive role for government is essential. It follows that if a government is unwilling or unable to play such a role, then the government itself can be considered a barrier to development or a fundamental cause of poverty.

Political Stability

To begin with, governments must be able to create and maintain a stable environment for modern enterprises, whether public or private. At a minimum, civil war, sustained insurrection, or invasion by hostile forces must be avoided. It is an obvious point but one frequently forgotten in discussions of the nature of development. Prolonged instability connected with civil war and foreign invasion goes a long way toward explaining why China failed to enter into modern economic growth prior to 1949. By extension, the creation of a stable environment after 1949 helps to explain why growth began then. More recently Vietnam with a civil war raging, was obviously not in a position to develop its economy on a sustained basis in the 1950s and 1960s, and the same was true of Cambodia in the 1970s and 1980s. China, Cambodia, and Vietnam are extreme cases, but a much longer list of countries, including Bolivia, Pakistan, Ghana, Ethiopia, El Salvador, Somalia, Rwanda, and many others, have experienced prolonged domestic political instability of a kind that has inhibited growth. Bolivia, for example, has had 150 governments since independence in 1825. Investors will not put their money into projects that pay off only over the long run if, in the short run, a change of government could lead to the project's being confiscated or rendered unprofitable by new laws and other restrictions. Where instability is particularly rife, a common solution among the wealthy has been to stop investing in the local economy and to ship off a large part of their wealth to banks in the United States, Switzerland, or Singapore or to indulge in conspicuous consumption.

Political Independence

But a stable environment alone is not enough. Colonial governments were usually quite stable, often for very long periods of time. There were rebellions against British rule in India, French rule in North Africa, and Japanese rule in Korea, but these rebellions were generally short-lived or on the periphery of the colony. Furthermore, most colonial governments had a very specific interest in creating a stable environment for private business. Yet few, if any, European or Japanese colonies experienced anything that could be described as sustained economic development. Part of the explanation is that the stable environment created was often only for the benefit of a small number of traders and investors from the colonizing country, whereas the citizens of the colonies themselves received little such support. Probably a more important part of the explanation, however, is that most colonial governments made only limited investments in training local people, in developing electric power resources, or in promoting industry. Thus, in most cases political independence was necessary before modern economic growth was possible. Conceivably, colonial governments could have promoted genuine development, but for the most part they did not. Later in this chapter we shall return to the question of whether relations between rich and poor countries today continue to possess some of the features that characterized the colonial era.

The Politics of Development Policy

Achieving independence and ending civil war and other threats to government stability are only the first step toward a political environment that is conducive to economic development. All governments, including stable independent ones, face numerous political constraints on their actions. An original meaning of the word "policy" was the art of government. Economic policy is thus concerned with the art of government in the economic sphere, with politics as well as with economic analysis.

Bad economic policy can prevent economic growth from getting underway, and it can bring growth to a halt after it has started. The concept of **takeoff** is seen frequently in the development literature and is at the center of economic historian Walt Rostow's analysis of the stages of economic growth.[2] Often the term means simply that a country has entered into a period of modern economic growth, and it causes few problems when used that way. Frequently, however, the term has been used in ways that imply much more. Specifically, the term has been used to imply that development, once started, proceeds automatically along well-traveled routes until the country becomes a modern industrialized state.

The problem with the concept is that, once started, economic development does not necessarily proceed without interruption. Economic development itself, particularly in its early stages, can create enormous social and political tensions that can undermine the stability so necessary for growth. The classic example from the early part of the twentieth century is the case of Argentina. To many observers in the 1910s and 1920s, Argentina seemed well on its way to becoming a modern industrial state. At the time it was considered more advanced than Canada. But as urbanization and industrialization progressed, the expanding Argentinean working class became increasingly alienated from the country's leadership. Juan Peron was able to use this alienation to build a political organization that brought him to power in 1946. To keep his support, however, Peron carried out measures that were popular with his constituents, such as price control of food grains and enlarged military expenditures, but that stifled growth and divided society into sharply contending classes. More importantly, long after Peron left office, the forces he unleashed prevented the country from establishing a consensus behind any government that would maintain stability and promote growth.

More recent examples of similar connections between the early stages of economic development and political instability can be found in Pakistan and Iran. In the 1960s Pakistan experienced a decade of fairly rapid industrialization, but most of this industrialization was concentrated in the western half of the country. East Pakistan made few gains, and the people there felt that the west was developing at their expense. It matters little now whether West Pakistan exploited East Pakistan; the people in the east perceived that they were the losers. The result was a civil war, the splitting of an already geographically divided country in two with the formation of Bangladesh, and the subsequent instability and economic stagnation in Bangladesh.

Iran presents a variation on the same theme. Oil revenues in the 1950s and 1960s fueled rapid industrial development, which accelerated even more dramatically after the quadrupling of the price of oil in 1973. Oil revenues, however, were also used extravagantly in the purchase of weapons, in large capital-intensive projects such as the Teheran subway, and in fueling corruption among Iran's elite. Iran's new wealth, far from buying stability, increased the alienation of the great majority of the people, who felt that the nation's wealth was being monopolized by the corrupt few. When combined with other deeply felt grievances, such as those of the religious fundamentalists led by Ayatollah Khomeini, the result was a

2. W. W. Rostow, *Stages of Economic Growth,* (2d ed.; New York: Cambridge University Press, 1971; 1st ed., 1960).

year of rioting and demonstrations, culminating in the fall of the Shah and his army.

Examples such as these have brought home to development economists as well as others that an understanding of political context is an essential element in effective economic policy making. Understanding the political context in turn starts from a recognition that governments are led by politicians, not philosopher kings. Philosopher kings can ignore the special interests of various groups within the country and, with the help of competent engineers and economists, design development programs that maximize the benefits to society as a whole. Politicians must first take steps to ensure that the groups of people who put them into office will continue to support them. Or they must worry about avoiding policies that will create new opposition groups or invigorate old ones.

That politicians in a democracy must pay attention to the special interests of their supporters requires little elaboration. But authoritarian governments also have their constituencies. The power of President Park Chung Hee in the Korea of the 1960s and 1970s rested on the dual pillars of the Korean army and the conservative farmers of the southeastern provinces. The political power of Argentina's Juan Peron rested on well-organized urban labor unions. The government bureaucracy can itself be a basis of authoritarian political power, and government bureaucracies have their own special interests or goals.

These various constituencies come into play whenever difficult economic policy choices must be made. In fact, more often than not, it is the desires and goals of these constituencies that make the choices difficult in the first place. Economic growth may require improved management of state-owned enterprises, for example, or the removal of large food subsidies causing a government budget deficit. Removal of food subsidies for urban workers frequently leads to widespread urban rioting. Such riots occurred in Egypt in 1977, in Zambia in 1990, and in numerous other countries before and since. Stopping inflation usually involves stopping the rapid rise in the money supply, which in turn requires the government to cut expenditures and increase revenues in order to eliminate the government deficit that is causing the rise in money supply. But in much of Latin America, as elsewhere, organized interest groups mobilize to prevent the government from cutting "their" expenditures or raising "their" taxes. The result is that the deficit is not cut and chronic inflation continues.

Currency devaluations can be a powerful tool for countries with severe balance-of-payments problems, a common phenomenon in developing countries. Devaluing the currency, as explained more fully in Chapter 19, raises the cost of imports and the price of exports, and so leads to a contraction of the former and an expansion of the latter. In Ghana in 1970, just such a devaluation was carried out for the purpose of closing a large unsustainable excess of imports over exports. But most imports were luxury goods consumed by the urban elite including the army. Two weeks later, using the sharp rise in the cost of luxury goods as an excuse, the army took over the government in a coup d'etat.

In recent years scholars and practitioners of economic policy reform have attempted to incorporate politics into their analysis in a more systematic way. One important issue has been whether or not to institute a full range of reforms all at once, what is sometimes referred to as the **big-bang approach** to economic reform. Poland in 1989–90 was the best example of the big-bang approach. As part of an effort to end spiraling inflation, the Poles cut out virtually all subsidies to consumers, many of which had been in place for decades. Producer subsidies to state-owned enterprises were also sharply curtailed, and an effort was begun to privatize production as rapidly as possible.

Price stabilization is often best handled by the big-bang approach. After a long period of rapid price increases, the population is frequently in a mood for any change that will end them. Drastic action becomes politically acceptable. When the drastic action works to stop the price rise, the government's credibility as a good manager of the economy is enhanced and continued fiscal discipline gains critical support. A gradual approach, in contrast, does not really solve the problem, and the population quickly tires of halfway austerity measures that inflict some pain but seem to do little long-term good.

Structural adjustments such as privatization of state-owned enterprises, however, do not lend themselves so readily to the big-bang method. In a country such as Poland, these enterprises have been used to following the dictates of planners who guaranteed inputs to the enterprise and sales by the enterprise. If the enterprise suddenly has to buy all its inputs on a market and sell its output on that same market, it may not know how to do this. It takes time, perhaps years, for managers to learn how to behave in the new environment. If government support is withdrawn immediately and totally, the enterprise may go bankrupt before managers learn the new ways. Workers will be thrown out of work and political support for reform will erode. In these circumstances a more gradual approach to reform may be required. These issues of the transition from a planned to a market economy will be discussed at greater length in Chapter 5.

Politics is, therefore, central to what impedes development and what makes development possible. Politics is in turn deeply rooted in the culture of a society. The social structure and politics of East Africa have little in common with the social structure and politics of East Asia. The political and social systems of Central America differ significantly from each other and even more from those of Central Africa or South Asia. To understand why some countries have experienced sustained economic development and others have not, therefore, the scholar and policy analyst must understand the politics as well as the economies of those countries.

International Obstacles to Development

Up to this point our analysis of the obstacles to development has concentrated on political obstacles that are internal to the less-developed world. To the extent that these internal conditions are the main reasons that economic growth did not occur in the past, successful development will depend on internal solutions to these internal problems. But some economists and others argue that the main barriers to development today are conditions external to the developing world. Specifically, the existence of already rich and industrialized countries, it has been argued, creates international political and economic pressures that hamper the growth efforts of today's poor countries.

Before reviewing the various arguments that stress the political and economic costs of relations between rich and poor countries, it is useful to present a brief synopsis of some of the beneficial economic aspects for poor countries in a world in which some countries are already rich. These positive economic elements are less controversial, and with them in mind, one can ask whether they are outweighed by the negative side of the ledger.

One important part of any argument about the positive side of rich-poor relations is based on the concept of gains from trade. Since these gains are considered in some detail in Chapter 17, only a brief listing will be attempted here.

Gains from Trade: A Preliminary View

To begin with, the **theory of comparative advantage** states that nations with different endowments of capital, labor, and natural resources will gain by specializing in those areas where their relative costs of production are low and importing in those areas where their relative costs of production are high. Further, the greater the difference in endowments between countries—and the differences between rich and poor countries are great indeed—the greater these gains from trade are likely to be. In certain extreme cases, but ones that occur in the real world, a country possesses one resource or factor, such as land or oil, in such abundance that it is impossible to make effective internal use of all of that resource. Trade makes it possible to use this surplus resource because the country can export what is not needed at home to purchase things that are needed. Saudi Arabia could not possibly use all the petroleum it is capable of producing, or Canada all the wheat from its great plains. Trade thus becomes what is sometimes referred to as a **vent for surplus.**

Developing countries also gain from trade because capital resources can only be transferred from rich to poor countries (and vice versa) through trade. In addition, some countries' export-producing enterprises are among their most progressive businesses because they have to be to survive international competition. The example set by these progressive firms then influences the operation of domestic enterprises.

Drawing on Experience

The gains from trade, however, encompass only a part of the economic advantages of poor nations that exist in a world where some countries have already achieved sustained development. The term used by Gerschenkron to describe this broader phenomenon is the "advantages of backwardness." Developing countries are in a position to learn from the experience of already-advanced nations. The most obvious area in which these advantages exist is the realm of science and technology. But the advantages are not confined to science and technology.

By the middle of the twentieth century, advanced countries had acquired a great deal of experience with management of enterprises, with national economic policy making, and even with widely different kinds of economic systems. In the late eighteenth century, laissez-faire capitalism was probably the only system capable of achieving modern economic growth in England. During World War I, however, wartime conditions led Germany and others to experiment with close state management of the economy. In the 1930s the Soviet Union, building on the World War I experience of others, developed what we know today as the Soviet-type or socialist system of planned economy. When China opted for a fully socialized economy in the 1950s, Chinese planners were able to draw on Soviet experience, often to the extent of simply translating Soviet planning rules and regulations into Chinese and then putting them into effect. The Chinese later modified the Soviet planning system to make it more suitable to Chinese conditions, but the point is that without prior Soviet experience, China would have had to move much more cautiously in setting up a centrally planned economy. In a similar fashion, South Korea learned much from the experience of Japan about how to operate a privately owned but state-managed economy.

There are situations, of course, where having a wide range of choices makes it possible for a country to make the wrong choice. Some nations would be better off if they had no range of options and instead had to follow a single optimal or at least feasible development path. But other nations have benefited from being able to make choices that took into account their own local economic, political, and social conditions.

Imperialism

While almost everyone acknowledges the potential advantages of learning from the experience of others, many have argued that this potential is seldom realized in practice because advanced countries create barriers to the progress of poor countries. Many economists and other scholars have attempted to explain the nature and sources of these barriers imposed on the less-developed world, but the largest group of theorists in one way or another owe an intellectual debt to Karl Marx and to Lenin, the architect of the Russian revolution.

Marxian Approaches to Development

One of the centerpieces of Karl Marx's theory of capitalist development was the view that the rate of profits on capital inevitably declines as growth takes place.[3] These profits were produced by labor from the surplus, or the excess, of what was needed to meet the subsistence needs of that labor. Competition in the face of this declining rate of profit leads to the stronger capitalists swallowing up the weaker, who then join the ranks of the proletariat, or workers. Economic crises or depressions become more severe as development proceeds, and the wages of workers may actually decline as capitalists squeeze them harder in a desperate attempt to keep profits up. The end result is a revolution that overthrows the rule of the capitalist class.

By the late nineteenth and early twentieth centuries, there was little evidence to support the view that the rate of profit was declining, and it was clear that real wages were rising. At the same time, however, the capitalist powers of Europe were vigorously expanding their colonial empires. The question then became whether there was a connection between the two phenomena. Workers in the colony also produced a surplus. If the imperial power could drain off enough of that colonial surplus, it could maintain profits at home and perhaps have enough left over to raise the wages of workers so that they would not become restless.

Conversely, from the colonial country's point of view, its development was severely inhibited because its surplus was being drained off abroad. In the absence

3. Karl Marx. *Das Kapital,* the first volume of which was published in 1867.

of this surplus, the colony had few resources of its own to invest while at the same time it was receiving only small amounts of investment from abroad.

In this form the basic propositions of the theory can be tested empirically. The issue is mainly whether the flow of surplus, or profits and tax revenues, from the colonial to the imperialist country was large enough to keep the profit rate in the capitalist country high or to keep the rate of investment in the colonial country low. The issue is not whether this drain of surplus made a few people of England and others very rich, but whether it accounted for a large share of the total profits of the capitalist world. More important from the point of view of development, was the drain of surplus large enough relative to the national product of the colonial country to have a significant impact on the investment, and hence development, prospects of that country? Even many early proponents of this Marxian viewpoint recognized, however, that it was difficult to find quantitative data with which to support the argument in this form.

The end of colonialism in much of the world did not by itself necessarily reduce the drain of surplus. Capitalist countries could continue to accomplish much of what was achieved by colonialism through private investment activities abroad. But there was also little quantitative evidence to support this hypothesis.

A different tack taken by other scholars is that what was lost was a potential, rather than actual, surplus. The drain of profits from the developing world might not be large, but measures taken by the capitalist countries may have prevented the developing countries from producing the surplus that would have existed in the absence of capitalist pressures from abroad. Some argued, for example, that free-trade policies imposed on the developing world made it impossible to protect infant industries, and hence those industries did not develop. The resources that would have gone to produce industrial output and funds for further investment instead lay idle. It is argued that free trade, leading to imports of manufactured cloth and the like, also destroyed local handicrafts and thereby further contributed to the unemployment of domestic resources. Still other scholars have argued that the drain of profits was real enough, but hidden by the way prices were set for goods transferred from the industrial to the developing nation. Multinationals, it is argued, charge much higher prices when they sell to developing countries than when they sell the same product at home.

Modern Theories of Imperialism

Modern theories of imperialism or of the nature of relations between rich and poor countries continue to use many of these older themes, but there has been a definite shift of emphasis. There are also many differences in analysis and emphasis among scholars writing about imperialism. Broadly, however, these scholars share the view that slow growth, extreme inequality, and high levels of unemployment in developing countries arise out of unequal relations of power both between rich and poor countries and between classes within the poorer developing countries. Furthermore, a solution to these problems of poverty requires a fundamental change in these power relations usually involving the elimination of capitalist class structures and values.[4]

4. Keith Griffin and John Gurley, "Radical Analyses of Imperialism, the Third World, and the Transition to Socialism," *Journal of Economic Literature,* 23, no. 3 (September 1985), 1090–91.

As to why capitalist countries are inherently imperialistic, the important point is not so much a declining rate of profit shored up by returns from abroad as it is the need of capitalist firms to secure a reliable supply of natural resources and markets. Capitalist firms, therefore, are interested in protecting their investments abroad, and to that end they want a large military force at home and abroad capable of providing that protection. But workers in capitalist societies also benefit from this large military force even though they gain nothing, or less than nothing, from foreign investments. In the absence of such military expenditures, scholars like Stanford economist Paul Baran argued, there would be a great depression and large-scale unemployment in capitalist countries.[5] This belief is based on a Keynesian-like analysis of the sources of unemployment. In addition to avoiding unemployment, workers in the large defense industries benefit directly from military expenditures. Thus the presence of democracy in the capitalist world does not prevent imperialism because large numbers of voters in that world see imperialism, at least indirectly, as being in their interests.

For poor countries attempting to develop, the emphasis has shifted away from the role of a direct drain of surplus to collusion between advanced-country capitalists and antigrowth forces within the developing country. The issue is not so much the drain of surplus abroad as it is the misuse of that surplus at home.

There are many variations on this basic theme. Some scholars argue that it is in the interest of advanced-country capitalists to keep raw materials flowing from developing countries. Industrial growth within the developing country would be harmful to both goals since local industrial products would compete with imports and would also bid for local raw materials. The old ruling classes made up of landlords and other feudal elements also have no interest in promoting the rise of industrial capitalists who would compete with them for power and who might find it in the interest of industry to advocate such measures as land reform. Although some commercial capitalists exist in such societies, it is argued that they too tend to side with foreign investors and the feudal ruling classes because they make their living from the existing pattern of trade and do not want competition from newer patterns. Capitalists with this orientation are sometimes referred to as "compradores." Even the workers in modern establishments share this viewpoint, because their wages are so much higher than the average. The end result is an alliance of foreign investors backed by their governments, feudal landlords, and merchant capitalists and their workers, who together keep a government in power that does little to promote development.

Income Inequality and the Demand for Luxury Products

Another variation on this theme is that put forward by the prominent Brazilian economist Celso Furtado.[6] Furtado starts from the proposition, for which there is much evidence, that poor countries in the early stages of development tend to have a very unequal distribution of income. As a result demand for industrial

5. Paul Baran, *The Political Economy of Growth* (New York: Monthly Review Press, 1957).

6. Celso Fuirtado, "The Brazilian 'Model' of Development," in Charles K. Wilber (ed.), *The Political Economy of Development and Underdevelopment* (New York: Random House, 1979), pp. 324–33.

products in these societies tends to be concentrated on luxury products such as automobiles, since the poor have little money left over after purchasing food and housing. It is precisely luxury goods such as automobiles that are usually either imported from abroad or produced domestically by foreign firms. Local enterprises and investors lack the capital or know-how to produce such sophisticated products in the early stages of development. Foreign investors have an interest in keeping the distribution of income unequal because that is what keeps up demand for products only they can produce. The local ruling class has the same interest because they are the beneficiaries of this unequal distribution. Growth is slow because foreign investors only invest the minimum necessary to maintain control of the local market.

A key link in this argument is the connection between income inequality and the demand for luxury products. It is a link that can be tested empirically by observing what happens to demand in a given country when income is redistributed in a way to achieve greater equality. Although the tests are not conclusive because of the limitations of the data used, the results so far indicate that a major redistribution of income does not lead to large shifts in the structure of demand. The demand for a luxury good such as automobiles might fall, but there is little change in the demand for steel, cement, and machine tools, to mention only a few important items.

The common theme of these theories of imperialism, therefore, is that local elites combine with foreign capitalist powers to keep a government in power that pursues policies that put obstacles in the way of economic development. The differences among the theories are mainly over the reason why this collusion of anti-growth forces exists, not whether it exists.

There is also variation in emphasis about which policies, when forced on the poor of the developing world, most inhibit their prospects for a rise from poverty. Some continue to stress how in the developing world, the imposition of free-trade policies leads to an overemphasis on investment in natural resources and an underinvestment in industry. Others argue that foreign investment in developing countries, far from enriching those countries, is later returned to the industrialized world through repatriated profits, artificially low prices for developing-country exports, and high interest payments on developing-country debt. More will be said about these specific policies in later chapters.

While there are variations on how the imperialism of the industrialized world and the dependency of the developing world stifle growth and promote inequality, scholars who make these arguments share a common view that progress for a developing country is possible only if its ties to the international capitalist system are severed. It is this claim for universality, however, that is the weakest point in these analyses of the relationship between rich and poor countries. It is simply too easy to demonstrate that some countries with close ties to the capitalist world economic system have achieved rapid economic growth and, in a few cases, even a reduction in inequality. Taiwan is the clearest case in point, where both rapid growth and falling inequality have been achieved by increasing the island's integration into the international economic system, not by decreasing that involvement. A much longer list of countries has achieved rapid growth by exporting more to the capitalist world—growth in which most have shared in the benefits but not on an equal basis.

If the claim to universality is dropped and the argument is simply that some countries are hurt by becoming entangled in the capitalist economic system, few would object. The issue then becomes one of how, and under what circumstances, to become involved in world trade and capital movements, not whether to become involved at all. Few economists today, for example, would argue with the proposition that Mexico and Brazil would be better off if they had avoided becoming so dependent on loans from Western banks in the 1970s.

In a similar vein, Ethiopia under the rule of Emperor Haile Selassie was afraid of many key development-oriented reforms precisely because they would undermine the government's domestic sources of support. Certainly the Selassie government's ability to stay in power was also reinforced by continuing support from such countries as the United States. Similar situations involving external political support from France, Britain, and others can be found elsewhere. On the other hand, when Ethiopia overthrew Haile Selassie and switched its main international ties from the United States to the Soviet Union and Cuba, the country's economy continued to stagnate and suffer from famine. Even in the case of Ethiopia, poverty was only in part the result of the country's ties to the capitalist economic and political system.

Clearly international influences operating through politics as well as economics can have a profound impact on the course of a country's development. Warfare is an extreme form of the negative influences that are possible, but there are many subtler effects on both the positive and negative side of the ledger. Which effects are likely to predominate in any given country depends on the particular historical circumstances in which that country finds itself.

The one clear conclusion is that there is no single cause for why some countries took longer to initiate growth than others or for why some have yet to enter into sustained modern economic growth even today. Nor is there any single set of explanations that applies to all countries. Instead there are a wide variety of reasons for the continued poverty of countries, some of which apply in certain cases but not in others. The list of elements, both internal and external, that may have some negative influence on the prospects for development is a long one. And yet many countries have managed to enter into sustained periods of economic development, and the number of such countries is growing. The political and social barriers to development are being overcome among an ever-widening proportion of the world's people.

3

Growth and Structural Change

Once started, economic development proceeds along paths that vary somewhat from country to country. The United States and Germany, for example, did not follow slavishly the patterns of development set by England, the first developing country. The economic growth strategies of China and India were different from those of Europe or Japan.

There are some features of the development process that are common to all countries, however. The next sections of this chapter introduce a framework of analyzing why some growth rates are higher than others and for explaining what we know about the patterns of development that have occurred in the past and are likely to occur in the future. Attempts to determine the basic sources and patterns of growth have followed two very different approaches—one empirical and the other theoretical. One group of economists, best represented by Simon Kuznets of Harvard and Hollis B. Chenery formerly with the World Bank, has attempted to discern patterns of development through an analysis of data on the gross national product and the structure of that product for dozens of countries around the world and through time. The search has been for patterns that are common to all countries, or more realistically, to a large subgroup of countries.

The second approach has been to construct theories of how the structure of a country's economy could be expected to change given various assumptions about the conditions facing that country. This theoretical approach has a long tradition stretching back to Adam Smith and David Ricardo of the eighteenth and nineteenth centuries. In the 1950s and 1960s theorists of growth and structural change included such economists as Roy Harrod, Evsey Domar, Robert Solow, W. Arthur

Lewis, John Fei, and Gustav Ranis. In the 1980s and 1990s, the **new growth economics** theorists and modern proponents of neoclassical growth theory included Paul Romer, Robert Lucas, Robert Barro, Dale Jorgenson, and many others.

In economics the ultimate objective is to develop theories whose validity can then be tested with the data available. Therefore, the empirical or data-based approach and the theoretical approach are not two different ways of looking at a given problem, but are two parts of what is really a single approach. Increasingly in practice these two approaches are being combined, but to simplify the exposition that follows, the two approaches will be presented separately.

Estimating Gross National Product

Kuznets and Chenery approach the analysis empirically. Before we can talk about the empirical approach to an analysis of the sources of growth and of the patterns of development, however, it is important to understand both the strengths and particularly the weaknesses of the data used to measure those patterns. In essence the analysis of patterns of development involves relating trends in gross national product per capita to trends in the various components of gross national product. **Gross national product** (GNP) is the sum of the value of finished goods and services produced by a society during a given year and excludes **intermediate goods** (goods used up in the production of other goods, such as the steel used in an automobile or the chips that go into a computer). GNP counts only income earned by citizens of the country including wages and profits earned by them outside the country. **Gross domestic product** (GDP) is similar to GNP except that it counts all income produced within the borders of a country, including income earned by resident foreigners, but excludes wages and profits earned by citizens of the country from sources abroad.

The share of a sector or component of GNP such as manufacturing or agriculture is measured by the value added by that sector. **Value-added** refers to the addition to the value of the product at a particular stage of production. Thus the value-added of the cotton textile industry is the value of the textiles when they leave the factory minus the value of raw cotton and other materials used in their manufacture. Value-added, in turn, is equal to the payments to the factors of production in the textile industry: wages paid to labor plus profits, interest, depreciation of capital, and rents for buildings and land.

The great advantage of the GNP concept is that it encompasses all a country's economic activity in a few mutually consistent summary statistics. The alternative of describing growth in terms of tons of steel and kilowatt-hours of electricity either leaves out much economic activity or, in an effort to be inclusive, involves the hopelessly complex discussion of thousands of individual products. The analysis of individual products in physical terms can be misleading, particularly in the measurement of broad economic change over time. Cotton textile output, for example, may fall over time, but the output of textiles made from artificial fibers may be increasing by more than enough to offset that fall. Gross national product provides a consistent technique for adding these two different trends together.

If the concept of gross national product has certain advantages, it also has certain important limitations, particularly when comparing patterns of development in a wide variety of developing countries. One difficulty is that poor countries usually have poor statistical services; data from certain sectors of poor countries, such as agriculture and handicrafts, are the worst of all. Estimates of the gross national product of many developing nations are based on fairly reliable statistics of modern industrial and mining enterprises combined with estimates of rural-sector performance based on small samples or outright guesses.

In addition to data limitations, there are basic methodological issues that get in the way of reliable estimates.

What Is Included in GNP?

To begin with, there is a problem with the definition of gross national product. The proper way to calculate GNP is to add up all the goods and services that are produced by a country and then sold on the market. In adding up steel and mangos, one can use either the prices at which steel and mangos were sold on the market **(GNP at market prices)** or one can use the cost of all factor inputs (labor, capital, land) used to produce a ton of steel or a bushel of mangos **(GNP at factor cost).** Many valuable contributions to society are therefore excluded from gross national product. When housework and child care are performed by paid servants or day-care employees, for example, they are included in GNP, but when they are performed by unpaid members of the household, they do not enter GNP. In developing countries a very large number of activities do not enter the market. Much of what is produced by the agricultural sector, to take the most important example, is consumed by the farm household and never reaches the market. Strictly speaking, one cannot meaningfully discuss the changing share of agriculture in GNP but only the changing share of the marketed agricultural product in GNP. Because this strict definition of GNP would severely limit the usefulness of comparing structural change among countries in which agriculture is the dominant sector, the usual practice is to include farm output consumed by the producer, with that produce valued at the prices of marketed farm produce. While making GNP a more meaningful indicator of the productive capacity of a developing economy, this procedure turns GNP into a somewhat arbitrary concept. If nonmarketed agricultural produce is included, for example, why not include household-provided child care services? A related issue that works in an opposite way from subsistence agriculture is the treatment of nonrenewable resources such as petroleum or silver. The value-added of mining products includes the original value of the ore as well as the value-added of the labor and capital needed to mine that ore. But the original value of the ore was not produced by the economy and hence does not really belong in GNP. We shall return to the issue of nonrenewable resources in Chapter 17.

Exchange-Rate Conversion Problems

A second methodological problem arises when attempting to convert the GNP of several different countries into a single currency. To compare the changing economic structure of several countries as per capita income rises, one must measure the per capita income figures in a common currency. The shortcut to accomplishing this goal is to use the official exchange rate between U.S. dollars and each national currency. For example, to convert Pakistan's GNP from rupees into U.S. dollars, the official exchange rate between rupees and U.S. dollars (over 31 rupees per U.S. dollar in 1995) is used. One problem with this procedure is that exchange rates, particularly those of developing countries, are frequently highly distorted. Trade restrictions make it possible for an official exchange rate to be substantially different from a rate determined by free trade.

But even an accurate estimate of the exchange rate that would prevail under a free-trade regime would not eliminate the problem. A significant part of GNP is made up of what are called **nontraded goods and services,** that is, goods that do not and often cannot enter into international trade. Electric power, for example, can be imported only in rare cases from an immediate neighbor with a surplus to sell (the United States imports some electricity from Canada, for example). For the most part electric power must be generated within a country, and it makes little sense to talk about the international market or the international market price for electric power. By definition, internal transportation cannot be traded, although many transport inputs, such as trucks, can be imported. Wholesale and retail trade or elementary school teachers are nontraded services. The wages of workers in these nontraded services are less influenced by any international market.

Gross national product converted to U.S. dollars by exchange rates that are determined by the flow of traded goods alone will give misleading comparisons if the ratio of prices of nontraded goods to prices of traded goods is different in the countries being compared. The way around this problem is to pick a set of prices prevailing in one of the countries and use that set of prices to value the goods of all countries being compared. In effect what one is doing is calculating a **purchasing power parity** exchange rate. The essence of the procedure can be illustrated with the simple numerical exercise presented in Table 3–1. The two economies in the table are called the United States and India, and each economy produces one traded commodity (steel) and one nontraded service (measured by the number of retail sales people). The price of steel is given in U.S. dollars in the United States and rupees in India, and the exchange rate is based on the ratio of the prices of the traded good (in this case, steel). The value of the services of retail sales personnel is estimated in the most commonly used way, which is to assume the value of the service is equal to the wages of the service personnel. The two methods of converting Indian GNP into U.S. dollars are presented in the table. Clearly, one gets very different results depending on which method is used.

Systematic estimates using the two different methods on a select group of countries are presented in Table 3–2. While many of the differences in results between the two methods are not as great as in our numerical illustration, they are still substantial. Furthermore there is a reasonably systematic relation between the degree to which the exchange-rate conversion method understates GNP and the level of development of the country. For Germany and the United States, whose per capita GNPs were not far apart in 1992, the exchange-rate conversion is a reasonable approximation of what is obtained when converting German GNP into U.S. dollars using the better method. For Kenya, however, the ratio between the two results is 4.39 to 1. With differences of that magnitude, exchange-rate conversions are misleading.

Other Index-Number Problems

The issue being discussed here is part of a larger group of issues generally referred to as **index-number problems.** Index-number problems arise not only in

TABLE 3–1 Exchange Rate versus Purchasing Power Parity Methods of Converting GNP into a Single Currency

	United States			India		
	Quantity	Price (U.S. dollars)	Value of output (billion U.S. dollars)	Quantity	Price (rupees)	Value of output (billion rupees)
Steel (million tons)	100	200 per ton	20	8	6,000 per ton	48
Retail sales personnel (millions)	2	5,000 per person per year	10	4	30,000 per person per year	120
Total GNP (local currency)			30			168

Official exchange rate, based on steel prices, = 6,000/200, or Rs 30 = U.S. $1.

1. Indian GNP in U.S. dollars calculated by using the official exchange rate:

   168/30 = U.S. $5.6 billion.

2. Indian GNP in U.S. dollars calculated by using U.S. prices for each individual product or service and applying that price to Indian quantities:

Steel	8 million × $ 200	= $ 1.6 billion
Retail sales personnel	4 billion × $5,000	= $20 billion
GNP		= $21.6 billion.

3. Ratio of 2 to 1:

   21.6/5.6 = 3.9.

TABLE 3–2 Gross Domestic Product* per Capita in 1992 (U.S. Dollars)

	Using official exchange-rate conversion (1)	Using dollar prices for each individual product (2)	Ratio 2 to 1 (3)
United States	23,240	23,120	.99
Germany	23,030	20,610	.89
Japan	28,190	20,160	.72
United Kingdom	17,790	16,730	.94
South Korea	6,790	8,950	1.32
Mexico	3,470	7,490	2.16
Colombia	1,330	5,760	4.33
Indonesia	1,905	2,970	1.56
Bolivia	680	2,270	3.34
Ghana	450	1,890	4.20
Kenya	310	1,360	4.39
India	310	1,210	3.90

* Gross Domestic Product (GDP) is similar to Gross National Product (GNP). GDP can be derived from GNP by subtracting payments to a country's own factors (capital and labor) from abroad and adding payments to foreign factors remitted abroad. In brief, GDP includes everything produced within a country no matter who receives the income, but excludes income from abroad by residents of the country.

Source: These figures were derived from *World Development Report 1994*, pp. 162–63, 220–21.

the comparison of two countries using two different currencies, but also in the study of the growth of a single country over a long period of time. As growth occurs, it usually happens that relative prices change; that is, the prices of some commodities fall while the prices of others rise. If the country is experiencing **inflation,** which is a sustained increase in the general price level, all prices are rising, but some rise faster than others so that relative prices still change. To eliminate the impact of inflation on the statistics, economists measure *real* increases (actual growth) rather than nominal increases (where the prices also grow) in GNP. The proper procedure is to recalculate GNP in each year using the prices of only one year. But which year should we pick? Estimates of the growth rate will differ as one uses the prices of different years, just as the ratio of Indian to U.S. GNP will vary if one uses Indian prices to value both countries' GNPs in one case and U.S. prices in another.

A hypothetical illustration of the impact of base-year versus current-year prices is presented in Table 3–3. In this example a higher growth rate is achieved using base-year rather than current-year prices. This happens because the relative price of the industrial product (television sets) is higher in the base year (when TV sets were scarce) than in the current year (when they are more abundant), and thus the faster-growing industrial product accounts for a larger share of total product when base-year prices are used. In most countries the industrial sector is growing faster than the agricultural sector, and hence a set of prices that gives the industrial sector a larger weight in national product will result in a higher GNP growth rate.

Data problems are, therefore, pervasive whenever one studies the aggregate performance of an economy as it evolves over time or compares the aggregate performance of two different economies. When comparing the steel ingot output of two countries, it is possible to say precisely how many more tons of steel one of the countries produces when compared with the other. There is no comparable precision when one compares large aggregates such as GNP. A certain ambiguity is always present when these figures are used to measure the sources of growth or to search for similarities in the development patterns across countries or over time.

The emphasis here has been on data issues connected with the estimation of

TABLE 3–3 Base-Year versus Current-Year Price Calculation of GNP

	Base year (1972)		Current year (1994)	
Product per year	Quantity	Price (U.S. dollars)	Quantity	Price (U.S. dollars)
Television sets (millions)	1	300	50	100
Wheat (million tons)	100	100	200	150

1. GNP index using base-year prices:

$$100 \times \frac{(50 \times 300) + (100 \times 200)}{(1 \times 300) + (100 \times 100)} = 340.$$

2. GNP index using current-year prices:

$$100 \times \frac{(50 \times 100) + (150 \times 200)}{(1 \times 100) + (150 \times 100)} = 232.$$

GNP, but it should also be noted that increases in GNP are not synonymous with improvements in the welfare of the population. Welfare, for example, may be raised markedly by improvements in public health, but those health advances may have only a modest impact on the level of GNP. These and related issues will be taken up at greater length in Chapter 4.

One-Sector Growth Models

In Parts 2 and 3 we shall analyze how the quality and quantity of labor and of savings and investment are mobilized and used to promote economic development. The theory explaining the relationship between these inputs and the growth in national product is based on the **production function.** At the individual firm or microeconomic level, the production function tells how much the output of a firm or factory, such as a textile mill, will increase if the number of workers or the number of spindles and looms rises by a given amount. These are mathematical expressions, often derived from engineering specifications, that relate given amounts of physical inputs to the amount of physical output that can be produced with those inputs. Often, for convenience, microeconomic production functions are expressed in money values rather than in physical quantities.

At the national or economywide level, production functions describe the relationship of the size of a country's labor force and its stock of capital with the level of that country's gross national product. These economywide relationships are called **aggregate production functions.** They measure increases in the value of output or national product, given the value of increases in such inputs as the stock of capital and the labor force. Because both inputs and outputs are measured in aggregate terms (national capital stock, GNP), index-number and other measurement problems of the kind just described do introduce some ambiguity into the interpretation of economywide production functions. Still, it is the one tool we have for relating inputs and output at the national level within a consistent framework. For that reason, it is useful to see what this aggregate production function can tell us about how inputs contribute to growth before turning in later chapters to how those inputs can be mobilized.

The Harrod-Domar Model

The simplest and best-known production function used in the analysis of economic development was developed independently during the 1940s by economists Roy Harrod of England and Evsey Domar of MIT, primarily to explain the relationship between growth and unemployment in advanced capitalist societies.[1] But the Harrod-Domar model has been used extensively in developing countries as a simple way of looking at the relationship between growth and capital requirements.

The underlying assumption of the model is that the output of any economic unit, whether a firm, an industry, or the whole economy, depends on the amount of capital invested in that unit. Thus if we call the output Y and the stock of capital

1. Roy F. Harrod, "An Essay in Dynamic Theory, " *Economic Journal,* 1939, pp. 14–33, and Evsey Domar, "Capital Expansion, Rate of Growth, and Employment," *Econometrica*, 1946, pp. 137–47, and "Expansion and Employment," *American Economic Review,* 37 (1947), 34–55.

K, then output can be related to capital stock by

$$Y = K/k, \tag{3–1}$$

where k is a constant, called the capital-output ratio. To convert this into a statement about the growth of output, we use the notatation Δ to represent increases in output and capital and write

$$\Delta Y = \Delta K/k. \tag{3–2}$$

The growth rate of output g is simply the increment in output divided by the total amount of output, $\Delta Y/Y$. If we divided both sides of Equation 3–2 by Y, then

$$g = \Delta Y/Y = (\Delta K/Y) \cdot 1/k. \tag{3–3}$$

For the whole economy, ΔK is the same as investment I, which must equal savings S. Hence, $\Delta K/Y$ becomes I/Y, and this is equal to S/Y, which can be designated by the savings rate s, a percentage of national product. Equation 3–3 can then be converted to

$$g = s/k, \tag{3–4}$$

which is the basic Harrod-Domar relationship for an economy.

Underlying this equation is the view that capital created by investment in plant and equipment is the main determinant of growth and that it is savings by people and corporations that make investment possible. The **capital-output ratio** is simply a measure of the productivity of capital or investment. If an investment of $3,000 in a new plant and new equipment makes it possible for an enterprise to raise its output by $1,000 a year for many years into the future, then the capital-output ratio for that particular investment is 3:1. Economists often use the term **incremental capital-output ratio,** abbreviated ICOR, because in studying growth, one is mainly interested in the impact on output of additional or incremental capital. The incremental capital-output ratio measures the productivity of additional capital while the (average) capital-output ratio refers to the relationship between a country's total stock of capital and its total national product.

For economic planners, given this simple equation, the task is straightforward. The first step is to try to come up with an estimate of the incremental capital-output ratio (k in Equation 3–3) for the country whose plan is being drawn up. There are two alternatives for the next step. Either planners can decide on the rate of economic growth (g) they wish to achieve, in which case the equation will tell them the level of saving and investment necessary to achieve that growth. Or planners can decide on the rate of saving and investment that is feasible or desirable, in which case the equation will tell planners the rate of growth in national product that can be achieved.

This procedure can be applied to the economy as a whole, or it can be applied to each sector or each industry. Incremental capital-output ratios, for example, can be calculated separately for agriculture and industry. Once planners decide how much investment will be allocated to each sector, the Harrod-Domar equations determine the growth rates to be expected in each of the two sectors.

Production Functions

At the heart of this kind of analysis is the explicit or implicit assumption that the incremental capital-output ratio is a fixed number. This assumption is consistent with a production function that employs fixed proportions of capital and labor and constant returns to scale, like that depicted in Figure 3–1. Output in this figure is represented by **isoquants,** which are combinations of inputs (labor and capital in this case), that produce equal amounts of output. Only two isoquants are shown in this diagram. The L-shape of the isoquants indicates production processes that use fixed proportions of capital and labor. For example, it takes capital (plant and equipment) of $10 million and 100 workers to produce 100,000 tons of cement. If more workers are added without investing in more capital, output will not rise above 10,000 tons per year. Because the diagram is also drawn with **constant returns to scale,** if capital in the cement industry is doubled to $20 million and labor is doubled to 200 workers, output also doubles to 200,000 tons per year.

Most economists, however, believe that the production function (often referred to as the **neoclassical production function**) for many industries, and for the economy as a whole, looks more like that depicted in Figure 3–2. In this figure, if one starts with output of 100,000 tons at point *a,* using $10 million of capital and 100 workers (not shown in the figure), the industry could be expanded in any of three ways. If industry planners decide to expand at constant factor proportions and move to point *b* on isoquant II, the situation would be identical to the fixed proportions case of Figure 3–1. The capital-output ratio at both point *a* and point *b* would be 2:1. But production of 200,000 tons could be achieved by using more labor and less capital, a more labor-intensive method, at a point like *c* on isoquant II. In that case the incremental capital-output ratio (ICOR) falls to 1.4:1 if the price of cement is $50 a ton. Or if a more capital-intensive method is desired, such as the production technique given by *d* on isoquant II, the ICOR would rise to 2.8:1.

If the production function facing a country is neoclassical, then the capital-output ratio becomes a variable that is to some extent under the control of policy makers in the government. Considering production functions like those in Figure 3–2 from the industry level, policy makers in developing countries in which capi-

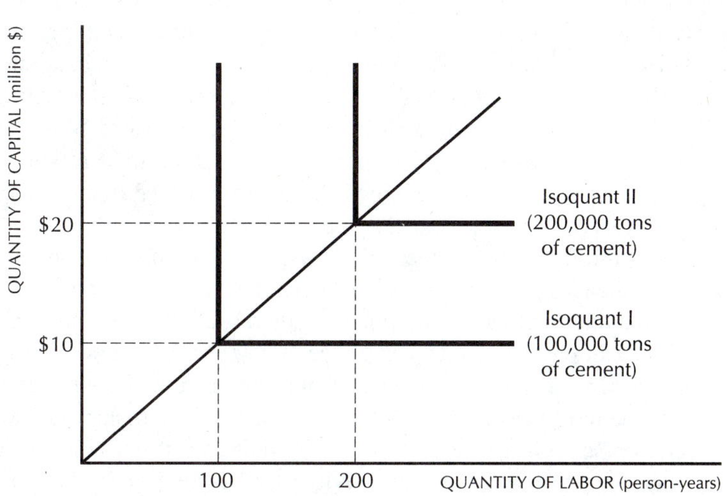

FIGURE 3–1 Production Function with Fixed Coefficients. With constant returns to scale, the isoquants will be L-shaped and the production function will be the straight line through their minimum-combination points.

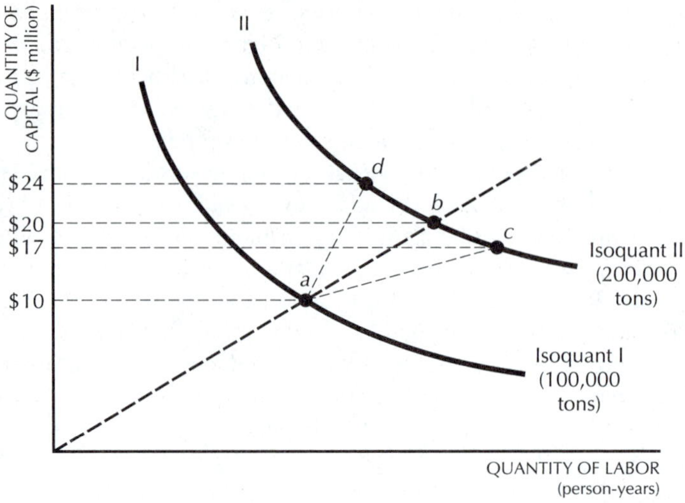

FIGURE 3–2 Neoclassical (Variable Proportions) Production Function. Instead of requiring fixed factor proportions, as in Figure 3-1, output can be achieved with varying combinations of labor and capital. This is called a **neoclassical** production function. The isoquants are curved, rather than L-shaped.

tal is scarce can try to induce manufacturers and farmers to employ more labor-intensive technologies. Then, for a given amount of saving and investment, both growth and employment can be higher. At the level of the whole economy, policy will encourage labor-intensive technologies as well as investment in the more labor-intensive industries, and so reduce the demand for investment and saving on both counts. The kinds of tools that policy makers may use to accomplish this reduction in the capital-output ratio are discussed in depth in several chapters of this text, especially Chapters 8, 13, and 17.

The appropriate incremental capital-output ratio will vary among countries and, for a single country, over time. Poor countries, with low savings rates and surplus (unemployed and underemployed) labor, can achieve higher growth rates by economizing on capital and utilizing as much labor as possible. As economies grow and per capita income rises, savings rates tend to increase and the labor surplus diminishes. Thus the ICOR shifts upward. In the more-advanced countries it can be higher than in the developing countries without sacrificing growth. And resource-rich developing countries, such as those exporting petroleum, can afford more capital-intensive development than other LDCs. These shifts in the ICORs can come about through market mechanisms as prices of labor and capital change in response to changes in supplies. As growth takes place, savings become relatively more abundant and hence the price of capital falls while employment and wages rise. Thus all producers increasingly economize on labor and use more capital. Alternatively, in Soviet-type and other planned economies, the planners can allocate investment in ways that move the economy toward an appropriate ICOR. Finally, technological change and "learning by doing" can play important roles. Both can contribute to increased productivity of all factors of production, which reduces the ICOR. In Figures 3–1 and 3–2, increased factor productivity can be represented by a shifting inward of each isoquant toward the origin.

Data on incremental capital-output ratios for a few selected countries are presented in Table 3–4. These ratios vary from under 3:1 to 7:1 and even higher. Some of these differences can be explained by the point made earlier that richer countries such as the United States, Norway, and Japan tend to have higher ratios because capital is less expensive relative to labor than in poorer countries in the early stages of development. Other differences, however, such as those between Korea and India, have little to do with differences in the relative scarcity of capital. These differences are more likely to be the result of the differences between countries in the efficiency with which capital and other inputs are managed.

Sources of Growth

The simple Harrod-Domar production function, therefore, obscures some of the basic differences in growth performance between countries. One wants to know much more about why the capital-output ratio varies so much. To that end, economists such as Robert Solow and Edward Denison have attempted to explain the sources of growth with a different form of the production function, one that allows the analyst to separate out the various causes of growth rather than subsume all these other causes in the capital-output ratio.

The production function used in this analysis is neoclassical like that depicted in Figure 3–2. However, more factors of production are included. The function relates increases in output to increases in inputs of capital, skilled and unskilled labor, and other variables. This method also attempts to separate out the contribution made by rises in the efficiency with which inputs are used. The production function takes the form

$$Y = f(K, L, R, A), \qquad [3\text{–}5]$$

TABLE 3–4 Selected Incremental Capital-Output Ratios*

	Incremental capital-output ratios*		
Country	1970–1981	1978–1987	1988–1992
United States	6.6	5.6	9.6
Japan	7.4	5.1	7.5
South Korea	3.3	4.0	4.4
Indonesia	2.6	5.5	5.2
India	6.0	5.7	4.7
Argentina	13.3	†	9.1
Brazil	2.8	4.8	†
Venezuela	6.8	†	4.6
Ivory Coast	4.2	8.2	†
Kenya	4.0	5.9	6.6
Tanzania	5.2	10.1	6.9

* These ratios were derived by dividing the average share of gross domestic investment in gross domestic product by the rate of growth in gross domestic product.

† Because there was little or negative growth in these countries during this period, the incremental capital-output ratio was around 100 or approaching ∞.

Sources: World Bank, *World Tables,* Vol. 1, Economic Data (1983), pp. 9, 23, 39, 85, 87, 95, 101, 103, 123, 175, 239, 247, 257; *World Tables* (1988), pp. 34–37, 62–65; and World Bank, *World Bank Tables 1994,* pp. 22–25, 58–61.

where Y = output or national product,
K = stock of capital,
L = size of the labor force,
R = stock of arable land and natural resources,
and A = increases in the productivity or efficiency with which inputs are used.

The next step is to convert this production function into a form that makes measuring the contribution of each input possible. The derivation of this new form of the equation involves calculus and so is presented in the appendix to this chapter. The resulting equation is

$$g_Y = a + W_K g_K + W_L g_L + W_R g_R \qquad [3\text{–}6]$$

where g = growth rate of any variable,
W = share in income of any input (e.g., the share of wages),
Y = national product,
K = capital stock,
L = labor,
R = arable land and natural resources,
and a = variable measuring the shift in the production function resulting from greater efficiency in the use of inputs.

Data for each of these variables can be found in the statistical handbooks of many countries and the contribution of each of these variables to growth can thus be measured and identified.

A simple numerical example illustrates the way in which this equation is used. Assume the following values for the variables in the equation:

$g_Y = 0.06$ (GNP growth rate of 6 percent a year)
$g_K = 0.07$ (capital stock rises at 7 percent a year)
$g_L = 0.02$ (labor force increases at 2 percent a year)
$g_R = 0.01$ (arable land is rising by 1 percent a year).

The share of labor in national income is 60 percent ($W_L = 0.6$), the share of capital is 30 percent ($W_K = 0.3$), and the share of land is 10 percent ($W_R = 0.1$). By substituting these figures into Equation 3–6, we get

$$0.06 = a + 0.3(0.07) + 0.6(0.02) + 0.1(0.01).$$

Solving for a, we get $a = 0.026$. What these figures tell us is that productivity growth is 2.6 percent a year and thus accounts for just under half the total growth of GNP of 6 percent a year.

Growth accounting or **sources of growth analysis,** as this method has been called, has been carried out for many countries. Because of variations in the way different economists carry out growth accounting, it is not possible to summarize the results of these calculations in a simple table. Two conclusions that have arisen from this empirical work, however, provide an important basis for much of the analysis in subsequent chapters.

First, most efforts to measure the sources of growth have indicated that increases in productivity or efficiency (a in Equation 3–6) account for a much higher proportion of growth than was believed to be the case before these calculations were made. Increases in the capital stock frequently account for less than half the increase in output, particularly in rapidly growing countries. Second, while capital does not contribute as much to growth as assumed in early growth models, capital does play a large role in the growth of today's developing countries. Furthermore, some of the increases in efficiency or productivity involve advances in technology that are embodied in capital equipment. Thus mobilization of capital remains a major concern of policy makers in developing countries and is the subject of four chapters in this text (Chapters 11 to 14), but mobilization of labor and improvements in the quality of that labor are also important (Chapters 9 and 10).

Edward Denison, Dale Jorgenson, and others have attempted to measure in a more precise way the contribution of these and other elements to rising productivity. Thus labor is divided into different categories based on the amounts of formal education that that labor has received. A worker having a high school education and earning \$20,000 a year is treated as the equivalent of two people having only primary school educations and earning \$10,000 a year each. Similar procedures are used to measure the increase in productivity that occurs when workers shift from low-productivity occupations in rural areas to higher-productivity occupations in urban areas. Other methods are used to measure improvements in the quality of capital and increasing use of economies of scale. Price distortions and other data problems, however, cause difficulties in the calculation of some of these measures for developing countries. Few developing countries, for example, have reliable measures for differences in quality of alternative capital inputs.

Another approach, associated with what has been called the **new growth economics,** has moved away from the kind of production function used by Solow. Instead of constant returns to scale, this approach often assumes that the national economy is subject to increasing returns to scale. These newer approaches also assume the presence of important **externalities.** The gain from education, for example, is not just determined by how much a scientist's or manager's productivity is raised by that individual's investment in his or her own education. If many scientists and managers invest in their own education, there will then be many educated people who will learn from each other. An isolated scientist working alone will not be as productive as one who can interact with dozens of well-educated colleagues. It is this interaction that constitutes the externality. Because the new growth economics typically uses equations based on differential calculus that are more complex than the Solow growth equation, a more formal presentation of the new growth economics approach will not be attempted here.

Most measures of the sources of growth, for all of their limitations given the quality of developing-country data or uncertainties about the precise nature of the production function, make clear that productivity growth as well as capital formation are both critical to achieving high rates of growth in per capita GNP. The sources of differences in productivity and capital formation that occur in the developing world are a recurring theme throughout this book.

The Changing Structure of Output

Structural change in the course of economic development thus involves rises in productivity and also increases in the capital stock relative to other inputs such as labor. Structural change also involves major shifts between the sectors that make up the output side of the production function equation. These shifts in the structure of output or national product are the subject of the remainder of this chapter. In this chapter we are mainly concerned with the relationship between these sectors as growth takes place. In later chapters (notably Chapters 18 to 20) we shall look at development within each of these sectors individually.

One clear pattern of changing economic structure in the course of economic development is that, as per capita income rises, the share of industry in gross national product rises also. Although it is possible to conceive of a situation in which a country moves from a condition of poverty to one of wealth while concentrating on agriculture, this kind of growth has yet to occur. Every country that has achieved a high per capita income has also experienced a population shift, in which the majority moves from rural areas and farming to cities and industrial jobs. All have also experienced an increase in industrial value-added in gross national product.

There are two principal reasons for this. The first is **Engel's law.** In the nineteenth century Ernst Engel discovered that as incomes of families rose, the proportion of their budget spent on food declined. Since the main function of the agricultural sector is to produce food, it follows that demand for agricultural output would not grow as rapidly as demand for industrial products and services, and hence the share of agriculture in national product would decline. This relationship holds for all countries that have experienced sustained development.

A second reason has reinforced the impact of the first: productivity in the agricultural sector has risen as growth has progressed. People require food to survive, and if a household had to devote all its energies to producing enough of its own food, it would have no surplus time to make industrial products or to grow surplus food that could be traded for industrial products. In the course of development, however, increased use of machinery and other new methods of raising crops have made it possible for an individual farmer in the United States, for example, to produce enough food to feed, and feed very well, another 70 to 80 people. As a result only 3 percent of the work force of the United States is in farming, while the others have been freed to produce elsewhere.

The rising share of industry also helps to explain why, as incomes rise, an increasing percentage of every country's population lives in cities rather than in the countryside. There are **economies of scale** in the manufacture of many industrial products. The existence of economies of scale implies that output per unit of input rises as the firm size increases; that is, a large industrial enterprise in an industry such as steel will produce more steel per dollar cost (made up from the cost of coal, iron ore, limestone, labor, plant machinery, and electricity) than will a smaller enterprise. Furthermore it makes sense for many different kinds of industrial enterprises to locate in the same place so that common support facilities, such as electric power stations, transport, and wholesalers, can also operate at an efficient level. The result is that industry leads to the growth of cities, and the growth of cities itself tends to increase the share of manufacturing and some services in gross national product. In the rural economies of most poor countries, for example, food processing is done in the home and is not usually included in gross national product calculations at all. In urbanized countries, in contrast, food processing is often done in large factories, and the value-added produced by these factories is included in the share of the manufacturing sector.

Even though the rising share of manufacturing in gross national product and the declining share of agriculture is a pattern common to all countries, it does not follow that the rates of change are the same in each country. In fact planners around the world have been plagued by the question of how much to emphasize agriculture versus industry during the course of development. The Chinese in the 1950s, for instance, tried to follow the Soviet example of putting most of their investment into industry, hoping that agriculture would somehow take care of itself. Disastrous harvests in 1959 through 1961 forced the government to put more resources, notably chemical fertilizer, into agriculture, but machinery, steel, and related industries continued to receive the lion's share of investment. Food production grew, but only just fast enough to hold per capita consumption constant since population grew at 2 percent a year. When wages and farm incomes began to rise in the late 1970s, however, constant per capita output was perceived as being insufficient, and the government once again greatly increased the share of investment going to agriculture. In the 1980s it took the even more radical step of abandoning collectivized agriculture in what proved to be a successful move to raise agricultural production at an accelerated rate.

For a decade and more after independence some African countries also felt that agriculture required little help. Increased food requirements could be met by the simple expedient of expanding the amount of land under cultivation. But population continued to grow, at rates over 3 percent a year in many countries, and the supply of readily available arable land became exhausted. On the edge of the Sahel desert the overuse of fragile land has contributed to severe ecological damage that, together with a change in weather patterns, has brought about widespread famine in the region.

In fact, virtually every government in the developing world has struggled with the question of the proper relationship between agricultural and industrial development. Would a greater awareness of the historical relationship between agriculture and industry in countries undergoing development improve performance in these countries? If planners knew that the share of agriculture in national product always remained above 40 percent until per capita income rose above $500, those planners would have a target to aim at. Investment in agriculture could be kept at a level to ensure that the share did not fall below 40 percent. But what if there were no consistent patterns among countries at comparable levels of development?

Hollis Chenery and his coauthors, for example, found that there was no single pattern for the changes in shares and that to talk meaningfully about consistent patterns at all, the countries of the world had to be divided into three subgroups: large countries, meaning countries with a population over 15 million in 1960; small countries that emphasize primary (agriculture plus mining) exports; and small countries that emphasize industrial exports.[2]

Subsequent work in this same tradition has divided nations into very large (with populations over 50 million in 1980), large (populations of 15 to 50 million in 1980), and small (under 15 million people). The patterns for these three categories of countries are presented in Figure 3–3. The figure also includes the individual country patterns for the years 1960 to 1982 or 1983 for 11 of the largest nations. As is apparent from this figure, the average performance of the very large, large,

2. Hollis B. Chenery and Moises Syrquin, *Patterns of Development, 1950–1970* (London: Oxford University Press, 1975), and Hollis B. Chenery and Lance J. Taylor, "Development Patterns: Among Countries and over Time," *Review of Economics and Statistics,* November 1968, pp. 391–416.

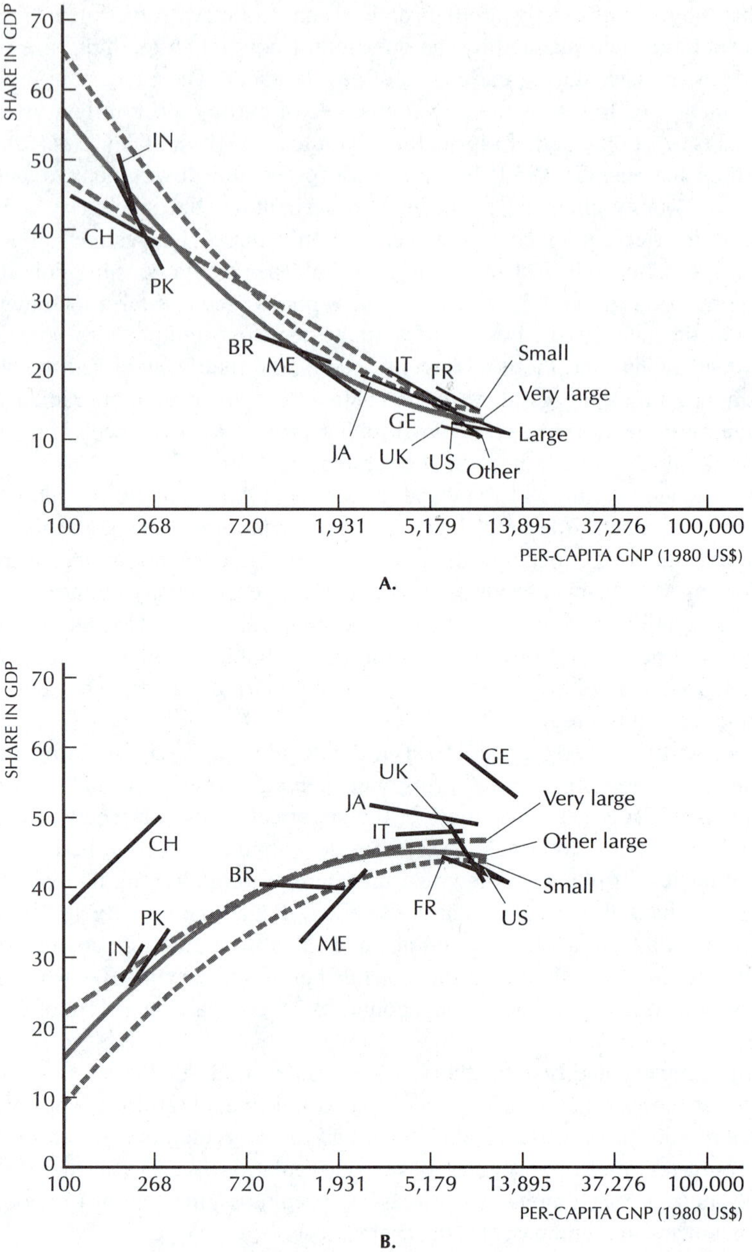

FIGURE 3–3 Development Patterns. In this figure the Chenery methodology for making cross-country comparisons is used to compare the patterns of the share of industry and agriculture in GNP for very large (over 50 million people), large (15 to 50 million people), and small (under 15 million people) countries. Part A depicts the share of agriculture and part B the share of industry. The very large countries for which individual country trends are given are China (CH), India (IN), Pakistan (PK), Brazil (BR), Mexico (ME), Japan (JA), West Germany (GE), Italy (IT), United Kingdom (UK), France (FR), and the United States (US).
Source: Dwight H. Perkins and Moshe Syrquin, "Large Countries: The Influence of Size," in Hollis B. Chenery and T. N. Srinivasan (eds.), *Handbook of Development Economics,* Vol. 2 (Amsterdam: North-Holland, 1989), pp. 1725–26.

and small nations is similar although the share of industry begins rising at a lower per capita GNP in large countries than in small ones. An individual country's performance, however, can deviate substantially from these average trends at least for a period of two decades and longer. No one of the 11 very large countries in Figure 3–3 is right on the average trend line for industry's share in GNP.

Chenery and his coauthors once spoke of the trends they estimated as being the **normal pattern** of development for large (or small) countries. The term has contributed to a good deal of misunderstanding and misuse of the results. Planners have compared these estimated trends with the actual performance of their country, and if their own industrial share has grown more rapidly than the trend, they have congratulated themselves for a good performance. Or if their share has grown at a rate below the general trend line, they have concluded that something had to be done to correct a poor performance. In either case a deviation from the trend was seen as a cause for concern. But these patterns are nothing more than the average results obtained from comparing many diverse patterns. They are not a guide to what a country ought to do. Perhaps someday we shall be in a position to say that one trend makes more efficient use of a nation's resources than another or leads to a faster overall growth rate. Today all we have are data and estimates that give us a general idea of the trends to expect as economic development occurs. Under the circumstances it is better to drop the term "normal pattern" from the vocabulary and speak of **average pattern.** On the average the primary share (agriculture plus mining) of GNP in large countries falls from 32 percent at $600 per capita (in 1983 prices) to 19 percent at $1600 per capita, but the variation around that trend is so great that these patterns provide only the crudest of guides for planners.

Two-Sector Models

Long before the concept of GNP was invented or economists had many statistics of any kind to work with, they recognized the fundamental importance of the relationship between industry and agriculture. To better understand the nature of that relationship, they began to design simple models to explain the key connections between the two sectors. The best known of the earlier models appeared in David Ricardo's *The Principles of Political Economy and Taxation,* published in 1817. In his model Ricardo included two basic assumptions that have played an important role in two-sector models ever since. First, he assumed that the agricultural sector was subject to **diminishing returns:** given increases in inputs lead to continually smaller increases in output. The reason is that crops require land and land is limited. To increase production, Ricardo felt, farmers would have to move onto poorer and poorer land, and thus it would be more and more costly to produce a ton of grain. Second, Ricardo put forward the concept that today is called **labor surplus.** Britain in the early nineteenth century still had a large agricultural work force, and Ricardo felt that the industrial sector could draw away the surplus labor in the rural sector without causing a rise in wages in either the urban or rural areas.

The concept of labor surplus is closely related to concepts such as **rural unemployment** and underemployment or disguised unemployment. Rural unemployment is formally much the same as urban unemployment. When there are people who desire to work, are actively looking for work, and cannot find work, they are said to be **unemployed.** Very few people in rural areas of developing countries are unemployed in this sense. While most rural people have jobs, those jobs are not very productive. In many cases there is not enough work to employ the entire rural work force full time. Instead members of farm families all work part time and share what work there is. Economists call this **underemployment** or **disguised unemployment,** because some members of the rural work force could be removed entirely without a fall in production. Some remaining workers would simply change from part-time to full-time effort.

Underemployment and other features of developing-country labor markets will be discussed at greater length in Chapter 8. Here we are mainly interested in how an agricultural sector with diminishing returns and surplus or underemployed labor affects the development of the industrial sector. Put differently, if the industrial sector grows at a certain rate, how fast must the agricultural sector grow in order to avoid a drag on industry and on overall economic development? And will accelerated population growth help or make matters worse? To answer these and related questions, we shall develop a **simple two-sector model.**

The modern version of the two-sector labor-surplus model was first developed by W. Arthur Lewis.[3] Lewis, like Ricardo before him, pays particular attention to the implications of surplus labor for the distribution of income, and hence it is the Lewis version of that labor surplus model that is most relevant to the discussion in Chapter 4. The concern in this chapter, however, is with the relationship between industry and agriculture. The model we use to explore that relationship is one developed by John Fei and Gustav Ranis.[4]

The Production Function

Our starting point is the agricultural sector and the **agricultural production function.** A production function, as indicated earlier, tells us how much output we can get for a given amount of input. In our simple agricultural production function we assume two inputs, labor and land, produce an output, such as grain. The production function of Figure 3–4 differs from that of Figure 3–2, because instead of showing two inputs, labor and capital, on the axes, it shows output and one input, labor. Because increases in labor must be combined with either a fixed amount of land or with land of decreasing quality, the production function indicates diminishing returns. Put differently, the **marginal product of labor** is falling; this means that each additional unit of labor produces less and less output.

The next step in constructing our model is to show how rural wages are determined. The standard assumption in all labor surplus models from Ricardo to the present time is that rural wages will not fall below a minimum level. Thus in its more general form the concept of labor surplus includes not only situations in which the marginal product of labor is zero, but also situations in which the marginal product of labor is above zero but less than the minimum below which rural wages will not fall. In the Fei-Ranis model and in other labor surplus theories the usual assumption is that rural wages do not fall below the **average product** of

3. W. Arthur Lewis, *The Theory of Economic Growth* (Homewood, Ill.: Irwin, 1955).

4. Gustav Ranis and John C. H. Fei, *Development of the Labor Surplus Economy* (Homewood, Ill.: Irwin, 1964).

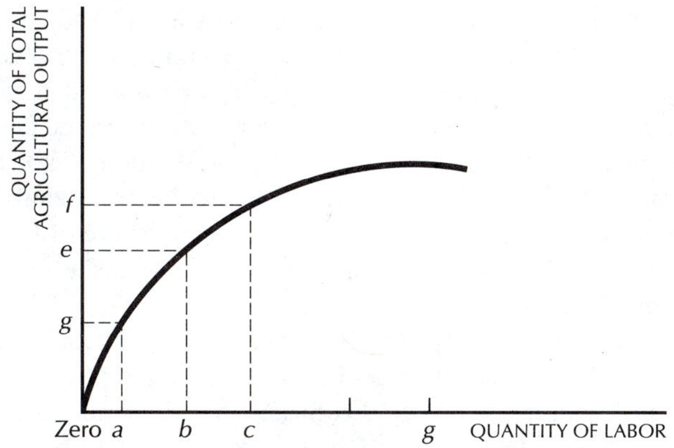

FIGURE 3–4 The Production Function. In this figure, a rise in the labor force from *a* to *b* leads to an increase in output of *de;* an equal in labor from *b* to *c* leads to a smaller rise in output. At point *g* further increases in the amount of labor used do not lead to any rise in output at all. Beyond point *g* the marginal product of labor is zero or negative, so additional labor causes no increase or a reduction in output.

farm labor in households with a labor surplus. The logic behind this view is that a laborer in a farm household will not look for work outside the household unless he or she can earn at least as much as he or she would receive by staying at home. These concepts in diagrammatic form are presented in Figure 3–5.

Figure 3–5 can be derived directly from Figure 3–4. The *total product* per unit of labor in Figure 3–4 is converted into the *marginal product* per unit of labor of Figure 3–5. The concept of a minimum wage (represented by the dotted line *hi*) is then added to the diagram. This minimum wage is also sometimes called an **institutionally fixed wage** to contrast it with wages determined by market forces. In a perfectly competitive market, wages will equal the marginal product of labor for

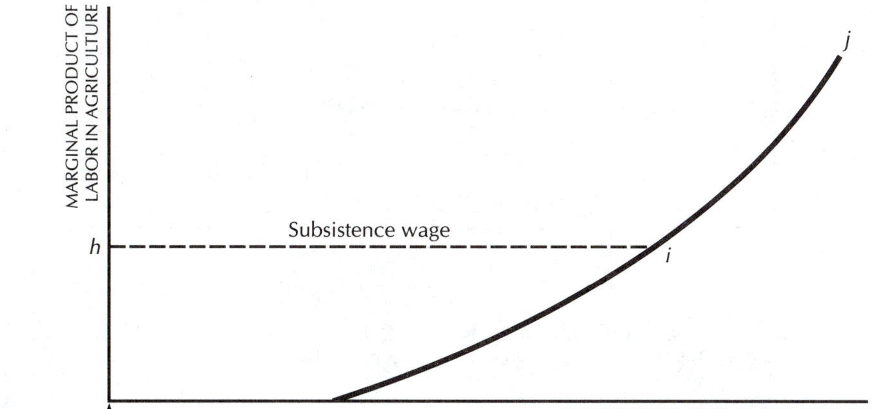

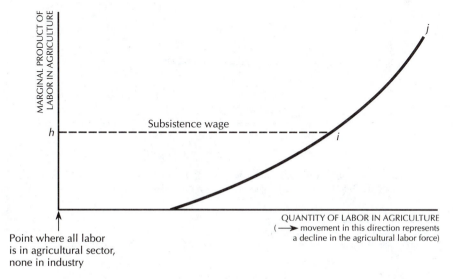

FIGURE 3–5 Marginal Product of Labor in Agriculture. As the quantity of agricultural labor decreases, the marginal product increases.

reasons that will be discussed at greater length in Chapter 8. Thus once labor is withdrawn from agriculture to a point where the marginal product rises above the minimum wage (point *h* in Figure 3–5), wages in agriculture will follow the marginal product curve. To hire away from the farm, factories in the city will have to pay at least as much as the workers are earning on the farm. Thus the line *hij* in Figure 3–5 can be thought of as the **supply curve of labor** facing the industrial sector. Actually the usual assumption is that the supply curve of labor in industry is a bit above the line *hij* because factories must pay farmers a bit more than they are receiving in agriculture to get them to move.

The key feature of this supply curve of labor is that unlike more common supply curves, it does not rise steadily as one moves from left to right but has a substantial horizontal portion. Formally this means that the supply curve of labor up to point *i* is **perfectly elastic. Elasticity** is a measure of responsiveness. Technically, it is the percentage change occurring in one variable (in this case, the supply of labor) arising from a given percentage change in another variable (in this case, wages).[5] Perfect elasticity occurs when the ratio of these two percentages equals infinity. From the point of view of the industrial sector this means that that sector can hire as many workers as it wants without having to raise wages until the amount of labor is increased beyond point *i*.

The final steps are to add a demand curve for labor in the industrial sector (Figure 3–6) and then to combine the three figures into a single model. As we see in Figure 3–6, this demand curve can be derived from the industrial production function. To simplify our model, we ignore this step and draw in the demand curve *mm′*. The supply curve in Figure 3–6 is derived from Figure 3–5. 0*k* in

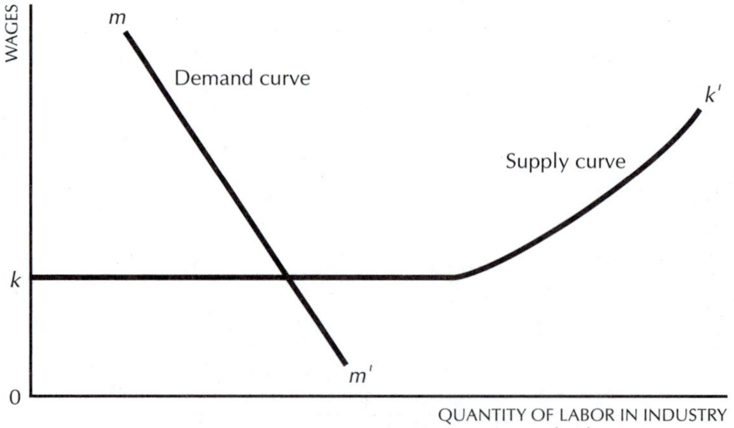

FIGURE 3–6 The Supply and Demand for Industrial Labor. The supply curve *kk′* is drawn directly from Figure 3–5. Demand *mm′* is derived from the industrial production function.

5. The term **"elasticity"** refers to the percentage change in one variable that results from a percentage change in another variable and is presented as a ratio. In the case discussed here, the elasticity is the ratio of the percentage change in the supply of labor ($\Delta L/L$) to the percentage change in the wage rate $\Delta W/W$.

$$\text{Elasticity} = \Delta L/L \div \Delta W/W.$$

In the case of perfect elasticity, this ratio approaches infinity.

Figure 3–6 is assumed to be slightly higher than the subsistence wage in Figure 3–5. The supply curve of labor to industry turns up when withdrawal of labor from agriculture can no longer be accomplished without a decline in the agricultural output (when the marginal product of labor rises above zero) because at that point the relative price of agricultural produce will rise, and this will necessitate a commensurate rise in urban wages. The demand curve for labor in industry is determined by the marginal product of labor in industry, and hence the demand curve can be derived from the industrial production function.[6]

To combine Figures 3–4, 3–5, and 3–6, one additional piece of information is needed, the size of the country's labor force. Many models use total population rather than the labor force, and this switch has little effect if the labor force is closely correlated with total population. The size of the labor force in Figure 3–7 is represented by the line zero to *p*, as labeled in part A. In order to combine the three figures, Figure 3–4's relation to the others is made clearer if it is flipped so that an increase in labor in agriculture is represented by moving from right to left rather than the reverse. Handled this way, a movement from left to right represents both a decline in the agricultural labor force and a rise in the industrial labor force, that is, a transfer of labor from agriculture to industry.

If a labor-surplus economy starts with its entire population in agriculture, it can remove a large part of that population (*pg*) to industry or other employment without any reduction in farm output. Industry will have to pay that labor a wage a bit above subsistence (the difference between $p''k$ and $p'h$) to get it to move, but as long as there is some way of moving the food consumed by this labor from the rural to the urban areas, industrialization can proceed without putting any demands on agriculture. Even if agriculture is completely stagnant, industry can grow. As industry continues to grow, however, it will eventually exhaust the supply of surplus labor. Further removals of labor from agriculture will lead to a reduction in farm output. A shift in industrial demand to *mm* will force industry to pay more for the food of its workers; that is, the *terms of trade* between industry and agriculture will turn against industry and in favor of agriculture. It is this shift in the terms of trade that accounts for the rise in the supply curve of labor between g'' and i''. Industry must pay more to get the same amount of food to feed its workers.

The Fei-Ranis model can be used to explore the implications of population growth and a rise in agricultural productivity, among other things. To simplify, if one assumes that there is a close relationship between population and the labor force, then an increase in population from, say, *p* to *t* will not increase output at all. The elastic portion of both the urban and rural labor supply curves will be extended by $p't'$ and $p''t''$ respectively and thus postpone the day when industrialization will cause wages to rise.[7]

This point where wages begin to rise is sometimes referred to as the turning point. Most important, if population rises without any increase in food output, the

6. A factory owner under competitive conditions is willing to pay up to but no more than what a laborer contributes to increase the volume of output of the factory. The increase in output value contributed by the last laborer hired is by definition the marginal revenue product of that laborer.

7. In the industrial labor supply and demand part of Figure 3–7, Part C, it is also necessary to move the labor demand curves to the left since the zero point on the horizontal axis has been moved to the left. These new demand curves, $s's'$, $m'm'$, and $n'n'$, therefore, are really the same as *ss*, *mm*, and *nn*. That is, the quantity of labor demanded at any given price is the same for $s's'$ as *ss*, and so on.

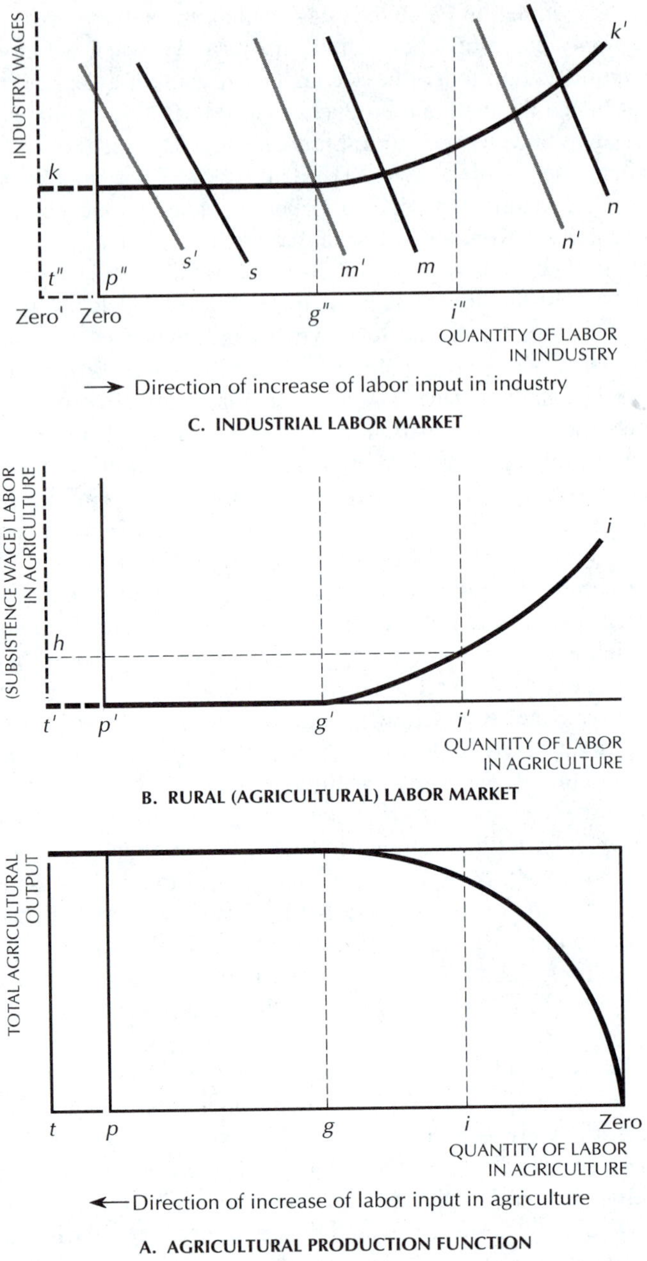

FIGURE 3–7 **The Two-Sector Labor-Surplus Model.** The limit imposed by the country's population (zero to p in Part A), coupled with the agricultural production function, allows us to analyze the effects of industry wages on the mix between agricultural and industrial labor.

average amount of food available per capita will fall. From the standpoint of everyone but a few employers who want to keep wages low and profits high, population growth is an unqualified disaster. Wages may actually fall in the urban areas, and the welfare of the great mass of farmers will certainly fall. It is a model such as this, even if only imperfectly understood, that people often have in mind when they speak of population growth in wholly negative terms.

How fast agricultural production must grow depends on what happens to a number of different variables. If industry's demand for labor is growing very rapidly, for example, agricultural productivity must grow rapidly enough to keep the terms of trade from turning sharply against industry and thereby cutting into industrial profits and slowing or halting industrial growth.[8] On the other hand, as long as there is a surplus of labor and no population growth, it is possible to ignore agricultural productivity growth and concentrate one's resources on industry.

David Ricardo, using similar although not identical reasoning, was concerned with keeping population growth down to avoid using poorer and poorer land in order to get a sufficient food supply. He also feared the impact of increasing wages, which he saw as leading to a twofold disaster. Following Thomas Malthus, he argued higher wages would lead to workers having more children. Further, they would cut into the profits that initially had provided the funds for investment in capital and that had allowed the rural surplus labor to move to cities and be employed in industry. Modern labor-surplus theorists would not agree with Ricardo's harsh policy prescriptions, but they would see the problems facing today's developing countries in a similar light.

The Neoclassical Two-Sector Model

By changing many of the assumptions in the labor-surplus model, many of its implications can be explored. Here we take up the implications of one assumption, the labor-surplus assumption. Many economists simply do not agree that a surplus of labor exists in today's developing countries, even in India or China. These economists have developed an alternative two-sector model that is sometimes referred to as a **neoclassical model.**

The framework developed in Figure 3–7 can also be used to explore the implications of the neoclassical assumptions. A simple neoclassical model is presented in Figure 3–8.

The implications of population or labor force growth in the neoclassical model are quite different from what they were in the labor-surplus model. An increase in population and labor in agriculture will raise farm output (see dotted line *t* in Figure 3–8A), and any removal of labor from agriculture will cause farm output to fall. That is, the neoclassical model is different from the labor-surplus model; the marginal product of labor is never zero, and wages, instead of being set above the marginal product of labor, are equal to it. Thus in a neoclassical model population growth is not such a wholly negative phenomenon. The increase in labor is much less of a drain on the food supply since that labor is able to produce much or all of its own requirements, and there is no surplus of labor that can be transferred without a consequent reduction in agricultural output.

If industry is to develop successfully, simultaneous efforts must be made to ensure that agriculture grows fast enough to feed workers in both the rural and urban sectors at ever-higher levels of consumption and to prevent the terms of trade from turning against industry. A stagnant agricultural sector, that is, one with little new investment or technological progress, will cause wages of urban workers to rise rapidly and thereby to cut into profits and the funds available for industrial

8. Agricultural productivity in the model presented here refers to a shift in the agricultural production function causing a given amount of labor input in agriculture to produce a larger amount of agricultural output.

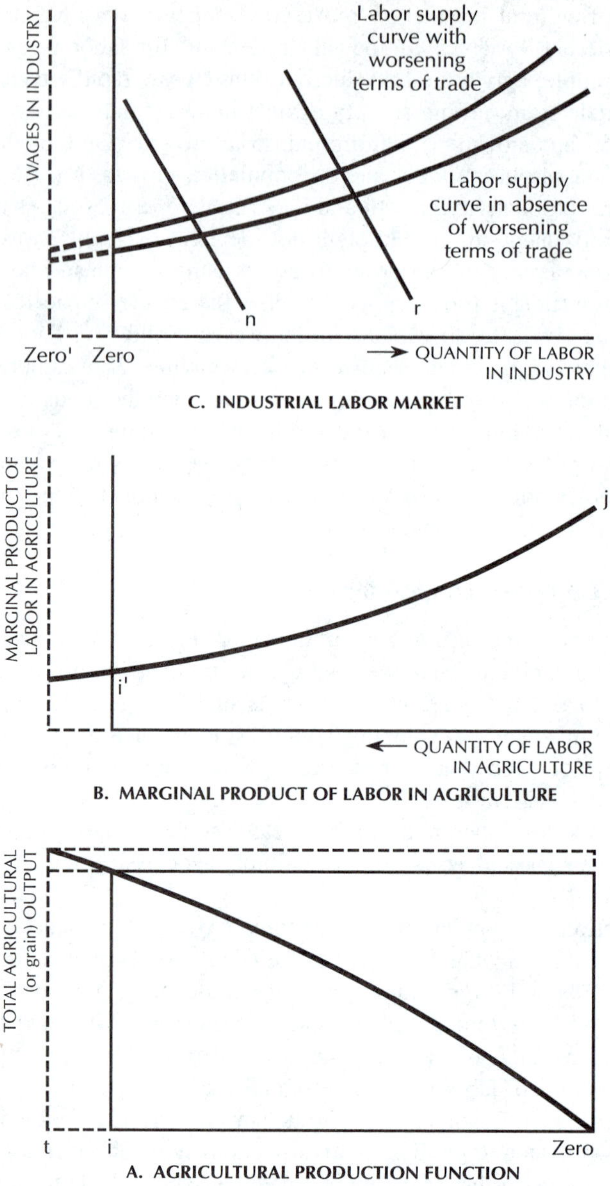

FIGURE 3–8 Neoclassical Two-Sector Model. The key difference between Figures 3–7 and 3–8 is the agricultural production function (Figure 3–8A). Limited land resources do lead to slightly diminishing returns in the agricultural sector, but the curve never flattens out; that is, the marginal product of labor never falls to a minimum subsistence level, so there is no minimum subsistence or **institutionally fixed** wage in Figure 3–8B. Instead wages are always determined by the marginal product of labor in agriculture. Finally, the supply curve of labor to industry no longer has a horizontal section. Since the removal of labor from agriculture increases the marginal product of labor remaining in agriculture, industry must pay an amount equal to that marginal product plus a premium to get labor to migrate to the cities. The supply curve of labor to industry rises for another reason as well. As labor is removed from agriculture, farm output falls; and in order to extract enough food from the agricultural sector to pay its workers, industry must pay higher and higher prices for food. Only if industry is in a position to import food from abroad will it be able to avoid these worsening terms of trade. If imports are not available, rising agricultural prices will lead to a higher value of output and hence higher wages for workers in agriculture. As in the labor-surplus case, industry will have to pay correspondingly higher wages to attract a labor force.

development. Where in the labor-surplus model planners can ignore agriculture until the surplus of labor is exhausted, in the neoclassical model there must be a balance between industry and agriculture from the beginning.

Two-sector models of both the labor-surplus and neoclassical type can become very elaborate, with dozens or even hundreds of equations used to describe different features of the economy. These additional equations and assumptions will also have an influence on the kinds of policy recommendations an economist will derive from the model. But at the core of these more elaborate models are the labor-surplus and neoclassical assumptions about the nature of the agricultural production function.

These same points can be made in a less abstract way by turning to Chinese and African examples of the relationship between industry and agriculture during economic development.

Labor Surplus in China

In China by the 1950s most arable land was already under cultivation, and further increases in population and the labor force contributed little to increases in agricultural output. Urban wages rose in the early 1950s, but then leveled off and remained unchanged for 20 years between 1957 and 1977. If allowed to do so, tens of millions of farm laborers would have happily migrated to the cities despite urban wage stagnation. Only legal restrictions on rural-urban migration, backed up by more than a little force, held this migration to levels well below what would have been required to absorb the surplus. Population growth that averaged 2 percent a year up until the mid-1970s continued to swell the ranks of those interested in leaving the countryside. In short, China over the past three decades was a labor-surplus country.

As pointed out earlier, China did invest in agriculture, but only enough to maintain, not to raise, per capita food production. The rural-urban migration that did occur was not fast enough to eliminate the agricultural labor surplus, but it was enough to require farmers to sell more of their production to the cities. Thus the prices paid to farmers for their produce were gradually raised, while the prices paid by farmers for urban products remained constant or fell; that is, the rural-urban terms of trade shifted slowly but markedly in favor of agriculture.

To get out of this labor-surplus situation, Chinese planners in the late 1970s had both to accelerate the transfer of workers from agricultural to urban employment and to take steps to keep the agricultural pool of surplus labor from constantly replenishing itself. Accelerating the growth of urban employment was accomplished by encouraging labor-intensive consumer goods (textiles, electronics, etc.) and service industries (restaurants, taxis, etc.). In order to feed this increase in urban population, the government increased food imports, shifted more investment funds to agriculture, and allowed a further improvement in rural-urban terms of trade.

To keep the rural pool of surplus labor from replenishing itself, planners slowed those kinds of farm mechanization that had the effect of reducing the agricultural demand for labor. Most important, planners attacked the surplus at its source by a massive effort to bring down the birth rate. By 1980 the population growth rate in China had slowed from 2 to 1.2 percent a year, and the rate stayed below 1.5 percent throughout the 1980s and the first half of the 1990s. By the mid-1980s rapid industrial and services growth in and around the cities and in the countryside itself was absorbing nearly 10 million new workers a year. But because of past population growth, the work force in the 1980s and 1990s was still growing by 15 million new entrants each year, so the surplus in agriculture was not yet falling in absolute numbers.

Labor Surplus in Africa

Africa, as already pointed out, had low population densities relative to the availability of arable land. In nations such as Kenya, increases in population could be readily accommodated in the 1950s and 1960s by opening up new land or by converting land to more intensive uses (for example, from pasture to crops). Therefore, increased population was more or less matched by rises in agricultural production. Food output, at least in the richer countries such as Kenya, kept up with the needs of both the expanding rural population and with the even more rapidly growing urban sector. Planners felt little pressure either to improve the rural-urban terms of trade or to increase state investment in agriculture. In short, until recently Kenya fit reasonably well the assumptions of the neoclassical model.

Because Kenya's land resources were not unlimited and because population growth continued at the extraordinarily high rate of close to 4 percent per annum, by the late 1970s Kenya was beginning to acquire some of the characteristics of a labor-surplus economy, and planners were having to adjust to the policy implications (more investment and better prices for agriculture, a greater effort to reduce population growth) of these new conditions. But throughout the 1980s and early 1990s Kenya's population grew at 3.6 percent per year while agricultural output growth lagged behind at 2.9 percent per year. Per capita agricultural output in 1992 was thus 8 percent less than it was in 1980.

This discussion of the relations between the agricultural and industrial sectors during the process of economic development has gone as far as we can productively go at this stage. Analysis of the patterns of development using data on shares of the two sectors of GNP provided an insight into the patterns that have occurred in the past and might be expected to recur in the future. Two-sector models have made it possible to go a step further and to acquire an understanding of some of the reasons why different patterns of industrial and agricultural development might occur. In later chapters the validity of the labor-surplus versus neoclassical assumptions for today's developing world will be explored at greater length. There will also be extended discussions of the nature and problems of industrial and agricultural development that will include further consideration of the nature of relations between the two sectors.

To know precisely which industries would develop at each stage in a country's growth would be a very valuable piece of information for economists. Plans could be drawn up that could concentrate a country's energies on particular industries at particular stages. If all industrial development began with textiles, for example, then planners could focus their attention on getting a textile industry started and worry about other sectors later. Similarly, if only countries with high per capita incomes could support the efficient production of automobiles, planners in countries beginning development would know that they should avoid investing resources in the automobile industry until a later stage.

Empirical Approaches

Chenery and Taylor have used the terms early industries, middle industries, and late industries.[9] **Early industries** are those that supply goods essential to the populations of poor countries and are produced with simple technologies, so that their manufacture can take place within the poor country. In statistical terms the share of these industries in GNP rises at low levels of per capita income, but stops rising when income is still fairly low and stagnates or falls thereafter. Typically included in this group are food processing and textiles. **Late industries** are those whose share in GNP continues to rise even at high levels of per capita income. This group includes many consumer durables (refrigerators, cars) as well as other metal products. **Middle industries** are those that fall in between the other two categories.

Unfortunately, it is frequently difficult to decide in which category a particular industry belongs. For many industries the nineteenth-century experience of European nations or of the United States is a poor guide because many industries that are important today did not even exist then. The nuclear power industry, for example, did not exist prior to World War II, and even the chemical-fertilizer sector as we think of it today did not really begin until well into the twentieth century.

A way around the problem of changing technologies over time is to use data for countries at different levels of development at a given point in time. Data of this sort are called **cross-section data,** and, while they solve the one problem, they introduce others. In several Arab states petroleum accounts for a large share of GNP because these nations have unusually rich underground resources. In Malaysia soil and climate have been favorable to producing rubber, palm oil, and timber. Singapore and Hong Kong, which have no natural resources to speak of, have taken advantage of their vast experience in foreign trade to develop textiles, electronic equipment, and other manufactures and services for export. In short, the share of particular industries in the GNP of individual countries is determined by endowments of natural resources, historical heritages of experience with commerce and trade, and many other factors. There is no single pattern of industrial development, or even two or three patterns, that all nations must follow as they progress out of poverty. Some industries where the techniques used are easier to master, such as textiles, are more likely to get started in the early stages of devel-

9. Chenery and Taylor, "Development Patterns."

opment than others, such as the manufacture of commercial aircraft. And there is some regularity in the patterns of what people consume as they move from lower to higher incomes. Engel's law has already been mentioned as a part of the explanation for the declining share of agriculture in GNP. The same law has much to do with why the share of food processing within industry falls as per capita income rises. But before planners can decide which industries to push in one country, they must know the particular conditions facing that country as well as these more general patterns.

Theoretical Approaches

Economists' debates on balanced and unbalanced growth predate much of the quantitative work on patterns of development. **Balanced-growth** advocates such as as Ragnar Nurkse or Paul Rosenstein-Rodan argued that countries have to develop a wide range of industries simultaneously if they are ever to succeed in achieving sustained growth.[10] What would happen in the absence of balanced growth has often been illustrated with a story of a hypothetical country that attempted to begin development by building a shoe factory. The factory is built, workers are hired and trained, and the factory begins to turn out shoes. Everything goes well until the factory tries to sell the shoes it is producing. The factory workers themselves use their increased income to buy new factory-made shoes; but of course they are able to produce far more shoes than they need for themselves or their families. The rest of the population is mainly poor farmers whose income has not risen, and hence they cannot afford to buy factory-made shoes. They continue to wear cheap homemade sandals. The factory in turn, unable to sell its product, goes bankrupt, and the effort to start development comes to an end.

The proposed solution to this problem is to build a number of factories simultaneously. If a textile mill, a flour mill, and a bicycle plant, and many other enterprises could be started at the same time, the shoe factory could sell its shoes to the workers in these factories as well. In turn, shoe factory workers would use their new income to buy bicycles, clothing, and flour and thus keep the other new plants solvent. This kind of development is sometimes referred to as **balanced growth on the demand side** because the industries developed are determined by the demand or expenditure patterns of consumers (and investors). Balanced growth on the supply side refers to the need to build a number of industries simultaneously to prevent supply bottlenecks from occurring. Thus, in building a steel mill, planners need to make sure that iron and coal mines and coking facilities are also developed, unless imports of these inputs are readily available. At a more aggregated level, it is also necessary to maintain a balance between the development of industry and agriculture. Otherwise, as pointed out earlier, the terms of trade might turn sharply against industry and thereby bring growth to a stop.

One problem with the balanced-growth argument is that in its pure form it is a counsel of despair. A poor country with little or no industry is told that it must either start up a wide range of industries simultaneously or resign itself to continued

10. Ragnar Nurkse, *Problems of Capital Formation in Underdeveloped Countries* (New York: Oxford University Press, 1953), and Paul N. Rosenstein-Rodan, "Problems of Industrialization of Eastern and Southeastern Europe," *Economic Journal,* June–September 1943, reprinted in A. N. Agarwala and S. P. Singh (eds.), *The Economics of Underdevelopment* (New York: Oxford University Press, 1963).

stagnation. This across-the-board program has sometimes been referred to as a **big push** or a **critical minimum effort.** By whatever name, it is discouraging advice for a poor country that is taxing its managerial and financial resources to the limit just to get a few factories started.

In the discussion of patterns of industrial development, however, we pointed out that there is little evidence that all countries have to follow a set pattern. Some countries have emphasized one set of industries while other countries concentrated on different ones. Proponents of unbalanced growth, especially Albert Hirschman, recognize these differences and use them to suggest a very different pattern of industrial development.[11] Nations, they say, could and did concentrate their energies on a few sectors during the early stages of development. In most cases there was little danger of producing more shoes than could be sold.

Certain industrial products have ready markets, even among the rural poor and even in the absence of a big push toward development. A worker in a nineteenth-century factory, for example, could produce 40 times as much cotton yarn per day as a peasant with a spinning wheel in a dark rural cottage. From the peasant's point of view, therefore, it made sense to buy factory yarn and to concentrate effort on a more productive activity, such as weaving that yarn into cloth. Initially much of this yarn was imported into places like India and China from factories in Britain, but it was not long before entrepreneurs in China and India discovered that cotton yarn could be produced more cheaply at home than purchased as an import. Thus they substituted domestic production for imports. **Import substitution,** as this process is called, is one way a nation can find a ready market for one of its own industries. The market is already there, and all a country's planners have to do is ensure that the domestic industry can compete effectively with the imported product. How this can be done is a subject to which we shall return in Chapter 16. Here the main point is that import substitution is one way of beginning industrialization on a limited and selective basis rather than with a balanced big push. Another way is to rely on exports, as England did during the Industrial Revolution. If it is impossible to sell all a factory's product at home, it is often possible to sell the product abroad, assuming that product could be produced at a cost that is competitive. Some of the most rapidly developing nations from the 1960s through the 1990s have begun exporting manufactures at a very early stage in their development process.

Backward and Forward Linkages

Unbalanced growth advocates such as Hirschman, however, did not content themselves with simply pointing out an escape from the dilemma posed by balanced-growth proponents. Hirschman developed the unbalanced-growth idea into a general interpretation of how development ought to proceed. The central concept in Hirschman's theory is that of **linkages.** Industries are linked to other industries in ways that can be taken into account in deciding on a development strategy. Industries with **backward linkages** make use of inputs from other industries. Automobile manufacturing, for example, uses the products of machinery and

11. Albert O. Hirschman, *The Strategy of Economic Development* (New Haven, Conn.: Yale University Press, 1958).

metal processing plants, which in turn make use of large amounts of steel. The building of an automobile manufacturing plant, therefore, will create a demand for machinery and steel. Initially this demand may be supplied by imports, but eventually local enterpreneurs will see that they have a ready market for domestically made machinery and steel, and this demand stimulates them to set up such plants. Planners interested in accelerating growth, therefore, will emphasize industries with strong backward linkages because it is these industries that will stimulate production in the greatest number of additional sectors.

Forward linkages occur in industries that produce goods that then become inputs into other industries. Rather than start with automobiles, planners might prefer to start at the other end by setting up a steel mill. Seeing that they had a ready domestic supply of steel, entrepreneurs might then be stimulated to set up factories that would make use of this steel. In a similar way successful drilling for oil will encourage a country to set up its own refineries and petrochemical complexes rather than ship its crude oil to other countries for processing.

Both forward and backward linkages set up pressures that lead to the creation of new industries, which in turn create additional pressures, and so on. These pressures can take the form of new profit opportunities for private entrepreneurs, or pressures can build through the political process and force governments to act. Private investors, for example, might decide to build factories in a given location without at the same time providing adequate housing facilities for the inflow of new workers or roads with which to supply the factories and transport their output. In such cases government planners might be forced to construct public housing and roads.

While on the surface the balanced- and unbalanced-growth arguments appear to be fundamentally inconsistent with each other, when stated in less extreme forms they can be seen as opposite sides of the same coin. Almost everyone would agree that there is no single pattern of industrialization that all countries must follow. On the other hand, quantitative analysis suggests that there are patterns that are

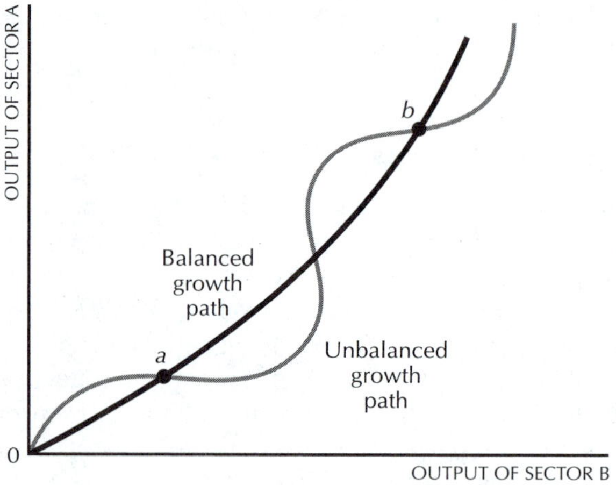

FIGURE 3–9 Balanced- and Unbalanced-Growth Paths. The solid line between points *a* and *b* is shorter than the dotted line, but because of the impact of linkages, a country traveling along the dotted line may get from point *a* to *b* in less time than a country traveling along the solid line or balanced-growth path.

broadly similar among large groups of countries. While countries with large amounts of foreign trade can follow an unbalanced strategy for some time, a country cannot pick any industry or group of industries it desires and then concentrate exclusively on those industries throughout the country's development, cannot follow in effect an extreme form of an unbalanced-growth strategy. The very concept of linkages suggests that extreme imbalances of this sort will set up pressures that will force a country back toward a more balanced path. Thus the ultimate objective is a degree of balance in the development program. But planners have a choice between attempting to maintain balance throughout the development process or first creating imbalances with the knowledge that linkage pressures will eventually force them back toward the balance. In terms of Figure 3–9, the issue is whether to follow the steady balanced-growth path, represented by a solid line, or the unbalanced-growth path, represented by a dashed line. The solid line is shorter, but under certain conditions a country might get to any given point faster by following the dashed line.

Appendix: Deriving the Sources of Growth Equation

There are six steps to deriving the sources of growth equation from the standard aggregate production function. To simplify the presentation, we shall assume that there are only two factors of production, capital and labor.

1. Assume an aggregate production function:

$$Y = F(K, L, t), \qquad [3\text{–}7]$$

which is continuous and homogeneous to degree 1,

where Y = national income or product,
K = capital stock,
t = time (shift in basic production function),
and L = labor force.

2. Differentiate this production function with respect to time.

$$\frac{dY}{dt} = \left(\frac{\delta F}{\delta K} \cdot \frac{dK}{dt}\right) + \left(\frac{\delta F}{\delta L} \cdot \frac{dL}{dt}\right) + \left(\frac{\delta F}{\delta t} \cdot \frac{dt}{dt}\right) \qquad [3\text{–}8]$$

where the symbol δ is used to represent the partial derivative.

3. Divide through by Y, and insert L and K in the equation.

$$\frac{1}{Y} \cdot \frac{dY}{dt} = \frac{1}{Y}\left(\frac{\delta F}{\delta K} \cdot \frac{dK}{dt} \cdot K \cdot \frac{1}{K} + \frac{\delta F}{\delta L} \cdot \frac{dL}{dt} \cdot L \cdot \frac{1}{L} + \frac{\delta F}{\delta t}\right). \qquad [3\text{–}9]$$

4. Rearrange terms.

$$\frac{dY/dt}{Y} = \frac{(\delta F/\delta K)K}{Y} \cdot \frac{dK/dt}{K} + \frac{(\delta F/\delta L)L}{Y} \cdot \frac{dL/dt}{L} + \frac{\delta F/dt}{Y}, \qquad [3\text{–}10]$$

where $G_Y = \dfrac{dY/dt}{Y}$ = growth rate of income,

$G_K = \dfrac{dK/dt}{K}$ = growth rate of capital,

$$G_L = \frac{dL/dt}{L} = \text{growth rate of labor force,}$$

and $$W_K = \frac{(\delta F/\delta K)K}{Y} = \text{share of product of capital in national income.}$$

5. Assume perfect competition, so that wages and the interest rate equal the marginal product of labor and capital respectively. If

$$\frac{\delta F}{\delta L} = \text{wage rate,}$$

then $$W_L = \frac{(\delta F/\delta L)L}{Y} = \text{share of wages in national income,}$$

and if $$\frac{\delta F}{\delta K} = i \text{ (rate of interest),}$$

then $$W_K = \frac{i \cdot K}{Y} = \text{share of income of capital in national income}$$

and $$a = \frac{\delta F/\delta t}{Y} = \text{increase in output as share of income not explained by increase in factors.}$$

6. Substitute G_Y, G_L, G_K, W_L, W_K, and a into Equation 3–10, which then gives one the sources of growth equation:

$$G_Y = (W_K \cdot G_K) + (W_L \cdot G_L) + a. \qquad [3\text{–}11]$$

This equation can also be rewritten in the form

$$a = \text{(the residual)} = G_Y - (W_K \cdot G_K) - (W_L \cdot G_L). \qquad [3\text{–}12]$$

Countries with reasonably good statistical systems regularly publish data on the growth rate of national product (G_Y) and the labor force (G_L). Data on the growth rate of the capital stock (G_K) are more difficult to find because estimates of the capital stock are readily available only for industrialized nations. Economists who work with developing-country data, therefore, sometimes rewrite the $W_K \cdot G_K$ component of Equation 3–11. By not inserting K into Equation 3–10, that part of Equations 3–10 becomes

$$\frac{\delta F}{\delta K} \cdot \frac{dK/dt}{Y},$$

where $$\frac{\delta F}{\delta K} = \text{the interest rate as previously assumed}$$

and $$\frac{dK/dt}{Y} = I = \text{the share of gross domestic investment in gross domestic product.}$$

The share of gross domestic investment (I) or capital formation in gross domestic product is regularly calculated for most countries.

Data on the shares of labor income in national income (W_L) are the total wages and salaries paid to workers plus the inputted wages of farmers. The share of capital income in national income (W_K) is made up of interest income and profits. In a two-factor model, W_K would encompass all property income, including the rent on land.

When economists such as Edward Denison calculate the sources of growth, they generally use more than two factors of production. Labor, for example, is usually divided into unskilled and skilled labor of various types. Foreign exchange earnings are sometimes treated as a separate factor of production from capital, and so on. There often is an attempt to break down the residual measure of productivity increases (a) into its various components. Some of these refinements can be used in estimating the sources of growth in developing countries, but others cannot because of the limited availability of relevant developing-country data.

4

Development and Human Welfare

Since 1980, many developing countries have experienced declining per capita income while quite a few others have been able to achieve economic growth in either modest or generous measure. This chapter is about how the presence or absence of growth affects the material well-being of the 4.5 billion citizens of the developing countries, particularly about what happens to the relative welfare of different groups (**inequality**) and the well-being of the poor (**poverty**).

Logically, economic growth is a necessary but not sufficient condition for improving the living standards of large numbers of people in countries with low levels of GNP per capita. It is necessary because if there is no growth, people can become better off only through transfers of income and assets from others. In a poor country, even if a small segment of the population is very rich, the potential for this kind of redistribution is severely limited. When GNP per capita is $1,000 (PPP), the most a country can do through static income redistribution is to create shared poverty in which each citizen receives $1,000 a year.[1] Economic growth, by contrast, enables some or even all people to become better off without anyone necessarily becoming worse off.

Economic growth is not a sufficient condition for improving mass living standards, however, because the distribution of the income created is also important. For at least three reasons, it would be wrong to assume that higher per capita GNP necessarily means higher incomes for all, or even most, families.

1. There is, however, a view which argues that if assets are redistributed first, faster growth will result. This is taken up in the last section of this chapter.

First, governments promote economic growth not just to improve the welfare of their citizens but also, and sometimes primarily, to augment the power and glory of the state and its rulers. Much of the wealth of ancient Egypt was invested in the pyramids. Modern LDCs may buy ballistic missile systems, develop nuclear weapons, or construct elaborate capital city complexes in deserts and jungles. When the gains from growth are channeled to such expensive projects, they provide little immediate benefit to the country's citizens.

Second, resources may be heavily invested in further growth, with significant consumption gains deferred to a later date. In extreme cases, such as the Soviet collectivization drive of the 1930s, consumption can decline dramatically over long periods. When the Soviet Union fell in 1991, its consumers were still waiting, with growing impatience, for the era of mass consumption to arrive. Normally, the power to suppress consumption to this extent in the name of economic growth is available only to totalitarian governments.

Third, income and consumption may increase, but those who are already relatively well-off may get all or most of the benefits. The rich get richer, the old saw says, and the poor get poorer. (In another version, the poor get children.) This is what poor people often think is happening. Sometimes they are right.

The question of who benefits from economic growth is not new. In Victorian England, rising inequalities in income and wealth and persistent poverty among the lower classes were widely perceived and frequently discussed. Social philosophers like Karl Marx and novelists like Charles Dickens made these issues their major themes. Defenders of the status quo responded either by denying that things were as bad as the critics charged or by arguing that the conditions they deplored were a necessary part of a process of change that would ultimately benefit all strata of society.

Despite the efforts of a few nineteenth-century statistical pioneers and those of later economic historians, the precise dimensions of nineteenth-century inequality and poverty cannot be measured. What is clear is that improvement occurred during the late nineteenth and early twentieth centuries in England and other countries that we now consider developed. These gains came as real wages rose and governments enacted reforms (antitrust legislation, progressive taxation, unemployment insurance, social security, and, after 1930, stabilizing monetary and fiscal policies) that helped to mitigate the worst inequalities and assure some minimal living standard for all members of society. Contrary to Marx's prediction of ever-worsening inequality and social instability leading to the collapse of the "bourgeois system" itself, workers in the rich capitalist countries ultimately did reach an era of mass consumption that allowed them to share in the gains from economic development.

What concerns us here is the prospects of those millions of Asians, Africans, and Latin Americans who remain desperately poor by the standards of the ordinary citizen of a rich Western country, or even by those of "transitional" (post-Communist) Central and East European societies. As industrialization proceeds and their nations' GNPs rise, what will happen to their individual economic welfare? When can they hope to reach an era of mass consumption?

During the early years of the current period of interest in economic development, roughly 1950 to 1965, development specialists ignored the problems of inequality and poverty, tacitly assuming that when per capita GNP rises everyone becomes better off. Evidence that certain sections of the population were not benefiting from growth was sometimes shrugged off with assurances that in due course the benefits of economic development would "trickle down" to them. The lack of statistics on income distribution in developing countries at this time made it easier to ignore the distributive issue.

The question of whether economic development was really helping the poor arose first in India around 1960. By the late 1960s enough data had been compiled for developing countries to rock the complacent. These numbers confirmed that, as some had already suspected, income inequality is generally higher in poor countries than in rich ones. Further, they suggested that inequality was rising in many developing countries and the mass of people in some countries were receiving no benefits at all from development. Finally, and more controversially, some writers claimed that the poor were actually becoming worse off, at least in certain large and very poor countries such as India and Bangladesh.

Interest in problems of inequality and poverty waned in the 1970s and all but vanished in the 1980s. Sadly, interest diminished not because these problems had been solved but rather because they were eclipsed by seemingly larger and more immediate difficulties. With economic growth slowing or even being replaced by decline for several years, the most pressing need in many African and Latin American countries seemed to be to deal with the factors that had brought growth to a halt: the foreign debt crisis in the case of Latin America and a host of troubles, much debated, in sub-Saharan Africa.

More recently, interest in poverty—but not inequality—has revived. East Asia, an area of rapid growth, has seen a dramatic decline in the extent and severity of poverty. Meanwhile, in sub-Saharan Africa, where economic decline has become more common than growth, critics have charged that economic stabilization programs cause poverty to deepen as social services and subsidies to the poor are cut back. Particular concern has been expressed about the impact of these policies on children and women. The critics have been challenged, however, by others who have asked whether poverty is really getting worse and, if so, whether economic stagnation or decline (the "disease") should not be blamed, rather than stabilization programs (the prescribed "cure").

While the level and nature of interest has thus changed over the years, the relationship between economic growth and human welfare remains a vital topic. The following pages review our knowledge of inequality and poverty in the developing countries. They deal first with concepts of economic welfare, then with the recent historical record, next with theories about the causes and effects of inequality and poverty, and finally with policies to help ameliorate inequality.

CONCEPTS AND MEASURES

Income Distribution

There are two important types of income distribution: the functional and size distributions. The **functional distribution of income** shows how national income is divided among the factors of production, traditionally identified as land, labor, and capital. It can be used to measure the productive contributions made by the different factors. The **size distribution of income** shows the amounts of income of all functional kinds received by rich, poor, and middle-class individuals or families and is often interpreted as a direct measure of welfare.[2]

The functional and size distributions of income are interrelated. Since the size distribution depends on ownership patterns of the productive factors (including the value of the labor services that one "owns") and the role each factor plays in the production process, the functional distribution of income has a major effect on welfare. For example, if ownership of land and capital is highly concentrated, then anything that enhances the returns to these factors will make the size distribution of income more unequal. Conversely, higher wages for unskilled labor, the most widely distributed factor of production, will lead to a more equal size distribution. In the discussion that follows, we emphasize the size distribution, but its relationship to the functional distribution of income should be kept in mind.

Many practical problems are involved in measuring the size distribution of income. Ideally, average income over several years should be used since earners in developing countries often experience wide income fluctuations as a result of the vagaries of nature, markets, and their own governments. Cumulated lifetime income would be an even better measure, because earnings vary systematically with age. But such refinements are seldom practical, and most studies are based on estimated income in a particular recent period, usually a year. Other practical issues are precisely how to define income and collect data.

Usually a sample survey of households is undertaken. Even when great care and ingenuity are exercised, the resulting statistics are likely to be of questionable accuracy. Respondents may not know what their true income is, or they may be afraid to disclose it, perhaps thinking that their taxes will go up. Generally, reported incomes are understated. If a household income survey is projected over all households, the total ought to equal the aggregate household share of national income implied in the national income estimates.[3] In practice a shortfall of "only" 15 or 20 percent of national income is regarded as a good result for a household income survey. In general, the uncertainties of these statistics require the analyst to tread cautiously when trying to interpret them.

Once the data have been collected, they must be analyzed. Most procedures begin by ranking respondents (either individuals or households) by income size. The best ranking criterion is household income per capita, since family members in LDCs usually pool their incomes; welfare is thus enhanced by an increase in total household income received and reduced when a larger number of family members must be supported.

The data can be arranged in various ways. The most common method is the **Lorenz curve,** shown in Figure 4–1. To draw a Lorenz curve, income recipients are arrayed from lowest to highest income along the horizontal axis. The curve it-

2. One could argue that the distribution of consumption or wealth should be measured instead. Consumption measures the volume of goods and services actually consumed, so it could be equated with material welfare. But income represents potential consumption, including a part of the potential that is not realized in the current period because it is saved to yield higher consumption later on. Wealth, finally, defines the potential to earn and to consume, especially when human capital is included in the definition of wealth (see Chapters 9 and 10). But the distribution of wealth is notoriously hard to measure, and statistics on wealth distribution are rare.

3. **National income** equals gross national product less depreciation and indirect taxes; the household share of national income would also exclude profits retained (not distributed as dividends) by corporations.

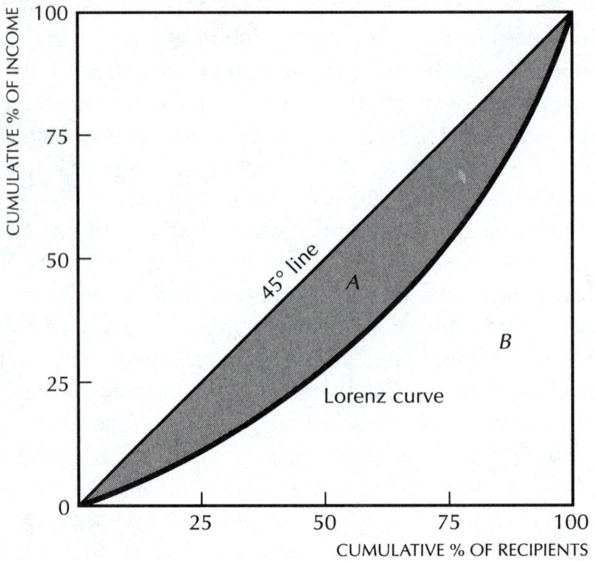

Figure 4–1 Lorenz Curve. The farther the Lorenz curve bends away from the 45-degree line, the greater is the inequality of income distribution. Dividing the shaded area (*A*) by the total area under the 45-degree line (*A* + *B*) gives one measure of inequality, the Gini concentration ratio.

self shows the share of total income received by any cumulative percentage of recipients. Its shape indicates the degree of inequality in the income distribution. By definition the curve must touch the 45-degree line at both the lower left corner (0 percent of recipients must receive 0 percent of income) and the upper right corner (100 percent of recipients must receive 100 percent of income). If everyone had the same income, the Lorenz curve would lie along the 45-degree line (perfect equality). If only one individual or household received income, the curve would trace the lower and right-hand borders of the diagram (perfect inequality). In all actual cases, of course, it lies somewhere in between. Inequality is greater the farther the Lorenz curve bends away from the 45-degree line of perfect equality (the larger the shaded area *A*).

Inequality Measures

Statisticians have long sought to define a single number that would express the degree of overall inequality present in an income distribution. Such simple measures as the range and standard deviation have serious flaws. The most frequently used statistic, the **Gini concentration ratio,** is derived from the Lorenz curve. This ratio is most easily understood as the value of area *A* divided by area *A* + *B* in Figure 4–1. That is, the larger the share of the area between the 45-degree line and the Lorenz curve, the higher the value of the Gini concentration ratio. One can see from Figure 4–1 that the theoretical range of the Gini ratio is from 0 (perfect equality) to 1 (perfect inequality). In practice, values measured in national income distributions have a much narrower range, normally from about .25 to .60. Some examples are shown in Table 4–1.

Like all other indicators that have been proposed to measure inequality, the

TABLE 4–1 Income Distribution in Selected Countries*

Country	% of income received by: Lowest 40%	Highest 20%	Gini concentration ratio†
Low-income countries			
Ethiopia	21.3	41.3	.312
Tanzania	8.1	62.7	.572
Bangladesh	22.9	38.6	.280
India	21.3	41.3	.311
Kenya	10.1	61.8	.551
Pakistan	21.3	39.7	.301
Ghana	18.3	44.1	.358
China	17.4	41.8	.351
Sri Lanka	23.0	39.3	.294
Indonesia	20.8	42.3	.322
Zambia	15.2	49.7	.422
Middle-income countries			
Ivory Coast	19.2	42.2	.338
Bolivia	15.3	48.2	.411
Philippines	16.6	47.8	.377
Peru	14.1	51.4	.443
Bulgaria	24.3	36.2	.252
Colombia	11.2	55.8	.474
Tunisia	16.3	46.3	.391
Thailand	15.5	50.7	.426
Poland	23.0	36.1	.229
Brazil	7.0	67.5	.610
Malaysia	12.9	53.7	.473
Venezuela	14.3	49.5	.429
Hungary	25.7	34.4	.227
Mexico	11.9	55.9	.493
South Korea	19.7	42.2	.331
High-income countries			
Hong Kong	16.2	47.0	.400
Singapore	15.0	48.9	.422
Australia	15.5	42.2	.374
United Kingdom	14.6	44.3	.393
Canada	16.5	40.2	.343
France	17.4	41.9	.354
Germany‡	18.8	40.3	.329
United States	15.7	41.9	.369
Sweden	21.2	36.9	.279
Japan	21.9	37.5	.282
Switzerland	16.9	44.6	.388

* Dates of the surveys underlying these estimates vary by country; they range from 1981 to 1992. Countries are categorized and ranked by their GDP per capita (PPP) in 1990.

† Approximate Gini concentration ratios calculated from grouped data (that is, from data that have been aggregated by income-size groups).

‡ Data refer to West Germany in 1988 (before unification).

Source: World Development Report 1994.

Gini concentration ratio has its problems. For one thing Lorenz curves can intersect. It is even possible for curves with different shapes to generate the same Gini ratio. This happens when one distribution is very unequal in one part of its range—say, from the bottom to around the middle—while another is unequal in a different part—say, in terms of the income shares of the very richest families. Another problem is that the Gini ratio's extreme reference standard, perfect equality, makes the measure generally insensitive to changes in distribution. This insensitivity is greatest for changes in the incomes of low-income groups, which may be small in relation to total income but important in relation to the income of the poor households themselves; such changes may also be an important form of redistribution in policy terms.[4]

Any measure that tries to encompass the entire Lorenz curve in a single statistic must be arbitrary to some degree. One way around this is to look only at a particular part of the curve. Thus if we are most interested in how the poor are faring, we might examine the absolute and relative incomes of the poorest 30 or 40 percent of the distribution. Conversely, if our main concern is the concentration of wealth near the top of the distribution, then the top 5, 10, or 20 percent could be studied. This tells what we want to know for particular purposes, but at the cost of generality; it ignores what is going on in the rest of the distribution.

Some of these points are illustrated in Table 4–2, which compares two hypothetical income distributions. In one country, income is equally distributed both within the lower half of the income distribution and within the upper half, but mean income differs greatly between the two halves. In the other country, people in the lower three-quarters of the distribution receive the same income while people in the upper one-quarter receive a larger sum. These two distributions turn out to have the same Gini coefficients (.35), but their Lorenz curves are of different shapes and cross, as shown in Figure 4–2.

Poverty Measures

While inequality is clearly a matter of relative incomes, the concept of **poverty** focuses on the low absolute incomes received by certain households. An objective definition of poverty is surprisingly hard to formulate. Calculations of the minimum income level necessary for physical survival indicate that one can get by on very little if one chooses.[5] Efforts to link poverty to its specific manifestations—starvation, severe malnutrition, illiteracy, substandard clothing and housing—are also inconclusive. The fact is that poverty is not just a matter of absolute incomes; it also implies something about relative incomes. In social terms, the poor are those who must live below what most people in a particular time and place regard

TABLE 4–2 Comparison of Two Hypothetical Income Distributions

Income group	Distribution No.1	Distribution No. 2
Lowest 25%	7.5	13.3
Next 25%	7.5	13.3
Next 25%	42.5	13.3
Highest 25%	42.5	60.0
Gini Coefficient	.35	.35

4. In the Philippines in 1970–71 the lowest 20 percent of the income distribution received only 5.2 percent of total income while the top 10 percent of households got 38.5 percent of total income. Taking 1 percent of total income from the richest group and giving it to the lowest 20 percent would raise the incomes of the poor by 19 percent, a meaningful increase. Yet it would lower the Gini concentration ratio only from .461 to .445, assuming that the redistributive gain is shared equally by the lowest two deciles.

5. George Stigler calculated that Americans could purchase a physiologically adequate diet for $8 per month per person (in 1950 prices) by limiting themselves to a diet of wheat flour, evaporated milk, cabbage, spinach, and dried navy beans. See George Stigler, *The Theory of Price* (Rev. ed.; New York: Macmillan Co., 1952), p. 2. The fact that very few choose to do so indicates the importance of the psychological and social aspects of poverty.

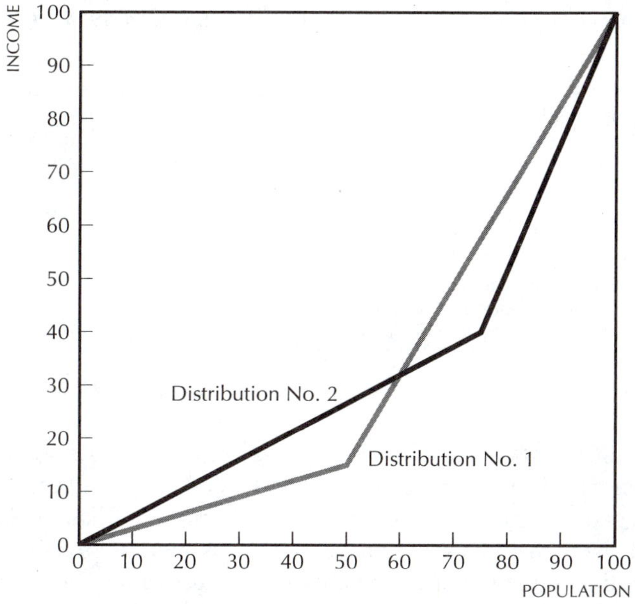

Figure 4–2—Two Hypothetical Lorenz Curves. Although these two income distributions differ substantially, the fact that their Lorenz curves cross permits them to yield the same measures of relative inequality (Gini coefficient = .35).

as the minimum acceptable standard. Thus while almost everyone in the United States receives a higher income than almost everyone in, say, Chad, there are still (relatively) poor people in the United States and (relatively) nonpoor people in Chad. Different standards apply in the two places. Psychologically, the poor are those who feel deprived of whatever is enjoyed by other members of the society of which they consider themselves to be a part (their reference group). Reference groups are probably expanding as education and communication improve. Formerly, peasants may have compared their own status with that of the village elites at most. Now they are becoming more aware of how urban elites in their own countries live, and even of the standards that prevail in rich countries. The sense of deprivation may well be growing.

Those interested in measuring the amount of poverty existing in a country usually begin by drawing a poverty line. Ideally, this line is defined in terms of household income per capita. Households with per capita incomes below the poverty line are defined as poor while those with incomes above the line are not poor. The simplest and most common measure of poverty (the "poverty headcount") is the percentage of all households that are poor. A better measure, however, would also take account of the extent to which the incomes of the poor fall below the poverty line. A reduction in poverty would then be measured through a fall in the percentage of poor households in the total number of households and also through increases in the absolute incomes of the poor.

Table 4–3 illustrates these points, using as an example one of the most successful cases of poverty and inequality alleviation. Sri Lanka in 1953 had a low per capita income, relatively great inequality (as measured by the Gini ratio), and a large population of poor people (defined here as receiving a monthly per capita income below 100 rupees in 1963 prices). Over the succeeding two decades in-

TABLE 4–3 Changes in Income Distribution and Poverty in Sri Lanka, 1953–1973

Measure	1953	1963	1973
Income shares of quintiles			
Bottom 20%	5.2	4.5	7.2
Second quintile	9.3	9.2	12.1
Third quintile	13.3	13.8	16.3
Fourth quintile	18.4	20.2	21.6
Top 20%	53.8	52.3	42.9
Gini concentration ratio	.46	.45	.35
Mean monthly income per capita (rupees)*	117	134	150
Mean monthly income of bottom 40% (rupees)*	42	46	72
Percent of households below 100 rupees/month*	63	59	41

* In 1963 prices.
Source: Gary S. Fields, *Inequality and Development* (London: Cambridge University Press, 1980), p.197.

equality declined and outstanding progress was made in reducing poverty, as can be seen from the rise in the mean income of the bottom 40 percent of the income distribution and from the sharp decline in the percentage of households below the poverty line. Note that this was achieved with only modest growth in average income; according to the statistics, monthly income per capita rose only 28 percent in 20 years, while the average income of households in the lowest four deciles of the distribution rose by 71 percent. Few developing countries have been able to duplicate this achievement.

The poverty analyst can apply similar or different standards across varying times and places. World Bank publications sometimes refer to the quantity and distribution of "absolute poverty" in the world; these calculations are made using a simple global poverty line of about $1 per capita per day.[6]

Equality and Equity

Equality means simply that everyone gets the same income (or owns the same wealth). Although this never occurs in practice, the concept provides an objective standard against which any actual distribution can be judged. Equity, on the other hand, is a normative (ethical) concept: what is equitable depends on one's sense of right and wrong. Many Americans, for example, believe in equality of opportunity but think that considerable inequality of results may be justified by interpersonal differences in ability, effort, training, willingness to take risks, and stage in the life cycle. Even societies that favor greater equality of income and wealth find that they must offer extra rewards for hard work, education, saving, and ability in order to achieve economic growth. Most concepts of equity therefore allow for some degree of inequality in the distribution of income.

Basic Human Needs and Social Indicators

Some students of development, including many from disciplines other than economics, reject definitions of poverty based on income. Of course, they say, higher

6. For a probing discussion of these measurement problems, see Amartya K. Sen, *On Economic Inequality* (New York: Norton, 1973). A good short discussion is provided in Richard Szal and Sherman Robinson, "Measuring Income Inequality," in Charles R. Frank and Richard C. Webb (eds.), *Income Distribution and Growth in the Less-Developed Countries* (Washington, D. C.: Brookings Institution, 1977), pp. 491–533.

incomes *help make it possible* for people to live better and longer, but why not ask directly whether these changes actually occur? Efforts to measure a wide variety of **social indicators** go back many years. More recently interest has centered on seeing whether **basic human needs** are satisfied. Lists of basic human needs vary, but most include minimal levels of nutrition, health, clothing, shelter, and opportunities for individual freedom and advancement. Some of these, at least, can be measured.

The World Bank periodically publishes data on social indicators obtained from various sources. Table 4–4 summarizes part of this information. Some of the indicators listed—infant deaths, life expectancy, child malnutrition, and adult literacy—reflect the degree to which basic human needs are satisfied in countries at different levels of GNP per capita. Other indicators are less directly related to welfare. Some, such as energy consumption and newspaper circulation, measure the sophistication of the economy and society. Still others, represented in Table 4–4 by the provision of physicians and hospital beds, indicate levels of services that may contribute to basic needs satisfaction, which is itself measured more directly by other indicators.[7]

Two interesting points emerge from an examination of Table 4–4. One is that improvement in social indicators generally goes hand in hand with a rise in per capita GNP. Nearly every time we move to a higher-income group in Table 4–4, the average value of each social indicator for the countries covered by the World Bank's data changes in the expected direction.[8] But the second point is that, within each income class, variations among countries are large. This is demonstrated by the high values for standard deviations shown in the table.[9]

Overall Indicators of Development

Social indicators are hard to combine into an overall measure of a country's social development. In 1979, an effort to do so was made by the Washington-based Overseas Development Council (ODC). The ODC's physical quality of life index (PQLI) was based on three widely available indicators of the basic-human-needs variety: life expectancy at age one, infant mortality rate, and literacy rate.[10] Each indicator was assigned a scaled value from 0 to 100, with the best and worst known cases setting the limits of the scale. An unweighted average of the three indicators was then taken. The PQLI was interpreted by its promoters to suggest

7. Besides being an approach to measuring welfare, the satisfaction of basic human needs is also a strategy for welfare-oriented development. This aspect is discussed in the last section of this chapter.

8. In other words, "good things" like life expectancy and access to safe water rise, while "bad things" like infant deaths and malnutrition fall. The sole exception is the decline in availability of hospital beds from the $5,000–$10,000 income class to the over-$10,000 income class. This anomaly occurs because several ex-socialist countries in the former income class report very large numbers of hospital beds relative to population.

9. The standard deviation is a measurement of the average variation among observations. It can be defined as

$$(d^2/n)^{1/2},$$

where d is the deviation of each observation from the mean and n is the number of observations. A large standard deviation indicates a wide spread among the observations, while a small one suggests that most observations have values close to the mean. In a normal, or bell-shaped, distribution, over 60 percent of all observations lie within one standard deviation of the mean.

10. See Morris David Morris, *Measuring the Condition of the World's Poor. The Physical Quality of Life Index* (New York: Pergamon Press for the Overseas Development Council, 1979).

TABLE 4–4 Illustrative Social Indicators for 1990*

	GDP per Capita (PPP)				
	<$1,000	$1,000–$2,000	$2,000–$5,000	$5,000–$10,000	>$10,000
Infant deaths/1000 live births	115 (21)	80 (32)	42 (22)	22 (14)	9 (5)
Life expectancy at birth (years)	49 (5)	57 (7)	67 (5)	70 (3)	76 (2)
Physicians/1000 inhabitants	7 (4)	31 (31)	165 (152)	201 (149)	230 (95)
Hospital beds/1000 inhabitants	96 (72)	156 (86)	506 (432)	1587 (3590)	718 (345)
Access to health care (% of population)	48 (21)	56 (30)	88 (13)	94 (10)	100 (2)
Access to save water (% of population)	44 (17)	53 (18)	71 (21)	87 (10)	98 (3)
Energy consumption per capita (kg of oil equivalent)	46 (33)	189 (159)	977 (955)	2029 (1469)	4857 (2472)
Malnourished children under 5 (% of total)	35 (14)	25 (13)	20 (13)	12 (7)	n.a.
Adult literacy (%)	44 (18)	56 (19)	76 (15)	87 (10)	94 (9)
Newspaper circulated/1000 inhabitants	5 (4)	28 (35)	79 (91)	125 (83)	328 (170)

* Data points vary. Most are in the 1987 to 1992 range, but some are from 1980 to 1985. Figures in parentheses are standard derivations.

Sources: United Nations Development Program, *Human Development Report 1994* (New York: Oxford University Press, 1994), and World Bank, *Social Indicators of Development 1994* (Baltimore: Johns Hopkins Press, 1994).

that the richest countries do not always enjoy the highest quality of life and that at least a few countries (for example, Sri Lanka, Cuba, Guyana, and South Korea) had achieved a comparatively high quality of life at levels of per capita income well below those of the industrialized nations.

In 1990 the United Nations Development Program (UNDP) introduced a **human development index** (HDI), which combines measures of life expectancy, educational attainment (encompassing mean years of schooling and adult literacy), and GNP per capita in the manner of the PQLI.[11] Like other such indexes, the HDI is somewhat arbitrary and may reflect the political opinions of its compilers. For example, the HDI disregards increases in GDP per capita above about $5,300 per capita (PPP); this suggests that raising per capita income from the level of Colombia or Lithuania to that of Switzerland contributes nothing to human development.

Rankings of countries according to their HDI and PQLI values correlate fairly well with their per capita GNP or GDP rankings, especially when the purchasing power parity measure is used.[12] The largest deviations are for obvious cases such

11. United Nations Development Program, *Human Development Report 1990* (New York: Oxford University Press, 1990). The *Human Development Report* has appeared annually since then, and minor adjustments have been made to the HDI. The description in the text refers to the latest (1994) version.

12. In the data set that underlies Table 4–5, 59 percent of the intercountry variation in HDI is "explained" by variations in GDP per capita (PPP). Explained variation drops to 37 percent if GNP per capita is converted to U.S. dollars by the exchange rate method.

as the oil-exporting countries, which have high per capita income (at least in years when oil prices are high) but low values on the social development indexes. Table 4–5 gives recent values of all three measures for a number of countries.

Although further efforts to develop new ways of measuring and comparing wel-

TABLE 4–5 Comparison of per Capita Income and Human Development Index for Selected Countries, 1992

	GDP per capita (PPP, 1992)	GNP per capita (exchange rate)	Human development index
Low-income countries			
Ethiopia	340	110	.249
Tanzania	630	110	.306
Zambia	1,890	450	.382
India	1,010*	390	.352
Bangladesh	1,210	310	.382
Kenya	1,230	220	.309
Nigeria	1,360	310	.434
Ivory Coast	1,440	320	.348
Ghana	1,640	670	.382
China	1,910	470	.644
Lower middle-income countries			
Cuba	2,000	—	.666
Pakistan	2,130	420	.393
Bolivia	2,270	680	.530
Philippines	2,480	770	.621
Sri Lanka	2,810	540	.665
Indonesia	2.970	670	.586
Peru	3,080	950	.642
Poland	4,880	1,910	.815
Bulgaria	5,130	1,330	.815
Tunisia	5,130	1,720	.690
Brazil	5,250	2,770	.756
Colombia	5,760	1,330	.813
Thailand	5,890	1,840	.798
Upper middle-income countries			
Hungary	5,740	2,970	.863
Russia	6,220	2,510	.858
Mexico	7,490	3,470	.804
Malaysia	8,050	2,790	.798
Chile	8,090	2,730	.848
Venezuela	8,790	2,910	.820
South Korea	8,950	6,790	.859
Oman	9,630	6,480	.654
High-income countries			
Saudi Arabia	11,170	7,510	.742
Singapore	16,720	15,730	.829
United Kingdom	16,730	21,970	.911
Australia	17,350	17,260	.926
Sweden	17,610	27,010	.928
France	19,200	22,260	.927
Canada	19,720	20,710	.932
Hong Kong	20,050	15,360	.875
Japan	20,160	28,190	.929
Germany	20,610	23,030	.918
Switzerland	22,100	36,080	.931
United States	22,120	23,240	.925

* 1991.
Source: World Development Report 1994 and United Nations Development Program, *Human Development Report 1994.*

fare in different countries can be expected in the future, we can safely predict that universally acceptable measures will never be found. Development brings about many changes, and an evaluation of its effect on welfare inevitably depends on the importance one attaches to each type of change. Varying degrees of emphasis on growth, inequality, and poverty lead to differing assessments. A particular measurement scheme can express one evaluator's values, but the values of other observers may well diverge. There is, however, general agreement that successful development (in welfare terms) requires rising per capita output, reduced poverty, and improved health and longevity, with at least no dramatic worsening of inequality.

Patterns of Inequality and Poverty

Kuznets' Inverted U

In his 1955 presidential address to the American Economic Association, Simon Kuznets suggested that the relationship between per capita GNP and inequality in the distribution of income may take the form of an inverted U. That is, as per capita income rises, inequality may initially rise, reach a maximum at an intermediate level of income, and then decline as income levels characteristic of an industrial country are reached.

Kuznets based this proposition on the mere fragments of data available at the time for estimating income distributions in a few rich and poor countries and on trends in distribution over time in a few European countries. His insight has been both supported and challenged by later studies based on much larger bodies of data. Income distribution has now been estimated for more than 70 countries, but some of these estimates are outdated or of dubious quality. Table 4–6 summarizes reasonable estimates made for 65 countries since 1980. Inequality can be measured in this table in three different ways: as the share of total income received by the poorest 40 percent, the share of the top 20 percent, and the Gini concentration ratio. By all three measures, inequality first rises, then peaks, and finally falls, just

Table 4–6 Estimates of Inequality and Poverty in Relation to GDP per Capita (PPP)*

Country groups†	Number of countries included	Percentage of income received by: Lowest 40%	Highest 20%	Gini concentration ratio	Mean income of lowest 40% (dollars PPP)	GDP per capita (dollars PPP)
Low-income countries	8	17.7	46.4	.379	300	690
Lower-middle-income countries	25	14.9	50.6	.430	830	2,270
Upper-middle-income countries	9	12.9	54.3	.460	2,170	6,570
High-income countries	20	18.1	40.6	.340	7,940	17,340
East European countries	3	24.3	35.6	.236	3,090	5,040

* Unweighted average within groups.
† For purposes of this table, low-income countries are those with GDP per capita of less than $1,000 (PPP) in 1990. Lower-middle-income countries are in the $1,000–$5,000 range, upper-middle-income countries in the $5,000–$10,000 range, and high-income countries in the over-$10,000 range.
Sources: Same as Table 4–1.

as Kuznets predicted in 1955. This result has often been obtained in studies of cross-section data. Less frequently noted, however, is its heavy dependence on the Latin American countries, most of which are in the middle-income group and generally have high inequality. If these countries were removed from the data set, the U-shaped relationship might disappear.

Cross-section data like those in Table 4–6 (that is, estimates made for a number of different countries at about the same time) provide most of the available evidence on the relationship between income levels and inequality. **Time-series data** (comparable estimates at different times for particular countries) are rarer. For many countries there is still only one good estimate of income distribution (at most!). Even where two or more surveys have been made, differences in survey design and execution may make comparisons of results misleading.

Nevertheless, there are now successive estimates for enough countries to fuel speculation about trends in inequality over time. In some cases, the pattern hypothesized by Kuznets is discernible, but in others it is not. One recent survey indicated that while inequality has tended to increase over intervals for which changes can be measured in developing countries, it has been almost equally likely to do so in developed countries.[13] Another study concludes agnostically that "rapid growth in a mixed economy is consistent with unchanged, or even improved, income distribution, even at early stages of development."[14]

In summary, the inverted-U relationship discerned by Kuznets has received some support (especially from cross-section analyses) but remains controversial. Even in cross-section data such as those shown in Table 4–6, however, the hypothesized curvilinear relationship explains only a small fraction of the intercountry variation in Gini coefficients. A calculation based on data for the 65 countries shown in Table 4–6 yields

$$G = -1.072 + 0.395 \log Y - 0.026 \log Y^2, \qquad [4\text{–}1]$$

where G = the value of the Gini coefficient and $\log Y$ = the natural logarithm of GDP per capita in 1985 according to the purchasing power parity measure.[15] The R^2 (share of variation explained) of this equation is only .15.

Other Influences on Inequality

Many individual countries have substantially more or less inequality than might be expected at their per capita income level. Sri Lanka is often cited as an example of relatively equal income distribution in a low-income country (see boxed example), while South Korea and Taiwan are famed for their ability to combine rapid growth with relatively equal income distributions. Latin American countries are known for high inequality, but inequality in Argentina and Uruguay has been measured in the past as far below the normally high levels for the region. Developing countries with unusually high inequality include Tanzania, Kenya, Zambia, Peru, Colombia, Thailand, Brazil, Malaysia, Venezuela, and Mexico.

13. Gary S. Fields, "Changes in Poverty and Inequality in Developing Countries," *World Bank Research Observer,* 4, no. 2 (July 1989), 176.

14. Gustav F. Papanek and Oldrich Kyn, "The Effect on Income Distribution of Development, The Growth Rate and Economic Strategy," *Journal of Development Economics,* 23 (1986), 55–56.

15. Robert Summers and Alan Heston, "The Penn World Table (Mark 5): An Expanded Set of International Comparisions, 1950–1988," *Quarterly Journal of Economics,* 106, no. 2 (May 1991), 327–68.

Transitional economies (such as Bulgaria, Poland, and Hungary in Table 4–1) tend to have low inequality. Among developed countries, New Zealand, Hong Kong, Singapore, the United Kingdom, and Switzerland have considerably more inequality than the average for their income level.

Efforts to identify factors other than per capita income that might explain the amount of inequality present in a given country have had mixed results. One influential study concluded that higher enrollment rates in primary and secondary schools and a higher GNP growth rate are associated with less inequality, given the level of GNP per capita, while a higher growth rate of population goes with more inequality.[16] However, no one has been able to explain much more than half the intercountry variation in inequality, and some of the results obtained have been contradictory. We still lack a general explanation of income distribution in relation to economic growth that closely conforms with the known facts.

Irma Adelman and Cynthia Taft Morris tried to identify the types of societies (in social and political as well as economic terms) where inequality is likely to be high or low. They concluded that income distribution is typically relatively equal in two kinds of countries: very poor countries dominated by small-scale or communal (jointly farmed) agriculture and well-developed countries in which major efforts have been made to improve human resources.[17] This conclusion both qualifies the Kuznets hypothesis and suggests some of the factors that may be associated with the inverted-U pattern. Very poor countries may be quite egalitarian, it says, but only if their economies are dominated by small peasant farms and not by large farms or mines. Countries with intermediate income levels are likely to have considerable inequality. Adelman and Morris found the income share of the poorest 60 percent of the income distribution to be smallest where well-entrenched foreign or military elites control the most productive economic sectors and receive most of the benefits of development.

How Growth Reduces Poverty

Logically, if the income share of the poor rises with growth, their absolute income must also rise, since they then receive an increasing share of an increasing total. But what if their share declines, as it may in the early stages of development? Even in this case, poverty alleviation is closely associated with per capita GNP or GDP. The mean income of the poor in a given society is very closely associated with GDP per capita ($R^2 = .93$), as the following equation based on the data in Table 4–5, suggests:

$$\log Y_p = -1.406 + 1.056 \log Y, \qquad [4\text{–}2]$$

where $\log Y_p$ = the natural logarithm of the mean income of the poorest 40 percent of families and $\log Y$ = the natural logarithm of GDP per capita (PPP).

The share of the population living in poverty is also closely related to per capita GDP ($R^2 = .80$), at least if we adopt a global poverty line (in this case $370 per

16. See Montek S. Ahluwalia, "Income Inequality: Some Dimensions of the Problem," in *Redistribution with Growth,* Chenery et al., pp. 3–37, and Montek S. Ahluwalia, "Inequality, Poverty and Development," *Journal of Development Economics,* 3 (1976), 307–42.

17. See Irma Adelman and Cynthia Taft Morris, *Economic Growth and Social Equity in Developing Countries* (Stanford, Calif.: Stanford University Press, 1973).

capita, expressed in 1985 PPP), the poverty line used in the *World Development Report 1990*. The equation, again based on the data in Table 4–5, is

$$P = 4.942 - 1.116 \log Y + 0.063 \log Y^2, \qquad [4\text{–}3]$$

where P = the percentage of households with less than \$370 per capita and $\log Y$ = the natural logarithm of GDP per capita in 1985.

In summary, while people may be poor for many different reasons, the most important one is that they live in poor countries.[18] Assuming that what we see in cross-section data will hold up over time as countries develop, these calculations lead us to expect that raising per capita income will almost certainly increase the absolute income of the poor and will probably also reduce the proportion of the population living in poverty, as measured by a global poverty line.

Another indication that poverty and low national income per capita go together is the geography of world poverty. In 1990, nearly half the world's more than 1 billion poor (defined as per capita income below \$370 in 1985 purchasing power parity dollars) lived in the low-income countries of South Asia (Table 4–7). Worldwide, more than 80 percent of the poor in 1990 lived in low-income countries with per capita GNP of less than \$1,000 (PPP).[19] There were of course absolutely poor people in other regions, but their numbers were much smaller.

While most poor people continue to be found in the poorest countries, sharp differences in rates of economic growth are causing the incidence of poverty to fall in Asia but rise in sub-Saharan Africa. Asia's share in world poverty is still large, but it is declining (East Asia's especially rapidly), while sub-Saharan Africa's share is rising. The World Bank projects that between 1985 and the year 2000 the number of poor people in East Asia will fall from 280 million to fewer than 100 million and the number in South Asia from 520 million to fewer than 400 million. Over the same period, poverty in sub-Saharan Africa is expected to rise from 180 million to more than 250 million. The gradual shift of world poverty from faster-growing Asia to virtually stagnant Africa is further indication

TABLE 4–7 Geographical Distribution of World Poverty, 1990

Region	Number of poor (millions)	% of region's population	% of world poor
East Asia and the Pacific	169	11	15
Eastern Europe	5	7	—
Latin America and the Caribbean	108	25	10
Middle East and North Africa	73	33	6
South Asia	563	49	50
Sub-Saharan Africa	216	48	19
All developing countries	1133	30	100

Source: World Bank, *Implementing the World Bank's Strategy to Reduce Poverty. Progress and Challenges* (Washington, D.C.: World Bank, 1993), p. 5.

18. See also Ahluwalia, "Income Equality" and "Inequality, Poverty, and Development."
19. *World Development Report 1990*, p. 29.

that economic growth reduces poverty while economic stagnation or decline allows poverty to rise, especially when it is accompanied by rapid population increases (see Chapter 7).

In all third-world regions and countries, poverty is more prevalent in rural than in urban areas. World Bank estimates suggest that in most Asian and African countries 80 percent or more of the poor lived in rural areas in the 1980s. In Latin America, which is more urbanized than Africa or Asia, the urban poor are a larger share of the total, but the prevalence of poverty (the percentage of the population that is poor) is still greater in the countryside. Although many countries have urban slums, urbanization is clearly an important part of the poverty reduction process.

Two qualifications must be attached to our strong conclusion that poverty is associated with low national per capita income and tends to be eradicated as per capita income rises. First, it applies to absolute poverty measured using a global poverty line. Relative poverty is far more persistent. Few people live on $370 a year in the United States, but many receive incomes far below a reasonable U.S. standard. Second, some time-series studies for particular countries have shown stagnation or even decline in the incomes of the poor and increases in the number of poor people or both. Many of these findings have been challenged, but they do at least warn us not to assume complacently that economic growth will necessarily or rapidly eliminate poverty.

Income Distribution Models

The most ambitious way to study the determinants of income distribution and the effects of various policies on it is to build a comprehensive model of income distribution as it is generated by the overall workings of an economy. In one of the best-known studies, quantitative economists Irma Adelman and Sherman Robinson modeled the South Korean economy.[20] Their computable general equilibrium (CGE) model (see further discussion in Chapter 6) specifies price and quantity adjustments in both factor and product markets and allows for substitution possibilities in production and consumption in response to changes in relative prices. A dynamic version of the model projects investment by sector on the basis of profitability, expectations, and government financial policies.

The model predicted that economic growth would continue in Korea, but most of the gains would go to the urban population and the income distribution would steadily worsen. Experimental runs of the model to simulate the effects of various policy packages showed that most policies would have little effect on income distribution. Some supposed antipoverty policies actually gave disproportionate benefits to the high-and middle-income groups. The best policies for bettering income distribution were those that either improved relative prices received by agricultural producers (their internal terms of trade) or encouraged rural-to-urban migration. Foreign trade policies, working largely through these two factors, had significant impacts on inequality and poverty.

Four case studies help to round out the picture of world poverty created by the global statistics and research that we have been discussing. If they achieve nothing else, these case studies show that one should be cautious in generalizing about

20. Irma Adelman and Sherman Robinson, *Income Distribution Policy in Developing Countries. A Case Study of Korea* (Stanford, Calif.: Stanford University Press, 1978).

development, inequality, and poverty. Much depends on the circumstances of the individual country and the type of development pursued.

South Korea

South Korea has continued to enjoy an extraordinarily high rate of economic growth (per capita income growth averaged 8.5 percent a year from 1980 to 1992), which has helped to alleviate poverty and satisfy basic needs. The Korean development pattern has been highly equitable, compared with virtually all other developing countries, for two reasons. First, assets, especially land, were distributed relatively equally before rapid growth began; second, Korea pursued a pattern of development that did not greatly concentrate income or wealth. When Korea emerged from Japanese colonial rule at the end of World War II, the many large production units that had been Japanese-owned were either nationalized or broken up and redistributed. Two land reforms subdivided the larger agricultural holdings and virtually eliminated tenancy (in which land is owned by one person but farmed by another, who pays rent for its use).

The rapid economic growth that began in the early 1960s emphasized the modernization of small- and medium-sized firms (although by the 1970s, large-scale firms were formed). Foreign ownership was held to a minimum. Manufacturing for export boomed and absorbed a larger share of labor-force growth than in almost any other country. The Korean educational system, which accommodated all children at its lower levels and then rigorously selected the few best performers for continuation to its higher levels, supported both equity and growth. All these factors contributed to a rapid decline in poverty. Inequality has risen slightly as the country transformed itself economically and began to emphasize growth in larger firms, but it has remained lower than in other developing countries and comparable to inequality in the most developed Western countries. Korea, then, is a clear-cut case of rapid growth with equity.

Brazil

Brazil has grown faster during some periods than most other Latin American countries, but the consequences for human welfare have been somewhat equivocal. A large, naturally rich country, Brazil has made impressive strides toward the creation of a modern, diversified economy. Some of its industries and modern cities bear comparison with those in the rich countries. Brazilian agriculture has also progressed in important areas, such as the development of soybeans as a major export crop alongside coffee and other traditional items. But economic growth has been uneven in both time (there have been several stop-and-go phases) and space.

Whole sections of the country, such as the poor northeast, have been largely excluded from development. Even the big, modern cities in the south (Rio de Janeiro, São Paulo, Belo-Horizonte) have appalling urban slums, sometimes located right next to luxurious, architecturally impressive, new constructions. Many of the factors that have led to equitable growth in Korea are reversed in Brazil: asset ownership is highly concentrated; there has been no land reform; access to education is uneven and heavily influenced by wealth; production, both manufacturing and agricultural, is concentrated in large production units; and technologies adopted have tended to be capital-intensive. The results are very high inequality and little progress toward poverty alleviation, despite some increases in the real incomes of the poor.

Sri Lanka

Sri Lanka has grown at low or average rates through most of its history. As a result of the country's open democratic system of government and the articulateness of its well-educated electorate, all Sri Lankan governments since independence in 1948 have had to be populist to survive. A system of social benefits that included cheap staple foods and free schooling and medical services helped to produce a healthy, literate populace. Inequality was kept relatively low, and despite low income levels, the worst manifestations of poverty (premature deaths, malnutrition, illiteracy) were avoided to a remarkable degree. The trouble was that economic growth was too slow to provide either adequate financing for the welfare system or employment for the growing labor force, especially the educated youths seeking white-collar jobs. Chronic popular dissatisfaction led to repeated changes in government at the polls and an unsuccessful youth revolt in 1971. In 1977 a new government inaugurated an effort to accelerate growth by emphasizing labor-intensive manufacturing, irrigation, and tourism. This led to accelerated economic growth, but also rising income inequality. Tragically, conflict between the island's majority Sinhalese community and the minority Tamils has severely limited the benefits realized from the post-1977 growth strategy.

India

India, like Brazil, is a big country with areas of both dynamism and stagnation. Also like Brazil, it has emphasized inward-looking development to build a self-sufficient, subcontinental economy. Like Sri Lanka, India is a poor country, which has generally not grown very rapidly. There has been substantial development in some regions, such as Bombay and the Punjab, through either industrialization or successful adoption of the Green Revolution in food-grain production. Other areas, like Bihar state, remain desperately poor. One southern state, Kerala, has a Sri Lanka-like pattern of high basic-needs satisfaction together with low income and growth. Overall inequality measures for India usually come out rather low because there are so many poor people and relatively small classes of the comfortable or rich. About 50 percent of the population lives below the officially defined poverty line, and this proportion has changed little over the years. Recently, there have been market-oriented policy reforms, but their effects on poverty and inequality are not yet evident.

THEORIES OF INEQUALITY AND POVERTY

During the classical period of economic thought, poverty and inequality and their relationship to economic growth were a principal concern of theorists. This is particularly evident in the work of David Ricardo, who wrote in the early 1800s, when England was a developing country.

Ricardo's Two-Sector Model

We saw in Chapter 3 that Ricardo pioneered the two-sector model of development. His analysis suggested that if England did not abolish the corn laws, which protected grain farmers from foreign competition, and allow imports of food to fuel its industrial revolution, income would be redistributed from capitalists to landlords. (Wages, he assumed, would remain at the subsistence level.) Since Ricardo regarded landlords as spendthrifts and believed that economic growth was financed by the savings of the thrifty capitalist class, he concluded that this redistribution would harm economic growth.

Although his theory was innovative and internally consistent, all Ricardo's predictions about income distribution and economic growth turned out to be wrong. Rent (income to landlords) has not taken a growing share of national income in industrializing countries but instead has remained a rather small share. The profit share (income to capitalists) has not been squeezed out. And wages have not been held to the subsistence level but have risen, at least in the later stages of industrial development; the share of wages in national income, if anything, has tended to increase. There are several reasons why actual trends have not matched those predicted in Ricardo's model. One is that England did adopt free trade, as Ricardo wanted. But even if it had not, diminishing returns would probably have been largely offset by technological change, which would have made it possible to grow increasing amounts of food on land of given quantity and quality. Ricardo also overestimated the strength of the Malthusian population mechanism (see Chapter 7), which he thought would hold wages at the subsistence level.

Marx's View

Karl Marx also believed that capitalist development would create an increasingly unequal distribution of income. Capitalists, he thought, had an incentive to create a "reserve army of the unemployed," whose brooding presence would ensure that the wages of employed laborers stayed at the subsistence level. (Marx hotly rebutted the Malthusian theory that demographic forces created the labor surplus, calling this line of thinking an insult to the working class.) In Marxian thought, the owners of capital dominate both the economy and the "bourgeois state." But as capitalism develops, the rate of profit falls and crises occur and cause firms to fail and industrial concentration to rise. Eventually, in a final apocalyptic crisis, capitalism itself collapses, to be replaced by socialism. Only then, according to Karl Marx, can the lot of the workers improve.

Although Marx was enormously influential as a critic of capitalism and revolutionary prophet, his prediction of how income distribution would evolve over time was no more accurate than Ricardo's.

Neoclassical Theory

The dominant theory used today to explain income distribution in developed countries was worked out in the late nineteenth and early twentieth centuries. The **neoclassical (marginal productivity) theory** postulates that all factors of production (now more numerous than land, labor, and capital, to take account of quality differences) are in scarce supply and that their rates of return are set equal to their marginal products in competitive factor markets. This theory is also relevant to developing countries, but its applicability there is more debatable because the theory's assumption that product and factor markets are perfectly competitive is less valid in such a setting.

Labor-Surplus Model

An alternative to the neoclassical theory for analyzing income distribution in developing countries is provided by the labor-surplus model of W. Arthur Lewis. It was Lewis who first observed that conditions in less-developed countries are in some ways more similar to those that prevailed in the industrialized countries before the Industrial Revolution than they are to conditions in those same countries today. A useful theory to analyze the workings of a low-income economy, therefore, might be built on classical rather than neoclassical assumptions. This insight led Lewis to his celebrated model of "economic development with unlimited supplies of labor," which utilized the Ricardo-Marx assumption that labor is available in unlimited quantity at a fixed real wage, rather than being a scarce factor of production that must be bid away from other uses, as in the neoclassical theory. The implications of the labor-surplus model for the importance of agricultural development and the role played by population growth were discussed in Chapter 3. Here we seek to bring out the model's implications for the distribution of income.

The labor-surplus model suggests that inequality will first increase and later diminish as development takes place. It is thus consistent with Kuznets' generalization about what has actually occurred. Lewis gives two reasons why an initial rise in inequality might be expected. One is that the income share of the capitalists (i.e., those who control capital, including state-owned enterprises) rises as the size of the modern, or capitalist, sector increases. The second reason is that inequality in the distribution of labor income also rises during the early period, when increasing but still relatively small numbers of laborers begin to move from the subsistence wage level to the capitalist-sector wage level, which Lewis says tends to run about 30 percent higher in real terms.

If this seems counterintuitive, imagine that there are no wage differentials within either sector of the dual economy but a 30 percent differential between the two sectors, as Lewis assumes. In this case, inequality in the distribution of labor income would be zero at the beginning of the development process, when all the workers were employed in the low-wage sector, and zero again at the end of the process, when all the workers are employed in the high-wage sector. At all points between these two extremes, there would be some inequality in the distribution of labor income. In our simple model, inequality in the distribution of labor income would rise up to the point at which half the labor force is employed in the high-wage sector and then decline.

The tendency for inequality to rise during the early stages of development is strongly reversed (as explicitly depicted in the Fei-Ranis extension of the Lewis model; see Chapter 3) when all the surplus labor is finally absorbed into modern-sector employment. At that point, labor becomes a scarce factor of production, and further increases in demand require increases in real wages to bid labor away from marginal uses. The model suggests that the resulting rise in the general wage level brings about not only an eventual downturn in inequality but also the long-awaited abolition of poverty, at least by former standards.

In the Lewis version of the labor-surplus model, inequality is not just a necessary effect of economic growth; it is also a cause of growth. A distribution of income that favors high-income groups contributes to growth because profit earners save to obtain funds for expanding their enterprises. The more income they receive, the more they invest. Their saving and investment are essential for increasing productive capacity and thus bringing about output growth. In a famous quotation, Lewis says that "the central problem in the theory of economic development is to understand the process by which a community which was previously saving and investing 4 or 5 percent of its national income converts itself into an economy where voluntary saving is running about 12 to 15 percent of the national income or more."[21] The answer, he argues, lies with the 10 percent of the population which receives 40 percent or more of national income in labor-surplus countries. Growth occurs when the well-off save more, not because their marginal propensity to save increases but because their aggregate income and share in total income go up. This happens because the profit share of income increases with the growth of the modern sector while the wage share remains constant.

Not only does inequality contribute to growth according to Lewis, but attempts to redistribute income "prematurely" run the risk that economic growth will be stifled. As in Ricardo's theory, anything that raises urban wages cuts into profits, and hence into savings, investment, and economic growth. Factors that could have this effect include a rise in the price of food relative to the price of manufactured goods and actions by trade unions or government to bargain for or legislate increased modern-sector wages. Such efforts would gain little anyway because, as noted earlier, in poor countries there is little to redistribute; everyone will benefit in time, Lewis suggests, if they wait for the development process to run its course. A temporary increase in inequality is the price that must be paid for these gains.

The implications of the labor-surplus model have been presented at some length because this has been the dominant paradigm for nearly 40 years. It is far from universally accepted, however, and has often been challenged. Several questions have been raised about the model. Will the capitalists save or will they indulge in luxury consumption? If they do save, will they necessarily invest at home or will they seek higher rates of return abroad? How fast will the capitalist (modern) sector absorb labor, particularly since it may be using capital-intensive technology imported from the developed countries and inappropriate to the factor endowment of a poor labor-surplus economy? (See Chapter 8 for discussion of this issue.) Finally, can governments in today's developing countries afford to wait for the accumulation process to work and for the benefits of growth eventually to be distributed throughout the society? Or do poverty, population growth, and political instability require interventions to redistribute income sooner?

There are no firm, categorical answers to these important questions. Some capi-

21. W. Arthur Lewis, "Economic Development with Unlimited Supplies of Labor," *Manchester School,* 22 (May 1954), 155.

talists will save and invest their savings locally, while others will consume their high income or invest abroad. What they do probably depends on a complex set of factors relating to the characteristics of the upper-income group in a particular country and to the local investment climate. Nor does making the government the capitalist necessarily solve the problem. Few governments have been able to follow the Soviet model of rapid accumulation under a system of state capitalism; most of those that tried were unable to evolve the combination of discipline and incentives needed for publicly owned enterprises to generate surpluses.

Strategies for Growth with Equity

Countries in Asia, Africa, and Latin America have demonstrated the difficulties of trying to redistribute before growing. "Socialism" has been a popular slogan in many countries, connoting immediate redistribution through direct controls on economic activity, elaborate social service networks, consumer subsidies, reliance on cooperatives, and other populist devices. Especially when undertaken by "soft states," which find it hard to enforce their own mandates on the populace, these measures have often slowed economic growth without achieving their redistributive objectives. Burma under Ne Win, Ghana under Kwami Nkrumah, and Jamaica under Michael Manley are three examples among many in recent history. Even when carried out relatively successfully, directly redistributive policies often succeed in redistributing income only in a rather narrow sense. For example, the Peruvian "national revolution" of the 1970s redistributed income to the urban working class but left the poorest elements of society (Andean peasants, mainly of indigenous origin) almost untouched.

Is there then no alternative to the stern trade-off between growth and equality postulated by Lewis? Contemporary development thinking and experience have in fact suggested three alternative models. If Lewis' classical model may be characterized as "grow first, then redistribute," the alternatives could be described as a radical "redistribute first, then grow" model and two reformist models: "redistribution with growth" and "basic human needs."

Redistribute First, Then Grow

The radical model is epitomized by the experience of the Asian socialist economies, especially the People's Republic of China, prior to their recent conversion to more market-based policies. Socialist development in these countries began with the expropriation of capitalists and landlords. Their property was then either subdivided among small-scale producers or, more often, placed under a system of collective ownership. Confiscation has two kinds of effects on income distribution. The immediate impact is to eliminate the property income of the previous owner and assign it either to the state or to the new owners of the subdivided property. This can substantially alter income distribution if the profit or rent share is large. In the longer run, however, the second effect of confiscation is likely to be more important. This works through the productivity of the confiscated asset (factory, farm, etc.) under its new management. If the asset is managed at least as efficiently as under the prior ownership, then the initial redistributive effect holds up in the long run. If, however, the asset is less productive under the new arrangement, then some or all of the redistributive effect is dissipated. The old owner has lost the property income, but the new owners have not gained as much as the old owner lost. The management of a confiscated asset is thus an important determinant of its redistributive effect.

Countries that pursue a radical pattern of development are not exempted from the need to amass a surplus and reinvest it productively if they wish to grow. Development in the Soviet Union, which followed a basic-industry strategy, involved a concerted effort to hold down consumption and squeeze a surplus out of the general population, particularly the peasants. Inequality was limited because most property income accrued to the state, but the system came under fire and ultimately broke down because it could not substantially improve the consumption standards of the Soviet people.

The People's Republic of China followed a more balanced development pattern. While it also aimed at building up heavy industry, it simultaneously paid attention to smaller scale, decentralized, and more labor-intensive production units. By thus "walking on two legs" and not stinting on basic human services, China was able to achieve a more equitable pattern of development than existed in the Soviet Union, and in a much poorer country.

By the late 1980s, however, dissatisfaction with the radical approach to economic development had become nearly universal. In the Soviet Union, Mikhail Gorbachev launched *perestroika* (restructuring) in an attempt to introduce market principles into the Soviet economy. This failed to prevent the breakup of the Soviet Union itself in 1991. Now its successor republics are trying to undo much of the Soviet structure and establish market-oriented systems. China's government has also freed up markets, so far avoiding political collapse. It shifted responsibility for farm production decisions from collectives to families and permitted foreign investors to establish factories in some regions. These reforms accelerated production growth so dramatically that China became the world's fastest-growing economy, but they created large income gaps among individuals and regions, which reportedly led to political strains. Since the Chinese Communist Party clearly has no intention of relinquishing political control, incidents such as the Tienanmin Square crisis of June 1989 raise doubts about whether economic reform will be sustained if it is seen as a serious threat to the existing political system.

Although many of the radical redistribution policies followed by the Chinese Communists in their earlier phase are probably available only to a strong regime that gained power through a revolution, a modified version of the redistribute-then-develop approach has been used in Taiwan and South Korea, where large rural landholdings were broken up shortly after World War II, and development has proceeded rapidly and comparatively equitably.

Redistribution with Growth

The desire to avoid both the extremes of concentrated industrial development as depicted by the Lewis model and radical restructuring of asset ownership has naturally led to a search for a middle way—"redistribution with growth," as a study sponsored by the World Bank called it. Is there, in other words, a way in which the gains from economic growth can be redistributed, so that over time the income distribution gradually improves—or at least does not worsen—as growth proceeds?

The basic idea of redistribution with growth (RWG) is that government policies should try to shape the pattern of development so that low-income producers (in most countries, located primarily in agriculture and small-scale urban enterprises) see improved earning opportunities and simultaneously receive the resources necessary to take advantage of them. According to the World Bank study group, seven types of policy instruments can be employed to this end:

1. Measures to make labor cheaper relative to capital and thus encourage the employment of more unskilled labor
2. Dynamic redistribution of assets by encouraging the creation of assets that the poor can own, such as improved agricultural land or small shops
3. Greater education to improve literacy, skills, and access to the modern economy
4. More progressive taxation
5. Public provision of consumption goods, such as basic foods, to the poor
6. Intervention in commodity markets to aid poor producers and consumers
7. Development of new technologies that help make low-income workers more productive

The way in which these elements could be combined into an effective national policy package will naturally vary with a country's circumstances. A rural-based, equity-oriented development strategy is often proposed for large, predominantly rural countries such as India.[22] For these countries, it is argued, the time required for the modern sector to soak up all the surplus labor existing in the traditional sector would be far too long for any reasonable standard of equity to be achieved or political stability to be maintained. A strategy that emphasizes rural development, it is hoped, will bring about a much more equitable pattern of development than could ever be attained through emphasis on urban and industrial growth. (Rural development is discussed in Chapter 18.)

On the other hand, countries in which the modern sector is larger relative to the traditional sector face a less severe trade-off. These nations can hope to create an integrated, modern economy in a much shorter period and in the meantime have a much larger surplus available to redistribute to the traditional sector through social services and rural development projects.

The RWG approach has attracted a lot of interest among those who want to see the welfare of the third-world poor improve without violent social revolution. Indeed the reader may note that many of the ideas included in the RWG package are treated sympathetically in this book. In practice, RWG is the approach used by most developing-country governments that regard poverty reduction as a serious policy objective. Yet one must accept that the changes brought about by such a strategy will occur slowly in most countries. Development is almost always a gradual business, and even the changes in equality and poverty projected by the World Bank's study group, which was intellectually and emotionally committed to the approach, struck many readers as disappointingly small and gradual.

22. For example, see John Mellor, *The New Economics of Growth. A Strategy for India and the Developing World* (Ithaca, N.Y.: Cornell University Press, 1976).

Basic Human Needs

Pessimism about how fast economic development, even when it is poverty-focused, can improve the well-being of the poor in most developing countries promotes interest in the **basic human needs** (BHN) approach. Although advocates of RWG and BHN share the same objectives, they differ on the best means of achieving them. While RWG stresses increases in the productivity and purchasing power of the poor, BHN emphasizes the provision of public services, along with entitlements to the poor to make sure they get access to the services provided.

The BHN strategy aims at providing the poor with several basic commodities and services: staple foods, water and sanitation, health care, primary and nonformal education, and housing. The strategy requires two important elements for success. First, financing must be adequate to ensure that commodities and services needs can be provided at costs affordable to the poor. Second, service networks are needed to distribute these services in forms appropriate for consumption by the poor, especially in areas where the poor live.

The possibility of using fiscal policy to ameliorate poverty is discussed in Chapter 12. Redistribution of income through a combination of progressive taxation and public expenditures on social service programs has been an important part of twentieth-century reform movements in Western industrial countries. The potential of this form of redistribution for less-developed countries used to be downplayed because the public sector is smaller in these countries and thus has less revenue-raising power; because the government pursues multiple objectives in its tax and expenditure policies and thus cannot devote itself wholeheartedly to redistribution; and because there are many difficulties in identifying, designing, and implementing public consumption and investment projects that can affect the incomes of the poor.

However, there is a more positive side to the picture. Many LDCs now collect 20 percent or more of their GNPs in government revenues. While the room for progressive taxation is often limited in developing countries, their tax systems can at least be made less regressive, even when direct (income) taxes are paid by only a small fraction of the population. Indirect taxes, such as customs duties, excises, turnover taxes, and sales taxes with exemptions, can lend a modest element of progressivity. Finally, much can be done on the expenditure side of the budget to improve the distribution of benefits from public services. Some of these possibilities will be discussed in Chapters 9 and 10, which deal with education and health.

For BHN programs to redistribute income, basic services must be subsidized. Otherwise redistribution will not work because the poor will either spend too much of their meager incomes on the services offered or be deterred by high user charges and not take advantage of them at all. If the poor fail to use the services offered, the income transfer provided by subsidies can be perverse. In many countries, for example, government-run universities admit selectively only the well-qualified secondary school graduates, yet charge low fees, and thus subsidize the well-to-do. For the poor to be reached, appropriate forms of service must be emphasized: primary schools over universities, village clinics over intensive-care units in urban hospitals. Second, the system must be extended to the poor in their villages and urban slums. There must be schools and clinics with teachers and primary health workers where the poor live. So far most LDC social service networks have not met this challenge, although there are some honorable exceptions.

Much of the appeal of BHN derives from its link to the notion of investment in human capital. Many kinds of education, health, and other social expenditures can improve the quality of human resources. When such expenditures are directed particularly toward the poor, as for instance in primary education or rural community health programs, they become ways to reduce poverty by increasing the productivity of the poor.

The World Bank's review of the problem of third-world poverty in its *World Development Report 1990* spotlights two basic actions for poverty reduction: policies to increase the productivity of the main resource owned by poor—their labor—and the provision of basic social services to the poor. This supports the importance of satisfying basic needs as a complement to a RWG-influenced strategy, but not as an alternative. Countries that are not achieving economic growth usually find it extremely difficult to satisfy basic human needs.

Structural Adjustment and the Poor

Many of the countries in sub-Saharan Africa, Latin America, and elsewhere that experienced slow economic growth or none at all in the 1980s have undertaken programs of "structural adjustment" in cooperation with the IMF and World Bank. As explained in Chapter 5, these countries agreed to make major policy changes—correcting macroeconomic imbalances and reforming macro and sectoral policies—in exchange for external assistance. The transitional costs of these programs, for example, the termination of consumer and producer subsidies, can be substantial, and critics charge that they fall disproportionately on the poor. The impact of structural adjustment on the children of the poor was documented by a group of analysts assembled by UNICEF, the United Nations Children's Fund. Their report called for "adjustment with a human face," a set of policies that would permit growth to resume, raise the productivity of the poor, improve the equity and efficiency of social services, compensate the poor for deficits in nutrition and health services during adjustment periods of limited duration, and improve monitoring of the conditions of effected low-income groups, particularly children.[23] "Adjustment with a human face" can be regarded as an adaptation of the BHN and RWG ideas to fit the circumstances of the 1980s, especially in sub-Saharan Africa.

While macroeconomic adjustment programs can undoubtedly be carried out in ways that give more attention to the plight of the poor, the analysis of this chapter suggests that a more fundamental solution to the problem of poverty in third-world countries that have not been growing is a resumption of economic growth itself, combined with the provision of basic social services to the poor and policies that seek to increase their participation in the development process.

Growth and Equity: Key Policy Issues

Probably the single most promising way of achieving greater equity during growth under the reformist approach is to put more emphasis on employment creation. By appropriate price incentives and other measures to absorb more labor in relatively productive forms of employment, the inequality generated by the

23. See Giovanni Andrea Cornia, Richard Jolly, and Frances Stewart (eds.), *Adjustment with a Human Face,* 2 vol. (London: Oxford University Press [Clarendon], 1987).

Lewis-type employment shift can be mitigated and the labor surplus can be eliminated in a shorter time, as discussed in detail in Chapter 8.

The other touchstone of equitable growth is the relationship between the prices of rural and urban outputs. If farm prices are held down to depress urban wages and increase the investible surplus, then the majority of the poor who live in the rural areas and depend mainly on agriculture for a living will suffer. (There are also likely to be food supply problems; see Chapter 18.) Of course, if farm prices rise too high, growth will be choked off. But a concern for equity rules out the squeeze-the-farmer approach that has often been attempted in the past and remains in effect in some LDCs (for example, many in Africa) today.

Finally, one can ask whether governments of less-developed countries will in fact take advantage of these opportunities to reduce inequality arising during the course of economic growth. This is an important question of political economy. Marxists argue that governments are controlled by particular social classes and act in the best interests of those classes. Certainly, many third-world governments are heavily influenced by civilian or military elites and for this reason are much less likely to undertake egalitarian reforms than to talk about them. But political motivations are perhaps more mixed than Marxists believe. Some governments may be inclined to make limited reforms for essentially conservative reasons: to forestall upheavals or demands for more radical changes. Others may be motivated toward reform by a different kind of political incentive: in countries where ethnic, tribal, or religious distinctions form an important basis for political activity, it may not be the rich but rather a large, less-wealthy social group whose interests are primarily reflected in government policy. In such cases—for example, the Malays of Malaysia—ambitious redistributive programs may be launched even by relatively conservative governments.

PART 2

GUIDING DEVELOPMENT

5

Guiding Development: Markets versus Controls

Market forces can propel the processes of development described in the last three chapters. But skillful policies can accelerate these changes and virtually all governments have attempted to push development faster than market forces might have allowed. Two sets of policy tools are available. The first depends on a **capitalist** or **market economy** and its competitive energies, but tries to make the market work more efficiently and comprehensively. The second rejects the autonomous, self-regulating nature of a market economy and substitutes government controls, resulting in a **socialist** or **command economy.** In this chapter we compare these two very different systems for guiding development, and then show why and how governments have moved away from controls toward market-based policy tools in the last decade or so.

Managing Development

From World War II until the 1980s, capitalism and socialism competed for adherents throughout the world, and nowhere more intensely than in the developing countries. Neither of these systems was ever pure. All market economies were managed by their governments and for that reason were sometimes labeled **mixed economies.** And all command economies were tempered by unregulated and often illegal markets. In the 1980s, and especially after the fall of the Berlin Wall in 1989, even the socialist countries began adopting market systems. By the end of the decade, the command economy in its pure form was rapidly disappearing.

Debates about economic management still range over a continuum of market mechanisms versus controls, but largely within the context of a mixed economy. Still, it is useful to keep in mind the capitalist-socialist dichotomy that marked the postwar world.

Market Economies

Most countries depend on market mechanisms, rather than government controls, to allocate most goods, services, and factors of production. Three arguments favor market allocation. First, the market can allocate thousands of different products among consumers, reflecting their preferences, and thousands of productive inputs among producers, getting the maximum output from available inputs.[1]

These complex allocative tasks, if handled by the state, require enormous governmental responsibility with attendant high costs for decision making and control. Second, markets are frequently more flexible than governments and better able to adapt to changing conditions, automatically providing incentives for growth, innovation, and structural change that governments either cannot manage or are slow to achieve. Third, reliance on markets encourages private economic activity, providing greater scope for the dispersion of economic power. Economic pluralism, in turn, is one element tending to encourage democratic government and individual liberties.

Despite these substantial advantages, there are some circumstances in which markets do not perform well on their own. Economists have identified a number of such **market failures.**

1. Modern economies are marked by growing concentration and **monopoly** or **oligopoly power,** where one or a few sellers gain control of a market. In developing countries, **economies of scale** (the decline of unit costs as output rises) may be so large relative to market size that monopoly is inevitable in some industries, while oligopoly is the rule in many others. Truly competitive markets, where no one seller or buyer has any influence over market prices, typically exist in agriculture, fishing, handicraft industries, construction, transportation, retail trade, personal services, and sometimes in banking. In much of mining, manufacturing, utilities, airlines, communications, and wholesale trade, monopoly or oligopoly are common. One or a few firms are able to raise their prices, and consequently their profits, by restricting output, so that consumers pay more and obtain less than they would in a competitive market. In large economies, governments can try to limit the exercise of monopoly pricing in some sectors by regulating the size of firms and by breaking up the largest ones. In all economies, competing imports—actual or potential—curtail monopoly power in manufacturing industries and in some services by forcing domestic firms to meet competition from abroad. However, this antimonopoly weapon is seldom used in developing countries. Price controls are often employed instead. If government cannot prevent monopoly pricing, it can capture some of the benefits from monopolists by taxing the resulting profits at high rates.

2. **External economies** are the benefits of a project, such as a hydroelectric dam, that are enjoyed by people not connected with the project, such as the downstream farmer whose production rises because the dam prevents floods. External

1. The principles of market economies underlying these allocations are familiar to those who have taken an introductory course in microeconomics.

economies are important benefits in many **overhead** investments, such as dams, roads, railroads, and irrigation schemes. Although in principle the beneficiaries could be charged for all external benefits, in practice they cannot be. It may be difficult and costly to control access to the facilities and difficult even to identify the beneficiaries or the extent to which they benefit. Hence a private investor would not be able to realize revenue from this aspect of the project's output. Because private investors cannot easily charge for externalities and because such projects take large investments with long repayment periods, private investors are unlikely to undertake them. Governments do so instead. Another kind of external economy is central to the balanced growth strategy discussed in Chapter 3. If several industries are started at the same time, the resulting labor force may be large enough to create an internal market for the output of all industries and backward linkages may create adequate markets for producer goods industries. But a single private investor who depended on these newly created markets would not invest without strong assurances that the other investments would take place simultaneously. Government must intervene to ensure that these external benefits can be realized.

3. **External diseconomies** are costs not borne by the firm. The pollution of air and water is a widely recognized problem in the industrial world, and increasingly so in developing countries. Polluters could bear all the costs of reduced emissions and effluents, but they benefit only as average members of the population of the affected area, so have little incentive to control pollution on their own. The same situation arises with **common resources,** such as forests, fisheries, or open grazing land, which can be used by many people who do not own them. For example, the first cattle to graze on open range land find abundant grass, so costs to the herders are low. But as more cattle graze, there is less grass for each and herders must go farther afield to find it. The *tragedy of the commons* is that overgrazing so degrades the rangeland that fewer and fewer cattle can be fed there, yet each private herder continues to have an incentive to graze cattle on the open range. Both pollution and common resources require some kind of intervention by government as discussed in Chapter 7.

4. Markets may not accommodate the changes in economic structure required for development. The most frequently cited example is the **infant industry,** one brand-new to a society, whose productivity increases and whose costs fall over time because managers and workers are "learning by doing." Although the industry can become profitable over several years, investors may be too shortsighted to finance the new firms. This can justify a **protective tariff** (a tax on competing imports) or **initial subsidy** (where the government bears some start-up costs) to make an infant industry more profitable in the short run. But the long-run gains in productivity may only be realized if the tariff or subsidy is gradually reduced and the new industry is eventually forced to compete with imports (or other domestic firms). The infant industry argument has even greater force for the economy as a whole because experience in all industries creates a more skilled and productive labor force, and this makes all activities more attractive for investors. This "infant economy" phenomenon is closely akin to the balanced growth strategy because it also depends on external economies: as trained, experienced workers leave one employer to work for another, the second firm benefits from the training provided by the first. Sectorwide (or even economywide) protective tariffs could be justified by this effect, although a depreciated exchange rate combined with offsetting

taxes on traditional exports would be a superior intervention, for reasons that will be explored in Chapter 20.

5. **Underdeveloped institutions** exclude large numbers from the market. In developed economies consumers "vote" with their dollars for the goods the economy should produce. But in developing economies, remoteness, poverty, and illiteracy prevent many subsistence farmers, rural laborers, and their families from "voting" in goods, services, and financial markets, so these groups have little influence on the types of goods and services supplied. Special efforts are required to bring them into the monetary economy. Even for those in the monetary economy there is **inadequate information** about markets and products, so many consumers remain ignorant about the goods and services being offered, workers know little about job opportunities, and producers cannot easily learn about changing market conditions. Perhaps the best example is in banking, which generally remains urban-based and employs standards of services, modeled on Western banking methods, that exclude most of the rural and much of the poor urban population. Similarly, investors, producers, and traders find it difficult to hedge against the **risks** of doing business in changing circumstances, because financial, commodity, and insurance markets are underdeveloped or missing altogether. Government may have to encourage or establish some of these missing institutions to help markets function better.

6. Economywide markets for labor, credit, and foreign exchange do not always adjust rapidly enough to balance supply and demand as conditions change, and **macroeconomic imbalances** characterize every modern economy. Wages that adjust slowly, low short-run elasticities of supply or demand, and misinformed expectations cause shortages and surpluses that can require government interventions such as monetary management, fiscal policy, exchange rate adjustments, and incomes policies. We will hear more about such **macroeconomic management** tools through this book, particularly in Chapter 21.

7. To a considerable extent market economies require intervention not only because of inherent market failures but also because societies impose on them **national goals** that even well-functioning markets cannot satisfy. Establishing policies that favor poorer majorities over entrepreneurially accomplished minorities is one example. If ethnic Chinese in Malaysia and Indonesia or ethnic Indians and Pakistanis ("Asians") in Kenya and Tanzania, already dominate the production and distribution system of those countries, then unguided economic growth may improve their relative position over time. To expand the role of the indigenous majority and allow it to "catch up" requires government intervention. Markets can be very effective in stimulating rapid growth that automatically generates demands for the output of small farmers and the self-employed, creates jobs to absorb poor workers, and generally helps to relieve poverty. Nevertheless, these market forces are often led by—and hence favor—people and firms that are already successful. Thus market-oriented growth may concentrate incomes initially, as we saw in the discussion of Kuznets' proposition in Chapter 4, even while relieving poverty. It is only after growth has been rapid for some time that the income distribution begins to equalize. But the reduction of inequality is often considered too urgent to await the operation of market forces, and intervention is considered necessary. This may be true for other goals as well, such as greater employment creation or reduced dependence on foreign goods, capital, technol-

ogy, and skills. Even accelerated growth, typically served well by market economies, may require intervention if savings levels are initially low.

These market failures provide some of the reasons that governments intervene in market economies. The particular interventions chosen are not always ideal. Worse, they often work against the goals they are supposed to achieve. The most egregious examples will be explored in later chapters: legislation on wages, pensions, and job security that concentrates incomes and reduces employment; interest rate ceilings that reduce and bias investment; tariffs and import controls that intensify dependence on imports; and food price controls that discourage farm production. Nevertheless, because markets are imperfect and governments have political goals that markets must serve, intervention is the rule. Usually interventions work best and avoid undesired side effects if they are aimed to improve the functioning of markets and to work indirectly through prices to alter supply and demand, rather than operating directly through controls. A central aim of development policy in a mixed economy is to structure these interventions to achieve their aims with minimal incidental costs.

Socialist Economies

Socialism can be defined as government ownership and control of the means of production. Whether a country is socialist or not is a matter of degree. The clear examples have been the Communist countries—the Soviet Union, the Eastern European countries until 1989, China, North Korea, Vietnam, and Cuba—in which government ownership and control dominated industry and services and strongly influenced agriculture. Some Western European countries, such as Sweden and Great Britain, were for a time governed by socialist political parties that nationalized key industries. Many other countries have large state-owned enterprise sectors, but these economies retain the market character of mixed economies.

What distinguished the Soviet and other command economies was government control over production. Whereas *in mixed economies the market sets prices as* signals for production and consumption, *in Soviet-style economies central planners controlled the quantities* produced and consumed. Official prices became irrelevant to production and investment decisions. But prices, along with quantity rationing, still regulated demand, because no government is able to give directives to each household about its complete consumption basket. Prices also served an accounting function; they determined how much income was transferred from households to government-owned producers (and vice versa, through wage payments), among producers, and from producers to the government.

In order to manage a Soviet-style economy, it was necessary to begin with a plan. Typically, governments operated with one-year plans for controlling current output and five-year plans to guide major investment projects. The planning methods used in the Soviet Union and until the 1980s in China were similar to the planning models developed in mixed developing economies, as described in the next chapter. What separated a centrally planned economy from the others was the way in which plans were carried out. Once broad goals and quantitative targets for individual industries had been decided, planners gave direct orders to firms on how much to produce and the quantity of inputs that could be used in production. Firms could not buy the necessary inputs in a market, but had to apply to government organizations for the delivery of needed items. The firm paid for these items, but willingness to pay did not determine whether it got them. Only if the plan said it should receive a certain amount of steel, for instance, was that amount delivered.

In reality, the Soviet-type system did not follow the plan quite so rigidly. A variety of both legal and illegal devices, including markets, provided some flexibility. Nevertheless many allocations that were handled by impersonal market forces in mixed economies were decided by the commands of bureaucrats in centrally planned economies. The command system therefore needed large numbers of people trained to manage the complex tasks of deciding which firms ought to get particular inputs. Hundreds and even thousands of different kinds of inputs had to be parceled out to tens of thousands of individual enterprises. If the inputs got to the wrong enterprises, those enterprises would have surpluses piling up in their warehouses while other enterprises operated below capacity. Large inventories were characteristic of this kind of system.

The advantage of the command system was that it gave central planners a high degree of control over the economy and, with that control, the power to restructure key sectors. The system, however, did not put a high premium on the productive use of resources. The problems of inefficiency increased if people with skills adequate to manage such a system were in short supply, as has often been the case in developing countries. Even though China had sufficient numbers of such people or was able to train them with Soviet help in the 1950s, after 1978 China began to experiment with greater use of market forces in order to reduce inefficiency.

The leaders who designed the Soviet economic system began from the premise that prices determined by the market could not be relied on to guide production. This basic view of the market was reinforced by the pronounced emphasis in the Soviet Union, and later in China, on machinery and steel as leading sectors in their industrialization programs. Since neither economy had much of a steel or machinery industry to begin with, planners were faced with an extreme form of the infant industry problem and with very large external economies, because the main demand for steel was from a machinery sector that did not yet exist. In general the price system is less effective when the change in economic structure being contemplated is rapid and massive. What the Soviet Union desired in the 1930s when it introduced this system and what China wanted in the 1950s was precisely such a rapid and massive restructuring of economies that were fundamentally agricultural into ones that were based on machinery and steel.

Recent history has demonstrated the limitations of the centrally planned economy. It was effective in mobilizing resources in the early days of communism: few countries have ever industrialized as rapidly as the Soviet Union. The heavy industrial base so created contributed to the Soviet Union's ability to make the weapons that helped throw back the German invasion in World War II. But the Soviet system was not efficient in allocating the myriad goods, services, and factors of production among thousands of competing uses. It was particularly ineffective in producing consumer goods. And, once the economy became more industrialized, the command system was unable to adjust easily to changes in the economic environment. Pressure built up in the 1980s in both Eastern and Central Europe and the Soviet Union as stagnant economies had to be propped up with increasing amounts of international debt. Wages and consumption grew hardly at all, and thereby fed worker and consumer discontent. When President Gorbachev made it known that the Soviet army would no longer prop up the Communist-party-dominated governments then in power throughout Eastern and Central Europe, most of these governments collapsed and were replaced by leadership that was democratically elected. Soon thereafter the Soviet empire itself collapsed and was replaced by a number of republics of which Russia was by far the largest. It wasn't just the political system that collapsed. The Council for Mutual Economic Assistance (Comecon), the organization that governed trade between the Soviet Union, Eastern Europe, and Vietnam, also collapsed, and so all these nations were forced to develop new foreign trade relationships.

Many of the democratic governments that came to power in Eastern Europe after 1989 were determined to dismantle the Soviet command economies as rapidly as possible and replace them with market systems much like the ones they observed in Western Europe. Poland was the boldest in attempting to create a market economy almost overnight by what came to be called **shock therapy.** Hungary, having begun to move toward a market system long before 1989, moved more cautiously to introduce further market reforms. Under President Boris Yeltsin, Russia also attempted to move rapidly toward a market system by freeing prices and introducing across-the-board privatization of much of the state-owned economy. For reasons that we shall go into later in this chapter, however, the move to a market system proved to be more difficult than many of the reformers anticipated. Recessions in the economies of the countries of Eastern Europe and the republics of the former Soviet Union were long and deep. The resulting hardships for many individuals, although by no means for everyone, created political resistance to reforms that led to votes for many antimarket parliamentarians in the elections of 1993 and 1994.

Among developing countries with per capita incomes of less than $2,000, only China, Vietnam, North Korea, and Cuba ever succeeded in introducing the full Soviet-style command system, although a few other countries not ruled by Communist parties, notably Tanzania, tried. China, Vietnam, and North Korea arguably had the administrative and decision-making capacity to control production through central planning without the use of market forces, and they did achieve sustained increases in gross national product for a time under this system. But discontent with the inefficiency and slow growth of the command system led China to begin moving toward a market system after 1978, and Vietnam to do so after 1986. North Korea and Cuba, both of which resisted moves toward the market into the mid-1990s, experienced economic stagnation and declining standards of living.

Tanzania was one of the few countries in Africa to attempt to introduce parts of a command system, one patterned in large part after the model of China. In the 1970s, Tanzania, avowedly socialist, placed the majority of modern industries under public ownership, nationalized much wholesale and retail trade, and attempted to socialize its agriculture. Nevertheless the government did not try to set output targets and most units, public or private, continued to respond to market-determined prices. Interventions in setting these prices, though substantial, were not markedly greater in socialist Tanzania than in many nonsocialist developing countries such as Bolivia, Kenya, and Indonesia. India based its first development plans on Soviet models that emphasized investment in capital goods and other heavy industries and espoused public ownership of these sectors. Yet even when India's economy was ostensibly socialist, less output was produced in public enterprises than in avowedly capitalist South Korea.

THE MARCH TOWARD MARKETS

It is clear from the perspective of the 1990s that all kinds of governments—capitalist and socialist, industrial and developing—have been reducing the scope of controls and adopting market mechanisms instead to guide their economies. What explains the popularity of controls before reforms became common? And what explains this historic march away from controls toward market mechanisms?

The Appeal of Controls

We have already given two reasons that governments might want to resort to controls to hasten development. Controls may be essential if policy makers desire large structural changes, as did the leaders of the Soviet Union before World War II and China after 1949. And within a mixed economy, controls can be used to correct for market failures that might otherwise retard development, make it unsustainable, or yield politically and socially undesirable outcomes. After World War II, a confluence of historical factors pushed many governments of developing countries to employ controls rather than market mechanisms as a means to accelerate economic development.

The Great Depression of the 1930s had destroyed confidence in market capitalism. The antidote to depression offered by John Maynard Keynes—and accepted for decades by most economists and governments—was active intervention to stimulate the economy through fiscal policy. Price controls and quantity rationing helped guide the U.S. economy through the Second World War. In the 1930s and 1940s, when trade wars and real wars made export-oriented development strategies almost impossible, building one's own industrial capacity behind high tariff walls seemed to make sense. After the war, European recovery was substantially aided by the U.S. Marshall Plan. The U.S. government not only provided vast amounts of capital (equivalent to 1.5 percent of its GNP over four years), but also encouraged governments of wartorn economies to plan for public investment in postwar recovery.

In Asia and Africa, economies had been highly regulated by the colonial powers before and after the war. After independence in 1947, India's new leaders followed the interventionist tendencies of Fabian socialism and the British Raj to a planned and regulated economy. As other countries in Asia and Africa emerged from colonialism over the next two decades, many of them emulated India. The Soviet Union's rapid industrialization under communism also impressed the leaders of these newly emerging countries. The older countries of Latin America, especially Argentina, Brazil, and Mexico, had taken advantage of the war to build their own industries to supply goods once imported from the United States. After the war, Argentine dictator Juan Peron and others built on this base a highly protected manufacturing system that spurred industrial growth for a time. Even in the capitalist United States, as in Western Europe, government intervention in markets was the norm, from the New Deal of President Franklin Roosevelt during the depressed 1930s to the Great Society of President Lyndon Johnson in the 1960s.

Economic thought encouraged these tendencies. Underlying the views of many thinkers, ancient and modern, is the view that markets lead to outcomes that are arbitrary, capricious, or worse. Karl Marx's belief in the chaotic nature of markets had a major influence on those who designed the economic systems of the Soviet Union and China. In more recent times, as described in Chapter 3, there were Paul Rosenstein-Rodan's 1943 theory of the big push and Albert Hirschman's 1958 retort, the strategy of unbalanced growth. Both strategies assumed that markets would not work adequately for rapid development and both invited some form of government intervention. Latin American economist Raul Prebisch and European economist Hans Singer were influential in arguing that world demand could not grow fast enough to accommodate the rapid growth of food and raw material exports, on which most developing countries depended.[2] This **export pessimism** was taken as strong support for a strategy of **import substitution,** which required government intervention to protect local manufacturers. Perhaps the most influential article of all was W. Arthur Lewis' 1954 theory of the labor-surplus economy, also explained in Chapter 3. Though Lewis did not advocate intervention, one implication of his theory was the need to transform a developing economy rapidly away from traditional, stagnant agriculture toward dynamic industry. This, as the Soviet Union and China appeared to show, could be accomplished by a command economy. These treatises and others like them set the tone for development economics at least until the mid-1960s. Even if national leaders did not know about these works, their economic advisers were strongly influenced by them.

These historic and intellectual tendencies influenced many governments to try a range of interventions in search of economic development. By the early 1970s, the vast majority of third-world countries could be characterized as mixed economies with a strong dose of controls. A development adviser, flying into almost any developing country picked at random, could expect to find high protective tariffs and quantitative restrictions over imports, strict controls over foreign exchange dealings, ceilings on interest rates and floors under wages, government-set prices of vital commodities from food grains to fuel, restrictions on private investment, many government-owned firms displacing private companies, harassment of people operating in the informal sector, and many other interventions.

Resurgence of the Market

Most of these interventions are still visible in the developing world, but they are no longer so ubiquitous and many countries have begun to shed many of these controls. The pronounced trend of the 1980s and 1990s was toward economic reform that substituted market mechanisms for controls in many aspects of economic policy. No corner of the world has been immune. Deregulation was a byword of economic policy in the United States under President Jimmy Carter in the 1970s, although the approach was later associated with President Ronald Reagan. Western Europe moved toward open, integrated markets throughout the 1980s and came close to full economic integration in 1992. The Uruguay round of

2. United Nation (by Raul Prebish), *The Economic Development of Latin America and Its Principal Problems* (Lake Success, N.Y., 1950), and Hans W. Singer, "The Distribution of Trade between Investing and Borrowing Countries," *American Economic Review,* 40 (1950), 470–85. See also Ragnar Nurkse, *Equilibrium Growth and the World Economy* (Cambridge, Mass.: Harvard University Press, 1961).

negotiations further freeing up worldwide international trade was completed successfully in 1994. The roll call of developing countries undertaking market reforms, including Chile, Bolivia, Ghana, Kenya, Tanzania, India, South Korea, and Indonesia, grew throughout the 1980s and 1990s. In the communist world, China led the way after the death of Mao Zedong in 1976. The changes in Central and Eastern Europe after 1989 have already been described.

Many factors combined to stimulate market reforms in the developing world. First was a series of negative causes: controls and other market interventions just did not work very well. Protection and import substitution spurred industrial growth at first, but then industrial development sputtered in country after country. Price interventions generally had unintended consequences: high protective barriers bred inefficient manufacturing; interest rate ceilings suppressed the evolution of financial systems, depressed monetary savings and encouraged unproductive investment; minimum wages, if they had any impact at all, stifled employment growth and exacerbated inequalities; and ceilings on food prices and taxes on agricultural exports discouraged farmers and retarded productivity growth in agriculture.

Controls by government engendered just political and bureaucratic reactions by private entrepreneurs and managers, instead of the innovative and competitive behavior needed for sustained development. Regulations created higher-than-necessary profits, which economists call **rents,** for those able to gain favorable treatment from bureaucrats or to evade the rules. Widespread corruption and other forms of **rent seeking** diverted the energies of entrepreneurs, investors, managers, and traders from productive activities, wasted scarce resources, and reduced economic growth.[3] The almost universal proliferation of public enterprises extended ineffectual bureaucratic behavior into activities that private enterprises could have handled more effectively and more efficiently.

The consequences of these interventions were apparent as early as the end of the 1960s. In 1970, influential studies by economists at Williams College and Oxford University chronicled the failures of import substitution and all the interventions that generally accompanied it.[4] The explosive rise of oil prices in the 1970s, then their precipitate fall in the 1980s, and the accompanying accumulations of unserviceable debt exposed the failures of some interventionist development strategies. These swings in economic fortune required flexible, creative responses from all economies. But regimes mired in controls were too rigid to cope with the unstable economic environment.

The near stagnation of many developing economies in the 1970s and 1980s stood in stark contrast to the rapid and sustained growth of four East Asian "newly industrialized countries" during the same period. South Korea, Taiwan, Hong Kong, and Singapore, all of which grew by 8 to 10 percent a year for 20 years or more, provided the positive reasons for the conversion to economic reforms. Hong Kong and Singapore had economies governed largely by market forces. In South Korea and to a lesser degree Taiwan, however, government intervened forcefully. What these four had in common was a strategy of depending

3. Anne O. Krueger, "The Political Economy of Rent-Seeking," *American Economic Review,* 64, no. 3 (1974).

4. Henry J. Bruton, "The Import Substitution Strategy of Economic Development," *Pakistan Development Review*, 10 (1970), 123–46, and Ian Little, Tibor Scitovsky, and Maurice Scott, *Industry and Trade in Some Developing Countries* (London: Oxford University Press, 1970).

heavily on export growth to lead development. This "outward-looking" strategy is explored in Chapter 20. In essence, by inducing private firms to seek markets overseas, these countries took advantage of the large world market and simultaneously exposed their manufacturing firms to the discipline of competition in international markets. It was this competitive industrial base that permitted the four East Asian countries to sail through the economic crises of the 1970s and 1980s with relative ease.

Development economists of the **neoclassical school** began to promote the virtues of market-oriented, outward-looking development even before the oil and debt crises. Chicago economist Theodore Schultz won his Nobel Prize partly for his work in the early 1960s showing that so-called traditional farmers were rational decision makers whose techniques were well adapted to the conditions and constraints they faced. One implication was that market incentives, accompanied by new technologies, would induce farmers to change their methods and raise productivity.[5] The promise of a dynamic agriculture was realized with the coming of the Green Revolution in Asia. The 1970 studies of import substitution, that were mentioned above, suggested the obvious alternative strategy of more open, market-oriented economies. By the late 1970s, a series of country studies by trade economists Bela Balassa, Jagdish Bhagwati, and Anne Krueger, had established a strong empirical case that outward-looking strategies work better than import substitution.[6] We will further explore the reasons for this in Chapter 20.

At the core of the argument for market-guided development is the proposition of neoclassical economics that markets create competition and competition stimulates the growth of productivity. The discussion of growth accounting in Chapter 3 showed how the growth of income per capita can be attributed to two sources: growing supplies of the productive factors, especially capital available to each worker and increases in the productivity of all factors used in production. Rapid capital accumulation—high investment rates—has been achieved for sustained periods by both well-functioning market economies (Japan and the four newly industrialized countries of Asia) and command economies (the Soviet Union and China). But when it comes to raising **factor productivity**—the productivity of capital, labor, land, and other resources—some market economies do quite well while command economies have a notoriously poor record. In mixed economies, greater market orientation—less government intervention and more openness to world markets—appears to promote gains in factor productivity.

There are several reasons why this should be so. In market economies, competition and the profit motive force producers—farmers, industrial firms, service industries, and individual workers—to operate as efficiently as possible and to reduce costs (raise productivity) whenever they can. Those who cannot use their resources efficiently or cannot find profitable markets for their output earn less than others who can, and their businesses may fail. These individual attempts to operate more efficiently, compelled by market forces, translate into a more pro-

5. Theodore W. Schultz, *Transforming Traditional Agriculture* (New Haven, Conn.: Yale University Press, 1964).

6. Bela Balassa, "Exports and Economic Growth: Further Evidence," *Journal of Development Economics,* 5, no. 2 (1978), 181–89; Jagdish Bhagwati, *Foreign Exchange Regimes and Economic Development: Anatomy and Consequences of Exchange Control Regimes* (Cambridge, Mass.: Ballinger Press, 1978); and Anne O. Krueger, *Foreign Exchange Regimes and Economic Development: Liberalization Attempts and Consequences* (Cambridge, Mass.: Ballinger Press, 1978).

TABLE 5–1 Impact of Outward Orientation on Growth*

		GDP growth	Total factor productivity growth	
	Countries	1950–83	1960–70	1970–82
Primary-oriented	55			
Inward-oriented	37	3.9	1.1	0.4
Outward-oriented	28	5.0	2.0	−0.2
Manufacturing-oriented	41			
Inward-oriented	23	4.7	2.2	0.2
Outward-oriented	18	5.5	2.4	0.9

*Growth rates in percent per year.
Source: Moshe Syrquin and Hollis B. Chenery, "Three Decades of Industrialization," *World Bank Economic Review,* 3, no. 2 (1989).

ductive economy so long as the market failures are compensated. When market forces do not guide production decisions, the incentive for productivity gains is weaker. Price distortions draw labor, capital, and other factors into less productive employment, for example, from efficient export industries into protected import-substituting ones. Government regulations establish incentives for rent-seeking and bribery; entrepreneurs and managers then spend more time dealing with and influencing government officials and less time making their plants run more efficiently. Protection behind high tariffs, other import barriers, and investment restrictions insulates firms from competition, both foreign and domestic, and so permits them to earn profits even when they use resources inefficiently. When governments themselves enter into production through state-owned enterprises, the profit motive of their managers is diluted by political and bureaucratic concerns: noneconomic goals are imposed by government; bureaucratic rules and procedures govern key decisions on investment, finance, and wages; and managers' careers often depend more on their ties to government leaders than on their firms' performances.

There is some empirical support for the proposition that markets, particularly foreign markets, within which firms are exposed to competition contribute to factor productivity growth. A cross-country comparison by economists Moshe Syrquin and Hollis Chenery suggests that outward orientation has some impact on the growth of both gross domestic product and total factor productivity.[7] The results for 106 countries are summarized in Table 5–1. For Syrquin and Chenery, outward orientation means that a country has a higher-than-average ratio of exports to GDP given its per capita income and population. They also distinguish between **primary-oriented** countries, which have higher-than-average shares of primary good (agricultural and raw material) exports to total exports, and **manufacturing-oriented** countries. Regardless of this classification, outward-oriented countries had significantly higher GDP growth rates than inward-oriented ones from 1950 to 1983 (column 1).

The impact on factor productivity is not so clear-cut, however. For the primary-oriented countries, openness did lead to substantially higher productivity growth during the relatively stable decade of the 1960s. During the 1970s, however, when

7. Moshe Syrquin and Hollis B. Chenery, "Three Decades of Industrialization," *World Bank Economic Review,* 3, no. 2 (1989), 145–81. See also World Bank, *The East Asian Miracle* (Oxford: Oxford University Press, 1993), Chap. 6.

oil prices forced major readjustments and other commodity prices first rose and then fell, all countries' productivity growths were much lower. The outward-oriented primary exporters then had lower productivity growth than their inward-oriented counterparts, perhaps because they had more severe adjustments to make. In contrast, there was very little difference in productivity growth among manufacturing-oriented countries during the 1960s, but the outward-oriented economies did better when major adjustments were required in the 1970s. However, in manufacturing-oriented countries, where resource endowments matter less and trade strategies matter more, there seems a clear if moderate margin in favor of outward orientation.

A more recent study by Harvard economists Jeffrey Sachs and Andrew Warner confirms the importance of market orientation in economic growth.[8] They establish two sets of criteria for market-based economic policies: the security of property rights, defined as the absence of socialist economic structures, civil or external war, and extreme deprivation of civil or political rights, and economic openness, defined as a low proportion of imports covered by quantitative restrictions and a free market exchange rate that is within 20 percent of the official rate. Sachs and Warner identify only 13, out of 75, countries meeting all these criteria over the period from 1970 to 1989. Of those 13, 11 had growth rates of income per capita over 3 percent a year and the other two had rates over 2 percent. Of the 75 countries that did not meet all these criteria, only 6 grew by more than 3 percent a year and 51 grew by less than 2 percent a year.

These studies suggest that market orientation is important for rapid growth of incomes and productivity. But market-based policies are not sufficient to ensure growth, nor do these studies rule out the possibility that growth can be achieved through other policy regimes. Market orientation is not the only factor contributing to growth; entrepreneurial talent, educated workers, and well-run governments are also important. Several countries that are open in the sense of having high ratios of exports to gross national income may lack other requirements for growth, while some inward-looking countries may have them in abundance. Under the circumstances, the apparently narrow differences in productivity growth in the Syrquin-Chenery data and the stronger results on income growth in the Sachs-Warner study support the proposition that openness contributes to economic growth. Economists believe that openness works because it introduces competition (as well as wider markets and the ability to attain economies from larger-scale production). Then, by extension, we conclude that markets, which create competition, also work to raise productivity.

Implementing Market Reforms

Over the past several decades, therefore, a strong case has been built favoring a greater role for market forces in the management of the economy. But how does a country used to widespread government intervention wean itself from overuse of bureaucratic commands in favor of more market influence? Is it simply a matter of dismantling the government's role in the economy and allowing market forces to take over? Or do market-oriented reforms require a different role for government, not necessarily a lesser role?

8. Jeffrey Sachs and Andrew Warner, "Economic Convergence and Economic Policies," Harvard Institute for International Development, Development Discussion Paper No. 502, March 1995.

To make the transition from a regulated economy to a well-functioning market economy, five conditions need to be met, each of which will be explored in greater depth in subsequent sections.

1. *Prices must become reasonably stable* and the macroeconomy should be close to equilibrium. Macroeconomic instability—large budget deficits, rampant inflation, and a severe drain on the balance of foreign payments—discourages productive activity and invites widespread government interference with market forces.

2. *Most goods and services must be bought and sold through market mechanisms,* and not allocated through administered arrangements such as import licensing, output quotas, ration shops, government agencies, and public enterprises. Before the 1990s, most developing countries and all socialist countries allocated a significant share of goods and services through nonmarket mechanisms.

3. *There must be competition,* either within the domestic market or from abroad, if productivity gains are to be achieved. In some cases the economy is too small to sustain more than one firm in an industry and government restrictions on imports eliminate competition from foreign firms. In other instances there are several firms in the industry but their own collusion or government allocation of quotas for critical inputs effectively removes competitive pressure. Centrally planned economies favor monopolies in part because it makes planning easier.

4. *Relative prices should reflect relative scarcities* in the economy. It is possible to have a market system with highly distorted prices, but it is not possible to have an efficient market system under such circumstances. Price distortions have been pervasive in many developing economies and "getting prices right" is a major objective of most market-oriented reforms.

5. *Firm managers, farmers, and other decision makers must be able and willing to respond to market signals.* Firms must maximize profits by increasing their sales or cutting their costs, or they must follow some rule that is a close approximation of profit maximization. Economists tend to assume that firms will maximize profits because it is in their own interest to do so. But when economies are riddled with government interventions, profits are obtained by extracting greater subsidies, price supports, and the like from the government, not by increasing the economic efficiency of the firm.

These five transitional requirements incorporate two market failures discussed earlier: macroeconomic stability is in both lists and competition is the antidote to monopoly power. Other market failures are also relevant to reform. Prices that reflect relative scarcities suggest taxation or other corrections for external costs and benefits as discussed in Chapter 7. And economies in transition from controls to market mechanisms are deficient in the market institutions, especially those for diversifying risk and conveying information, that are necessary to make markets work efficiently. Though essential to long-term development, corrections for these market failures are usually not addressed in transitional reforms and are mentioned only incidentally in the next sections.

1. Stabilization of the Macro Economy

In theory a market can work while prices are rising rapidly. In practice price increases above a certain level will trigger government interventions in the form of general price freezes or specific price controls. If price controls are put in place without first curing the underlying causes of inflation, the result will be excess demand for the goods whose prices were frozen. To deal with this excess demand, the government must either introduce rationing or stand by while long lines form at shops selling the goods in short supply, an informal kind of rationing. Either way the goods end up being distributed by some nonmarket mechanism, through ration coupons or to those who are first into line and most willing to wait. In the Soviet Union it was normal for citizens to carry shopping bags with them at all times on the chance that some shop had just gotten a new supply of some scarce item. Under rationing, those who first obtain scarce goods frequently turn around and sell them in the **parallel or black market,** where prices are higher than in the official market and can exceed the prices that would prevail in an uncontrolled market.

What is the level of inflation that triggers this kind of intervention? The answer is in part political. Some societies such as those in South America are accustomed to very rapid inflation and rates of 20 or 30 percent a year are considered relatively stable. Other societies, China for example, consider any rate above 20 percent intolerable, while Germans feel uncomfortable with inflation of 5 percent a year.

Inflation leads to distortions in relative prices and the decisions based on them. Groups that are organized to wield political power, such as unionized labor, large firms, the military, and civil servants, compete intensely to protect their shares of the national income. The result is a distortion of relative prices away from scarcity values to reflect instead the outcome of these political struggles. Relative prices themselves become volatile, and so reduce the information they convey to participants in the economy. For example, **real interest rates** (interest rates corrected for inflation) often become negative; this reduces the supply of long-term funds for investment. Exchange rates usually become **overvalued:** the central bank offers, for instance, too few pesos (the local currency) to people with dollars to sell, and this discourages exports and encourages imports.

These distortions and the uncertainty about future rates of inflation cause people to acquire land, gold, and other assets whose prices will rise with inflation, rather than productive assets, or to transfer their financial wealth overseas. With rapid inflation, entrepreneurs and managers spend more time trying to profit from inflation and devote correspondingly less energy to producing more efficiently. After all, large and sustained productivity gains might reduce costs by 3 to 5 percent a year, not much compared to rates of inflation from 10s to 100s of percent a year.

There is impressive evidence that macroeconomic stability is necessary—though far from sufficient—to promote economic growth. Figures 5–1 and 5–2 assemble data on rates of inflation, exchange rate overvaluation, and economic growth for 29 countries from 1980 to 1992. They show that none of the countries with rapid inflation, such as Ghana, Zambia, and several in Latin America, were able to generate growth in per capita income. Conversely, all the countries with very rapid growth, especially those in East and Southeast Asia, had low rates of inflation. Similarly, all countries with per capita income growth greater than 2 percent a year kept their official exchange rates within 20 percent of the free market rate. But low inflation and low exchange rate overvaluation were not always sufficient to generate growth, as evidenced by Kenya and Cameroon.

More comprehensively, MIT economist Stanley Fischer compiled data for 80

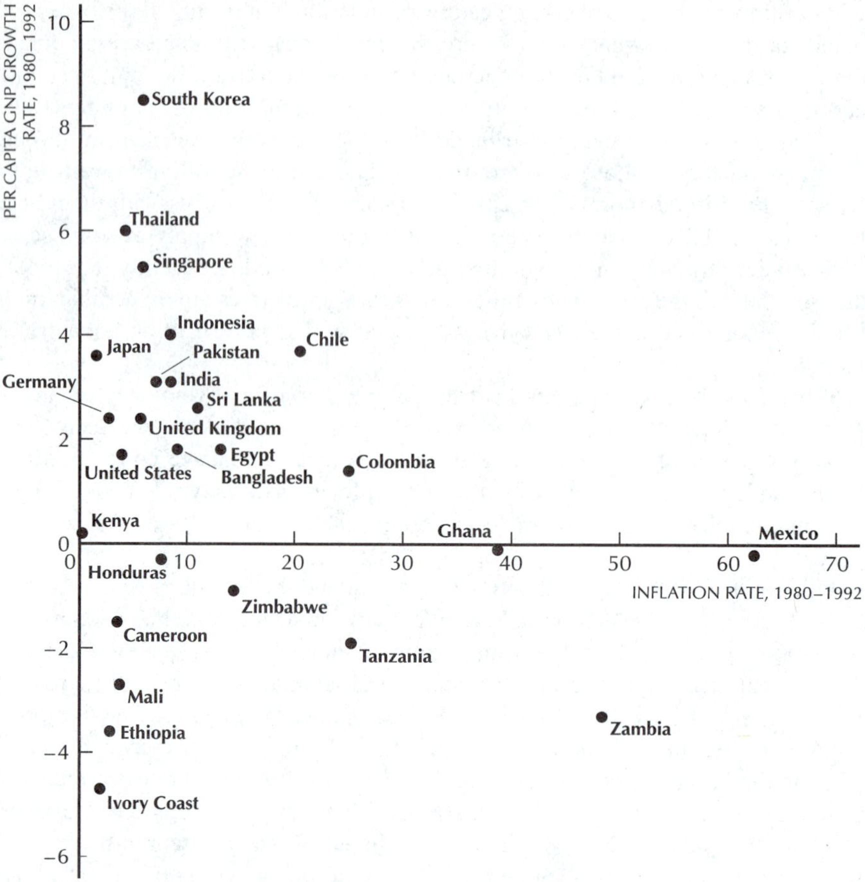

FIGURE 5–1 Inflation and Economic Growth, 1980–1992. All countries with per capita income growth greater than 2 percent a year kept inflation below 20 percent a year and the most rapidly growing countries all kept annual inflation below 10 percent.

countries over 25 years, covering the early 1960s to the middle 1980s. His regressions demonstrate that higher inflation, higher budget deficits, and more overvalued exchange rates are closely correlated with reduced economic growth. And there is some indication that the macroeconomic imbalances cause slower growth, not the other way around.[9]

Stabilization programs are designed to stem inflation and correct the other imbalances associated with it, notably deficits in the government budget and in the balance of foreign payments. Often it is the International Monetary Fund that works with the country to introduce a package of stabilization policies. At the core of the package is the notion that inflation is caused when the supply of money increases faster than the demand for it. To correct this and other imbalances, a typical program will contain some or all of the following remedies. (1) A reduction in the government's budget deficit, through higher taxes and reduced

9. Stanley Fischer, "The Role of Macroeconomic Factors in Growth," *Journal of Monetary Economics*, 32 (1993), 485–512. Exchange rate distortions are measured by the percentage deviation of the parallel market exchange rate from the official rate.

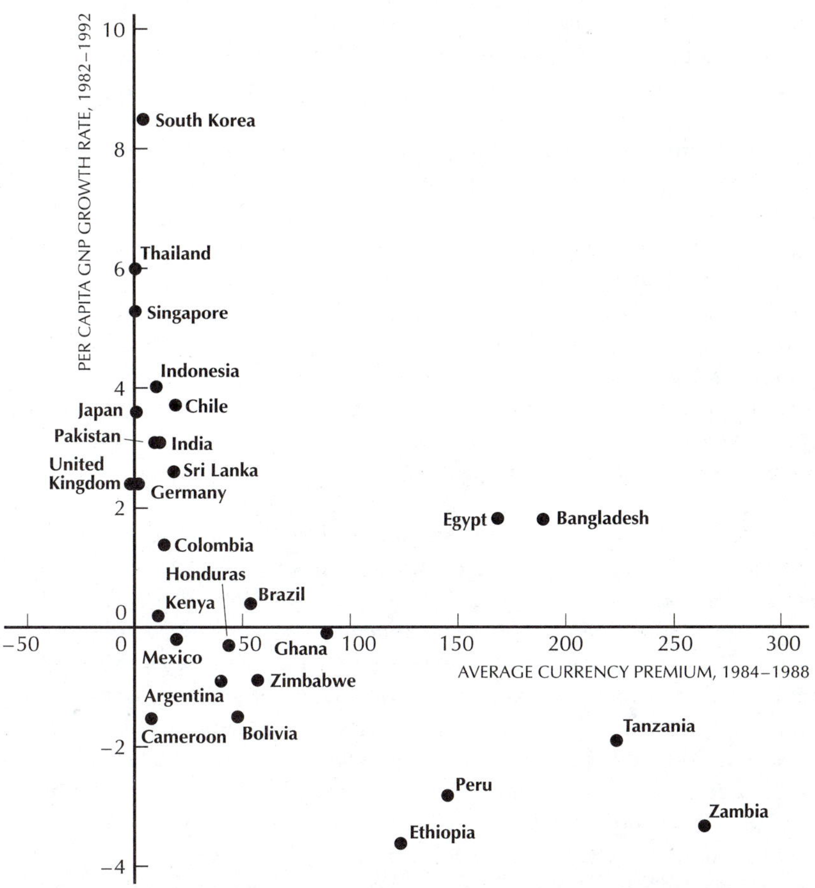

FIGURE 5–2 Exchange Rate Overvaluation and Economic Growth, 1980–1992. All countries with per capita income growth exceeding 2 percent a year had exchange rate premia (excess of free market over official market rates) of less than 20 percent, while most countries with high premia suffered declines in average income.

expenditure, is needed because deficits are financed either by money creation or by borrowing from private savers, which "crowds out" private investment. (2) To control growth of the money supply, restrictive targets are set for central bank credit to the government and the commercial banks. (3) The exchange rate may be devalued. This raises the price of foreign exchange in domestic currency and helps to correct a balance-of-payments deficit by stimulating exports and restraining the demand for imports. (4) Price controls may be removed so that markets can reduce the distortions in relative prices; administered prices may be adjusted for the same reason. Interest rates, food prices, utility rates and transport fares are often affected. (5) Targets are set for restraining wage increases. If wages increase faster than productivity, they push up the cost of production and thus contribute to inflation. We discuss macroeconomic stabilization further in Chapter 21.

When deficits in the budget or balance of payments occur, they must either be reduced through economic adjustment or be financed from overseas. To assist in financing deficits, the IMF may help the government to reschedule its foreign debt payments, especially those due to commercial banks. The IMF itself offers loans—called **standby credits**—for three to five years at moderate interest rates to help close the balance-of-payments gap. This is intended to ease the pains of stabilization by permitting the corrective measures to be less drastic than they would otherwise have to be. However, disbursement of the loan (as well as debt relief) is contingent on successful implementation of the measures designed to stabilize the economy. This *quid pro quo*—loans and debt relief in return for policy reform—is known as **conditionality.**

The IMF stabilization package is controversial. Most economists accept that imbalances, particularly budget deficits, have to be corrected and inflation curbed if growth and development are to be sustained. One issue, however, is the speed of adjustment. Stabilization is likely to require some rise in unemployment and a decline in income for some groups, although the imbalances themselves might have caused similar problems. The more abruptly these measures are enforced, the greater will be the dislocations. Yet a gradual implementation may undermine the government's credibility and make it more difficult to complete the stabilization.

When control of inflation has to be combined with a major restructuring of the economy, the dislocations can be particularly severe. This situation, in essence, was the case in much of Central and Eastern Europe, Russia, and Vietnam during the first half of the 1990s. The structural changes there led to both a loss in revenue, as existing sources of tax revenue disappeared, and an increase in government expenditures to bail out the many loss-making state enterprises—losses due in large part to the difficulties these enterprises were having in adjusting to a market system. Formally these enterprises received loans from the central bank, but since no one expected the loans to be repaid, they were in reality subsidies from the government budget. Closing down the loss-making enterprises would have reduced expenditures and hence inflation pressure, but it would also have thrown large numbers of people out of work. Russia was unable or unwilling to face the political consequences of what the leaders believed would be large-scale unemployment, so inflation continued at 10 to 20 percent per month (300 to 900 percent per year). Vietnam, with a much smaller state enterprise sector, did cut back sharply on subsidies to state enterprises and thereby reduced inflation from around 70 percent a year in 1990 and 1991 to well under 20 percent a year in 1992 and 1993.

Even where the restructuring of the economy is less drastic than what has been attempted in Russia or Eastern Europe, inflation may be more difficult to bring down than many orthodox economists believe. A school of heterodox economists, led by Lance Taylor of the New School for Social Research, believes that many wages and other prices are set by predetermined, nonmarket rules. For example, in inflation-prone countries in Latin America, labor agreements sometimes adjust wage rates to compensate for inflation, a practice called **indexing.** And many firms set their prices by calculating a fixed percentage, or margin, over the costs of production, a practice called **markup pricing.** To the extent that these practices prevail, a reduction in the growth of the money supply will not reduce inflation for some time, as unions and firms continue their habit of raising wages and prices to make up for past losses to inflation and to protect against future inflation. Instead, with prices rising faster than the money supply, the result is layoffs and bankruptcies. Eventually, perhaps, the unions and firms will adjust their expectations and inflation will abate, but it can take years and may require more than the economic measures contained in stabilization packages. Fundamental agreements among employers, workers, and government may be needed to change the entrenched habits of indexing and markup pricing; sometimes these "agreements" are forced by coercive measures, often by military governments.[10]

Ultimately this is an empirical matter: are prices **flexible,** moving up and down with demand, or **fixed** and insensitive to reductions in demand? Most economies have a mixture of both kinds. Prices for most agriculture, many services, and some manufactured goods are flexible. But in some industries, especially those with a few large-scale firms, fixed pricing may prevail. In countries with entrenched and politicized labor unions and concentrated industries, prices are more likely to be inflexible. When, in addition, the income distribution is very unequal, a government is often unable to win a broad consensus on stabilization measures. These conditions seem characteristic of some Latin American countries, where the experience with stabilization programs has been mixed, with many notable failures, such as Brazil and Argentina in the 1980s, and some successes, notably Bolivia in 1985 (see box). In Asia, governments have been better able to use stabilization packages to correct budget and payments imbalances and control inflation.

Stabilization That Worked: Bolivia, 1985–1986[11]

From August 1984 to August 1985, prices in Bolivia rose by 20,000 percent, the most rapid inflation in Latin American history. During September 1985, inflation was stopped cold and prices actually began to fall. How did this happen?

The hyperinflation of 1984–85 was the culmination of events under the regime of President Siles Zuazo, which in 1982 became Bolivia's first elected government in 18 years. Declining foreign aid and commercial bank lending, combined with rising international interest rates and debt payments, led to a growing payments deficit: net resource flows into Bolivia declined by 10 percent of GDP over three years to a net outflow of $190 million in 1983. To compensate for this loss of revenue, the government resorted to central bank credit, and thus increased the money supply. This, combined with wage increases granted to organized labor, caused accelerating inflation. Rising prices caused a precipitate decline in tax revenues, from 9 percent of GDP in 1981 to only 1.3 percent in 1985, and led to a rapid depreciation of the exchange rate, both of which fed back into higher inflation. By 1985 the public had lost all confidence in the *boliviano* and most transactions were denominated in dollars.

In August 1985 the newly elected government of President Victor Paz

10. For a review of these controversies, see Tony Killick (ed.), *The Quest for Stabilization: The IMF and the Third World* (London: Heinemann Education Books 1984); Lance Taylor, *Varieties of Stabilization Experience: Toward Sensible Macroeconomics in the Third World* (London: Oxford University Press, [Clarendon], 1988); and John Williamson (ed.), *IMF Conditionality* (Washington, D. C.: Institute for International Economics, 1983). The Taylor book is for advanced readers.

11. This account is drawn from Juan Antonio Morales and Jeffrey D. Sachs, "Bolivia's Economic Crisis," in Jeffrey D. Sachs (ed.), *Developing Country Debt and the World Economy* (Chicago: University of Chicago Press, 1989), pp. 57–79, and Jeffrey D. Sachs, "The Bolivian Hyperinflation and Stabilization," *American Economic Review,* 77, no. 2 (May 1987), 279–83.

Estenssoro took power and instituted a radical stabilization program along orthodox lines. The *boliviano* was devalued and made fully convertible into dollars; a sharp rise in the prices of goods and services sold by government corporations, together with a freeze on public sector wages, immediately cut the budget deficit; a tax reform was proposed and later enacted to increase revenues and avoid future deficits; the treasury went on a cash flow basis, spending no more than its incoming cash revenues. The elimination of the deficit reduced the need to obtain central bank credit, and so restricted the money supply; this in turn curbed price increases and stabilized the new exchange rate. In contrast to other Latin American stabilizations, no price controls were employed and some existing controls were eliminated. The stabilization was aided by a standby agreement with the IMF and the subsequent resumption of lending by the aid donors, including the World Bank. But the moratorium on debt payments to commercial banks, begun under the Siles government, was maintained.

The abrupt elimination of the government's deficit and its ability to stabilize the exchange rate made its program credible to the public. The Paz government's task was easier because the previous government's policies had been completely discredited and the economy was in a shambles. The government was even able to carry out the kind of unpopular measures that might have toppled other regimes, notably the layoff of 21,000 workers employed by the inefficient government tin mining company, COMIBOL, and the sharp curtailment of government expenditures. After the first few months of dramatic reform, inflation did resume, but at levels of 10 to 15 percent, some of the lowest rates in Latin America.

2. Dismantling Controls

Once stabilization has been achieved, or even while it is being achieved, the other four elements of a well-functioning market system must be put in place. Many of the measures designed to accomplish this task come in the category the World Bank calls **structural adjustment.**

A critical step at the outset is to make as many goods as possible available for purchase on the market rather than through some allocation mechanism of the government bureaucracy. Thus an important element in trade reform is to remove government quotas on imports. Import licensing is a way of transferring allocations from the market to the government. In many developing countries firms starting up a new factory must get licenses to purchase land, to get foreign exchange for imports of capital equipment and intermediate inputs, and even to buy electricity. Negotiations to acquire these licenses can drag on for years. In the agricultural sector, fertilizer and pesticides are sometimes distributed through a state commercial network in amounts determined by government, rather than by farmers' willingness to purchase and use these inputs. Most of these interventions in mixed economies were justified at their origin by the market failure and distributional arguments outlined at the beginning of this chapter. Others, restrictions on foreign investment for example, are justified on political or security grounds. When restriction is piled on restriction, however, the cumulative effect is to remove large parts of the economy from participation in the market.

In command economies, such as those of China, the Soviet Union, and Vietnam, allocation of goods through the market, except for retail sales to consumers, was rejected altogether. Industrial and agricultural inputs were allocated by government bureaus to enterprises in accordance with a central plan. If an enterprise needed more of one kind of input, it had to go back to the central planners or the government bureau to get an increased allocation. Buying the item on the market was not possible because no such market existed.

Dismantling such controls over production, marketing, and consumption, in both mixed and command economies, is a central feature of structural adjustment packages. Reforms that end controls are called **liberalization** or **deregulation.**

3. Ensuring Competition

In many developing countries competition has been avoided. Foreign competition in particular is considered "unfair" because foreign firms have years more experience than the country's new domestic firms. The solution is often to prohibit entry into the domestic market by foreign firms. Competition between domestic firms is also seen to waste resources. Why have three firms when one or two can produce all that is required? Fewer firms can achieve economies of scale, and produce at lower average cost. Competition is disorderly, so the argument goes, and some firms will fail, and put people out of work.

Waste caused by the bankruptcy of a company is visible to all, but waste is not so apparent if caused by lack of pressure to produce more efficiently. Hardly anyone noticed that the U.S. automobile companies had largely ignored the demand for smaller cars until the Japanese came along with their compacts and subcompacts. Competition is the force that pressures everyone to do better. The desire to produce goods that were competitive in international markets was one reason for the rapid growth of the four East Asian tigers. State-owned enterprises are often inefficient in part because the state frequently awards monopoly control of their market to these enterprises. With monopoly control they can set prices high enough to cover their high costs and can sell goods of inferior quality. Under the circumstances, why bother working hard to lower costs? Industries built behind a wall of protection from foreign imports may never be able to compete in foreign markets. Managers in these industries, as already pointed out, will put most of their energy into lobbying to maintain that protection, rather than learning how to meet the competition.

Centrally managed economies, such as those of the Soviet Union and China before the recent reforms, allowed little real competition among enterprises. In China in the 1970s even small-scale county-owned enterprises were given a monopoly over the local county market. When demand in the local market for the output of the small enterprise was saturated, production was stopped and the enterprise retooled to produce something else. In this kind of system the government allocates inputs and tells firms how much to produce. Pressure to surpass the targets set by the state provides some impetus to produce more efficiently, but this kind of pressure is a poor substitute for competition between firms where the loser will have a smaller market share, lower profits, and fewer employees, and may go out of business. Command economies are notorious for their profligate waste of resources.

Reform programs attempt to introduce competition into markets where it has been limited or absent. In larger countries, or in industries with few economies of scale, there can be several firms in any industry. Competition between these domestic firms can be fostered simply by dismantling import or investment licensing, quotas over output, controls over prices, or other government interventions that give some firms advantages over others. In China one of the first reform steps was to abolish all regional or local monopolies, and thus force enterprises in different regions to compete with each other.

If the domestic market is small and one or a few firms dominate the industry or if domestic firms fail to compete vigorously, the only viable competition comes from abroad, in the form of competing imports. Thus the deregulation of import controls and reduction of tariffs provide the competitive stimulus for improved productivity and higher quality. Another way to infuse domestic industry with competitive urges is to bias the entire structure of incentives toward exports, away from domestic sales. Import liberalization should be part of this strategy, but it also encompasses exchange rate devaluation, direct and indirect subsidies, preferential credit, investment in ports and other infrastructure, and many other measures to support exporters. In order to take advantage of more profitable sales in foreign markets, domestic firms must improve both their quality and their productivity and learn to market aggressively. This is the outward-looking approach used by the four East Asian "tigers."[12]

4. Moving toward Scarcity Prices

While competition creates the stimulus for firms to maximize profits and improve productivity, **relative prices** are the signals that tell firms how to manage their resources to earn the highest rewards. If the relative prices reflect the real scarcities in the economy, firms that maximize profits and consumers who maximize their utility will automatically act to make the most out of all resources on behalf of the economy as a whole. This is called **static efficiency.** Scarce resources, such as capital or energy, should have relatively high prices to conserve their use; abundant resources, such as unskilled labor in poor economies and educated workers in rich ones, should receive relatively low wages so they will be used more intensively in production. When market prices dictate these allocations of scarce and abundant resources, a greater value of output can be achieved for any given expenditure on inputs.

Despite these advantages of market-determined prices, governments have regularly intervened to set prices and shield them from market influences. In principle these price controls were designed to correct for market failures and thus to bring prices in line with real scarcities. In reality, price setting was generally a process based on political and not economic objectives. More often than not, government intervention led prices further away from real economic scarcities.

A major objective of structural adjustment reforms, therefore, is to reduce or remove these distortions generated by government intervention. In the majority of developing countries, the list of distorted prices is a long one. (1) Tariffs raise the price of imports and competing domestic goods. If tariffs were at a uniform rate on all imports, the distortions would not be so great. But tariffs typically vary

12. Not all the measures listed are always advocated for outward-looking strategies. Subsidies and preferential credit, though they do promote exports, also distort the economy away from scarcity prices.

from 0 to 50 percent, and rates of 200 percent are not uncommon. (2) Interest rates on loans are frequently held well below market rates in a misguided attempt to promote investment by reducing the cost of finance. Low rates discourage saving, however, and this reduces the availability of finance. Also cheap loans meant for the poor are usually syphoned off by the well-connected rich, while the poor pay very high rates on the loans that are available to them through informal credit markets. (3) Small numbers of well-organized urban workers can sometimes pressure governments to support demands for high wages and nonwage benefits or to restrict layoffs. Poorer, unorganized workers in both the urban and rural areas continue to receive lower, market-set wages. The larger factories, faced with higher labor costs, cut back on employment and substitute machines where they can. (4) Gasoline and other fuels are often sold at prices below those of the world market; this encourages the wasteful use of energy and generally favors well-off consumers. (5) Food prices are frequently kept low for urban workers even though this can mean that the poorer rural people get paid less for their crops.

The political nature of price setting is readily apparent. For every government-determined price, there are winners, who receive more for their output or pay less for their inputs, and losers. Price distortions most often occur when the beneficiaries of a price change are few and concentrated, while the losers are large in number and dispersed. A tariff on bicycles, for example, will raise the profits to the owners of a country's handful of bicycle factories. A small increase in prices may mean very large increases in profits. Those paying the higher price will number in the millions in a large country, but they will be scattered unevenly across the country and are unlikely to organize to protest the increase. Since the tariff is built into the price of the bicycle, these consumers may not even be aware that government intervention caused the higher prices. The producers will know, however, and will be in positions with their increased profits to help those who helped them. Where the beneficiaries of price distortions are large in number, as in the case of food price subsidies, other kinds of political pressures can arise. Removal of a food subsidy frequently triggers rioting that can topple governments.

Structural adjustment reforms designed to correct price distortions, therefore, frequently run into stiff resistance. Nowhere is this more true than in the former command economies of Central and Eastern Europe, Russia, and China. In these countries most state enterprises saw themselves as beneficiaries of state price controls because it meant that they received key inputs at artificially low prices. To get around the resistance of large state enterprises, China created a dual price system where steel going to a large enterprise in accordance with the annual plan was charged a low state-set price, while all other steel was sold on the market at much higher market-determined prices. This dual system overcame much of the political resistance to price reform, but it also created opportunities for corruption by those who could use their influence to buy at the low state price and quickly resell at the high market price—corruption which contributed to the discontent that fueled the demonstrations on Tiananmen Square in 1989. Many of the other socialist and former socialist countries, from Russia to Vietnam, therefore, opted for eliminating state-set prices altogether and using one market-determined price for most goods and services.

There is no question that removing the distortions in prices caused by state intervention will normally raise the welfare of the nation as a whole even as it hurts select groups and individuals. But how large are these welfare improvements?

There is no easy answer to this question. Potentially in the former socialist economies the gain should be very large given the size of the previous distortions, but only China and Vietnam have experienced unequivocal benefits in the form of high growth rates, while in Russia and much of Eastern and Central Europe price reforms were followed by deep recessions. Some economists argue that the gains from price reforms in most developing countries are quite modest. Others suggest that, where distortions are large, as was true in much of the developing world in earlier decades, the gains will be large and are the very essence of reform. Because structural adjustment reforms such as those in Russia and China or in Latin America involve much more than the freeing up of prices, however, it is usually not possible to separate out the impact of efforts to correct price distortions from the effects of the four other elements that make markets work. Most successful reform packages, therefore, involve a combination of reforms of which removing price distortions is only one.

5. Responding to Market Signals

Perhaps the least understood of the reforms needed to make markets work are those that induce producers to act in accordance with market signals. The rule is simple enough: producers should maximize profits by cutting their costs or increasing their sales. Economists typically assume that producers automatically maximize profits.[13] A firm's owners try to earn high incomes for themselves. But what happens when the firm is run by managers who are hired by the owners? What happens if the firm is owned by the state and managers are appointed to their posts by the government?

Some of the early socialist theorists, the Polish economist Oscar Lange for example, thought this problem could be solved by simply ordering managers of state-owned enterprises to maximize profits. These orders would be necessary because, with the state receiving the profits, higher profits no longer necessarily mean higher incomes for the managers. It is to the credit of these early theorists that they recognized that the issue had to be solved. If firms did not maximize profits, getting prices right would not necessarily lead to a better allocation of resources. Prices work by raising profits to producers of goods in short supply. The prospect of earning higher profits stimulates producers to increase production of scarce items. But if the producers are not rewarded by higher profits, they may not respond to higher prices. The early theorists had correctly diagnosed the problem, but their solution—ordering managers to maximize profits—was insufficient.

Increasing the role of the market often works most easily in agriculture. As Theodore Schultz emphasized, farmers, like owners of small businesses, are profit maximizers.[14] If prices are raised on a particular crop, say coffee in Kenya, farmers will plant more land in coffee but less in maize, because by doing so they will raise their income. Reform can therefore be effective simply by freeing up prices of agricultural products so that prices reflect society's demand for those products and by making inputs such as fertilizer available through the market rather than through state trading companies. Family farmers respond to deregulated prices and supplies because it is profitable for them to do so.

13. But recall the structuralists, led by Lance Taylor, who assume firms mark up their prices to cover costs plus a percentage profit; this is not the same as maximizing profits.

14. Shultz, *Transforming Traditional Agriculture.*

A key reason for the success of the Chinese and Vietnamese reform efforts was that both countries began with reforms in agriculture and small-scale trading. The collective farms and communes were broken up, and the land was turned over to be farmed by individual profit or income-maximizing households. The crops raised on this land could then be sold on the freed up rural markets. In both China and Vietnam, farm output increased dramatically after these reforms were introduced, and so added credibility to the overall reform effort.

Small-scale industrial and commercial enterprises behave much like family farmers. Managers and owners are the same people and increased profits go directly to the managers. In developing countries, this direct link between ownership and management holds even for moderately large firms, which are often owned by one or a few families. But as firms increase in size and complexity, the direct link is broken. Owners hire professional managers whose ownership stake in the firm is limited. Incentive bonuses based on profits can help motivate managers, but are not a perfect substitute for direct ownership. Single or family owners give way to many stockholders whose control over managers is diffuse and often ineffective. In the United States, boards of directors often do not restrain managers and many large shareholders, especially pension funds and other institutions, are not even represented on the boards.

In the case of **state-owned enterprises,** even the owner has goals other than profit maximization. Government-appointed managers are often directed to keep their prices low to help consumers, to employ more people than needed, to invest and locate in less-developed (and less profitable) regions, to contribute to the political campaigns of the ruling party, and much else. Profits and efficiency may not even be a specified goal.

A more fundamental problem is that state-owned enterprises are owned by all of the people in the country; this usually means that no individual or group of individuals feels any real sense of ownership. It is left up to the state to make sure that the enterprise doesn't waste its assets or sell off its output to a favored few at below market prices. But the state is often a rather remote entity that has little real knowledge of what is going on within the enterprise. State rules with special auditors to enforce them can prevent theft but they can also tie up an enterprise in so much red tape that it cannot respond to market signals and hence loses money. To help get around this problem, many state enterprises are required to sign performance contracts in which the state specifies the goals that managers are expected to achieve and managers' rewards if they do achieve them. But performance contracts do not always elicit the kinds of changes in managerial behavior that are required. The limitations of the ownership problem have led many countries to implement more radical changes including outright privatization.

One critical issue is how to create **property rights** or a full sense of ownership for those who have decision making authority over the enterprise. **Property rights,** to be meaningful, must be **well defined** and **exclusive.** If they are neither, then others will lay claim to the property and no one will know who really has decision making authority. Property rights must also be **secure** for long and indefinite periods. Otherwise those who have these rights will take a very short-term view knowing that they won't be around to reap either the rewards or the punishments for long run success or failure. Normally property rights must also be **transferable** through sale or lease for much the same reason. If an enterprise decision maker can sell the enterprise, that decision maker will want to maintain its value and not lower its price by running the enterprise into the ground. And property rights must be **enforceable** usually through a well-established legal system, although there are other enforcement mechanisms.[15]

Most state enterprises fail to meet these property rights requirements. Neither the managers nor the supervising ministry officials have well-defined, secure, and transferable rights to the enterprise in most cases. They can be removed from control by the stroke of a pen of some higher government official. Only the voting public or a small oligarchy, if it is an authoritarian system, have any real property rights, and they are usually too remote to exercise effective control.

Increasingly in the 1980s and 1990s privatization of all or most state-owned firms is seen as the solution to the property rights problem. There have been efforts to privatize state-owned firms in both mixed economics and in the former Soviet-style command economies. In some cases, usually in mixed economies, enterprises are sold off one by one over a long period. In other cases, the effort has been rapid and across-the-board.

The Russian privatization program of the first half of the 1990s is one of the more interesting cases of the latter approach. Vouchers were given to four groups: the general public, local governments, managers of privatizing state enterprises, and workers of those same enterprises. These vouchers through an auction system could then be used to purchase a share of ownership in enterprises undergoing privatization, which by 1994 represented more than two-thirds of all state-owned firms.

Russia represented a particularly severe case of an absence of property rights prior to privatization. The central government was too weak to protect the state assets. Workers, managers, and local governments had little incentive to help the center because there was nothing in it for them. So workers and managers who had temporary control of state assets took the opportunity to sell them for personal profit. Privatization was thus designed to end this theft of assets by giving those with control over them a stake in their preservation and efficient use.

Privatization may not always be necessary in order to create the required property rights. China's county, township, and village enterprises, for example, are often owned by the county, township, or village. In many cases the local government officials at this level behave as profit-maximizing entrepreneurs and the township population as a whole clearly sees the relationship between the effectiveness of the local enterprise and its own personal rewards. Public pension funds and other forms of public mutual funds may also serve as effective owners of state firms if those funds are clearly profit oriented and have the right to hire and fire enterprise managers by electing their representatives to the enterprise board of directors. Experiments of this sort are underway in places as diverse as Central Europe, China, and Malaysia.

Whether or not privatization is necessary, it is almost never sufficient. Privatization that creates secure and transferable property rights but does nothing to force the enterprise to compete will not create efficient enterprises capable of sustaining high productivity growth. A firm sold to a cousin of the country's president, who then gets monopoly rights over the sale of its product and state

15. Theodore Panayotou, *Green Markets: The Economics of Sustainable Development* (San Francisco: ICS Press, 1993), pp. 35–37.

subsidies of various kinds, will be no more efficient than a state-owned enterprise with similar forms of protection.

Whether public or private, the umbilical chord tying the enterprise to the government must be cut. Management energy, as already pointed out, must go into raising sales and cutting costs, not into generating more government support. Government reform, therefore, is often an integral part of making both state and private enterprises work better. If a tax system removes all or most discretion from the tax collector, then the enterprise does not have to spend time negotiating with or bribing the collector for favorable treatment. The government must also disengage from setting the firm's prices or from providing other kinds of subsidies, such as import quotas when the firm gets in trouble. Only then will the enterprise, whatever its ownership, be a truly independent, competitive firm capable of playing a leading role in the development effort.

The Transition to a Market System

The implementation of stabilization and structural adjustment measures raises another set of issues for a reforming government: the credibility of the whole reform package, the timing of measures, and the magnitude of change.

Success in reforming an economy depends crucially on the **credibility** of the entire package.[16] If budget deficits remain high or for any other reason money creation is not slowed, the public will anticipate continued or higher inflation. If the real exchange rate is allowed to appreciate because inflation outruns nominal devaluations, as happened in Chile and elsewhere, export industries become unattractive to investors. If import liberalization is undertaken tentatively or if past attempts are reversed, investors will put their money into the old protected industries. To establish credibility, governments need to manage their reform programs decisively, despite their complexity. They may also need to "lock in" reforms by making commitments that are difficult to reverse. Many reforms, especially in Africa, now start by freeing the exchange rate and foreign exchange flows from all controls; this forces the government to reduce its deficit and contain money supply growth to avoid massive depreciation and capital outflows. One of the more decisive government efforts to establish the credibility of trade liberalization was the decision by President Carlos Salinas of Mexico to negotiate and sign the North American Free Trade Agreement (NAFTA). Opponents desiring to reverse these reductions in trade barriers must first contend with an international treaty.

Credibility also depends on the public's perceptions about stabilization and liberalization. In judging the effects of policies, the public is most likely to compare situations before and after, when the proper comparison is with and without. A stabilized economy may look worse than the observed precrisis economy, but could well be an improvement over the situation that might have developed without stabilization, which of course cannot be observed. Leaders and officials in many countries have a deep-seated statist bias towards controls and often main-

16. Political scientist Joan Nelson has explored issues of credibility, timing, and magnitude as director of a multi-country study of stabilization programs. See "The Political Economy of Stabilization: Commitment, Capacity and Public Response," *World Development,* 12, no. 10 (1984), 983–1006.

tain an illusion that government controls are effective when they are not. These perceptions by government and the public make it more difficult to plan and implement reforms. Disappointing results with past stabilization and reform efforts make it more difficult to convince the public to support new initiatives.

The influence of foreign aid institutions on credibility is two-edged. The International Monetary Fund and the World Bank provide additional resources that can ease the transition to an open economy and help to protect incomes during the transition. Foreign aid can enhance the position of reforming elements within a government and can be used by government to sell stabilization programs to the public. However, additional resources also make the crisis seem less intense and reforms less necessary. Moreover, an IMF presence has increasingly become a focal point for opposition to economic change. Although governments of countries such as Egypt and Zambia have deflected public ire by ceasing to negotiate with the Fund, the result has only been to delay stabilization, not eliminate its necessity.

Public debt plays a similarly dual role. To a point, the need to pay off foreign creditors can be used to steel the public to a degree of austerity. But at some point debt becomes a liability, as the public begins to wonder why their standard of living should decline so that foreign bankers' profits can be maintained. In the long run, it probably requires convincing arguments about the population's own well-being to sustain either stabilization or reform efforts.

Implicit in the discussion of credibility are the questions of **timing** and **magnitude.** Should reforms be pushed through quickly or phased in gradually? There are times in a country's history when economic and political forces provide a brief opportunity for dramatic reforms. Probably the single most convincing observation on timing, by political scientist Joan Nelson, is that the beginning of a new regime is the time to act.[17] Recently elected regimes have the momentum of popular support, used to good effect by President Jayawardana in Sri Lanka in the late 1970s and dramatically by President Victor Paz Estenssoro in Bolivia in 1985 (see boxed example, pp. 117–18). New regimes of any kind have a brief initial period when they can blame problems on the previous government. Early success obviously has political benefits for the regime. But as time goes on, growing ties between government and its supporters in the private sector *(clients)* make policy change increasingly dangerous for any regime. In these circumstances, credibility is probably served by rapid, decisive, comprehensive action.

But the more complex and multifaceted the reform process becomes, the more difficult it is to act in a way that achieves across-the-board changes. The main task in Bolivia in 1985 was to stop rampant inflation in what already was a market economy. The task in Russia, Vietnam, and much of Central and Eastern Europe was to control inflation, but it was also to create a complete market economy where little or none had existed before. Enterprises, private or public, had to learn how to act in a completely different environment. Property rights had to be established where none had existed before, and a supporting legal system had to be designed and then made to work.

Poland, in what came to be called **shock treatment** or the big-bang approach to reform, tried to do everything at once. Early reform efforts in Russia associated with Yegor Gaidar attempted to do something similar. The approach called for an

17. Nelson, "The Political Economy of Stabilization."

immediate halt to inflation by stopping the growth in the money supply, freeing up all prices, and privatizing the state-owned sectors of the economy. In terms of economic theory, abstracted from politics, doing everything at once made sense. If all of the elements of a market system are in place, the market will work better than if only some of the elements are in place.

In practice shock treatment, at least in its initial form, proved impossible to implement. State enterprises could not adjust to the new situation quickly so many of them ran deeply into the red. Rather than letting these enterprises go bankrupt, thus throwing large numbers of people out of work, the central bank, as pointed out earlier in this chapter, kept the enterprises alive by giving them large loans which no one expected them to pay back to the bank. Increased loans raised the money supply and so kept inflation at high levels. Freeing up prices put goods back on the shelves of stores, but left those with incomes that didn't adjust to inflation in a difficult situation. This is, in essence, what happened in Russia in the first half of the 1990s. Some former socialist countries did better, others worse.

In virtually all of Central and Eastern Europe and the republics of the former Soviet Union, there were deep declines in gross national product that lasted for years. The problems of introducing a market system were compounded by the need to downsize the overblown military establishment and to establish new trading relationships after the breakup of the Communist trading bloc Comecon. Recession brought parties to power promising to slow the reform or even to reverse it.

China and Vietnam in the 1980s and early 1990s demonstrated, for some countries at least, that there was a more gradual approach to replacing a command system with a market system. Both began by freeing up prices and reestablishing household-based farming in the agricultural sector. They then freed up inputs and prices to the industrial sector and so created the conditions, in China at least, for a boom in small- and medium-scale industries. These industries in turn put competitive pressure on the large enterprises to become more effective at marketing their products and lowering their costs. While these changes were going on, Chinese GNP grew at an average of 9 percent a year, and Vietnamese GNP rose to over 7 percent a year by 1992 through 1994. China's and Vietnam's experience does not, however, prove that gradualism is the right answer for all countries. The large-scale state enterprise sector, the most difficult to reform, was a much smaller share of the economy in China and Vietnam than it was in Russia or Poland. China and Vietnam could afford to delay the full marketization of the large-scale state sector while they transformed the other three-quarters of the economy. In Russia and much of Eastern Europe, the large-scale state sector constituted most of the economy. Delaying reform of that sector meant delaying the entire effort to introduce a market economy.

Most developing economies, however, have at least some elements of a market system in place, and few have economies completely dominated by large-scale state enterprises. In these economies, piecemeal reform of one sector rather than the whole economy is often possible. Import liberalization can occur across the board, or it can begin with a few commodities and then spread to others. Customs procedures can be streamlined even if many tariffs remain high, and quotas can be abolished and replaced with tariffs. There is a danger that political resistance to gradual change will build because the costs may be more apparent than the benefits, but this could happen with across-the-board liberalization as well. What is feasible in individual countries will depend on the nature of the government and the base of its political support.

Even in market-dominated economies, however, structural adjustment reforms may not always be able to be carried out gradually over time and in a piecemeal fashion. In many Latin American countries, for example, trade liberalization is difficult if one cannot control inflation. And controlling inflation is difficult because the government is committed to supporting large vested interests at a level that cannot be paid for from existing sources of revenue; thus there is a rise in the money supply and more inflation. Many of these vested interests are the very workers and capitalists who own and work in the import-substituting industries that will be hurt by trade liberalization. Structural impediments to reform of this type are deeply rooted in the social and political systems of the country and may not be changeable without some radical across-the-board restructuring.

Some argue that the structural barriers to rapid reform are more economic than political. For a devaluation to improve the balance of payments, for example, people must cut back their consumption of imports and producers of exports must be able to move quickly to expand production and sales. In technical terms the **demand elasticities** for imports and the **supply elasticities** for exports must be large. If they are low, even if they are only low in the short run, the response to devaluation will be slow and the economy is more likely to be disrupted. Rapid change, to avoid disruption, requires elastic responses. Much of the resistance to reform comes from "elasticity pessimists" who feel that reform will cut back on key inputs without eliciting a dynamic production response that will overcome the impact of the reduction in inputs on incomes and employment. Sometimes elasticity pessimists create self-fulfilling prophesies by not carrying through with reforms that would allow producers to respond with alacrity.

For all the complexity involved in meeting these conditions for efficient markets, an increasing number of countries are making the effort to do so. Some of the most successful efforts have been in Asia. Hong Kong and Singapore were relatively free market economies from the beginning. South Korea used government controls extensively in the 1970s but systematically dismantled many of the controls in the 1980s and 1990s. Taiwan has based its remarkable growth on small firms guided by market forces. China was one of the first avowedly socialist developing economies to introduce market reforms, first into agriculture and, after 1984 with less complete success, into industry. Indonesia moved from a government-regulated industrial and financial system in the 1970s to a more market oriented economy in the 1980s and 1990s (see boxed example).[18]

In Latin America, many market reforms have stumbled over failed stabilization programs, including those in Argentina and Brazil during the 1980s. Among the exceptions, Bolivia's successful stabilization and reform has already been described. In its almost two decades of stabilization and structural adjustment, Chile took many wrong turns but seems to have found a workable formula during the 1980s and 1990s. Mexico has been deregulating its trade and industry in recent years while meeting large debt payments—a process now reinforced by the signing of the North American Free Trade Agreement. In Africa, the most notable reforms have been attempted in countries such as Ghana, Uganda, Tanzania, and

18. David Lindauer and Michael Roemer, *Asia and Africa: Legacies and Opportunities in Development* (San Francisco: ICS Press, 1994).

Zambia, which had fallen into stagnation or even economic anarchy before righting themselves, and in The Gambia, whose government had to rationalize its economic management to avoid being swallowed up by Senegal. The Ivory Coast and Kenya, never in such dire straights, have flirted with mild reforms which produced marginal results.

Stabilization and Deregulation, Indonesia 1986–1990

Indonesia is an oil-producing country that suffered major losses when, from 1984 to 1986, world oil prices fell by half. Indonesia's annual export earnings were cut by $6 billion, about a quarter of total export revenues. At the same time, with export revenues denominated in dollars and much of its debt denominated in Japanese yen, the falling dollar added nearly 40 percent to Indonesia's annual debt service payments. These two external shocks forced the Indonesian government first to stabilize its economy and then to make it less dependent on oil exports for both foreign exchange earnings and government revenues.

The government of President Soeharto had been in office for two decades when the crisis struck and had already laid the groundwork for stabilization and reform. Indonesia's currency, the rupiah, had been fully convertible into foreign currencies since 1970. Devaluations in 1978 and 1983 had kept the rupiah in reasonable alignment with the dollar. Government was prevented by law from financing budget deficits from domestic sources, though it could, and did, borrow overseas. A tax reform enacted in 1983, which introduced a 10 percent value-added tax, had already begun to shift the burden of government revenues from oil exports to domestic taxes. When the oil market collapsed in 1985–86, the government acted quickly to correct imbalances: civil service salaries were frozen for four years; overall government spending net of debt service fell by 6 percent of GDP; and a 33 percent devaluation of the rupiah in September 1986 enhanced the competitiveness of nonoil exports, on which export growth now depended. Because budget deficits were kept small and not financed by bank credit, money creation and hence inflation could be kept under control. Despite the devaluation, prices rose by only 9 percent a year in 1986 and 1987, then by around 6 percent in the next two years.

With the economy stabilized, policy makers instituted a strong but gradual five-year reform, called a "deregulation," of Indonesia's international trade regime and its financial markets. In 1985 the president responded to corruption and costly delays in the customs service by bringing in a foreign private firm to manage customs, a bold and unprecedented reform. In 1986 exporters were exempted from paying duties on imported inputs and allowed to buy them without regard to existing import restrictions. From 1986 to 1988, a series of deregulation "packages" eased the nontariff barriers to many imports. Financial reform packages in 1988 and 1990 allowed banks to determine their own deposit and lending rates, phased out subsidized credit, and otherwise deregulated financial markets. In some respects the banks have been slow to respond to market signals, but they have competed vigorously for savers' deposits and have vied to open new branches to serve customers all over the country, in urban and rural areas. Restrictions on domestic and foreign investment were reduced substantially in 1989, and the Jakarta stock exchange, now encouraged by government, experienced a boom in 1989 and 1990.

These reforms showed results almost immediately. The dollar value of nonoil exports rose by 22 percent a year from 1985 to 1989 and from 32 to 61 percent of total export earnings. As money flowed into the bank deposits, domestic credit expanded from 15 percent of GDP in 1985 to 32 percent in 1989. Government revenues rebounded. And GDP growth resumed, averaging nearly 7 percent a year between 1989 and 1993. A long-serving government, with shrewd policy leadership and a history of cautious reform, had acted quickly to adjust to a major external shock, then took deliberate steps to transform its economy into one of the more dynamic export-led developers in Asia.

6

Planning Models

Although economic planning and controls have given way to market forces as the primary vehicle of development, governments still devote considerable effort to national planning and economists still work on mathematical planning models. There are a number of reasons for this. First, economic models can be useful, and sometimes essential, to the policy makers concerned with macroeconomic management and stability. Second, models of economic structure can give a rough picture of an economy's potential to achieve long-run development goals such as income growth, employment creation, and poverty alleviation. Such models can also evaluate the outcomes to be expected from alternative strategies under consideration. Third, cost-benefit models have been developed to guide governments toward public investments that maximize the economic returns for a given expenditure or that minimize the economic costs of achieving social and economic goals. Fourth, if markets are to guide private activities toward development goals, governments need to correct or compensate for inherent market imperfections; this requires some coordination and planning. Finally, comprehensive models force economists to marshal all extant data on an economy, test the internal consistency of the data, and establish a research agenda to gather additional information on crucial but poorly understood mechanisms in the economy.

Six planning models are covered in this chapter: a simple Keynesian macroeconomic growth model, interindustry (input-output) analysis and its extension, the social accounting matrix, linear programming, computable general equilibrium models, and cost-benefit analysis.[1]

1. Readers who are shy of mathematics should be able to comprehend the basic concepts of this chapter without mastering the mathematical treatments.

PLANNING MODELS (Ch. 6)

Models can yield outcomes that are **consistent** or **optimal.** The distinction can be illustrated with a simple example. A traveler who has a two-week vacation and a budget of \$5,000 to spend wants to travel to Kenya to see as much big game as possible. The tourist is offered three itineraries by the travel agent. The consistency problem is, simply, which of these itineraries is *feasible* within the constraints of \$5,000 and two weeks? The consistency problem becomes an optimality problem if asked another way: Which of the feasible itineraries will enable the traveler to *maximize* satisfaction by seeing the most species of game?

A consistent plan can be illustrated in terms of the **production possibility frontier** of Figure 6–1. The production possibility frontier shows the maximum feasible output of two goods, X (say, necessities) and Y (say, luxuries), in an economy with a given endowment of productive resources or a given period such as 1, 5, or 20 years. The more of good Y the economy wants to produce, the less of X it can produce, because resources (land, labor, and capital) must be taken from the production of necessities (X) to be used in production of more luxuries (Y). Consistency models ensure that any plan resulting from them would place the economy *within* its frontier, at a point like *A*, or at best *on* the frontier, at a point like *B*. Any point, like *C*, beyond the frontier is unobtainable.

To illustrate an optimal plan it is necessary to review the concept of **indifference curves,** illustrated in Figure 6–2. The individual's indifference curve assumes that a single consumer may purchase two goods, X (necessities) and Y (luxuries), in various combinations. If the consumer were to purchase quantities X_a and Y_a, he or she would achieve a certain level of satisfaction. Other combinations of purchases, such as X_b and Y_b, may yield the same level of satisfaction to the consumer. If so, then points *a* and *b* lie on the same indifference curve, labeled II in the diagram. Indifference curve II is the locus of all combinations of the two goods that give the same satisfaction to the consumer as does the combination X_a

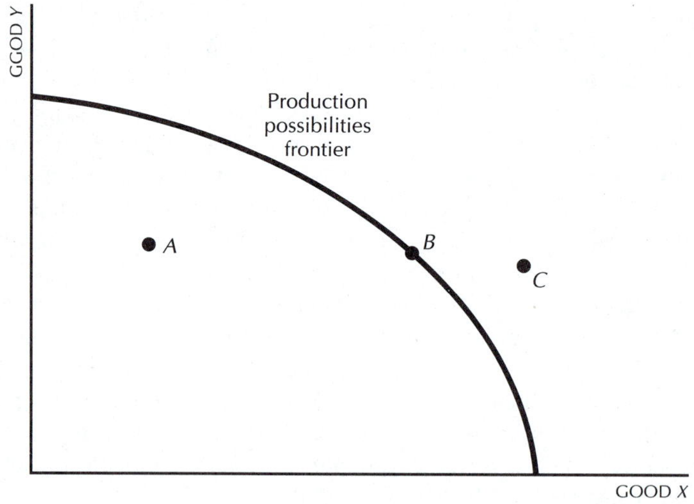

FIGURE 6–1 Consistency. Consistency as shown by the production possibilities frontier. Points such as *A* or *B*, below or on the frontier, are consistent with this economy's endowment. Point *C*, beyond the frontier, is not.

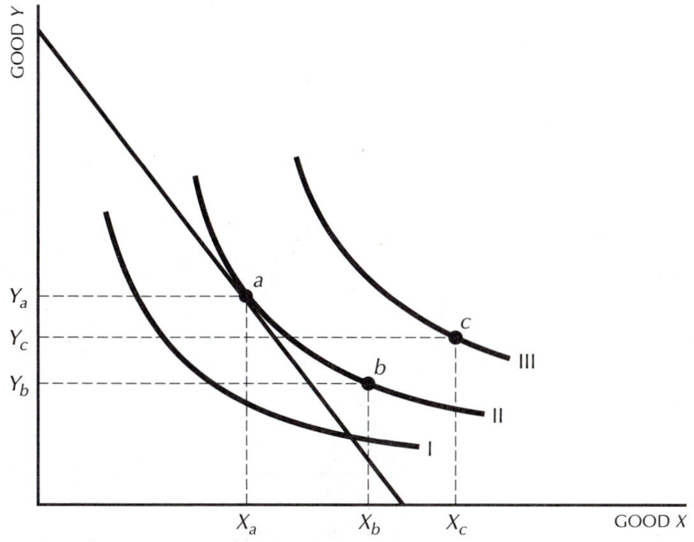

FIGURE –2 Indifference Curves and the Budget Constraint. Each indifference curve traces out a series of points that yield an individual the same level of satisfaction. The budget line shows the possible purchases of both goods for a given income and relative price. A consumer's highest possible level of satisfaction occurs at the tangency of the budget line and an indifference curve.

and Y_a. Any indifference curve to the northeast of II, such as curve III, contains combinations of the two goods that yield greater satisfaction to the consumer than does any point on curve II. That is, the combination X_c and Y_c is preferred by the consumer to X_a and Y_a (or to X_b and Y_b). Similarly, combinations along curve I, to the southwest of curve II, are inferior to those along curve II.

Introduction of the **budget line** (or **constraint**) completes the picture. The budget line gives the combination of goods X and Y that can be purchased by the consumer within the limits of the person's income. The slope of the budget line gives the relative price of one good Y in terms of the other X; the intercepts are the points where the consumer's entire income is spent on either good X or good Y. The consumer can maximize his or her level of satisfaction by consuming at point *a,* where the budget line is tangent to indifference curve II. The consumer cannot reach any other point on curve II, such as *b,* and still satisfy the budget constraint. (Nor would the consumer want to, since he or she is indifferent between combinations *a* and *b*.) Any combination of purchases on higher indifference curves, such as point *c* on curve III, would require more income than the consumer has. And there is no need to accept less satisfaction on a curve such as I, even though it lies partly within the budget constraint, since greater satisfaction is achievable at point *a.*

It takes very restrictive assumptions to use indifference curves, which are valid for individuals, to represent the consumption choices for an entire community or country. However, the concept of **community indifference curves** is useful—and often used—to demonstrate many theories in economics. Figure 6–3 shows a set of community indifference curves superimposed on the production frontier of Figure 6–1. In planning models, society's welfare is represented by an **objective** or **welfare function** that measures the country's development goals in a way that

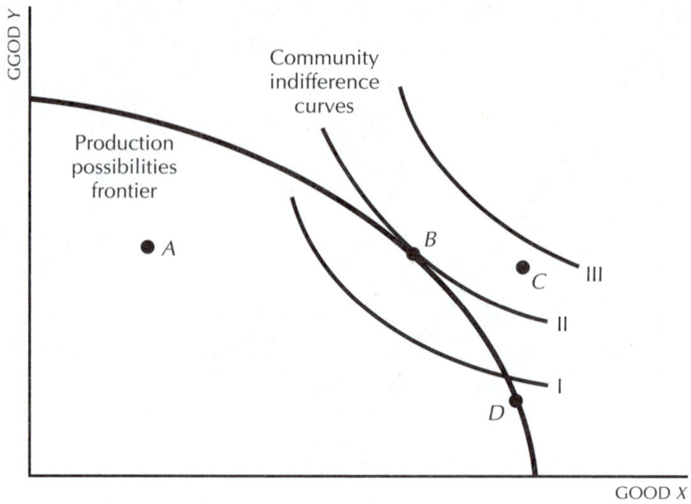

Figure 6–3 Optimality as Shown by the Production Possibilities Frontier. Indifference curves I, II, and III represent the consumption preferences for an entire community, analogous to those for an individual. The production frontier is analogous to the individual's budget constraint. The optimal combination of the two goods X and Y is given by point *B*, where indifference curve II is tangent to the production frontier. The country cannot achieve a higher level of satisfaction, such as indifference curve III, given its resource and production contraints.

will be explained later in this chapter. The community indifference curves of Figure 6–3 can also represent increasing values of this objective function. The production frontier is to society what the budget constraint is to the individual: society's resources and technologies permit it to consume only the quantities of X and Y on or to the southwest of the frontier. An optimal planning model seeks solutions like point *B* in Figure 6–3, for which the value of the objective function is at its maximum given the resource (and hence the production) constraints on an economy.

Keynesian Models

The simplest and best-known consistency model for planning is the Harrod-Domar model, introduced in Chapter 3:

$$g = s/k, \qquad [6\text{–}1]$$

in which g is the annual growth rate of gross domestic (or national) product, s is the saving rate, and k is the incremental capital-output ratio. If k is known, then planners can decide on a target rate of growth (g) and calculate the consistent rate of saving (s) needed to obtain that growth. Alternatively, they can determine a feasible rate of saving and calculate the growth rate consistent with it.

The Harrod-Domar equation is the basis of many macroeconomic growth models, some of which can be quite elaborate. To illustrate these models, a still quite simple version would begin by turning the Harrod-Domar investment relationship, Equation 6–1, into a more realistic form, such as

$$\Delta Y_t = Y_t - Y_{t-1} = (1/k)\Delta K_{t-1} = (1/k)(I_{t-1} - \delta K_{t-1}), \qquad [6\text{–}2]$$

which can be written as

$$Y_t = Y_{t-1} + (1/k)(I_{t-1} - \delta K_{t-1}). \qquad [6\text{–}3]$$

In Equation 6–2, Y is the gross domestic (or national) product, K is the capital stock, I is the gross investment (that is, it includes an allowance to replace depreciated capital), k is the ICOR of Equation 6–1, and δ is the rate of depreciation of existing capital stock. The subscripts refer to the current year t and the previous year $t - 1$. Note that here we simplify by assuming it takes investment just a year before it can produce output. This is the entire supply side of our elementary model and indicates how much the economy can produce.

The demand side of the model, showing how output is used, can be contained in five equations, all in the spirit of Keynesian macroeconomic (multiplier) analysis:

$$S_t = sY_t \qquad [6\text{–}4]$$
$$I_t = S_t + F_t \qquad [6\text{–}5]$$
$$M_t = mY_t \qquad [6\text{–}6]$$
$$M_t = E_t + F_t \qquad [6\text{–}7]$$
$$C_t = Y_t - I_t + F_t. \qquad [6\text{–}8]$$

The new variables are S = gross domestic saving, F = foreign saving (the same as foreign aid plus foreign investment), M = imports of goods and services, E = exports of goods and services, and C = consumption. The parameters are s, the domestic saving rate, and m, the import rate, known as the propensity to import. They, like k, are assumed to be known values. Equation 6–4 is a Keynesian saving function, in which saving is a constant proportion s of income. Equation 6–5 says that gross investment must be financed by domestic saving and foreign saving. Equation 6–6 determines imports as a constant fraction m of income, whereas, Equation 6–7 says that imports must be financed by export earnings and foreign capital (saving). Equation 6–8 determines consumption as a residual between income and saving, but puts it in terms of domestic investment and foreign saving, using Equation 6–5.

Any system of independent, linear equations, such as the six of our model (Equations 6–3 through 6–8), can be solved if the number of equations equals the number of unknowns. In this model, however, there are ten variables (Y_t, Y_{t-1}, K_{t-1}, I_t, I_{t-1}, S_t, F_t, M_t, E_t, and C_t), four too many. Three of them, the so-called "lagged" variables, Y_{t-1}, K_{t-1}, and I_{t-1}, are considered to be known, because they represent values from an earlier year for which we presumably have data. A fourth, E_t is usually estimated separately, because exports depend on factors outside the model, mainly domestic supply capacity for export goods and the state of world markets. That leaves just six unknowns to be found from the six equations, and the model can be solved for all variables.

Suppose, however, that another variable, F_t, the flow of foreign saving (aid plus foreign investment), were also estimated independently of the model. This is quite realistic since foreign aid is a matter for negotiation and private foreign investment in LDCs is not always closely related to domestic economic variables. Then we have a model with only five unknowns (Y_t, I_t, S_t, M_t, and C_t), but six equations, so the model is **overdetermined:** one of the six equations cannot be satisfied, except by chance. Put another way, one of the equations—and we are not sure yet which one—is not necessary for the model; it is **redundant.** This kind of redundancy is characteristic of planning models.

To see which equations might be redundant, let us trace through the working of the model. Potential national income (measured, let us say, as GNP) is already known from the first equation, since it depends only upon lagged variables, those determined in the previous year. Thus both saving (Equation 6–4) and imports (Equation 6–6) can be found directly. However, each of these variables also appears in another equation. Saving helps determine investment from Equation 6–5. But what if government has a target income growth rate? Then to make income grow at the target rate in the following year, $t + 1$, investment must be

$$I_t = k(Y_{t+1} - Y_t) + K_t. \qquad [6\text{–}9]$$

This is merely a rearrangement of Equation 6–3, with a change of subscripts to the next period, which says that gross investment must be adequate to increase income from Y_t to Y_{t+1} and to cover depreciation of the existing capital stock, K_t. With foreign capital fixed, the target level of investment from Equation 6–9 might require national saving more or less than that forthcoming from Equation 6–4. If more, then the economy will not grow at the target rate, because Equation 6–4 sets a limit to the level of saving, a level inconsistent with the growth target. Saving becomes a **binding constraint** on investment growth. If Equation 6–9 requires less saving than available, the growth target is consistent with saving behavior and the saving (Equation 6–4) is redundant.

Imports might present another problem. Imports include both consumer and producer goods, the requirements of which are determined by national income (Equation 6–6). But what if the separately estimated level of exports and foreign capital give a different level of financeable imports from Equation 6–7? If more can be financed, then Equation 6–7 is redundant and the model is consistent. If, however, the sum of exports plus foreign capital is less than necessary imports, then income cannot reach the target level of Y_t; it would have to be lower to get along with fewer imports. In this case the foreign exchange equation (Equation 6–7) becomes a binding constraint on production. Moreover, since most capital goods are imported (an important feature left out of this simple model), the shortage of imports would prevent investment from being high enough to attain the growth target.

This fairly primitive macroeconomic planning model—Equations 6–3 to 6–8—is one version of the **two-gap model** developed by Stanford University economist Ronald McKinnon, Harvard University economist Hollis Chenery, and others.[2] The two gaps refer to Equation 6–5, which balances investment against domestic and foreign saving, and Equation 6–7, which balances imports against export earnings and foreign saving. Under the model's rigid assumptions, only one of these equations will be in balance on the basis of previously determined values of the variables. This becomes the binding constraint; the other is redundant. After the fact, both equations will be in balance, but the redundant one will balance because of subsequent adjustments in the variables, as, for example, a

2. Ronald McKinnon, "Foreign Exchange Constraints in Economic Development," *Economic Journal,* 74 (1964); 388-409, and Hollis B. Chenery and Alan Strout, "Foreign Assistance and Economic Development," *American Economic Review,* 56 (1966); 679–733.

drop in exports or in investments. Targets are consistent with resource constraints (the two balance equations, 6–5 and 6–7) only if one is just balanced and the other redundant, in which case no greater growth can be achieved without some structural change in the economy or a greater influx of foreign resources, or if both are redundant, in which case higher targets can be achieved.

Models like this one can be made much more complicated by **disaggregating** some of the relationships, breaking them into component variables and relationships; by separating the economy and model into sectors, such as agriculture, industry, and services; and by adding factors of production, such as various categories of labor, natural resources, kinds of imports, and so forth. Each new factor of production adds a resource balance or constraint equation, so that these become multigap models. But the basic principles of solution and of planning remain the same.

INTERINDUSTRY MODELS

Macroeconomic models, such as the Keynesian models, lack detailed information on the many agricultural, industrial, and service industries that make up an economy. The interactions—or **linkages**—between these sectors are of crucial significance for planners, who simultaneously need to keep overall macroeconomic balances in view to ensure consistency. The tool designed to accomplish these tasks is the **input-output** or **interindustry table.** Its two inventors suggest its flexibility and usefulness. The Russian-born economist Wassily Leontief developed input-output tables at Harvard during the 1930s to help understand the workings of a modern economy and later to help with postwar planning in the United States. About the same time, though working independently, the Russian economist Leonid Kantorovich developed the same tool, allowing both for final demands and for the use of intermediate products within industry to help planners in his country set quantity targets for Soviet production. The two economists eventually won Nobel Prizes for their efforts.

Input-Output Analysis

The essence of an input-output table is to display the flow of output from one industry to another and from industries to final users (consumers, investors, and exporters). A highly simplified example is shown in Table 6–1, which contains only four sectors: primary products, manufactured consumer goods, manufactured producer goods, and services. Sectors shown in rows are producing industries, whereas those shown in columns are users. For example, row 1, "Primary industry," indicates that agriculture, forestry, and mining produced $20 (million, billion, or whatever unit is convenient) worth of products used within the sector (for example, feed for livestock); it produced $65 worth sold to consumer goods manufacturers (such as wheat for bakeries or cotton for textiles), $50 worth sold to producer goods industries (for instance, wood for pulp or iron ore for steel), and $10 worth sold to services (perhaps meat for restaurants). These intermediate uses totaled $145 (column 5). Final products, such as corn for consumption or cocoa for export, were valued at $245, so total output was $390. Similarly, producer

TABLE 6–1 **Simplified Input-Output Table (Flow Matrix), Value in Dollars**

	As users						
As producers	1. Primary industry	2. Manufactured consumer goods	3. Manufactured producer goods	4. Services	5. Total inter-mediate uses	6. Final use	7. Total use
1. Primary industry	20	65	50	10	145	245	390
2. Manufactured consumer goods	0	30	0	0	30	260	290
3. Manufactured producer goods	50	60	70	15	195	50	245
4. Services	40	15	50	70	175	200	375
5. Total purchases	110	170	170	95	545		
6. Value-added	280	120	75	280		755	
7. Total output	390	290	245	375			1,300

goods manufacturers sold $60 worth of output, such as chemicals, to consumer goods manufacturers (row 3, column 2), and so on.

Each producer is also a user of intermediate goods, and its purchases are shown in the columns of the input-output table. For example, consumer goods manufacturers (column 2) bought $65 worth of primary products, which we know from inspecting row 1, and also $30 from within the sector (for example, textiles used in clothing), $60 from producer goods industries (such as chemicals or paper used in printing), and $15 from services (for instance, banking services or transportation of goods). Total purchases for this sector, given in row 5, were $170. These industries added value of $120, including wages, rents, depreciation, interest, and profits, so total output was valued at $290. This must be equal to the total output shown in row 2 for manufactured consumer goods. Each row shows output allocated according to uses (including final demand), whereas each column shows the costs and profit of producing the output. Rules of accounting tell us that these must give the same total. This applies to the total columns (5, 6, and 7) and rows as well. Column 6, "Final use," gives the sum of consumption plus investment plus exports less imports by sector. Add these and the result must be the gross national product, $755. Row 6 gives value-added by sector, and the sum of its entries which must also yield GNP.

National input-output tables are much larger than the example shown here. Small ones may have 15 to 20 sectors, while those developed for the United States economy have close to 500 sectors. Moreover, the columns giving final uses and the rows giving value-added may be broken down into their components and considerably refined. Quantities of capital, labor, and essential imports (goods not produced in the country) can be added as rows to the bottom of the table and show the investment, labor, and foreign exchange requirements of expanded output. In this form, the input-output table is also called a **flow matrix.**

To turn the input-output flow matrix into a usable tool for planning or analysis, a crucial assumption is required. Interindustry tables are based on observations of a single year's activity for each sector, merely a snapshot of the economy. If it is assumed that the ratio of purchases and value-added to total production is fixed for every industry and will prevail in the future, then this accountant's snapshot of costs becomes an economist's production function with fixed coefficients. It says that for any industry, inputs and costs must expand proportionately with output. Table 6–1 can be converted into a matrix of ratios, called **input-output coefficients;** this is done in Table 6–2. Each column in Table 6–1 has been divided through by its total, so that the second column, for example, now gives the ratios of inputs to output for consumer goods industries: each unit requires 0.23 of primary goods, 0.10 of consumer goods, 0.21 of producer goods, 0.05 of services, and 0.41 of value-added.

The resulting table of coefficients, known as the **A-matrix,** can be seen as a set of production functions for each sector shown in the columns. These fixed-coefficient production functions are often called **Leontief production functions.** The **elements** (coefficients) of input-output tables are usually designated a_{ij}; the subscripts referring to the row (i, for input) and column (j) in that order. Thus, a_{12} is the output of primary products needed per unit of consumer goods, a value of 0.23, while a_{43} is the 0.20 unit of services needed to produce 1 unit of manufactured producer goods.

The input-output matrix is particularly suited to solving the following kind of problem: starting with a target growth rate for an economy over five years, planners can estimate a bill of final goods—those commodities and services purchased by private consumers, investors, government, and foreign importers—that will be demanded at the higher income level. Approximately how much output will be required from each branch of industry to produce that set of final goods? If we can estimate the required output, then it should be possible to determine roughly the amount and kinds of investment needed to produce it.

The answer to the central question, how much of each good, is not immediately obvious. Let us say that 100 units of manufactured consumer goods will be needed. We know from Table 6–2 that this will require, for example, 21 units of producer goods (coefficient $a_{32} \times 100$). But the story does not end there, because to manufacture those inputs, producer goods industries will in turn purchase, for example, 4.2 units of primary goods (21 units needed for consumer goods times a_{13}, or 21×0.21). To produce this 4.2 units, primary industries require 0.55 units (4.2×0.13) of producer goods, and so on, through an endless chain of outputs and inputs. How can we solve the problem?

Start by asking a simple question: for any level of output of the four products, which we now label X_1 through X_4, how much of one product, primary goods X_1, will be required? The answer is

$$X_1 = a_{11} X_1 + a_{12} X_2 + a_{13} X_3 + a_{14} X_4 + F_1. \qquad [6–10]$$

Table 6–2 Coefficients Matrix

	1. X_1	2. X_2	3. X_3	4. X_4
1. Primary goods (X_1)	0.05	0.23	0.20	0.03
2. Consumer goods (X_2)	0.00	0.10	0.00	0.00
3. Producer goods (X_3)	0.13	0.21	0.29	0.04
4. Services (X_4)	0.10	0.05	0.20	0.18
5. Total purchases	0.28	0.59	0.69	0.25
6. Value-added	0.72	0.41	0.31	0.75
7. Total output	1.00	1.00	1.00	1.00

This says that enough X_1 must be produced to cover the input needs of each of the producing sectors, given by the input-output coefficient times the level of output, or $a_{ij} X_j$, plus the amount of X_1 needed for final demand F_1. The same is true for each of the other products, so the complete model is:

$$X_1 = a_{11} X_1 + a_{12} X_2 + a_{13} X_3 + a_{14} X_4 + F_1 \quad [6\text{–}11]$$
$$X_2 = a_{21} X_1 + a_{22} X_2 + a_{23} X_3 + a_{24} X_4 + F_2 \quad [6\text{–}12]$$
$$X_3 = a_{31} X_1 + a_{32} X_2 + a_{33} X_3 + a_{34} X_4 + F_3 \quad [6\text{–}13]$$
$$X_4 = a_{41} X_1 + a_{42} X_2 + a_{43} X_3 + a_{44} X_4 + F_4. \quad [6\text{–}14]$$

We already know the values for F_1 through F_4, because these are the final goods required by our growth targets. Since we have four equations (Equations 6–11 through 6–14) and four unknowns (the values of total output, X_1 through X_4), we can solve this set of linear simultaneous equations for each of the outputs and get our answer that way. This is a mechanical process that any student of intermediate algebra (or a computer) can easily complete.[3]

This basic calculation, yielding the total production needed for any bill of final goods, was at the heart of planning in the former Soviet Union, where it was called the method of **materials balances,** and in other command economies. When the requirements of total production are checked against the capacity in each sector, it becomes a test of consistency: Is present capacity adequate for projected final uses, industry by industry? If not, as is likely in any growing economy, plans must provide enough investment in additional capacity so that each sector can produce the required output. The resulting requirement for investment can then be checked against available savings and foreign investment, one of the constraints of the macroeconomic model. Similarly, requirements for labor of varying skills, for imports (foreign exchange), and for other scarce factors of production can be measured against anticipated supplies. One of these constraints, **labor requirements,** has received considerable attention from education planners who utilize input-output techniques to project the demands for education implied by growth targets.

Thus the input-output table can provide a comprehensive but detailed model of the economy, one capable of tracing through the implications for all resources of any output or growth target. This is the most complete form of consistency planning that has been done, although only a minority of developing countries including South Korea, Malaysia, India, and Mexico have used it in this way. Despite its power, the input-output model has some serious drawbacks. First, the assumption of fixed coefficients rules out the real possibility that targets may be met not by proportional growth of all factors of production but through the substitution of abundant factors, like unskilled labor, for scarce ones, like capital. This possibility was suggested in Chapter 3 when the Harrod-Domar model was contrasted with a neoclassical production function. The concept of substitution is central not only to neoclassical economic theory, but also to much real-world economics. The fuel crisis of the 1970s, for example, was solved partly by substitution of more abundant fuels, like coal, for oil. Solutions to the greenhouse effect and other environmental problems will also require substitution of cleaner-burning fuels or solar energy for coal and oil.

The fuel crisis and environmental concerns also suggests the need for **techno-**

3. For those who know matrix algebra, this set of equations can be solved by inverting $I - A$, where I is the identity matrix and A is the input-output matrix of Table 6–2. The result is a matrix of **direct plus indirect** input coefficients, usually labeled r_{ij}. The matrix is call the **Leontief inverse.**

logical innovations, or improvements, another possibility not handled easily by interindustry methods. Any time new technologies appear, new coefficients are required in the Leontief table. If planners anticipate such changes, they can make approximate allowances by adjusting the initial coefficients, for example, by reducing petroleum inputs relative to outputs as oil prices rise. Nor can tables of fixed coefficients handle economies of scale and learning by doing, both of which increase factor productivity with growth.[4]

Social Accounting Matrix

As complex as an input-output matrix can become, it describes only a portion of an economy and leaves many essential policy concerns untouched. An innovation of the 1970s, the **social accounting matrix,** or SAM, amplifies the Leontief model to accommodate far more economic data. Table 6–3 shows a simplified schematic diagram of a typical social accounting matrix. The SAM is laid out as an input-output table. Rows represent amounts received by suppliers of goods, services, and factors of production; these are the producers of the interindustry matrix, Table 6–1. Columns represent expenditures, amounts paid out by users of goods and services, the users in Table 6–1. Each row and column taken together can be seen as an account for each entity, covering receipts and expenditures, so that each row and column must balance.

To see how the matrix works, follow down column 1, "Activities," which are productive units such as the steel industry or the restaurant industry. In row 2 we find that the activities account purchased intermediate inputs from the commodities account, such as coke and iron ore for the steel industry or food for the restaurant industry; this is the interindustry core of the input-output matrix of Table 6–1, subsumed into one cell of our simplified SAM. Row 3 shows the payments by activities to factors of production—land, labor, and capital. Add indirect taxes (sales and excise taxes) paid to government (row 6), and the total represents payments to all suppliers or total cost of production. Follow across row 1, representing receipts (sales) by these same activities, and we find that they receive payments from domestic sales (under column 2, "Commodities"); from exports (column 8, the "Rest of world"); and from "Government" (column 6) if export subsidies are paid. The sums of column 1 and row 1 must be equal, because total payments must equal total receipts; profits are implicitly included under factor payments.

The information contained in rows and columns 1 to 3 can be found in most input-output tables. The major innovation of the social accounting matrix is the addition of a row and a column representing each of the institutions that make up the economy: enterprises, households, and government. In addition, the matrix adds an account for capital and one for the rest of the world. Now we find that commodities (row 2) are sold to activities (intermediate demand, column 1), for household consumption (column 5), for government consumption (column 6), and for investment (column 7); the total represents domestic demand. Reading down column 5, we learn that households pay for (consume) commodities (row 2), pay direct or income taxes (row 6), and save (row 7).

The SAM is a comprehensive account for the entire economy. Each of the na-

4. For an introductory text on input-output analysis, see Hollis B. Chenery and Paul Clark, *Interindustry Economics* (New York: Wiley, 1959).

tional accounting aggregates can be found in the table. Gross domestic product at factor cost can be found as the sum of either row 3 or column 3. Gross domestic expenditure (consumption plus investment plus exports minus imports) can be read from elements of the commodities and rest-of-world accounts. Account 6 presents the government budget; the row gives revenues and the column shows expenditures. Row 7 shows the sources of savings, which must be matched by column 7, its uses as investment. Account 8 provides the balance of payments and shows the sources of foreign exchange (column 8) used to purchase imports (row 8).

Table 6–3 is a highly simplified SAM. These accounts can be subdivided in many ways. You already know that accounts 1 and 2 can be broken into many industrial sectors, covering all producers of goods and services in an economy. By dividing households into different income categories and firms into different types and sizes (publicly owned versus private firms, large versus small firms, corporations versus partnerships or family-owned businesses), we could obtain a detailed picture of who owns and supplies the different factors of production, who receives various kinds of income and how much, in what kinds of industries and organizations workers of various skills are employed, and so forth. This detail gives a comprehensive picture of how production in an economy results in the observed income distribution among households (or, in the jargon of mathematically minded economists, how production relationships **map** into income distribution).

Social accounting matrices serve four purposes in economic planning. At the most basic level, SAMs provide comprehensive and consistent frameworks to organize masses of economic data, including the national accounts, balance of payments, household budget surveys, government acounts, income tax information, financial market accounts, and other sources. Once organized into a SAM and added up in the relevant rows and columns, these data can be checked to ensure internal consistency. Second, when this has been done, the SAM provides a detailed and comprehensive picture of the economy. Third, the SAM highlights areas where data are missing and thus defines an agenda for research. Fourth, when this economic picture has been completed, the SAM can be converted into a dynamic model of the economy and used to determine how various interventions might affect the economy in detail.[5]

Linear Programming

Input-output analysis is useful for answering the question: Do we have adequate resources to achieve our targets? Planners often ask a different question: Given our resources, how can we use them to achieve our goals to the greatest extent possible? That is, instead of planning a merely consistent use of resources, we would like to plan an optimal allocation of resources. Linear programming is a technique used to answer the second question. At the core of a linear programming model is the same input-output table used in consistency planning. It also includes a set of resource constraints, as in consistency models. The major difference is in the treatment of goals. Consistency models start with specific values for one or more goals, which we called targets. Linear programming uses a **welfare** or **objective function** instead.

5. Social accounting matrices were introduced by Graham Pyatt and Eric Thorbecke in *Planning Techniques for a Better Future* (Geneva: International Labour Office, 1976).

Table 6–3 Simplified Social Accounting Matrix

	Expenditures								
Receipts	1. Activities	2. Commodities	3. Factors	4. Enterprises	5. Households	6. Government	7. Capital	8. Rest of world	9. Total
1. Activities		domestic sales				export subsidies		exports	total sales
2. Commodities	intermediate demand				household consumption	government consumption	investment		total demand
3. Factors	factor payments								value-added
4. Enterprises			gross profits			transfers			enterprise income
5. Households			wages	distributed profits		transfers		foreign remittances	household income
6. Government	indirect taxes	tariffs	factor taxes	enterprise taxes	direct taxes				government receipts
7. Capital				retained earnings	household savings	government savings		net capital inflow	total saving
8. Rest of world		imports							imports
9. Total	total payments	total absorption	value-added	enterprise expenditure	household expenditure	government expenditure	total investment	foreign exchange	

Source: Sherman Robinson, "Multisectoral Models," in Chenery and Srinivasan, *Handbook of Development Economics,* Vol. 2, p. 897. [Reprinted with permission.]

An objective function is simply an algebraic expression that contains one variable for each of the goals that must be taken into account. To combine these into one formula, each goal must have a **priority** or **welfare weight,** which expresses its importance relative to other goals. Such weights are arbitrary because economics provides no scientific guidance for selecting values for priority weights. Thus, for example, a government may hold three quantifiable economic goals important: (1) increase in national income (G_1), (2) employment creation (G_2), and (3) additional income for the poorest 40 percent of society (G_3). Say the first goal is arbitrarily given a weight of 1. If the additional value of wages paid to new jobholders is considered half again as important, then its weight w_2 would be 0.5; and if redistribution, expressed as increases in income to the poorest 40 percent, is considered 75 percent more valuable than income increases on average, then its weight w_3 would be 0.75. Thus the objective function would be

$$W = w_1G_1 + w_2G_2 + w_3G_3 = G_1 + 0.5G_2 + 0.75G_3. \qquad [6\text{–}15]$$

A linear program would choose the activities or quantities of output that would maximize the value of the objective function, subject to two sets of constraints. First, production of each good must satisfy the input-output relationships of the Leontief inverse matrix. In order to obtain high values for Equation 6–15, the model will emphasize production in those activities that give rapid growth, high employment, and income for the poor. But whatever activities it selects, it must provide for enough output of each commodity and service to ensure that the required intermediate inputs are produced. Second, the production of these goods and services must satisfy the resource constraints and not use more factors of production than the economy has available. In practice, and because this is a model of linear equations, only one of the resources will be used fully, and its supply exhausted. Other resources will generally not be fully employed; these are redundant.

The model works, in effect, by trying out a first solution, consisting of outputs and resource inputs that are consistent. This set of values results in a trial value for the objective function. The model (or more correctly, the computer program that simulates the model) then searches for a set of variables which, while still consistent, will improve the value of the objective function. Eventually the program will find a value of the objective function on which it cannot improve. This is the solution, the set of outputs and resource inputs that maximizes the welfare function. The process can be viewed in terms of Figure 6–3 as a search from within the production frontier (a point as *A*) to find the point of tangency of the objective function with the production frontier (point *B*).

Linear programming is a step forward in sophistication from input-output analysis. It depends upon the same assumptions, however, and is therefore limited in the same ways. Programming has been widely and effectively used in certain microeconomic applications in agriculture and industry, such as combining nutrients to feed livestock for maximum biological growth or planning industrial processes to minimize costs. Its use as a sectoral or national planning tool has been limited to experiments, principally by academic economists, to apply the technique and draw general lessons about economies such as Brazil, Chile, India, Israel, Mexico, and South Korea.

These experiments have shown that linear programming is useful not so much for its detailed portrayal of optimal resource allocations, but, perhaps paradoxically, for the macroeconomic picture it provides, based on detailed analysis. Its particular strength is in measuring the trade-offs among different development strategies. Its major weakness lies in its linear equations, which tend to give unstable and extreme results. To avoid these, it is necessary to insert artificial limiting conditions that have no counterparts in real economies and thus make it difficult to interpret the results.[6]

Computable General Equilibrium Models

Linear programming models have severe limitations as representations of mixed economies where markets determine outcomes and substitution is important. To represent the complex market-based interactions of mixed economies and the kinds of policy interventions that are feasible, economists have developed the **computable general equilibrium model** or CGE. CGEs come in many forms, from relatively simple models of a few equations to models as comprehensive as the social accounting matrix, on which they can be based.

The key technical innovation of CGEs is that they escape the constraints of linearity. The Leontief and linear programming models would represent production of a commodity X_j as

$$X_j \leq a_{ij}X_i, \qquad X_j \leq b_jK_j, \qquad X_j \leq c_jL_j, \tag{6–16}$$

where X_i is one or more commodity inputs in the production of X_j; K_j is the capital used in the X_j industry and L_j is its labor force; and the coefficients *a, b,* and *c* are the required inputs of the commodity, capital, and labor, respectively, used in producing $X_{j.}$ The is the **fixed-proportions production function** pictured as an L-shaped production isoquant in Figure 3–1; it comes directly from the *a* coefficients matrix of an input-output table, such as that shown in Table 6–2. We have already discussed the shortcomings of a model employing these linear relationships.

A CGE model, in contrast, uses the **neoclassical** (or **variable-proportions) production function,** depicted in Figure 3–2, to represent some input-output relationships. With this innovation, not only can the interindustry format be represented, but the possibilities of factor substitution, productivity increases, and economies of scale can also be included. A fairly simple neoclassical function would be

$$X_j \leq a_{ij}X_i, \qquad X_j \leq L_j^{\alpha j}K_j^{\beta j}. \tag{6–17}$$

The input-output relation is unchanged from the linear production function, but the contributions of labor and capital to value added can be variable. Moreover, economies of scale can be accommodated by having the sum of the coefficients, $\alpha_j + \beta_j$, exceed 1. Productivity increases could be represented by inserting a time trend into Equation 6–17. Similarly, a CGE would contain consumption functions that permit substitutability among consumer goods, such as

$$p_jX_j = \eta_jY_d, \tag{6–18}$$

6. The standard text on the economic theory of linear programming is Robert Dorfman, Paul Samuelson, and Robert Solow, *Linear Programming and Economic Analysis* (New York: McGraw-Hill, 1958).

which says that consumers spend a constant proportion η_j of their disposable income Y_d on good X_j; if p_j, the price of the good, rises, consumers will buy a proportionately smaller quantity of X_j. This very simple demand equation yields a map of indifference curves like that of Figure 6–2.

CGEs can become quite complex and represent each cell of a disaggregated SAM model as a nonlinear expression such as Equation 6–17 or 6–18. These are **behavioral relationships,** the supply and demand functions that describe in mathematical terms the ways in which producers utilize factors and consumers respond to market prices. In addition, the model must contain equations representing constraints on the availability of each of the factors used in production, and **balance equations** representing each of the accounting relationships of the rows and columns in the SAM. Because a CGE can incorporate substitution, productivity increases, and economies of scale, it can be a much better representation of real economies than its linear predecessors, without resort to the artificial constraints that are needed to make a linear programming model behave.

This major improvement in economic modeling has a cost: a sophisticated computer program is required to solve these complex models. However, such programs exist and can now be handled routinely by an experienced operator with a modern desktop computer. Once a CGE model has been built, it can be tested and run repeatedly at low cost: as a consistency model; as a simulation model, tracing out many different solutions with varying specifications of the model; or as an optimizing model. With the development of the CGE, it has become feasible to test hypotheses about economic development and to try out policy recommendations within a general equilibrium framework, accommodating the many interactions that mark a real economy.[7]

PROJECT APPRAISAL

The models discussed so far have ranged from the macroeconomic treatments such as the Harrod-Domar model to disaggregated treatments of sectors (agriculture, industry) or of industries (rice farming, plastics manufacturing). One of the most commonly used tools of planning, **cost benefit analysis** or **project appraisal,** refers to a still more disaggregated activity, the investment project, such as an irrigation system, a single plastics factory, a hydroelectric dam, or a road. This technique has its genesis in the kind of analysis done by private firms on their alternative investment prospects. When a firm lays out its investment plans (called capital budgets), it tries to select investments that will yield the highest profit for a given amount of finance. The firm's calculation involves three steps, as explained in the next section.

Present Value

The first step in the firm's investment decision is to forecast the **net cash flow** of an investment. Net cash flow measures the difference between the cash revenues from the sale of the product and the cash outlays on investment, material inputs,

7. Advanced students should consult Kemal Dervis, Jaime de Melo, and Sherman Robinson, *General Equilibrium Models for Developing Countries* (London: Cambridge University Press, 1982), and Sherman Robinson, "Multisectoral Models," in Hollis B. Chenery and T.N. Srinivasan (eds.), *Handbook of Development Economics,* Vol. 2 (Amsterdam: North-Holland, 1989).

salaries and wages, purchased services, and so forth. Costs that do not deplete the cash resources of the firm, of which depreciation is the most prominent example, are not counted.

The second element involves the observation that cash received in the future is less valuable than cash received immediately, because in the interim the firm could earn interest (or profits) on these funds by investing them in bonds or savings accounts (or in additional, revenue-earning production facilities). For example, a firm or individual, asked to choose between $1,000 today or $1,000 next year, would take the money now and place it in a savings account earning, say, 8 percent a year. Then after one year the interest payment would boost the savings account balance to $1,080. So the prospect of $1,000 a year from now should be evaluated as equivalent to only $1,000 ÷ 1.08 = $926. This process, reducing the value of future flows because funds earn interest over time, is called **discounting.** Because interest is also earned on previous interest, discounting must allow for **compound interest.** In the second year another 8 percent would be earned on the balance of $1,080, and increase it to $1,166. The payment of $1,000 two years from now would then be discounted to yield a **present value** of only $1,000 ÷ 1.166 = $858. A general expression for the present value *P* is

$$P = F/(1 + i)^n \qquad [6\text{–}19]$$

where F is the value to be realized in the future ($1,000 in our example), i is the interest rate (8 percent), and n is the number of years. As the interest rate or the delay in payment increases, the present value decreases.

An investment project will result in a series of net cash flows over time: they flow out in the early years as investments are made; then they become positive, perhaps gradually, as the new facilities begin to generate revenue in excess of recurrent costs. Such a **time profile** of net cash flow is depicted in Figure 6–4; it is

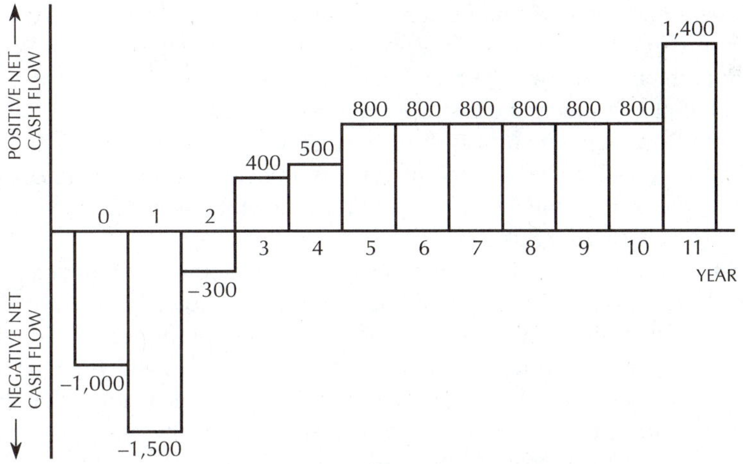

FIGURE 6–4 Time Profile for Investment: Net Cash Flow. The cash flow of a project can be represented by a bar diagram. Cash outflows are shown by bars below the horizontal axis, inflows by bars above the axis. Years 0 and 1 show investment in construction and equipment, and hence negative cash flows; year 2 is the start-up period; years 3 and 4 show gradually increasing output and cash inflows; years 5 through 10 show steady output and cash inflows; and the project is assumed to end in year 11, when the salvage value of equipment swells the cash inflow.

the most common of several possible profiles. To summarize the value of this net cash flow in a single number, each year's net cash flow is multiplied by the respective discount factor and the resulting present values are added to give the **net present value** (NPV). Thus,

$$\text{NPV} = \sum_{t=0}^{n} (B_t - C_t)/(1 + i)^t, \qquad [6\text{–}20]$$

where B_t and C_t are the benefits (revenues) and costs, including investment, in each year t; i is the discount rate; and n is the life of the project. For a firm, the correct discount rate is the average cost at which additional funds may be obtained from all sources, the firm's cost of capital.

If the net present value of a project, discounted at the firm's average cost of capital, happens to equal zero, this implies that the project will yield a net cash flow just large enough to repay the principal of all funds invested in the project and to pay the interest and dividends required by lenders and shareholders. In that case, when NPV = 0, the discount rate has a special name, the **internal rate of return** (IRR). If the net present value is positive, then the project can cover all its financial costs with some profit left over for the firm. If negative, the project cannot cover its financial costs and should not be undertaken. Clearly the higher the net present value, the better the project.

Another measure of project desirability is the **benefit-cost ratio,**

$$\text{BCR} = \sum_{t=0}^{n} B_t(1 + i)^{-t} \Big/ \sum_{t=0}^{n} C_t(1 + i)^{-t}. \qquad [6\text{–}21]$$

When NPV = 0, BCR = 1, so desirable projects have an NPV greater than zero or a BCR greater than one. Although the BCR can be useful, it has the disadvantage that its precise value depends on sometimes arbitrary decisions about which cash flows to include in the numerator, and which in the denominator. Neither the NPV nor the IRR calculation suffers from this ambiguity. However, the IRR has a different problem: there will be more than one IRR for a cash flow if at any time after the initial investment the cash flow again turns negative.

The cash flow of Figure 6–4 is discounted at a rate of 12 percent in Table 6–4, using Equation 6–20. The net present value is a positive $518; this indicates that the investment project will earn enough to repay the total investment ($2,500 over years 0 and 1) with a surplus of $518.

We come now to the final step in project appraisal, comparison among projects. We already know that a project should be considered for investment only if its net present value is positive. But how to choose among many projects, all with positive NPVs? The answer is to select that set of projects which will yield the highest total net present value for the entire investment budget. This assumes that the firm has a set of alternative projects to consider at any one time and an investment budget that can accommodate several but not all of these.

Opportunity Costs

A country wishing to derive the greatest possible future income (or consumption) from the resources available for investment faces the same problem as the invest-

TABLE 6–4 Net Present Value

Year	Cash flow * from Figure 6–4 (dollars)	Discount factor † at 12%	Present value ‡ (dollars)
0	−1,000	1.000	−1,000
1	−1,500	0.893	−1,340
2	−300	0.797	−239
3	400	0.712	285
4	500	0.636	318
5	800	0.567	454
6	800	0.507	406
7	800	0.452	362
8	800	0.404	323
9	800	0.361	289
10	800	0.322	258
11	1,400	0.287	402
Net Present Value§			+518

*Cash flow = $(B_t - C_t)$ from Equation 6–17.
†Discount factor = $1/(1+i)^t$ from Equation 6–20. In this example, i = 12 percent; t takes the value of each year, 0 to 11. Discount factors for a range of discount rates are readily available in discount tables. (See, for example, the appendix table in Michael Roemer and Joseph J. Stern, *The Appraisal of Development Projects* [New York: Praeger, 1975]).
‡Present value = cash flow x discount factor.
§Net present value = algebraic sum of the present values.

ing firm. The only difference is that the country is interested in resource flows and their **opportunity costs,** rather than cash flows. When any project in the public or private sector uses goods and services, it denies these to other possible projects. For example, investment in a dam requires utilization of savings that could otherwise be invested in a rural road or a textile factory, cotton used in that factory could otherwise have been exported to earn foreign exchange, or the labor used to build the road might have otherwise been used to build the dam or to grow cotton. For society, the cost of undertaking a project is the value of the resources—goods and services—used to invest in and operate the new facilities. The value of these resources is measured in terms of the net benefits they would have provided if used in some alternative project, the opportunity cost.

A simple illustration should capture this point. A textile factory is built and hires labor away from the rural areas. For the textile firm, the cost of labor is the wages paid. For society, however, the cost is the reduction in the value of production, net of costs, in the rural areas. If ten laborers migrate to take jobs in the new factory, their opportunity cost would be the reduction in agricultural output due to their leaving the farm, net of the nonlabor recurrent costs of producing that output. This reduction in net output is the value of the marginal product of price theory and is the opportunity cost of labor in this situation.[8] Similarly, if the investment in the textile mill means that savings will be drawn away from other projects that would on average have earned a return of 12 percent, then the opportunity cost of capital is 12 percent, and this should be used as the discount rate in evaluating the textile mill. Because project appraisals are most conveniently done at **constant prices,** netting out inflation, the discount rate is a **real rate of inter-**

8. The value of the marginal product of a factor of production can be defined as the price of a commodity multiplied by the additional physical ouput that results when one unit of the factor is added to the production process with all other factors held constant.

est, net of inflation. If, in this example, inflation were 10 percent a year, the corresponding nominal interest rate, the rate observed in the market, would be 23 percent.[9]

Foreign exchange plays a special role in cost-benefit analysis. Most developing countries face a shortage of foreign exchange, in the sense that export revenues and foreign investment are not adequate to finance the imports needed to achieve growth and other development targets. When a project requires imports, such as capital equipment or raw materials, it reduces the foreign exchange available to other projects. If it yields additional foreign exchange, by exporting its output or by substituting domestic production for imports, it benefits other projects by providing more foreign purchasing power. Thus, the opportunity cost or benefit of any good that could be imported or exported should be measured as the net amount of foreign exchange the good represents. For example, the cotton used in the textile mill might have been exported otherwise; if so, its opportunity cost would be the foreign currency it would have earned as an export. If the cloth produced by the mill would have been imported in the absence of the project, its opportunity cost (a benefit in this case) would be the foreign exchange that would otherwise have been spent on cloth imports.

Shadow Prices

The opportunity costs of goods and services are estimated for the economy as a whole and are called **shadow prices** or **social opportunity costs.** The first approximation of a shadow price—for land, labor, capital, foreign exchange—is the price paid by private participants in the market. Many interferences in the market distort market prices from their social opportunity cost: taxes and subsidies of all kinds, monopoly power, minimum wages, interest rate controls, tariffs and import quotas, price controls, and so forth. Prices that are observed in the market need to be adjusted for these effects before a good approximation of shadow prices can be found. A simple example is the wage of textile workers. If the government imposes minimum-wage regulations, the factory will probably have to pay a wage above the opportunity costs of rural migrants and urban workers who are outside the formal, protected urban wage sector.

Estimation of shadow prices is a research task that requires intimate knowledge of the workings of an economy, both its macroeconomic relationships and the microeconomic behavior of its factor markets. It is a task to be undertaken by a planning agency, which then instructs other planning units—ministries, public enterprises, regional and local governments—in the application of these economy-wide shadow prices to the appraisal of development projects. Not only does shadow price estimation help improve the selection of development projects, but the estimation of these opportunity costs teaches the researchers a great deal about the working of the economy, an important by-product for a planning agency.

9. The formula relating these is $1 + i = (1 + r)(1 + p)$, where i is the nominal rate of interest, r is the real rate, and p is the rate of inflation. Normally we know the nominal rate and need to calculate the real rate:

$$r = \frac{1 + i}{1 + p} - 1 = \frac{i - p}{1 + p}.$$

For small values of p, r can be approximated by $r = i - p$.

Although there remains much controversy among economists on the precise estimation of shadow prices, some general results have emerged for a wide range of developing countries. First, and most significant, the shadow foreign exchange rate tends to be higher than the official rate in terms of local currency per dollar, perhaps 10 to 50 percent higher. This reflects the widespread use of import duties and quotas, as well as the reluctance of many countries to devalue their exchange rate despite the inflation of domestic prices.[10] As a consequence, any export project that earns more foreign exchange than it uses or any import-substituting project that saves more than it uses gets a boost from the shadow exchange rate. In terms of the net cash flow profile of Figure 6–4, application of the shadow rate to such projects will raise the positive net cash flows of years 3 through 11 proportionately more than it raises the negative flows of years 0 through 2, giving the project a higher net present value at the same discount rate.

Although salaries and wages of skilled employees probably require no adjustment from market to shadow prices, it is frequently true that the opportunity cost of unskilled workers is lower than the wage in formal, urban labor markets. Thus any project using unskilled labor, especially if it is located in a rural area, gets a boost because the shadow wage reduces costs without changing benefits.

The social discount rate can represent either the opportunity cost of investment and saving in the private sector or the rate at which policy makers wish to discount future benefits. The first method yields discount rates of 10 to 15 percent for developing countries. The second approach usually employs a lower discount rate, but entails a shadow price of investment that raises the effective cost of capital. In either case discounting at social rates treats capital as a very scarce factor and so discourages any project with high initial investment costs, long gestation periods, and low net cash flows in the productive years. This system favors projects that generate their net benefits early, because these can be reinvested in other productive projects for continued growth, and projects that use abundant resources, especially labor, instead of scarce ones, like capital.

Project Appraisal and National Goals

Project appraisal using social opportunity costs is a simple and powerful device to further certain national goals. Its underlying tenet is that saving should be allocated to investments yielding the greatest future income or consumption, and thus automatically accommodate the goal of efficient resource use to promote maximum growth. This further implies that scarce resources, like foreign exchange, are more highly valued than the market would indicate. The subsidiary goals of improving foreign exchange earnings or reducing dependence on imports are also built in, because any project that efficiently increases exports or reduces imports is given a correspondingly higher net present value by the shadow exchange rate. Once the planners establish a system of appraisal with shadow prices, every agency that designs, evaluates, and proposes investment projects is automatically incorporating these national goals in its work.

An illustration of the power of shadow pricing is contained in Table 6–5. It depicts two projects with identical cash flows. However, one project (the textile mill) earns more foreign exchange than the other (a telecommunications system),

10. When countries undertake market reforms, as described in Chapter 5, these distortions are reduced and the official exchange rate becomes a closer approximation of the shadow rate.

TABLE 6–5 Effects of Shadow Pricing on Cost-Benefit Analysis

1. Take two projects with identical cash flows, but project A earns more net foreign exchange and uses more labor than project B:

Project	Invesment (first year)	Net annual cash flow (next 5 years)	Net present value at 10%
A. Textile mill of which:	−1000	+300	+137
Net foreign exchanged earned	−500	+400	
Wages paid	−350	−100	
B. Telecommunications system of which:	−1000	+300	
Net foreign exchange earned	−800	0	
Wages paid	−100	−50	+137

2. *Shadow wage* is 75% of market wage, so all wage costs reduced by 25%. This results in the following net cash flows:

	Investment	Net annual flow	NPV (10%)
A. Textile mill	−913	+325	+319
B. Telecommunications system	−975	+313	+212

3. *Shadow exchange rate* is 20% above official rate, so net foreign exchange flow is raised by 20%. This results in the following net cash flows:

	Investment	Net annual flow	NPV (10%)
A. Textile mill	−1100	+380	+340
B. Telecommunication system	−1160	+300	−23

net of foreign exchange expenditures, and also uses more labor. Because the shadow wage rate is below the market rate, the economic net present value of both projects is raised, but the more labor-intensive textile project benefits more (part 2). When the shadow exchange rate is applied, the net present value of the exchange-earning textile mill is raised considerably, but that of the telecommunications system, which is a net user of foreign exchange, falls and becomes negative (part 3).

Not all national goals can be conveniently incorporated into project appraisal, however. Two are of particular concern. The use of low shadow wages for unskilled workers will encourage employment creation but only insofar as this is efficient, in the sense that the workers' opportunity cost is below the net benefit they would produce in the project. Government may, however, want to encourage employment beyond this point, because a job is the most significant way that people can participate in development and employed workers may be deemed politically more stable than the unemployed. If projects such as rural public works employ people inefficiently for the sake of employment, then the role of cost-benefit analysis is to estimate the cost of the employment in terms of the greater net benefits that might be earned if investment and labor were allocated to other projects that employ fewer people.

A second class of goals, income redistribution or poverty alleviation, can also be served by project appraisal, because low shadow wages encourage the employment of low-income labor. The impact may be weak, however, because distributional goals are still subordinate to efficient growth in the cost-benefit framework. Situations requiring structural change and large investments to alleviate poverty may not measure up to the high efficiency standard of project analysis in the short run. For this reason some economists have suggested, and some governments have considered, using welfare weights in a project analysis. These would place a higher value on net additional income to certain target groups, such as families in the lower 40 percent of the income distribution. (We have already seen such a welfare weight: w_3 of the linear programming objective function, Equation 6–14, gave an additional value of 75 percent to any income going to the poorest 40 percent of society.) Then projects generating such incomes would have higher NPVs than otherwise and would tend to be selected more frequently.

The method is potentially powerful, but has its dangers as well. The welfare premiums are arbitrary weights, subject to planners' or politicians' judgments. This in itself is not bad, but these weights can so overwhelm economically based shadow prices that project selection comes down to a choice based almost entirely on arbitrary weights. This gives a false sense of precision.

Shadow prices based on existing economic conditions are not value-free, either. They imply a welfare weighting scheme that accepts the existing income distribution and the resulting pattern of demand. A compromise is to keep the two goals separate, make measurements of net present values using only the economic variables, and then identify separately the redistributional benefits of projects. The two can then be compared; this gives decision makers a trade-off to consider and the opportunity to make clear choices of goal priorities.

We have skirted an issue of terminology. When a firm undertakes investment analysis, it can be called **commercial project appraisal,** which uses *market prices.* Traditionally, once *shadow prices* are introduced to reflect the goal of efficient growth and the real scarcities of productive factors, it has been called **social project appraisal.** The implication may be too large, however, because only economic, and not other social, goals are incorporated. The World Bank, which undertakes a large fraction of the project analysis done in the world, has shifted to a more accurate terminology. It calls the second form **economic project appraisal.** The term "social appraisal" is reserved for a third stage, in which welfare weights are applied to reflect distributional goals. But readers should be wary, because this distinction has not been universally accepted.

Transforming Market Prices into Shadow Prices

If governments undertake projects on the basis of economic appraisals, using shadow prices, an implementation problem arises. A firm, whether public or private, can only be financially sound if it covers costs and earns a profit at market prices. The shadow prices of planners exist only on paper; no one pays them or receives them in the marketplace. For example, consider a public enterprise producing paper; its investment is encouraged by the planning ministry because it employs many workers whose opportunity cost is low. However, the enterprise must pay its workers not the low shadow wage, but the higher minimum wage set by the government. If this causes the firm to lose money, it could go bankrupt, in which case the economic benefits to the country would be lost. (A private firm, of course, would never undertake such an investment.) Hence if the government wants the project implemented, it would have to compensate the enterprise. The most effective compensation would be a direct subsidy to wages, up to the difference between the shadow and minimum wages. Not only would this improve the firm's cash flow, but it would also give the firm an incentive to use more labor because its wage costs would be lower. This is precisely what government wants: to employ more workers, an abundant resource with low opportunity costs, and less of other, relatively scarce factors of production, like capital and foreign exchange.

The same holds for any production factor that is shadow priced: labor, capital, foreign exchange, and specific commodities. Whenever shadow prices push projects that are commercially unprofitable into the realm of the economically profitable, a subsidy may have to be paid to induce a firm to undertake the project. And, conversely, if economically undesirable projects are nevertheless profitable at market prices, government should consider imposing taxes to discourage firms from undertaking such projects.

This leads to a more general point about shadow prices. They represent the opportunity costs that ideally functioning markets should be generating to give the right price signals to private producers and consumers. Market prices deviate from shadow prices for two reasons. First, government interventions—controls and taxes—cause artificial price distortions. These *policy failures* can be reduced substantially (though not entirely) through market deregulation and tax reform, as discussed in Chapter 5. Second, inherent *market failures* such as externalities, natural monopolies, infant industries, and institutional deficiencies cause price distortions that require counteracting policies by government. If government can correct its own policy failures and intervene to counteract market failures, then resources would be used efficiently, that is, according to their relative scarcities; this would promote economic growth.

7

Sustainable Development

An abundance of natural resources should be an advantage in economic development. Well-endowed countries such as Brazil, Nigeria, and Indonesia should be able to exploit their natural capital—climate, soils, natural forests, fisheries, and mineral deposits—to generate income in the early stages of development. If a large share of that income is saved, natural wealth can be converted into human-made capital such as an educated workforce, roads, power and telecommunications systems, productive agriculture, modern industry, growing cities, and the other assets of developed countries. If, instead, the resource-rich country chooses to preserve its natural capital for future generations, it should be no worse off in development than resource-poor countries such as Korea or Taiwan that have nevertheless managed to grow very rapidly. In either case, it should be feasible to sustain development over long periods.

Yet many if not most resource-rich countries, especially those in the tropics, have grown more slowly than countries with scarce natural resources.[1] And, if we allow for the depletion of the resource base with development, as national income accounting systems do not, the performance of resource-rich developing countries would be even worse. Yet a few resource-rich countries, notably Botswana, Indonesia, and Malaysia, have converted natural wealth into rapid economic

1. Based on regressions with more than 70 countries over 20 years, Harvard economists Jeffrey Sachs and Andrew Warner ("Natural Resources and Economic Growth," Harvard Institute for International Development, February 1995) conclude that a 10 percent rise in the share of natural resource exports in total exports causes a cumulative decrease in GDP of 6 percent over 20 years. The effect is independent of changes in the world price of exports.

growth. How should developing countries manage their resources to use them most productively in the short term and to convert natural wealth into sustainable economic growth and development in the long term?

A country's environment—its air, water, diversity of biological species, and natural surroundings—are also valuable natural resources. To some extent all economic activity uses the environment as a dump for waste products. Economic growth, as conventionally measured, might be more rapid if such environmental pollution is not inhibited by regulations or other policies. But there is a limit to the capacity of air, water, and natural surroundings to dispose of waste within tolerable limits, and the acceptable level of pollution tends to decline as income rises. So rapid but polluting growth today reduces welfare and incurs clean-up costs in the future. Is it rational for developing countries to pollute now and pay later? Can growth be sustained if it depletes the natural environment?

These questions take on greater meaning when the whole planet is considered. The issues are familiar to any reader of newspapers and magazines in the 1990s. Are we depleting the world's fisheries and cutting down its rainforests so fast that neither can regenerate and large numbers of species are becoming extinct? Will the world run out of minerals, especially fuels, before our ingenuity can develop technologies to harness renewable sources of energy and develop alternative materials? Is humankind polluting the air and contaminating water supplies faster than these resources can absorb our waste and cleanse themselves by natural processes? Are we heating earth's atmosphere so much with emissions of carbon dioxide from burning fossil fuels that economic development will change the world's climate, with dramatic and unpredictable effects on human welfare? And will these uses of our natural resource base have cumulative effects that are irreversible if we do not act soon enough?

In this chapter we try to answer these questions. At the national level, it is not difficult to design policies that promote sustainable development, although governments often find it difficult to implement them. For the earth as a whole, the answers are more speculative and there are few mechanisms to enforce solutions to environmental problems.

Market Failures

The central theme of this chapter, and the main thrust of economists' approach to sustainability, is that, within a single country, properly working (efficient) markets can be the most effective mechanism available to promote efficient resource use, reduce environmental degradation, and generate sustainable development. At first blush, that proposition may be hard to accept. In Chapter 5 we developed the idea that competition among private producers, disciplined by markets, is more likely to promote rapid economic development than an economy dominated by government intervention. But Chapter 5 also discussed the conditions that cause markets to fail, when market prices deviate from scarcity values and lead private agents to make decisions that would maximize their earnings but cause uncompensated losses for others and for society as a whole.

Prominent among these conditions are *externalities*—*costs* that are borne by the population at large but not by individual producers, or *benefits* that accrue to society but cannot be captured by producers. And the most important externalities are those caused by the depletion or degradation of natural resources, including the environment. If resources are depleted at rates faster than they can be replenished or substituted by human-made capital, development will be **unsustainable,** either nationally or globally. If markets fail in this fundamental way, how can they promote sustainable development? To resolve this apparent conflict, we need first to analyze in greater depth the reason that markets fail to allocate natural resources efficiently.

The Commons

During the eighteenth century, as the Industrial Revolution began in England, cows still grazed on the commons of many villages in England and its American colonies. The essence of a village commons was **open access,** free of charge, to any member of the village. The first villagers to take advantage of open access would have ample grazing for their livestock; their only cost was the time it would take to herd their animals to the commons, allow them to graze, and herd them home. But the amount of land was fixed and the quantity of grass was limited by soil fertility and climate. As more villagers used the commons, the grass became sparse, so the animals took longer to feed or, in the case of open rangeland, the herder was forced to travel farther to find forage, so that everyone's costs rose. The rising average cost to each herder did eventually discourage grazing on the commons. But none of the new entrants had to pay the rising costs to each of the previous entrants and more grazing took place than was in the interests of the village as a whole. Eventually, overgrazing destroyed the commons as a useful source of feed.

The disappearance of the grazing commons from eighteenth-century villages was probably inevitable and certainly not a global tragedy. But the dilemma of the commons is a widespread phenomenon, applicable to any limited resource to which access is unlimited by fee or regulation. Grazing on open range, whether in the U.S. west or the African savannah, has the same outcome. Open access to timberlands or access at fees well below social costs results in overlogging and the destruction of native forests in Brazil, Ghana, Thailand, and many other tropical countries. Open access to fishing grounds in the North Atlantic, in Peru's Pacific waters, and in some inland lakes in Africa has already depleted fish stocks beyond their ability to regenerate. Free use of water from a stream benefits upland farmers, who have first access to the water, at the expense of downstream farmers, who get less water. Even traffic congestion in a city like Bangkok, Mexico, or New York fits the description of a common property: city streets, to which access is free, are the common resource; each new vehicle causes worse traffic jams, forcing all previous entrants to drive more slowly.

The earth's environment, on which life depends, is itself composed of several common resources: air and the atmosphere, fresh water and the oceans, Earth's soils and minerals, and the diverse plant and animal species that live in this biosphere. Access to the environment is free. When manufacturers and farmers vent their waste into the air or water or create toxic dumps in the ground, they create health problems for the affected population, reduce the value of land in the affected area, destroy recreational potential, and generally reduce the welfare of people who value a clean environment. When lumber companies cut down a rainforest, they destroy the habitat of plant and animal species that are of value to others, including local populations that may harvest them or ecotourists who simply like to see them. They may also alter local climates, change patterns of water availability to surrounding farmers, and cause soil erosion. When we include the environment as a common resource, then much private activity generates external costs and market failure becomes a very general phenomenon.

Externalities: A Closer Look

External costs and benefits are at the core of the common resource problem. A new producer creates higher costs for all previous entrants, or all producers impose external costs on the general population. In either case, in the absence of regulation or taxes, external costs are not borne by the producers who cause them and the prices of their products do not reflect the social costs of production. Thus more of these resource-depleting or polluting goods and services are produced and consumed than would be the case if prices reflected external costs. Hence societies pollute more than their people would choose if markets reflected all social costs.

Figure 7–1 shows this. In a market with competitive producers, the supply curve S represents private marginal costs. Market equilibrium occurs at price P_1 with output Q_1. But if this is a polluting industry, the external costs would make the social marginal cost, SMC, higher. If these costs were reflected in the market, the price would jump to P_2 and demand, and thus output, would be reduced to Q_2. As less of the offending product would be grown or manufactured, there would be less environmental degradation.

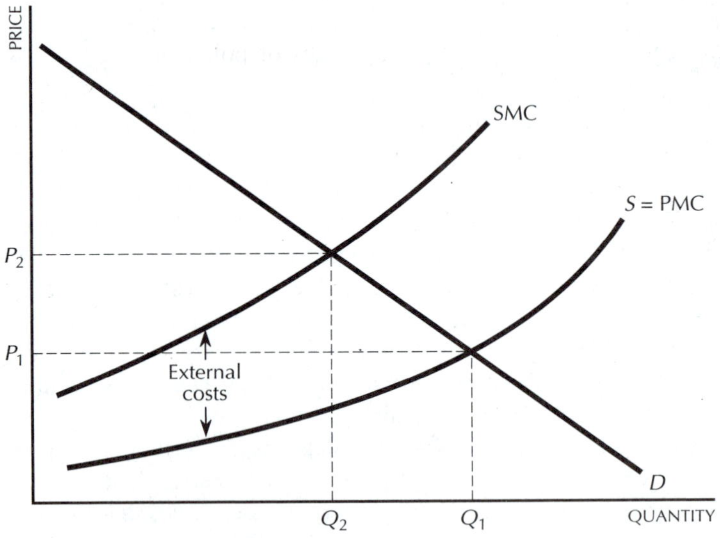

FIGURE 7–1 External Diseconomies. Polluters impose costs on others. If these external costs were reflected in the firms' costs, the social marginal cost curve, SMC, would prevail, the market price would be P_2, and output would be Q_2. But, because the firm does not bear these costs, their private marginal cost curve, PMC, is lower, so more, Q_1, of the polluting product is produced and consumed.

Soil Erosion in Java, Indonesia[2]

Soil erosion in the uplands of Java is thought to be the main determinant of downstream siltation, water flow irregularities, and agrochemical run-off. Because the costs to low-lying areas from upland conservation are external to the upland farmers, taking on additional costs to conserve soil would not be economically sound for upland farmers. Costs for soil conservation include time spent during the dry season constructing terraces and the cost of paid labor to complete the work, which takes far more time than a single farmer can spend. Assuming a four-month dry season and a holding of an acre, a single farmer could provide a maximum of 100 person days each dry season for soil conservation. The time required for terracing a plot of this size ranges from 375 person-days for gradual slopes and up to 900 person-days for steep slopes. If the farmer intends to add an intensive livestock system with the terracing, there are costs for adding a grass cover to the terraces and for the livestock itself. For slopes steeper than 45 to 50 percent, where the preferred method of soil conservation is to take land out of annual food-crop production to produce tree crops for cash income, there are both planting costs of around US$100/hectares in 1982 and opportunity costs while the trees mature. Unless compensated, the upland farmer will not undertake these measures.

Sustainable Harvests

Most common resources are **renewable resources:** they can regenerate themselves, given time. The village common or open rangeland reproduces grass each year. Fish breed new stocks, wild animals replenish their herds, and forests reseed themselves. Air and water cleanse themselves of pollutants through biological, chemical, or mechanical transfers. It is possible to exploit renewable resources sustainably if annual harvests do not exceed the annual growth of the stock. The difference between the rate of harvest and the rate of growth is called the **rate of depletion.** The faster these resources can be replenished, the greater the rate of economic growth that can be sustained indefinitely.

For renewable resources, three questions arise: What is the maximum sustainable harvest? What is the economically optimal harvest? And what is the danger of overexploiting the resource to the point of irretrievable loss or extinction? To answer these questions, it is convenient to explore a simple model of a fishery. Fish stocks are renewable within a relatively short period. Anything we can conclude about fisheries must apply with greater force to forests or the environment, which take longer to regenerate.

Before fishing begins, the stock of fish (in a lake or an ocean fishery) is large and cannot grow rapidly because its supply of food is limited. When fishing begins, food becomes relatively more abundant, the fish can replenish their numbers more rapidly, and the sustainable catch rises. But as the fishing effort increases, this process reaches a peak, after which the annual growth of the stock declines

2. From Edward B. Barbier, *Economics, Natural Resource Scarcity and Development* (London: Earthscan Publications Limited, 1989), pp. 160–80.

and so does the sustainable catch. If the fishing effort continues to grow, the fish stock may be so small or so scattered that reproduction cannot replace the catch at any level; this leads to extinction. The fishery model is an alternative way to describe the common resource problem. With the village common, we assumed that more entrants raise the cost for all. With the fishery, even if the costs of operating a boat are constant, the catch per boat, and hence fishermen's revenues, decline.

Fishermen's total costs and revenues are shown in Figure 7–2, which gives total revenue for the fishery on the *y* axis and the total effort by all fishermen on the *x* axis. Assuming a constant price for fish, the total revenue curve *TR* first rises with effort, then peaks and begins to fall. At some point, overfishing depletes the stock so much that the fish cannot reproduce at the rate of extraction and become extinct. The total cost of fishing *TC* is assumed to rise linearly: each boat puts to sea at the same cost, so total cost is simply the unit cost times the number of boats. Note that costs include the minimal profit necessary to keep fishermen in business.[3]

If fishing is done by small, independent operators who have open access, the level of effort will increase as long as new entrants earn some net revenue over costs and necessary profit. Fishermen earn net revenues up to E_1, the point where *TC* intersects *TR*. The last boat to enter the fishery just balances costs and revenues. Note that, because these are total revenue and cost curves, once the marginal boat is in the fishery, there are no net revenues for any of the fishing units. The external costs of exploiting the common fishery have caused this result.

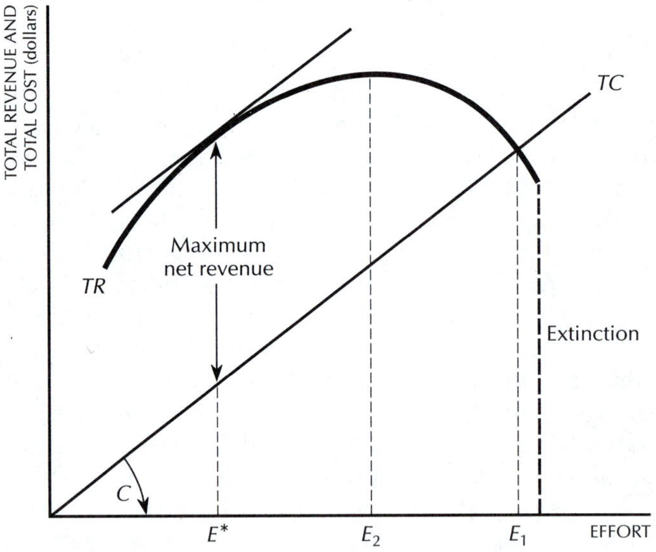

FIGURE 7–2 Fishery Economics. As the level of fishing effort increases, sustainable total revenue (*TR*) at first rises, then peaks at E_2 and begins to fall, until the fish cannot reproduce fast enough to replace the catch and extinction occurs. The total cost of effort is *TC*, assuming each boat puts to sea at the same unit cost. With open access, effort reaches E_1. The optimal outcome would maximize the net revenue from the fisheries—the difference between *TR* and *TC*—at E^*, where marginal revenue (the slope of *TR*) equals marginal cost (the slope of *TC*).

3. For a complete discussion of the fisheries model, see any of a number of texts on natural resources, listed in the readings at the end of the book. This abbreviated version is based on Tom Tietenberg, *Environmental and Natural Resource Economics* (Glenview, Ill. Scott, Foresman, 1988).

In Chapter 6 we learned that a society wishing to maximize its economic welfare will utilize resources to the point where net present value is maximized for any activity. In the fishery case, that rule is equivalent to maximizing the net revenue to all fishermen, the difference between total revenue and total cost.[4] We know from microeconomic principles that maximum net revenue is achieved by equating marginal cost and marginal revenue. In Figure 7–2, the marginal cost is the slope of the total cost line. Marginal revenue is the increase in the catch for a unit increase in effort, valued at a constant price, which is the slope of the *TR* curve at any point. The slope of *TR* is the same as the slope of *TC* at level of effort E^*. This level of effort, maximizing net revenue, would be achieved by a fishing company that had exclusive rights to the fishery or by a government that regulated access by individual fishermen.

Another term for net revenue in this case is **resource rent.** A rent is a return to producers in excess of that necessary to keep them in production. Because the total cost curve in Figure 7–2 includes necessary profit, any revenue in excess of *TC* is a rent. Thus the rule to optimize the exploitation of a natural resource—maximize net revenue—is equivalent to prescribing the maximization of resource rents.

Note that the optimal level of effort E^* is much lower than E_1, the effort expended by fishermen with open access. The economically optimal effort is also less than that needed to achieve the biologically determined maximum catch E_2. So long as there is some cost to fishing effort, the economically optimal effort occurs where the *TR* curve has positive slope, to the left of E_2. It is not in society's interest to extract the maximum sustainable yield from the fishery or from any renewable resource; a society gains maximum welfare by extracting less than the maximum yield.

Can profit-maximizing fishermen cause extinction? This could happen in an open access fishery if the unit cost were so low that the *TC* line intersected the *TR* curve along the dashed line, where the stock had become too small to replace the annual catch. It could also happen at a lower level of effort, such as E_1, if environmental conditions caused a reduction in fishes' reproduction rates for a time, so that what had been a sustainable catch became unsustainable. Once overfishing has become apparent, fishermen might adjust by reducing their effort. However, consider a lake fisherman in Africa: once he has a boat and net, his cost of fishing is only the opportunity cost of his time, which is probably quite low, while the benefits of withdrawal accrue not to him but to other fishermen. Hence there is little incentive to withdraw from the industry. The exhaustion of fisheries in the North Atlantic, in the Humboldt Current off the coast of Peru, and in some lakes in Africa shows that overfishing is not just a theoretical possibility.

Similar models can be used to describe the exploitation of other renewable resources. The application to game hunting is clear. Where hunting is effectively controlled, as is deer hunting in the United States or the hunting of large cats in many African countries, stocks can be maintained. Where hunting is less effectively controlled, extinction becomes a real possibility, because the cost of hunting is so low. For poachers of elephant and rhinoceros in Africa, costs are low, the value of tusks or horns is very high, and poachers place little value on sustaining

4. It is assumed implicity that the discount rate is zero, so that net benefits tomorrow have the same weight as those today. We will relax that assumption in the next section.

stocks into the future. The African tourist industry benefits from big game and tries to conserve it, but the poachers do not share in the benefits from this lucrative industry. The reduction in earnings from tourism slows economic growth.

Natural forests regenerate over much longer periods than fish or mammals, and second-growth forest is likely to be different from native stands. Tropical rainforest species can take seventy years or so to grow to harvestable maturity, and economic rotations of northern species such as Douglas fir are about the same length.[5] Moreover, if harvesting greatly alters the habitat, regeneration can take longer or become impossible. In parts of Indonesia, clear-cutting the forest allows the generation of a grass, called *alang-alang,* that has no economic value and prevents both reforestation and farming; forest land is literally laid to waste.

Environmental amenities, such as clean air and water, have similar properties. Waste can be dumped in them and water can be consumed without permanent impairment, so long as these uses do not exceed the capacity of air and water to cleanse themselves or of rainfall to replace ground water. But, at least until environmental regulation became common over the past two decades, air and water were common properties with virtually free access. The extreme air pollution of cities such as Los Angeles, Mexico, Bangkok, and Jakarta testify to the overuse of this common resource. Industrial pollution of many waterways in North America, the "killing" of the Aral Sea in Uzbekistan by excessive irrigation that reduced its supply of river water, and the dumping of household waste in Asian rivers are examples of burdening water resources beyond their medium-term abilities to cleanse themselves. Private and public wells have seriously depleted aquifers in many places, sometimes to the point of permitting the incursion of seawater, which renders them permanently useless.

The Value of Time

So far, we have skirted the issue of time by discussing sustainable harvests as if all years were of equal value. That is unrealistic and especially difficult to sustain in talking about exhaustible resources. We know from the discussion of discounting in Chapter 6 that benefits and costs realized in the future have less present value than those that are realized immediately. If the discount rate (the real interest rate) is r percent per year, then in any future year n, the present value placed on resource flows is $1/(1 + r)^n$.[6]

The more productive is capital and the scarcer are savings that finance investment, the higher is the discount rate and the lower is the value placed on future benefits and costs. In developing countries we expect real discount rates of 10 percent a year or so; at that rate, a benefit of \$100 accruing 10 years from now would be worth only \$38 today ($1/1.10^{10} = 0.38$). This indicates that people are not so willing to wait long for benefits from their investments. The more developed a country becomes, the lower is the likely return on new investments (because the capital stock has become larger), the more can be saved (because incomes are higher), and the more willing is the population likely to be to wait for future benefits; hence the appropriate discount rate is lower. If an industrial country's dis-

5. Tietenberg, *Environmental and Natural Resource Economics,* p. 245.
6. See page 147.

count rate were 5 percent a year, the value of $100 of benefits received in ten years would be $61.

To see how discounting affects the allocation of scarce resources over time, consider an oversimple but instructive hypothetical example. Zambia has a copper deposit that is expected to last two decades and the government is trying to decide how much copper to extract and export in each of the first and second decades. Zambia's output is large enough to affect the world price. For each decade, the higher the rate of extraction and the more Zambia exports, the lower it will drive the price of copper on world markets. If extraction costs are constant, then in each decade the net revenue from copper exports (world price less mining cost) will decline as more ore is extracted. How much should be mined in each decade?

The answer depends on the **marginal net benefit** (MNB), or the additional revenue net of additional costs from producing one more unit (mining one more ton of copper ore), in each period. The rule for maximizing net benefits over time is to equate the marginal net benefit for each period; that is, $MNB_1 = MNB_2$. If marginal net benefit is higher in period one than in period two, it pays the country to mine more copper in period one and less in period two, until the net benefits are equal at the margin. If Zambia values benefits in period two the same as benefits in period one and if the demand and cost schedules remain the same in both periods, it will mine the same quantity of copper in each decade.

But Zambia is a developing country with scarce capital, low income, and an expectation of higher income in the future if it can save and invest more today. It therefore places a lower value on benefits received in the second decade than in the first. The net benefit received in the second decade must be discounted by $1/(1 + r)$, so the maximizing rule becomes $MNB_1 = MNB_2/(1 + r)$. (In this example, r is the discount rate between decades, not years.) This rule can only be satisfied if MNB_1 is less than MNB_2. Because the price and thus MNB decline as output rises, net benefits are maximized over both decades if Zambia mines and exports more copper in the first decade than in the second.[7]

This highly simplified example has important implications for resource management. First, even though the current generation, mining in decade one, is concerned about the welfare of the next generation, it will consume some of the nonrenewable resource. Second, the current generation should consume more of the resource than the next generation so long as time has value and the discount rate is positive. This will be the case whenever there are profitable investments to be made and savings to finance them, so that the next generation will have higher income than the current one. Third, the higher the discount rate and the higher the expected level of future incomes, the more should be exploited by the current generation.

This two-period example can easily be extended to the more realistic case of annual discounting over many years or generations, for both renewable and nonrenewable resources. Discounting applies with particular force to the harvesting and regeneration of natural forests. Assume that a large area of forest is owned by a private firm with secure rights long into the future, and for simplicity ignore the nontimber products of the forest. The timber company has three choices. It can

7. If Zambia's exports of copper were too small to affect world market prices, this result would still hold if the marginal cost of mining increased with the quantity mined in each period, as it well might.

fell all the marketable timber now for immediate profit and then invest the proceeds in another business. It can wait for some future time to do the same thing. Or it can harvest the timber continuously over time. These three options are depicted in Figure 7–3.

Felling all trees now brings in revenue, net of costs, shown in rectangle *A*. Because this is done in the present, no discounting is necessary. Waiting until some future time to harvest the entire forest yields the revenue in rectangle *B*. Because world timber prices have been rising at about 2 percent a year in real terms and because the trees may produce more volume in the future, the company can expect to earn higher current revenues by waiting, as indicated by the dotted rectangle. But to compare future revenues *B* with current revenues *A*, future revenues must be discounted; this yields the crosshatched rectangle at *B*. The decision to harvest continuously is shown by option *C*, the dotted line rising continuously over time as prices rise and trees grow; its discounted value is the crosshatched area under the solid line.

If the discount rate exceeds the rate of price increase plus the rate of timber growth, the value of option *A* will exceed the discounted value of either *B* or *C*. Immediate harvest is likely to be the optimal choice for mature forests, with little or no potential timber growth. But if the forest is not mature, so that potential growth is substantial, and if the discount rate is not very high, discounted net revenues from future harvest at *B* or continuous harvest, option *C*, may exceed those at *A*.

Any of these options can result in a sustainable harvest. Whether trees are logged all at once or continuously, the natural forest can regenerate itself if there are nearby forests to provide seeds and if the logged land is protected from encroachment by loggers, fuelwood gatherers, herders, and farmers. For some forests, clear-cutting large tracts, as under options *A* and *B*, are compatible with sustainable harvesting. For others, selective and continuous logging may be more sustainable. The period for complete regeneration can be long, however. In the Indonesian rainforest, it takes up to 70 years for trees to mature, though it may not be economically efficient to wait for full maturity.

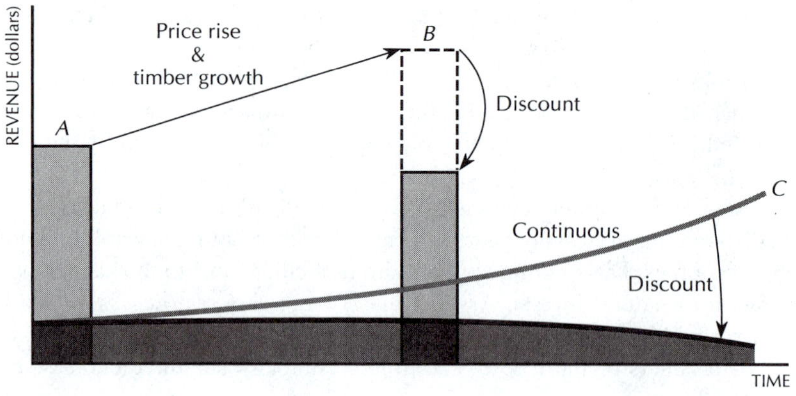

FIGURE 7–3 Discounted Value of Forest Harvest Options. Option *A* is to cut all trees now. Option *B* is to wait for benefits from tree growth and rising real prices, but discounting reduces the present value of future net revenues. Option *C* is a continuous harvest, made more attractive by rapid tree growth and price rises, but less so by a high discount rate.

Environmental protection has the same time dimension. Cleaning up a degraded environment or forgoing pollution altogether entails current costs or the loss of current output, in favor of greater environmental benefits in the future. The most serious deterrents to such investments are that the benefits of clean air and water and more attractive scenery are external to the firm and most environmental benefits cannot easily be valued or marketed. But leaving this aside, high discount rates—implying a low regard for the future compared to the present—also work against environmental protection or cleanup.

This is one reason that poorer countries, with high discount rates, may place less emphasis on environmental amenities than do richer countries. High discount rates can help to explain why Brazil and Malaysia cut down their tropical rainforests at unsustainable rates and why authorities in Mexico City and Bangkok appear less concerned about air pollution than authorities in Los Angeles. Economists have also suggested that, because of their higher discount rates, poorer countries may be more willing to accept polluting industries than are richer countries.

POLICY SOLUTIONS

The market failures that lead to overexploitation of natural resources stem from external costs that are not borne by producers. Even in a well-functioning market economy, externalities require government intervention to reach efficient market outcomes. Government can bestow property rights on private users, regulate access to common resources, impose taxes that reflect external costs, and issue tradable access rights. We discuss each in turn.

Property Rights

Common properties generate external costs because no one owns or controls the right to exploit them. For some resources, a simple solution would be to confer ownership, which economists call **property rights,** on a single individual or company. As long as the owner is a profit maximizer and sells output in a competitive market, the socially optimal outcome will be achieved without further government intervention.[8] Nor does the owner have to be the producer to achieve optimal resource use. If the owner rents the resource to some of the same producers who previously had common property access, she will maximize profits by charging rents that limit access and production to the optimal level.

Property rights, to be effective, must be exclusive and well defined, leaving no doubt to the owners and possible competing claimants about what has been conferred and to whom. Rights need to be secure, so that the risk of loss through legal challenge or expropriation is reduced, and enforceable through the judicial system. Ownership must be valid over a long enough horizon that the owners have a stake in the long-term, sustainable exploitation of the resource. Longevity converts the resource into an asset for the producer, who can reap the benefits from

8. If the owner is a monopolist in the product market, output would be below, and the price above, the social optimum. With the possible exception of a few minerals such as diamonds, markets for the products of common resources are fairly competitive (i.e., firms face elastic demand), especially when close substitutes are considered.

investments in improving and sustaining its productivity. And the rights must be transferable, so the owner can realize the benefits of the resource asset by selling the property at any time.[9]

For some resources, such as forests, rangeland, or mineral deposits, the application of property rights is straightforward. The resource is a tangible property and exclusive ownership is enforceable. Government can privatize the asset by granting or selling rights to private producers. If the right is granted, then the producer gains all the resource rents. If it is sold for a fixed fee, government shares part of the rent. But if the property right is auctioned, potential owners will bid up the price to the point where they can still earn a reasonable profit on their investment of capital and labor,[10] but have forgone most or all of the resource rents, which are then captured by the government. Concessions to exploit the tropical rainforest are common in Indonesia and Malaysia, though the terms are badly flawed and do not result in optimal regeneration. Most timberland in the United States is privately owned and harvested and replanted on a sustainable basis, though the result is often plantations of uniform species rather than regenerated natural forest.

Property rights can be held by communities. If local populations have traditional access to the forest, for example, and can enforce this right, it is in their interest to achieve optimal output because they benefit from the resulting rents. The struggle over property rights in Brazil's Amazon is in part a conflict between local communities that have traditionally exploited the rainforest sustainably (though perhaps not optimally) and modern companies whose incentives are to overexploit this resource. In Kenya, county councils have been given property rights to some of the game parks that attract international tourists in large numbers; the entry fees charged give local governments an incentive to preserve these assets against poaching and grazing by cattle. Communal tenure has worked to preserve natural forests in Papua New Guinea.[11]

Communal Forest Management in India[12]

In the village of Arabari in West Bengal, officials began in 1970 to experiment with a form of communal management of the forest that had some of the desirable characteristics of property rights. Villagers had been cutting the forest and earning much of their income from the sale of fuelwood. The Arabari experiment employed villagers in planting trees and grass and provided fuelwood and construction materials to the village from outside sources at cost. Villagers also received 25 percent of the sales of mature trees. In return, villagers were asked to prevent encroachment of the forest. After 15 years, the forests had been restored and village incomes were higher than before the experiment. The Forest Department expanded the arrangements to cover 700 village groups and so rehabilitated some 170,000 acres of forest.

9. Theodore Panayotou, *Green Markets: The Economics of Sustainable Development* (San Francisco: ICS Press, 1993), pp. 35–37.

10. Remember that rents are defined as revenue net of costs and that costs include the profits necessary to keep capital engaged in the industry.

11. Reported in Panayotou, *Green Markets*, pp. 20–21.

12. Ibid., pp.118–19.

For some common resources, however, it is difficult or impossible to convey property rights as these are usually understood. Both law and ease of access make it impractical to own an ocean or lake fishery. Nor can a company own the air and water that accommodate its waste, because the polluter cannot exclude other users and thus cannot charge for access to clean air and water. Nevertheless, governments can create property rights even in these common resources by legislating, granting, and enforcing quotas, access permits, licenses to operate, and other legal instruments that give some agents the right to fish, harvest, pollute, or otherwise use a common resource. Because these instruments convey only limited access, they have value to the holder and can be treated as any other asset.

Government Regulation

As an alternative to conveying private property rights, governments can themselves act as the owners of common resources and directly regulate their use. Governments can limit the quantity of a hunter's kill, a fisherman's catch, a logger's haul, a rancher's herd, or a polluter's emissions. And they can regulate the kinds of equipment that can or must be used: some kinds of fishing nets, boats, or navigation equipment have been banned; hunters may be restricted in their choice of weapons; polluters are required to install equipment that scrubs gas emissions and treats wastewater.

Quantity regulations raise two issues. First, how do the regulators know the optimal levels of access and output? If property rights can be conveyed, efficient outcomes will be approached through market forces and no government judgments are needed. But if regulation replaces the market, regulators need to estimate the characteristics of both producers' costs and users' demand for the products of a common resource. To get a sense of these information requirements, consider the regulation of air pollution.[13]

The external costs of pollution are manifest in the reduced welfare of others: poor health, unsightly environment, lower property values, fewer and more expensive recreational possibilities, and possibly reduced productivity and income. If these costs could be measured, they would be depicted by a curve such as MEC in Figure 7–4, which shows the marginal external cost of pollution (measured along the horizontal axis). Any reduction in pollution means a reduction in this cost or, equivalently, an increase in the marginal external benefit of abatement.

However, there is a cost to abating pollution. The polluting firm, say a petrochemical plant, can reduce its effluents either by changing its production process, by installing abatement equipment such as gas scrubbers and water treatment plants, or by reducing output. Schedule MAC traces these marginal abatement costs. At any point along MAC, the cost shown is that of the lowest-cost method of abatement. Moving from right (high pollution) to left (lower pollution), MAC rises because it becomes increasingly costly to clean up air or water the stricter the standards or the lower the level of contamination. It is important to recognize that these costs of abatement, though borne by the petrochemical firm, are also costs to society because they involve either less consumption of steel or savings spent on abatement that might otherwise have been spent on investment in other

13. This approach to the economics of pollution abatement is based on the treatment by David W. Pearce and R. Kerry Turner, *Economics of Natural Resources and the Environment* (Baltimore: Johns Hopkins Press, 1990), Chaps. 4–7.

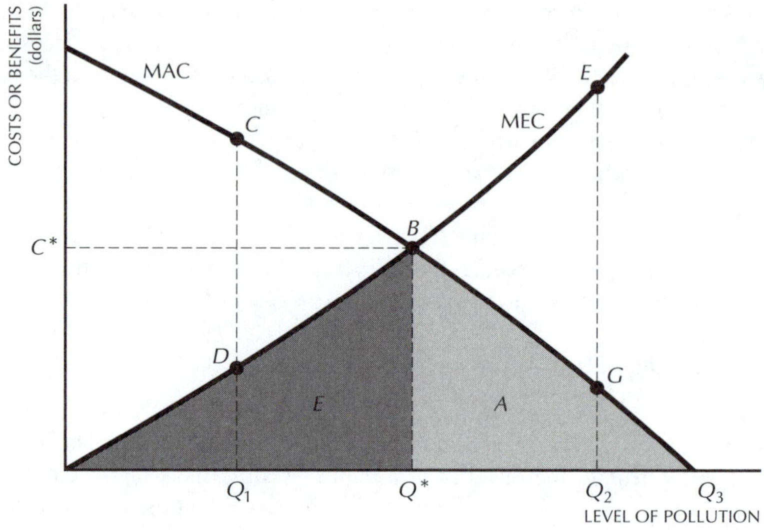

FIGURE 7–4 Optimal Level of Pollution. The marginal external cost of pollutants, borne by the population, is given by MEC; the marginal cost of abatement, borne by the firm, is MAC. The total cost to society (the crosshatched area *E* plus *A*) is minimized and pollution is optimal at Q^*, where MEC = MAC.

goods or services that people want. These abatement costs thus have equal weight to the benefits gained by reducing pollution.

Society's (and thus government's) aim should be to minimize the combined costs of pollution and its abatement. This is achieved at Q^* in Figure 7–4, where MEC = MAC; $Q_3 - Q^*$ of pollution has been abated (assuming for convenience that Q_3 is the maximum amount of pollution), and Q^* of pollution remains. Because these are marginal cost curves, the total external cost of pollution is the crosshatched area *E* under MEC from 0 to Q^*. And the total cost of abatement is given by the crosshatched area *A* under the MAC curve between Q^* and Q_3. With less pollution, such as Q_1, the marginal abatement cost exceeds the marginal external cost of pollution and the total cost of additional abatement, Q_1Q^*BC, exceeds the net gain from reduced pollution, Q_1Q^*BD. If more pollution is permitted, such as Q_2, the additional external cost, Q^*Q_2EB, exceeds the reduced cost of abatement, Q^*Q_2GB.

Thus society is better-off, in that it suffers minimal costs, with some pollution than with none, just as society gains from some exploitation of natural resources, even nonrenewable ones. But how do the regulators, who wish to achieve this optimal level of pollution, know what it is? To find Q^*, they would have to know all the external costs of pollution as a function of the levels of contaminants in the air, water, and soil. This implies some method of finding the values placed by the affected individuals on environmental amenities such as clean air, water, and soil. Survey and other methods are being developed to measure such valuations, but these are still experimental and beyond the scope of governments in many developing countries.[14] The regulators need also to know the costs of abatement. Yet

14. Paul R. Portney, "The Contingent Valuation Debate: Why Should Economists Care?" *Journal of Economic Perspectives* 8, no. 4 (Fall 1994), 3–17.

firms subject to regulation have an incentive to overstate these costs in the hope of being allowed to emit more pollutants and avoid abatement costs.

In the absence of such knowledge, regulators must, and do, set arbitrary standards based on studies estimating the impact of pollutants on human health, animal survival, forest dieback (from acid rain) and regeneration, and presumed climate changes. Because of the large uncertainties in such estimates and the conflicting objectives of environmental policy, these standards become political issues, subject to contention by interest groups speaking for the environment, the public, industry, and developers. These policy struggles, the establishment of compliance staffs in both the government and polluting firms, and the ensuing law suits all add significant costs to the imposition of environmental standards, and so reduce the gains to society. In developing countries where rent-seeking is an important feature of political and legal systems, polluting industrialists are likely to use their financial and political muscle to thwart environmental regulation.

The second question raised by regulation is its efficiency compared to other methods. Governments have imposed many different methods for restricting access to common resources. They have specified hours or days of access to fisheries; completely barred access to some forests or fisheries; set quotas for individual hunters, loggers, and fishermen; limited the specific levels of pollution for each plant in a region; prohibited particularly efficient equipment such as gill nets or even, in Alaska for a time, motorized boats;[15] mandated the use of abatement equipment; and shut off electricity to conserve water in hydroelectric sites. These methods may get the economy closer to the optimal rate of use, but are unlikely to achieve it. Even if they did, the outcome would not be optimal for society because the controls themselves impose costs on producers and consumers.

In Figure 7–4, regulators might achieve output Q^* by requiring certain equipment for each plant or by setting output quotas for each producer. But while the MAC curve assumes that each polluter makes the most efficient choice of technique for abating pollution, regulators are unlikely to know the costs of each option and have little incentive to find the most efficient way to reduce emissions. So their required method of achieving Q^* is likely to raise the MAC schedule above its minimum, and so unnecessarily raise the costs borne by society. In controlling the fisheries depicted in Figure 7–2, regulators might achieve optimal catch E^* by enforcing certain practices or prohibiting certain equipment, and so raise the cost of fishing to each entrant. But the higher costs would dissipate the rents available from the optimum level of effort and these rents would no longer be available to society for other uses.[16]

Taxation

In principle, government could also achieve optimal rates of resource use by imposing taxes that reduce the incentive for producers to enter common properties or to manufacture polluting products. A tax might be imposed on output that represents the external costs of production, so that the private marginal cost schedule shifts up to equal the social marginal cost schedule.[17] This might take the form of

15. Tietenberg, *Environmental and Natural Resource Economics,* p. 271.
16. Ibid., p. 270.
17. In Figure 7–1, the tax would shift the PMC schedule up to coincide with the SMC schedule.

a tax on each ton of steel or petrochemicals at a rate representing the external cost of pollution or a tax on gasoline to cover the costs of both pollution and traffic congestion. A tax, equal to the maximum resource rent, could be levied on the level of effort or on the quantity harvested by fishermen or foresters, so that their private costs would induce them collectively to take the optimal harvest.[18]

If the tax is on output or level of effort, the incentive is to reduce production of the good with external costs. If the tax can be levied on the externality itself, there is an additional incentive to invest in reducing external costs. For example, a tax on the quantity of pollutants would give petrochemical plants an incentive to abate pollution, because the tax would then be reduced. Malaysia has had success with emissions fees on its palm oil industry (see the boxed example). It may not always be practical to tax emissions, however, especially in developing countries where monitoring would be difficult and tax avoidance easy. An alternative might be to tax the polluting product but to reduce or eliminate the tax if pollution abatement equipment is in operation.

Taxes that internalize external costs have one important advantage over regulation: they allow the producer to choose the method of reducing access to a common resource, so that rents are not dissipated in wasteful expenditures forced by regulators. An optimal tax, however, requires the same information as optimal regulation: in the case of pollution, knowledge of the relation between pollution and output, of the cost of abatement, and of the external costs to the population. If, however, there is a consensus that pollution is too great or a common resource is being overexploited, government can move in the right direction by imposing some tax, observing outcomes, and adjusting the tax rate if necessary.

Reducing Water Pollution from Palm Oil Mills in Malaysia[19]

Between 1970 and 1989, Malaysia's output of palm oil, a major export, grew twelvefold. Unfortunately, the processing of palm oil in rural mills generates 2.5 tons of waste water for every ton of crude palm oil produced. By the late 1970s, effluents from the mills had severely polluted over forty rivers in Malaysia, mainly by depleting their oxygen. Pollution killed freshwater fish, endangered mangroves on the coast that are essential for traditional marine fisheries, contaminated the major source of drinking water for many rural Malays, and emitted a stench that made several villages uninhabitable.

Water pollution became so serious that in 1974 the government passed the Environmental Quality Act and in 1975 established the Department of the Environment (DOE). In 1977 the DOE announced standards for the quality of effluents from palm oil mills that were to become increasingly stringent over time. To provide the reluctant mills with incentives to comply, the DOE established a two-part licensing fee with a constant charge per unit of effluent plus an excess fee that varied with the oxygen-depleting potential of the discharge. Thus the mills could choose their least-cost

18. In Figure 7–2 a tax equal to the maximum resource rent would move the cost schedule up to *TC′* and induce fishermen to expend the optimum effort E^*.

19. From Jeffrey R. Vincent, "Reducing Effluent While Raising Affluence: Water Pollution Abatement in Malaysia," Harvard Institute for International Development, March 1993.

option: either pay the costs of reducing and treating their effluent or pay the higher fees for discharging waste that exceeded the environmental quality standard.

The industry responded by developing and installing improved treatment technologies; by developing commercial products, such as fertilizer and animal feed, from their waste products; and by recovering methane that could be used to generate electricity. Over time, the economic incentives became less important as inflation eroded their value, and direct controls became more important. Nevertheless, the market-oriented regime set in motion a sharp reversal of polluting practices. By 1989, even though palm oil production had reached an all-time high, three out of four mills complied with the stringent sixth-generation standards and the oxygen-depleting potential of emitted waste was only 1 percent of its mid-1970s level.

Marketable Permits

A fourth intervention is to create a property right where none exists by issuing **marketable permits**, granting the holders the right to harvest a common resource up to a given limit or giving producers a license to pollute the environment up to specified amounts. Although environmentalists sometimes scoff at the notion of a "right" to pollute or exploit resources, in fact these permits may be the most efficient way to reduce pollution and resource overuse.

Figure 7–5 shows how a pollution permit works.[20] The MAC and MEC curves

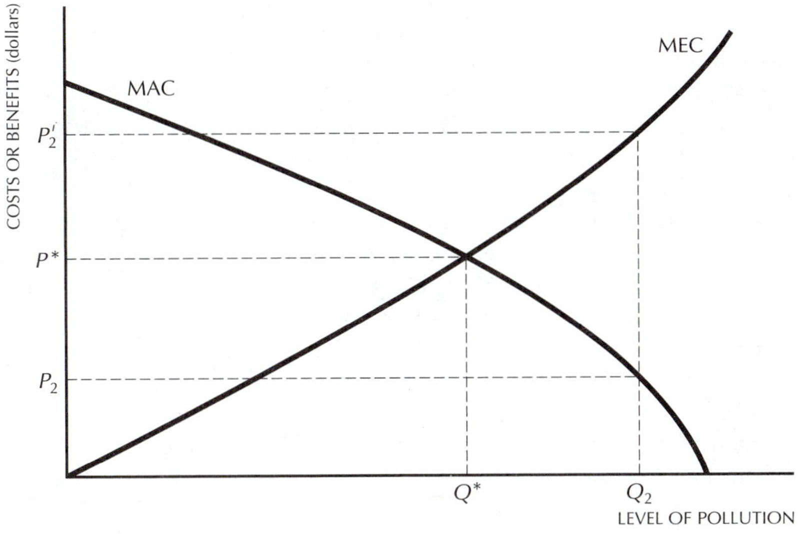

FIGURE 7–5 Marketable Permits to Pollute. The MAC schedule shows the demand for pollution rights. If rights are issued to pollute up to Q_2, these are worth P_2 to polluters, but the public places a value of P_2' on reducing pollution. This could be the basis for a bargain to reduce pollution to the optimal level Q^*.

20. This figure is adapted from Pearce and Turner, *Economics of Natural Resources,* pp. 110–13, and Tietenberg, *Environmental and Natural Resource Economics,* pp. 319–20.

are copied from Figure 7–4. Say that government knows the optimal level of pollution and auctions off emissions permits totalling Q^*. Any firm polluting without a permit would, if detected, be fined or shut down. (Thus permits have the same enforcement requirements as regulations or taxes.) If MAC represents the cost of pollution abatement for all firms in the market, they would bid up the price of permits to P^*. The MAC schedule shows that firms can reduce pollution from Q_3 to Q^* at costs less than P^*. Without permits, however, they would have to reduce pollution below Q^* at costs higher than P^*. Thus the MAC schedule is the demand curve for permits. Either government can issue a given number and observe the auction price paid for them, or it can set a price and issue whatever number of permits is demanded by polluters.

What if government overshoots and either issues Q_2 of permits or offers permits at a price P_2? There would be more pollution than the public would like, as indicated by the MEC schedule; with Q_2 permits, the public's marginal cost due to pollution is P_2'. If there is an effective market for permits, sufferers from pollution could offer to buy permits from producers. At first, they should be willing to offer a price of P_2', the marginal benefit to them of less pollution. This would be more than enough to induce a polluter to sell a permit and reduce his emissions at a cost of only P_2. Such bargains would continue, until the public's benefits, given by MEC, just equalled the polluters costs, MAC, which would occur at the optimum level of pollution Q^*, where permits would sell for P^*.

Economist Robert Coase theorized that this is precisely what could happen, even in the absence of government-issued permits.[21] But the requirements of the Coase theorem are stringent and probably not often met in practice. In particular, the suffering public would have to incur the costs of organizing to make their bargaining power effective and would have to mobilize funds to match the benefits they would gain from reduced pollution. But as many of those benefits, such as improved health, better recreational facilities, or more attractive scenery, have no market price, it would be difficult to convert them into cash that could compensate polluters. And in poor societies or among the poor in any country, it seems highly unlikely that the demand for an improved environment could be made effective in a permits market.

Some environmental groups, which are organized to solicit contributions for environmental causes, could overcome these obstacles and behave as Coase predicted. They could, for examaple, purchase and then withdraw tradable emission permits from the market. Conservation groups have purchased fishing rights in New Zealand and other countries to reduce the catch. And the programs of the Nature Conservancy and other groups to purchase rainforest land in tropical countries, while using a different mechanism, has the same effect of expressing consumer interests in an improved environment through the market.[22]

Even if the market between polluters and sufferers is not fully effective, the

21. Robert Coase, "The Problem of Social Cost," *Journal of Law and Economics,* 3 (October 1960), 1–44.

22. In one version of this transaction, an environmental group will buy some of the host country's debt from disappointed bondholders on the international market, usually at a heavy discount, and then agree not to seek repayment of the loans from the host government. In return, the host country sets aside a negotiated area of rainforest to be preserved as a national park. These are called "debt-for-nature swaps."

market among polluters can be highly effective in minimizing the costs of meeting any government-imposed standard for emissions or other limitations to resource use. Assume that the government issues an arbitrary quantity Q_p of permits to pollute that would reduce emissions below their current level, and divides these among existing firms by any method, for example, in proportion to their output. Firm 1, with old technology, would find it very costly to reduce its emissions to the new standard represented by the permits. Firm 2, built recently, is capable of reducing its emissions below the level of its permits at low cost. Here is the basis for a bargain between the two firms that would benefit society. Firm 1 sells some of its permits to Firm 2 at a price above its marginal abatement cost but below the MAC of Firm 2. Both firms are better-off: Firm 1 has earned revenue in excess of its costs of abatement while Firm 2 has paid less than it would have to reduce its pollution. The public is also better off because the reduced emission standard has been met, but at a lower total cost than would have been incurred had the initial allocation of permits been enforced.

This powerful result is quite general. It suggests that, whenever there is a limitation to be imposed on private activity, the creation of a marketable property right can achieve an efficient outcome with minimal government intervention. It is for that reason that economists recommend that traditional property rights to natural resources, such as forest concessions or licenses to fish and hunt, should be marketable. The use of marketable permits is in its infancy. Considerable experience has been gained in the United States with pollution permits issued to public utilities. In developing and transitional economies, where policy dependence on market forces is a more recent phenomenon, marketable permits have hardly been tried, but hold promise for the future if the problems of enforcement can be overcome.

Policy Failures

Although some government intervention is necessary to correct for the market failures associated with natural resources, it is equally true that, all over the world, government policies frequently contribute to wasteful use of resources and the degradation of the environment. We have seen that, when production has external costs, one approach is to internalize those costs by taxing output or by granting marketable property rights. But governments commonly suppress the prices or subsidize the production of commodities that degrade natural resources and often compromise property rights in ways that encourage rapacious exploitation. Examples are not hard to find.

Forestry policy has been especially destructive in many tropical countries. Brazil subsidizes ranching and other activities that encroach on the Amazon rainforest (see the following box). Indonesia grants logging concessions for only 20 years, which encourages wasteful logging practices because regeneration times are 70 years; charges no fees for the concessions; discourages transfers of the concessions; imposes inadequate taxes and fees that do not encourage conservation; and is ineffective in policing the regulations aimed at conservation. Thailand's policies were so wanton that its rainforest has all but disappeared, and the Philippines is on the same path.

Trade policy has been equally destructive. Ghana, Indonesia, and Malaysia, for example, placed bans on log exports as a means of promoting wood-processing industries. Export bans drive down the domestic price of tropical hardwood, and so make it profitable for sawmills and plywood mills to purchase logs and export semifinished products. But these industries have been inefficient and have consumed resource rents in higher production costs. Because timber companies cannot export tropical hardwoods, such as ebony and mahogany, as logs, these valuable species are used along with low-value timber to make inexpensive products, such as plywood sent to Japan to make forms for pouring cement! The role of self-imposed log export bans in destroying rainforests should be a warning to northern countries that want to preserve tropical forests by imposing their own import bans on these same logs.[23]

Subsidized Deforestation of the Amazon[24]

The government of Brazil, wishing to promote development in the Amazon, has been subsidizing ranchers to cut down the vast rainforest. Three to four thousand square miles of the Amazon was deforested each year throughout the 1970s and almost a quarter of the Amazonian state of Rondonia was converted from rain forest to pasture from 1970 to 1985. Not only does pastureland replace the rain forest, but rain-forest occupations provided more jobs than the ranching that replaced them. Despite this, the government provided new ranchers with 15-year tax holidays, investment tax credits, exemptions from export taxes and import duties, and loans with interest substantially below market rates. Although a typical subsidized investment was estimated to yield a loss to the economy equivalent to 55 percent of the initial investment, a private rancher was able to earn a return, due to subsidies, equivalent to 250 percent of the amount invested.

Energy pricing is another common policy failure. In oil-rich countries like Nigeria and Venezuela, energy has been kept cheap as a stimulus to industrialization and diversification. This has multiple adverse effects. It encourages wasteful domestic consumption, and reduces the country's petroleum and gas reserves and its export earning potential. It encourages the use of cars and minibuses, and so adds to congestion. Cheap energy promotes industry that is ill-suited to the country's endowments. Firms and consumers have little incentive to adopt energy-saving technologies. Because burning oil is an important source of air pollution, all these overuses contribute to environmental degradation. Not all oil exporters underprice energy. Indonesia now values its fuel at world prices and has begun to recognize environmental externalities as a factor in domestic oil pricing. But some oil importers, such as Egypt, Argentina, China and India, have subsidized petro-

23. On forest policies, see Robert Repetto and Malcolm Gillis (eds.), *Public Policies and the Misuse of Forest Resources* (Cambridge, U.K.: Cambridge University Press, 1988), and Jeffrey Vincent, "The Tropical Timber Trade and Sustainable Development," *Science*, 256 (1992), 1651–55.
24. From Panayotou, *Green Markets*, pp. 14–15.

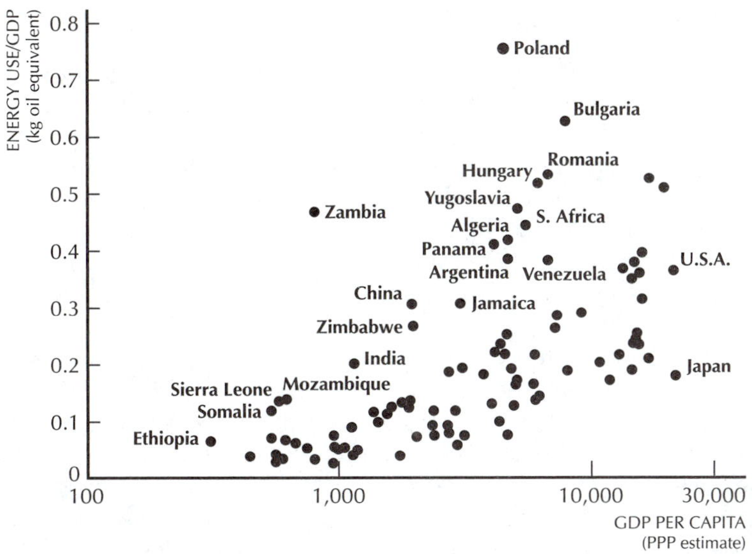

FIGURE 7–6 **Energy Use and Income.** Although energy use as a share of GDP generally rises with income per capita, some countries have especially high energy use, in many cases because of distorted prices and subsidized energy.

leum products by as much as 50 percent of the world price, and so encouraged imports they cannot afford, industries that cannot compete in world markets, and environmental degradation that market pricing would have discouraged.[25]

Figure 7–6 shows commercial energy use per unit of GDP (using the purchasing power parity estimates for 1990) for almost ninety countries. The variance, even among poor countries, is notable. Countries with especially high energy use are labeled in the diagram; the United States and Japan are also labeled for comparison. Among the high energy users, mistaken energy policies are not entirely to blame, but must be suspected in countries like Zambia, India, Argentina, South Africa, and Venezuela, where market prices have been generally distorted until the economic reforms of the 1980s and 1990s; even today, Venezuela prices gasoline at about 25 U.S. cents a gallon. The consequences of price distortions are particularly notable in the former communist countries, China, Poland, Bulgaria, Hungary, and Romania, where markets played very little role in resource allocation until recently. Among industrial countries, Norway and Canada stand out as particularly high users of energy. The United States, often castigated as a wanton consumer of fuel, does not show an especially high rate of use for its income, partly because energy is priced at or above world market levels.

Investment in infrastructure is a third area of widespread policy failure. In forestry and energy pricing, governments typically underprice the resource and fail to force private operators to account for external costs. In infrastructure investment, governments often create new external costs and fail to account for them in project planning. Environmental groups have focused much of their fire on investments in power dams, irrigation and flood control systems, roads, and

25. Bjorn Larsen and Anwar Shah, "World Fossil Fuel Subsidies and Global Carbon Emissions," World Bank, Working Paper WPS 1002, October 1992, especially Chart 1.

Kerosene Subsidy in Indonesia[26]

From 1972 to 1984, the government of Indonesia heavily subsidized the consumption of kerosene and other fuels. The kerosene subsidy was justified as an aid to poor rural dwellers, who were thought to use it for cooking, and as a disincentive to harvest fuelwood. The cutting of fuelwood was denuding mountain slopes and causing soil erosion on Java, Indonesia's most densely populated island. But research subsequently discovered that rural families used kerosene predominantly for lighting, not for cooking, so that only about 50,000 acres of forest land was protected each year by the subsidy at a cost of almost U.S.$200,000 a year per acre. Replanting programs, in contrast, cost only $1,000 per acre. Moreover, most kerosene turned out to be consumed by the wealthy, not the poor. And the low price of kerosene made it necessary to subsidize diesel fuel as well, because the two fuels could be substituted in truck engines, and this caused greater environmental damage. Recognizing the costs of this policy, the government sharply reduced its subsidy on kerosene and now prices most fuels at world market levels.

power plants that damage their environments. Dams that flood their upstream areas displace local populations, who seldom fare as well in new locations, and destroy natural habitat. Egypt's huge Aswan Dam controlled the floodwaters of the Nile. But those same floodwaters had beneficial effects, replenishing soils and leaching out unwanted salts, so the dam may have reduced agricultural productivity over the long run. Irrigation schemes in Africa encourage diseases such as schistosomiasis and river blindness. Roads into the rainforest in Brazil and elsewhere not only destroy habitat along the right of way, but encourage overexploitation of the forest and surroundings.

Project analysis, discussed in Chapter 6, can to some extent accommodate the external costs of large projects. The commercial value of land, forests, and inland fisheries can be calculated and added to the costs of projects. More controversially, the cost of illness from some kinds of environmental change can be estimated. Recreational benefits and costs might also be quantified (see the following box). To the extent possible, the inclusion of these costs and the use of cost-benefit analysis in public investment decisions would help to avoid environmentally damaging projects or to change designs and reduce external costs. However, many environmental costs cannot be quantified so readily, although attempts are being made. Probably more critically, too many governments do not take project appraisal at all seriously. The World Bank, under considerable pressure from environmental groups, now undertakes impact analyses of the investments it finances. This practice is likely to spread.

26. Malcolm Gillis, "Indonesia: Public Policies, Resource Management and the Tropical Forest," in Robert Repetto and Malcolm Gillis (eds.), *Public Policy and the Misuse of Forest Resources* (Cambridge, U.K.: Cambridge University Press, 1988).

Valuing a Recreational Facility in Bangkok, Thailand[27]

For environmental amenities, valuation techniques are either market-oriented or survey-oriented. Market-oriented techniques use information on observed behavior, especially market prices. Survey techniques ask affected populations about their willingness to pay for amenities or to accept compensation for losses. Lumpinee Public Park in downtown Bangkok provides many benefits to its users. Because no admission fee is charged, no direct expression of its value can be observed, so two survey techniques have been employed. The first, called the "travel cost approach," uses the money and time costs of getting to the park as an estimate of the demand schedule for environmental amenities associated with the park. The value of the park is calculated as consumer surplus, the area under the estimated demand curve. The second approach, called "hypothetical valuation," asks users how much they would contribute annually to the upkeep of the park if the government could no longer maintain it. The two approaches gave similar results: the park's services were valued at about 13 million baht in 1980, or 650,000 U.S. dollars using the 1980 exchange rate. Capitalizing these annual benefits at a discount rate of 10 percent per annum in perpetuity gives an asset (or present) value of US$6.5 million.

In one important respect, then, the economic reform agenda discussed in Chapter 5 is also an agenda for more sustainable development. The core of structural adjustment is to depend as much as possible on markets to determine prices and allocate resources. As part of this, subsidies and protective tariffs are to be reduced or eliminated. Where this agenda is implemented, all resources, including marketable natural resources and sources of pollution, will bear prices that are closer to their true scarcity costs. That is the first step toward an incentive regime to promote sustainable resource use. Because external costs and benefits are not reflected in market prices, it is not the only step. Marketable property rights and permits, taxes, or even regulation will also be necessary to internalize the externalities and complete the incentive regime. But it is important to recognize that there is no necessary conflict between economic reform and sustainable development.

MEASURING SUSTAINABILITY

Most societies and their governments aim to increase incomes as rapidly as possible over long periods. How do they ensure that economic growth does not depend unsustainably on the consumption of natural resources? This chapter has so far answered this question in terms of the markets for individual resources such as fisheries, forests, mineral deposits, and the environment. If a government wished to track the country's success in sustaining its growth, what concepts could it use and how would these be measured?

27. From John A. Dixon and Maynard M. Hufschmidt (eds.), *Valuation Techniques for the Environment* (Baltimore: Johns Hopkins Press, 1986), 121–40.

Natural Capital

SUSTAINABLE DEVELOPMENT (Ch. 7)

The economic growth models presented in Chapter 3 show that rising incomes depend on increases in the capital stock and in the productivity with which labor and capital produce goods and services. In those models, and in most economic analysis, capital stock has meant **human-made capital:** machines, buildings, and infrastructure (**made capital**), as well as the education and experience of the labor force (**human capital**).[28] What if, however, production also consumes natural resources? The productivity of made capital and labor will decline as natural resources are depleted, unless more resources are discovered, greater amounts are invested in made capital, or technological change increases productivity. This suggests that natural resources ought also to be included in economic growth models and in measures of national output.

To incorporate natural resources in our thinking about economic growth, economists have developed the concept of **natural capital**, analogous to that of made capital. Natural capital is the value of a country's existing stock of natural resources, including fisheries, forests, mineral deposits, water, and the environment. Natural capital produces goods and services, just like labor and made capital. It can be, and usually is, depleted in the process of production, just as made capital is depreciated. It can also, through natural growth of renewable resources and investment in discovery of new reserves, be augmented, just as investment augments the stock of made capital.

The concept is clear, but how can natural capital be measured? Made capital is measured as the cost of investment: if a factory cost $30 million to build and equip, that is the value of the capital stock recorded in the national accounts. In any year, such as 1995, the *gross capital stock* of a country is the sum of such investments over the previous many years, with each year's investment adjusted for inflation. Because the capital stock wears out in the course of production, the stock is reduced each year by a percentage called *depreciation.*[29] Thus each year the beginning capital stock is increased by the value of investment and decreased by depreciation to calculate the *net capital stock.* If the economy is to grow sustainably, net capital stock must grow at the same rate.

Obviously there is no analogous way of valuing natural capital. But there is an alternative and economically preferable way of valuing made capital that can be applied to natural capital. Capital of any kind produces goods and services into the future. A measure of the net benefits from producing these goods and services is the difference between their market price and the cost of the other inputs—materials and labor—used to produce them. The capital can then be valued as the sum of these future benefits, discounted by the appropriate interest rate. That is, the capital is valued as the *net present value* of the future stream of value added by the capital.

This approach can be used to value natural capital. If a forest is harvested, the logs have a market value determined by their price less the costs of harvesting, that is, their resource rent.[30] The cost of harvesting includes materials, wages, and

28. Economists have defined *human capital* as the value of learning and experience embodied in workers, which, like made capital, increases productivity and income. Chapter 10 deals with this important concept.

29. The rate of depreciation varies with the kind of asset. It is usually low, say 2 percent, on buildings and infrastructure, around 10 percent on equipment, and perhaps 20 percent on vehicles.

30. Strictly speaking, the resource rent should be measured using the *marginal* cost of extraction.

the minimum necessary return to made capital, that is, the opportunity cost of made capital engaged in logging. The market price of timber will vary depending on the quality and volume of the timber, something that can be roughly estimated from the characteristics of the forest and logging practices. Then the value of the forest can be calculated as the discounted present value of the future resource rents, using the prevailing interest rate (see Equation 6–19). The annual depletion of the forest is simply the volume of logged timber valued at the same resource rent. The annual growth of the forest can be valued in the same way as investment.

The application of this approach to fisheries, water supplies, mineral deposits, and soil fertility is straightforward. The estimation of the recreational value of an urban park is discussed in the box on page 177. But the valuation of clean air and water and other environmental amenities is not so simple. The physiological impacts of particular pollutants on human well-being are complex, indirect, and not completely understood. Many of these impacts do not have market values. And environmentalists suspect that pollution has cumulative, nonlinear effects that are not easily estimated, such as climate change due to the venting of carbon dioxide into the atmosphere (the *greenhouse effect*). Until scientists and economists understand more about the costs of environmental degradation, the valuation of natural capital is likely to be confined to marketable resources like fish, timber, minerals, and water supplies.

A Concept of Sustainability

If an economy consumes natural capital in producing current income, then the economy's capacity to generate income will decline in the future unless the natural capital is replaced. For the moment, consider a constant population. A test for a sustainable economy is its capacity to maintain consumption at a constant level indefinitely. To achieve this, the depletion of natural capital must be replaced by made capital, technological change must be generated to increase the productivity of all capital and labor, or both must be done. This suggests an alternative, if partial, criterion for sustainability: the maintenance of the total stock of capital, both natural and made.[31] The depletion of natural capital must be compensated for by net investment in made capital.

Thus sustainability can involve the depletion of natural resources and the eventual decline of farming, fishing, forestry, mining, petroleum, and other sectors dependent on natural resources. As these industries decline, others grow: manufacturing, utilities, construction, finance, transportation, telecommunications, trade, health, education, and other services. Indeed, this transformation is what most people have in mind when they speak of development. When an economy develops from a natural resource base, it is the net benefits or rents from the primary sectors that provide much of the finance for secondary and tertiary industries. And some of the finance may go into research and development of new technologies that will increase productivity.

One other kind of transformation should be noted. In countries almost entirely dependent on natural resources for income, such as oil exporters Kuwait and Brunei, there is little scope for transforming resource rents into other productive

31. Human capital could be included in this criterion.

capital within the economy. Instead, these countries invest their resource rents in bonds and stocks in the international capital markets or even in the industries of other countries. Brunei, for example, has invested in cattle ranching in Australia and hotels in the United States. As the oil runs out, these countries begin increasingly to live off their investments. They become *rentier* economies, another path to sustainability.

The transformation to made capital does not justify the wanton use of resources. Resources should be exploited efficiently, in ways described earlier in this chapter. The substitution of made capital for natural capital may not be productive or even possible forever. Natural resources are also used in manufacturing and services, as raw materials, fuels, and waste sinks. Unless technology continues to reduce this dependence on raw materials, it is possible that a country, or even the planet, may run out of needed resources. Further, if population is growing and if a society wants its income per capita to grow as well, then it becomes necessary to invest more than resource rents in order to continuously increase the total capital stock. Within these limits, however, some societies may choose to accelerate resource depletion in favor of investment in other industries and can do it sustainably if resource rents are invested productively.

Resources and National Income

The concept of sustainability as the transformation of natural into made capital can be reflected in the national accounts. Chapter 3 defined **gross national (or domestic) product** (GNP or GDP) as the sum of value added in the production of finished goods and services in an economy. GNP is *gross* because it makes no allowance for the depreciation or consumption of capital. Another income measure, **net national product** (NNP), is equal to GNP less the depreciation of made capital (D_m):

$$\text{NNP} = \text{GNP} - D_m. \qquad [7\text{–}1]$$

Net national product is an appropriate measure of the resources available for consumption once allowance has been made for the consumption of capital. Because GNP consists of consumption (C) and national saving (S),

$$\text{NNP} = C + S - D_m. \qquad [7\text{–}2]$$

As long as saving equals or exceeds depreciation, consumption is less than net product and can be sustained indefinitely. In effect, the stock of capital together with labor produces NNP each year; if enough is saved to replace the worn-out capital, production is sustainable.

Once there is a measure of the stock of natural capital, its annual depletion (D_n) can be estimated and included in net product. The result has been called **adjusted net national product** (ANNP):

$$\text{ANNP} = \text{GNP} - D_m - D_n = C + S - D_m - D_n. \qquad [7\text{–}3]$$

This corrected definition of net product has the same implication as NNP. If enough is saved each year to cover the depreciation of both made and natural capital, the economy can sustain its level of consumption.

Estimates of ANNP and of net saving are given in Table 7–1 for several resource-rich countries. Note the high estimated rates of resource depletion (D_n) for

TABLE 7–1 Adjusted Net National Income

Country	GNP	S	D_m	D_n	Net S	ANNP
Costa Rica	100	21	3	8	+12	89
Indonesia	100	30	5	17	+8	78
Brazil	100	21	7	10	+4	83
Philippines	100	18	11	4	+3	85
Nigeria	100	23	3	17	+3	80
Mexico	100	17	12	12	−7	76
Malawi	100	2	7	4	−9	89

Sources: Saving rates (S), *World Development Report 1994,* Table 9 (for 1992); and depreciation of made and natural capital (D_m and D_n), David Pearce and Giles Atkinson, "Measuring Sustainable Development," unpublished paper, 1993 (year of estimate unspecified).

Indonesia and Nigeria which were, however, more than balanced by high saving rates. Measurement of natural capital depletion is still experimental and these estimates should be considered highly approximate. Even the standard depreciation of made capital (D_m) is estimated only approximately, if at all, for most developing countries. Partly for that reason, neither NNP nor ANNP have been used much in official estimates and they have hardly affected policy discussions. Yet even rough allowances for natural depletion would be an improvement on current estimates of national product and should lead to better policy.[32] The United Nations and the World Bank are, however, encouraging countries to begin keeping resource and environmental accounts as satellites to their standard national income accounts.[33] As more experience is gained, resource and environmental accounting may become an integral part of the standard national income accounts of many countries.

Sustainable Development in Malaysia[34]

Malaysia has used its rich natural resource base—oil, tin, timber, and fertile tropical land—to transform its economy and generate rapid growth in per capita income, averaging 3 percent a year from 1965 to 1990. Has it done so sustainably? To find out, Harvard economist Jeffrey Vincent estimated natural resource depletion for three parts of the country: the Malay Peninsula, on mainland Asia, and Sabah and Sarawak, two timber-rich Malaysian states on the nearby island of Borneo. In Peninsular Malaysia, with a diverse resource base and rapidly growing industry, adjusted net domestic product (ANDP) has equaled or exceeded consumption in every year from 1970 to 1990. That had also been the pattern in the outlying

32. The omission of natural capital depletion is not the only important fault with standard national accounts. Among others, failure to include the services provided by unpaid housewives and children causes underestimates of gross income similar in size to the overestimates of net income from the omission of natural depletion.

33. See the collection by Ernst Lutz (ed.), *Toward Improved Accounting for the Environment* (Washington, D.C.: World Bank, 1993).

34. From Jeffrey Vincent and Rozali bin Mohamed Ali, *Natural Resources, Environment, and Development in Malaysia: An Economic Perspective*, unpublished manuscript, 1994, Chap. 2, and Vincent and Yusuf Hadi, "Deforestation and Agricultural Expansion in Peninsular Malaysia," Harvard Institute for International Development, Development Discussion Paper No. 396, September 1991.

state of Sarawak until the late 1980s, when the situation reversed. Sabah, however, has been consuming unsustainably for the entire 20-year period; from 1970 to 1980 ANDP was only about half of consumption, which declined over those 10 years. Peninsular Malaysia was making a highly successful transformation while Sabah was in effect consuming its rainforest.

The development of Peninsular Malaysia shows how resource use and industrialization can interact to generate sustainable growth. The expansion of plantations in rubber (during the first 60 years of the century) and oil palm (in the 1960s and 1980s) caused rapid rates of deforestation, felling most of Malaysia's original, species-rich lowland forest, but leaving about half the country's forest, mostly on hillsides. Rubber and palm oil exports were profitable to the private growers and earned positive returns to the economy and contributed importantly to its growth. Government policies and structural change in the economy combined eventually to end deforestation. Property rights to plantation land were secure; government invested in infrastructure and promoted crop research, which was financed by charges to the growers; and it avoided subsidies that would have encouraged overexpansion of plantations. Consequently, after 1980 growers had incentives to invest in the intensification of production on existing land, rather than to further expand the area under cultivation.

Growing plantation exports supported investment in economic diversification. Rapid, export-oriented industrialization was encouraged by open market policies akin to those described in Chapter 5, expanding employment opportunities at rising wages. Industrialization led to the migration of workers from rural to urban areas, raising rural wages and further encouraging intensification of agriculture. In textbook fashion, natural capital had been converted into made capital that fueled Malaysia's continuing development, while setting in motion forces that eventually limited the further depletion of natural resources.

Global Sustainability

Is economic development sustainable? For any one country, given appropriate economic and resource policies, the answer is "yes," because any single, well-managed country can draw on resources, saving, and technology from other countries. The answer becomes less certain when the whole planet is considered. Scientists are developing complex models to predict whether our economies will exhaust the earth's minerals, soils, forests, and fisheries or cause irreversible damage to the environment, including changes in climate. But the existing models give uncertain, sometimes unstable, and often conflicting results. In this state of uncertain scientific knowledge, what are the biases for gloom and for hope?

Malthusian Views

In the early nineteenth century, the famous English demographer Thomas Malthus predicted that growing populations would exhaust the earth's capacity to produce food, until rising death rates and falling birth rates would harshly keep populations in check.[35] Malthusian ideas remain influential in the late twentieth century, although the focus has shifted from land and agriculture to all natural resources and the global environment.

The heart of the Malthusian view is the notion that the demand for natural resources is based on the exponential growth of both populations and incomes, while the supply of resources is either absolutely limited or can increase only linearly. No matter how slow the growth rate, any exponentially expanding demand must eventually overwhelm any fixed or linearly increasing supply, as shown in Figure 7–7. Historically, human societies have been able to avoid the Malthusian trap in three ways. First, science and technology have moved fast enough to increase the productivity of land and other natural resources. Second, when resources became scarce, such as wood in England in the seventeenth century or coal in the nineteenth, substitutes (coal, then petroleum) were found. Third, people have chosen to reduce family size and thus population growth.

The question is whether these processes can continue indefinitely to avoid Malthusian scarcity. Though world population growth is slowing, it remains high enough to expect a doubling of the world's population by the middle of the next century.[36] As development proceeds, especially in populous Asia and in Latin America, a rising share of this expanding population will aspire to the consumption standards of the northern middle class, which suggests more intensive consumption of resources and pollution of the environment. As nonrenewable fuels run out and the environment becomes saturated with waste, alternative sources of materials or new technologies may be substantially more costly than current ones, and so growth may be slowed. And, if the impacts of resource depletion and pol-

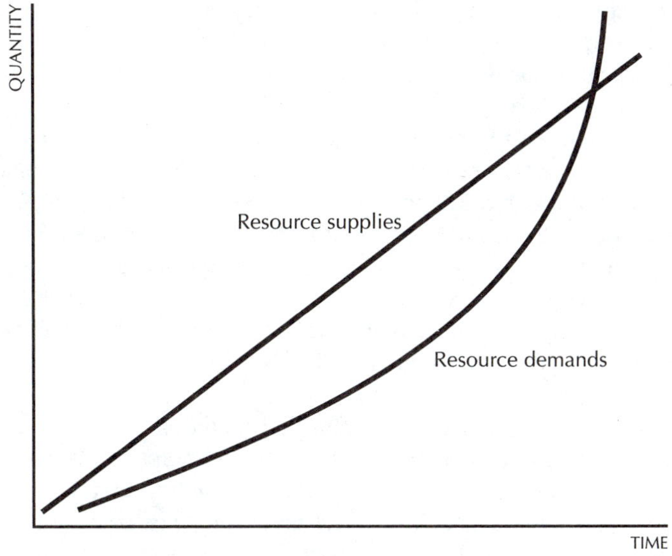

FIGURE 7–7 Global Resource Balance. The Malthusian view is that resource supplies rise at a linear rate, at best, while demand rises exponentially. If so, demand must eventually exceed supply.

35. Malthus is discussed in Chapter 8.
36. *World Development Report 1992,* p. 26.

lution accelerate and become irreversible, it may be beyond the capabilities of humans to develop new technologies fast enough to compensate.[37]

Neoclassical Views

The basis for optimism lies in both history and economics. Human societies have in fact been able to evade the Malthusian trap. The hopeful interpretation of this experience comes from neoclassical economists, who argue that the growing resource scarcity has itself been the main inducement to changes in behavior and technology. As one country or the entire earth runs out of resources such as wood and then petroleum for fuel or supplies of fresh water or clean air, either the market price of these resources rises or, in the case of unpriced amenities, the cost of using them increases. Higher costs, which are often anticipated, become a signal for several changes that ameliorate the growing resource scarcity.

Rising costs of fuels and raw materials make it profitable to search for new deposits and to exploit less-accessible deposits with higher extraction costs. The fuel crisis of the 1970s led to new finds of oil and natural gas deposits: proven reserves rose from 50 billion tons of oil equivalent in 1950 to over 250 billion tons in 1990, despite consumption of 100 billion tons during those 40 years. Estimates of ultimately recoverable reserves are 600 times current rates of usage.[38] Higher costs also mean greater rewards from research into new technologies that increase the productivity of waning resources or make it cheaper to use alternative materials. Even if the costs of using alternatives cannot be reduced, substitutes may become economic as the prices of exhaustible resources go up. Solar energy is technically feasible today but too expensive. If fuel deposits become more expensive to tap, solar energy would be relatively more attractive even at current costs, and more research would be undertaken to reduce these costs. It is estimated that solar energy is already competitive with the use of natural gas for generating electricity during peak loads and that, on current trends, it could become competitive with fuel oil for base load generation by 2020.[39]

Increased scarcity also forces users to conserve. World energy consumption fell substantially as a result of the oil crises of 1973 to 1980. In 1971 a dollar of world GNP required more than a kilogram of energy (in oil equivalents); by 1992 the same output could be produced by a third of a kilogram.[40] Much of the decline was due to improved technologies, such as improvements in automobile engines, that reduced fuel consumption without any reduction in output or changes in consumers' behavior. In the United States, the stock of cars in 1973 averaged 13 miles per gallon of gasoline; by the mid-1980s average mileage had almost doubled.

As with resource use, so with environmental pollution. Even though many environmental amenities are not marketed, pollution entails costs that are felt by producers and consumers. Some of these work through the market, for example, as land values fall in polluted areas. Others may have to be artificially imposed by government policies, of the kinds discussed in this chapter, that impose external

37. These views are discussed by Edward B. Barbier, *Economics, Natural-Resource Scarcity and Development* (London: Earthscan Publications Ltd., 1989).

38. *World Development Report 1992,* p. 115.

39. Ibid., p. 123.

40. *World Development Report 1994,* p. 171.

costs on producers or consumers. As these costs are felt, the demand rises for new technologies or for behavioral changes that reduce pollution. Gas scrubbers seemed to be a costly imposition on industry at first, but they have become economic and less costly as societies become willing to pay for cleaner air.

None of this guarantees that the resource barriers, cumulative effects, and irreversibilities emphasized by Malthusian views can be overcome. Perhaps the economic behavioral and technological mechanisms of the past will be swamped by global resource exhaustion. But predictions of exhaustion that ignore proven adaptive mechanisms are just as likely to be wrong as predictions of sustainable growth that ignore possible irreversibilities. And the cost of acting on wrong predictions, in either direction, can be large.

From an economics perspective, the soundest strategy for global sustainability would be to move quickly toward more effective markets, including property rights, marketable permits, and taxes, so that real resource scarcities will be reflected in the prices people pay for all commodities and services. An end to subsidies on fuels, fertilizers, pesticides, water, timber, land clearing, and other destructive uses of resources would be a major step toward sustainability. Most countries are far from this ideal market environment and can reduce resource wastage without jeopardizing economic growth.[41] While this is happening, we need to invest in better scientific observations and models to see how close humankind really is to exhausting the earth.

Poverty and the Environment

The two major threats to the earth's capacity to sustain living standards are seen to be growing populations, especially of poor people in developing countries, and rising consumption standards, especially of the expanding middle class. The middle class, wherever it prospers, not only consumes more resources, but eventually wants, and exerts political pressure to get, a cleaner and more sustainable environment. Whether these opposing tendencies are balanced enough to promote sustainability remains to be seen.

What about the poor? Asian, African, and Latin American farmers and migrants use slash-and-burn techniques to clear land for farming; African herders graze their livestock on deteriorating common land; poor, rural households throughout the developing world encroach on the forest to obtain wood for charcoal, their most common fuel; local fishermen in Africa deplete inland fisheries; and the rivers of densely populated Asia are used simultaneously as common sewers and sources of water. The poor have little margin for subsistence. Struggling to survive today, they heavily discount the future and choose consumption over conservation. In countries where the majority of people are poor enough to exert such pressure on the environment, it is both infeasible and unfair to regulate and tax the access of the poor to common resources. Development itself is then seen as a solution to resource degradation: as incomes rise, the poor will move away from the margin of subsistence and open opportunities for more sustainable resource use.[42]

Although there is considerable truth to this view of poverty and resource use, it

41. These ideas are developed in Panayotou, *Green Markets.*

42. See, for example, World Commission on Environment and Development (the Brundtland Commission), *Our Common Future* (New York: Oxford University Press, 1987), pp. 3, 28, and *World Development Report 1992,* pp. 23, 30.

is not the whole story. The poor are also victims of resource degradation and have a stake in efficient resource use. Land in central Kenya is exquisitely planted to derive the maximum output from small plots, farmers of arid land in Sudan have developed techniques to make the most of the occasional rainfall, and complex irrigation systems are effectively managed by small farmers in Indonesia. Photographs from the semiarid Machakos District of Kenya show evidence of better soil conservation and more trees today than in the 1920s.[43] Small, poor farmers in the Philippines have organized to prevent the destructive logging of nearby rainforest. The murder of Chico Menendez, who organized local rubber tappers to protect the Amazon from commercial exploitation, made headlines everywhere. Greenbelt and other grassroots organizations have sprung up in Africa and Asia to protect the environment.[44]

Although extreme poverty undoubtedly makes resource conservation more difficult, the principles of resource policy seem as applicable to poor producers and consumers as to rich ones. Where poor farmers, foresters, or fishermen are invested with secure property rights, they will act in their own interest to use resources sustainably. Where poor nomads, migrants, and the landless have no properties to protect, they are more likely to degrade the environment.

Rich Nations and Poor Nations

Today the industrial countries are pressing for global action for sustainable resource use. The developing countries, with more untapped resources, higher discount rates, and greater pressures for rapid economic growth, resist. Industrial countries would like to preserve tropical rainforests for their many environmental amenities and productive uses. The tropical countries see timber as an important export of growing value and forest land as an opportunity for agricultural expansion. Northern countries are concerned about global warming, produced mainly by the burning of fossil fuels. Southern countries wonder why they, at lower incomes, have to slow development to help compensate for a problem caused, until now, mainly by industrial growth in the North. China wants to use its abundant coal to fuel rapid income growth for a fifth of the world's population, a vanguard of which is already moving into middle-class consumption patterns. Environmentalists in Europe and North America shudder at the idea of so much production and consumption growth fueled by the most-polluting source of energy in the world.

Thus the North places a high value on resource and environmental sustainability, while the South is more concerned about rapid economic growth. These are the conditions for a bargain. Industrial countries should be willing to help finance programs to preserve resources and the environment and permit developing countries to invest in growth. Debt-for-nature swaps, in which environmental groups from rich countries have paid off poor countries' debts in return for the protection of natural habitats, have been one popular example of such bargains. National and multilateral aid agencies condition their assistance on the kinds of market reforms

43. Mary Tiffen and Michael Mortimore, "Malthus Controverted: The Role of Capital and Technology in Growth and Environment Recovery in Kenya," *World Development,* 22, no. 7 (July 1994), 997–1010.

44. Robin Broad, "The Poor and the Environment: Friends or Foes?" *World Development*, 22, no. 6 (June 1994, 811–22).

that promote more efficient resource use, but they could do this in a more focused way. They are also taking more explicit care about the environmental impacts of large projects. Industrial countries might finance the use of new technologies that use resources more efficiently and reduce industrial effluents.[45]

The sustainability of global development may thus require a transfer of financial and made capital from the industrial to the developing countries in return for the preservation of natural capital in the South, which will also benefit the North. The measure of the North's sincerity in promoting efficient global resource use will be its willingness to make these transfers. But increased efficiency and greater sustainability in resource and environmental management will be beneficial to the developing countries themselves and should be undertaken whether or not a bargain can be struck.

45. Theodore Panayotou, "Financing Mechanisms for Agenda 21," Harvard Institute for International Development, 1994.

PART 3

Human Resources

8

Population

The chapters in Part 2 deal with the human factor in economic development. People play a dual role in the development process: on the one hand they are its ultimate beneficiaries; on the other they provide the most important input into the process of production growth and transformation that is called "economic development."

In view of this dual role, what attitude should one take toward the growth of population at the family, national, and global level? Should population growth be limited on the ground that it creates more mouths to feed and bodies to clothe, frequently in households and societies that are having trouble feeding the mouths and clothing the bodies that they already have? World population projections and estimates of natural resource availability can make frightening reading. Yet each new individual can also bring additional labor power and, even more important, additional human spark and creativity to help solve the many problems that society faces. The argument for some form of population limitation is strong, but agreement is not universal, and there are important social, political, and moral issues to be weighed.

The decision of how many children to have is an intimately personal one. Traditionally, it has been left to the choice of the couple involved, but all societies condition these individual decisions in many ways. Arguments for conscious policy intervention to limit population growth depend either on the rationale that couples do not know how to achieve their desired family size or find it too expensive to do so, and thus must be helped to achieve it, or alternatively on the belief that individual reproductive choices impose excessive social costs at the national or international level. A few governments have intervened to *promote* reproduction; they have argued that the national interest requires that more children be born than people would have if left on their own. Arguments *against* intervention in reproductive decision making may appeal either to the value of freedom for the individual or to the supposed advantages of a larger population for a nation or social group.

The view of humans as an economic resource has quantitative and qualitative dimensions. In the past, economic theory often emphasized the quantitative aspect while downplaying or ignoring the qualitative aspect. Many economic models assumed that labor is homogeneous (undifferentiated) and thus can be measured satisfactorily by counting bodies or hours or days of work. Other models made only a broad distinction between skilled and unskilled labor. Few took account of the importance of gender. Such models, although useful for revealing particular truths, are extreme simplifications, since the study of economic development clearly demonstrates that the qualitative aspects of the human contribution to production are at least as important as the quantitative aspects.

In the past thirty years, however, interest in the quality of human resources as a contributor to economic growth has increased. Development specialists now talk about "developing human resources" or "investing in human capital." The analogy to natural resources and physical capital is appropriate in many ways. But it should not be taken to imply that the nature of "human resources" and their contribution to production are as fully understood as the contributions of a lathe, a road, or a ton of bauxite. The role of human resources is far more complex and mysterious than any of these. To what extent, and in what ways, human resources can be created through an investmentlike process are questions to be addressed in Chapters 9 to 11. This chapter lays a foundation for the later discussion by reviewing some of what is known about population and development.

DEMOGRAPHIC MEASURES

Demography, the study of population, has its own specialized vocabulary. The **birth rate,** also called the **crude birth rate,** is births per thousand of population. Similarly, the (**crude**) **death rate** is deaths per thousand of population. The **rate of natural increase** is the difference between the birth rate and the death rate, but it is conventionally measured in percentage terms (per hundred rather than per thousand). Say a developing country has a population of 10 million at the start of a given year. During that year it experiences 400,000 births and 150,000 deaths. If net international migration is zero (that is, if the number of immigrants equals the number of emigrants), its population at the end of the year will be 10,250,000. The midyear or average population is used to calculate the birth rate, death rate, and rate of natural increase, which in this case turn out to be 39.5, 14.8, and 2.47 respectively.

The growth potential of a population can be expressed through its **doubling time.** For a population rising at a constant rate, doubling time is approximately 70 divided by the growth rate. Thus growth at 1 percent a year doubles the population in about 70 years, while steady 2 percent annual growth doubles it in just 35 years and 3 percent growth in 23 years and a few months.[1]

Crude birth and death rates reflect the interaction between the *age structure* of a population and its *age-specific fertility and death rates*. Comparisons of crude birth and death rates across populations with different **age structures** (different shares of various age groups in the total population) can be misleading. For example, some LDCs have crude death rates as low as those in the developed countries, yet more people die each year in all age groups in these LDCs. The reason is that LDC populations are much younger on average and emphasize age groups (older children and youth) in which death rates are low.

Thus for some purposes it is important to use age-specific demographic rates. One such rate, the **infant death rate,** differs sharply between rich and poor countries. It is defined as deaths in the first year of life per thousand live births. Thus if 40,000 of the 400,000 babies born in our hypothetical country die before reaching their first birthdays, the infant death rate is 100. Similar age-specific death rates can be calculated for other age groups, using mean population in the age group as a base.

Life expectancy is the number of additional years that the average person of a given age will live if age-specific death rates remain constant. It is a purer measure of mortality than the crude death rate because it is unaffected by the age distribution of the population. **Life expectancy at birth** is the most frequently used version of this measure.

The **fertility** of a population refers to its propensity to have children. An **age-specific fertility rate** is the average number of children born each year to women in a particular age group. The **total fertility rate** is the sum of the age-specific fertility rates applying to a particular group (cohort) of women as they move through their reproductive years. In other words, it is the number of children the average woman will have in her lifetime if age-specific fertility rates remain constant.

A Brief History of Human Population

Concern is frequently expressed over high rates of population growth and rising population densities in places such as Egypt, Mexico, and Bangladesh. But rising population densities are a very old story. For years people have been saying, "This cannot continue"; yet it does. How do current demographic trends fit into the history of human experience?

1. The formula for exponential growth is

$$P_t = P_0 e^{rt}$$

where P_0 = population in the base year, P_t = population t years later, e = the base of the natural logarithm (2.7183), and r = the annual growth rate. If $P_t = 2P_0$, then

$$2P_0 = P_0 e^{rt}$$
$$2 = e^{rt}.$$

It turns out that $2 = e^{.7}$ (approximately). This means that rt, the product of the growth rate (expressed as a decimal) and the number of years, must equal 0.7. At 2 percent annual growth, for example, $0.02 \times 35 = 0.7$.

World population has been growing more or less continuously since the appearance of life on earth, but the rate of growth was accelerating from 200 years ago until very recently. Four eras of demographic history can be distinguished.[2]

The Preagricultural Era For perhaps half a million years, humans lived a precarious existence as hunters, gatherers, and sometimes cannibals. Population density (the number of people per square kilometer) was necessarily very low, since a given population required a vast extent of land to sustain itself. The birth rate was probably high, but the death rate was nearly as high and the rate of natural increase was very low. When this unimaginably long era ended with the introduction of settled agriculture about 12,000 years ago, the world's population was perhaps no more than 100 million.

From Settled Agriculture to the Industrial Revolution The introduction of settled agriculture revolutionized the earth's capacity to sustain human life. During the years leading up to the Industrial Revolution of the late eighteenth and early nineteenth centuries, the food supply grew and became more reliable. The death rate fell, life expectancy increased, and population growth gradually accelerated to around 0.5 percent a year. This growth, however, was set back at intervals by plagues, famines, and wars, any of which could wipe out as much as half the population in a given area. As late as the fourteenth century, the Black Death (bubonic plague) killed one-third of the population of Europe. Nevertheless, by 1800 the world's population was about 1.7 billion.

From the Industrial Revolution to World War II The Industrial Revolution, which marked the start of modern economic growth, further expanded the earth's population-carrying capacity. Innovations in agriculture matched innovations in industry, permitting labor to be transferred to industry while the productivity of the remaining agricultural laborers rose fast enough to feed the growing urban population. Transcontinental railroads and fast, reliable ocean shipping further boosted world food output in the late nineteenth century, making it possible to grow more basic foodstuffs in the areas best suited for this activity and get supplies to food-deficit areas quickly in emergencies. Famines decreased in frequency and severity. Food prices fell. Meanwhile, modern medicine, sanitation, and pharmaceutical production began to develop. All these factors helped to reduce the death rate. Population growth accelerated, reaching about 1 percent per annum by World War II. When this third demographic era ended in 1945, the population of the world was slightly less than 2.5 billion.

The third demographic era saw major shifts in the location of world population. Between 1846 and 1930, more than 50 million people left Europe to settle in other parts of the world. The United States received the bulk of them while smaller numbers went to Canada, Brazil, Argentina, Chile, South Africa, Australia, and New Zealand. The proportion of world population that was of European stock grew from an estimated 22 percent in 1846 to 35 percent in 1930, when the Great Depression ended mass international migration.[3] During the same period millions of laborers and merchants from densely populated India and China moved to more

2. Based on Lester R. Brown, *In the Human Interest* (New York: Norton, 1974), pp. 20–21; for an informative and enjoyable longer presentation, see Carlo Cipolla, *The Economic History of World Population* (7th ed.; New York: Barnes & Noble, 1978).

3. For discussion, see Cipolla, *Economic History.*

sparsely settled areas in Southeast Asia, Africa, the South Pacific, and elsewhere. The existence of colonial empires facilitated this movement.

The Post-World War II Period After the war there were further dramatic improvements in food supply and disease control. Techniques introduced in the developed countries during the preceding era spread throughout the globe. People became more aware of famines and epidemics in "remote" parts of the world and less willing to tolerate them. The result was a veritable revolution in death rates and life expectancy. Plummeting death rates in many areas raised rates of natural increase to 2 or even 3 percent. As its doubling time shortened drastically, world population passed 5 billion in 1987 and now exceeds 5.5 billion.

It appears that this fourth demographic era, with its dramatic acceleration of population growth, will be short-lived. Population growth is slowing down in most parts of the world as many developing countries follow the industrial countries in a **demographic transition**. Initially, countries experiencing this transition have high birth and death rates. Then they experience a fall in the death rate, which raises the rate of natural increase. Some years later, this is followed by a drop in the birth rate, which cuts natural increase to around 1 percent. The demographic transition as it occurred in England and Wales is depicted in Figure 8–1.

Some of the developing countries that experienced their own demographic transitions have seen far more rapid change than occurred in England and Wales. Shortly after World War II, for reasons discussed in Chapter 11, death rates started

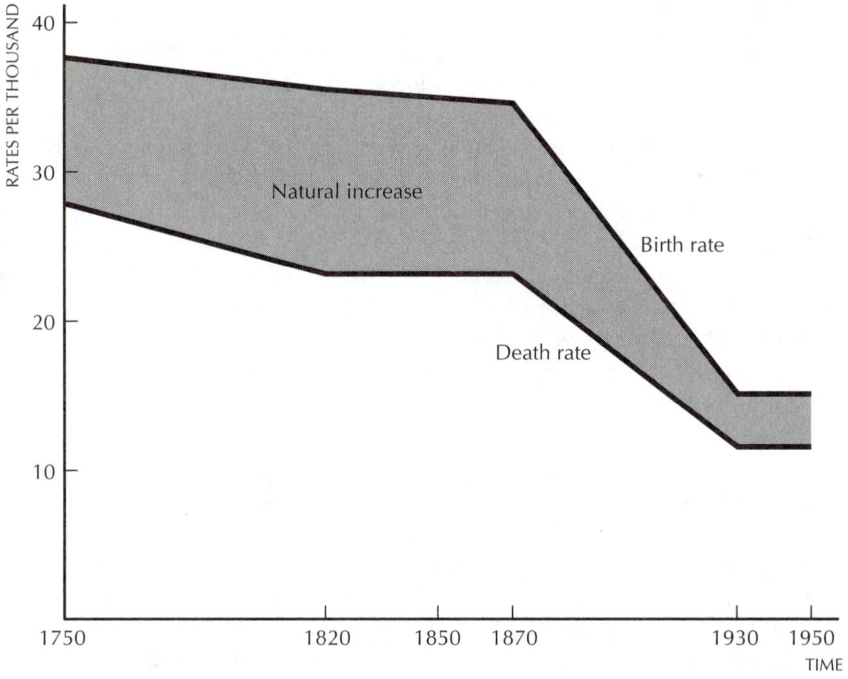

FIGURE 8–1 The Demographic Transition in England and Wales, 1750–1950. The decline in the death rate preceded the decline in the birth rate; this created a period of fairly rapid (about 1 percent per annum) natural increase in the late eighteenth and early nineteenth centuries. After 1870 the birth rate fell more rapidly; this sharply reduced the rate of natural increase. *Source:* Cipolla, *The Economic History of World Population.*

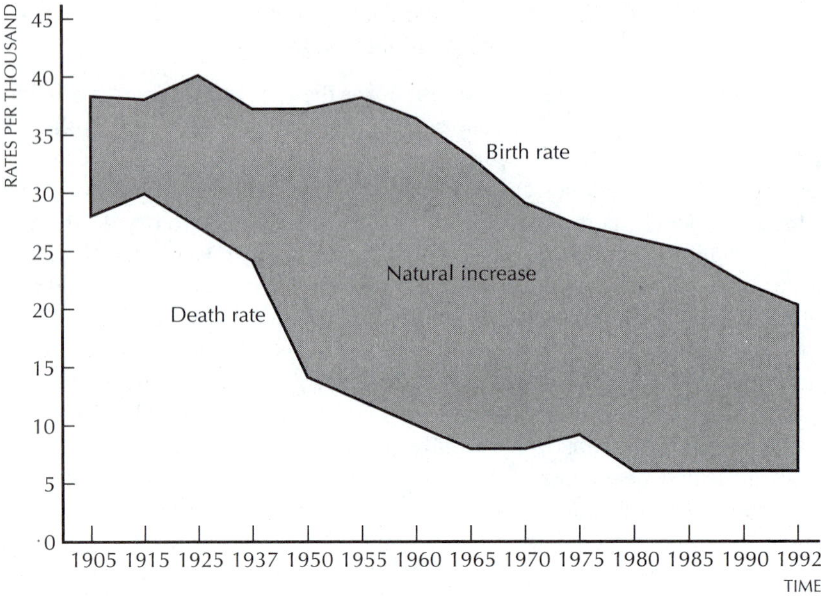

FIGURE 8–2 **The Demographic Transition of Ceylon (Sri Lanka).** The death rate fell very sharply after 1920 but the birth rate remained high until about 1960. Very high rates of natural increase were experienced in the 1950s and 1960s. Later, however, the crude death rate bottomed out as the population aged, and permitted the continuing birth rate decline to bring down the rate of natural increase.

to fall almost everywhere. In the developing countries, the mortality decline began at much lower levels of per capita income and fell much faster than it had earlier in the developed countries. An example is given in Figure 8–2 (drawn to the same vertical scale as Figure 8–1), which depicts the demographic experience of Ceylon (now Sri Lanka) during the twentieth century. These early and sharp death rate declines, which by now have been achieved for practically the entire population of the world, were not always followed by such rapid decline in the birth rate as occurred in Sri Lanka after 1955. But as time goes by, it is becoming increasingly evident that the phenomenon of falling birth rates is widespread. A "new demographic transition" has become visible in most of the developing world, although it will probably continue to differ in important ways from the classic demographic transition experienced earlier by the developed countries.

THE PRESENT DEMOGRAPHIC SITUATION

Although recent data provide strong evidence that fertility is now falling almost everywhere (see Table 8–1), rates of decline differ greatly among countries and regions. Western Europe and North America have completed the demographic transition and now have crude birth rates below 20 and rates of natural increase well under 1 percent. Their aging populations and low total fertility rates suggest that natural increase will contribute little if anything to their future population growth.[4] In several developed countries current fertility is already too low to re-

4. But demographic behavior does sometimes surprise the experts. They were confounded, for example, by the post-World War II "baby boom" in the United States.

TABLE 8–1 **Changes in Total Fertility Rate by Region and Level of GDP per Capita (PPP), 1970–2000**

	1970 (Actual)	1992 (Actual)	2000 (Projected)
Region			
Sub-Saharan Africa	6.6	6.1	5.6
Asia & Pacific	5.7	2.9	2.5
Eastern Europe & Central Asia	3.0	2.2	2.0
Western Europe	2.7	1.8	1.7
Middle East & North Africa	6.9	5.0	4.1
U.S. & Canada	2.5	2.1	2.1
Latin America & Caribbean	5.3	3.1	2.5
Income Group			
Below $1,000	6.3	6.3	6.0
$1,000–4,000	5.9 (6.2)	3.3 (4.4)	2.9 (3.7)
$4,000–6,000	4.6	3.0	2.6
$6,000–10,000	3.7	2.4	2.1
Above $10,000	2.5	1.8	1.8
World	5.1	3.1	2.8

Note: Figures in parentheses exclude China and India.
Source: World Development Report 1994, pp. 212–13.

place the existing population.[5] Zero population growth (ZPG), promoted by some as a desirable target in view of limitations on natural resources, may soon be a reality in the industrialized countries.

The great majority of developing countries now show unmistakable signs of fertility decline.[6] Among countries with GDP per capita of $1,000 or more (PPP) in 1992, all but a few had undergone a fall in the total fertility rate by 1992. Experience among those poorest countries that lie below this income level was more mixed, but most of them are expected to join the movement toward lower fertility in the period 1992 to 2000.

Although nearly everyone is thus joining the movement to lower fertility, rates of fertility decline vary considerably across regions. The drop has been fastest in Asia, which by no coincidence has also seen the most rapid economic growth. Asian women now have fewer than three children on average, and women in Latin America and the Caribbean are only slightly more fertile (Table 8–1). While women in sub-Saharan Africa still have six children on average, and those in the Middle East and North Africa five, even they have participated in the birth rate decline. Only the very poorest countries,[7] most of which are located in sub-Saharan Africa, still have birth rates of 40 or more (Table 8–2). Crude death rates in these countries, although higher than those in richer countries, have fallen in re-

5. Clearly, women must have at least two children each during their childbearing years for the population to replace itself. Allowing for infant and child mortality, the replacement level of total fertility is around 2.1. In 1992, 18 developed countries (out of 24 for which data were available) had TFRs below 2.1 while another 3 were right at the replacement fertility level. An additional 14 countries not yet considered developed also had less than replacement fertility; most of these were located in Eastern Europe. *World Development Report 1994,* p. 233.

6. The data are summarized in Table 8–1 and presented country by country in the *World Development Report 1994,* pp. 212–13.

7. Those with GDP per capita (PPP) of less than $1,000 in 1992.

TABLE 8–2 Demographic Characteristics of Countries by Region and Level of GDP per Capita (PPP), 1992

	Crude birth rate (per 1000)	Crude death rate (per 1000)	Rate of natural increase (%)	Infant death rate (per 1000 live births)
Region				
Sub-Saharan Africa	44	15	2.9	99
Asia & Pacific	25	9	1.6	52
Eastern Europe & Central Asia	16	11	0.5	22
Western Europe	14	10	0.4	13
Middle East & North Africa	34	8	2.6	58
U.S. & Canada	16	9	0.7	9
Latin America & Caribbean	26	7	1.9	44
Income Group				
Below $1,000	45	16	2.8	112
$1,000–4,000	27 (33)	9 (10)	1.7 (2.3)	58 (70)
$4,000–6,000	23	8	1.5	40
$6,000–10,000	19	9	1.0	23
Above $10,000	14	9	0.5	8
World	25	9	1.5	60

Note: Figures in parentheses exclude China and India.
Source: World Development Report 1994, pp. 212–15.

cent years and caused population growth to approach three percent.[8] Even a slightly higher income level produces a better situation, however, as Table 8–1 shows. In countries with $1,000 to $4,000 per capita (PPP),[9] women now have only three or four babies in their lifetimes (versus six or more on average as recently as 1970) and the rate of population growth is around 2 percent.

These widespread fertility declines are causing world population growth to slow down. As Table 8–2 shows, world population grew at a rate of 1.5 percent in 1992, an average which masks large differences in regional population growth rates. These regional differences are altering the global population distribution (Table 8–3). 85 percent of humanity lives in developing countries. Nearly 60 percent lives in low-income countries, and 56 percent lives in Asia. Only 10 percent are sub-Saharan Africans, but this share will rise sharply in the future. As these population-share figures indicate, further reductions in world population growth depend heavily on demographic behavior in the developing countries.

Table 8–2 reveals some demographic characteristics of countries at different levels of GNP per capita. With only a few aberrations, such as those caused by the atypically low birth rates of India and China, birth rates decline steadily as one moves up the income scale from the poorest countries, with per capita incomes below $1,000 (PPP), to the richest, with annual incomes of $10,000 or more. Death rates, however, are sensitive to per capita income only below $1,000 per capita; almost all countries above that level now have relatively low death rates. The highest rates of natural increase are now in the low-income countries. (Formerly, the middle-income countries had the highest rates, but their birth rates

8. Whether the AIDS epidemic, which is severe in parts of Africa, could materially increase the overall death rate and thus significantly reduce the rate of population growth rate is a matter of current debate.

9. Those with GDP per capita (PPP) of $1,000 to $4,000 in 1992.

TABLE 8–3 World Population by Region and Development Category, 1992

	Total Population			
	Number (millions)	% of total	Population density (per square km)	Annual growth rate 1980–1992 (%)
Region				
Sub-Saharan Africa	543	10	22	3.0
Asia & Pacific	3042	56	102	1.8
Eastern Europe & Central Asia	416	8	18	0.7
Western Europe	440	8	91	0.6
Middle East & North Africa	261	5	24	3.2
U.S. & Canada	283	5	15	1.0
Latin America & Caribbean	454	8	22	2.0
Development category				
Developing countries	4611	85	45	1.9
Low-income countries	3192	59	82	2.0
Middle-income countries	1414	26	23	1.8
High-income countries	828	15	26	0.7
World total	5439	100	41	1.7

have now fallen enough to cut down their rates of natural increase.) The infant death rate is a particularly sensitive measure of death rate decline; it falls by 94 percent from the poorest group of countries in Table 8–2 to the richest group. Table 8–4 gives similar information for selected countries and thus provides some idea of the range of intercountry variation.

The high birth rates still found in most low-income countries give them populations in which children make up large shares of the total—44 percent on average in the poorest countries, versus only 21 percent in high-income countries (see Table 8–5). Elderly people are a more significant (and growing) component of the

TABLE 8–4 Demographic Characteristics of Selected Developing Countries, 1992

	Crude birth rate (per 1000)	Crude death rate (per 1000)	Rate of natural increase (%)	Total fertility rate	Infant death rate (per 1000 live births)
Latin America					
Bolivia	36	10	2.6	4.7	82
Brazil	23	7	1.6	2.8	57
Chile	23	7	1.6	2.7	17
Colombia	24	6	1.8	2.7	21
Peru	27	7	2.0	3.3	52
Africa					
Ghana	41	12	2.9	6.1	81
Kenya	37	10	2.7	5.4	66
Tanzania	45	15	3.0	6.3	92
Asia					
China	19	8	1.1	2.0	31
India	29	10	1.9	3.7	79
Indonesia	25	10	1.5	2.9	66
South Korea	16	6	1.0	1.8	13
Malaysia	28	5	2.3	3.5	14
Pakistan	40	10	3.0	5.6	95
Sri Lanka	21	6	1.5	2.5	18

TABLE 8–5 Population Characteristics of Countries by Region and Level of GDP per Capita (PPP), 1992

	Population below 15 years (% of total)*	Growth rate of urban population 1980–1992 (%)	Urban population (% of total)
Region			
Sub-Saharan Africa	44	3.7	29
Asia & Pacific	34	3.9	33
Eastern Europe & Central Asia	25	n.a.	n.a.
Western Europe	22	1.3	76
Middle East & North Africa	44	4.4	55
U.S. & Canada	22	1.2	76
Latin America & Caribbean	39	2.9	73
Income Group			
Below $1,000	44	5.4	20
$1,000–$4,000	34	4.1 (4.8)	30 (36)
$4,000–$6,000	35	3.7	62
$6,000–$10,000	31	2.9	74
Above $10,000	21	0.9	78
World	32	2.8	38

*Figures are for most recent population census, taken in various years.
Sources: United Nations, *Demographic Yearbook 1993* (New York: United Nations, 1994), and *World Development Report 1994*, pp. 222–23.

population in developed countries, although China and a few other developing countries that have rapidly depressed fertility will soon see their populations age rapidly. A country with a large share of either young or elderly population is said to have a high **dependency ratio**, or ratio of nonworking-age population (conventionally defined as 0 to 14 and 65 and over) to working-age population. A high dependency ratio depresses per capita income by requiring the output of a given number of producers to be shared among a larger number of consumers.

The spatial distribution of population is another concern in many low-income countries. **Urbanization** is a well-known concomitant of development. In low-income countries, the great majority of people live in rural areas; in middle- and high-income countries, most live in towns and cities (Table 8–5). Fears that migration from the countryside is causing urban areas to grow too fast and creating serious social problems are frequently expressed. Yet when third-world governments have tried to stanch the flow, they have enjoyed little success. The reason is that people have found they can better themselves in several ways by moving to the cities. They earn higher incomes than in the rural areas and gain access to better schooling for their children and social services of other kinds. This is what people seek in rural-urban migration, and studies have shown that by and large they find it.

This raises an important question: if rural-urban migration is good for the people who move, can it really be bad for society? It is true that there are external social costs associated with the migration process: congestion may make it harder to provide adequate urban infrastructure (housing, roads, sewers, etc.) and social services. This can be seen as a problem of **common property**. We all benefit from having fresh air to breathe, and we all lose when the air becomes polluted, but as individuals we have little incentive to avoid polluting because doing so has little

TABLE 8–6 Population Characteristics of Selected Developing Countries, 1992

	Population below 15 years (% of total)	Growth rate of urban population 1980–1992 (%)	Urban population (% of total)
Latin America			
Bolivia	41.5	4.0	52
Brazil	38.1	3.3	77
Chile	32.3	2.1	85
Colombia	36.1	2.9	71
Peru	41.2	2.9	71
Africa			
Ghana	45.0	4.3	35
Kenya	48.3	7.7	25
Tanzania	46.2	6.6	22
Asia			
China	27.7	4.3	27
India	39.5	3.1	26
Indonesia	36.5	5.1	32
South Korea	29.9	3.4	74
Malaysia	39.0	4.8	45
Pakistan	44.5	4.5	33
Sri Lanka	35.2	1.5	22

effect on the air that we ourselves breathe. Is not some form of social intervention therefore needed to limit pollution so that we all may have fresher air to breathe?

Probably, but many of the social costs of urbanization arise because governments feel obliged to provide facilities for urban populations that they do not provide for rural populations. If they choose to provide better facilities in the cities than in the villages, they can hardly complain when people avail themselves of the opportunity to get improved educational, health, and recreational services. The common perception of urbanization as a problem contains an element of class bias. Ruling elites sometimes feel threatened by rapid growth in the number of poor people who live, so to speak, within marching distance of the palace.

Some third-world governments have tried to accelerate the development of secondary towns or backward regions of the country. To the extent that these policies attempt to counteract the existing pattern of incentives affecting the location of population and economic activity, they frequently fail. To make them succeed, governments have to commit large amounts of their own resources to the backward areas in the form of infrastructure and public facilities. It would take nothing less than a radical shift in development strategy to a genuine emphasis on the intensification and diversification of the rural economy to do the job.

THE DEMOGRAPHIC FUTURE

When extrapolated into the future, even modest-seeming population growth rates soon generate projected total populations that may seem unthinkable. Continued growth at the 1.7 percent rate that prevailed in the period 1980 to 1992 would bring world population to 6.2 billion by the year 2000 and 14.5 billion by 2050.

This type of projection, beloved by popular writers, is frightening to many. It is hard to imagine life in a world with two or three times as many people as there are today. How will this expanded population live? How will the globe's finite supplies of space and natural resources be affected? Should population growth be slowed down? Can it be slowed down? These are obviously vital questions that concern everyone.

In the first place linear extrapolations of current trends are invalid because, as we have seen, after accelerating for more than two centuries world population growth is now beginning to slow down. While the demographic transition is clearly spreading to the developing countries, however, the speed of future birth rate decline remains uncertain. As Table 8–1 shows, the total fertility rate fell in all regions of the world between 1970 and 1992, and is projected by the World Bank to decline further during the remaining years of the present century. What will happen after 2000 is less clear and depends to a large degree on the rates of economic growth that poor countries are able to achieve.

Despite all these fertility declines, world population growth has not yet stopped. That it will continue for some time yet is assured by the phenomenon of **demographic momentum.** Fertility reduction does not immediately bring population growth to a halt because populations that have been growing rapidly have large numbers of people in, or about to enter, the most fertile age brackets. Even if all the world's couples were to start today having only enough children to replace themselves in the population—what is called the replacement level of fertility—growth would continue well into the next century. One projection is that the replacement level of fertility will be reached for the world as a whole around the year 2025. If so, world population will stabilize at about 10 billion near the end of the twenty-first century.[10]

The Causes of Population Growth

So world population growth will continue for at least another 100 years. The bulk of this growth will occur in the developing countries, with an increasing share in Africa. Viewpoints on this prospect vary widely, and discussions of world population often turn acrimonious. Questions of whose population is to be limited and by what means are clearly sensitive. Before we can confront such issues intelligently, we must consider what is known about both the causes and the effects of rapid population growth. In particular, a course on economic development must concern itself with the two-way relationship between the growth of population and the rise in average income levels and structural change that we term "economic development." We deal first with economic development as a cause of population growth.

Malthus and His World

The most famous and influential demographic theorist of all time was Thomas R. Malthus (1766–1834). His pessimistic view of the principles underlying human reproduction and the prospects of economic development is well known. Malthus

10. See Thomas W. Merrick, "World Population in Transition," Population Bulletin, 41, no. 2 (January 1988), 8–16.

believed that "the passion between the sexes" would cause population to expand as long and far as food supplies permitted. People would generally not limit procreation below the biological maximum. Should wages somehow rise above the subsistence level, workers would marry younger and have more children. But this situation could only be temporary. In time, the rise in population growth would create an increase in labor supply, which would press against fixed land resources and eventually, through diminishing returns, cause wages to fall back to the subsistence level. If this process went too far, famines and rising deaths would result. Malthus did not think that the growth of the food supply could stay ahead of population growth in the long run. In a famous example he argued that food supplies grow according to an arithmetic (additive) progression while population follows an explosive geometric (multiplicative) progression.

We can see that in the grim Malthusian world, population growth is limited primarily by factors working through the death rate, what he called "positive checks." In this deceptively mild phrase Malthus included all the disasters that exterminate people in large numbers: famines, wars, and epidemics. It was these phenomena, he believed, that generally constitute the operative limitation on population. Only in the late editions of his famous *Essay on the Principle of Population* did he concede the possibility of a second, less drastic, category of limiting factors: "preventive checks" working through the birth rate. What Malthus had in mind here were primarily measures of "restraint," such as a later age of marriage. Unlike latter-day "Malthusians" he did not advocate birth control, which as a minister he considered immoral. Although he grudgingly admitted that humanity might voluntarily control its own numerical growth, Malthus invested little hope in the possibility.

The gloominess of the Malthusian theory is understandable when one considers that its author lived during the early years of the Industrial Revolution. In all prior history (that is, through the first two demographic eras outlined above) population had tended to expand in response to economic gains. Now with unprecedented economic growth underway in the world he knew, what could Malthus expect except an acceleration of natural increase as death rates fell? That indeed was happening during his lifetime.

Malthus did not live to witness the rest of the European demographic transition. As we saw in Figure 8–1, the early decline in death rates was followed, with a lag, by a fall in fertility; beginning in the middle of the nineteenth century, wages began to increase dramatically. Why did all this happen? Wages rose, despite accelerating population growth, because capital accumulation and technical change offset any tendency for the marginal product of labor to decline. It appears that the death rate fell through a combination of the indirect effects of higher incomes (better nutrition and living conditions) and the direct effects of better preventive and curative health measures. The fall in the birth rate is harder to understand. There are both biological and economic reasons to expect, as Malthus did, that fertility would rise, not fall, as income went up. Healthier, better-fed women have a greater biological capacity to conceive, carry a child full term, and give birth to a healthy infant. Also, people marry earlier when times are good, and better-off families have the financial capacity to support more children. Why then do increases in income seem to lead to declines in fertility? An answer to this question must be sought in post-Malthusian demographic theory.

Mechanisms for Reducing Birth Rates

The first stage of the demographic transition is marked by a decline in the death rate, particularly a reduction in deaths among infants and young children. This in itself is a very good thing and no humane person or government would wish to reverse the trend. The question of how to reduce the rate of population growth therefore narrows down to ways of lowering the birth rate.

Three kinds of demographic change affect the crude birth rate. The first is change in the population shares of different age groups and sexes. A rise in the share of people of reproductive age (roughly 15 to 45) increases the birth rate, as we saw earlier in the discussion of demographic momentum. Conversely, if the proportion of older people in the population goes up, as is happening in many industrial countries today, the birth rate drops. Similarly, unbalancing the sex ratio (for example, through migration of males) reduces the birth rate, whereas correcting a previously unbalanced ration increases it. However, these structural effects are quantitatively important only in rather special circumstances.

The second demographic mechanism that influences the birth rate is change in the share of people of reproductive age who are married. This in turn is affected by the proportion who marry at some time in their lives, by the average age of first marriage, and by the divorce rate.

The third factor is marital fertility, the rate at which married couples reproduce. Historical birth rate declines have come about mainly because of declines in marital fertility. Later age of marriage has also been important in some cases, for example, in the drop of the Irish birth rate after the potato famine of the 1840s.

It has been suggested that there are three basic preconditions for a significant decline in marital fertility. (1) Fertility must be subject to conscious choice; it must be socially acceptable for a couple to decide how many children they want to have. (2) Reduced fertility must be seen as advantageous; there must be perceived social and economic benefits to having fewer children. (3) Effective techniques of fertility reduction must be available; couples must know about them and agree to employ them.[11] Some theorists regard the first and third preconditions as merely facilitating influences. The active force working for lower birth rates, they argue, is perceived incentives for individuals to have fewer children.

Modern Theories of Fertility

Modern theories of fertility try to explain how people use the available mechanisms for determining the number of births. Many of these theories employ a supply and demand framework. Looked at this way, family planning programs work mainly on the supply side. They can reduce the birth rate by making it easier and cheaper for people to regulate the number of births and come closer to their desired family size. They may also affect the demand side of this equation (the number of children people want to have) through propaganda, but probably not much. The social motivations that lead governments to undertake family planning programs—perceived crowding and strain on national resources, perhaps some pressure from foreign aid organizations—are unlikely to carry much weight with individuals. Couples are unmoved by general, remote-sounding arguments.

11. Michael S. Teitelbaum, "Relevance of Demographic Transition Theory for Developing Countries," *Science*, 188 (May 2, 1977), 420–25.

Why, then, do people have children? Is it because they are moved by Malthus' "passion between the sexes" and do not know how to prevent the resulting births? Or do they have many children because they are tradition-bound, custom-ridden? Or is it perhaps rational in some social settings? All three positions have some merit. The case for the first one was stated by a Latin American doctor at an international conference a few years ago. "People don't really want children," he said. "They want sex and don't know how to avoid the births that result." This viewpoint captures the element of spontaneity that is inevitably present in the reproductive process. Yet the evidence suggests that all societies consciously control human fertility. In no known case does the number of children that the average woman has over her childbearing years even approach her biological capacity to bear children. All societies practice methods of inhibiting conception, aborting pregnancies, and disposing of unwanted infants, even societies that have had no contact with modern birth control methods.

It has been said that many children are the social norm in traditional societies, that society looks askance at couples who have no or few children, that a man who lacks wealth can at least have children, and that a woman's principal socially recognized function in a traditional society is to bear and rear children. Such norms and attitudes are important, but they are probably not the decisive factors in human fertility. Fertility is evidently determined by a complex combination of forces, but social scientists in recent years have given increasing credence to the elements of individual rationality in the process. Simply stated, they believe that most families in traditional societies have many children because it is rational for them to do so. By the same token people in modern societies have fewer children because that is rational behavior in the settings in which they live. It follows that to reduce fertility in developing countries, it is necessary to alter the incentives.

Although some would regard it as a cold, inhumane way of looking at the matter, it is nevertheless true that children impose certain costs on their parents and confer certain benefits. To the extent that couples are influenced by these benefits and costs, are able to calculate them, and are capable of carrying out their reproductive plans, it follows that to reduce the birth rate, it will be necessary to raise the ratio of costs to benefits.

The benefits of having children can be classified as economic and psychic. Within a few years of their birth, children may supplement family earnings by working. On family farms and in other household enterprises there is usually something that even a very young child can do to increase production. And in many poor societies large numbers of children work for wages outside the home. In the longer run children also provide a form of social security in societies that lack institutional programs to assist the elderly. In some cultures it is considered especially important to have a son who survives to adulthood; if infant and child mortality is high, this can motivate couples to keep having children until two or three sons have been born, just to be safe. Besides these economic benefits, which are probably more important in a low-income society than in a more affluent one, children can also yield psychic benefits, as all parents know.

The costs of children can also be categorized as economic and psychic. Economic costs can be further divided into explicit (monetary) and implicit (opportunity) costs. Children entail cash outlays for food, clothing, shelter, and sometimes for hired child-care services and education. Implicit costs arise when child care by a member of the family (usually, but not always, the mother) involves a loss of earning time. Psychic costs include anxiety and loss of leisure-time activities. Some of the costs felt by parents parallel the costs of population growth experienced at the national level. For example, more children in a family may mean smaller inheritances of agricultural land, an example of a natural resource constraint operating at the family level. Similarly, it may be harder to send all the children in a larger family to school; this reflects the pressures on social investment that are felt when population growth is rapid.

Viewing childbearing as an economic decision has several important implications. (1) Fertility should be higher when children can earn incomes or contribute to household enterprises at a young age than when they cannot. (2) Reducing infant deaths should lower fertility because fewer births will then be needed to produce a given desired number of surviving children. (3) The introduction of an institutionalized social security system should lower fertility by reducing the need for parents to depend on their children for support in their old age. (4) Fertility should fall when there is an increase in opportunities for women to work in jobs that are relatively incompatible with childbearing, essentially work outside the home. (5) Fertility should be higher when income is higher because the explicit costs are more easily borne.

The first four theoretical predictions have received substantial support from empirical studies. The fifth, however, conflicts sharply with observed reality. In the real world, fertility is usually negatively related to income, not positively related as simple theory predicts. The negative relationship shows up both in time-series date (that is, fertility usually declines through time as income rises) and in cross-section data (fertility is generally higher in poor countries than in rich countries; also, in most societies middle- and upper-income families have fewer children than poor families).

Several theorists have wrestled with this anomaly. Gary Becker of the University of Chicago, a pioneer of "the new household economics," views children as a kind of consumer durable that yields benefits over time. Couples maximize a joint (expected) utility function in which the "goods" they can "buy" are (1) number of living children, (2) "child quality" (a vector of characteristics including education and health), and (3) conventional goods and services. The constraints faced by parents in Becker's model are (1) their time and (2) the cost of purchased goods and services. Becker explains the fall in fertility as income rises over time by saying that the cost of children tends to rise, especially because the opportunity cost of the parents' time goes up. He believes that the spread of contraceptive knowledge also plays a part. Given the rising cost of child *quantity*, Becker argues that many parents opt to invest in child *quality* and spend more money on a decreasing number of children.[12]

Whereas Malthus erred in basing his theory of population on the assumption that people would always be driven by their passions, Becker has been charged with going too far in the opposite direction and exaggerating the extent to which couples consciously select their family sizes using a cost-benefit calculus. Others argue that socially conditioned changes in tastes and values are an important part of the demographic transition, but Becker regards tastes as given.

Rivaling Becker's purely economic model of fertility is the more eclectic framework of University of Pennsylvania demographer Richard Easterlin, who di-

12. See Gary Becker, *A Treatise on the Family* (Cambridge, Mass.: Harvard University Press, 1981).

rectly addresses people's motivation to use the available means of fertility control. He says this is determined by two factors. One is the demand for children, defined as the number of surviving children a couple would have if fertility regulation were costless; this is essentially a matter of tastes, which Easterlin, unlike Becker, believes do change over time. The second factor influencing people's interest in fertility control is natural fertility, which Easterlin defines as their potential number of children if fertility were not deliberately limited; this is determined partly by biology and partly by culture. Besides motivation to limit fertility, Easterlin believes the cost of controlling fertility is another important influence on the use of means to limit births. To Easterlin, cost includes not only market costs, such as the cost of contraceptives, but also psychic costs deriving, for example, from social disapproval of particular fertility limitation practices. Easterlin thus explains declining fertility in the real world as the combined effect of changing tastes and the declining cost of fertility control.

For the population policy maker, Becker's theory emphasizes the importance of changing incentives to have children if one wishes to reduce fertility, while Easterlin's approach points to the need to change tastes and reduce the market and psychic costs of practicing birth control.[13]

The demographer John Caldwell explains the demographic transition in somewhat different terms that are still consistent with the general idea of rational choice. He argues that the main reason why large families are rational in traditional societies is that extended family relationships cause net intergenerational wealth transfers to flow from younger to older generations. According to Caldwell, as nuclear families become more common and the emotional and economic ties between generations weaken in the course of modernization, the direction of the intergenerational flow of wealth reverses. Since parents must now transfer net wealth to their children, rather than receiving net wealth from them, they opt to have fewer children.[14]

Analyzing the Effects of Rapid Population Growth

Two questions are important for population policy. What are the effects of population growth on development and human welfare? And if population growth is thought to have harmful effects, how can these harmful effects best be reduced or eliminated?

Optimum Population

The theory reviewed in the preceding section implies that at the family level population tends toward an optimum, in the sense that people have the number of children they consider beneficial to their overall welfare. Yet when asked, many parents in developing countries say that they would rather have fewer children than they have. Also, several studies show that rates of sickness and death are higher among children in large families, especially those born later. So perhaps

13. See Richard Easterlin, "Modernization and Fertility: A Critical Essay," in R. Bulatao and R. Lee (eds.), *Determinants of Fertility in Developing Countries,* Vol. 2 (New York: Academic Press, 1983), pp. 562–86.

14. See John C. Caldwell, "Toward a Restatement of Demographic Transition Theory," *Population and Development Review,* 2, nos. 3–4 (September–December 1976), 321–66.

spouses' judgments about optimal family size change after they become parents and form a more realistic appraisal of the costs and benefits of children.

When we consider the relationship between population and welfare at the national level, the main question is whether individual preferences should be allowed to determine how large a population a country has. What are the effects of population growth on development and human welfare? Is there a case for the state to intervene to curb, or in some instances perhaps to encourage, human reproduction?

We can begin to attack this issue by considering the relationship between per capita income and the size of a country's population. Would per capita income be higher or lower if the population were larger than it is? In dynamic terms, which are more relevant for policy, the question is whether the future growth of per capita income would be faster or slower if the rate of population growth were increased or reduced.

An answer to this question can be reached through successive approximations. The oldest and simplest answer is that with every mouth comes a pair of hands. This implies that economic activity is scale neutral, that per capita income is unaffected by the size or growth rate of the population. But this ancient piece of folk wisdom is all too obviously oversimplified. It ignores the role of nonlabor resources and particularly the possibility (which so concerned Ricardo and Malthus) that diminishing returns will be encountered as population expands.

A somewhat more sophisticated approach that meets this objection is the optimum population theory: for any given country with a fixed supply of nonlabor resources at any particular time, there is a unique population size at which per capita income is maximized. The idea is that at suboptimal levels of population, per capita income is lower than it could be because there is not enough labor to utilize the available nonlabor resources efficiently, whereas at levels above the optimum, per capita income is also lower than it could be because there is too much labor and diminishing returns set in. This relationship is graphed in Figure 8–3.

Optimum population theory is consistent with the intuition that there can be underpopulated countries and overpopulated countries. It is not hard to believe that immigration into the United States, Canada, and Australia during the nineteenth century raised per capita income in those countries. (It is harder to think of underpopulated countries in today's world, although some in East and Southern Africa might qualify.) Nor is it implausible to think that Bangladesh's per capita income would rise if some millions of its population could somehow be made to disappear. The trouble with the approach is that it is a static framework and can take only limited account of dynamic factors. Capital accumulation, technical change, and natural-resource discoveries make it possible simultaneously to raise per capita income and increase the optimum population over time.

Dynamic Models of Population Growth

Figure 8–3 depicts what economists call comparative statics. The optimum population theory shows how income per capita is determined at a point in time, given population, stocks of other resources, and technology. It also indicates how income per capita is affected by, say, a one-time improvement in technology, but it does not show what would happen through time as population and capital stocks

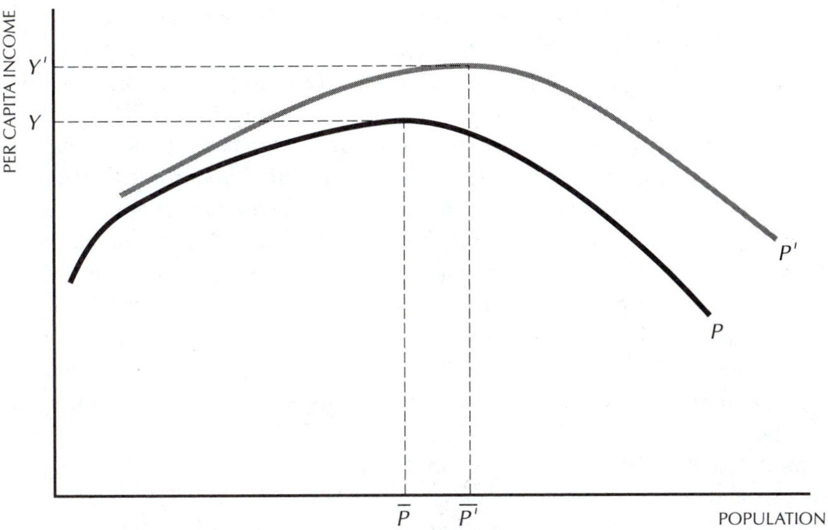

FIGURE 8–3 The Theory of Optimum Population. Curve *P* shows that, at levels of population below *P*, an increase in population leads to an increase in income per capita, but beyond *P*, more population reduces average income. $\bar{P}$ is the optimum level of population. Discoveries of new resources, capital accumulation, or technological change can shift the curve upward to *P′*, with a new, higher optimum population $\bar{P}'$.

grow, as resource supplies stabilize or decline, and as technology changes. A dynamic model would try to do that.

The pioneering work in dynamic modeling of population's effect on material welfare was published in 1958 by Princeton University demographer Ansley Coale and Duke University economist Edgar Hoover, who created a macroeconomic model of population growth and development in India.[15] According to their analysis, a reduction in the Indian birth rate would help raise per capita income in two important ways. First, slower population growth would lower the dependency ratio, reducing consumption and increasing saving at any given level of income. Second, as labor force growth slowed about 15 years later, the amount of investment needed to provide a constant amount of capital per worker for a growing number of workers (called "capital widening") would go down and permit more investment to be used to increase capital per worker ("capital deepening"). These two kinds of benefit from slower population growth would be felt both at the household level and at the national level.

Concern about the Effects of Population Growth on Development

Later model builders have generally supported the findings of Coale and Hoover and thus endorsed the long-standing view that rapid population growth impedes development. During the 1970s the U.S. Agency for International Development, the World Bank, and other international aid agencies gave heavy emphasis to population policy as a criterion for judging the seriousness of the development effort

15. Ansley J. Coale and Edgar M. Hoover, *Population Growth and Economic Development in Low-income Countries: A Case Study of India's Prospects* (Princeton, N.J.: Princeton University Press, 1958).

of a potential aid recipient. A comprehensive review of population change and development conducted by the World Bank in 1984 found that rapid population growth depresses private savings, necessitates more capital widening, and discourages capital deepening that would raise productivity and per capita income.[16] In addition, many writers called attention to the deleterious effects of population growth on the environment. They noted that rising population densities have contributed to deforestation in many parts of the third world as rural people move up the hillsides in search of more agricultural land and firewood. Indeed, depletion of all nonrenewable resources is accelerated by rapid population growth. Maintaining a stable or rising per capita food supply has been less of a problem than Malthus anticipated, but it has proven difficult in wide areas of sub-Saharan Africa. The World Bank, among many others, has also pointed to the impact of growing total population on urbanization, which brings with it extra costs that society must bear.

The proposition that population growth retards increases in per capita income has obvious appeal in developing countries (including many in Asia, Egypt, and most Caribbean islands) where population density is already so high in relation to land and other natural resources that diminishing returns have probably set in. Even in areas where population density is lower, however—certain land-rich areas in sub-Saharan Africa and South America—rapid population growth can press on scarce capital resources and inhibit capital deepening and efforts to improve public services. It thus can be argued that it reduces the growth of per capita income in both types of LDCs.

Recall from the earlier discussion of fertility determinants that although some of the pressures created by high population growth and density are felt by individuals, others are not. For example, excessive growth in the number of school-age children makes it difficult for society to provide schooling of adequate quality for everyone. Although a reduction in the average number of children per family would contribute to a solution of this problem, particular couples would not find publicly financed educational facilities any better if they had fewer children (although they would be better able to meet the private costs of schooling). One argument for policy intervention to bring about a more moderate rate of population growth is that such social diseconomies can be avoided.

It is also contended that rapid population control in particular countries produces external diseconomies at the international level. There are nationalistic reasons, related to prestige and sometimes also to military power, why particular states may want to have larger populations. But this can disrupt international relations and injure other countries. Policies to expand national populations may raise the likelihood of war by making larger armies possible and heightening competition for land and other resources. They may create pressures for migration from densely populated countries to other countries whose population growth is under control. For all these reasons there is a case for an international effort to limit world population. The main problem is to decide whose population is to be limited. Possibilities for doing much about population at the global level are limited by the linkage of the population problem to other issues of international politics and by the locus of population policy, which is at the national level.

16. See *World Development Report 1984,* pp. 51–206.

Doubters and Dissenters

Despite the arguments for limiting population growth in developing countries, the results of population modelers, and the views of powerful aid organizations, there have always been dissenters from the majority opinion that rapid population growth is harmful to economic development in the third world. These contrary views have received some support recently from empirical researchers who have found it difficult to identify or measure population growth's deleterious effects.

Here are some examples of analysts who have doubted that faster population growth retards growth in per capita income or even claimed that it is beneficial.

1. The Australian economist Colin Clark was one of the first to note the lack of empirical support for the proposition that population growth impedes economic growth. He claimed that the empirical relationship between the growth rate of population and that of per capita income was in fact positive.[17]

2. The Danish economist Ester Boserup concluded from her historical studies of agricultural development that population growth serves as a stimulus to agricultural intensification and technological improvement.[18]

3. Julian Simon of the University of Illinois has mustered a variety of arguments in favor of population growth, notably that a larger population is likely to contain more entrepreneurs and other creators, who can make major contributions to solving the problems of humanity. He calls human ingenuity the "ultimate resource" that can overcome any depletion of other resources.[19]

4. Rati Ram of the University of Illinois and Theodore W. Schultz of the University of Chicago have pointed out that the longer life spans that accompany falling death rates and faster population growth in the LDCs increase the incentives for investment in human capital and make labor more productive.[20]

5. A 1986 review of population and development sponsored by the National Academy of Sciences addressed a series of assertions about the negative effects of population growth and generally found that empirical evidence to support them is weak.[21]

Conclusion: A New Consensus?

Despite these doubts and dissents, most analysts still believe that in the circumstances of nearly all LDCs, slower population growth would permit per capita income to rise more rapidly. But the issues are complex, and evidence for the notion that slower population growth by itself would create large benefits is not strong. The authors of the National Academy of Sciences report put it this way: "On balance, we reach the qualitative conclusion that slower population growth would be

17. See Colin Clark, "The 'Population Explosion' Myth," *Bulletin of the Institute of Development Studies*, Sussex, England, May 1969, and Colin Clark, "The Economics of Population Growth and Control: A Comment," *Review of Social Economy,* 28, no. 1 (March 1970), 449–66.

18. See Ester Boserup, *The Conditions of Agricultural Growth* (Chicago: Aldine, 1965).

19. See Julian L. Simon, *The Ultimate Resource* (Princeton, N.J.: Princeton University Press, 1981), and Julian L. Simon, *Theory of Population and Economic Growth* (Oxford: Basil Blackwell, 1986).

20. Rati Ram and Theodore W. Schultz, "Life Span Savings, and Productivity," *Economic Development and Cultural Change,* 27, no. 3 (April 1979), 394–421.

21. See National Academy of Sciences, *Population Growth and Economic Development: Policy Questions* (Washington, D.C.: National Academy Press, 1986).

beneficial for most developing countries. A rigorous quantitative assessment of these benefits is difficult and context-dependent."[22]

As emphasis on the role of population growth in retarding economic development declines, it has been suggested that a "new consensus" on the relationship between population growth and economic development may be forming.[23] Analysts may now be slower to blame population growth for development problems and more cautious about assertions that individuals' reproductive decisions create heavy social costs. Political and institutional factors intermediate the relationship between population growth and development. A high rate of population growth does not necessarily slow down economic growth, and a lower population growth rate will not necessarily accelerate it. The new consensus would reject casting population growth as the "villain" in the story of third-world development, although it may be the "accomplice."

Population Policy

Most LDC governments today are on record as favoring slower population growth and have formulated policies, usually family planning programs, for attempting to achieve it. The strongest commitments have generally come from Asian governments. In Latin America, governments may provide family planning services officially or permit private organizations to do so, but their actions are usually rationalized as efforts to promote the welfare of mothers and children. Some African governments are committed to population growth limitation, while others have been indifferent or even hostile (see boxed example on Kenya). The population policies of Communist regimes have varied among countries and from time to time. China has achieved what is probably the most effective control over population ever attained by any government through its "planned births" campaign (see boxed example).

Population and Family Planning in Kenya

Kenya is an African country with relatively low population density but a high population growth rate and explosive demographic potential. Until the early 1980s, Kenya's total fertility rate was eight and its population growth rate well above 3 percent, both among the highest in the world. A survey taken in the late 1970s found that Kenyans regarded eight children as an ideal family size, up from six in the 1960s. Nevertheless, fertility began to fall in the 1980s. The total fertility rate dropped to 6.9 by 1988 and 5.4 in 1992. Although population is still growing at 2.7 percent, fast enough to double in 26 years, some type of demographic transition is clearly underway.

Why were Kenyans so very fertile, and why are they now becoming less so? The recent decline seems to have resulted from a combination of economic and social change and the increased availability of family planning services. Although Nairobi, the capital, is a prosperous, modern city,

22. Ibid., p. 90.
23. Merrick, "World Population in Transition."

the country is still 78 percent rural. The per capita GDP of $1,360 (PPP, 1992) is very unequally distributed. Water shortages severely restrict the cultivatability of much of Kenya's land, and in some of the fertile areas there are large farms. Many Kenyans, therefore, must make a living from holdings that are either too small or too poorly watered to ensure an adequate income.

Although the Kenyan government adopted a policy of population limitation as early as 1966, the national family planning program received only tepid political backing before the 1980s. The late President Jomo Kenyatta, who issued the 1966 policy statement, later refused to lend public support to family planning. Kenya's keen tribal rivalries made the issue a sensitive one, since each group feared that if it adopted birth limitation it would become weaker relative to its competitors. In recent years, however, as the dangers of continued rapid population growth have become both evident and imminent, President Daniel Arap Moi's government has actively supported a revived family planning effort, which is widely regarded as having contributed to the fertility declines observed since 1980.

Population and Family Planning in China

Since 1971, China has made spectacular and unique progress toward controlling the growth of its massive population. By doing so, it has not only made a large numerical impact on world population growth but has also provided important lessons to other low-income countries interested in fertility reduction. But some of the techniques used to reduce the number of births in China may not be transferable to other political and cultural settings, and others would not be widely acceptable because of the loss of personal freedom they involve.

Population policy in China has been anything but constant. After the Communist takeover in 1949 Chairman Mao Zedong repeatedly asserted that "revolution plus production" would solve all problems, with no need to limit population growth. China's first census, conducted in 1953, revealed such a large population (nearly 600 million) that it shook this complacency. But birth control campaigns from 1956 to 1958 and from 1962 to 1966 had only limited results and were interrupted by Mao's famous policy reversals, the Great Leap Forward of 1960 and the Cultural Revolution of the late 1960s. Only in 1971 was a serious and sustained effort launched. At that time the crude birth rate, already reduced by the disruptions of the Cultural Revolution, stood at 30. By 1983 it had been cut to 19.

The "planned births" campaign of 1971 was reportedly launched at the personal initiative of Premier Zhou Enlai. It established three reproductive norms (*wan xi shao*): later marriage, longer spacing between births, and fewer children. To implement these norms, the highly committed post-Mao leadership set birth targets for administrative units at all levels throughout China. The responsibility for achieving these targets was placed in the hands of officials heading units ranging from provinces of 2 to 90 million people down to production teams of 250 to 800. The national government held information and motivation campaigns to persuade people to have fewer children, but it was left to local officials to fill out many details of the program and finance much of its cost. A wide range of contraceptives was offered, and family planning was closely linked to efforts to improve child and maternal health care.

While national spokespeople maintained that participation in the program was voluntary, local officials with targets to fulfill often applied pressure. At the production-team level, birth planning became intensely personal, as couples were required to seek approval to have a child in a particular year. (The application might be accepted, or they might be asked to wait a year or two.) Such extreme methods seem to have worked and been reasonably well accepted in China, presumably because of its cohesive social structure and strong government authority from the national down to the neighborhood level.

The most popular form of birth limitation in China has been the intrauterine device (IUD). Two other major forms have been abortion and sterilization of both women and men.

The *wan xi shao* campaign lowered fertility, but population projections continued to cause concern and in 1979 the "one child" campaign was promulgated. Couples were now told that "only children are better children" and urged to take a pledge to stop at one. Those who do so often receive special incentives, such as an income supplement, extra maternity leave, and preferential treatment when applying for public housing. The "one child" campaign flew in the face of traditional son preference by asking half of China's couples to stop reproducing before they had a male child and appears to have been associated with some resurgence of female infanticide or neglect of girl babies, but it did succeed in reducing fertility to the replacement level by the mid-1980s. There is now hope that China's population will stabilize early in the twenty-first century.

Although some aspects of China's population program will doubtless remain unique, countries interested in strengthening their own programs could learn from China's strong information activities, its use of a wide range of contraceptive methods, and its decentralization of many aspects of planning and implementation to local authorities.

Population policy has raised political, moral, and religious issues in a number of countries. Some countries are pronatalist for nationalistic reasons, perhaps because they want to have enough people to hold areas of low population density against external challenges. Others (Guyana, Lebanon, Nigeria, Malaysia, and Singapore, to name a few) have internal racial, tribal, religious, or ethnic divisions that make population policy a sensitive matter, since it involves the balance of power among the various groups. Still other countries have provoked adverse political reactions by adopting methods of population control regarded as excessively zealous, offensive to local belief, or callous in their disregard of individual rights. Indira Gandhi's surprising defeat in India's 1977 general election was attributed in part to the population policy of her emergency government. Despairing of controlling population growth by conventional means, the government added male sterilization to its list of promoted family planning methods. Incentives were offered to those who agreed to be sterilized, and quotas were assigned to officials charged with carrying out the program in different parts of the country. Problems arose when force was allegedly used against low-status individuals by officials anxious to fill their quotas. The result was a setback not only for Indira Gandhi's government but also for Indian family planning.

The thinking about population and development reviewed here casts light on both the rationale for population policy in the LDCs and the proper design of programs to reduce fertility. Population policy must be grounded in a consideration of the effects of rapid population growth in a low-income country. Its design should pay attention to the modern theories of fertility determination.

There are two main rationales for the promotion of family planning in an LDC. One is that, through information dissemination and access to contraceptives, couples can be helped to realize their reproductive plans. The second rationale is that high fertility has social costs that are not taken into account by individuals but should be offset by government on behalf of society by subsidizing family planning, penalizing couples who have many children, or both. The first argument enjoys wide support; the second is more controversial. The World Bank's 1984 *World Development Report* supported both arguments,[24] but the National Academy of Science's recent review called into question the magnitude of population growth's social costs.

Policy Alternatives

A policy maker who wishes to reduce population growth can consider family planning, population redistribution, more drastic measures like abortion or sterilization, and policies that alter reproductive incentives.

In essence, **family planning programs** do two things: they make one or more forms of contraception more widely or cheaply available or both, and they undertake information and propaganda activities to urge people to use them. These programs have achieved good results in some cases but had little or no discernible effect in others. They appear to work best where there is a preexisting desire for smaller families, at least in some parts of the population. Most of the family planning programs that have been relatively successful in reaching a large number of acceptors and retaining a large stock of current users over time are to be found in countries that are rapidly attaining higher literacy, reduced infant death rates, and more widespread female employment outside the home.[25] In countries where these factors are absent, family planning tends to catch on among the relatively well-off, the urbanized, and the educated, but it spreads very slowly among the rest of the population.

The record, however, is not clear-cut. In some parts of rural Indonesia, family planning has had a measurable effect on the birth rate, despite comparatively low levels of income, education, and health services (see the following boxed example). Integrating contraceptive services with other services, especially maternal and child health services, seems to help. Even if population growth is not reduced,

24. See *World Development Report 1984,* pp. 51–206.

25. This list of factors is based on empirical research. Some of the reasons why these factors should be influential were suggested earlier.

enabling women to improve the spacing of births has health and welfare benefits that women recognize and that contribute to acceptance of the program.

Population and Family Planning in Indonesia

Indonesia is the world's fourth most populous country. Its 184 million people (1992) inhabit a chain of islands stretching some 3000 miles along the equator. Yet two-thirds of all Indonesians cluster on Java and Bali, small islands that make up only 7 percent of the land area. In rural sections of Java and Bali, population densities are among the highest in the world, land holdings are small and shrinking, and decent jobs remain hard to find, even after more than two decades of rapid economic growth.

For many years transmigration to the less fertile but relatively uncrowded outer islands of Sumatra, Kalimantan, and Sulawesi was promoted as a way of easing population pressure in Java and Bali. But the program was unable to make a significant impact on population growth in these core islands, let alone reduce existing densities. Indeed, about as fast as migrants were moved to available agricultural land in the outer islands, others flocked to Java's cities, where the best income-earning opportunities were concentrated.

Indonesia's population policy reversed gears in the late 1960s. Sukarno, the ardent nationalist who was president from 1945 to 1966, often avowed that Indonesia had too few people, not too many. "We have rich natural resources," he said. "We need more people to exploit them." Yet Sukarno's government failed to develop the country's resources, and by the mid-1960s Indonesia's masses were desperately short of food, clothing, and medical care.

Suharto, the second president, tried to rebuild the economy. He also declared approval of population limitation, and in 1970 an official family planning program was launched. Although most people in Indonesia remain poor and ill educated, this program has succeeded beyond anyone's expectation. Greatest attention was paid to, and greatest success achieved in, the rural parts of Java and Bali. The program was imaginatively conceived, well managed, and implemented largely through existing village institutions. Pills were used as the main method of contraception. By 1980 fertility in key areas had fallen by 15 to 20 percent. In other areas fertility remained high; in still others it was low, but only because of low female fecundity resulting from ill health and malnutrition.

During the 1980s fertility reduction in Indonesia was further spurred by rapid expansion of educational opportunities. Parents came to see greater possibilities for sending their children to high school and college, and began to limit the number of children they had as a way to save more and thus realize these dreams. Between 1970 and 1992, the total fertility rate fell from 5.5 to 2.9. This reduction is in line with a goal adopted in the early years of the family planning program—to cut fertility in half by the year 2000—which was then regarded as highly ambitious. Indonesia's experience thus shows what an effective family planning program launched by a determined government can achieve, even in circumstances that experts considered quite unfavorable for family planning.

A second broad approach to population policy would try to move people from one part of the country to another to improve the fit between population and the availability of land and other resources. *Population redistribution* may help to accommodate a growing total population in limited circumstances, but the magnitude of the effect is unlikely to be great. First, there must be empty but habitable space into which people can be moved. Then, particularly if the government is going to organize the movement, considerable investment and formidable organizing capacity will be required. It is hard to move enough people to make a real difference, as experience in Brazil, Indonesia (see boxed example), and elsewhere shows. We have already noted that the kind of mass international population redistribution that was common in the nineteenth century is unlikely to occur in today's world, although smaller movements of people (motivated by political as well as economic considerations) still take place.

Methods of population control more drastic than contraception, such as abortion and sterilization, have played an important part in the slowdown of population growth in several European, South American, and East Asian countries. These methods are often regarded as objectionable on moral grounds. When forced on resisting populations, as in India during the emergency of the mid-1970s, they can backfire. Yet when acceptable to local mores, they may help to bring about a rapid decline in fertility.

Besides family planning, many other government policies indirectly influence fertility levels by *altering incentives to have children*. Some governments have used these policies to complement the effects of their family planning efforts. The policies include increased education for girls, especially the attainment of basic literacy for all women in countries that have not yet reached this target; increased job opportunities for women outside the home; formal social security systems—a realistic option only for middle-income countries; a ban on child labor; compulsory schooling up to a certain age; and improvement in the status of women, which will give them greater control over their own lives. The use of monetary incentives and disincentives geared to the number of children per family has also been advocated. The trouble with these measures is that although they may discourage parents from having an additional child, they frequently penalize those children already born. For example, levying higher charges for the medical care and schooling of third and subsequent children may indeed cause parents to have fewer children, but it may also result in lower quality care for children who, through no fault of their own, are born late into large families.

Reduction of infant mortality can be also be considered an indirect population policy. According to the child replacement thesis, the number of children that a couple has is geared to the number it expects to survive; accordingly, if survival prospects improve, then the birth rate—if not necessarily the rate of natural increase—will fall.

A country that once emphasized policies to provide disincentives for large families, albeit in rather special circumstances, is Singapore. There 60 percent of the population lives in public housing, and nearly everyone is heavily dependent on the government for a variety of social services. In its campaign to limit population growth, the government of Singapore discriminated among users of public services on the basis of how many children they have. People with large families paid higher maternity fees, got lower priority in school selection, and received no extra income tax deductions or housing space. Abortion and sterilization (both male and female) were made available on demand at nominal fees. All this was backed up by a determined information campaign. Singapore's tough policy contributed to a dramatic fall in population growth, although rapid economic and social change in the Southeast Asian city-state probably had an even greater impact. In fact, the campaign was so successful in reducing fertility that the prime minister later reversed himself and urged educated women to have more children so that the quality of the population could be maintained!

A final idea for indirectly influencing fertility is that *improvement in the distribution of income* will cut the birth rate. (The complementary proposition, that unequal income distribution leads to higher fertility, has also been advanced.) This makes sense, since poor households have perhaps three-quarters of the babies born in a developing society and it is their income that must rise if an increase in income is to bring about a decline in fertility. A related notion is that a generally equitable pattern of development, including improving social services for the poor, will convince people that their lives are improving and they are gaining increasing control over their own destinies, and lead to an especially rapid decline in fertility. These are attractive hypotheses and there is some evidence to support them, but it is not conclusive.

Family Planning versus Development?

Some people, with diverse perspectives, argue that governments should worry less about population policy, concentrate more on *economic development,* and leave it to the demographic transition to bring about a decline in fertility. At the first United Nations World Population Conference, held in Bucharest in 1974, a popular slogan was, "Take care of the people and the population will take care of itself." There and elsewhere, verbal wars have been waged between "family planners" and "developmentalists." Ideology often becomes entwined in the debate. Marxist spokespeople routinely contend that population pressure in capitalist countries is merely one more manifestation of class conflict. In a socialist society the problem will disappear because it will be possible to organize society "scientifically," and thus provide full employment and satisfaction of everyone's basic needs. In the meantime, capitalist efforts to promote family planning are seen as just one more futile attempt to stave off the coming revolution. Interestingly, the United States delegation to the second World Population Conference, held in Mexico City in 1984, provided a mirror image of this argument by contending that population would be less of a problem if LDC governments gave freer rein to private enterprise.

The earlier review of facts and theories suggests that family planning *versus* development is a false dichotomy. The fertility decline that completes the demographic transition can be hastened *both* by family planning *and* by economic development. Family planning alone is unlikely to reduce the birth rate; we have seen that it seldom works well in settings where there has been little development. Moreover its effects on marital fertility need support from a trend toward a higher age of marriage, and this is also more likely to come about in a more rapidly developing society.

Yet family planning has made its own independent contribution to LDC fertility decline in recent years, as studies have shown.[26] Both in Latin America and the Caribbean and in Asia, more than 50 percent of married couples now practice family planning.[27] In reality family planning and development are more complements than substitutes.

26. W. Parker Mauldin and Bernard Berelson, "Conditions of Fertility Decline in Developing Countries, 1965–75," *Studies in Family Planning,* 9, no. 5 (1978). See also "Fertility and Family Planning Surveys: An Update," *Population Reports,* Series M, no. 8, Baltimore, Johns Hopkins University, September–October 1985.

27. Based on "most-recent estimates" reported in World Bank, *Social Indicators of Development 1989* (Baltimore: Johns Hopkins Press, 1989).

9

Labor's Role

The dual role of people as both the beneficiaries of economic development and a major productive resource is particularly evident in discussing labor and employment. Labor employed in economic activity is likely to be costly (that is, have an alternative use, as discussed below) in the same way that the use of other scarce resources is costly. But employing the available labor supply offers two important benefits. First, because of market imperfections, it may be possible to increase production through policies that encourage better use of available labor and the adoption of technologies more appropriate to the factor endowments of less-developed countries. Second, even if total output does not rise, increased employment of poor people can be an effective and relatively low-cost way to increase their share of total income, and thus diminish poverty and distributive inequality.

A perplexing problem is how best to measure the quality of labor used in production. Given the supplies of capital and natural resources available, as well as a range of applicable technologies, the level of GNP attainable depends on the amount of labor available. But what is the "amount of labor available?" We could simply count the number of people potentially available for work—the number of people who are not underage, overage, or infirm—but this could be misleading. Labor productivity, or quality, varies widely in the real world, depending on several factors.

One of these is people's attitudes and values. How highly do they value the goods and services that can be earned by working? Are people willing to abandon traditional social settings and take up jobs in unfamiliar environments, such as factories, mines, and plantations? Do they come to work on time? Do they exert themselves on the job? Can they tolerate routinized operations? Is saving for the future important to them or do they live for the moment? Although economic theories usually abstract from the effects of values and attitudes on productivity, in the real world they are significant. Values and attitudes are acquired, not inborn. The work of sociologists and psychologists indicates that they are shaped by experiences in the home, in school, and on the job. In a sense they are thus a consequence of economic development, but they are also one of its causes. The subject is not yet well-enough understood for values and attitudes to be readily manipulated as a means of promoting development, although many governments try to do so.

A second set of influences on labor productivity is made up of the skills possessed by the population. If values and attitudes refer to the way people look at the world, skills are what they know how to do. Some skills are widely usable; others are specific to particular environments. One needs to know different things to work effectively in an Asian rice field, a Detroit auto factory, or an Arctic fishing community; skills that are vital in one of these settings may be useless in another. Compared to attitudes and values, skills are acquired in a more straightforward and easily understood manner. The process can be called "education," although the term is used here in a broader sense than is usual.

Finally, labor productivity is affected by the health and nutrition of the working population. People must possess the physical and mental stamina necessary, first to learn economically useful skills and then to apply them in the workplace. Education and health merit extended treatment and are taken up in Chapters 10 and 11. Here we concentrate on quantitative aspects of the human factor in development.

Analyzing Employment Issues

Quantitative aspects of labor's role include growth in the number of laborers, patterns of employment, structure of labor markets, and methods of measuring labor supply and its utilization. We take up these issues in turn.

Growth of Labor Supply

A major difference between the development challenge faced by developing countries today and the one overcome by the industrial countries in the early phase of their own development is that the growth rate of labor supply is much faster in the developing countries. In most low-income countries the number of people who want to work is currently increasing at more than 2 percent a year. Since nearly all adult males and many adult females seek work outside the home, the rise in the number of potential workers is closely related to the increase in total population. Labor force growth lags population growth by 15 to 20 years, depending mainly on how long children stay in school. When health improves and more children survive from infancy to adulthood, population growth accelerates; this leads to faster labor force growth after 15 to 20 years. Similarly, a fall in the birth rate leads to reduced labor force growth, but only after 15 years or so. During the 1980s, labor force growth began to slow down in Asia and Latin America, but not in Africa or the Middle East (Table 9–1). The remainder of this century is expected to see further deceleration, except in sub-Saharan Africa,

TABLE 9–1 **Growth of Labor Force, 1970–2000***

	Actual		Projected
	1970–1980	1980–1992	1992–2000
Sub-Saharan Africa	2.5	2.5	2.8
Asia & Pacific	2.2	2.0	1.4
Eastern Europe & Central Asia	n.a.	n.a.	n.a.
Western Europe	0.8	0.1	0.1
Middle East & North Africa	2.8	2.8	2.7
United States & Canada	2.4	1.0	0.8
Latin America & Caribbean	3.2	2.5	2.3
All developing countries	2.3	2.2	1.7

*Weighted averages based on labor force size in 1992.
Source: World Development Report 1994, p. 210.

where the delay in achieving a demographic transition means that growth in the labor supply will actually speed up in the period 1992 to 2000.

Patterns of Employment

One of the best-known characteristics of labor in developing countries is that most people work in agriculture. Agriculture's share of the labor force is highest in the poorest countries and declines systematically as GNP per capita rises. The shares of both industrial and service workers rise to offset this decline (Table 9–2). Individual countries generally follow this pattern with case-to-case variations, as depicted in Table 9–3.

Another well-known fact about LDC labor is that wages are generally low by the standards of industrial countries. In developing countries labor is plentiful relative to the supply of complementary resources that could raise its productivity and permit higher wages to be paid. Nearly all complementary resources tend to be scarce: capital equipment, arable land, and foreign exchange, as well as those less tangible but important resources, entrepreneurship and managerial capacity. Thus, low wages are easily understood from the perspective of an elementary supply-demand analysis.

It is not demeaning to LDC workers, however, to note that another cause of low productivity and pay is the characteristics of the workers themselves. Through no fault of their own, few have the education and work experience required for high productivity. Indonesia's 1980 population census revealed that only 32 percent of adults had completed primary school, a mere 10 percent had gone on to secondary education, and a microscopic 0.5 percent had been to a university. Few indeed had ever worked in a factory or had other good opportunities for on-the-job training. In many developing countries these proportions are even lower. All too many LDC workers lack even the capacity to do sustained physical labor because their health and nutritional status is low. Yet developing countries also have in their work forces persons of consummate learning and outstanding abilities.

Another characteristic of LDC labor is that differentials among the wages received by different skills and education levels are wider than in developed countries. Skilled manual workers in developed countries may earn 20 to 40 percent more than their unskilled counterparts. In Asia, they are likely to earn 40 to 80 percent more, in Latin America 70 to 100 percent, and in Africa the skill differen-

TABLE 9–2 Employment Shares at Different Levels of Development, 1980–1992*

Level of GDP per capita (PPP), 1990	Percent of labor force employed in:		
	Agriculture	Industry	Services
Less than $1,000	74	8	18
$1,000–$2,000	65	13	22
$2,000–$5,000	38	22	40
$5,000–$10,000	24	32	44
More than $10,000	6	29	65

* Data are for different years in the 1980 to 1992 range, depending on the latest available source (usually a national population census). Weighted averages have been taken within income classes.
Source: United Nations Development Program, *Human Development Report 1994*, pp. 162–63, 194.

TABLE 9–3 Employment Shares in Selected Countries, 1980–1992*

	Percent of labor force employed in:		
Country†	Agriculture	Industry	Services
Low-income countries			
Ethiopia	88	2	10
Mali	85	2	13
Tanzania	85	5	10
Bangladesh	59	13	28
Ghana	59	11	30
Kenya	81	7	12
Nigeria	48	7	45
Sengal	81	6	13
India	62	11	27
Honduras	38	15	47
Boliva	47	19	34
Cameroon	79	7	14
Pakistan	47	20	33
China	73	14	13
Egypt	42	21	37
Middle-income countries			
Indonesia	56	14	30
Philippines	45	16	39
Sri Lanka	49	21	30
Peru	35	12	53
Argentina	13	34	53
Colombia	10	24	66
Hungary	15	31	54
Russia	20	46	34
Mexico	23	29	48
Malaysia	26	28	46
South Korea	17	36	47
High-income countires			
United Kingdom	2	28	70
Japan	7	34	59
Germany	3	39	58
United States	3	25	72

* Data are for different years in the 1980 to 1992 range.
† In ascending order of GDP per capita (PPP) in 1990. "Low-income" means less than $2,000, "middle-income" means $2,000–$10,000, and "high-income" means over $10,000.
Source: United Nations Development Program, *Human Development Report 1994*, pp. 162–63, 194.

tial can be 100 percent or more. Earnings differentials attributable to higher levels of education are also much larger in developing countries. In part these large earnings differentials exist because the rarity of skills and schooling attracts a larger market premium. Other factors may be segmented labor markets and "efficiency wage" considerations, discussed in the following section.

A final characteristic of labor in the poorest economies is widespread underutilization of the available labor supply. For reasons discussed below, much of this underutilization takes the form of **disguised unemployment**, rather than the visible unemployment familiar in industrial countries. That is, people do have some kind of a job, and may even work long hours, but their contribution to output is small. With some reallocation of resources and improvement of institutions, their labor could be made more productive. This is a major challenge for development policy.

To recapitulate, low wages and productivity, large wage differentials, rapid growth of labor supply, and underutilization of the existing supply of labor all characterize developing countries. There are, however, many intercountry variations. As we saw earlier, labor-force growth is now declining in most Asian countries but still accelerating in sub-Saharan Africa. The degree of labor underutilization also varies greatly, depending mainly on the supply of arable land and other complementary resources in relation to the working-age population.

The Structure of Labor Markets

It is useful to think of labor services as being bought and sold in markets like other goods and services. In the economist's "perfect market," given certain assumptions, prices are set to cause goods to be allocated efficiently. But labor markets are notoriously imperfect, and none are more so than those of the LDCs. Wages (the "price" of labor) are not entirely determined by competitive forces. This section describes a pattern of segmented labor markets, which may help to explain wage and employment determination in the LDCs.

A "typical" developing country could be represented by a three-tiered employment structure, consisting of an urban formal sector, an urban informal sector, and rural employment. Figure 9–1 is a schematic representation of these three markets.

The **urban formal sector** is where almost everyone would like to work if he or she could. It consists of the government and large-scale enterprises such as banks, insurance companies, factories, and trading houses. People welcome the opportunity to work in a modern facility and be associated with a prestigious name, but the main attractions of formal-sector employers are that they pay the highest wages and offer the steadiest employment. One reason they pay more is that they hire virtually all the university- and secondary-school-educated labor in the country. But they also tend to pay more for given types of labor than the smaller firms pay—more, indeed, than they would have to pay just to attract the number of workers they need.

Why do formal-sector firms pay as much as they do, when there are many unemployed people who would work for less? Sometimes formal-sector firms pay more because the government presses them to do so (for example, through minimum wage laws or pressures to be model employers), but often they do so quite voluntarily. The efficiency wage theory postulates that worker productivity is a

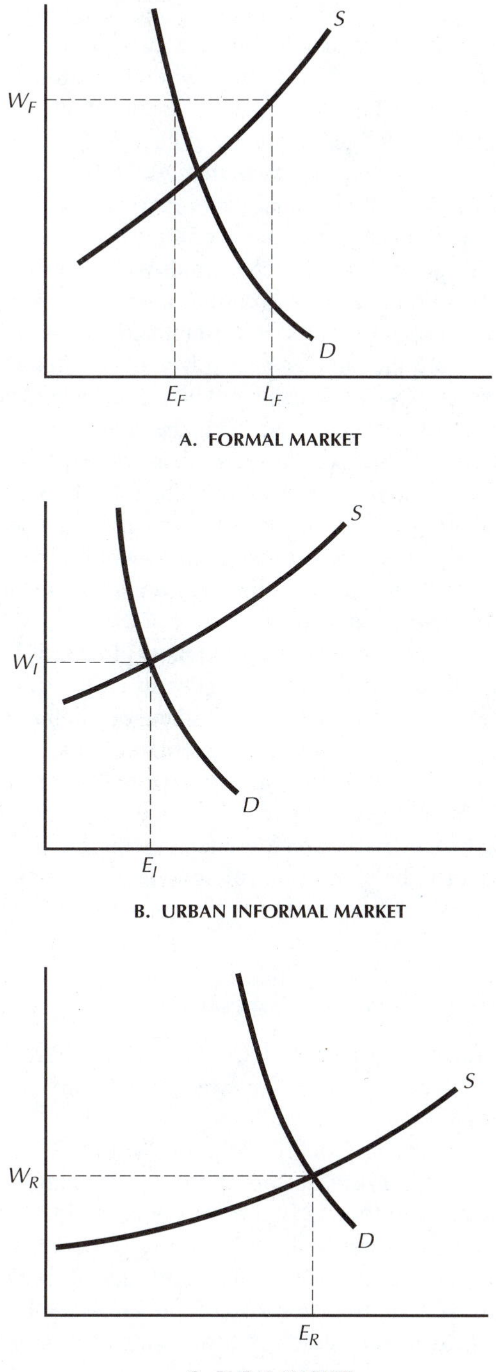

FIGURE 9–1 The Three-Tiered Employment Structure. In the formal market (A) the wage (W_F) is too high for the market to clear; not everyone can find work and there is a queue ($L_F - E_F$) of job applicants. In urban informal sector (B), the wage (W_I) clears the market but is lower than the formal-sector wage (W_F). Finally, in the rural labor market (C) the wage (W_R) also clears the market but is lower yet; the supply of labor to this sector is highly elastic.

positive function of the wage paid.[1] For several reasons, better-paid workers may be more productive. First, they may be better nourished, and therefore physically better able to work. Second, they may be inherently better workers, since firms that pay higher wages can be more selective about whom they hire. Next, they may stay where they are longer, learn by doing, and reduce the firm's labor turnover. Finally, higher wages may make them work harder because they fear to lose such a good job. With wages held above market-clearing levels by some or all of these factors, there is always a queue of workers ($E_F - L_F$ in Figure 9–1A) waiting for jobs with urban formal-sector employers. A routine job-opening announcement may attract hundreds, or even thousands, of applicants.

Alongside the large urban formal-sector establishments—or, more likely, in the alleys behind them—are the smaller enterprises of the **urban informal sector**. These shops and curbside establishments produce and trade a wide range of goods and services. Sometimes they compete with the larger enterprises; more often, they meet market demands that formal-sector firms do not find it profitable to satisfy. Often the urban informal sector provides jobs for migrants who have come to town from the rural areas to seek work in the urban formal sector but have been unable to find it. However, studies in several third-world cities indicate that many of the people who earn their income in this way are long-time urban residents and veterans at their particular lines of work.

The urban informal sector can be easy to enter; often one can become a street hawker or enter dozens of other lines of work with only a tiny amount of capital. For those who lack even the 10 to 100 dollars of capital needed to be self-employed, there is always the opportunity to work for others, although frequently at low wages and in harsh working conditions. Domestic servants form one such group, a large and important one in every low-income country (servants then disappear gradually as wages rise in middle-income countries). The urban informal sector can provide incredible amounts of low-wage employment and a useful array of goods and services (see box).

The Urban Informal Sector in Indonesia

Although the informal sector is hard to define, there is no denying its importance as a source of jobs, income, and a wide array of goods and services in many developing countries.

In-depth studies carried out in Jakarta by the Center for Policy and Implementation Studies under the direction of Harvard anthropologist Marguerite S. Robinson focused on three specific activities that are important in the Indonesian capital: becak driving (a becak is a three-wheeled pedal rickshaw); scavenging of waste materials such as metal, rags, and glass; and curbside retailing (hawking). The studies showed that these activities provide jobs for hundreds of thousands of workers at earnings lev-

1. On efficiency wage theory, see Joseph E. Stiglitz, "Economic Organization, Information, and Development," in Chenery and Srinivasan, *Handbook of Development Economics,* Vol. 1, pp. 93–160; George A. Akerlof and Janet L. Yellen (eds.), *Efficiency Wage Models of the Labor Market,* (Cambridge, U.K.: Cambridge University Press, 1986), "Introduction," pp. 1–21; and Lawrence F. Katz, "Efficiency Wage Theories: A Partial Evaluation," *NBER Macroeconomics Annual 1986* (Cambridge, Mass.: National Bureau of Economic Research, 1986), pp. 235–76.

els that compare favorably, on average, with what the same workers could earn in the formal sector. Informal-sector workers are often migrants from rural areas who regularly remit substantial sums to relatives left behind in the villages. They produce low-priced goods and services (e.g., short-distance transportation, inputs for small-scale industries, and small-lot retailing) that help to hold down the cost of living for working-class households and, ironically, permit formal-sector employers to pay lower wages. Jakarta's scavengers recycle a variety of waste materials with an efficiency that modern industrial societies, which lack an equally efficient technology (at their high wage rates) for separating different types of materials so that they can be reprocessed, should envy.

Although informal-sector entrepreneurs provide many benefits to their families, their numerous employees, and their customers, they are often viewed negatively by the municipal authorities. Their activities are frequently suppressed, and efforts to help them are often misguided (for example, new markets may be developed at sites less favorably located than those habitually used by traders; the authorities then wonder why many of the new sites remain empty whereas traders who do move to them may fail to repay their government loans!). More-enlightened policy must be based, not only on empathy for people who are struggling to survive, but also on an understanding of how their enterprises really contribute to development.

Because it is easily entered, the urban informal-sector labor market tends to be in equilibrium (Figure 9–1B). New entrants can generally find something to do, even if their presence tends to drive down wages slightly for all participants.

Although in visualizing the urban informal sector one tends to think first of massive urban agglomerations such as Mexico City, Lagos, and Calcutta, smaller cities and towns also provide significant amounts of urban informal-sector employment. Market towns often draw rural workers to participate in activities linked to the farm economy: marketing and processing of local agricultural produce, distribution of basic consumer goods and farm inputs, transportation, and repair services.

Even the urban informal sector is likely to pay higher wages than the **rural labor market**, employment outside the cities. In part this wage differential is illusory because urbanites have to pay higher prices for food and housing than rural residents, and they are often forced to buy things (water, fuel, building materials) that are obtainable free (that is, without monetary cost although large expenditures of time and effort are often required) in rural areas. But even after allowance has been made for differences in living costs, surveys indicate that most urban residents, even recent rural-urban migrants, are better off than all but the wealthiest rural residents.

As assumed by dual-economy models of development (presented in Chapter 3), rural employment in low-income countries commonly means work by family members, not for wages but for a share in the output of a family enterprise. Yet there is almost always a market for hired labor, particularly in seasons of peak labor demand. Depending on the amount of population pressure and the prevailing pattern of land tenure, there will be a large or small number of people who are forced to depend on wage employment because they have no land to farm or not enough to support their families. These agricultural laborers typically make up the very lowest income stratum in a poor country. Even when there are few agricultural laborers as such, rural households commonly trade labor back and forth at different times of the year, sometimes on a cooperative or barter basis but more often for wages in cash or kind. While rural people work primarily in agriculture, they often rely on small-scale nonagricultural activities such as trade, services, and handicrafts to provide important supplements to agricultural income.

Measuring Labor Supply and Utilization

The structural complexity of labor markets in developing countries makes it hard to apply concepts that are relatively straightforward in developed countries. In both types of countries, policy makers want to measure the supply of labor available to the economy and determine how fully the available labor supply is being utilized.

In developed countries labor supply is measured through the **labor force** concept. The labor force includes everyone who has a job or is actively looking for work. Its size is determined by three factors: (1) the size of the population; (2) its composition in terms of age groups and sexes; and (3) the labor force participation rates of these groups, which reflect social factors such as educational patterns and the willingness of women to work outside the home. The short-term responsiveness (elasticity) of labor supply can be large under unusual circumstances, as when women in many countries went to work in factories for the first time during World War II, but normally it is low. Developed countries experiencing full employment, as many European nations did during the 1950s, can easily have their economic growth constrained by the available supply of labor.

In LDC conditions, the size of the labor force is generally not a constraint on development, although skilled labor and management can be very scarce. Typically, more people would like to work than are working, and many who are working are underutilized. Moreover, the meaning of "having a job" or "actively looking for work" is harder to pin down in the context of most developing countries, where multiple job holding, part-time work, and work for one's own family all tend to be more common than in a developed country. The number of "discouraged workers" (those who have stopped looking for work because they believe none is available) is also likely to be greater in less-developed than in developed countries. Using the conventional definitions, women participate increasingly in the labor force as development proceeds and the number of jobs outside the home rises. This suggests that at low levels of development there is a large reserve of female labor not apparent in the statistics, but ready to come forth when reasonably attractive work opportunities open up. In fact, of course, these women are already working hard in the home, where by convention they are not counted as part of the labor force.

In developed countries, labor underutilization is measured primarily through the concept of **unemployment**. The unemployed are defined as those who do not have a job but are actively looking for one. The familiar **rate of unemployment** is total unemployment as a percentage of the labor force. In industrial countries this rate is a closely watched indicator of economic performance.

In developing countries the rate of unemployment understates labor underutilization, often by a large factor. Surveys have indicated that India has a lower rate of unemployment than the United States. Yet most observers would agree that underutilization of labor supply is much greater in India than in the United States. Semideveloped countries with per capita income levels much higher than India's (for example, Malaysia, the Philippines, or almost any Latin American country) have also been measured in surveys as having far higher rates of unemployment than very poor countries. One reason for these anomalies is suggested by analyzing the types of people who are reported as unemployed when labor force surveys are carried out in developing countries. Many of them are young and live in urban areas; they are far better educated than the population in general, and many have never worked before. The inference is clear. The unemployed, as measured in these surveys, tend to be those who can afford to remain unemployed while they search for the type of job, undoubtedly in the urban formal sector, that they want and for which they believe their educational attainments qualify them. They are in fact likely to come from the better-off families in society and to be supported by their parents through an extended period of search for the "right" job.

The very poor may appear less often in the unemployment statistics of developing countries, and when they are caught by the labor force surveys, they do not remain unemployed for long. Because they lack resources, they cannot be without work for more than a brief period or they and their families may starve. Therefore, the poor must accept almost any job that becomes available. It has been ironically observed that in a poor country unemployment is a luxury. Unemployment is usually part of a job search that can be long and costly. Those best situated to make this search are the relatively privileged. Because LDCs lack unemployment insurance and other forms of social support common in the developed countries, job seekers must be supported either by their families (which sometimes make large sacrifices for the purpose) or by such casual work as they can find.

If the standard concept of unemployment is an inadequate measure of labor underutilization in developing countries, what better measure might be devised? This is a complex matter because, in fact, several different kinds of underutilization are common in developing countries (Table 9–4) and it is hard to encompass them all in any single measure.

It has been argued that disguised unemployment (the lower right-hand quadrant of Table 9–4) is the major form of labor underutilization in poor countries. Workers in this category are fully but unproductively employed in the rural sector or urban informal sector. Standard examples include the street vendor who sits for hours just to make one or two small sales, the shoe-shine hawker, and the goatherd. These people, it is argued, contribute little or nothing to production. Like those classified as unemployed, they could be put to work somewhere else in the economy at little or no opportunity cost. We will discuss the merits of this argument as a guide to development policy later. The important point here is that although this category of labor underutilization may be large and important, it is exceedingly difficult to define and measure precisely.

TABLE 9–4 Types of Labor Underutilization in Developing Countries

Type	Unemployment	Underemployment
Visible	Mostly urban new entrants	Rural labor; seasonal
Invisible	Mostly women ("discouraged workers")	Rural + urban informal sector ("disguised unemployment")

One country profile of labor underutilization, based on a framework similar to that of Table 9–4, was provided by the 1970 International Labor Office (ILO) employment mission to Colombia.[2] Visible unemployment in urban areas was running at 14 percent of the labor force, but the mission estimated that when discouraged workers and the underemployed (those involuntarily working short hours) were taken into account, urban labor underutilization rose to at least 25 percent. Adding disguised unemployment, as indicated by extremely low income, raised it to one-third of the labor force. In rural areas everyone was apparently employed at the peak season, but at least one-sixth of the labor force earned incomes low enough to be characterized as disguised unemployment.

The many difficulties of defining and measuring labor utilization make it uncertain just how the overall degree of labor utilization varies with the level of economic development. The highest rates of visible unemployment, often reaching 10 to 20 percent of the labor force, have been measured in the urban areas of low- and middle-income countries. According to broader definitions of underutilization, still larger shares of the labor force are underutilized and overall underutilization is probably greatest in the poorest countries. Disguised forms of underutilization are relatively more important in the poorest countries than in the somewhat richer ones. In the semideveloped countries covered by labor utilization surveys, disguised unemployment was significant but quantitatively somewhat less than open unemployment.

Nor is it easy for trends to be established with certainty. In the 1960s it was widely feared that accelerated population growth would lead to massive unemployment in the developing countries. During the decade of the 1970s, many observers thought that the degree of labor underutilization in most LDCs was increasing. However, a careful review of the data showed that this was probably not the case.[3] The point is that nearly everyone in developing countries must work to live. The main issue, therefore, is not how many job seekers find employment, but rather what kind of work they find to do—how productive they are and how good an income they earn.

Labor Reallocation

We cannot talk about employment policy in developing countries without broaching an issue that has been debated extensively by development theorists: how can underutilized labor be used in a development strategy? In theoretical writings of the 1950s it was frequently asserted that large numbers of people engage in work which adds nothing to national output. Two well-known writers who emphasized this idea and made it a cornerstone of their analyses of how development proceeds were the Finnish economist Ragnar Nurkse and Nobel laureate W. Arthur Lewis.[4] Nurkse saw the reallocation of surplus labor to more productive uses, especially labor-intensive construction projects, as a major source of capital formation and

2. International Labor Office, *Towards Full Employment* (Geneva: ILO, 1970), pp.12–28.

3. Peter Gregory, "An Assessment of Changes in Employment Conditions in Less-Developed Countries," *Economic Development and Cultural Change,* 28, no. 4 (July 1980), 673–700.

4. Ragnar Nurkse, *Problems of Capital Formation in Underdeveloped Countries* (Oxford: Blackwell, 1957; first published in 1953), and W. Arthur Lewis, "Economic Development with Unlimited Supplies of Labour," *Manchester School,* 22 (May 1954), 139–91.

economic growth. Lewis envisaged a similar reallocation process, but he pictured the "capitalist sector," essentially industry, as the principal employer of the surplus labor. (Chapters 3 and 4 discuss Lewis' theory in detail.) Both theorists regarded the labor reallocation process as nearly costless, but they worried about how to capture from the agricultural sector the food necessary to feed the reallocated laborers.

This approach to development theory opened up a debate on two issues: what extra laborers actually contribute to LDC agricultural production and how readily any excess labor can be mobilized in industry or in construction projects. Three conclusions emerged from this debate. First, extra laborers do increase agricultural production, contrary to Nurkse's and Lewis' assumption. The marginal product of labor is almost always positive, not zero, but it may be very low in densely populated countries. At least this is true on a year-round basis. If there is really such a thing as zero marginal product labor, the condition is likely to be seasonal. Second, even if forgone output were zero or negligible, there would be other costs associated with the physical movement of labor from agricultural pursuits to industry or construction. These will be discussed shortly. Third, although long-term growth consists of reallocating labor to more productive uses, there are no free, or even very easy, gains to be had in the short run.

A more positive restatement of this conclusion is that in almost all countries and times there are opportunities to work at some positive wage and marginal product, although these may be very low. If workers remain unemployed despite such opportunities, the most likely reason is that they reject the wage offered as too low to compensate for their loss of leisure or chance to search for a better-paid job.

Costs and Benefits of Reallocating Labor

Given these findings, how should an LDC government look at an employment-creating development project? In Chapter 6 we saw that any development project can be evaluated using social cost-benefit analysis. An important part of the social cost of any input is its **opportunity cost**, its value in its next best alternative use. Labor hired for an urban formal-sector project might well be drawn from the urban informal sector. The worker who moves out of the urban informal sector may in turn be replaced by someone from the rural sector. In this example, the output lost is that of the worker who was formerly in the rural sector the worker at the end of the employment chain. For this reason, some analysts believe that the wage paid to casual agricultural laborers provides a good measure of the social cost of unskilled labor.

However, this measure, although a good indicator of output forgone through labor reallocation, probably understates the true social cost of employing labor, which has other components that are likely to be significant.

One such component is **induced migration**. An influential model of rural-urban migration, developed by John R. Harris and Michael P. Todaro and described more fully in the following section, implies that migrating workers are essentially participants in a lottery of relatively high-paid jobs in the towns.[5] When new urban jobs are created, the lottery becomes more attractive to potential

5. John R. Harris and Michael P. Todaro, "Migration, Unemployment and Development: A Two-Sector Analysis," *American Economic Review*, 60 (March 1970), 126–42.

migrants. Depending on their responsiveness to this improved opportunity, it is possible that more than one worker will migrate for each job created. If so, the output forgone may be that of two or more agricultural workers, not just one. Family ties may multiply this effect. If a male worker migrates and brings his family with him, additional output may be lost because the wife and children find fewer employment opportunities in the town than in the rural areas; for example, they do not have land on which to grow food.

In addition to forgone output, certain **costs of urbanization** should be included in computing the social cost of urban job creation. Some of these costs are internalized by the worker and presumably taken into account in the migration decision: the higher cost of food, housing, and other items in the town. Other costs are external and must be borne by society as a whole: social services that are provided only to the urban population or that are more expensive in the town, pollution, congestion, and additional security requirements. It is these costs that make many third-world governments frown on urbanization, however much they may desire industrialization.

Finally, there is the possibility of a reduction in national savings, which has worried development theorists and Soviet-style economic planners alike. If labor that has been adding little to agricultural output but has been consuming a larger share of that product is withdrawn from the sector, who controls the food thus freed up? Government planners may want to transfer the food that the rural worker was consuming to feed the same worker in the city. Their fear is that the remaining rural population will simply increase its per capita consumption. Since the urban labor force must be fed—from imports, if not from domestic production—the planners' concern is that aggregate national consumption will rise and national savings will fall and reduce the growth of GNP. The problem is exacerbated when the new urban workers get higher wages and thus want to consume more food than they were consuming in the rural areas.

During the 1930s this concern moved Soviet planners to drastic measures to extract a surplus from a resistant rural population. Governments of developing countries generally have neither the means nor the desire to suppress food consumption, so they may indeed experience some decline in savings. This is far from pure loss, however, because the added consumption is a gain to some members of society. In any case there are better ways to increase saving than through coercive controls on food consumption.

The primary benefit of urban employment is added output. A highly productive project can easily repay all the costs discussed above, but low-productivity make-work projects in urban areas may incur costs with few offsetting benefits. Labor-intensive projects in rural areas, especially those employing seasonally underutilized labor, may also waste resources but are likely to be more beneficial on a net basis because they do not require workers to migrate. These projects are discussed near the end of this chapter.

A secondary benefit of urban job creation is the training it may provide. In developing countries opportunities to learn skills useful in the modern economy are concentrated in urban areas. For example, the ability to operate and repair machinery of all kinds is typically rare. A worker who comes to town can acquire these skills. In doing so, the worker may benefit and obtain higher wages if employment as a skilled worker can be found. But the worker also confers an "external benefit" on society because everyone gains when bus drivers, auto mechanics, appliance repairpeople, and others who work with machinery learn to do their jobs better. The gainers include both employers, who can hire labor from a more-skilled pool, and consumers, who get better service at lower prices.

It is thus evident that developing through the reallocation of low-productivity labor is a more complex business than Nurkse and Lewis imagined in the 1950s. Nevertheless, employment expansion remains vital, both for increasing output and for redistributing income. Economies that can create jobs with a marginal product of labor above its social cost, taking into account all the elements discussed here, can achieve both these objectives simultaneously. Output rises and more income goes to unskilled workers from low-income families. Less-productive forms of employment creation, in which the social cost of labor exceeds its marginal product, can be acceptable as redistributive measures if income redistribution is desired and other ways of achieving it are unavailable. But they achieve more equity only by sacrificing growth.

Internal Migration

Most of the internal labor migration that occurs in the course of economic development is from rural to urban areas. Theorists have long argued that economic factors dominate the decision to migrate. Some early writers distinguished between "pull" and "push" factors, saying that rural-urban migration can result either from favorable economic developments in the town or from adverse developments in the countryside. The Harris-Todaro model of rural-urban migration, introduced above, integrates these two sets of factors by positing the urban-rural wage differential as the motivating force behind migration. Yet there is something to the older notion. Just as eighteenth-century English cottagers were pushed into the town by the Enclosure Movement, so peasants in eastern India move to Calcutta primarily because of wretched conditions in the surrounding countryside, rather than outstanding income or employment opportunities in Calcutta itself. By contrast, the growth of dynamic third-world cities such as Sao Paulo and Nairobi could be attributed at least partly to pull factors.

The Harris-Todaro model is an important formulation of the role of economic incentives in the migration decision. The model assumes that migration depends primarily on a comparison of wages in the rural and urban labor markets. That is,

$$M_t = f(W_u - W_r), \qquad [9\text{–}1]$$

where M_t is the number of rural to urban migrants in time period t, f is a response function, W_u is the urban wage, and W_r is the rural wage. Since there is unemployment in the town (assume that there is none in the countryside) and every migrant cannot expect to find a job there, the model postulates that the expected urban wage is compared with the rural wage. The expected urban wage is the actual wage times the probability of finding a job, or

$$W_u^* = pW_u, \qquad [9\text{–}2]$$

where W_u^* = expected urban wage and p = probability of finding a job.

A simple way of defining p is

$$p = \frac{E_u}{E_u + U_u}, \qquad [9\text{–}3]$$

where E_u = urban employment and U_u = urban unemployment. In this formulation all members of the urban labor force are assumed to have equal chances of obtaining the jobs available, so W_u^* becomes simply the urban wage times the urban employment rate. Migration in any given time period then depends on three factors: the rural-urban wage gap, the urban employment rate, and the responsiveness of potential migrants to the resulting opportunities.

$$M_t = h\,(pW_u - W_r), \qquad [9\text{–}4]$$

where M_t = the migration in period t and h = the response rate of potential migrants.

As long as W_u^* exceeds W_r, the model predicts that rural-urban migration will continue. It will only stop when migration has forced down the urban wage or forced up urban unemployment sufficiently that $W_u^* = W_r$. It is also possible that W_r is greater than W_u^*, in which case there will be a flow of disappointed urban job seekers back to the countryside.

An interesting feature of this model is that an increase in the urban wage (W_u) requires an increase in unemployment to restore equilibrium. In other words, an increase in the demand for labor or anything else that raises wages in the cities is likely to induce more migration and thereby worsen urban unemployment.

Critics of the Harris-Todaro model point out that the equilibrium condition specified by the model is seldom attained. It is common for urban wages to be, say, 50 to 100 percent higher than rural wages and for urban unemployment to run at 10 to 20 percent of the labor force. If the figures stay in this range, the expected urban wage (W_u^*) remains above the rural wage (W_r). Migration in practice does not seem to close the gap between W_u^* and W_r as the model predicts. The model can be rescued, however, by assuming (realistically) that not all urban jobs turn over, that is, are available in the "lottery." In this case, the probability of a migrant not finding a job is lower than the employment rate. For example, if the unemployment rate is 20 percent, the probability of a migrant's finding a job might actually be 50 percent or less, not 80 percent as implied by the simplest version of the model.

Reverse migration from town to country is significant in many countries. Although Harris and Todaro interpret such movement as disappointed urban job seekers returning home in despair, much of this two-way or *circular* migration is clearly intentional. Young, unattached males are particularly likely to migrate temporarily to towns, mines, or plantations, there to work for a while and amass savings, which they then take back to the rural areas to invest in land, farm improvements, or marriage. This pattern of cyclical migration has been especially common in parts of Africa, perhaps because in many African cultures women customarily tend the crops after the men have planted them. The opportunity cost of absent males outside the planting season is thus low.

Economic factors are not the only important influences on migration decisions. Studies show that distance and social ties are also significant. Migrants to expanding urban areas tend to come from nearby rural regions, and peasants pushed out of their native districts by a calamity are likely to go to the nearest large town. People often move to areas where members of their family, village, or ethnic group have settled.

Although most internal migration in developing countries is from rural to urban areas, interregional differences in economic opportunity can bring about substantial rural-to-rural movement as well. Countries fortunate enough to possess lightly settled yet cultivable regions may try to bring about such movement as a matter of public policy, as we saw in Chapter 8. Unless there are massive physical or legal barriers to the settlement of relatively empty areas, however, such interregional movements tend to occur spontaneously. This happened in Nepal, for instance, where farmers moved from the densely packed Kathmandu Valley into the southern *terai* region, and in many parts of Africa and South America. Unforced movements of population from one region of a country to another are likely to be socially beneficial. People make these moves to improve their own living standards and those of their families. Even in the most congested slums of such major LDC cities as Sao Paulo, Lagos, and Jakarta, migrants report that they are better-off than they were in the rural areas and generally do not want to go back.

Society is likely to benefit as well from an improved spatial allocation of labor relative to other resources. But two factors could make social costs greater than benefits. First, distorted incentives, such as artificially high wages and subsidized urban services, can inflate private benefits. Second, external costs such as congestion, pollution, and crime are borne equally by migrants, who benefit from migration, and by their predecessors, who do not. If these distortions and externalities are large, social costs may exceed benefits.

International Migration

International migration, which has continued at a high level in recent years,[6] is frequently regarded as a different matter altogether. To bring a degree of cool rationality to this often-heated subject, it is helpful to distinguish between unskilled labor and skilled or educated labor. This distinction may not matter when we look at the problem from the global point of view: it has been argued that world GNP is maximized when everyone works where the salary, and therefore presumably the productivity, is greatest. But it is important from the viewpoint of the developing countries because skilled and unskilled labor have different opportunity costs.

There are two reasons why the migration of educated, highly skilled labor is abhorrent to most developing countries and has been stigmatized as the "brain drain." One is that such people represent one of the LDCs' scarcest resources. The other is that in most cases their education has been time-consuming, expensive, and heavily subsidized by the state. If they depart for foreign lands, not only are their services lost but a high cost must be incurred to train replacements. Yet if they are so productive, why are they not paid enough to keep them at home? The answer may be nonmarket influences on the salary structure. For example, if most doctors and engineers work for the government and their salaries are held down to avoid politically embarrassing salary differentials, it is not surprising that many of them seek an opportunity to emigrate. International agencies, which recruit in a worldwide labor market, typically pay far more for the same skills than national governments. This is why one finds Pakistani experts working in Egypt, for example, even as Egyptian experts are employed in Pakistan, although both groups could probably work more effectively in their own countries.

6. From 1985 to 1990 eight developing countries each supplied 200,000 or more net emigrants: Mexico, the Philippines, China, Lebanon, Pakistan, India, El Salvador, and Colombia. The United States was by far the largest receiving country with nearly 3 million net immigrants, including an estimate of illegal entrants. Australia, Canada, and Saudi Arabia each admitted more than 300,000 in this period. See Fred Arnold, "International Migration: Who Goes Where?" *Finance and Development,* 27, no. 2 (June 1990), 46–47.

Although it surely does raise world GNP, international migration of the educated worsens the distribution of income between rich and poor countries. To offset this effect, Jagdish Bhagwati of Columbia University has proposed a tax on the brain drain, to be collected by the governments of developed countries to which professional and technical personnel from underdeveloped countries have migrated.[7] The proceeds of the tax would be transferred to the poor countries of origin as compensation for their loss of talent.

In contrast, international migration of unskilled labor can be beneficial to the country of emigration. Unskilled workers are more plentiful, so their loss is likely to be felt less keenly by the sending economy. There are even significant offsetting benefits. One is remittances: unskilled migrants are less likely to take their families along and are thus more likely to send money back. This makes labor a kind of national export. Countries such as Turkey, Algeria, and Egypt have long relied on worker remittances as a significant source of foreign exchange earnings. A second potential benefit is training. Unskilled workers who go abroad generally return to their native lands after a few years and bring back usable skills acquired abroad.

Some LDC governments have begun to look more favorably on worker emigration. Despairing of generating enough employment at home, they have begun to encourage their people to go abroad, at least for a while. South Asian countries, for example, took advantage of lucrative employment opportunities in the Middle East in the 1970s and 1980s. When education is particularly cheap, even the emigration of trained personnel may be encouraged. The Philippines has been exporting doctors and nurses in quantity for years.

EMPLOYMENT POLICY

The main cause of the employment problem in the developing countries has been the rapid growth of the population and labor force relative to the natural resource base and sometimes also the stock of physical capital. But there have also been problems on the demand side of the labor market. Even when capital stock has risen faster than labor force, it has often been deployed in ways that kept labor absorption well below its potential. It was once thought that import-substituting industrialization (ISI) would readily solve the employment problem in most LDCs. This was the premise, for example, of India's first two 5-year plans. But experience has shown that although industrial-sector employment has grown rapidly in many cases of ISI, it has been unable to absorb the expanding labor force. A simple example will help to explain why this is so.

Labor Absorption through Industrialization

Industrial sectors in developing countries typically grow rapidly from a low base. In low-income countries between 1965 and 1983, value-added in industry (defined to include manufacturing, utilities, and construction) grew at an average rate of 7.1 percent a year. Yet employment growth in the sector was only 60 percent as

7. Jagdish Bhagwati and Martin Partington, *Taxing the Brain Drain: A Proposal* (Amsterdam: North-Holland, 1976).

fast, or 4.3 percent a year. The amount of industrial employment growth expected from a given rate of output growth can be expressed by

$$\Delta E_i = \eta g\,(V_i)S_i, \qquad [9\text{–}5]$$

where ΔE_i = annual employment growth in industry, expressed in percentage points of labor force growth; η = an elasticity relating the growth of employment to the growth of value-added; $g(V_i)$ = growth in industrial value added, expressed in percentage points; S_i = industrial employment as a fraction of total employment. Industry absorbed 9 percent of the labor force in low-income countries in 1965, so

$$\Delta E_i = 0.6 \times 7.1 \times 0.09 = 0.4. \qquad [9\text{–}6]$$

This means that only 0.4 of 1 percent of the labor force was absorbed by industrial expansion each year. Yet the labor force grew at 2.1 percent a year from 1965 to 1983. Thus, fewer than one-fifth of the workers entering the labor force found jobs in industry. The rest had to do the best they could in primary production or in the service sector.

Is this too pessimistic a depiction of the problem? On the brighter side it can be noted that only direct employment creation in industry has been taken into account. Some additional **indirect job creation** can be expected in sectors with either forward or backward linkages to the industrial sector, such as service activities that distribute its products and agricultural and mining activities that supply its inputs (linkages within the industrial sector are already accounted for in the calculation). Indirect job creation can be significant in some circumstances, as when the capacity to process domestically produced primary commodities is expanded, but it is frequently limited for industrialization of the import-substituting type, which has few forward or backward linkages. Chapter 16 will discuss this in detail. **Secondary job creation** also occurs as workers employed in high-paying industrial jobs spend their incomes. Businesses supplying them with consumer goods of various kinds prosper, and this creates additional employment.

Since industrial jobs are often among the most productive and best paid in the economy, it is important to ask what can be done to improve industrial-employment creation. In the formula given above, raising ΔE_i requires increasing η, $g(V_i)$, S_i, or some combination of them. Industry's share in employment (S_i) will rise only gradually through time. In the medium term, industrial labor absorption can be increased by raising either the growth rate of sectoral value-added $g(V_i)$ or the employment elasticity η.

When economic growth slowed down in the 1980s, particularly in many Latin American and African countries, the labor market situation tended to deteriorate. Governments and private formal-sector employers shed workers in some cases and trimmed the wage premiums that they had traditionally paid in others. One result was accelerated growth of the urban informal sector.

A few countries were able to expand industrial employment much faster than average. These are the nations that achieved most success in exporting labor-intensive manufactured products. This path to industrial job creation was pioneered by South Korea, Taiwan, Hong Kong, and Singapore, known collectively as the *four tigers*. More recently, Malaysia, Thailand, and even Indonesia and coastal areas of China have followed in their footsteps, along with a few other countries including tiny Mauritius. Many other developing countries in all regions are now eager to join the trend. It is thus important to understand what, exactly, is involved.

There were two separate aspects to the four tigers' achievement. First, by breaking into the export market, they were able to reach higher growth rates of industrial output $g(V_i)$, because they freed themselves from dependence on growth of the domestic market for manufactured goods. Second, they achieved high values of η because the goods they chose to export, at least at the start of their export drives, were those which used large amounts of their most plentiful resource, labor. These countries have experienced values of η of around 0.8 instead of the more typical 0.4 to 0.6. Thus South Korea after 1963 was able to absorb as much as half its total labor force growth in manufactured exports alone, at a time when most LDCs were absorbing less than 5 percent of their labor force growth in this activity.[8] How many other LDCs will be able to take lessons in employment policy from South Korea and the other tigers? We take up this question in the next section.

The employment performance of industry in most developing countries has been particularly distressing when one recalls that this sector should not only be soaking up a good share of labor force growth, but also gradually drawing labor away from less productive forms of employment in peasant agriculture, petty services, and cottage industries. When industry fails to do this, employment in these less productive sectors must rise rather than fall. This can lead to stagnant, or even declining, levels of worker productivity and income. There is evidence that wages and productivity are in fact stagnating or declining in a number of the poorer and less dynamic countries, both in manufacturing and more broadly.

Although the above discussion was couched in terms of manufacturing, it can be extended to the entire urban formal sector. Large trading companies, financial organizations, transport and communication facilities, public utilities, and the like may collectively be even more important for intersectoral labor transfer than manufacturing. And they, too, often fail to increase their employment fast enough to employ the growing labor force.

Elements of a Solution

In principle the problem of labor underutilization could be attacked on either the supply or the demand side. In practice, however, little can be done to bring about a supply-side adjustment. Labor supply grows steadily from year to year. It is hard to discourage people from seeking work. Nor would most policy makers wish to do so, given the advantages of employment creation as a means of income redistribution and the psychological and political advantages of enabling everyone to participate in the economy. The only realistic supply-side potential is to reduce the growth of labor supply in the long run by limiting population growth.

At one time it was widely believed that increasing the supply of certain types of skilled labor would produce a strong expansionary effect on employment generally through the increased absorption of complementary unskilled labor. Thus India in its early post-independence years tried to eliminate a perceived labor bottleneck by expanding the supply of engineers, on the supposition that employment in construction and other activities could be increased in this way. The number of

8. Susumu Watanabe, "Exports and Employment: The Case of the Republic of Korea," *International Labour Review,* 106, no. 6 (December 1972), 495–526.

Indian engineers increased rapidly. The effect on general employment is hard to determine, but the effect on the engineers was clear-cut: there were soon far too many of them, and many were unemployed. The moral is that although skill shortages can constrain employment and output growth, they can sometimes be eliminated relatively quickly and easily through the expansion of education and training programs or through migration. In other countries, where education is less developed, skill formation may be much more difficult and time-consuming.

Given the limited potential for correcting the labor market disequilibrium by working on the supply side, policy must concentrate on the demand side of the equation. Many different kinds of policy affect the economy's ability to create jobs for a growing labor force. Wage, industrial promotion, fiscal, foreign trade, and education policies all have important implications for employment.

Earlier we identified two different approaches to employment creation. One is to stimulate output, especially in relatively high-productivity and high-wage sectors of the economy. The other is to try to increase the amount of labor used to produce a given amount of output. The first approach will be discussed in Chapters 17, 18, and 20, which deal with the growth of exports, agriculture, and industry. The second is examined here.

In general, there are two ways to make production more labor-intensive. One is to alter relative prices and thus create incentives for businesses to substitute labor for capital. The other is to develop technologies more appropriate to the factor proportions prevailing in developing countries.

Factor Price Distortions

The prices of labor and capital faced by modern-sector firms in less-developed countries are frequently distorted in ways that make capital artificially cheap relative to labor. This distortion can inhibit labor absorption at several levels. At the sectoral level it can promote the growth of sectors that are technologically better suited to capital-intensive production (for example, basic metals) and hinder the growth of sectors that tend to be more labor-intensive (for example, textiles). At the level of interfirm competition, it can promote the appearance and growth of plants using relatively capital-intensive technologies (these may be large scale, foreign-owned, or both) and accelerate the decline and disappearance of more labor-intensive units. At the plant level it can promote the use of machines in place of people.

These factor price distortions usually result from some form of government action. Artificially high wages may be imposed on modern-sector firms by minimum-wage laws intended to protect workers' incomes, by government support of trade union demands, or by pressure (especially on foreign- and state-owned enterprises) to be model employers. Some governments levy payroll or social security taxes on modern-sector payrolls and thus raise the cost of labor to the employer. In Latin America, restrictions on firing workers are frequently so severe that employers think twice before hiring them in the first place. When jobs once done by foreigners are taken over by citizens, nationalist pressure can cause salaries to be kept at their previously high, internationally competitive levels.

All these policies promote the welfare of relatively small groups at the expense of much larger ones. Minimum-wage laws and similar measures, if effectively enforced (and often they are not), can improve wages and working conditions for those workers fortunate enough to get jobs in modern-sector firms. But by raising the cost of labor, these measures limit the ability of existing firms to absorb more workers and inhibit the creation of more enterprises like them. In this way, they harm the much larger group of workers who either are unemployed or work in the informal and rural sectors.

Why do governments of countries with serious employment problems enact such measures as minimum-wage laws? The answer is that relatively small but well-organized, vocal, and visible groups of modern-sector workers, nearly always located in urban areas, have enough political power to lobby effectively for enactment of these laws, or for increases in the statutory minimum wage once a system of minimum wages is established. In some Latin American countries, minimum wages are indexed to inflation; this ensures that they remain high in real terms. Under a minimum-wage system the government accepts direct responsibility for the earnings of workers in the protected sectors. If it resists a strongly backed demand for a rise in the minimum wage, it is inviting political trouble. Of course the government is also responsible for the welfare of those who lose from the wage increase because their chances of ever getting a job in the protected high-wage sector are reduced. But their loss is less easily perceived than the wage gain of the protected workers, and the government is less likely to be held accountable for it.

Artificially cheap capital reinforces the effect of artificially expensive labor. In many developing countries, interest rate ceilings make capital equipment cheaper for those preferred customers who can obtain the credit necessary to buy it. (For the rest, of course, capital may become more expensive, or even unobtainable, as banks and other financial institutions direct the available funds to their preferred customers.) Overvaluation of the domestic currency in terms of foreign exchange can have a similar effect. It forces the imposition of a licensing system for foreign exchange, imports, or both, and this in turn makes artificially cheapened capital goods available to those who can obtain the necessary licenses.

Like minimum wages, interest ceilings, foreign exchange control, and import licensing all serve the interests of influential minorities. New York University economist Lawrence White has shown how preferred access to imports and credit in Pakistan led to the increasing concentration of industry and commerce in the hands of an elite group known as the *twenty families.*[9] Licensing systems also receive strong support from officials of the license-granting authorities, who can earn substantial illicit income from the bestowal of their favors.

Another way governments make capital artificially cheap is by gearing investment incentives to the amount of capital invested. Often a firm that invests $50 million is given a longer tax holiday or a shorter write-off period than one that invests only $5 million. This creates incentives for capital-intensive industries to be established in the country and for firms facing a range of possible technologies to select more capital-intensive modes of production.

Correcting Factor Price Distortion

What can be done to correct these factor price distortions? The most straightforward approach is for governments to avoid the kinds of price-distorting policies mentioned above, or if they have already instituted them, to deregulate as soon as

9. Lawrence White, *Industrial Concentration and Economic Power in Pakistan* (Princeton, N.J.: Princeton University Press, 1974).

possible. While there has been a trend toward liberalization in recent years, many governments remain reluctant to deregulate, out of either concern for the welfare of workers already holding modern-sector jobs or fear of the political power of those who benefit from artificially high wages or artificially cheap capital and foreign exchange.

Price distortions that cannot be removed can in theory be offset by taxes or subsidies. Economists have argued that the artificially high labor costs faced by modern-sector employers should be countered by a wage subsidy. While this advice has rarely been followed, a few countries have adopted investment incentives that depend in part on the number of jobs an investor creates.

An important question about all proposals for correcting factor price distortions is exactly how much employment they are likely to create. Technically speaking, this depends on the **elasticity of substitution**, which can be defined as

$$\sigma = \frac{\Delta(K/L)\,(w/r)}{\Delta(w/r)\,(K/L)},$$

where K is the amount of capital, L is the amount of labor, W is the wage rate, r is the cost of capital, and Δ signifies a change. The elasticity of substitution is thus the percentage change in the capital/labor ratio, $\Delta(K/L)/(K/L)$, that results from a given percentage change in the ratio of the price of labor to that of capital, $\Delta(w/r)/(w/r)$. (The expression w/r is also called the **wage-rental ratio**.) Thus, if a 10 percent decline in the wage-rental ratio leads to a 5 percent fall in the capital-labor ratio, then the elasticity of substitution is 0.5. In these circumstances a 10 percent decline in the wage-rental ratio would mean that in the future it would take 5 percent less investment (capital) to employ a given amount of labor; alternatively, a given amount of investment would employ 5 percent more workers.

Debates over the efficiency of employment creation through the correction of factor price distortions range elasticity optimists against elasticity pessimists. The optimists argue that the employment effects are likely to be large because investors tend to be rational profit maximizers who have a range of possible outputs and technologies open to them. When faced with cheaper labor relative to capital, they will therefore adjust by (1) concentrating on goods that can be produced relatively efficiently using a lot of labor relative to capital and (2) using more labor-intensive technologies in some or all of their operations. (The optimists assume that investors have a "shelf" of appropriate technologies available to them, an issue to be explored in the following section.)

The pessimists, on the other hand, contend that the response to a change in the wage-rental ratio may be small or nonexistent. They note that in some modern industries, technology permits little substitution of labor for capital. Examples include **process industries** such as petrochemicals and wood pulp. In such industries, highly capital-intensive technologies may be absolutely more efficient than any less-capital-intensive alternatives. That is, they may use less capital per unit of output as well as less labor. In many cases these technical characteristics are linked to economies of scale: to be efficient, a plant must be very large, as well as highly capital-intensive. An LDC government should think twice before establishing such an industry, but it would be ill advised to try to make it either small scale or labor-intensive.

Elasticity pessimists also point out that many firms sell in protected markets and therefore do not necessarily have to maximize profits; that they may prefer the most modern (capital-intensive) technologies for their own sake; and that they may produce goods mainly for middle-class consumption, to which capital-intensive technologies are better suited than labor-intensive technologies. For all these reasons, the pessimists argue against the policies advocated by the optimists. They would expect, for example, that a wage subsidy would do more to increase business profits than to expand employment.

Figures 9–2 and 9–3 show the differences between what the pessimists and the optimists have in mind. Which is the better depiction of the real world? It might seem simple to calculate the elasticity of substitution in developing countries and settle the argument once and for all. Indeed, many econometric estimates have been made. Quite a number of these studies have found the value of σ to range from 0.5, not a dramatically high value but high enough to encourage the elasticity optimists, up toward 1.0. But other writers have criticized these estimates on various grounds: they assume labor and capital to be **homogeneous**, that is, of uniform quality, when in fact they are not; they ignore the roles of other factors of production, such as management; they often deal with industries that are defined so broadly as to encompass a variety of outputs; and so on. Modest changes in assumptions, the critics note, can lead to large differences in conclusions.

Thus the debate between the optimists and the pessimists is not so easily resolved. However, there remain good reasons for believing that the relative prices of labor and capital can make a significant difference for employment creation. First, whatever the range of technologies available for producing a particular item, factor prices can have an important influence on employment by affecting the choice of goods to be produced. Recall the example of the successful exporters of

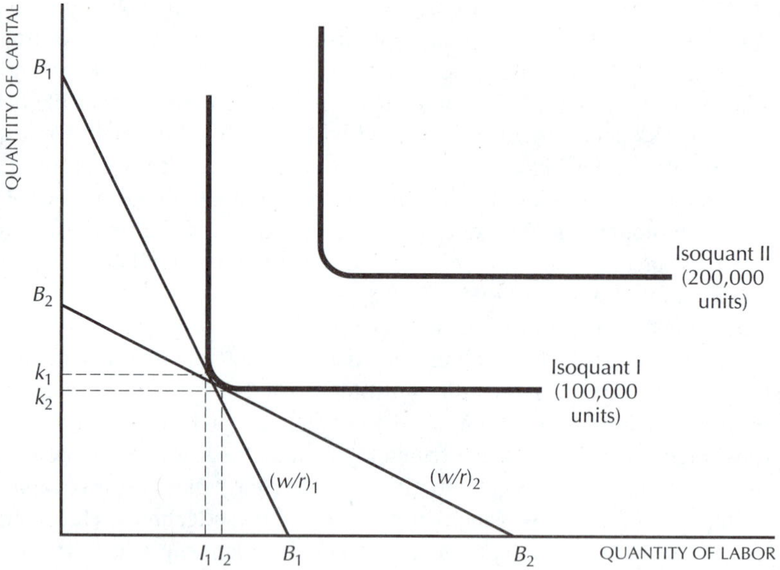

FIGURE 9–2 Factor Substitution with Relatively Fixed Factor Proportions (Low Elasticity of Substitution). Possibilities for producing given levels of output with different factor combinations are severly limited. When the wage-rental ratio falls from $(w/r)_1$ to $(w/r)_2$, there is little effect on the amounts of labor and capital used to produce 100,000 units of output.

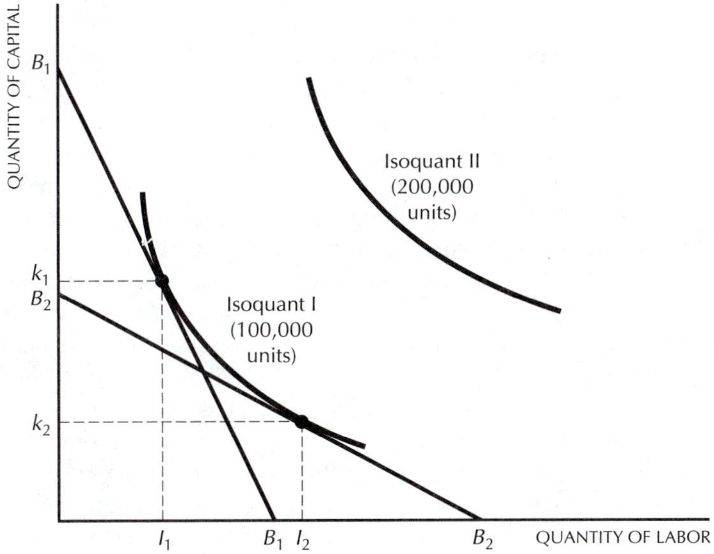

FIGURE 9–3 Factor Substitution with Relatively Variable Factor Proportions (High Elasticity of Substitution). Possibilities for producing given levels of output with different factor combinations are much greater than in Figure 9–2. When the wage-rental ratio falls, the amount of capital used is sharply reduced while employment expands significantly.

labor-intensive manufacturers mentioned earlier. Second, even if the technology of a core production process is fixed and capital-intensive, opportunities exist for using large amounts of labor in subsidiary operations such as materials handling. Similarly, in construction some operations are best done by machines at almost any wage-rental ratio, but others lend themselves to labor-intensive methods if labor costs are low enough.

Third, employers are far more responsive to relative factor prices when they are forced to sell their products in competitive markets than if they can sell in protected markets. An important study conducted in Indonesia by Harvard Business School professor Louis Wells showed that while the nonmaximizing behaviors cited by the elasticity pessimists are real enough, business executives indulge them much more freely in protected markets.[10] When competition forces them to seek the most-profitable technologies and factor proportions, both domestic and foreign business executives find ways to economize on capital and substitute more labor in labor-rich, capital-scarce countries.

A broad conclusion that emerges from these three points is that open competition promotes appropriate factor choices. Increasing the degree of competition, both within a given economy and among economies (as we will see in Chapters 16 and 17), can go far toward validating the assumptions of the elasticity optimists and making it possible to promote employment by reducing factor price distortions.

10. Louis T. Wells, "Economic Man and Engineering Man: Choice of Technology in a Low-Wage Country," in Peter Timmer et al. (eds.), *The Choice of Technology in Developing Countries: Some Cautionary Tales* (Cambridge, Mass.: Harvard University Center for International Affairs, 1975), pp. 69–93.

For the employment problem to be solved, or even significantly ameliorated, technology appropriate to the factor endowments of the low- and middle-income countries is clearly needed. How can such technology be acquired?

The LDCs face a paradoxical situation: they must depend on the developed countries to provide the great bulk of their modern technology, yet most of what these countries have to offer is inappropriate for use in countries with plentiful labor and scarce capital and skills. Since the beginning of their industrialization processes, the United States and Europe have had a scarcity of labor relative to other factors of production. Nearly all their innovations accordingly aimed at saving labor. The result in almost every productive sector has been a sequence of increasingly mechanized and automatically controlled technologies, each more appropriate than the last for a country with scarce labor and plentiful capital, but less and less appropriate for a country with the opposite factor endowments.

Excessive capital intensity is only one dimension of the inappropriateness of developed-country technology for the developing countries. Since the economies of even the smaller industrial countries are generally much larger than those of even the most populous developing countries, technologies are frequently designed to be efficient at a much larger scale of operation than the developing countries can hope to attain in the foreseeable future. In addition, borrowed technology may necessitate the use of skills that are unavailable in poor countries, and thus may require the importation of foreign technicians. Finally, it may be designed to produce the wrong type or grade of product: for example, no-iron synthetic fabrics in countries where cotton is cheaper and there is plenty of labor to wash and press cotton garments.

Despite all these dimensions of inappropriateness, rich countries remain the main source of technology for poor countries. Well over 90 percent of the world's expenditure on technology research and development takes place in rich countries. Third-world countries invite multinational corporations to invest in their leading sectors. They obtain equipment through official aid programs. The investors and aid givers can only provide what they know and have available. In the absence of appropriate policies in the developing country, the result is often the transfer of inappropriate technology.

Technology Policies

How can technology available from developed countries be adapted to LDC needs? Four possible methods have been suggested.[11] First, LDCs can use developed-country technologies but make peripheral modifications, for example, in materials handling. Second, they can borrow old technologies from the industrial countries. The U.S. technology of twenty, thirty, or even fifty years ago may be more appropriate to the setting of, say, India, than the methods and machines used in the United States today. A third possible source of appropriate technology is selective borrowing from the industrial countries. Former British, French, U.S.,

11. See Frances Stewart, "Technology and Employment in LDCs," in Edgar O. Edwards (ed.) *Employment in Developing Nations* (New York: Columbia University Press, 1974), pp. 83–132, and Henry Bruton, "Technology Choice and Factor Proportions Problems LDCs," in Norman Gemmell (ed.), *Surveys in Development Economics* (Oxford: Blackwell, 1987), pp. 236–65.

and Dutch colonies in Southeast Asia gradually learned after independence that Japanese equipment was often better suited to their needs than the machines they had formerly imported from the metropolitan country. Now machines from Korea, Taiwan, and mainland China are replacing Japanese equipment. Fourth, LDCs can do their own research and development to evolve technologies specifically designed to fit local conditions. Sometimes indigenous technologies developed over the years by local farmers, craftsmen, and fishermen provide a promising basis for this work.

Making these types of appropriate selections and adaptations is neither simple nor straightforward. The U.S. economist Larry E. Westphal has suggested that what is needed is a broad-based "acquisition of technological capacity," which can only be developed through "learning by doing."[12] The Republic of Korea purposively set out to acquire technological capability in several industries in which it thought it could develop a comparative advantage. Making the ability to export increasing amounts, initially with the aid of government subsidies, its criterion for continued support, Korea succeeded in developing industries that could hold their own in international competition without further subsidization. Some economists have argued that this result can also be achieved through judicious import substitution.[13] Either way, the key point is that productivity must be raised through learning by doing; this will permit the industry in question to stand on its own after a few years.

Despite this potential, few countries have succeeded in making the development of appropriate technology a dynamic force in their economic development. One important reason has already been suggested: when competitive pressures are absent, incentives to adapt technology to local conditions are weak. Barriers to communication are also significant. It is hard for someone sitting in Surabaya or Sao Paulo to know just what technologies—new and modern, or older vintages—are available in New York or Nagasaki. Finally, it must be said that most third-world governments have not yet fully awakened to the need to promote local research and development. Their universities are usually preoccupied with teaching, and official research institutes established in various fields are often slow to develop, in part because of severe staffing difficulties. Sometimes in these circumstances the most useful research and development work is done by foreign firms with long histories of operations in the country.

The British economist Frances Stewart has identified three broad schools of thought on technology policies for third-world countries. The first group, which she calls the **price incentive school**, stresses "getting the prices right," because it believes that factor prices that reflect social costs will not only lead to the selection of the most efficient techniques out of the currently available range but will also create incentives for more appropriate technologies to be developed. The opposing **technologist school** believes that this mechanism of induced innovation

12. See Larry E. Westphal, Linsu Kim, and Carl J. Dahlman, "Reflections on the Republic of Korea's Acquisition of Technological Capability," in Nathan Rosenberg and Claudio Frischtak (eds.), *International Technology Transfer: Concepts, Measures, and Comparisons* (New York: Praeger, 1985), pp. 167–221, and Howard Pack and Larry E. Westphal, "Industrial Strategy and Technological Change. Theory versus Reality," *Journal of Development Economics,* 22 (1986), 87–128.

13. See Larry E. Westphal, "Fostering Technological Mastery by Means of Selective Infant-Industry Protection," in Simon Teitel (ed.), *Trade, Stability, Technology and Equity in Latin America* (New York: Academic Press, 1982), pp. 255–79, and Bruton, "Technology Choice and Factor Proportions Problems in LDCs."

cannot be relied on to do the job and urges that a conscious decision to invest more in technological development be taken. Finally, a **radical reform school** takes a broader view of the matter. It argues that both the array of goods produced and the methods used to produce them are inherent features of social systems. How can one expect anything but capital-intensive methods and products targeted for middle-class consumption from the multinational corporations? The creation of appropriate technologies and use of appropriate factor proportions, this last group argues, require that production be reoriented toward a multitude of cheap items for mass consumption. This in turn requires massive redistribution of income, which cannot be achieved without a social revolution. Hence the problem of inappropriate technology and inadequate job creation can only be solved in the context of a radical reform of society.

As Stewart sensibly concludes, there is a degree of truth in each school of thought. Evidence for the efficacy of radical reform comes from the experience of China, which was able to find social and technological solutions that permitted that nation's vast labor force to be employed more fully and productively than ever before. Chinese industry "walks on two legs," combining large-scale, relatively capital-intensive production units with smaller, more labor-intensive and decentralized plants. Large-scale public works projects, such as dams and irrigation channels, have been another important form of labor absorption. Finally, intensified agricultural technologies using much larger amounts of fertilizer and other modern inputs have made it possible to increase agricultural employment productively. Appropriate technology is combined with strong production organization at the local level. The rural commune contrives to provide full employment for all its members in a combination of agricultural and nonagricultural activities.

Other socialist developing countries have had trouble deciding just which way they want to go. Different conceptions of African socialism prevalent in Tanzania in the early 1970s stressed decentralized small-scale industry, increased processing of domestic raw materials, and creation of a modern, self-sufficient, state-run economy, but did not show how these ideas could be reconciled.

Other Employment Policies

Some theorists have argued that *improving income distribution* would accelerate job creation. According to this argument, goods consumed by poor people tend to be more labor-intensive than items consumed by those who are better-off, so redistribution of income in favor of the poor would make the pattern of demand more favorable to employment creation. Unfortunately, most of the studies undertaken to evaluate this proposal have concluded that the amount of employment generated by such a shift in demand would not be very great. A major stumbling block seems to be that although the goods consumed by the middle- and upper-income groups are indeed more capital-intensive than those consumed by the lower-income group, the better-off groups also consume more services, many of which are almost pure labor, such as household services. Moreover, goods consumed by the rich and poor often use the same intermediate inputs, for example, steel. Thus a shift in the pattern of final demand may have only a limited impact on the structure of production.

One useful approach to employment creation is to seek out *investments that complement labor* rather than substitute for it. Such investment opportunities probably exist in every sector of the economy. In agriculture, for example, mechanization of the planting and harvest functions may displace massive quantities of labor, but investments in irrigation actually create employment by making it possible to cultivate the same land more intensively and through a greater proportion of the year. A different kind of complementary investment, discussed earlier, is training to fill skill bottlenecks.

Even though capital is scarce in low-income countries, paradoxically their stocks of capital equipment are often underutilized. In many countries factories produce at only 30 to 60 percent of capacity, shift work is rare, tractors sit idle in fields, and bulldozers rest by roadsides. If a way could be found to *increase capacity utilization* and put this idle capital to work, there would be a sharp upswing in the demand for labor, achievable in the short run, without having to wait for new investments to be made and mature. Unfortunately, this appealing prospect is hard to realize. There are many reasons for unused capacity, including fluctuations in demand and inadequate supplies of materials. Despite the scarcity of capital, distorted prices in some developing countries may make it cheaper for firms to let equipment stand idle part of the time than to use it more intensively.

Generally speaking, *small informal-sector establishments* use less capital and more labor to produce a given type of output than larger formal-sector firms. One reason may be that small firms face prices for labor and capital that are closer to their social opportunity costs. Minimum-wage laws, unions, and payroll taxes all have little or no application to informal-sector firms. And not being preferred customers of the banks—indeed, often not dealing with banks at all—they have no access to rationed credit at artificially low interest rates. This situation has led many governments and international agencies to pay special attention to small-scale industry, as further discussed in Chapter 20.

Small firms often provide much-needed jobs to workers who cannot find work in larger firms. This valuable social function is sometimes impeded by government policies that discriminate against small firms. Such policies range from overvalued exchange rates and investment incentives available only to large firms to regulatory harassment and disruptively selective enforcement of tax and licensing requirements. Although discrimination against small-scale industry is obviously inappropriate, the long-term potential of small-scale industry is more debatable. Normally the relative importance of small firms declines in the course of economic development (see Table 9–5). Small firms that survive the transition to industrialization are progressive enterprises that have adapted to changing economic

TABLE 9–5 Share of Small Establishments in Total Manufacturing Employment, 1980s (percent)

GNP per capita ($)	Distribution of employment by size class (%)			
	1–4 workers	5–19	20–99	100+
$100–$500	64	7	4	25
$500–$1,000	41	12	10	37
$1,000–$2,000	11	13	14	61
$2,000–$5,000	8	11	17	64
Over $5,000	4	6	20	70

Source: Donald R. Snodgrass and Tyler S. Briggs, *Industrialization and the Small Firm: Patterns and Policies,* forthcoming.

conditions and found ways to use resources just as productively as large firms. In some countries, such as Japan historically and Taiwan in recent decades, small-scale industry has continued to play a major role in industrial employment and value added up to high levels of per capita income. These small firms have been able to flourish in a competitive environment, unlike the subsidized and protected small-scale industry of India, which has stagnated and remained a drain on the exchequer.

When all else fails, governments may institute **food-for-work programs** to provide at least part-time or temporary employment to groups that are particularly distressed or well placed to give the government trouble if their needs are not looked after. Many of these programs have been financed by foreign food aid, either by paying the participants with food or by selling the food and using the counterpart funds thus earned to help pay the cost of the program.

Food-for-work programs promise to combine construction of a socially useful facility with income redistribution to some of the poorest elements in society. It has been discovered, however, that the promise has been fulfilled only occasionally in the dozens of such programs that have been undertaken.[14] Many food-for-work programs have been plagued by bad management, and in some countries local elites have found ways to capture most of the benefits; sometimes they have even forced peasants to labor at low wages to provide a road or irrigation ditch that only increases the value of the landlord's property. Implementing an effective food-for-work program is a challenging task, best undertaken by governments (such as China's) that possess both a strong commitment to economic and social equity and the capacity to enforce that commitment.

Employment Creation Strategies

The desirability of accelerating the creation of productive employment, especially in countries hoping to combine a reasonable measure of equity with economic growth, is evident. Its feasibility is much less straightforward. Many different types of public policy impinge on employment creation. It is not really possible to draw up an employment plan for a developing country, only a general development plan stressing employment as one in a set of interrelated objectives.[15] The importance of employment as an objective of development policy and planning has received full recognition only since 1970. Policy makers and scholars alike are still learning what is involved in increasing productive employment in developing countries.

What is clear is that the context of the particular developing country—its size and economic structure—makes a difference for the kind of employment creation strategy to be pursued. South Korea and Singapore were able to solve their em-

14. J. W. Thomas et al., "Public Works in Developing Countries: A Comparative Analysis," World Bank Staff Working Paper No. 224, February 1976.

15. This did not prevent the ILO, under its World Employment Programme, from preparing a series of such plans through the use of visiting missions for Colombia, Sri Lanka, Iran, Kenya, the Philippines, and the Sudan. While useful as a means of publicizing the goal of employment creation and as illustrations of how employment-oriented development planning can be carried out, these plans have not in any literal sense been implemeted by the governments concerned.

ployment problems by emulating the Japanese pattern of whirlwind industrialization based largely on the export market. Medium-sized, semi-industrialized countries like Malaysia and the Philippines may be able to follow a similar path, with modifications permitted by their richer natural-resource endowments. Larger, more agricultural countries must take a more-balanced approach. At best they may be able to develop rapidly following a continental model, as Brazil seems to be doing. At worst, as in Bangladesh and the other very poor countries, a long period of reliance on job creation in agriculture and other rural activities will be required.

10

Education

The previous chapter discussed labor as a homogenous resource in economic development, a quantity of human power available to produce goods and services. But numbers of workers cannot tell the whole story. Attempts to attribute economic growth to growth in the factors of production always leave an unexplained residual, as we saw in Chapter 3. One important explanation for that residual is the improvement in the quality of human resources that leads workers to be more productive. Labor quality may be enhanced by education of either children or adults, as well as by improved health and nutrition for children and working adults, by migration of workers to places with better job opportunities, and by fertility reduction.

Some of these activities are discussed in other chapters. At this point we want to stress their common characteristics. In each case someone—either the community as a whole, employers, the individuals concerned, or their parents—makes a decision to use scarce resources to improve the productivity, present or future, of human beings. In an influential presidential speech to the American Economic Association in 1960, Nobel laureate Theodore Schultz suggested that such activities should be considered a process of accumulating capital, which could later be drawn on to increase a worker's productivity and income. He called this "investment in human capital." This form of investment, said Schultz, is every bit as important as investment in physical capital, but until his speech it had largely been neglected by academics and policy makers alike.[1] Subsequent work by Schultz

1. See Theodore W. Schultz, "Investment in Human Capital," *American Economic Review,* 51 (January 1961), 17.

and others elaborated the idea of investment in human capital, applying it to all the human resource development activities mentioned above. A fuller idea of what the concept implies should emerge from discussion of it in the context of education later in this chapter.

Studies sponsored by the World Bank lend further support to the idea that human resource development has an important bearing on economic growth.[2] There is reason to believe that the relationship is two-way and mutually supporting. On the one hand growing economies can and do devote increasing resources to improvement of educational, health, and nutritional standards. But it is also apparent that investment in human resources helps to accelerate economic growth. It does this by increasing labor productivity, encouraging greater physical investment, and reducing the dependency burden of the population. These contributions to growth are especially evident in the case of education.

TRENDS AND PATTERNS

Education can be defined broadly as all forms of human learning or more narrowly as the process that occurs in specialized institutions called "schools." It is unquestionably the most important form of human resource development, in several senses.

First, there is tremendous popular demand for education, particularly for schooling, in virtually all countries, developing and developed alike. Often in developing countries the number of people seeking admittance to schools far exceeds the number of places available. In Indonesia (see boxed example) there was a tremendous popular response when the government made primary schooling widely available. Obviously, people everywhere believe that education is beneficial for themselves and their children.

Education in Indonesia

In 1973, as he was working on his country's second 5-year plan, the chairperson of Indonesia's National Development Planning Board registered displeasure at statistics received from the Ministry of Education. The data showed that only 54 percent of 7- to 12-year-olds were enrolled in primary school. Worse, the ministry projected no rise in the percentage of children enrolled over the next five years. The major reasons were: too few of Indonesia's 60,000 villages had primary schools, trained teachers were in short supply, textbooks were scarce and expensive, and many poor rural households were unable to pay even the modest fees charged to attend school. The chairperson decided that something drastic had to be done.

The solution was a special program to improve rural children's access to schools by cutting red tape and building primary schools in villages that did not yet have them. These new schools were then staffed with

2. See many World Bank publications, including *World Development Report 1980* and the working papers cited therein, as well as George Psacharopoulos and Maureen Woodhall, *Education for Development. An Analysis of Investment Choices* (New York: Oxford University Press, 1985).

newly trained teachers and provided with millions of just-printed library books and textbooks. Meanwhile, school fees were abolished at the primary level. The program was funded through loans from the World Bank and the high oil revenues that Indonesia was fortunate to receive during the 1970s. Would rural parents respond to the improved opportunity by sending their sons and daughters to school? They did. By 1983, after more than 60,000 new schools had been built and over 100,000 existing schools rehabilitated, 95 percent of 7- to 12-year-olds had signed up for school. The program was a great success.

But every development success brings new problems in its wake. In the 1980s the Indonesian government struggled to cope with the rising tide of primary school graduates who wanted to go on to secondary school and eventually university. By then oil prices had fallen, and the government could not afford to build enough public high schools to accommodate all who wanted to attend them. Many parents could not afford to send their children to private schools. To this day, therefore, enrollment in secondary and higher education remains restricted largely to the minority of students from better-off families who can afford to pay. Nor is it clear where the farmers of the future will come from, since virtually everyone who has completed primary school wants to leave farming and seek a living elsewhere.

A second reason for believing that education is important is that education and income are highly correlated at both the individual and the societal level. Figure 10–1 shows typical patterns relating age, educational attainment, and earnings in two developing countries. Although not all high school graduates, for example, earn more than all who completed only primary school, the majority do, and on average their earnings are much higher. People the world over intuitively recognize this correlation and consequently try to obtain the largest possible amount of schooling for themselves and their children.

The correlation between national income levels and educational attainments is also strong. As we saw in Chapter 1, illiteracy is rife in the very poorest countries and diminishes steadily as one goes up the income scale (see also Table 10–1). Mass education is still a relatively recent phenomenon in the poorer countries. When most adults now living were children, schooling was far less prevalent than it is today. Yet all but the very poorest countries currently educate rather large fractions of their school-age populations (middle columns of Table 10–1), so the educational attainment of the adult population is rising fast.

The relationships shown in Figure 10–1 and the top part of Table 10–1 are averages. There are many contrary cases: of rich individuals and societies that have received little schooling and of well-educated individuals and highly schooled societies whose incomes are relatively low. Some of the intercountry variations are showing the bottom part of Table 10–1. On average, however, the correlation between education and income is strong. But does this necessarily mean that education *causes* a person's or a country's income to rise? Could causation not flow in the opposite direction, indicating merely that richer countries and families spend more on education, as they do on goods and services? Or, finally, are higher in-

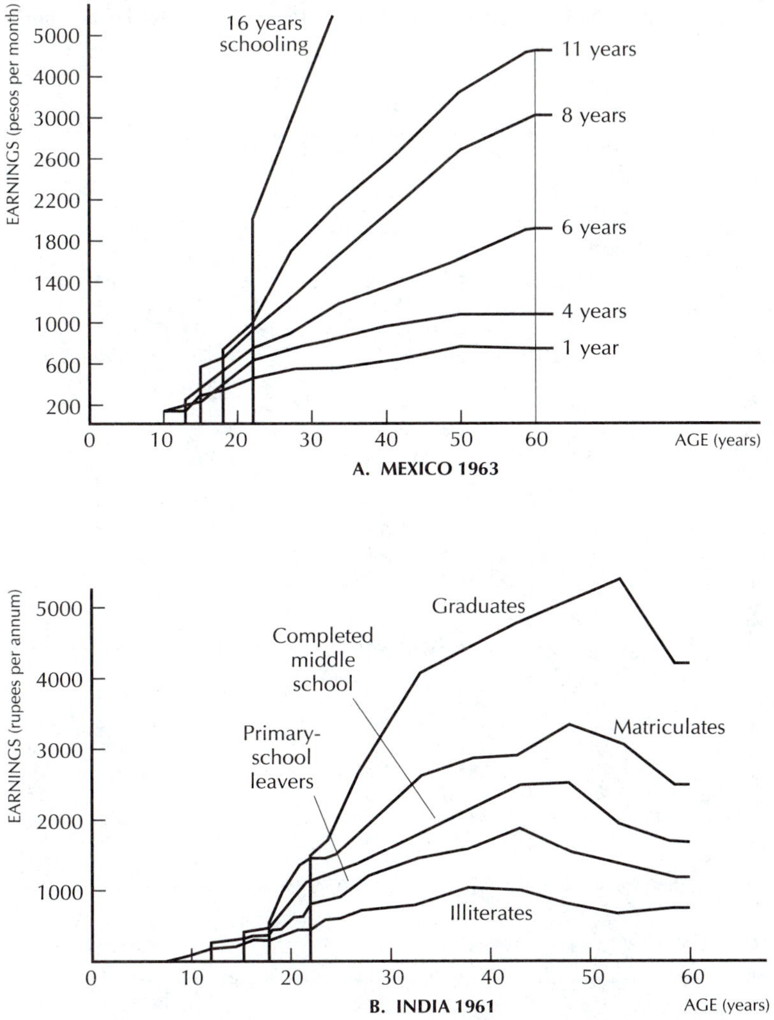

FIGURE 10–1 Age Earnings Profiles in Mexico and India. The lines of the graph represent mean earnings at different ages of people with varying amounts of formal education. On average, people who stay in school longer earn higher incomes.
Sources: Martin Carnoy, "Rates of Return to Schooling in Latin America," *Journal of Human Resources,* Summer 1967, pp. 359–74, and M. Balug, R. Layard, and M. Woodhall, *Causes of Graduate Unemployment in India* (Harmondsworth, England: Allen Lane, Penguin Press, 1969), p. 21.

come and education perhaps the common results of some unidentified third factor? These questions are explored later in the chapter.

A third reason why education is important is that large sums are spent to acquire it. Education is a big item in both household and national budgets. Because their people want it, and to some extent also because they think it will stimulate national development, governments of developing countries devote a substantial fraction of their resources to the creation and operation of school systems. Table 10–1 indicates that the expenditure of 3 to 5 percent of GNP in public funds was

TABLE 10–1 Education Statistics in Relation to GDP per Capita and for Selected Countries (around 1990)*

GDP per capita (PPP)	% of illiterate adults	Enrollment ratios† Primary school Gross	Primary school Net	Secondary school Gross	Higher education Gross	Public expenditure % of GNP	Per pupil ($) Primary	Per pupil ($) Secondary	Per pupil ($) Higher
				A. By income group					
Below $1,000	58	66	47	13	2	2.3	35	101	1756
$1,000–2,000	46	88	70	33	6	4.4	84	172	1301
$2,000–$5,000	25	103	92	61	14	3.7	268	571	2540
$5,000–$10,000	15	104	89	64	18	3.1	451	616	1980
Above $10,000	5‡	102	96	92	38	3.6	4189	4340	7542
				B. For selected countries					
Tanzania	n.a.	69	47	5	0	n.a.	12	39	2940
Ghana	40	77	n.a.	38	2	3.6	25	68	1884
Kenya	31	95	n.a.	29	2	6.2	53	171	2353
India	52	98	n.a.	44	n.a.	0.4	33	37	26
Pakistan	65	46	n.a.	21	3	0.3	46	74	530
Bolivia	23	85	79	34	23	3.7	n.a.	n.a.	n.a.
China	27	123	100	51	2	n.a.	22	53	69
Indonesia	23	116	98	45	10	1.9	11	25	92
Sri Lanka	12	108	n.a.	74	5	1.4	n.a.	n.a.	n.a.
Peru	15	126	95	70	n.a.	n.a.	n.a.	n.a.	n.a.
Brazil	19	106	88	39	12	0.9	354	403	3386
Colombia	13	111	73	55	14	n.a.	128	181	484
Hungary	n.a.	89	90	81	15	1.8	823	1059	3292
Chile	7	98	86	72	23	2.9	261	241	784
South Korea	4	107	100	88	40	2.9	935	888	386
U.K.	2	104	100	86	28	5.2	2796	4721	7500
Japan	2	102	100	97	31	n.a.	3392	3666	1074
U.S.	2	104	99	90	76	0.4	3528	7430	4644

Sources: UNESCO Statistical Yearbook 1993 (Paris: UNESCO, 1994) and *World Development Reports 1992, 1993,* and *1994.*
* Year of most recent estimate varies by country.
† Enrollment ratios express enrollment as a percentage of the school-age population. Gross enrollment ratios relate total enrollment of students of all ages to the size of the age group that normally attends that level of schooling; they can exceed 100 percent. Net enrollment ratios show the percentage of the pertinent age group that is enrolled.
‡ Rough estimate; many high-income countries with very high literacy rates no longer publish statistics on literacy.

typical around 1990, except in the very poorest countries. Since the 1980s were a difficult decade for many developing countries, this indicates the strength of their commitment to development. Private expenditures on education, which are harder to measure, are omitted from most published statistics but are significant in many countries. Some 15 to 20 percent of the central government budget commonly goes for education, except in countries where regional and local governments bear the main responsibility. If education is regarded as an industry, one sees that it is one of the largest in all economies, ranked in terms of either value-added or employment.

Types of Learning

We have been treating the terms "education" and "schooling" as if they were synonymous, as one does in everyday parlance. Modern usage by specialists, however, applies the term "education" to a broader concept, akin to the notion of learning. This calls attention to the fact that there are several different forms of learning that are important and may substitute for each other in some circumstances. Usually three principal types of learning—education in the broad sense—are identified.

Formal education takes place in institutions called "schools." It usually involves young people who have not yet begun their working lives.

Nonformal education can be thought of as organized programs of learning that take place outside schools. Often the participants are adults. Programs of nonformal education are usually shorter, more narrowly focused, and more concerned with applied knowledge than programs of formal education. They may teach occupational skills or other subjects such as literacy, family life, or citizenship.

Informal education is learning that takes place outside any institutional framework or organized program. People learn many important things at home, on the job, and in the community.

Although other definitions of the three terms can easily be found, these formulations indicate the basic differences among them. In the rest of this chapter we will use them in the above senses.

Characteristics of Developing-Country Education

School systems in developing countries have expanded tremendously over the last four decades. Countries that emerged from colonialism after World War II usually inherited narrow-based systems designed to educate only the local elite and a small cadre of literate clerks. Most colonial regimes distrusted the educated "native" and feared the consequences of mass education. Even in Latin America, where most countries became independent early in the nineteenth century, a rigid class structure confined schooling essentially to the rural elite and better-off urbanites.

After independence, the political imperatives changed radically. Pledged to change so much in so short a time, newly independent governments found that one of the most popular things that could be done relatively quickly was to build schools. While a modern economy might be decades away, a modern-looking school system could be built in just a few years. Now the incentive was to expand schooling rapidly.

As Table 10–2 shows, school enrollments at all levels in developing countries grew from about 100 million in 1950 to 764 million by 1990. During the 1950s the number of students enrolled more than doubled. In the 1960s and 1970s the growth rate of enrollment tapered off, but the absolute number of students added each decade continued to rise. In the 1980s, with primary school enrollments approaching 100 percent in many countries and financial problems constraining expansion at higher levels, overall enrollment growth slowed further to 2 percent a year.

Enrollment growth came in waves. It hit the primary schools first. Then, as more children finished primary schooling, high school enrollment soared. Some time later, universities, technical colleges, and other institutions of higher education were affected. The spread of the system differed from country to country. A relatively westernized Asian country like Sri Lanka, which adopted a free-schooling policy at independence in 1948, was able to achieve practically universal primary schooling by the 1950s, and then press on rapidly with expansion of the higher levels until financial difficulties forced a slowdown of enrollment expansion in the 1960s. Other countries—in Latin America, India, and elsewhere—

Table 10–2 School Enrollment in Developing Countries, 1950–1990 (millions)

	1950	1960	1970	1980	1990
Primary					
Africa	7	17	30	59	79
Asia	71	164	234	319	356
Latin America	15	27	44	65	76
Total	93	208	308	443	511
Secondary					
Africa	—	2	4	14	24
Asia	6	12	66	124	174
Latin America	2	4	11	18	23
Total	8	18	81	156	221
Higher					
Africa	—	—	—	1	3
Asia	1	1	5	12	21
Latin America	—	1	2	5	8
Total	1	2	7	18	32
All Levels					
Total	102	228	395	617	764

Sources: UNESCO Statistical Yearbook 1993 and previous years.

began rapid enrollment expansion at the higher levels of schooling long before universal primary schooling was attained. Often this pattern resulted from a concentration of political power that gave more weight to elite interests than to those of the general population. Elsewhere, as in the more conservative Muslim countries, it was a consequence of reluctance to provide education for girls.

Rapid school expansion often created teacher shortages that led to increasing class sizes and the use of less highly trained teachers. Sometimes it proved possible to expand teacher training and overcome the worst of the shortages after a few years. In many countries, however, teacher shortages persist to this day, particularly in poor and remote regions where teachers, like other public servants, are reluctant to go.

Fiscal strains caused by the expansion of schooling began to appear as early as the 1960s. Few developing countries have been able to satisfy the social demand for education from public funds. African and Latin American nations that experienced slow economic growth, stagnation, or even declines in GNP per capita during the 1980s found it difficult even to maintain past educational standards. Nevertheless, as Table 10–3 indicates, enrollment ratios generally continued to rise during the 1980s. Gross enrollment ratios in primary schools did fall between 1980 and 1990 in 13 of the 22 sub-Saharan African countries for which data are available, but information gaps make it unclear whether this ratio rose or fell in sub-Saharan Africa as a region. For developing countries as a whole, government expenditures on education grew little during the 1980s, however (see the incomplete data cited in Table 10–3), so the quality of schooling probably declined in some of the more hard-pressed countries. It is also likely that private funding paid a larger share of the bill as private schools and colleges sprang up to offer places to disappointed applicants to the public institutions.

TABLE 10–3 Changes in Enrollment Ratios and Central Government Expenditure on Education during the 1980s

	Gross enrollment ratios						Central government expenditure as a % of:			
	Primary		Secondary		Tertiary		Government budget		GNP	
	1980	1990	1980	1990	1980	1990	1981	1990	1981	1990
Low-income countries	87	100	28	40	4	7	n.a.	n.a.	n.a.	n.a.
China	117	135	34	48	1	2	n.a.	n.a.	n.a.	n.a.
India	76	97	28	44	9	n.a.	2	3	*	1
Others	59	56	17	23	3	4	11	10	2	2
Lower-middle-income countries	100	108	38	58	11	16	12	13	3	3
Upper-middle-income countries	105	104	44	52	14	18	13	11	3	2
Developing countries in:										
Sub-Saharan Africa	71	65	14	18	1	2	15	17	4	4
East Asia & the Pacific	113	125	36	49	3	5	15†	13†	3†	2†
South Asia	74	89	26	40	8	12	2	4	*	1
Europe & Central Asia	n.a.	n.a.	n.a.	n.a.	n.a.	n.a.	n.a.	n.a.	n.a.	n.a.
Middle East & North Africa	90	99	43	60	9	12	15	17	5	5
Latin America & Caribbean	105	107	38	46	15	16	11	10	2	2
Severely indebted countries‡	88	88	29	38	8	10	12	12	3	3
All developing countries	85	87	31	40	7	11	14	13	3	3

*Means less than 0.5 percent.
†Excludes China and the Indo-China countries, for which no data are available.
‡As classified by the World Bank, includes 36 countries, mainly in sub-Saharan Africa and Latin America.
Sources: Based on data given in *World Development Report 1983, 1984, 1992 and 1993.*

Major reasons for the inefficiency of educational expenditures have been the high frequencies of **dropouts**, those who withdraw from schooling before completing an academically meaningful course of study, and **repeaters**, those who require more than the prescribed number of years to complete an educational program. Most educators believe that a child who does not complete at least five or six years of school gains little from attendance; yet millions fail to do so. In large measure these problems result from poverty. The various costs of keeping a child in school simply become too heavy an imposition on the poor household after a while.

In view of such problems, it is not surprising that learning achievements in developing country schools are often low. The World Bank reports that scores on standardized arithmetic and science achievement tests administered to fourth to eighth graders during the 1970s and early 1980s averaged 35 to 40 percent in low- and lower-middle-income countries, compared to 50 to 60 percent in high-income countries. In reading tests the difference was 49 percent versus 70 percent.[3] There is even evidence that those who master specific skills in school sometimes lose them in later life through lack of use. Functional literacy is likely to be retained only when one has access to written materials and some incentive to read and write daily. Many people in low-income countries have neither.

Severe inequalities among regions and social classes characterize most devel-

3. *Primary Education, A World Bank Policy Paper* (Washington, D.C.: World Bank, 1990), p. 13.

oping-country school systems. In many countries a child who lives in a major city or comes from a favored socioeconomic background is much more likely to receive schooling—and vastly more likely to get high-quality schooling—than a student from a rural area or a more ordinary socioeconomic setting. Since education frequently leads to a better job and a higher income, this pattern of educational provision worsens the distribution of opportunity and income. Some economists believe that an improved distribution of schooling could be a major force for achieving a more-equal distribution of income. Governments in developing countries have only begun to address these problems and potentials.

Another reason why limited learning seems to take place in developing-country school systems is what British scholar Ronald Dore calls the "diploma disease."[4] According to Dore and others, these systems are not primarily in the business of conveying knowledge and skills at all, but are more concerned with certification or credentialing. Dore argues that in late-developing countries an individual's fitness is often judged by the academic credentials that he or she possesses. And of course successful completion of a given level of schooling is the main qualification for admittance to the next highest level. In most developing countries, nationwide examinations are given at certain stages in the schooling process to determine the student's fitness for educational advancement or employment. These exams take on tremendous importance, and this causes teachers to bend their classroom efforts to the task of preparing students for them, and students to put in long hours outside school cramming for them. Dore contends that this perverts the true purpose of education and escalates the cost of a selection process that might be carried out more cheaply in other ways.

Some countries where enrollment expanded rapidly in the early years of independence soon experienced severe **educated unemployment**. India and the Philippines, two Asian pioneers in the expansion of secondary and higher education, acquired large pools of job-seeking graduates unable to find "suitable" employment. Sri Lanka, with its long-standing commitment to free schooling, found half its recent university graduates unemployed by the 1970s. A few lucky countries experienced a subsequent upswing in economic growth, which soaked up this pool of unemployed labor. One was South Korea, which had many frustrated out-of-work graduates in the late 1950s but began to experience a shortage of educated workers by the 1970s. In many less rapidly developing countries, however, educated unemployment became a far more persistent feature of society.

Lack of fit between school curricula and the needs of the job market seems to aggravate the problem. Harvard University education expert Russell Davis reported that in the 1970s the employment exchange in Calcutta was daily thronged with college graduates (some of them "firsts," recipients of top academic honors) in mathematics, English, and physics. Yet employers who approached the same office seeking workers skilled in air conditioning, silk-screen printing, or plumbing came away disappointed.[5] In such circumstances, graduates must eventually take jobs irrelevant to their education. College-graduate taxi drivers are said to be common in Manila. Employers then have to use on-the-job training to convey the skills that workers will need.

4. See Ronald Dore, *The Diploma Disease. Education, Qualification and Development* (Berkeley: University of California Press, 1976).

5. Russell Davis, "Planning Education for Employment," Harvard Institute for International Development, Development Discussion Paper No. 60, June 1979.

Nonformal education played little part in the inherited educational system. Significantly, however, many government departments that required technical skills conducted specialized training programs for their own staffs. This shows that needed skills were not being supplied by the formal education system. Nor were they available through informal education, since the limited experience with modern economic activities meant that accumulated on-the-job learning was necessarily low.

EDUCATION'S ROLE IN DEVELOPMENT

Education is many things to many people. Besides the economic benefits already mentioned, education up to a certain level is often seen as an inherent right. Education has also been promoted because it can socialize people. Through a common schooling experience, it has often been thought, people from different national, social, ethnic, religious, and linguistic backgrounds can be encouraged to adopt a common outlook on the world. Since many developing countries have diverse populations and must place a high premium on the attainment of greater national unity, this is often an important objective for them. Education is also thought to confer civic benefits. Some political scientists believe that at least a minimal level of schooling is a prerequisite for political democracy.[6]

Thinking about how education can be used to promote economic development has changed considerably over the years. During the 1950s much of the discussion centered on the need for trained manpower. Manpower planning, outlined below, became a popular way to analyze a developing country's human resource needs. Its emphasis on middle- and high-level trained personnel implies that it is secondary and higher education that are most in need of expansion. Yet as we have seen the 1950s was also a period of rapid growth in primary school enrollments. In 1959 a number of Asian governments subscribed to the **Karachi Plan**, which pledged them to provide at least seven years of compulsory, universal, and free schooling by 1980.

Disillusionment with this approach followed in the 1960s. Many governments found their budgets strained by the attempt to expand all levels of schooling simultaneously. Demand began to seem unquenchable; expansion of capacity at one level of schooling only increased the numbers applying for places at the next-higher level. Paradoxically, the continuing boom demand for schooling was accompanied by an apparent decline in its benefits to the individual. The rise of unemployment among the educated caused officials to wonder whether more and more resources should be devoted to expanding the school system, just so people could be unemployed. As shown in Figure 10–2, excess demand resulted from a market failure: because individuals lacked information about educational trends, they expected higher returns to investments in schooling than they were able to realize.

Growing cost consciousness fit well with a new method of analyzing educa-

6. Yet education does not guarantee the existence of democracy, as many examples of countries with educated populations but undemocratic governments attest. (The role of education in the recent upsurge of democracy in Latin America and Eastern Europe could be debated.) And there are examples of democratic systems in countries with relatively little education: India, Jamaica, Guyana, and Colombia. So the relationship of education to democracy is not clear-cut.

tional investments, introduced during the 1960s. Cost-benefit analysis, based on human capital theory, compares the costs and the benefits of education, as we shall see below; manpower analysis, in contrast, considers only the benefits. By the 1970s, however, disillusionment had spread to the human capital approach. A search for alternative concepts of education's role began, and is still underway.

Education remains tremendously important in developing countries. Indeed, larger numbers of people and sums of money are involved than ever before. Current concerns include how to finance the amounts of education that people want, how to improve the quality of schooling, and how to provide basic education to those who are still excluded, especially (in some countries) girls. In March 1990 four United Nations agencies sponsored the **World Conference on Education for All**, which focused on problems in basic education: more than 100 million children, including at least 60 million girls, with no access to primary schooling; more than 960 million adults, two-thirds women, who are functionally illiterate; more than one-third of all adults who have no access to printed knowledge; more than 100 million children who fail to complete basic education programs; and millions who satisfy the attendance requirements but do not acquire essential knowledge and skills. The conference tried to raise consciousness and mobilize resources to solve these problems.

Manpower Planning[7]

In any economy there is a tendency for people with given levels of education to hold certain types of jobs. In developing countries, for example, nearly all employed university graduates work at professional, technical, or managerial jobs, usually either in government or as independent professionals. People whose schooling ended at the secondary level tend to hold middle-level jobs in the clerical, sales, and service occupations. Half or more of the labor force in the typical developing country is made up of farmers and agricultural laborers who received little or no formal education.

It is tempting to jump from these observable facts to the assumption that a certain level of education is *required* if a person is to fill a particular occupational role. If this were the case, it would follow that a growing economy, which is expected to undergo a shift in occupational structure toward more professional, technical, and industrial workers, must follow a defined pattern of educational development to obtain the kinds of trained people it will need.

Manpower planning is based on this assumption. It presumes that the economy's need for educated labor can be predicted and the growth of the educational system planned to avoid both manpower shortages, which may retard economic growth, and manpower surpluses, which waste educational resources and may lead to educated unemployment or "brain drain."

Manpower planning starts with a prediction of manpower needs. This can be based on employer projections or an extrapolation of past trends, although both are highly unreliable. A more-sophisticated method, developed by Dutch Nobel laureate Jan Tinbergen and U.S. economist Herbert Parnes, tries to deduce the fu-

7. The term "manpower planning" refers to a specific analytical approach, which is described below. Since it covers female as well as male labor, the term is gender insensitive by contemporary standards. Unfortunately, there is no good gender-neutral synonym. "Human resource planning" is a more general phrase and does not refer to this specific approach.

ture employment pattern from a projection of GNP growth. It starts from a target growth rate of GNP during the planning period, which must be at least several years long, since the training of middle- and high-level manpower takes time. Next, it estimates the structural changes in output by sector of origin needed to achieve that overall growth rate. Third, employment by sector is estimated, using assumptions about labor productivity growth, or about the elasticity of employment growth relative to output growth, which is its inverse. Fourth, employment by industry is divided into occupational categories using assumptions about the "required" structure in each industry; these are then summed across industries to get the economy's required occupation mix. Finally, occupational requirements are translated into educational terms via assumptions about what sorts of education are appropriate for each occupational group.

These five steps lead to an estimate of manpower requirements in some future year. To project manpower supply in the same year, one first adjusts the current stock of manpower for expected losses through retirement, death, emigration, and withdrawal from the labor force. Next, one projects increases to manpower supply resulting from outputs of the school system, immigration, and labor force entry by nonworking adults. The projected manpower supply is then compared with projected requirements. If a gap results, it is usually assumed that it must be closed through accelerated school enrollments. Occasionally other ways of increasing manpower supply, such as upgrading less-skilled workers or bringing in foreign workers, are considered.

A major weakness of the manpower-planning approach is that the relationships it assumes fixed are often unstable and unpredictable in the real world. Labor productivity is affected by many factors, and often changes unexpectedly. The occupational mix also changes, for both exogenous (external) and endogenous (internal) reasons. For example, new technologies may be introduced and bring a new set of occupational requirements into being. Or a change in relative wages may induce employers to hire a different mix of workers; such price adjustments are assumed away in the model. In the long run, changes in the occupational mix occur as a direct result of changes in the supply of educated labor. People with more schooling increasingly do jobs that previously were done by less-educated persons. This can be called **educational deepening**.

Further undercutting the logic of manpower planning is the absence of a unique education-occupation linkage. The knowledge required to do virtually any job can be acquired through formal, nonformal, or informal education. Similarly, only a small fraction of what is learned in most educational programs is unique to a specific occupation; much more of it is applicable to a range of jobs.

Manpower planning also fails to account for the cost of education. Manpower "requirements" are assumed to be absolute, and the conclusion always seems to be that a projected gap should be filled through educational expansion, generally of secondary and higher formal education. Yet these types of schooling are relatively expensive in many developing countries (right-hand columns of Table 10–1). Alternative, possibly cheaper, ways of dealing with the problem, such as nonformal education or on-the-job training, are seldom considered.

These objections, plus the emergence of the competing cost-benefit approach, long ago doomed manpower planning to limbo as far as most academic specialists are concerned. However, the approach is still used by practical planners to gain at least a rough idea of what a developing country's possible manpower problems are. It often appeals to politicians, who like its apparent precision. They enjoy being told, say, that 125 architects need to be trained by the year 2000. As a matter of political economy, manpower planning is more likely to be heeded when it projects deficits than when it projects surpluses. Deficits offer an apparently strong rationale for expanding a particular type of education. In many developing countries, however, schooling has expanded so much that few manpower deficits can be legitimately projected. In these circumstances, society's demand for education and the political pressures that go with it generally ensure that the school system continues to expand at a faster rate than would be indicated by manpower planning, which tends to be ignored.

Cost-Benefit Analysis

The assumption underlying human capital theory is that the main reason why individuals, or their governments on their behalf, spend money on education, health, and other human services is to raise their incomes and productivity. The added income and output that result in future years then can be seen as a return on the investment made. Application of this idea to formal education begins with a set of **lifetime earnings curves**, such as those in Figure 10–1. These curves, which show average earnings at various ages for people with particular amounts of schooling, have been calculated for many populations. Nearly all of them have three characteristics. First, given the amount of schooling, defined in terms of either years of school or the highest level attained, earnings increase up to a maximum level that is reached around age 40 or later, and then level off or decline. Second, for those with larger amounts of schooling, the curve is higher, and steeper in its rising phase; although people with more schooling start work a bit later in life, they usually begin at a higher earnings level than those with less schooling who are already working. Third, more schooling leads to later attainment of maximum earnings and to higher earnings in retirement. All three features can be seen in the curves for Mexico and India shown in Figure 10–1.

Cost-benefit analysis, introduced in Chapter 6 as a planning tool and used in Chapter 9 to analyze employment, is frequently employed to calculate both the private and the social value of education. To understand the *private rate of return*, begin by imagining a set of parents faced with a decision on how much schooling to provide a child. They have a rough idea of what the lifetime earnings curves look like and regard them as a prediction of what their child could earn if he or she had different levels of educational attainment. Although it may strain one's credulity, it is necessary to think of these parents as calculating the discounted present value of the future earnings stream attached to each level of schooling and comparing it with the cost of attaining that level of school.

The present value of prospective earnings in any future year can be defined as

$$V_0^t = \frac{E_t}{(1+i)^t} \qquad [10\text{–}1]$$

V_0^t = the present value of earnings in year t, E_t = the earnings in year t, and i = the rate of interest (opportunity cost of the parents' capital). The earnings are discounted to the present, using the rate of interest i.

The discounted present value of the entire stream of earnings until year n is therefore

$$V = \sum_{t=1}^{n} \frac{E_t}{(1 + i)^{t'}}. \qquad [10\text{–}2]$$

This is the benefit side of the cost-benefit calculation. The private costs of schooling—those borne by private households—are of two types, explicit and implicit. **Explicit costs** involve actual outlays of cash. The most obvious example is tuition fees, but it is important to recognize that even "free"—that is, tuition free—schooling entails costs, explicit as well as implicit. Some cash outlays are almost always required for books, uniforms, transportation, and other purposes. Even such modest explicit costs can serve as a significant barrier to school attendance for children from poor families. Moreover, education has important **implicit costs.** These take the form of the forgone earnings of students who would be working, either as wage earners or as unpaid but productive workers on family farms and in family enterprises, if they were not in school. In general these opportunity costs are highest for older students and higher levels of schooling (since their earning potentials are greatest), but in settings where young children can work productively, opportunity costs may be a factor even at the primary level, particularly for the poorer households which need the modest income that young children can earn.

All the costs of schooling are typically incurred before any of its benefits can be reaped. Since benefits and costs occur at different times, cost-benefit analysis requires that **discounting** be used to make their values comparable. Whether a particular educational investment is worthwhile can be determined by comparing the discounted present values of the benefit and cost streams, as explained in Chapter 6. If discounted benefits exceed discounted costs, using a relevant rate of interest to discount both streams, then the investment should be made. If discounted costs exceed discounted benefits, the investment is not worth making. More commonly in educational analysis, however, the **internal rate of return** on the investment is calculated. This, as we saw in Chapter 6, is the discount rate that equates the discounted present values of the benefit and the cost streams. We can solve for the internal rate of return using

$$\sum_{t=1}^{n} \frac{E_t}{(1 + r)^t} = \sum_{t=1}^{n} \frac{C_t}{(1 + r)^{t'}}, \qquad [10\text{–}3]$$

or

$$\sum_{t=1}^{n} \frac{E_t - C_t}{(1 + r)^t} = 0, \qquad [10\text{–}4]$$

where C_t = the private costs (explicit and implicit) incurred in last year t and r = the internal rate of return. Using this approach, the family's rate of return on an investment in education would then be compared with the returns on other investments they might make. The family would invest in education if it offered a higher rate of return than, say, putting the money in the bank or expanding its herd of livestock.

There is also a **social** or **economic rate of return**, which is calculated using a more comprehensive measure of cost: all costs of education, public as well as private, are now included on the cost side of the calculation. In other words, public-sector outlays that are not reimbursed by tuition are added in here. Because income taxes are a cost to the individual but not to society as a whole, income should be measured after payment of income taxes when the private rate of return is estimated and before payment of income taxes when the social (economic) rate of return is estimated. This would make both benefits and costs higher in the social rate-of-return calculation than in the private rate-of-return calculation. Depending on the relative magnitude of the cost borne directly by the government and the income tax collected, the social (economic) rate of return to education could be either higher or lower than the private rate of return.

In practice, however, calculations done for developing countries generally measure income before taxes in estimating both the private and the social rates of return. This is done partly because personal income taxes are less important in developing countries than in developed countries and partly because tax data are difficult to obtain. If the same measure of benefits (income before taxes) is used in calculating both the private rate of return and the social rate of return, while a wider range of costs is included in the social rate-of-return calculation, it follows that the private rate of return must be higher than the social rate of return when this less satisfactory method of calculation is used (as in Table 10–4).

The usual form of social cost-benefit analysis of education is thus more comprehensive than private cost-benefit analysis only on the cost side. The many and varied social benefits of education that are not reflected in higher earnings are excluded from the calculation, even in social cost-benefit analysis. It would be better to include them, but benefits such as greater social cohesion and enhanced ability to participate in politics are hard to quantify.[8]

TABLE 10–4 Average Estimated Rates of Return to Education for Income Groups and Regions*

	Social			Private		
	Primary	Secondary	Higher	Primary	Secondary	Higher
		By income group†				
Low-income countries	23.4	15.2	10.6	35.2	19.3	23.5
Lower-middle-income countries	18.2	13.4	11.4	29.9	18.7	18.9
Upper-middle-income countries	14.3	10.6	9.5	21.3	12.7	14.8
High-income-countries	n.a.	10.3	8.2	n.a.	12.8	7.7
World	20.0	13.5	10.7	30.7	17.7	19.0
		By region				
Sub-Saharan Africa	24.3	18.2	11.2	41.3	26.6	27.8
Asia‡	19.9	13.3	11.7	39.0	18.9	19.9
Europe/Middle East/North Africa‡	15.5	11.2	10.6	17.4	15.9	21.7
Latin America/Caribbean	17.9	12.8	12.3	26.2	16.8	19.7
OECD countries	14.4	10.2	8.7	21.7	12.4	12.3
World	18.4	13.1	10.9	29.1	18.1	20.3

*Averages of latest estimates for countries in which rates of return have been calculated. Most estimates were made in the 1980s.

†Low income = $610 or less; lower middle income = $611–$2,449; upper middle income = $2,450–$7,619; and high income = $7,620 or more (exchange rate conversion method).

‡Excluding OECD countries.

Source: George Psacharopoulos, "Returns to Investment in Education: A Global Update," *World Development,* 22, no. 9 (September 1994), 1328.

8. One bold attempt to list and value some nonmarket benefits of education suggested that their total value may be roughly equal to that of the benefits reflected in higher earnings in the labor market. See Robert H. Haveman and Barbara L. Wolfe, "Schooling and Economic Well-Being: The Role of Nonmarket Effects," *Journal of Human Resources*, 19, no. 3 (Summer 1984), 377–407.

Many private and social rates of return to investment in education have been estimated for both developed and developing countries. Average results for countries at different per capita income levels and in different regions are displayed in Table 10–4. All the rates shown in the table are marginal rates. That is, they indicate the return on the additional investment needed to move from one level of educational attainment to the next-higher level.

Four principal conclusions emerge from Table 10–4 and similar calculations. First, rates of return to education in developing countries are generally high; often they are higher than the rates of return earned on investments in physical capital. Education looks like a good investment in most low- and middle-income countries. Second, the highest social rates of return are usually earned on primary schooling, particularly in countries where primary schooling is still far from universal. In countries where almost everyone has completed primary schooling, the rate of return at the primary level becomes indeterminate because there is no lower level with which to compare it. Third, the spread between private rates of return (where income is measured before taxes) and social rates of return can be large because the government sometimes bears most of the costs. When more of the costs of schooling are privately financed, as with higher education in OECD countries, the spread between the two rates of return is smaller. Fourth, returns to education tend to diminish as countries become more developed. The basic reason is that workers with a given amount of schooling become less scarce and thus command a smaller premium in the labor market.

Cost-benefit analysis can also be used to value the human capital created by the educational process. The value of human (or any) capital is derived from the stream of income that it will earn in the future. This income stream is capitalized by discounting it to the present. The formula for discounting the earnings created by a person's schooling—from primary school through the highest level attained—is given in Equation 10–5. E_t in the formula represents the additional sum earned each year, compared with someone who received no schooling. Conceptually, the value of human capital created by other forms of investment besides education could also be measured by discounting additional future earnings, but actually measuring the amount of human capital created would be more difficult in these cases because the added earnings are harder to measure.

$$\text{NPV} = \sum_{t=1}^{n} \frac{E_t}{(1 + r)^t}. \qquad [10\text{–}5]$$

Cost-Benefit Analysis in Educational Planning

Of what practical value are cost-benefit calculations of education? The idea is that private rates of return can serve as guides to individual educational choices whereas social rates can inform public investment and policy decisions. But doubts surround the validity of both claims.

From the private point of view, the main problem is predicting what the structure of earnings will be in the future. The procedure outlined above implicitly assumes that the current earnings structure provides an accurate guide to the future, but in fact relative earnings can change considerably for reasons originating on either the demand or the supply side of the labor market. In many developing countries in recent years the numbers of people possessing all kinds of academic credentials have increased much faster than the numbers of jobs traditionally held by people with these credentials. The result, discussed in Chapter 9, is that school leavers tend to be unemployed for a long period of time, following which they may have to accept lower salaries than their predecessors obtained. When such educational deepening is taking place, the incomes earned by previous school leavers become a poor guide to the future, since the rate of return to a particular level of schooling is likely to decline.

Despite this tendency, applicants continue to besiege the secondary schools and universities of most developing countries. How is this to be explained? Some observers interpret it as evidence that applicants for schooling are not motivated exclusively, or even primarily, by a desire for economic gains, but want more schooling mainly for social or psychological reasons (an economist would say that they value education as a consumption good). An alternative explanation is that when schooling is heavily subsidized by the government, the private rate of return can remain reasonably high, even when the social rate dips in response to educated unemployment and the ongoing devaluation of academic credentials. This latter thesis has been used to explain the continuing strong demand for secondary and higher education in countries such as India and Sri Lanka. It suggests that education can be simultaneously a good investment for the individual and a bad investment for society.

When the cost-benefit approach is used in educational planning, the starting point is again data on lifetime earnings by level and type of education, along with information on the total costs—explicit and implicit, private and public—of providing each level and type of education. The social rates of return on the various levels of education (primary, secondary, higher) and types of education (academic, vocational, nonformal, on-the-job) can then be calculated and compared. A rational government would expand those forms of education showing high social rates of return and cut back on those showing low rates of return.[9]

There are, however, a number of questions that can be raised about this procedure. As with manpower planning or any other planning methodology, its results are only as good as its assumptions, and some of these are questionable. Like the hypothetical parents discussed earlier, cost-benefit analysts must worry about how the structure of earnings may change in the future. In addition, they must weigh factors that are of no concern to the private decision maker.

If education is to be treated as an investment that must compete for scarce resources with roads and steel mills, it must be justified in terms of its contribution to national output. From the social point of view, higher earnings are not sufficient justification unless they are caused by higher productivity. The usual way of linking earnings to productivity is to assume that wages are equated to the marginal product of labor through the workings of a perfectly competitive labor market. This enables us to interpret wages as measures of marginal product. But if other factors—for example, the salaries paid to expatriates in colonial days; see Chapter 9—have a significant effect on the wages actually paid, then wages or earnings are not necessarily equal to marginal product and thus become unreliable indicators of social benefits. In theory, this problem could be dealt with by using

9. More precisely, activities showing a rate of return higher than the opportunity cost of capital (the return thought to be obtainable if the funds were invested outside the education sector) would be expanded and those with lower rates would be contracted.

shadow wages or opportunity costs (estimates of what wages would be under competitive conditions) instead of actual wages, but this is difficult in practice.

A second and closely related issue is whether the relationship between education and earnings is truly causal. Up to now we have in effect assumed that differences in average earnings are both associated with differences in education and also caused by these differences. This is not strictly the case, since both education and earnings are also partly the results of other factors, such as individual ability and socioeconomic origin. People who are more able or who come from favored backgrounds may do better both in school and in the workplace. According to the screening hypothesis, the main role of education is not so much to train people as to select those individuals who will do best in the job market.

Even if we agree that education raises earnings, there is a question of how this works. Do schools teach skills that turn out to have economic value, or do they only socialize people to work better—to be punctual in their attendance and conscientious in completing their assignments? These issues have been much debated, but recent research lends strong support to the view that underlies cost-benefit analysis of education: skills learned in school, especially literacy and numeracy, account for most of the differential in earnings associated with higher levels of schooling.[10]

The cost-benefit approach implicitly assumes that educational categories adequately specify the types of labor relevant to the labor market. In other words, it assumes that there is perfect substitutability within each educational category. This assumption is obviously crude, particularly when categories are specified only by level (primary, secondary, higher). Surely there are significant differences between graduates of academic and vocational high schools or between graduates of medical and legal faculties. Separate calculations should be made for these major different types of education, but even this fails to capture the quality dimension. In the real world, graduates of the "best" schools, which may be best solely or mainly in terms of popular perceptions, earn far more than graduates of the "inferior" institutions. Finally, alternatives to schooling—nonformal education and on-the-job training—tend to get left out of the comparison altogether. If the Ministry of Education is responsible for educational planning while training programs are provided by other ministries, there is a strong tendency to downplay them.

Like any planning tool, cost-benefit analysis can provide useful information, but it cannot be used mechanically to dictate solutions. It does furnish a useful measure of the productivity of the existing pattern of investment in education. If, for example, the social rate of return to primary schooling is high, this suggests that investment at this level is likely to be socially remunerative. Similarly, large differences between private and social returns may help explain patterns of educated unemployment, as we have seen. But the value of these calculations is always limited by the assumptions on which they are based. It is particularly hard to determine how fast the social rate of return will decline as a particular variety of education is expanded. To know this, we would have to calculate the elasticities relating earnings differentials to the relative supplies of different kinds of labor.

10. See M. Boissiere, J. B. Knight, and R. H. Sabot, "Earnings, Schooling, Ability, and Cognitive Skills," *American Economic Review*, 75, no. 5 (December 1985), 1016–30, and John B. Knight and Richard H. Sabot, *Education, Productivity, and Inequality. The East African Natural Experiment* (New York: Oxford University Press for the World Bank, 1990).

In spite of the attractiveness of its base in human capital theory—at least for those who admire neoclassical economic theory—the cost-benefit approach is of only limited use in practical educational planning. This brings us to the question of what alternatives might exist.

Educational Policy in Kenya and Tanzania and Its Results

Kenya and Tanzania are neighboring East African countries that are similar in size, colonial heritage, resource endowment, economic structure, and level of development. After gaining independence in the early 1960s, each country tried to provide all its children with seven years of primary schooling. When growth in the numbers of primary school graduates pushed the demand for secondary schooling beyond the governments' limited financial capacity to provide places in government secondary schools, however, the two countries' policies diverged. Influenced by manpower forecasts that projected limited need for secondary school graduates, Tanzania severely restricted its provision of secondary school places and rationed admissions on the basis of performance on a national examination. As in Kenya, government secondary schools were highly subsidized. Kenya also limited the creation of government schools (although less severely than Tanzania), but it permitted the establishment of private *harambee* (self-help) schools that met much of the excess demand that could not be satisfied by the government schools. As a result, by the 1980s Kenya had far more secondary school graduates than Tanzania.

The results of this policy divergence in otherwise similar circumstances have been intensively analyzed by researchers funded by the World Bank.[11] Their studies indicate that Kenya's educational policy performed much better than Tanzania's, both in raising labor productivity and in spreading education more equitably among the population. Although earnings differentials related to education narrowed as the supply of educated people increased and some of Kenya's secondary school graduates had to accept jobs beneath their expectations, Kenya's heavier investment in human capital paid off handsomely in productivity gains. Kenya's more permissive policy was also more equitable, particularly in permitting greater intergenerational mobility as students from farm or working class families had better opportunities to obtain secondary-level education. This was true even though access to Kenya's private secondary schools depended on ability to pay. By limiting access as it did, Tanzania created larger rents for those who were able to obtain secondary schooling. Those from favored backgrounds were able to perform better, on average, on the qualifying exam, and they received large subsidies once admitted.

Methodologically, the Kenya-Tanzania comparison supports the cost-benefit approach to analyzing educational decisions and casts doubt on the manpower planning approach. Although the Tanzanian planners were correct that their economy would not "need" the additional high school graduates that faster expansion of secondary schooling would have provided, the productivity benefits of an additional investment in secondary

11. Knight and Sabot, *Education, Productivity, and Inequality;* see also Arthur Hazelwood et al., *Education, Work and Pay in East Africa* (Oxford: Oxford University Press [Clarendon], 1990).

schooling would have more than repaid its cost. Given the Tanzanian government's well-known commitment to socialism, it is particularly ironic that the equity consequences of its educational policy were also less favorable than those of the policy followed by the capitalist-minded government of Kenya.

Alternative Viewpoints

Most educational policy decisions are made pragmatically, in response to whatever political pressures bear most strongly on the decision makers at any particular moment. Manpower projections and cost-benefit analyses are undertaken from time to time, but they seldom have more than a small impact on what actually happens. Because of the intellectual limitations of the two analytical approaches outlined above, more elaborate *formal modeling* has sometimes been attempted, but it has had even less influence. This was the case with several linear programming models of education and its relationship to the economy that were constructed in the 1960s and 1970s, as well as with efforts to synthesize the manpower and cost-benefit approaches.

Some economists and sociologists—*radical critics*—altogether reject the idea that education raises productivity. An element in their critique, mentioned earlier, is that education acts as a screen or sieve to select the fortunate few who are then "credentialed" to hold elite positions in society. To this the more radical critics add that those who pass through the sieve and receive the prized credentials tend strongly to be individuals who started from privileged positions in life. The school system, they say, essentially reproduces the class structure from generation to generation. Those not destined for elite positions receive a form of education intended to make them more amenable to playing a subservient role in society. They are taught diligence, punctuality, and respect for authority. The solution to all this lies not in any conceivable reform of the school system within the framework of capitalist society, but in the radical reform of the social structure and economic system. Less-conventional radical critics argue that efforts should be made to revamp schooling as we know it to permit true learning to take place or to use mass education as a means of raising the consciousness of the poor regarding their oppressed condition.[12]

In view of these criticisms and proposals, it is interesting to see how Communist regimes managed their school systems. They strongly emphasized universal attainment of basic literacy and numeracy, and then restricted secondary and higher education rather severely (or just higher education in the richer Communist states), while heavily emphasizing the attainment of specific vocational skills. In the Soviet Union and other East European countries, as in the West, opportunities to obtain the more restricted types of schooling went disproportionately to those from favored social positions. The Communist regime most noted for radical reform efforts was that of China, especially during the Cultural Revolution of the 1960s, but Chinese educational policy subsequently returned to something much closer to the Soviet or Western model.

12. Iconoclastic analyses of education in developing countries include Ivan Illich, *Deschooling Society* (New York: Harper & Row, 1970); Paolo Freire, *Pedagogy of the Oppressed,* translated from the Portuguese by Myra Bergman Ramos (New York: Seabury Press, 1970); and Ronald Dore, *The Diploma Disease.*

A very different critique and reform proposal argues for market-based reforms. Educational planning has failed, say these critics: all proposed methodologies are flawed and choices about what kinds of schooling to provide and whom to educate should therefore be left to market forces. An obvious objection to this proposal is that if the market gives the wrong price signal, it will only encourage people to respond in the wrong ways. As long as education is subsidized, people will tend to purchase too much of it relative to other goods and services. This bias could be corrected by reducing the degree of subsidization and charging people something much closer to the actual cost of providing schooling. But that would only serve to strengthen another objection to the market solution: that it takes no account of equity considerations. Proposed means of making a market system more equitable include liberal use of scholarships for the poor but deserving and—more far-reaching—creation of educational vouchers, a special currency that could be distributed according to any criteria deemed equitable and used to purchase any kind of schooling that the consumer thinks most beneficial.

Like the radical reform proposals, those coming from the right have been more discussed than implemented. Most governments prefer to retain a much tighter grip on educational activities than this type of reform would permit. The main role of the market in developing-country education, as noted earlier, is to provide places for those who are unable to gain admittance to public institutions, and even this is permitted only in certain countries.

An older reform proposal is that school curricula should be made more practical, for example by replacing schools that offer traditional academically oriented curricula with agricultural, technical, and **vocational schools** emphasizing the teaching of practical skills. Some vocational schools have succeeded and made valuable contributions to development, but many others have failed. In a well-known article, University of Chicago educationist Philip Foster traced a series of unsuccessful experiments in Ghana going all the way back to the middle of the nineteenth century. He attributed the persistent failure to "the vocational school fallacy," the idea that certain manual skills regarded as necessary for economic development should be stressed, when in fact the structure of incentives favors "impractical" academic training that opens the door to employment in the urban formal sector.[13] A major problem with government-run vocational schools is that they often fail to provide the skills actually required by private employers. Yet when adequately funded and run in close coordination with potential employers, vocational schools can make a real contribution to development.

A final reform proposal is to give much greater emphasis to **nonformal education.**[14] Proponents of nonformal education argue that it is more practical, cheaper, more flexible, and better able to reach lower-income groups than formal education. Although there have indeed been many successful nonformal education projects—in basic education (literacy and numeracy), family education (health, nutrition, child care, family planning), community education (cooperatives, community projects), and occupational training—it seems more realistic to regard

13. Philip J. Foster, "The Vocational School Fallacy in Development Planning," in C. A. Anderson and M. J. Bowman (eds.), *Education and Economic Development* (Chicago: Aldine, 1966), pp. 142-63.

14. Philip H. Coombs with Manzoor Ahmed, *Attacking Rural Poverty: How Nonformal Education Can Help* (Baltimore: Johns Hopkins Press, 1974).

nonformal education as a complement to formal education than as its rival. Nonformal training courses generally teach different skills and reach a different audience (mainly adults) from the schools. One criticism of nonformal education is that, like vocational schools, it perpetuates a two-tiered social system. Members of the favored class get into the schools, while the less-favored have to make do with the programs of nonformal education.

11

Health and Nutrition

The goal of improving health conditions in developing countries has often been accorded a low priority, both by the developing-country governments and by development specialists. In nearly every country the Ministry of Health has little bureaucratic clout and receives one of the smallest budget allocations. Development specialists have participated in this downgrading of health; as far as we know, ours was the first development economics textbook to include a chapter on health and nutrition.

Neglect of the subject has, however, been partially reversed in the past 25 years. Interest in health and development was boosted in the 1970s by the attention given to equity-oriented development strategies and later by concern about the effect that slower economic growth in the 1980s was having on the health of children, especially in Africa. Throughout the period, expenditures on health, like those on education, have increasingly been regarded as investments in human capital.

The health-development relationship is a reciprocal one. Economic development tends to improve health status, while better health contributes to economic development. But proponents of health-sector programs frequently warn that development alone cannot be relied on to cut morbidity and mortality, that special programs in nutrition, health care, and environmental sanitation are also needed. Occasionally they cite examples of how development can worsen health or argue that the provision of appropriate health programs can do the job by itself, even in the absence of significant overall development. Critics of this view stress the relationship of health status to income level and observe that the benefits of specific health measures are sharply reduced when the surrounding socioeconomic and physical environments remain unfavorable to health. We will return to this debate later in the chapter, as well as to the related issue of how health contributes to economic development.

HEALTH IN THE DEVELOPING COUNTRIES

What exactly is health? What determines whether an individual, or a society, is healthy or sick? Health is a surprisingly elusive concept. The World Health Organization (WHO), which is the United Nations agency responsible for programs to improve health standards, defines it as "a state of complete physical, mental and social well-being," but this goes far beyond what is normally meant by health. For most people, health is simply the absence of disease and infirmity. But even this commonsense definition can be hard to pin down in practice. Conditions such as infection with intestinal parasites or first-degree (mild) malnutrition, which are perceived as disease in countries with high health standards, may be so common in countries with lower standards that they are not even recognized as abnormal.

The health status of an individual can be determined through clinical examination by a qualified health professional. But this would be an expensive way to measure the health status of an entire population, so for that we usually rely on statistics. Health statistics attempt to measure **morbidity** (sickness) and **mortality** (deaths). Statistics on morbidity are seldom adequate. Not only is a clear-cut definition of sickness lacking, but many sick people in poor countries never consult a doctor or enter a hospital, so they fail to come into contact with the statistical system. Mortality data are considerably better: death seldom goes unnoticed, and most countries now have reasonably complete official systems of death registration, although significant gaps remain in some cases. Death statistics are most useful for assessing the health status of a population when they include detailed information on the person who has died (age, sex, place of residence, and so on) and on the cause of death. However, data on the cause of death are usually weak in low-income countries.

Patterns and Trends

Despite what one hears about famine, AIDS (acquired immune deficiency syndrome), and many other challenges to health in developing countries, the fact is that health conditions in these countries have been improving gradually for many years. Life expectancy rose everywhere as mortality declined in the 1950s and 1960s. Life expectancy is the average number of years members of a given population are expected to live. We cannot, of course, know how long any particular individual will actually live. But we can predict the average longevity of a class of people (for example, males age three), using the recent mortality experience of the relevant group (in this case, all males) as a guide. Life expectancy at birth is the form of the statistic most often cited, as in Table 11–1, but the concept really refers to expected years of *remaining* life and can thus be applied to people of various ages, as in Table 11–2.

Table 11–1 Life Expectancy at Birth by Income Group and for Selected Countries, 1960 and 1992

	Life expectancy	
	1960	1992
By income group (PPP)		
Below $1,000	37	50
$1,000–$2,000	45 (34)*	64 (56)
$2,000–$5,000	47	64
$5,000–$10,000	56	69
Above $10,000	69	77
In selected countries		
Latin America		
Bolivia	42	60
Brazil	56	66
Chile	56	72
Colombia	55	69
Africa		
Ghana	37	56
Kenya	43	59
Tanzania	37	51
Asia		
China	51	69
India	42	61
Indonesia	40	60
South Korea	53	71
Malaysia	52	71
Pakistan	42	59
Sri Lanka	61	72

Sources: World Development Report 1978 and *1994*.
*Figures in parentheses exclude India and China.

Table 11–2 Comparison of Male Life Expectancies in Bangladesh and Sweden

	Additional years a male is expected to live if he is now:				
	Newborn	Age 1	Age 5	Age 15	Age 65
Sweden (1976)	72.1	71.8	67.9	58.1	13.9
Bangladesh (1974)	45.8	53.5	54.4	46.3	11.6
Difference	26.3	18.3	13.5	11.8	2.3

Source: United Nations, *Demographic Yearbook, Historical Supplement* (New York: United Nations, 1979), pp. 553, 558.

The average crude death rate (CDR) for low-income countries is now 10 deaths per thousand population, far less than in earlier decades. However, this average is strongly influenced by the successful experience of China, where the CDR was 8 in 1992. In low-income countries other than China and India, where the CDR was 10, the crude death rate averaged 12 per thousand in 1992. In middle-income countries, the rate was 8, even lower than in high-income countries, where the CDR was 9.

Recall from Chapter 8, however, that the crude death rate is strongly affected by the age structure of the population. Young populations in developing countries pull down their CDRs. There are still big differences between rich and poor countries in life expectancy (see Table 11–1) and infant death rates (look back at Table 8–2, where we saw that the infant death rate falls from 109 per thousand in countries with GDP per capita of $1,000 or less measured in purchasing power parity to 8 per thousand in countries with $10,000 or more). The average male in a high-income economy lives 13 years longer than his counterpart in a low-income economy—19 years longer if we compare the industrialized economies with low-income economies other than China and India. Women live 6 years longer than men on average in developed countries, but in developing countries their longevity advantage is smaller (just 2 years on average in low-income countries). In parts of the developing world—China, South Asia, the Middle East, and North Africa—female life expectancy is less than would be expected.[1]

The correlation between income level and mortality, although strong, is far from perfect. The lower part of Table 11–1 shows life expectancy statistics for selected developing countries in 1960 and 1992. For a few of the countries listed in this table, life expectancy in 1992 was far longer than the average for their income group. China and Sri Lanka are particularly notable in this regard (see boxed example on pages 278–79). Every country listed in Table 11–1 raised life expectancy by 10 years or more between 1960 and 1992. Life expectancy in Indonesia rose by 20 years, a 50 percent increase. In Ghana, the 19 years of life gained on average increased longevity by more than one-half.

Such great gains in life expectancy come about mainly through reductions in mortality among the very young. This is dramatically illustrated in Table 11–2, which compares male life expectancies at various ages in Sweden and Bangladesh in the mid-1970s. These two countries differed enormously in life expectancy at birth. Yet for males who survived the early years of life, differences in remaining life expectancy fell sharply. Whereas in Sweden and other countries with high health standards expected years of further life decline steadily as a person ages, in Bangladesh a surviving five-year-old could actually expect to live eight more additional years than a newborn. As Table 11–2 shows, in 1974 the average newborn male in Bangladesh would not live to age 46 whereas a five-year-old could expect to survive to age 59. This is testimony to the terrible extent of infant and child mortality in the poorest countries.

The cross-section data in the upper part of Table 11–1 are consistent with the history of mortality in the industrial countries. Figure 11–1 shows how life expectancy has risen over the long run in different groups of countries. The early-developing countries experienced a slow, steady rise in life expectancy after 1850. Japan, a later developer, was able to extend life more rapidly and reach a level close to that of the early developers by about 1960. Less-developed countries have also been able to achieve rapid increases in life expectancy, particularly over the past 50 years. But these increases still leave their life expectancies far below that in the rich countries (Table 11–1), and the countries no better-off in many

1. A comparison of sex ratios in various national populations has led Harvard economist and philosopher Amartya Sen to conclude that "More than 100 Million Women are Missing." See his article of that title in the *New York Review of Books*, December 20, 1990, pp. 61–66. Females in these countries receive inferior nutrition and health care for a combination of cultural and economic reasons, and this adversely affects their longevity.

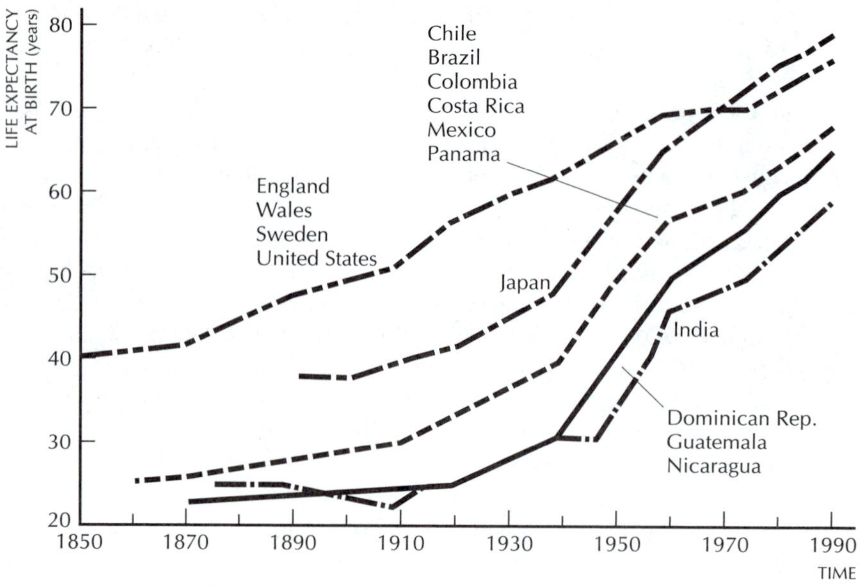

FIGURE 11–1 Trends in Life Expectancy in Selected Countries. Life expectancy rose gradually in Europe and the United States and more rapidly in Japan. It is rising rapidly in the LDCs, too, but they are still far behind the developed countries.
Sources: World Bank, *Health Sector Policy Paper* (2d ed.; Washington, D.C.: 1980), p. 10; updated using data from World Bank, *World Tables,* 1989–90 ed.

cases than the developed countries were in the early twentieth century (see Figure 11–1).

A reader who has heard concern expressed about serious and worsening child health problems, especially in sub-Saharan Africa and particularly during the slow-growth decade of the 1980s, might well ask whether the picture drawn here of improving global health status is not too rosy. Granting that there certainly are extremely serious health problems in Africa—and elsewhere—and also that African health statistics leave much to be desired, the impression given by the basic statistics published by the World Bank is that health measures in most of the nations of sub-Saharan Africa continued to improve, albeit slowly in many cases, during the 1980s and early 1990s.[2] Food supply was often perilous, however; average daily calorie intake declined between 1980 and 1989 in 19 of the 33 countries for which data are given in the *World Development Report.* Yet life expectancy continued to lengthen while infant death rate was reported to have fallen in most of these countries during the 1980s.[3]

Although large gaps remain between the health status of populations in rich and poor countries, the general picture is that these gaps have narrowed in recent decades and continue to do so. This contrasts with gaps in GNP per capita, which have continued to widen. Next we need to consider why.

2. World Bank, *World Tables,* 1989–90 ed., and *World Development Report,* various years.

3. Of 32 countries for which comparison is possible, 26 saw improvements in life expectancy between 1980 and 1990. Similarly, 27 countries reported declines in infant mortality. Countries where health conditions apparently worsened in the 1980s included Uganda, Tanzania, and Mozambique.

Interesting research by University of Pennsylvania demographer Samuel Preston shows that the cross-section relationship between income and life expectancy is parabolic in form and has been shifting upward during the twentieth century (Figure 11–2).[4] That is, at any given level of real income per capita, people are tending to live longer as time goes by. However, the relationship between income and life expectancy has become looser in recent decades. Preston found that rising income accounted for only 10 to 25 percent of the rise in life expectancy between the 1930s and 1960s. Other factors accounted for 75 to 90 percent of the increase.

What could explain this loosening of the relationship between income and life expectancy? Increasing literacy may have contributed. Preston stresses the international spread of health technology and a growing similarity of values regarding its application.

Although the international spread of health technology has been a major factor in the worldwide decline in death rates and rise in life expectancy that has occurred since World War II, its impact has sometimes been exaggerated. An early debate concerned a 43 percent fall in the crude death rate between 1945 and 1949 in Sri Lanka (then still called Ceylon). This improvement in mortality was initially attributed almost entirely to the control of malaria through the use of DDT. Later it became evident that DDT was only part of the story and that longer-run and more general factors such as rising income, widespread literacy, and availability of low-priced foodstuffs were also influential.

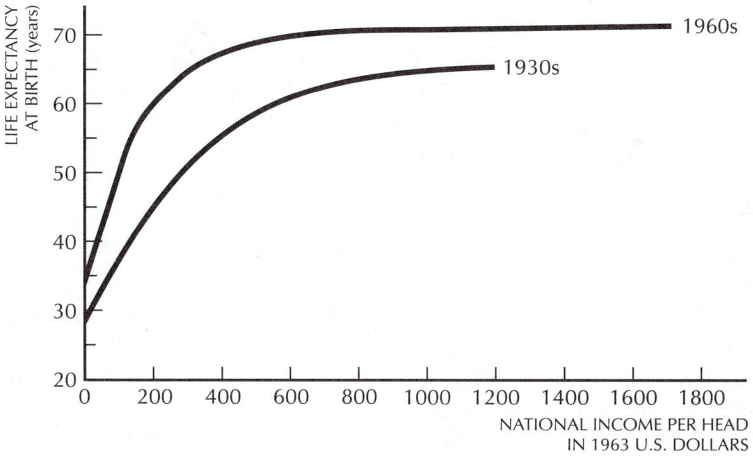

FIGURE 11–2 Relationship between Life Expectancy at Birth and National Income per Head. In both decades, people in richer countries could expect to live longer. Between the 1930s and the 1960s, the curve shifted up; citizens of countries with given real income levels lived longer on average. Note also that the curve for the 1960s is flatter than the curve for the 1930s; except for very poor countries (below $500), per capita income was no longer so important a determinant of mortality as it had been in the 1930s.
Source: Preston, "The Changing Relationship Between Mortality and Level of Economic Development," pp. 231-48, adapted from p. 235.

4. Samuel H. Preston, "The Changing Relationship between Mortality and Level of Development," *Population Studies*, 29, no. 2 (July 1975), 231–48. Continuing subsequent rises have been charted by the World Bank. See *World Development Report* 1993, p. 34, for the latest version.

Health in Sri Lanka

The small Asian country of Sri Lanka enjoys unusually good health and life expectancy compared with other low-income countries. This favorable experience is attributable to a combination of good fortune and the policies followed in the period since independence in 1948.

A small island located on the trade routes between Europe and East Asia, Sri Lanka had early contact with Western colonialism. The British, who controlled the island after earlier periods of Portuguese and Dutch domination, began to introduce modern medicine in the early nineteenth century. Campaigns to eradicate smallpox and yaws began in 1802. A civil medical department was started in 1858, a Contagious Diseases Ordinance enacted in 1866, and a medical school opened in Colombo, the capital, in 1870. In the early twentieth century Ceylon's tea, rubber, and coconut plantations were required to provide medical care for their workers and their families, and a school health program was started. In the 1940s a network of rural hospitals was built. The compact, self-contained nature of the island supported these efforts, and when it gained its independence in 1948, Ceylon already had unusually high health standards compared with other Asian countries.

Credit for continued improvement since 1948 belongs primarily to the government of Sri Lanka, which has consistently accorded a high priority to improving the health of its people. From the start medical care was free to all. More important, efforts were made to extend the service network to all parts of the island. These efforts were continuously hampered by shortages of funds. Sri Lankan hospitals have always been crowded, and the provision of additional beds ran only marginally ahead of population growth between 1950 and 1980. Efforts to train more doctors were partially offset by the emigration of physicians to countries where much higher incomes could be earned. The only dramatic change was in the supply of nurses and paramedics, which nearly tripled in relation to population between 1950 and 1980. This increase provided essential support for the extension of primary care to the rural areas.

Measures of mortality and morbidity show striking improvement in the past 50 years. Epidemics have been eliminated and diseases such as typhoid, tuberculosis, and malaria have declined sharply as causes of death. Crude and infant death rates have fallen, and life expectancy has climbed to 72 years. Sri Lanka has become, with China (where life expectancy at birth is 69 years), one of the rare examples of a country whose generally poor population is nearly as healthy as people in the high-income countries.

Not all the improvement in Sri Lankans' health is attributable to medical services. The island country is also unusually advanced in education. Near-universal literacy appears to have promoted better health conditions. Another positive factor is the comparative rarity of malnutrition, which results from a relatively equal distribution of income and a policy of subsidizing basic foods. Although average calorie intake in Sri Lanka is not very different from other countries at similar income levels (see Table 11–4), total available calories are probably better distributed among the population than in most other countries.

Medical services in Sri Lanka form a colorful mosaic. The indigenous ayurvedic system coexists with Western medicine and receives some official support. Psychological disorders are treated by trance dancers or exorcists in some cases and by Western-trained psychiatrists in others.

National statistics on causes of death, although weak, are good enough to permit comparison between rich and poor countries, and illuminate the historical pattern of death rate decline by cause. Important causes of death in poor countries, mainly affecting the young and accounting for more than half of all deaths, have included infectious, parasitic, and respiratory diseases such as diarrhea, pneumonia, malaria, whooping cough, polio, tetanus, and diphtheria. All these diseases—many of which have come to be known as tropical diseases in the twentieth century although they were major killers in temperate countries in earlier centuries—are now well controlled in rich countries, where diseases of the circulatory system and cancer have replaced them as major causes of death. Now infectious, parasitic, and respiratory diseases are being brought under control in developing countries as well. As people in these countries live longer, they too are succumbing in increasing numbers to heart disease and cancer, since they have been spared an earlier death from another cause.

Despite these improvements, a number of endemic and epidemic diseases continue to affect large populations in the developing countries. Some of these diseases—tuberculosis, malaria, cholera—are prominent causes of death. Others do not kill large numbers but limit people's lives and may contribute to a premature death which is officially ascribed to some other cause. One such kind of disease is parasitic conditions, which are almost universal in some areas. It has been estimated that perhaps one-fourth of the world's population has roundworms. Another is malnutrition, which is rare in its easily recognized clinical form but common at a subclinical level, where its effects, although destructive, are more subtle and difficult to detect.

Effects of Health on Development

Having considered the effect of development on health, it is now time to ask what better health can contribute to development. Can health expenditures legitimately be regarded as a form of investment in human capital? Before addressing this question, it is important to recognize that the validity of health services as a developmental activity does not rest entirely on our ability to prove that health expenditures increase national output. Better health is an important goal in its own right. Health increases human potentialities of all kinds and is rightly regarded as a basic human need. Everyone can benefit from better health in the present, and improved health for the young will lead to a healthier population in the future.

Like education, health services improve the quality of human resources, both now and in the future.[5] Better health for workers can provide direct and immediate benefits by increasing the workers' strength, stamina, and ability to concentrate while on the job. Better child health and nutrition promote future

5. For a comprehensive statement of the case for regarding health expenditures as investments in human capital, along with some U.S. examples, see Selma Mushkin, "Health as an Investment," *Journal of Political Economy*, 70, no. 5, part 2 (Supplement, October 1962), 127–57.

productivity growth directly by helping children develop into stronger, healthier adults. In addition they contribute indirectly by improving children's ability to acquire productive skills and attitudes through schooling. It has been shown that healthy, well-fed children have higher attendance rates and are able to concentrate better while they are in school. Moreover, children who enjoyed better health and nutrition in their preschool years achieve more after they enter school.

Unlike education expenditures, which increase only the quality of human resources, moreover, health expenditures also increase their quantity in the future by lengthening expected working life. This too complements educational investments, since other things being equal, returns to education will be higher if people can work and earn for longer periods.

Although expenditure on health thus promises several different kinds of private and social benefits, returns to investment in health are unfortunately even harder to quantify and verify empirically than returns to investment in education. For one thing there is no simple measure, analogous to years of schooling, for the amount invested in the health of any particular individual. The economic effects of better health are also hard to measure. The quantitative effects (extended working life) can be gauged in additional years worked, but what value should be put on them? In a private cost-benefit analysis expected additional earnings can be used, but in a social cost-benefit analysis the social marginal product of labor should be estimated to determine the value to society of extended working life. This recalls the complex question, already addressed in Chapter 9, of what the productivity of the marginal worker really is. In an economy in which marginal productivity is very low, the production benefits of extended working life are necessarily small. The qualitative effects of health expenditure (increased worker productivity and earnings) are also hard to measure because increases in productivity or earnings attributable to improvement in health may be difficult to identify.

Research to measure the effects of better health on labor productivity has yielded varying results. Several attempts have been made to measure the effects of improved health and nutrition on workers whose productivity can easily be measured (for example, plantation and road construction workers). While some of these studies have revealed the expected positive effects on productivity, others indicated smaller impacts than expected or none at all.[6] In some cases, people seem to find ways to adapt to wide ranges of ill health and malnutrition without greatly reducing their productivity. They may not feel well, but they can still work. In such cases, improving health will not necessarily increase productivity, but it remains desirable from a humanitarian point of view.

Besides increasing the quantity and improving the quality of human resources, health expenditures can also increase the availability or productivity of nonhuman resources. The clearest example is the large tracts of land rendered uninhabitable or unusable by endemic diseases. Malaria and yellow fever blocked access to

6. Two types of study have been undertake: (1) socioeconomic studies, in which the productivity effects of different health statuses are measured, controlling for other interpersonal differences, and (2) experimental studies, in which health improvement measures (e.g., iron supplementation) have been undertaken for one set of workers, whose productivity is then compared with that of a control group. The results of these studies are analyzed in Jere R. Behrman and Anil B. Deolalikar, "Health and Nutrition," in Chenery and Srinivasan, *Handbook of Development Economics*, Vol 1, pp. 631–711 (especially pp. 683–92), and Jere R. Behrman, "Health and Economic Growth: Theory, Evidence, and Policy," in *Macroeconomic Environment and Health* (Geneva: WHO, 1993), pp. 21–61.

many parts of Latin America, Africa, and Asia before these diseases were brought under relatively effective control in the twentieth century. Even today schistosomiasis makes it unsafe for people to enter lakes and streams in sections of Africa, and trypanosomiasis (African sleeping sickness) restricts the range of the livestock industry. So far no chemical means of control has been discovered for either of these diseases. China, however, has made progress against schistosomiasis through mass campaigns aimed at ridding lakes and streams of the snails that transmit the parasite. Improved control of ankylostomiasis (hookworm) and other parasitic conditions would increase resource availabilities in a different way. The effective productivity of resources devoted to food production would be increased.

Finally, better health can save money spent on curative health care. This frees up resources for other uses.

We have seen that the productive benefits of health expenditures, although easy to hypothesize, have proven difficult to verify empirically. But even the effects on health status are sometimes hard to measure. The main reason is the multiplicity of factors that go together to determine health status. For example, a study of the health effects of projects to provide safe water supplies to a number of villages in Lesotho found, surprisingly, that provision of a clean water source failed in many cases to lead to a significant reduction in the prevalence of waterborne and water-related diseases. One explanation was that waterborne diseases are also transmitted by other means, such as contaminated food, and the provision of a safe water source alone does not protect villagers from infection through other sources.[7]

Health improvement has one effect that could be considered a social cost: by reducing the death rate, it increases population growth. Admittedly, the decline in the death rate may in turn encourage a drop in fertility, which would reduce the overall positive impact on population growth; but studies indicate that the magnitude of this replacement effect, if it exists at all, is likely to be small. Another consideration at this point is a question of ethical values. Even if population growth is acknowledged to be injuriously high, universally espoused values make it unacceptable to reduce that growth by allowing persons already born to die when the means to save them are at hand. It follows that this "cost" should not be used as an argument against health improvements and that other means should be found to limit population growth if this is considered to be an important social objective.

Environmental Health

The health planner, like the physician, should carefully diagnose before he or she prescribes. Health planning must address the real health problems found in the developing countries. Some of the causes of sickness and premature death in the developing countries that deserve more careful examination are environmental health problems, malnutrition, and lack of medical care of adequate quantity, quality, and type.

The principal problem of **environmental sanitation** in low-income countries is the contamination of the water supply, and sometimes also of food and soil, with

7. Richard Feuchem et al., *Water, Health, and Development: An Interdisciplinary Evaluation* (London: Tri-Med Books, 1974), Chap. 9.

Table 11–3 Access to Drinking Water and Sanitation in Developing Countries, 1980* (percent of population)

<table>
<tr><th></th><th colspan="3">Drinking water</th><th colspan="3">Sanitation</th></tr>
<tr><th>Region</th><th>By house connection</th><th>By public standpoint</th><th>None</th><th>By sewer connection</th><th>Other</th><th>None</th></tr>
<tr><td>Urban population</td><td></td><td></td><td></td><td></td><td></td><td></td></tr>
<tr><td>Africa</td><td>29</td><td>37</td><td>34</td><td>11</td><td>43</td><td>46</td></tr>
<tr><td>Asia</td><td colspan="2">—— 64 ——</td><td>36</td><td colspan="2">—— 30 ——</td><td>70</td></tr>
<tr><td>Latin America</td><td>71</td><td>7</td><td>22</td><td>42</td><td>14</td><td>44</td></tr>
<tr><td>Rural population</td><td></td><td></td><td></td><td></td><td></td><td></td></tr>
<tr><td>Africa</td><td colspan="2">—— 22 ——</td><td>78</td><td colspan="2">—— 20 ——</td><td>80</td></tr>
<tr><td>Asia</td><td colspan="2">—— 31 ——</td><td>69</td><td colspan="2">—— 6 ——</td><td>94</td></tr>
<tr><td>Latin America</td><td colspan="2">—— 20 ——</td><td>80</td><td colspan="2">—— 20 ——</td><td>80</td></tr>
</table>

*Covers 51 countries.
Source: World Health Organization, *The International Drinking Water Supply and Sanitation Decade. Review of National Baseline Data, as at 31 December 1980* (Geneva: United Nations, 1984), p. 21.

human waste. This occurs in villages and cities alike. Although most urban residents have access to piped drinking water, the public water supply is often rendered unsafe by contamination in the distribution process as a result of a faulty or nonexistent sewage system. Few rural residents enjoy either piped water or decent sanitation. Table 11–3, although based on fragmentary data, gives some idea of the dimensions of the problem.

Many of the infectious, parasitic, and respiratory diseases that afflict poor countries are waterborne. Typhoid, dysentery, and cholera are leading examples. Their prevalence results in much sickness among adults and frequent deaths among infants and malnourished children. A second type of environmental sanitation problem arises from housing with insufficient space, ventilation, and access to sunlight. This situation, which is more likely to occur in urban than in rural areas, promotes the spread of airborne diseases such as tuberculosis.

Sanitary improvement programs primarily involve the problems of waste disposal and water supply, particularly the need to keep the one system from contaminating the other. In villages this means safe wells and properly constructed privies or latrines. Simple but effective technologies are available for such improvements. In urban areas matters become more expensive and complex. It will be a long time before all cities in the developing countries have decent sewage disposal and water supply systems, let alone adequate housing for their growing populations.

In the historical experience of the developed countries, improvements in sanitation were closely associated with reduction in diseases and became effective long before successful treatments were discovered. So far in the developing countries the experience has been mixed. Some projects to improve water supply and waste disposal methods have led to dramatic reductions in disease. Others, as noted earlier, have had no discernible effect.

MALNUTRITION

Malnutrition is a major source of ill health and premature death in the developing countries. Table 11–4 gives the most commonly cited nutritional statistic, average daily caloric intake. These figures are derived from **national food balance**

Table 11–4 Daily per Capita Caloric Supply for Income Classes, Regions, and Selected Countries, 1965 and 1989

	Total 1965	Total 1989	Percent change
Income groups (PPP)			
Below $1,000	2001	1890	−5.5
$1,000–$2,000	1982	2398	21.0
	(1936)*	(2026)	(4.6)
$2,000–$5,000	2115	2663	25.9
$5,000–$10,000	2420	2910	20.2
Above $10,000	3054	3338	9.3
Regions and selected countries			
Sub-Saharan Africa	2074	2122	2.3
Ghana	1937	2248	16.1
Kenya	2208	2163	-2.0
Tanzania	1831	2206	20.5
Asia and the Pacific	1960	2458	25.4
South Asia	1992	2215	11.2
India	2021	2229	10.3
Pakistan	1773	2219	25.2
Sri Lanka	2171	2277	4.9
East Asia and the Pacific	1939	2617	35.0
China	1929	2639	36.8
Indonesia	1791	2750	53.5
South Korea	2178	2852	30.9
Malaysia	2353	2774	17.9
Europe and Central Asia	n.a.	n.a.	n.a.
Western Europe	3074	3402	10.7
Eastern Europe and Central Asia	n.a.	n.a.	n.a.
Middle East and North Africa	2153	3011	39.9
North America	3224	3653	13.3
Latin America and the Caribbean	2445	2721	11.3
Bolivia	1868	1916	2.6
Brazil	2417	2751	13.8
Chile	2581	2581	0
Colombia	2179	2598	19.2
Peru	2323	2186	−5.9

*Figures in parentheses exclude India and China.
Source: World Development Report 1992, pp. 272–73.

sheets, accounts which estimate human food consumption by taking the total supply of food (production plus imports) and then subtracting other uses (exports; processing, spoilage, and rodent-infestation losses; livestock feed; and industrial uses). What remains must logically have been consumed by human beings. The resulting quantities of the various foodstuffs are then converted into nutrient values using standard equivalencies for the items concerned. These estimates of nutritional intake can be compared with minimum daily requirement figures, which purport to show how many calories and other nutrients a person would have to consume to maintain good health, given a certain body weight and at least a minimum level of daily activity.

The statistics in Table 11–4 indicate that average daily caloric intake rose between 1965 and 1989 in all major regions, in most (but not all) individual countries, and at all levels of GDP per capita (PPP) including the lowest. By 1989, estimated caloric intake exceeded the minimum daily requirement of approximately 2300 calories in nearly all countries with GDP per capita (PPP) of $2,000 or more and in most regions of the world. Countries with per capita GDP of less than $1,000, sub-Saharan Africa, and South Asia fell below the prescribed minimum. While this may appear to be a generally favorable situation and the shortfalls in the deficit income groups and regions, at 4 to 12 percent, may seem relatively small, one should be aware of two major pitfalls in interpreting these figures.

First, it must be recognized that the minimum daily requirement is not so simple a concept as it may appear. People can survive at lower levels of caloric intake, but to do so they must maintain a lower body weight and become less active. Such people generally do not appear ill, and it has even been suggested that some Asian groups, for example, should be regarded as "small but healthy." Arguing against this view, however, is considerable evidence that Asian workers who receive higher caloric intake and can maintain greater weight for height outperform their smaller counterparts at physical tasks such as farm work. It should be added that Asian smallness is not entirely genetic, but is at least partially attributable to inadequate nutrition in the past. When Asians regularly get enough to eat, as the Japanese have since World War II, and the Chinese and Koreans more recently, their average weight and height, and thus their caloric requirements, increase rapidly from one generation to the next.

The second problem is that these averages can make the situation look better than it actually is because available food may be very unequally distributed. Even in a country where the average daily intake is less than 2000 calories, there are at least a few people who eat as well as people in the developed countries (3500 calories or more). Meanwhile, as discussed below, large parts of the population are likely to experience significant caloric deprivation. The problem is that while the ample—even excessive—intake of the well-fed few raises the national average, it in no way diminishes the deficit suffered by those who cannot obtain the recommended minimum. Averages computed for large and diverse populations are particularly likely to understate the nutritional problem by offsetting surpluses against deficits in this misleading way.

Because of this problem, it may be more revealing to count malnourished people than to count calories. According to a World Bank estimate covering 87 countries but excluding China, 34 percent of all residents of developing countries received insufficient calories for an active working life in 1980; 16 percent were so poorly nourished that their bodily growth was likely to be stunted and their health seriously endangered.[8] By far the largest number of malnourished people in 1980, 470 million, were found to be in South Asia, where 50 percent of the population received insufficient calories. In sub-Saharan Africa 44 percent of the population was malnourished, and in Latin America 13 percent.

The prevalence of malnutrition and its injurious effects are greatest among children. In the early 1970s WHO estimated that 3 percent of developing-country children were afflicted by severe (third-degree) malnutrition, which gives rise to clinical conditions such as kwashiorkor, a protein-deficiency disease marked by bloated bellies and glassy stares, and marasmus, a condition brought on by shortage of both calories and protein. Another 25 percent suffered from moderate (second-degree) malnutrition, and a further 40 to 45 percent from mild (first-degree)

8. World Bank, *Poverty and Hunger: Issues and Options for Food Security in Developing Countries* (Washington, D.C.: World Bank, 1986).

malnutrition.[9] These conditions are indicated by substandard rates of physical development. Malnutrition was said to be present as a primary or contributing factor in more than half of all deaths among children under five in low-income countries. It can turn otherwise-mild childhood diseases, such as respiratory problems, gastrointestinal difficulties, and measles, into killers.

Most of the malnutrition in the world today is of the type known as protein-calorie malnutrition (PCM). Conditions caused by deficiencies of specific nutrients, such as rickets, scurvy, and beri-beri, have generally declined in importance. Among the remaining deficiency diseases the most important are vitamin A deficiency, which can cause blindness, and iron-deficiency anemia. At one time it was thought that shortage of protein was the principal nutritional problem of the developing countries, since protein is necessary for physical and mental development. Later, however, it was discovered that most of the children whose diets are protein deficient also suffer from a deficiency of calories, and if protein is added to the diet while calories remain insufficient, development is little affected because the added protein is used up as energy. Accordingly, calories are now regarded as the limiting factor in nutrition, and most programs attempt to supplement calories first and protein, vitamins, and minerals only secondarily.

The rising average calorie intakes shown in Table 11–4 have probably been accompanied by a fall in the extent of PCM. This should be measured directly, however, because of the tendency of these averages to mislead. Just as the upper half of Table 11–4 shows that national average nutritional levels are closely related to GNP per capita, different income groups within countries may also have very different consumption levels. If income distribution worsens, it is possible for the number of malnourished people to increase at the same time as the average caloric intake goes up.

Food Consumption

What causes malnutrition, and how could nutritional improvement contribute to economic development? The determinants of human nutritional levels can be analyzed using microeconomic consumption theory. The consumption of food, like that of other goods and services, can be thought of as determined by three elements: income, relative prices, and tastes. Engel's law, introduced in Chapter 3, says that households spend an increasing amount, but a decreasing proportion, of income on food as their incomes rise. Very poor households devote more than half their incomes to food and have relatively high income elasticities of demand for food; that is, a significant proportion of any additional income will be used to buy food. At higher income levels, the share of income devoted to food purchases falls to one-quarter or less, and the income elasticity of demand for food becomes quite low. Thus, income is an important determinant of food consumption levels, particularly at lower levels of household income. However, recent research has indicated that increases in income are less likely to raise calorie intake in the population as a whole than we previously thought, because people evidently

9. See Alan Berg, *The Nutrition Factor: Its Role in National Development* (Washington, D.C.: Brookings Institution, 1973), p. 5.

spend a large share of increased income on better quality or greater variety of food, rather than on more calories.[10]

Prices also have considerable influence, through income effects and substitution effects. A change in the price of the basic foodstuff—rice, wheat, or corn, depending on the country—can have a significant effect on the purchasing power of a poor household. If the household spends, say, 30 percent of its income on rice and the retail price of rice increases by 20 percent, this amount to a 6 percent cut ($0.3 \times 0.2 = 0.06 = 6$ percent) in the household's already-low purchasing power. For this reason staple food grain prices are a basic indicator of welfare levels among the poor—and also of political stability—in many low-income countries.

Substitution effects can also be significant. Even if people strongly prefer particular foods, large price differences can cause them to shift to cheaper substitutes for the more expensive foods that they prefer. This is especially true for the very poor. Hence it was possible to induce large numbers of people in East Pakistan (now Bangladesh) to consume U.S. surplus wheat instead of rice, the favored food grain, when there was a rice shortage during the 1960s. Similarly, desperately poor families are sometimes forced to "trade down" from the preferred food grain to a cheaper source of calories, usually either a hard grain like sorghum or a starchy root crop such as manioc (cassava).

A powerful argument for the influence of income on food consumption and nutritional status has appeared in recent discussions of famine. Most people associate famine with a precipitous drop in the overall food supply, usually as a result of crop failure, but Harvard economist Amartya Sen has shown that in several historical famines the total availability of food did not decline. The real problem, Sen argues, is likely to be people's food **entitlements:** their ability to obtain food, whether through purchase, rationing, or other forms of distribution.[11] Contemporary food policy analysts define their goal as **food security**, a situation in which all people, at all times, have access to enough food to permit them to lead active, healthy lives.

Both income and price influence the consumption of *food*, not necessarily or directly the consumption of nutrients derived from food. When people spend more on food, they may or may not obtain better nutrition. Some of their additional expenditure goes for a larger *quantity* of food, but much of it, especially above minimal income levels, goes for higher *quality*. Quality is defined subjectively by the consumer, following his or her tastes. Foods regarded as higher in quality need not be more nutritious than less-favored competitors, and they may even be nutritionally inferior. Every nutritionist can tell horror stories about the deterioration in nutritional standards as development proceeds: carbonated beverages replace natural drinks, commercial infant foods replace mother's breast milk, and various junk foods are increasingly consumed by children and adults. Statistics make it clear, however, that these cases run against the general pattern of improved nutrition in relation to increasing income. In general, people with higher incomes have at least a somewhat higher caloric intake and a more varied diet, which is superior in terms of nutrients other than calories.

Food beliefs and tastes can impede nutritional improvement. Every culture has

10. Behrman and Deolalikar, "Health and Nutrition."

11. Amartya Sen, "Ingredients of Famine Analysis: Availability and Entitlements," *Quarterly Journal of Economics,* 96, no. 3 (August 1981), 433–64.

beliefs about the health effects of various foods that are not supported by modern nutritional science. Traditional feeding taboos for infants and new mothers are particularly injurious in many developing countries. In most human environments one can point to nutritional potentials that remain underexploited for reasons of taste and habit. For example, soybean products provide a much cheaper source of protein than animal products, yet they are eaten in quantity only in East Asian countries where they are standard protein sources. Nutritionists can counter the economists' assertion that income is the main influence on nutritional status by demonstrating that even very poor households could eat more nutritiously if they had the necessary information and chose to do so.

Thus all three of the factors we have examined—income, prices, and tastes—are significant contributors to the determination of nutritional status. Emphasis on the role of each factor leads to a different approach to nutritional policy, as will be seen.

The distribution of food within a family is another important aspect of individual nutritional status. When there is not enough food to go around, children and older adults tend to find their rations disproportionately reduced.[12] It is understandable that in dire circumstances families channel scarce food to the working adults on whose continued health and strength the survival of all family members ultimately depends. This makes it hard to devise programs to improve the nutritional status of the more vulnerable family members, such as infants and new mothers, since if they get more food at a clinic, the family may compensate by giving them less at home. In the end, the net increase in the family's food supply may go to the breadwinner, rather than the intended recipients.

Nutritional Interventions

The first problem to be solved when designing a nutrition improvement program is to select a target group.

Infants and children face the greatest nutritional problem in the developing countries. Infants are usually adequately fed through the breast-feeding stage, but they may suffer a nutritional decline after weaning. If not corrected, this decline will reduce their energy levels and physical growth. This in turn may decrease their resistance to disease and impair their ability to learn in school. It has also been argued that malnutrition causes severe, even irreversible, retardation of mental development, but this assertion is now regarded as controversial at best. Even so, nutritional deficiencies among children in developing countries must be viewed as important because they are widespread and have such serious consequences.

Pregnant and lactating women also merit special attention because of their relationship to the child nutrition problem. While carrying or nursing a child, a woman has especially high nutritional requirements because she is "eating for two," as the saying goes.

Whether working adults should be specially targeted for nutrition intervention is more debatable. Conceivably, improved nutrition for this group could have the most direct and immediate effect on economic growth if its productivity were

12. Children with *high parity*—those born into families where there are several older siblings—are particularly likely to suffer. Studies have shown that such children have higher mortality rates, presumably because large families strain supplies of income, food, and parental attention.

thereby increased. But we have seen that there is mixed evidence on whether their productivity is reduced by the degrees of malnutrition prevailing in most developing countries and whether it would be improved by nutrition intervention. In any case, since working adults tend to get favored access to whatever food is available, it is not clear to what extent their food supply is cut when the family as a whole is short of food.

Several different types of nutrition intervention are possible. In the 1950s attention focused on the severely malnourished, who required hospital treatment. Later emphasis shifted to treatment of milder cases outside hospitals. Supplementary feeding programs were instituted in a number of countries. Their greatest difficulty turned out to be reaching the intended beneficiary group at reasonable cost. School lunch programs can be helpful, but the worst nutritional deficiencies are likely to be among preschool children. Even when the intended beneficiaries are reached and fed, evaluators of feeding programs suspect that substitution frequently takes place in the home: children are fed less to compensate for the school lunch, and the net increase in the family's food supply thus goes to the adults rather than the children.

The best way to get supplementary food to infants and small children is to integrate food distribution with **maternal and child health** (MCH) programs. These programs aim to provide health services to mothers and infants through local clinics while also providing nutritional surveillance. The food offered can serve as an inducement for mothers to bring their children into an MCH center regularly for weighing, examination, and treatment if necessary. Persuasion and linkage with other services that may be desired, such as family planning, also promote these programs. Without such efforts, very few mothers in developing countries bring their babies in for examination by a health professional unless they are obviously sick.

Other conventional nutrition improvement programs include the promotion of **backyard gardens** to provide dietary supplementation and **nutritional education** conducted in schools, adult education courses, and the like. Since these programs are inherently limited in scope, there have been attempts to develop broader, more general types of programs. **Food supplementation** (fortification) has sometimes had dramatic success in overcoming specific nutritional deficiencies, such as through the addition of iodine to the salt supply in goiter-prone areas. Fortification of bread and other basic foodstuffs to increase their protein content has been attempted in several areas, with mixed results. Still less successful have been efforts, some of them widely heralded for a time, to develop commercially compounded **new foods** whose exceptional nutritional values would overcome the problem of malnutrition. The high cost of new foods usually puts them beyond the reach of those low-income consumers who are likely to be malnourished.

Growing interest in malnutrition and the limited success of conventional approaches have led to increasing attention to still broader programs, such as **campaigns to increase national food production** and **food price subsidization** for low-income urban consumers. There is no doubt that food-growing peasants, such as small-scale rice or corn producers, eat better when their farms become more productive. Similarly, a price cut for staple food items—made possible by higher farm production and greater supplies—can provide a substantial boost in both purchasing power and nutritional status for the urban poor, as we have seen.

Staple-food subsidization programs pose two major problems: how to limit them to the intended beneficiaries and how to finance them. Recipients of subsidized foodstuffs (or food stamps, as in the U.S. program) may sell them to buy other goods which they prefer. While this practice is consistent with the idea of consumer sovereignty, it may defeat the purpose of nutritional improvement. Subsidy programs can be expensive, especially when their scope is broad. Egypt and Sri Lanka are two countries that have had food subsidy programs extending to nearly the entire population. In both cases subsidization of basic foodstuffs (wheat, beans, lentils, vegetable oil, meat, fish, and tea in Egypt; rice, wheat, and sugar in Sri Lanka) probably increased the real income of the poor and improved their nutritional and health status. But the cost of the program grew to around 15 percent of government expenditure in both countries and became a threat to fiscal stability. In both cases efforts to cut back on the subsidy bill led to political instability: riots in both countries, and in Sri Lanka the defeat at the polls of more than one government.

The cost-effectiveness of different approaches to nutritional improvement has been debated.[13] Targeted programs that deliver nutritional services to specific groups of beneficiaries—for instance, school lunch programs or baby-weighing programs—can involve high logistical and supervision costs per beneficiary served. More general programs, such as food fortification or food subsidies, may achieve a lower cost per recipient but entail a different kind of cost problem: leakage of program benefits to people other than the intended beneficiaries. Providing nutritional services, especially food subsidies, to large segments of the population can be costly, as the experiences of Egypt and Sri Lanka illustrate. Experience with World Bank–sponsored projects in Brazil, Colombia, Indonesia, and the Indian state of Tamil Nadu suggests that well-designed targeted programs can be more cost-effective than general programs.[14]

Medical Services

Most developing countries have too few health services, too poorly distributed. Public expenditures on health services are much smaller in developing than in developed countries, even as a percentage of GNP, as seen in Table 11–5. In terms of dollars per capita, these outlays are woefully inadequate. Governments in the poorest countries typically spend only a few dollars per capita, even when measured in purchasing power parity.[15] The inadequacy becomes clearer when we

13. Cost-effectiveness is a concept akin to the benefit-cost ratio, which was discussed in Chapter 6 (see footnote 8, page 284). But whereas in the benefit-cost ratio both benefits and costs are measured in money terms, cost-effectiveness uses a nonmonetary measure of benefits. In the case of a nutritional intervention, for example, greater cost-effectiveness would consist of achieving a larger amount of nutritional benefit for a given program expenditure. Alternatively, it could be defined as achievement of a given amount of nutritional benefit for less program expenditure.

14. Alan Berg, *Malnutrition. What Can Be Done? Lessons from World Bank Experience* (Baltimore: Johns Hopkins Press for the World Bank, 1987).

15. Conventional figures, which show government health expenditures of only \$1–\$2 per capita per year, are distorted by the extreme disparity in the pay of medical personnel, especially doctors, between rich and poor countries. The purchasing power parity adjustment used in Table 11–5 roughly triples the per capita expenditure figures for the poorest countries and doubles those for the somewhat-less poor. By any measure, however, the figures remain abysmally low. See Frederick Golladay, "Health Problems and Policies in Developing Countries," World Bank Staff Working Paper No. 412, August 1980.

TABLE 11–5 Health Personnel, Facilities and Expenditures (around 1990)

Country's GDP per capita (PPP)	Per 1000 population*			Public expenditures†	
	Hospital beds	Physicians	Nursing persons	Percent of GNP	Dollars per capita
Below $1,000	75	6	58	1.7	12
$1,000–$2,000	171 (143)	68 (36)	66 (95)	0.6 (2.4)	7 (46)
$2,000–$5,000	277	91	147	2.1	40
$5,000–$10,000	1291‡	142	161	1.3	75
Above $10,000	816	254	463	4.5	821

* Figures in parentheses exlude India and China.
† Figures in parentheses exclude India; no data on health expenditures are available for China.
‡ This average is inflated by the high figures reported by a number of exsocialist countries.
Sources: World Development Report 1992 to *1994*, and World Bank, *Social Indicators of Development 1994.*

consider that in developing countries, in contrast to the United States, the public sector finances the bulk of the modern, Western-style medical and health services.[16] Private doctors and hospitals are typically few and are patronized mainly by well-to-do urban residents. In most countries there are also indigenous practitioners of various kinds: herbalists, exorcists, and acupuncturists. Typically the masses of people consult both modern and indigenous healers, depending on the nature of the ailment and on their access to the various systems of medicine.

Low medical expenditures in the past have led to inadequate stocks of health facilities and personnel in most developing countries and particularly in the poorest ones, as Table 11–5 indicates. Medical training in many of the poorest countries may not benefit society because doctors are highly mobile, and once trained, many emigrate to seek higher income elsewhere (see boxed example on Cuba). In many cases, increasing the supply of nurses and other health auxiliaries may be a better way to improve services.

Health in Cuba

When Castro's forces took over in January 1959, Cuba was a middle-income country with reasonably plentiful but poorly distributed health care personnel and facilities. Average income was higher than in most other Latin America countries, life expectancy at birth was over 60 years, and the population was more than 50 percent urban. But inequalities were marked. Havana, with only 22 percent of the population, had 55 percent of the hospital beds in the country, whereas Oriente province, one of Cuba's poorest regions, had 35 percent of the population but only 15 percent of the hospital beds. There were 6300 doctors to care for a population of 8 million.

In the first three years after the revolution, 3000 physicians left the country; most emigrated to the United States. This is probably the first time in history when a country lost such a high percentage of its doctors in so short a time. Massive training efforts were inaugurated to make up this deficit. By 1971, 30 percent of all university students were studying

16. In the United States, total (public plus private) health expenditure in 1992 amounted to about 12 percent of GNP. Yet central government expenditure, as reported in the *World Development Report 1994,* was less than 4 percent.

medicine. By 1979, after more than 20 years of massive training efforts, the ratio of doctors to population was finally restored to about what it had been in 1958.

Despite having to cope with this massive problem of medical personnel, Cuba made major strides toward the achievement of high health standards for its entire population. To do so, it reorganized its health services and improved their distribution among social classes and regions of the country. A new system of hospitals and clinics was set up; it stretched from provincial hospitals serving areas of about 1 million people down to health centers serving communities of 25,000. Given the initial disparities, new facilities were constructed primarily in the rural areas. Thus while the number of hospital beds available in Havana increased by only 8 percent in the decade after the revolution, the increases in Camaguey and Oriente provinces were 184 and 147 percent respectively. Over half the new health centers built were allocated to rural areas which previously had no such facilities. Services in the new system were provided virtually free; this encouraged greater use by the public.

Medical personnel participated in the planning and management of health services, but the broad guidelines were laid down by the political leadership, dominated by the Communist party. After the introduction of local elections in 1976, community participation in health care planning increased.

Social and economic change have supported these improvements in medical services. Economic growth has generally been slow. Public policy has emphasized equitable distribution of basic necessities. Primary foodstuffs are rationed and price-controlled. Literacy is now estimated at 94 percent and elementary school attendance is universal (uniquely among Latin American countries). Housing problems have been chronic among Cuba's urban population, now 65 percent of the total, but are gradually being remedied by the construction of apartment houses.

Mortality indicators for Cuba have improved from good to excellent. The infant death rate was only 14 per thousand in 1992. Life expectancy at birth is 76 years. The total fertility rate is now 1.7, so although the population is still growing (at 0.8 percent a year), it can be expected to stabilize in the relatively near future. Family planning is not officially promoted because the country is perceived as suffering from a labor shortage, but contraceptives are freely available to those who want them.

In addition to being inadequately supplied, health services in poor countries are very unevenly distributed among the population. Capital cities and other major urban areas usually have several times as many doctors in relation to population as rural areas. Similar if slightly smaller disparities exist for hospital beds and primary health workers.

The usual public health service is organized on a referral basis, so in theory, patients from rural areas with acute medical problems are sent to better facilities in the towns and, if necessary, in the major cities, for care. Generally, however, this referral system works poorly. The lower reaches of the system seldom provide easily accessible services to the whole country. For large parts of the population in most low-income countries, even the most rudimentary public health facility is so far away that, given the prevailing poor transportation systems, it is in practice inaccessible. When patients do go to a government clinic or hospital, they often find that they have to wait many hours and possibly pay unauthorized fees before receiving any attention at all. Even then the care they obtain may be slipshod and halfhearted. As a result, rather than using the systems for routine services and referrals as intended, people tend to ignore it except in acute emergencies, and then go directly to a hospital.

Managerial and logistical problems overwhelm some developing-country health systems. Many of the vaccines administered, for example, have been rendered ineffective by age and exposure to heat, and sterile conditions for medical procedures are all but impossible to maintain. Reuse of needles without proper sterilization and other unsanitary procedures, always a means of spreading diseases such as hepatitis, now threaten to accelerate the spread of AIDS, which has appeared in many developing countries and already affects large parts of the population in some of them, particularly in Africa.

Medical resources are often distributed ineffectually among different types of ailments and forms of treatment. In many countries large fractions of tight health budgets have been devoted to acquiring state-of-the-art medical technologies for hospitals in the capital city or at the local medical school. Does it make sense for a country that is not providing even rudimentary medical care to sick infants to acquire the capacity to do open-heart surgery? For the cost of a single complicated medical procedure, basic attention could be provided to hundreds of rural patients. Why then do so many countries opt for what appears to be a severe maldistribution of their scant health resources? One reason appears to be urban bias, the general tendency in developing countries for urban populations to benefit disproportionately from government expenditures and policies.[17] Urban bias in the provision of medical services has many causes; one is that the powerful national elites centered in urban areas, especially the capital city, want good medical care for themselves and their families. A second reason is nationalism: "Our doctors are just as good as doctors in the advanced countries; they can do open-heart surgery, too." Yet a third reason is the technology-mindedness that many doctors share with engineers and other professionals. Medicine is often regarded as an outstanding example of the transfer of inappropriate technology from developed to developing countries. These three factors can interact, as when the self-interest of the elites prompts them to indulge the technology-mindedness of the doctors.

Still another shortcoming of public health services in most developing countries relates to the balance between preventive and curative services. Since, as we have seen, curing all the sick is beyond the means of many poor countries, the possibility that sickness and death can be reduced more cheaply through preventive measures deserves careful examination. Measures such as inoculation campaigns, mosquito spraying, and rat killing have produced dramatic improvements in health conditions in some low-income countries, most notably in China. Many developing countries still spend too much on curative services relative to preventive activities.

It is thus evident that inadequate, maldistributed, and inappropriate medical ser-

17. Urban bias has been defined and analyzed by Michael Lipton, *Why Poor People Stay Poor: Urban Bias in World Development* (Cambridge, Mass: Harvard University Press, 1977).

vices in poor countries are themselves contributors to sickness and premature death. What can be done about it?

Improved medical services depend on the extension of coverage to the entire population and on the development of service patterns more appropriate to the health needs and resource availabilities of a developing country. Many experts believe that a reformed health system would include (1) active and continuous promotion of community health, instead of intermittent treatment of specific conditions in individuals; (2) management of the system by nonphysicians; (3) training health care auxiliaries recruited from the community to diagnose and treat simple ailments; and (4) limited referral of difficult cases.

The health care systems evolved by socialist developing countries such as China and Cuba are sometimes taken as models by those interested in similar reforms. In 1976 China reported spending over 60 percent of its health care budget in rural areas and sending half its medical school graduates to assignments in the countryside. Like other developing countries it has experienced difficulty in getting health professionals to live in rural areas. China has countered this tendency, however, and through its well-known system of health auxiliaries, it is providing for the first time decent health care to its enormous peasant population. As of 1976 official sources reported that there were 1.5 million "barefoot doctors" working in the country, doing preventive work, treating patients at home and in the fields, assisting with mass health and sanitation campaigns, and disseminating information on family planning and maternal and child health care. In addition, some 3 million part-time health auxiliaries were said to be assisting in the same activities. These efforts have contributed to levels of health and life expectancy unusual for a country with China's still low income level.

The development and dissemination of simple cures for widespread health problems must accompany the spread of medical services into the rural areas. For example, at present about 10 percent of all children born in the developing countries die of diarrhea before reaching the age of 10. Yet there is a simple inexpensive technology that can prevent most of these deaths: oral rehydration therapy (ORT), which is nothing more than a solution of sugar and mineral salts in water. ORT counteracts dehydration, which is the direct cause of diarrhea deaths. A scientifically designed and tested ORT formula is being disseminated by organizations such as the United Nations Children's Fund (UNICEF), but even folk versions of the remedy, such as rice water and simple mixtures of sugar and table salt, may be effective. Sickness and early death among children in poor countries could be sharply curtailed by spreading knowledge and availability of this remedy throughout the world and developing others like it.

Health Services and the Market

We saw in this chapter that public health services in developing countries are severely underfinanced. The World Bank has observed that prices have generally played only a minor role, either in generating resources to finance health services or in determining who should have access to them.[18] According to the World

18. Emmanuel Jimenez, *Pricing Policy in the Social Sectors. Cost Recovery for Education and Health in Developing Countries* (Baltimore: Johns Hopkins Press for the World Bank, 1987).

Bank, only 7 percent of the cost of publicly provided services in developing countries is currently recovered through user fees. These observations led to proposals to increase fees charged for health services and institute charges for services currently provided free. The revenue thus generated would be used to expand health services. Since this is a textbook on the *economics* of development, it behooves us to conclude this chapter on health and development by considering the merits of this proposal to increase the role of prices in the provision of health care in developing countries.

In his analysis of the possibility of charging higher prices for educational and health services, World Bank economist Emmanuel Jimenez proposes that we distinguish between services that yield personal benefits enjoyed only by the individual recipient and those that have substantial external benefits for the broader society. When external benefits are large, the price charged for the service must be set below its cost, or else society will be deprived of valuable benefits. Broadly speaking, one would probably not want to charge for most preventive health services, but one might be more willing to place a reasonably high fee on many curative services. If there is excess demand for these services, fees could probably be raised without reducing the quantity of services provided. Additional revenues would be generated; if these were then reinvested in service provision, services could then be expanded, perhaps by enough to meet the previously unfulfilled demand. If there is no excess demand for services, the effect of a fee increase on revenues and the level of service would depend on the elasticity of demand for health services. Available evidence suggests that this demand is highly inelastic, since people regard at least some kinds of health services—particularly, one suspects, curative services in health emergencies—as necessities. Jimenez notes, however, that user fees for the highest-cost services can be brought close to the cost of providing them only if medical insurance is widely available, since few of the people unfortunate enough to require such services are likely to be able to afford them.

One should approach the possibility of financing expanded health services in developing countries through higher user fees with a critical frame of mind. There is little doubt that increasing expenditure on health services would benefit both economic growth and human welfare in the short run in most developing countries. Yet this kind of earmarked tax is neither necessarily the best way to raise the funding for such an expansion nor a sure way of garnering additional resources for this purpose (in a society that places a low priority on health, the funds might be diverted to other programs in any case). Serious objections can also be raised to fee charging, not only because of the external benefits mentioned by Jimenez but also on equity grounds.

As discussed above, the kinds of services the developing-country governments *should* be spending the bulk of their health budgets on are those that yield major benefits to society in general and particularly to poor people in rural and urban areas. One wishes to expand these services substantially in most countries, not to discourage their use through the imposition of substantial fees. Government expenditure on health and other social services cannot fulfill its potential for improving income distribution and lessening the grinding effects of poverty if it is accompanied by fees that discourage the use of these services by the very people we want to reach.

Health services may thus be one area where potentials for using the price system, so frequently advocated in this textbook, are limited. It should be noted, however, that this skepticism about the desirability of charging for health services is warranted only *if* the emphasis in health services is on primary and preventive services aimed at the masses of people, as advocated in this chapter. If, on the contrary, the services offered are primarily those which benefit the rich, then of course high fees should be charged. But this, as we hope to have made clear by now, is no way to run a public health service in a developing country.

PART 4

CAPITAL RESOURCES

12

Capital and Saving

Of all the approaches to development mentioned in Chapters 2 and 3, the emphasis on capital formation was perhaps the most influential and durable, for a number of reasons. First, it had respectable theoretical underpinnings—the simple but elegant Harrod-Domar model, discussed in Chapter 3. Properly viewed, the Harrod-Domar model provides insights into vital aspects of the development process, because it focuses on the difficulties involved in meeting the investment requirements for assuring substantial and steady growth without high rates of inflation or unemployment. However, more mechanistic interpretations of the Harrod-Domar model postulated a lockstep relationship between growth in investment and national income. The view that capital formation was the key to growth, called **capital fundamentalism,** was reflected in the development strategies and plans of many countries. The development problem was viewed essentially as one of securing investment resources sufficient to generate some chosen target rate of national income growth. The implications of target rates of income growth for employment and income distribution were rarely examined, as it was widely assumed that faster growth rates would in and of themselves ameliorate both unemployment and extreme income inequality.

Second, capital fundamentalism resonated with the aims and approaches of foreign aid donors of the 1950s and 1960s, by furnishing a readily explicable, apparently clear-cut basis for the justifying aid "needs." Capital shortage was then widely judged to be the single most important barrier to accelerated economic development, and a heavy premium tended to be placed on framing development plans that reflected this point of view. The best-crafted of such plans, such as Pakistan's third 5-year plan in the early 1960s, were able to show heavy initial capital requirements and a need for large early injections of foreign capital, especially foreign aid. Large initial contributions of aid, it was thought, would generate new flows of domestic savings, and reduce aid requirements in the long run.

Third, capital fundamentalism was durable because its framework was flexible enough to incorporate new economic ideas of the 1960s, especially the concept of human capital discussed in Part 3 of this book. The selective embedding of human capital considerations into the framework further strengthened the argument that capital formation was the linchpin of development. The incorporation of human capital into the framework was no minor embellishment, for the size of the human capital stock relative to the physical capital stock can be quite large. Estimates place the value of the human capital stock in the United States in the mid-1970s as roughly equal to that of the stock of physical capital.

High levels of capital formation made possible by initial abundance of savings matter little for income growth—much less for employment creation and improving income distribution—when capital is deployed in projects of low productivity. These include the much-ridiculed, large-scale showcase steel mills and thousands of inefficiently small hydroelectric plants; expensive higher education systems; and ultramodern cardiac care centers serving small elites in capital cities. Further, massive investment projects financed by foreign savings, however productive, may have little impact on income growth when host country policies are poorly suited for capturing an equitable share of the returns from such projects. Particularly before the mid-1960s, there were several instances in which host countries, especially those with sizable natural resource endowments, ultimately had little to show from major foreign investment projects other than the scrap content of equipment left behind at the end. We return to this problem in Chapters 15 and 19.

INVESTMENT REQUIREMENTS FOR GROWTH

The critical role of savings and capital in creating income growth has been well established in industrial societies. For example, the sources-of-growth analysis introduced in Chapter 3 has been employed to show that expansion of physical capital inputs alone was responsible for about half the growth in aggregate income of nine developed countries from 1960 to 1975. Similarly, the growth of East Asia's "Miracle Economies" has been shown to owe much to high levels of saving and investment in both physical and human capital.

Analyses of the relative contribution of capital to growth in developing countries are neither as numerous nor, owing to data limitations, as conclusive as those for the United States and other OECD members. However, the available sources-of-growth calculations suggest that the impact of capital formation on growth is considerable in those countries as well, particularly for the early stages of development; at higher levels of income, productivity growth appears much more important. Studies in middle-income countries such as Korea, the Philippines, and Mexico indicate that in the sixties and seventies, growth in the physical capital stock, quite apart from growth in the stock of human capital, may have contributed from one-fourth to one-third of income growth, with estimates' clustering toward the higher figure; the contribution is as much as one-half in poorer countries. None of these studies incorporate the contribution of human capital to income growth, so the results understate the role of capital formation, and therefore savings, in income growth.

In any case, although capital accumulation is no longer viewed as a panacea for poor countries, it is nevertheless clear that even mildly robust growth rates in incomes can be sustained over long periods only when societies are able to maintain investment at a sizable proportion of GDP. This proportion can rarely be much less than 15 percent and in some cases it must be as high as 25 or even 35 percent, depending on the environment in which capital accumulation takes place and the rate of income growth deemed essential to allow progress toward basic societal goals. In general, if developing countries seek a respectable 3 percent growth in real per capita income, then given rates of population growth in low-income economies of about 2 percent in the past decade (excluding China), the requisite rate of aggregate income growth would have to be at least 5 percent per annum.[1]

Effective Use of Capital

Given a goal of 5 percent growth in real aggregate income, annual investment requirements would then depend on both the volume of available savings and on the environment in which capital formation occurs. In developing countries where basic macro (economywide) prices (exchange rates, interest rates, wage rates) are approximately equal to scarcity values for factors of production, scarce capital is likely to be deployed where it can be applied most effectively with more abundant labor. In such circumstances a given addition to the capital stock can generate increments to output that exceed those in countries where production is more capital-intensive (see Chapter 3). Depending on the structure of basic macro prices such as interest rates and exchange rates and the orientation of public sector decision makers, the ICOR can vary from under 3:1 to 7:1 and even higher, as shown in Table 3–4. Consider the investment implications of an ICOR of 3.0 compared with an ICOR half again as high, or 4.5. For countries with an ICOR of 3.0, a necessary, but not sufficient, condition for achieving sustained aggregate growth in output of 5.0 percent per year is securing capital resources equivalent to 15 percent of GNP. However, countries with an ICOR of 4.5 will need to invest 22.5 percent of GNP to attain the same rate of output growth. Thus more efficient deployment of capital can substantially reduce the savings effort required for sustained growth.

Capital-Intensive or Labor-Intensive Investment: A Hypothetical Case

In the presence of immobilities of productive factors of the type discussed at the end of this chapter, a pervasive pattern of capital-intensive production in capital-short countries leads to lower rates of income growth, strong suppression of consumption, or both. To illustrate, consider two small low-income countries that are initially identical in all important respects: per capita income of $400 in 1995, population of 2.5 million, an investment ratio in 1995 of 15 percent, and similar

1. Strictly speaking, 5.1 percent growth is required. (1 + desired growth rate in real per capita income) × (1 + rate of population growth) = (1 + requisite aggregate growth rate). In this case, 1.03 × 1.02 = 1.0506.

patterns of exports, imports, agriculture, and industry. From 1985 to 1995, both followed essentially the same development strategy, which produced in an historic incremental capital-output ratio of 3.5 each. And each experienced a real GDP growth rate of about 5 percent over the ten-year period.

In 1995 new governments in both countries altered past development policies. For the next decade country A's government chose a strategy involving heavy outlays on large-scale, capital-intensive investments, such as oil refining, paper mills, and steel mills. As a result of this change, and supported by other government policies, the ICOR was expected to rise from 3.5 to 4. Country B, on the other hand, decided in 1995 to shift to a strategy emphasizing more labor-intensive investments in agriculture and industry, including textile mills, commercial firewood forests, coastal fisheries, and shoe manufactures. Decision makers in country B expect the ICOR to decline from 3.5 to 3 as a result. These two capital-output ratios are within the high range for developing countries given in Table 3–2. In this example we overlook contributions of other factors to growth.

We assume that both countries faced similar constraints on investment finance during the period 1995 to 2000. For both, resources available for investment (from both domestic and foreign sources) are most likely to expand by no less than 5 percent per year ("low") and by no more than 10 percent per year ("high"). The implications of these alternative investment availabilities for GDP growth are presented in Table 12–1.

A striking implication can be drawn from Table 12–1. The table shows that the efficiency with which capital is used can be much more important for GDP

TABLE 12–1 GDP and Investment under Two Different Strategies (millions of U.S. dollars)

	1995	Investment growth rate (%)	1996	1997	1998	1999	2000	Average annual growth (%)	2000 % of investment to GDP
Investment availability									
I. Low	150.0	5.0	157.5	165.4	173.6	182.3	191.4	5.0	—
II. High	150.0	10.0	165.0	181.5	199.6	219.6	241.6	10.0	—
GDP Country A Capital-intensive strategy (ICOR = 4)*									
I. Low	1000.0	5.0	1037.5	1076.9	1118.3	1161.7	1207.3	3.8	15.9
II. High	1000.0	10.0	1037.5	1078.8	1124.2	1174.1	1229.0	4.2	19.7
GDP Country B Labor-intensive strategy (ICOR = 3)*									
I. Low	1000.0	5.0	1050.0	1102.5	1157.6	1215.5	1276.3	5.0	15.0
II. High	1000.0	10.0	1050.0	1105.0	1165.5	1232.0	1305.2	5.5	18.5

*To simplify presentation, the example assumes that all investment resources in any given year are available by the beginning of that year and that there is only a one-year lag between the time investment resources are available and the time they begin to yield output.

growth than raising the volume of investment is. For the entire five-year period, the ICOR of country A is only 25 percent higher than that of country B. But after five years country B has a higher GDP than country A, even when investment resources grow at twice the rate in country A as in country B. At 5 percent growth in investment in country B, average annual GDP growth is also 5 percent, whereas in country A even 10 percent growth in investment leads to only a 4.2 percent average annual GDP growth. To accomplish this, by the fifth year country A must find investment resources equal to 19.7 percent of GDP. With an investment ratio of only 15 percent in 2000, country B can still grow faster than the maximum that is possible for country A.

On the other hand, if investment resources available to both countries were to grow at 10 percent per annum, aggregate income in country B would be 6 percent higher than in country A by 2000, even though they began at the same level. Although a 6 percent difference in total income after five years may not seem large, when placed in proper perspective it can be quite significant.

Few developing countries spend as much as 6 percent of GDP on education (Botswana, Kenya, and Lesotho were exceptions in 1992), and only a handful spend as much as 3 percent on public health. Merely because it uses capital more efficiently than country A, country B would, in the extreme, possess the capacity to more than double real outlays for education, or triple expenditures on public health programs. Alternatively, if both countries place a high premium on national autonomy and are therefore apprehensive over foreign participation in their economies, it is much more likely that country B will satisfy this goal since it will have less need to resort to foreign capital to finance a substantial share of its development effort. An investment ratio of 15 percent is clearly much easier to support from domestic resources than the 20 percent required for country A to attain the same level of GDP growth.

Investment Ratios in Developing Countries

The heavy emphasis on capital-intensive investment often found in developing countries is to some extent the unintended result of government policies. But it may also be attributed to a pervasive belief that only capital-intensive technology is efficient, and the choice of technology is not sensitive to relative prices of labor and capital. The discussion in Chapter 9 casts significant doubt on the notion that the choice of technique of production in developing countries is largely unaffected by price signals. Policies that result in underpricing capital and overpricing labor do seem to cause firms and government agencies to adjust by adopting techniques involving more capital and less labor than would be the case in the absence of such policies. However, Chapter 9 also reminds us that whenever found, bias toward capital intensity in investment cannot always, or even usually, be fully explained in terms of distorted price signals. Nor is it legitimate to assume that capital intensity always represents vice and that labor-using investment always denotes virtue. For example, those who would advocate a conscious, reverse bias in favor of labor-intensive methods of underground coal or tin mining have either never visited the hazardous labor-intensive facilities for these activities (for example, in Bolivia and Indonesia) or are unaware of the large surpluses available from capital-intensive mining that can be deployed for labor-intensive investments in other fields. Even in agriculture there are sound arguments, advanced in Chapter 16, for mechanization to increase both productivity and employment.

In the typical labor-surplus situation, 5 percent annual growth in real income cannot be sustained over extended periods in the absence of investment ratios of at least 20 percent (in the economies emphasizing more labor-intensive approaches) and 25 percent (in the capital-intensive strategies). Securing investment ratios of 20 percent or more has proven a difficult task for many developing countries, in particular for most of the 42 countries characterized as low-income economies by the World Bank.

Nevertheless, about half the countries in this group did manage to increase the share of gross domestic investment to gross domestic product between 1970 and 1992.[2] Whereas only nine low-income economies are known to have invested more than 20 percent of GDP in 1970, 16 countries reached this standard in 1992. The 46 lower-middle-income countries had a mixed experience over the 1970s and 1980s. More raised their investment ratios than lowered them, but data are lacking for many of these countries, especially those created out of the former Soviet Union. Yet at least 27 lower-middle-income economies invested 20 percent or more of GDP in 1992, compared to 13 in 1970. As a group, the 21 upper-middle-income economies found it harder to raise investment in 1970 to 1992. While 13 of them invested more than 20 percent of GDP in 1970, this number dropped to only five by 1992. Most of the developing countries that invested 30 percent or more of GDP in 1992 were among the world's fastest-growing economies, for example Thailand (40 percent), Indonesia (35 percent), and Malaysia (34 percent). China probably exceeded all of these, but precise figures are unavailable. Table 12–2 shows that developing countries as a group had, on average, higher investment ratios in 1992 than even the advanced industrialized countries.

Sources of Savings

Developing countries, particularly the poorest 42 nations, were able to finance their higher investment-GDP ratios by intensified saving mobilization efforts directed at savings from various sources, domestic and foreign, private and public. Before turning to an examination of recent patterns of investment finance, it will be useful to consider a simplified taxonomy of savings.

Taxonomy of Savings

The allocation of resources between present and future consumption (saving) is one of the most fundamental economic choices facing any economy. This choice affects not only the rate of economic growth a country can enjoy, but also the standards of living for future generations yet unborn.

For a country, the total supply of available savings S is simply the sum of domestic savings (S_d) and foreign savings (S_f). Domestic savings may be broken down into two components: government, or public-sector, savings (S_g) and private domestic savings (S_p). Government savings consists primarily of budgetary sav-

2. Twenty low-income countries did so, according to the *World Development Report 1994*, Table 9. Twelve countries experienced declining investment ratios, two had no change, and eight possessed insufficient data.

ings (S_{gb}) that arises from any excess of government revenues over government consumption, where public consumption is defined as all current government expenditure plus all capital outlays for military hardware. Examples of public sector consumption include expenditures for food subsidies; for meeting recurring costs such as salaries for civil servants and police; for purchasing stationery, fuel, and arms; and for maintaining roads and bridges, plus interest on the national debt. In focusing on this savings component, it is important to note that a country could still have positive public savings even when the overall government budget is in deficit, because budget expenditures include capital outlays, or investment, that represent uses of public savings. In a very few countries savings of government-owned enterprises (S_{ge}) have also contributed to public-sector savings (see Chapter 13). Private domestic savings also arise from two sources: corporate savings (S_{pc}) and household savings (S_{ph}). **Corporate savings** is defined as the retained earnings of corporate enterprises (corporate income after taxes minus dividends paid to shareholders). **Household savings** (S_{ph}) is simply that part of household income not consumed. Household savings includes savings from unincorporated enterprises (single proprietorships, partnerships, and other noncorporate forms of business enterprise). In most developing countries unincorporated business enterprise is by far the dominant form of business organization.

Foreign savings also comes in two basic forms: **official foreign savings** (S_{fo}) or foreign aid, and **private foreign savings** (S_{fp}), which may be broken down into two separate components. The first is **external commercial borrowing,** or *debt* finance, symbolized (S_{fpd}). Developing-country borrowers, including governments, agree to repay the amount of the loan (the principal) as well as interest on the loan, in accordance with prearranged schedules. The second major component of private foreign savings, **direct investment,** represents *equity* finance, symbolized (S_{fpe}). Returns to equity are called dividends and are paid only when profits are made.

To recapitulate, total available savings may be viewed in the first instance as

$$S = S_d + S_f = (S_g + S_p) + (S_{fo} + S_{fp}). \qquad [12\text{–}1]$$

For purposes of understanding saving patterns and policies, savings may be disaggregated further to

$$S = [(S_{gb} + S_{ge}) + (S_{pc} + S_{ph})] + (S_{fo} + S_{fpd} + S_{fpe}). \qquad [12\text{–}2]$$

Reliance on different sources of savings differs greatly among developing countries, depending not only on factors such as the level of per capita income, natural resource endowments, and sectoral composition of GDP, but also on the nature of saving mobilization policies adopted by particular governments. The balance of this chapter identifies the determinants of domestic saving and its various components. Chapter 15 will examine foreign saving, its patterns, and the controversies surrounding it.

Domestic Savings

Relative to 1965, developing countries as a group had by 1992 greatly intensified their efforts to mobilize domestic saving. Although many relied heavily on foreign savings as a source of investment finance, the rise in investment ratios depicted in Table 12–2 was accompanied by a roughly commensurate increase in the share of gross domestic savings in GDP. Although these averages mask some

TABLE 12–2 Gross Domestic Investment and Saving, 1965 and 1992

Country/Category	Gross domestic investment* (as % of GDP) 1965	1992	Gross domestic saving† (as % of GDP) 1965	1992	Resources gap‡ 1965	1992	Domestic saving as % of domestic investment 1965	1992
Ethiopia	13	9	12	−1	1	10	92	−11
Mali	12	22	4	5	8	17	33	23
Tanzania	15	42	17	5	−2	37	113	12
India	18	23	14	22	4	1	78	96
Bangladesh	11	12	8	6	3	6	73	50
Kenya	14	17	15	15	−1	2	107	88
Nigeria	19	18	17	23	2	−5	89	128
Senegal	12	13	8	7	4	6	67	54
Ghana	18	13	8	2	10	11	44	15
China	25	36	25	39	0	−3	100	108
Honduras	15	26	15	17	0	9	100	65
Low-income countries	*20*	*27*	*19*	*27*	*2*	*1*	*93*	*97*
(w/o China and India)	*14*	*17*	*13*	*8*	*1*	*9*	*94*	*49*
Pakistan	21	21	13	14	8	7	62	67
Bolivia	22	16	13	5	9	11	59	31
Cameroon	13	11	13	10	0	1	100	91
Philippines	21	23	15	18	6	5	71	78
Sri Lanka	12	23	13	15	−1	8	108	65
Indonesia	8	35	8	37	0	−2	100	106
Peru	34	16	27	13	7	3	79	81
Egypt, Arab Rep.	18	18	14	7	4	11	78	39
Lower-middle-income countries	*16*	*25*	*12*	*21*	*4*	*4*	*77*	*84*
Brazil	25	17	27	21	−2	−4	108	124
Hungary	26	19	25	18	1	1	96	95
Colombia	16	18	17	21	−1	−3	106	117
Argentina	19	17	23	15	−4	2	121	88
Mexico	22	24	21	17	1	7	95	71
Malaysia	20	34	24	35	−4	−1	120	103
Korea,Rep. of	15	39	7	36	8	3	47	92
Upper-middle income countries	*21*	*25*	*21*	*24*	*−1*	*1*	*102*	*95*
United Kingdom	20	15	19	14	1	1	95	93
Japan	32	31	33	34	−1	−3	103	110
Germany	28	21	29	28	−1	−7	104	133
United States	20	16	21	15	−1	1	105	94
Upper-income countries	*24*	*20*	*25*	*21*	*0*	*−1*	*101*	*105*

*Gross domestic investment is defined as all public- and private-sector expenditures for additions to the stock of fixed assets plus the net value of inventory changes.
†Gross domestic saving is calculated by deducting total consumption from gross domestic product.
‡Gross domestic investment minus gross domestic saving.
Sources: World Development Report 1987, Table 5, and *World Development Report 1994,* Table 9.

major differences in the saving performances of countries within each category, the general picture is one of some success in mobilizing additional domestic saving since 1965. Table 12–2 also depicts the evolution of saving and investment ratios for a group of 26 developing countries in Asia, Africa, and Latin America, chosen to represent a wide range in per capita income, natural resource endowments, and ideological orientation. Among countries in this table, domestic saving rates in 1992 ranged from a negative 1 percent to a positive 39 percent. Table 12–2 underscores the significance of income levels for saving mobilization efforts. Among the low- and lower-middle-income countries only China, India, and

OPEC members Nigeria and Indonesia had saving rates of 20 percent or more in 1992, while among the upper middle-income group four of the seven in the table have saving rates of over 20 percent. We would ordinarily expect a lower ratio of savings in poor countries relative to middle-income countries simply because there is less available for savings after subsistence needs are met.

It is also evident from Table 12–2 that the more prosperous developing countries tend to cover a larger share of their investment needs with local savings. Whereas seven of the low-income countries relied on foreign savings for more than one-third of their investment finance in 1992, only three of the middle-income countries in the sample exhibited that much dependence on foreign savings. Indeed, in four of the middle-income countries, domestic saving rates exceeded domestic investment rates in 1992. On average, the table also shows that although domestic saving rates increased appreciably from 1965 to 1992 in many low- and middle-income countries, the share of domestic saving in total investment finance rose little in developing countries in general and actually declined in a considerable number. In particular, the continuing strong saving performance of China and India in the group of low-income countries masks a serious decline in both saving rates and the share of investment financed locally in the other low-income countries.

Table 12–2 does not begin, however, to portray adequately the diversity of saving performances across more than 100 developing countries. In 1992, at least 12 developing countries had negative rates of domestic saving; in Guinea-Bissau, Nicaragua, Lesotho, and Jordan negative savings amounted to more that 10 percent of GDP. But in that same year, 16 developing countries, including the four depicted in Table 12–2, had positive saving rates of 25 percent or more per year.

Government policies have had a major impact on the ability of developing countries to mobilize domestic saving. We will see in the next three chapters that some countries have actively sought to deploy policies to encourage savings growth and have utilized instruments well-suited for that purpose. In still more countries, governments have been no less concerned with the promotion of domestic saving but have relied on policy tools ill-suited for saving mobilization. Finally, in a small group of countries, government policies appear to have been designed with little or no regard for their implications for domestic saving. As might be expected, saving has generally responded positively to policy initiatives in the first group of countries, less so in the second group, and has tended to stagnate or decline in the third.

Government Savings

Where present, government savings have arisen almost wholly from an excess of total tax revenues over public consumption expenditures (S_{gb}). Chapter 13 shows that in very few cases do savings by government enterprises (S_{ge}) ever materially contribute to aggregate government savings. Given the very minor role of S_{ge}, the discussion of government saving in this chapter is confined to budgetary savings.

During the 1950s and 1960s, one of the basic tenets of typical development strategies was that the investment expansion required for sustained income growth could not proceed in the absence of major efforts to increase the share of government savings in GDP. It was commonly held that growth in private savings was inherently constrained by such factors as low per capita incomes and high private consumption propensities among wealthy families with the greatest capacity for savings. Limited availabilities of foreign savings also led planners, as well as aid donors, to stress the necessity of programs for mobilizing government savings. In almost all cases, the preferred means for achieving this goal was to raise the ratio of tax collections to GNP (the tax ratio), through significant reform of the tax structure if possible or through increases in existing tax rates if necessary. Underlying this view was a belief that the propensity to consume out of an additional dollar of income was substantially less in the public sector than in the private sector. In this view diversion of income to the government should increase national saving rates. This engendered a prevailing view among many development planners that rising tax ratios were associated with successful development strategies, a view reinforced by policies of foreign aid donors. In the 1950s and 1960s many donors, including the United States, utilized tax ratios and tax effort indices as prime indicators of national commitment to belt-tightening in recipient countries. Countries willing to suffer higher domestic taxes were seen as more deserving of aid, other things being equal.

It is not easy to increase tax collections in developing countries. Except for those countries blessed with valuable natural-resource endowments, developing countries would not be expected to have tax ratios nearly as high as is common in the industrial countries, if for no other reason than their much lower per capita incomes, which allow a much smaller margin for taxation after subsistence needs are met. Whereas typical tax ratios for developing countries in 1992 ranged between 14 and 16 percent, the ratio of central government taxes to GNP in 1992 in the 21 wealthy member countries of the OECD averaged about 27 percent.[3]

Despite the difficulties involved, many developing countries have been able to raise their shares of taxes in GNPs since the 1960s. One study showed small advances in the average tax ratio for a group of 47 developing countries from 1950. For these countries as a group, the typical share of tax in GNP hovered at about 11 percent in the 1950s. By 1972 to 1976 the average tax ratio had risen to 16 percent.[4]

The average tax ratio has fluctuated about that level ever since; it increased to nearly 18 percent in the early eighties, when sharply higher world oil prices resulted in pronounced increases in tax collections in several oil-exporting developing countries such as Mexico, Indonesia, and Venezuela, and then slipped to about 15 percent during the subsequent period of depressed world oil prices (1982 to 1987). Table 13–4 suggests that the tax ratio tends to rise with per capita income, from about 16 percent of GNP in the poorest countries to 27 percent in the richest.

Particularly during the fifties and sixties, the conventional fiscal wisdom held that vigorously applied policies of savings mobilization through higher taxes would yield substantial improvement in the overall national savings rate. But higher taxes lead to higher savings only if the government's **marginal propensity to consume** (MPC) out of increased taxes is less than the private sector's propensity to consume out of the marginal income from which it pays increased

3. The range for central government tax ratios in 1992 in the high-income countries was from 14.5 percent in Japan to nearly 50 percent in the Netherlands. *World Development Report 1994*, Table 11.

4. Alfred Tait, Wilfred Gratz, and Barry Eichengreen, "International Comparisons of Taxation for Selected Developing Countries." *International Monetary Fund Staff Papers,* 26, no. 1, March 1979, 123–56.

taxes.[5] Government saving made possible through budget surpluses unquestionably played a major role in the early stages of Japan's economic development. But other success stories for saving mobilization through budget policy are difficult to find. Unfortunately, there is evidence that for most developing countries the government's MPC out of taxes has been sufficiently high that increased taxation may easily have resulted in less, not more, total domestic savings. This phenomenon has become known as the Please effect, after Stanley Please of the World Bank, who first brought it to widespread attention.[6] Whether or not the Please effect is widespread, we will see in Chapter 13 that higher taxes can and do displace some household and business savings in the private sector.[7] And experience over most of the past three decades does show rather strong consumption propensities on the part of governments.

While tax ratios in developing countries typically rose marginally over the 1960s and 1970s, before leveling off in the mid-eighties, the share of public-sector consumption expenditures expanded at rapid rates over the same period, generally in excess of GDP growth. In low-income countries (exclusive of India and China), the share of public-sector consumption expenditures in GNP rose from 8 percent in 1960 to 12 percent in 1983. By 1992 it had declined slightly to 11 percent. In middle-income countries the share of public-sector consumption in GDP has risen even more sharply over the past three decades: from 11 percent in 1960, to 13 percent in 1983, and to around 15 percent in 1992.[8]

This experience was widespread. It is worth emphasizing that in many countries much of the growth in public-sector consumption has been intended to promote development. Some governmental salary adjustments have been meant to keep and attract qualified civil servants, and many governments have strengthened their efforts to maintain roads, schools, health facilities, communication networks, and the like. But when higher government consumption has been traceable to rapid buildup of military purchases (which we will look at in the next chapter), excessive procurement of materials, or upkeep of a large government vehicle fleet dominated by Mercedes Benzes, the effects have been unhelpful to national development.

Nevertheless, rapid growth in public sector consumption over the past three decades, coupled with moderate increases in tax ratios, has meant that the growth in government savings has not been a major source of investment finance in most developing countries. And it will be evident from Chapter 15 that although foreign saving has been a growing share of investment finance in many low-income countries since 1960, this was not so for developing countries as a group, particu-

5. The marginal propensity to consume (MPC) refers to the amount of consumption out of each incremental (marginal) unit of income. Thus, if government spends $80 out of each additional $100 in tax revenue on consumption, the government's MPC is 0.80.

6. Stanley Please, "Savings Through Taxation: Reality or Mirage?" *Finance and Development*, 4, no. 1 (March 1967), 24–32.

7. Some analysts find a high degree of substitutability between government and private savings; others do not. See, for example, the exhaustive survey in Raymond F. Mikesell and James E. Zinser, "The Nature of the Savings Function in Developing Countries: A Survey of the Theoretical and Empirical Literature," *Journal of Economic Literature*, 11, no. 1 (March 1973), 1–26. One article surveyed in this contribution indicated that an additional 1 dollar of government savings is associated with a 57-cent decline in private savings. Another article indicates a positive relationship between public and private savings.

8. *World Development Report, 1985, 1990,* and *1994.*

larly the middle-income nations. We may wonder, then: What was the source of the additional savings required to cover significantly higher investment ratios (see Table 12–2) over that period? To answer that question we now look at the private sector.

Private Domestic Savings

Until fairly recently, economists, aid donors, and many decision makers in developing countries tended to view private domestic savings as decidedly secondary to government savings and foreign aid as a source of investment finance. There is, however, some evidence that in many developing countries private savings have come to play a major role in financing capital formation. Data compiled by the World Bank, summarized in Table 12–3, indicate that many developing countries have been able to restrain growth in private consumption over long periods, and thereby expand the pool of private savings. Among low-income countries, this was particularly true for China, where the share of private consumption in GDP declined from two-thirds to one-half between 1965 and 1990, as well as for India, where the drop was from three-quarters to two-thirds. This ratio declined in other low-income countries and in middle-income countries as well. But, here again, aggregate figures mask important differences among countries. Out of 31 low-income countries for which data are available, the share of private consumption fell in 14, rose in 15, and remained constant in 2. And among middle-income countries, the share of private consumption in GDP fell by more than 5 percentage points in 21 of 42 countries for which data are available. Although data on consumption growth are subject to large errors, the available evidence suggests that, except for a relatively small group of the poorest countries, growth in private consumption was held in check in most developing countries after 1965.

We have seen that the share of taxes in GDP rose only slightly in most developing countries over the past three decades. If higher taxes do not account for the drop in the share of private consumption in GDP, then the share of private saving must have increased. In any case, the most plausible source of a large share of finance for the rising investment ratios reported in Table 12–2 was private domestic savings. For developing countries in general, at least one of the components of private domestic savings must have risen at a fairly robust rate. But if so, it is difficult to determine which of the components played the more important role—

TABLE 12–3 Rates of GDP and Private Consumption Growth, 1970–1991

	Real GDP		Real private consumption		% share of private consumption in GDP	
	1970–80	1980–91	1970–80	1980–91	1970	1991
Low-income countries	4.2	6.8	4.1	5.6	70	62
Excluding China and India	3.1	2.9	4.4	1.7	75	73
Lower-middle-income countries	6.3	4.2	5.4	3.4	75	69
Upper-middle-income countries	6.6	3.7	6.1	3.3	69	66
High-income countries	3.2	2.9	3.5	2.9	59	61

Source: World Development Report 1993, Tables 2, 8, and 9.

household savings or business savings. To begin to answer this question and to gain further insights into fundamental relationships in the development process, it is useful to consider the economic theory of private-sector saving behavior.

DETERMINANTS OF PRIVATE SAVINGS

Theories of household saving behavior were initially developed as part of the postwar Keynesian revolution in economic thought to explain saving patterns in industrial countries. The applicability of these theories to the study of saving behavior in developing countries has been frequently called into question in recent years.[9] Nevertheless, current controversies over the determinants of saving behavior in developing countries are almost impossible to understand without reference to earlier studies developed for the analysis of private saving in industrial nations.

Household Saving Behavior

All theories of household saving behavior seek to explain the following three observed patterns: (1) within a particular country at a given time, higher-income households tend to save larger fractions of their income than lower-income households; (2) within a particular country over time, household savings ratios tend to be roughly constant, more so in industrial than in developing countries; and (3) across countries, household savings ratios vary with no clear relation to income. To help reconcile these "stylized facts," we will consider four alternative explanations of household saving behavior: the Keynesian absolute-income hypothesis, the relative-income hypothesis, the Friedman permanent-income hypothesis, and the Kaldor class-savings hypothesis.

Economists once widely believed in the general applicability of a simple income-savings relationship. Household savings was viewed as directly dependent on current disposable income (household income after direct taxes). The propensity to save out of current disposable income was thought to rise with income. This was known as the **Keynesian absolute-income hypothesis,** after the famed British economist John Maynard Keynes, who propounded the idea in the 1930s. In this view the savings-income relationship would be expressed as

$$S = a + sY^d, \qquad [12\text{–}3]$$

where S = savings, Y^d = current disposable income, a = a constant ($a < 0$), and s = the marginal propensity to save ($0 < s < 1$). The constant a is generally taken to be negative to signify that at low levels of income, savings will be negative. Under this formulation savings ratios (savings as a fraction of GDP) should be expected to rise over time in all countries where income is growing. But the historical record in both developed and developing countries provides very weak support for the Keynesian hypothesis.

At best the Keynesian formulation may depict saving behavior over the very short term, but it breaks down as a long-run proposition. The Keynesian formulation explains only the first household saving pattern, but not the second or third. An alternative view of the income-consumption relationship, the **relative-income**

9. See especially Angus Deaton, "Saving in Developing Countries: Theory and Review," *Proceedings of the World Bank Annual Conference on Development Economics*, Washington, D.C., World Bank, 1989.

hypothesis, focuses on the longer term. In its simplest form this hypothesis holds that consumption (and therefore saving) depends not only on current income but also on previous levels of income and past consumption habits. One form of the relative-income hypothesis, called the **Duesenberry hypothesis** after Harvard economist James Duesenberry, who originated the concept in the late 1940s, may be expressed as

$$C_1 = a + (l - s)\, Y_1^d + bC_h, \qquad [12\text{–}4]$$

where C_1 = consumption in period 1, Y_1^d = income in period 1, C_h = previous high level of consumption, $0 < s < 1$, and $0 < b < 1$. Thus under the relative-income hypothesis, the short-run consumption (saving) function in an economy tends to ratchet upward over time. As income grows over the long term, consumers adjust their spending habits to higher levels of consumption. But in the short run they are reluctant to reduce, and slow to raise, consumption levels should income fall, or rise, temporarily. The relationship between the Keynesian absolute-income hypothesis and the Duesenberry relative-income hypothesis is depicted in Figure 12–1.

The Duesenberry hypothesis was formulated as an explanation of consumption and saving behavior for the United States. Later researchers argued that it may also be applicable to developing countries. Some have suggested that a *demonstration effect* operates to cause consumption in developing countries to ratchet upward as incomes grow. Internationally mobile and worldly wise upper-income groups in the developing countries are thought to emulate high-consumption pat-

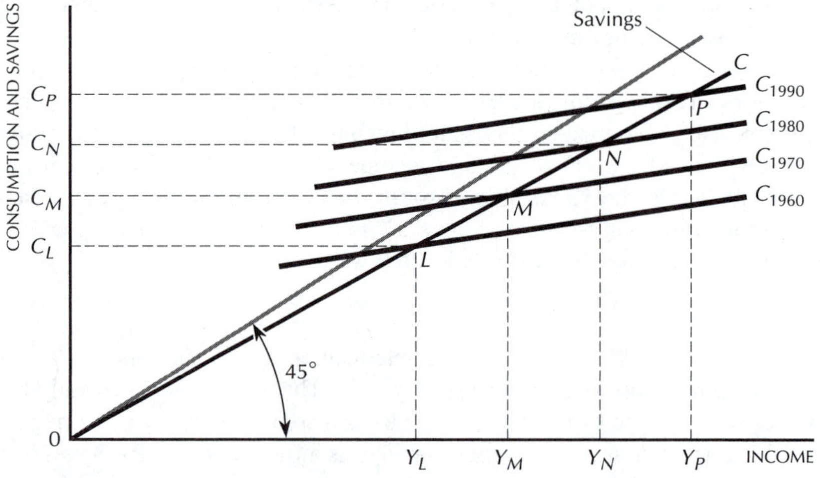

FIGURE 12–1 Consumption and Saving in the Short and Long Term with Rising Income over Time. The 45-degree line shows all points at which consumption is equal to income. Four short-run consumption functions are shown for each of the years 1960, 1970, 1980, and 1990 representing what people would have spent at various levels of income in those years. Consumption lines for each year plot Equation 12–3, with

$$C = Y_d - S = -a(1 - S)Y_d;$$

because $a < 0$, $-a > 0$. The flatness of these curves reflects consumers' reluctance to change consumption habits in the short run. In each of these years, actual (current) income was Y_L, Y_M, Y_N, and Y_P respectively. Thus actual consumption in each of those years was C_L, C_M, C_N, and C_P. The points *L* through *P* trace out a long-term consumption function. Consumption, and thus savings, tend to be a constant proportion of income over time.

terns of the wealthiest income groups in developed countries; successively lower income groups tend to emulate the patterns of higher-income groups, so that consumption in the society as a whole tends to be a high and stable function of income. Indeed, the British economist Nicholas Kaldor once estimated that if the richest families in Chile had the same consumption propensities as families at the same *relative* income position in developed nations (but at higher absolute levels of income), the Chilean savings rate in the 1950s could have been doubled.[10] The relative-income hypothesis explains all three of the observed saving patterns cited earlier.[11]

Other approaches developed to explain consumption and saving behavior in developed countries have been applied to developing countries. The most influential of these has been the **permanent-income hypothesis,** first formulated by Milton Friedman at the University of Chicago in the 1950s. In the Friedman view income consists of two components: permanent income and transitory income. The basic idea is simply that individuals expect to live for many years, they make consumption decisions over a horizon that includes the entire life cycle. The permanent-income component is not to be regarded as expected lifetime earnings. Rather it should be viewed as the mean income at any age regarded as permanent by the household, which in turn depends on both its time horizon and foresight. **Permanent income** is the yield from wealth, including both physical and human capital assets (education and so on) at the disposal of the household. Friedman held that individuals can predict with a reasonable degree of assurance the magnitude of these flows over their lifetimes and that they gear their consumption to what they perceive to be their normal, or permanent, income, which tends to be stable over time. Furthermore, in the most-restrictive variant of the permanent-income hypothesis, consumption tends to be a constant proportion of permanent income and to approach 100 percent of permanent income. Thus any saving that occurs will primarily be out of **transitory income:** unexpected, nonrecurring income such as that arising from changes in asset values, changes in relative prices, lottery winnings, and other unpredictable windfalls. In the most extreme version of the permanent-income hypothesis, individuals are held to save 100 percent of any transitory income. But econometric research since 1970 has called into question this assumption; some studies show a fairly high propensity to consume out of transitory income.

The permanent-income hypothesis may be expressed

$$S = a + b_1Y_p + b_2Y_t \qquad [12\text{–}5]$$

where S = savings, a = a constant, Y_p = permanent income, and Y_t = transitory income. As noted, in the most extreme version $b_l = 0$ and $b_2 = 1$, so all savings arises from the transitory component of income and all of this component is saved. Modified versions of the permanent-income hypothesis hold only that saving out of permanent income is constant over a person's lifetime, but can be positive, and that although the propensity to save out of transitory income is high, all

10. Nicholas Kaldor, "Problems Economicas de Chile," *El Trimestre Economico,* 26, no. 102 (April–June 1959), 193, 211–12.

11. More recent studies of factors affecting saving behavior among high-income elites in developing countries include Robert H. Frank, "The Demand for Unobservable and other Non-positional Goods," *American Economic Review,* 75 (March 1985), 101–16, and Philip Musgrove, "Income Distribution and Aggregate Consumption Function," *Journal of Political Economy,* 2, no. 88 (June 1980), 504–25.

transitory income may not be saved. Equation 12–5 can represent this version with $0 < b_1 < b_2 < 1$.

Several studies have sought to test the applicability of the permanent-income hypothesis to a variety of developing countries in Asia and Latin America. The results are far from conclusive, but in toto they do lend some support to the modified versions of the hypothesis: people do tend to save a higher proportion of transitory, as opposed to permanent, income.

A particularly interesting study by Angus Deaton in 1989, based on the framework of life-cycle permanent-income models, stresses the importance of precautionary motives in household saving behavior, particularly among poor rural families in developing countries. Deaton argues that for these groups saving is not so much a matter of accumulation as it is a method of smoothing consumption in the face of volatile income. Essentially, Deaton is saying that poor rural households dissave as often as they save and behave as if their primary motive for saving is to protect their living standards against disasters.[12] In general the permanent-income hypothesis has proven helpful in understanding all three observed saving patterns. Chapter 17 asseses the implications of modified versions of the permanent-income hypothesis in understanding the effects of fluctuating export income on growth.

One further model of household saving behavior merits attention: the **class theory** of the British economist Nicholas Kaldor. This approach views consumption (saving) habits to be sharply differentiated by economic class. Workers, who receive mainly labor income, are thought to have far weaker saving propensities than do capitalists, who receive primarily property income (profits, interests, rents). The class-savings hypothesis is represented as

$$S = S_w L + S_c P, \qquad [12\text{–}6]$$

where S_w = workers' saving propensities out of labor income, S_c = capitalists' saving propensities out of property income, L = labor income, P = property income, and $0 < S_w < S_c < 1$.

The class-saving hypothesis explains the first pattern and also explains the third pattern if factor shares (relative shares of labor and capital income) differ across countries. But the difference between the class-saving hypothesis and the permanent-income hypothesis may be more apparent than real. It is difficult to see why households, in their spending-saving decisions, treat labor income any differently than property income: a peso is a peso; a rupee of property income is no different from a rupee of labor income. However, property income of households, particularly that from unincorporated enterprises, tends to fluctuate more than labor income. The permanent-income hypothesis suggests that propensities to save out of variable income streams are higher than out of more-stable streams. In addition property income is more concentrated in higher-income groups. Thus studies of saving behavior based on the class model that show markedly higher saving out of property income may really be recording the effects of higher propensities to save out of higher fluctuating income.

All the hypotheses discussed above view income, whether current, relative, or permanent, as the principal determinant of saving behavior. But income is by no means the only determinant of aggregate private-sector saving behavior, particu-

12. Deaton, "Saving in Developing Countries," pp. 61–81.

larly in developing countries. As we will see in Chapter 14, the permanent-income hypothesis concedes a role for interest rates in affecting saving behavior. Beyond that, many economists have stressed the effects of such explanatory variables as the age structure and location (rural versus urban) of a country's population.

Changes in the age structure of a country's population are often found to have significant effects on private savings in several countries. In general, the proportion of any increases in income saved tends to be less in younger households than in older ones. Younger families are rearing children and accumulating belongings, but they earn lower incomes. To illustrate, the average ratio of savings to income for older households in Chile in 1964 was found to be twice that of younger households.

There is a strong tendency around the world for rural households to save higher fractions of their incomes than urban households with comparable levels of income—a phenomenon observed in a number of countries, including both Korea and Yugoslavia in the early 1970s. This behavior is also consistent with the permanent-income hypothesis, because farmers' incomes are more variable than those of urban wage earners.

The relative-income hypothesis and the permanent-income hypothesis provide a basis for understanding the lack of strong correlation across developing countries between per capita income and the ratio of private savings to GDP. Nonincome factors such as the age structure of the population and rural-urban differences, help explain why private saving ratios do vary across countries, even at comparable levels of per capita income.

Corporate Saving Behavior

We have seen that there is no shortage of hypotheses purporting to explain the determinants of household saving. There is, however, little consensus among economists about the determinants of corporate saving, particularly in developing countries. Indeed there is little general agreement on the determinants of corporate saving even in developed countries. For example, in the United States a major question in research on business finance has been to explain why U.S. corporations pay out such a high proportion of their after-tax income in dividends, despite strong tax and other incentives to retain earnings (save) within the firm.

In developed countries the share of corporate savings in total income is typically less than 5 percent, and the share of corporate saving in total net private saving is typically less than 25 percent. For example, over the period 1981 to 1985, corporate saving was 16 percent of the total in Japan, 10 percent in Belgium, about 21 percent in Canada and the United States, and close to 30 percent in West Germany and Britain. However, in Scandinavian nations, the corporate saving share tends to be much higher, 60 percent in Finland and 80 percent in Sweden, for example.[13] Such data are not available for large numbers of developing countries, but it is known that in only a few countries (Colombia, Pakistan, and Panama in the 1960s) have corporate savings represented a sizable share of total savings over any significant period.

13. Roger S. Smith, "Factors Affecting Saving, Policy Tools and Tax Reform: A Review," International Monetary Fund Working Paper No. 89/47, May 23, 1989, Table 2.

Corporate saving is relatively small in most developing countries primarily because the corporate sector is relatively small. For a variety of reasons there are fewer pressures and incentives in developing countries for doing business in the corporate form. The principal reasons for organizing as a corporation in the private sector are to limit the liability of enterprise owners to amounts invested in a business and to facilitate enterprise finance through the issue of equity shares (stocks). Although these advantages are substantial in developed countries with well-developed commercial codes, civil court systems, and capital markets, they are smaller in most developing countries, where the collection of commercial claims (for example, company debts) through the courts is relatively difficult and where, as shown in Chapter 14, capital markets are poorly developed when they exist at all.

As usual, however, there are important exceptions to these generalizations. In some developing countries corporations are both numerous and quite large. Each year since 1980, *Fortune Magazine*'s annual list of the 500 largest corporations outside the United States includes several dozen from developing countries.[14] Examples include conglomerates such as Bavaria (beverages and food processing) in Colombia and Hyundai (automobiles) in Korea and enterprises such as Alpargatus (textiles and shoes) in Argentina, the diversified firm Tata in India, and Villares (steel products) in Brazil. But, except in Korea and Brazil, even in middle-income countries such corporations are not numerous, do not ordinarily account for a large share of private-sector business activity, and clearly do not provide a high proportion of domestic savings.

In all but a few of the highest-income developing countries, the great bulk of private sector farming and commercial and manufacturing activity is conducted by unincorporated, typically family-owned enterprises, which will be discussed in Chapter 18. Some of these fall into the category of medium-scale establishments (from 20 to 99 workers). Very few are large-scale enterprises. The great majority are small-scale operations (fewer than 20 employees), which, in spite of their abundance, do not account for a sizable share of either value-added or savings.[15] Nevertheless the noncorporate sector manages to generate more than 50 percent of domestic saving in developing countries as a group, and this sector is the only consistent source of surplus in the sense that its savings exceeds its investment. Even for a high-income country like the United States, with a large corporate sector, income from unincorporated enterprise in 1976 was about double the value of corporate profits (after taxes). For those closely held, largely family-owned and -managed firms, enterprise profits become an important part not of corporate saving but of gross household income. The available evidence indicates, and economic theory suggests, that household savings account for the overwhelming share of private savings in developing countries and that the chief source of household savings is probably household income from unincorporated enterprises.

14. *Fortune Magazine*, "World Business Directory," annual.

15. One study for 21 developing countries in the 1960s shows that small-scale enterprises, although constituting 80 percent of industrial establishments, are responsible for an average of only 13 percent of industrial value-added. See Randev Banerji, "Small-Scale Production Units in Manufacturing: an International Cross Section Overview," *Weltwirtschafliches Archiv*, 114, no. 1 (1978). See also Donald Snodgrass and Tyler Biggs, *Industrialization and the Small Firm: Patterns and Policies* (San Franciso: ICS Press, forthcoming).

This chapter has focused primarily on patterns and determinants of domestic saving mobilization. The next two chapters examine policy options for mobilizing domestic saving, while Chapter 15 is concerned with issues in foreign saving. In practice, however, the distinction between domestic and foreign saving is rather more blurred than implied up to this point, to the extent that capital is mobile across national borders, particularly in the long run. The issue of the international mobility—or lack of mobility—of capital is one of the most important questions in economic policy; it is also one about which empirical evidence has been, at least until very recently, most scanty.

Short- and Long-Run Mobility

"In the long run we are all dead." With this pithy remark, the British economist John Maynard Keynes closed his landmark volume, *The General Theory of Employment, Interest and Money.* In doing so, Keynes sought to jolt governments into undertaking demand-side policy measures that would have the desired short-term effects of pulling the world economy out of the deep depression of the thirties. The statement was appropriate at the time, but ever since, the long run has had a bad press: Keynes's remark has been frequently employed as a verbal talisman against proponents of a longer-run focus on the effects of government policies on the economy. This has been particularly unfortunate in developing countries, inasmuch as it is the long-term effects of policies that are the most significant for growth and development. Furthermore, although it is indeed true that we are all dead in the long run when the long run is defined as sufficiently long, the long run in economic analysis is not always defined in terms of decades, or even years. The long run in some industries, such as mining of hard minerals, may be as long as ten years; in commercial chicken farming in the United States, the long run may be defined in terms of *months,* for that is how long it takes for new firms to enter and exit the business in responses to changes in poultry prices.

In any case, the distinction between the short and long run is among the most fundamental in economic analysis. Not a small share of the unintended, and usually perverse, effects of economic policies are traceable to failure to recognize that the short-term results of policies may be very different from the long-term results. The **short run** is defined as a period of time in which both capital and labor resources are locked into their present uses. The **long run** is defined as a period of time sufficiently long to allow economic agents (including resource owners) to adjust to changed circumstances, including economic policy changes that affect the returns to capital and labor. In the long run, resources may enter (or leave) an activity in response to higher (or lower) returns. Both capital and labor, then, tend to be much more *mobile* in the long run.

It is generally recognized that capital is particularly mobile across sectors of a given economy in the long run, even when highly immobile in the short run. For example, the enactment of price controls on wheat in 1995 ordinarily will not lead to a movement of capital from wheat farming in 1995 (the short run) even if low, controlled prices result in negative profits in 1995. But if the controls are extended through 1997, we would then expect some proportion of capital invested in wheat farming to have left. The longer such a policy remains in place, the more capital will tend to flow to other domestic activities not subject to price controls.

But what of mobility of capital across national boundaries? The degree to which capital is **internationally mobile** is a topic of considerable debate and has a profound bearing on possibilities for success in all economic policies in any given country, particularly so for these geared toward mobilization of savings. This is most apparent in the case of private foreign savings. Private capital abroad, whether it arrives in the form of direct foreign investment or borrowings from foreign banks, is obviously *inwardly* mobile, from the developing country perspective. Foreign-source capital is also clearly outwardly mobile in the long run: foreign debts are eventually repaid by most countries, on the basis of prearranged schedules, and dividends on foreign equity investment return capital to overseas investors when direct investments turn out to be profitable.

International capital mobility, however, is a two-way street. Domestic savings in developing countries, like domestic savings in wealthy countries, may be highly mobile internationally as well, both in the short and in the long run. The degree of short-run outward mobility is exemplified by such episodes of massive capital flight as plagued Mexico in 1981 and 1982 and Indonesia in 1983 and early 1986, just prior to an expected major currency devaluation in each country. In Indonesia in 1986, short-term capital flight reached nearly $100 million per *week* in a two-month period. Longer-term outward mobility is illustrated by the sizable outward migration of capital in Hong Kong in 1983 through 1985 and in the Philippines in 1985 and 1986. In the former, capital departed in response to uncertainties surrounding the 1982 announcement by the British of their plans to return the colony to Chinese sovereignty in 1997. In the latter, wealthy Filipinos sent capital abroad in large amounts as a hedge against the possibility of the assumption of political power by opponents of the Marcos government.

A high degree of international capital mobility, then, can be both a blessing and a curse for developing countries. Inward mobility expands opportunities for finance of domestic investment by foreign savings. But high *outward* mobility constrains the effectiveness of several policies intended to expand domestic saving mobilization. For example, in the short run, enactment of higher income taxes on corporations may allow higher government savings. But if capital is internationally mobile, the long-run result may well be to encourage domestic, as well as foreign, capital owners to dispatch their funds to other countries to restore the rate of return prevailing before the taxes were increased.

Evidence of International Capital Mobility

In the distant as well as the more recent past, policy makers and economists have tended to overlook the **domestic** policy implications of international capital mobility. One reason for this oversight has been the widespread existence of domestic controls on international capital movements and an equally widespread view that these controls were effective. It is true that official controls (both explicit and implicit) on capital flows abound in the world economy, particularly among developing countries. For example, in the five-year period 1978 to 1982, explicit controls on the international movement of capital existed in 72 percent of the 149 countries that are members of the International Monetary Fund (IMF).[16] Furthermore, even in those countries that employ no explicit capital controls, *im-*

16. Jeremy Grenwood and Kent Kimbrough, "Capital Controls and The World Economy," *Canadian Journal of Economics,* 19, no. 2 (1986), 111–16.

plicit controls may hinder the international mobility of capital. These include institutional restrictions that act as barriers to investments outside the domestic economy. In the United States, examples include laws that prevent savings institutions from investing in real estate abroad, and state government rules on pension funds that preclude such institutions from investing in overseas assets. Most developing countries have adopted similar regulations for the portfolios of their financial institutions.

The pervasiveness of controls on international capital movements would seem to indicate that international capital mobility may be quite limited in both the short and the long runs. There are, however, considerations that suggest otherwise. First, the number of countries having explicit controls on capital movements has been diminishing. Indonesia, for example, abandoned all official foreign exchange controls in 1970. Britain followed suit in 1979, as did France in 1986. With the implosion of communism in 1989 to 1990, several Eastern and Central European countries began to move to relax exchange restrictions. Second, controls may be evaded in whole or in part. There is no empirical evidence that capital controls are administered with anything close to 100 percent effectiveness, in either developed or developing countries, particularly in the latter.[17]

Third, there is a significant body of empirical evidence that suggests a fairly high degree of long-run international mobility of capital is sufficient to cause capital's real after-tax return to converge toward about 7.5 percent in both rich and poor countries.[18] The significance of this finding is that in the *absence* of moderate mobility, rates of return would be far higher in low-income countries, where capital is relatively scarce, than in high-income countries, where capital is relatively more abundant. Another 1985 study covered 115 countries, both developed and developing, and found significant evidence of a high degree of international capital mobility.[19]

In sum, although it is clear that capital is not perfectly mobile in or out of developing countries even in the long run, it is also clear that neither the design nor implementation of economic policies in developing countries may be based on the assumption that, given time, capital will not emigrate in response to policies that affect its return.[20]

17. Capital controls in such countries as Ghana (1963 to 1986) have been notoriously porous. Tight restrictions on the amount of dollars that could be removed from Ghana were easily evaded by several devices, including overinvoicing imports: the importer merely requests the exporter abroad to place a higher value on the goods than the true price. The exporter, on receipt of payment, merely deposits the excess in the importer's bank account in the exporter's country. Long-standing controls in Colombia before 1968, Argentina before 1979, India, and numerous other countries did not prevent the buildup of large resident-owned foreign currency holdings outside these countries in the past. Presumed stringency of capital controls did not prevent Indian multinational firms from exporting substantial capital while becoming significant foreign investors in Southeast Asia before 1975.

18. Arnold Harberger, "Vignettes on the World Capital Market," *American Economic Review*, 70, no. 2 (May 1980), 331–37.

19. Larry Summers, "Issues in National Savings Policy," National Bureau of Economic Research Working Paper No. 1710, Cambridge, Mass., September 1985.

20. For further discussion of the implications of the openness of economies and the growing international mobility of capital, see Joel Slemrod, "Tax Principles in an International Economy," in Michael Boskin and Charles E. McLure Jr. (eds.), *World Tax Reform: Case Studies of Developed and Developing Economies* (San Francisco: ICS Press, 1990), Chap. 2.

13

Fiscal Policy

The next two chapters focus on two sets of government policy instruments that operate across all sectors of an economy: fiscal policy and financial policy. Both sets of instruments can play critical roles, for good and ill, in the mobilization of domestic saving. Moreover, both types of policies have far-reaching effects on income distribution, employment, efficiency, and economic stability. In this chapter we focus on **fiscal policy,** which encompasses all measures pertaining to the level and structure of government revenues and expenditures. **Financial policy,** the subject of Chapter 14, includes monetary policy and a wide variety of policy measures affecting the growth and allocation of financial assets in an economy.

As the terms are used in this book, **government revenues** consist of all tax and nontax revenues flowing to the government treasury, including surpluses of public enterprises owned by governments and domestic borrowing by the treasury. **Government expenditures** are defined as all outlays from the government budget, including those for current expenditures such as civil service salaries, maintenance, military costs, interest payments, and subsidies to cover losses by public enterprise, as well as capital expenditures such as outlays for construction of irrigation canals, roads, and schools and for the purchase of nonmilitary equipment owned by government.

Fiscal policy operates through both the tax and expenditure sides of the government budget. The locus of decision making on fiscal policy in developing countries is typically split between two agencies: the Ministry of Finance (the Treasury Department) and the Ministry (or Board) of Planning. In most countries the

Ministry of Finance is assigned primary responsibility for the design and implementation of tax policy and for decisions concerning current government consumption expenditures. The Ministry of Planning sometimes holds sway on decisions concerning government capital expenditures. Some economists and policy makers reserve the term "fiscal policy" for that which is done by the Ministry of Finance and use the term "development policy" for that which is under the ultimate control of the Ministry of Planning. The present chapter focuses primarily on those aspects of fiscal policy which deal with government consumption expenditures and taxation. Criteria for decision making on public capital expenditures were considered in Chapter 6. But the distinction between public capital and consumption spending is essentially an arbitrary one, both in theory and in practice.

The Government Budget: General Considerations

Much of economic policy operates through the tax and expenditure sides of the government budget. To be sure, many government activities have an importance out of proportion to their relative significance in the overall government budget. This is particularly true for the conduct of financial policy; government regulation of competition, trade, and investment; and operations of public enterprises (except in countries where public enterprises receive heavy subsidies from the government budget). In any case, in this chapter, the term "public sector" refers only to that part of government operations reflected in the expenditure side of the budget.

All societies, from those organized under *laissez faire* principles to those organized under socialism, require a public sector, simply because even with the best of conditions, the market mechanism cannot perform all economic functions desired by households. Because of *public goods* and other types of *market failures* discussed at the beginning of Chapter 5, the market alone cannot satisfy all consumer wants, even when societies have a strong preference for decentralized decision making. For private goods, such as rice, saris, or TV sets, the signals provided by unfettered competitive market mechanisms guide producers to satisfy consumer demand efficiently. For pure public goods, the market fails entirely. There are few examples of pure public goods; national defense and lighthouses are generally cited as illustrations. The term "public good" refers to a good or service that exhibits two traits: *nonrival* consumption and *nonexcludability.*

In nonrival consumption, one person's use of a good does not reduce the benefits available to others. That being the case, no one has any incentive to offer to pay for the good: if it is available to one, it is available to all. Nonexcludability means that it is either impossible or prohibitively expensive to exclude anyone from the benefits once the good is available. In either case, the private market cannot provide the good; market failure is total. For most public goods the characteristics of nonrival consumption and nonexcludability are present but less pronounced and the market can function only in an inefficient way. Examples include vaccination against contagious diseases, primary education, police protection, and mosquito abatement. Therefore, it is evident that the appropriate role of the public sector is, to a significant degree, a technical issue. Extension of the public sector beyond that required to provide public goods and to correct for other market failures is an ideological issue, to be settled through a political process.

Most countries—industrial and developing—have extended the size of the public sector well beyond that required for technical reasons, to include income redistribution, provision of pension schemes, and ownership and operation of airlines, shipping, utilities, manufacturing enterprises, and banks.

Government Expenditures

In the late 1800s, the German political theorist Adolph Wagner propounded his famous *law of expanding state activity*. The thrust of Wagner's law was that the relative size of the public sector in the economy has an inherent tendency to grow as per capita income increases. Although few fiscal economists accept Wagner's law without several qualifications, it is nevertheless true that poor countries do have smaller public sectors than rich ones, when size of the public sector is measured as the ratio of government expenditure to GDP. As may be noted from Table 13–1, the overall proportion rises with per capita income, from about 17 percent in the lowest income countries (including India) to 23 percent in the middle-income countries, and 32 percent in the high-income economies.

Three classes of expenditure account for most of the difference between high-income and developing countries' outlays as a share of GNP. Military expenditures in the industrial countries, at 5 percent, are about double the share of national product in the developing countries. Expenditures on health are 1 percent or less in developing countries, but 4 percent of GNP in the high-income countries. But it is social welfare programs that account for most of the difference: these are 11 percent of GNP in the high-income countries, about half that in upper-middle-income countries, and only 1 percent in other developing countries as a group. However, the costs of economic services, which include direct government investments and subsidies to state-owned enterprises, are higher in the poorer market economies than in the richer ones.

Hundreds of books and articles have been written on the reasons for differences in government expenditure across countries and through time. The results of the studies often conflict. Although associated with income growth, these differences do not seem to be related in any systematic way to population growth, but may be strongly influenced by other demographic factors such as urbanization.

Table 13–1 Central Government Expenditures as Share of GNP, 1992

Spending category	Low-income countries	Excluding India	Lower-middle-income countries	Upper-middle-income countries	High-income countries
Military spending	3	2	3	2	5
Education	1	4	2	3	2
Health	0	1	1	1	4
Housing, social security, welfare	1	1	1	5	11
Economic services	3	8	5	4	2
Other	10	9	10	8	8
Total spending	17	24	22	23	32

Source: World Development Report 1994, Table 10, pp. 180–81.

Expenditure Policies and Public Saving

The effects of government capital spending on growth were long viewed as unambiguously positive. Critics have succeeded in demonstrating that not all public investment has contributed to growth, much less to development. But there is still a pervasive belief that public investment should have a higher priority than recurrent outlays, which are still widely considered to be unproductive. Recurrent costs of development programs are by convention labeled as government consumption; this implies that outlays for such purposes do not increase productive capacity. Yet some recurrent outlays, in education and health for example, are investments in human capital that can have major, long-term benefits to economic development, as discussed in Chapters 10 and 11. And although most governments focus their attention on new investments, they often do not make adequate provision for the recurrent operational and maintenance costs of previous investments. This gives rise to wasteful underutilization of public-sector capital, and in some cases to its rapid decay.

These observations notwithstanding, it is also true that in many countries there may be some scope for expanding public savings by curbing the growth of several types of recurrent expenditure. We will examine the main categories of recurrent, or "consumption," expenditures of government to determine how wide this scope may be.

Table 13–2 breaks down recurrent expenditure into five categories: (1) outlays for wages and salaries of civil servants, teachers, and the military; (2) outlays on nondurable goods and services, including equipment and materials for use by public sector employees, maintenance, and all spending on military equipment; (3) interest payments on the government debt; (4) subsidies and other transfers to individuals; and (5) transfers to subnational governments. The table shows a wide variance in the proportions of total expenditure devoted to each category. Some of this is related to the stage of development: richer countries have larger social welfare programs that cause subsidies and other transfers to be a much higher share of expenditures than in most lower-income countries. Some variations have to do with governmental structures: in India, Indonesia, Peru, Brazil, and Korea the central governments transfer 13 percent of more of their expenditures to subnational governments. Huge differences in interest payments on public debt reflect differing policy choices and alternative ways to manage—or mismanage—economies. And in some cases accounting practices may be responsible for differences in the way expenditures are reported.

Wages and Salaries

Wages and salaries constitute a large fraction of recurrent outlays of governments, especially in the low- and lower-middle-income countries: in Table 13–2, 6 of the 11 countries in this category devote more than a quarter of their current expenditures to wages and salaries.

The stereotypical image of public sector bureaucracies in developing countries is one of bloated payrolls and inefficient, corrupt, even indolent behavior. The evidence for this view is essentially anecdotal. Reliable international comparisons of civil service performance are almost nonexistent. It is easy to accumulate anecdotes involving bureaucratic snafus, stupidities, corruption, and shortsightedness in both developing and developed societies. No firm judgments can be made on

TABLE 13–2 **Composition of Government Recurrent Expenditure by Type** (share of total expenditure, %)

Country	Year	Recurrent share of total expenditure *	Wages and salaries	Other purchases of goods and services	Interest payments on public debt	Subsidies and other transfers †	Transfers to subnational governments
Low-income countries							
Ethiopia	1990	89	40	36	5	9	0
India	1993	74	9	10	23	11	21
Kenya	1994	80	32	18	25	5	0
Ghana	1993	85	28	17	16	23	0
Lower-middle-income countries							
Bolivia	1993	80	29	26	8	16	1
Cameroon	1991	77	41	13	6	18	0
Philippines	1992	83	28	13	31	4	6
Sri Lanka	1993	73	19	14	21	19	1
Indonesia	1993	52	18	8	12	1	13
Peru	1993	77	8	13	12	28	16
Egypt, Arab Rep.	1992	65	15	14	15	22	0
Upper-middle-income countries							
Brazil	1992	103	8	4	45	31	14
Hungary	1990	96	6	20	6	55	9
Colombia	1989	81	16	9	10	46	0
Argentina	1989	87	21	9	7	40	9
Mexico	1989	87	16	5	52	14	0
Malaysia	1993	77	31	14	17	12	3
Korea, Rep.	1994	76	11	16	3	17	28
High-income countries							
United Kingdom	1992	96	12	19	7	37	22
Germany	1992	93	7	23	6	51	6
United States	1993	96	10	15	14	46	11

* Subsequent columns are components of this column. Total expenditure is net of repayments of loans to government, so it is possible for recurrent expenditure to exceed 100 percent of the total, as it does for Brazil.
† Excluding transfers to subnational governments.
Source: IMF, *Government Finance Statistics Yearbook 1994*, pp. 46–47.

the extent of overstaffing of public agencies or overremuneration of officials or bureaucratic extravagance in developing countries relative to industrial countries: civil service payrolls in Massachusetts and New Jersey may be as bloated as in many developing countries. And although there are examples of gross venality and blatant use of political patronage in public sector hiring in segments of the civil service systems of some developing countries (and many U.S. cities), there are also examples of first-rate professionalism and codes of conduct that may rival those found in industrial countries, as in the Indian and Malaysian civil service systems.

There may be some countries in which the salary bill for civil servants could be compressed sufficiently to augment government savings. But in others, like Bolivia, Peru, and Kenya, civil service salaries remain so low relative to those available in the private sector that it has been difficult to attract and hold the type of qualified public-sector managers, secretaries, and technicians essential for efficient government operation.

About the only safe generalization that can be made about civil service systems in developing countries is that they appear no more, or less, responsive to the socioeconomic changes that accompany development than any other group in society. In the 1950s it was almost impossible to discuss Latin American development without hearing repeated mention of the "antidevelopmental" effects of the famous *mordida* (bite) then commonly demanded by civil servants for doing what they should—or should not—be doing. It was commonly believed then that such behavior was the result of both low civil service salaries and unalterable cultural habits. In the early 1960s many Western and Korean social scientists felt that widespread corruption and inefficiency in the Korean government were immutable, owing both to practices that became acceptable under decades of Japanese occupation and to the influence of the Confucian ethic. One hears much less of such claims today, whether for Latin America or Korea. Although civil service reformers may not wish to use the Colombian or South Korean experience as models for other countries, there can be no mistaking the palpable verve and professionalism displayed by substantial numbers of civil servants in those countries.

Purchases of Goods and Services

Governments need supplies, such as paper, computers, and fuel, to perform their functions, and they also purchase services, such as construction, transportation, and janitorial work, from private firms. If a road maintenance crew consists of employees of the Ministry of Works, their salaries come under the heading *wages and salaries* and their supplies are categorized as *other purchases* in Table 13–2. But if the ministry hires a private contractor instead, all the expenditure falls under *other purchases.* Two important items in this category are *maintenance and repair* and nonwage *military spending.*

If there is waste in government procurement in some areas, there are other areas where, for lack of funds, governments have been too miserly in appropriating funds, particularly with regard to **maintenance costs** for upkeep of the public-sector capital stock and for many vital operating expenses. The phenomenon is aptly characterized by Peter Heller:

> In Colombia, new tarmac roads have suffered rapid and premature deterioration for lack of maintenance. Throughout West Africa, many new schools have opened without qualified teachers, educational materials, or equipment. Agricultural projects are often starved for extension workers, fertilizer, or seeds. In the Sahel, pastoral wells constructed for livestock projects have fallen into disrepair. In Bolivia, doctors are often stranded at rural health centers for lack of gasoline for their vehicles.[1]

Underfinancing of recurrent costs is pervasive across countries, including the United States, where items such as bridge maintenance have long been postponed in many states. In developing countries, however, this pattern is exacerbated by the policies of aid donors, who strongly support capital projects, but as a matter of policy have been reluctant to support the recurrent costs of these projects. As a result, painfully accumulated public-sector capital stock tends to deteriorate rapidly until eventually it is beyond maintenance and requires new construction. Few

1. Peter Heller, "Underfinancing of Recurrent Development Costs," *Finance and Development,* 16, no. 1 (March 1979), 38–41.

countries are in a position to expand public savings by further compressing this category of recurrent expenditures.

The share of **military spending** in recurrent expenditures shows no trend as incomes rise (Table 13–3), but on average the low- and middle-income countries spend less of their national incomes (3 percent or less) on the military than do upper-income countries (4 percent). Israel and Jordan spend substantially more of their national income on defense than do any other countries in Table 13–3—a consequence of their position in the war-torn Middle East. Otherwise the high spenders are Pakistan, Singapore, and the United States, all at 5 to 6 percent of GNP.

Military spending is directed toward noneconomic goals, such as defense against external threats and internal instability. What is known about the impact of military spending on economic growth? Clearly, all countries could expand public savings significantly by reducing military spending. Beyond that, the topic is controversial. Nevertheless, research suggests that high military spending has many more negative effects on growth than positive ones, including the large contributions made by military spending to debt in some countries, the diversion of scarce resources from more productive civilian uses, and the effects of highly import-intensive military outlays on balance-of-payments deficits.[2]

TABLE 13–3 Military Expenditure as Share of Recurrent Expenditure and GNP (percent)

Country	Share of recurrent expenditure	Share of GNP	Country	Share of recurrent expenditure	Share of GNP
Madagascar	7.5	1.2	Turkey	11.3	3.3
Malawi	4.8	1.3	Brazil	3.0	0.8
Nepal	5.9	1.1	Iran, Islamic Rep.	10.3	2.0
India	15.0	2.5	Panama	4.9	1.5
Kenya	9.2	2.8	Hungary	3.6	2.0
Low-income			Thailand	17.2	2.6
countries	14.40	2.46	Uruguay	6.5	1.9
Excluding India	7.30	1.79	Mexico	2.4	0.4
			Malaysia	10.9	3.2
Pakistan	27.9	6.1	Chile	9.6	2.1
Bolivia	9.8	2.2	Korea, Rep.	22.1	3.9
Philippines	9.9	1.9	*Upper-middle-income*		
Sri Lanka	8.5	2.4	*countries*	8.55	1.87
Indonesia	6.8	1.3			
Morocco	12.8	3.8	Israel	22.1	10.0
Jordan	26.7	11.1	Singapore	22.1	5.0
Ecuador	12.9	2.1	United Kingdom	11.3	4.5
Lower-middle-income			Australia	8.6	2.4
countries	13.59	3.02	Netherlands	4.6	2.4
			Denmark	5 0	2.1
			France	6.4	2.9
			United States	20.6	5.0
			High-income		
			countries	14.17	4.02

Source: World Development Report 1994, Table 10.

2. Anita Bhatia, "Military Expenditure and Economic Growth," Washington D.C., World Bank, 1987.

Interest Payments

Interest on government debt is a major cost for many developing countries, ranging as high as a quarter of expenditures for India, Kenya, the Philippines, and Sri Lanka and about half of all outlays for the debt-ridden governments of Brazil and Mexico (Table 13–2). Chapter 15 discusses the debt crisis that was caused by overborrowing by developing countries, especially in Latin America and Africa. Because interest on government debt reflects past decisions about deficit finance and external borrowing, interest outlays are difficult to reduce in the short term, even if budgets are balanced and borrowing ceases. Debt payments can only be radically reduced if a government defaults on its debt obligations, as did Bolivia and Peru in the 1980s.

Subsidies

A variety of subsidies and other transfers accounts for substantial shares of expenditures in developing and industrial countries. In Table 13–2 the shares range from less than 10 percent in Ethiopia, Kenya, and Indonesia to 40 percent and more in Hungary, Colombia, Argentina, Germany, and the United States. This category includes subsidies to consumers, social welfare payments, and subsidies to loss-making state-owned enterprises.

Consumer subsidies are particularly common for basic foods. Countries such as Colombia, Egypt, India, Indonesia, and Sri Lanka have provided large subsidies on purchases of staple foods such as rice or wheat flour. A typical mechanism is to distribute price-controlled foods through state-owned entities and then to absorb losses in food distribution through budgetary transfers to these enterprises. When the world price of oil rose during the 1970s, most oil-producing countries (and a few oil importers) generously subsidized the domestic use of refined products; a few, such as Venezuela, still do. Budgetary subsidies have also been common for rural electrification (Malaysia and the Philippines), contraceptive devices (Indonesia), fertilizer (Indonesia and Sri Lanka), bank interest payments on savings deposits (Indonesia), and urban bus services (Colombia, Indonesia, and others).

As incomes rise, countries typically undertake social welfare programs that transfer funds to citizens for medical care and retirement. The high share of subsidies and other transfers for the industrial countries in Table 13–2 reflects programs such as Medicare, Medicaid, and Social Security in the United States. The transition economies took on heavy obligations of this sort under their communist regimes (note Hungary's 55 percent share in Table 13–2) and now find these obligations especially burdensome. Developing countries, especially middle-income economies, are also moving toward medical and pension plans that may swell their outlays on transfers in the future. Some of these will fund themselves through contributions from those who will benefit, as is true for some of the programs in the rich countries. But experience suggests that contributions will fall short of benefits and governments will bear part of the burden.

In virtually all developing countries employing budgetary subsidies, the stated purpose has been income redistribution. For foods, especially grains, the argument appears plausible, even if the ultimate effect is not always what was intended. Heavy subsidies on fertilizer use in Indonesia had a high payoff in greater rice production and rural incomes. The role of many other subsidies in securing goals of income redistribution is less clear, however, as we shall see. Whatever the ultimate impact of budget subsidies on income distribution, it is clear that in many countries substantial sums are involved and that efforts to remove or reduce them meet with strong resistance virtually everywhere. Riots have occurred following the reduction of food subsidies in Sri Lanka, Egypt, Turkey, Zambia, and other countries, and social disturbances followed the reductions of gasoline subsidies in Indonesia, Colombia, and Thailand when these were coupled with increases in urban bus fares. It is clear why governments often view proposals to reduce subsidies with even more reservations than proposals for tax increases. Yet by the late 1980s, the need to stabilize economies by reducing budget deficits had become so acute that many countries had been forced to shrink their subsidies.

State-Owned Enterprises

A significant portion of governmental outlays for subsidies and other transfers (Table 13–2) has been devoted to covering large deficits in state-owned enterprises (SOEs). Four decades ago, SOEs were not numerous in developing countries and were, with notable exceptions such as Turkey and Mexico, typically confined to a few sectors of their economies. Commonly, SOEs were limited to the so-called natural monopolies (decreasing-cost public utilities), monopoly production of sumptuary products such as liquor, beer, and tobacco, and so-called basic necessities such as salt and matches.[3]

With independence after World War II, there was a rapid expansion in the number and relative importance of state enterprises in developing economies. This was particularly so in Africa, where more than half the SOEs were established between 1967 and 1980; in Tanzania alone, the number of state enterprises increased tenfold from 1965 through 1985.[4] By 1980, SOEs were common, and often dominant, in manufacturing, construction, banking services, natural resource industries, and agriculture. Although SOEs were typically small-scale undertakings in most developing countries prior to 1950, many are now among the largest firms in their countries, and some are among the largest enterprises in their fields anywhere in the world.

The relative economic importance of state firms in developing countries is apparent from Table 13–3, which shows the percentage share of such firms in GDP for a number of non-oil-exporting developing countries. Major oil-exporting nations are excluded from the table (but not the discussion in subsequent sections) as outliers, given the extraordinarily high share of state oil companies in GDP and gross investment, especially in periods of high oil prices, such as 1974 to 1983 and 1989 to 1990. Although the share of the enterprises in GDP is, on the average, slightly lower than in industrial nations (9.6 percent), the average share in developing countries almost doubled during the 1970s, while that for industrial countries showed little change.[5] The average share of SOEs in total investment in developing countries, however, was nearly 2.5 times that in industrial countries at

3. For a good discussion of some of the reasons for the development of large public enterprise sectors in developing nations see R. P. Short, "The Rule of Public Enterprises: An International Statistical Comparison," IMF, Dept. Memo 83/34, Washington, D.C., 1983.

4. *World Development Report 1988.*

5. Short, "The Role of Public Enterprises," p. 1.

the end of the 1980s. And although the share of state firms in GDP is markedly higher in Africa than Asia or Latin America, the relative share of developing country SOEs in gross investment approaches or exceeds one-quarter of GDP in virtually all regions.[6]

Deficits in the state enterprises averaged 4 percent of GDP across all developing countries in the mid-1970s. The problem worsened in the period 1981 to 1984, particularly in such countries as Brazil, Costa Rica, the Dominican Republic, Ecuador, Egypt, the Philippines, Turkey, and Venezuela where SOE deficits have been between 3 and 12 percent of GDP. In all these countries, the rest of the public sector would have generated a fiscal surplus, excluding the net transfers to the state enterprises.[7]

Intergovernmental Transfers

Transfers from central to subnational governments are conventionally treated as recurrent expenditures, even though subnational governments (provinces, departments, counties, municipalities) may use the proceeds for capital formation such as construction of schools and hospitals. However, some countries, such as Indonesia, classify some transfers as capital spending and others as consumption, so international comparisons are difficult. Table 13–2 shows that transfers to subnational governments (including revenue sharing) constitute a sizable proportion of recurrent spending in a few countries (India, Indonesia, Brazil, Korea) and a very small share in most others. In a few cases subnational governments with small transfers have access to rich sources of revenue. This is true for Bolivia, where oil-producing provinces receive large oil royalties, and for Malaysia, where the state governments of Sabah and Sarawak earned substantial tax revenues from the export of tropical timber. In most unitary states, such as Chile, virtually all governmental affairs at all levels are run from the capital, and subnational units of government have few responsibilities to go with their limited sources of local revenue.

Elsewhere, including many federal countries, transfers of funds from the central government to subnational units are essential because the center has monopolized the most productive sources of tax revenue. In most cases, national governments impose income taxes because subnational governments lack the resources and skills required to administer such a complex tax, and could not do so effectively anyway because the income tax base can easily migrate within a country. Similarly, the major source of tax revenue for some developing countries—import duties—must necessarily remain a central government resource, since most countries have only a few serviceable ports.

We have just seen that there are few easy ways to reduce government recurrent expenditure to achieve higher public savings. The scope for doing so is often greatest in the areas of military spending and subsidies to cover deficits of state-owned enterprises. Together, these two categories of recurrent spending can account for 7 to 10 percent of GDP. Indeed, by the 1990s, several low- and middle-income countries, many francophone African countries, and the transitional countries of Eastern and Central Europe have moved to privatize many of

6. Malcolm Gillis, "Tacit Taxes and Sub-Rosa Subsidies," in Richard Bird (ed.), *More Taxing Than Taxes,* (San Francisco: ICS Press, 1991), Chap. 5.
7. *World Development Report 1988,* p. 171.

their SOEs at least partly as a means of reducing government subsidies. Interest payments, wages and salaries of civil servants, and transfers to subnational governments are not easily compressed in any country, particularly in very low income ones.

Despite the difficulty, developing-country governments have in recent years increasingly squeezed expenditures and raised public saving, often as part of comprehensive adjustment programs to deal with inflation and fiscal crises. One detailed study of 15 low- and middle-income countries revealed that real reductions in recurrent spending, averaging 5 to 6 percent, were achieved in the 1980s.[8] Such measures expand the scope for public saving, which is primarily intended to finance public investment. However, in this sample of 15 countries, public investment spending suffered even more from cutbacks: capital spending by government fell by more than 30 percent in real terms.

Tax Policy and Public Saving

For much of the postwar period, extending well into the 1970s, the most widely prescribed measures to boost public saving were policies to raise tax collections, especially increased tax rates and new taxes. This tendency was reinforced by policies of aid donors and the advice of foreign experts, who encouraged countries to generate high tax ratios, by making full use of their taxable capacity. **Taxable capacity** was defined in terms of an index composed of per capita income, mineral and oil exports, and the share of foreign trade in GDP. High values for these variables suggested higher taxable capacity, either because of a higher margin of income over subsistence (high per capita income) or because of the accessibility of the tax base in oil- and mineral-exporting economies and highly open economies. Exports and imports are easily taxed because they pass through bottlenecks (ports), where they are more easily tracked than are items in domestic trade.

By the mid-1980s, however, there was a wide consensus shared by development specialists and government officials, that high tax ratios were not necessarily a virtue, or low tax ratios a vice, in mobilizing domestic savings. Tax ratios reflect both opportunity and ideology. Sub-Saharan African countries in particular tend to tax themselves more heavily relative to their taxable capacities than do countries in Asia.[9] Ideology may be a factor, but a high tax ratio may also reflect the fact that opportunities for mobilizing other types of savings, especially private savings, are limited because of poorly developed and organized financial systems. Latin American countries tend to dominate any list of countries with low tax effort. This may merely reflect the relatively greater ease with which private savings can be mobilized through the financial system in Latin America. Since 1945, there

8. Norman L. Hicks, "Expenditure Reductions in Developing Countries," Washington, D.C., World Bank, 1988.

9. For the late 1970s, the average tax ratio for sub-Saharan African countries was 18.0 percent; that for Asia was but 15.0 percent. By 1985, tax revenues as a percent of GDP were about 23 percent in Africa, 16 percent in East Asia, and only 12 percent in South Asia. (See Vito Tanzi, "Quantitative Aspects of Tax Systems in Developing Countries," in David Newberry and Nicholas Stern (eds.), *The Theory of Taxation for Developing Countries* (London: Oxford University Press, 1987) and *World Development Report 1988,* p. 82.

have been extended periods of robust growth of organized financial markets in many Latin American countries, particularly in Mexico, Brazil, Argentina, and Chile and more recently in Colombia and Venezuela.

Tax measures can be used to expand public saving or to shrink a destabilizing government deficit only if the Please effect, discussed in Chapter 12, is weak or absent. And even when the government's marginal propensity to consume is significantly less than 1, there is no guarantee that the higher public saving made possible by higher tax revenues will result in an appreciable expansion of *overall* national saving; as shown later in this chapter, some part of any higher taxes will come out of private saving.

Where the Please effect is not a concern, a number of tax measures are available for increasing public saving or reducing destabilizing deficits. These include (1) periodic increases in rates imposed under existing taxes; (2) enactment of new taxes to tap previously unutilized sources of revenue; (3) improvements in tax administration that allow greater collection under existing taxes at present tax rates, by reducing tax avoidance and evasion; and (4) major reform of the entire tax structure, involving elements of options 1, 2, and 3. For many countries options 1 and 2 offer only slight hope for increased collections. Options 3 and 4 are perhaps the most difficult to implement, but if feasible, are much more likely to achieve the desired results

Recall from Chapter 12 that, as incomes rise, so does the share of GNP collected in tax revenues, from 16 percent on average for low-income countries to 27 percent for high-income countries. Table 13–4 shows that the composition of tax revenue also differs markedly between developing and developed countries. Taxes on commodities—including imports, a few primary exports, and domestically produced goods—account for over half of revenues in low-income countries but less than a fifth in high-income countries. Import and export duties in particular decline as incomes rise. In contrast, income, social security, and property taxes levied on households and corporations make up less than a fifth of total revenue in low-income countries but account for about two-thirds of revenues in the high-

TABLE 13–4 Composition of Tax Systems by Major Type of Tax, 1992

		Composition of Taxes (percent)				
	Total taxes share of GNP (percent)	Taxes on international trade	Domestic commodity taxes	Domestic income taxes	Social security taxes*	Other taxes†
Low-income countries	16.0	25.2	32.9	18.8	0.1	23.0
Excluding India	24.3	24.3	28.6	24.0	0.3	22.8
Lower-middle-income countries	19.0	17.8	28.3	31.5	1.7	20.7
Upper-middle-income countries	21.0	9.3	29.1	25.2	14.8	21.6
High-income countries	27.0	1.1	18.2	42.5	27.9	10.3

*Includes employers' and employees' social security contributions as well as those of self-employed and unemployed persons. Many developing countries have not yet introduced social security systems; this accounts for the small share of tax revenue collected through such taxes.

†Includes employers' payrolls or labor taxes, taxes on property, and taxes not allocable to other categories.

Sources: World Development Report 1994, Table 11, and *World Development Report 1993,* Table 12.

income economies. Some of the reasons for these variations are explored in the next sections.

Taxes on International Trade

Although reliance on taxes of foreign trade has diminished in recent years, particularly in middle-income countries, tax revenue structures in developing countries have historically depended heavily on import duties. Many low-income countries remain markedly dependent on import duties. This is particularly so for countries like Afghanistan, Sierra Leone, The Gambia, Uganda, Rwanda, Sudan, Togo, and Yemen, where at least half of total government revenue has come from taxes on imports. Dependence on import duties is much less marked in middle-income countries, which have developed alternative sources of tax revenue.

For most countries attempts to raise further revenues through higher duties is infeasible and undesirable on economic grounds. Higher import duties intensify the incentive for smuggling or evading tariffs. Various studies have shown that for countries with already high duty rates, the incentive to smuggle increases disproportionately with further increases, so that a 10 percent rise in duty rates can result in an increase in smuggling activity by more than 10 percent, as illustrated by the boxed example of Colombia. And in mountainous countries such as Afghanistan and Bolivia or archipelago countries such as Indonesia and the Philippines, borders are especially porous to smuggled imports.

Reliance on import duties for additional revenues may be infeasible for another reason. Except in open economies such as South Korea, Singapore, and Malaysia, the typical structure of import duties in developing countries is, as explained in greater detail in Chapter 19, heavily cascaded: the highest rates of duty in virtually all countries are imposed on consumer durable goods, particularly luxury goods (appliances, cameras, and so on); lower rates are applied on such intermediate goods as cement and leather; and the lowest duty rates are put on capital goods and imported items viewed as basic necessities (food, grains, fish, kerosene). When countries have sought additional revenues from tariffs, consumer goods already subject to high tariffs have been taxed even higher. Higher rates on necessities were considered inadvisable for equity reasons, and higher rates on capital goods and intermediate goods were deemed unacceptable because it was believed that this would retard industrialization programs. But the enactment of higher duties on consumer goods, particularly luxury consumer goods, generally did not produce higher revenue. The reason is simple: the price elasticity of demand is not zero for any consumer good, and for many already subject to very high duties, price elasticity is relatively high, in some cases −2.0 or more. For an import already subject to a 150 percent duty, such as stereos, and with a demand price elasticity of −2.0, a 10 percent increase in duty rates would actually decrease tax revenue on this item by about 2 percent.[10]

10. This result comes from applying the formula

$$\frac{dR/R}{dt/t} = 1 + E\left(\frac{t}{1 + t}\right),$$

where R = total duty collections on stereos
t = rate of duty
E = price elasticity of demand.

Tax Rates and Smuggling: Colombia

In Colombia before 1969, when the import duty rate on cigarettes was over 100 percent, it was virtually impossible to purchase duty-paid cigarettes. At such high rates, import duty collections on cigarettes were nil and the market was flooded with smuggled foreign brands. In 1969 the duty rate was reduced to 30 percent. Cigarette smuggling on the poorly policed Caribbean coast of that country continued, but duty-paid packages began to appear in the mountainous interior, and duty collections on this product soared. Smuggling profits possible under a 30 percent duty were no longer high enough to compensate smugglers for the risks of arrest. Similar phenomena have been observed in Indonesia, Bolivia, and elsewhere.

Export taxes are constitutionally prohibited in the United States and are extremely rare in other industrial countries. But export taxes are not uncommon in developing countries, particularly in tropical Africa and Southeast Asia. Taxes are ordinarily imposed on exports of raw materials such as timber (Ivory Coast and Liberia), tin (Malaysia), jute (Pakistan), and diamonds (Botswana) and on foodstuffs such as coffee (Colombia), peanuts (The Gambia and Senegal), cocoa (Ghana), and tea (Sri Lanka).

Twenty developing countries relied on export taxes for more than 10 percent of total tax revenue in the 1980s, but in only seven countries, primarily low-income African countries, do export taxes account for more than 20 percent of revenue. Export taxes are often imposed in the belief that they are paid by foreign consumers. That is, the taxes themselves are thought to be exported to consumers abroad, along with the materials. But the conditions necessary for exporting taxes on exports to foreign consumers are rarely present.

Export taxes are also employed to promote nonrevenue goals, including increased processing of raw materials within natural-resource-exporting developing countries. This is done by imposing high rates of export tax on unprocessed exports (cocoa beans or logs) and lower or zero rates of tax on processed items fabricated from raw materials (chocolate and plywood). In principle, this use of export taxes should increase local value-added on natural resource exports and thereby generate greater employment and capital income for the local economy. Unfortunately, in many cases the result has been that a government gives up more in export tax revenues than its country gains in additional local value-added, particularly when processed raw materials are exported tax free. One study documents several instances in Southeast Asia and Africa where the additional value-added gained in heavily protected local processing of logs into plywood was typically less than half the amount of export tax revenue that would have been collected had timber been exported in the form of logs.[11]

Personal and Corporate Income Taxes

Harried ministers of finance, perceiving slack in personal and corporate income taxes, often resort to rate increases in these taxes, with no change in the tax base.

11. Robert Repetto and Malcolm Gillis (eds.), *Public Policies and the Misuse of Forest Resources* (New York: Cambridge University Press, 1988), "Conclusions," Chap. 10.

The results are usually disappointing, particularly for the personal income tax. Even in middle-income countries, only a very small proportion of the population is covered by the personal income tax: only 2 percent in the 1970s in Ghana, Peru, and almost all other developing countries, though higher in Burma, Kenya, and Turkey. In contrast, about half the population in the United States filed income tax returns in 1980. Thus, few developing countries can rely heavily on the personal income tax for revenues. Whereas the personal income tax accounts for just over two-thirds of all federal tax in the United States, rarely does the personal income tax account for as much as 10 percent of total central government revenues in developing countries.

In Colombia, for instance, the personal income tax is as well developed as in any developing country. Yet even though this tax is typically responsible for as much as 15 to 18 percent of national government revenues, a large share of it is paid by a small number of people: in the early 1970s the top 4 percent of households paid two-thirds of the total tax.[12] In general, personal income taxes are paid largely by urban elites. Not only are these groups usually the most vocal politically, but over the years they have developed such a variety of devices for tax evasion and avoidance that rate increases stand little chance of raising additional revenues.

Rate increases for corporate taxes are not usually productive either. In only 16 of 82 developing countries did the corporation income tax account for more than 20 percent of total taxes in the 1980s. And in most of these countries, corporate tax collections usually originated with foreign natural-resource firms. Except for several middle-income countries such as Argentina, Korea, Taiwan, and Mexico, the corporate form of doing business covers but a small portion of the private sector. To be sure, most state-owned firms are corporations, but few such firms outside the natural-resources sector earn sizable taxable profits. Even fewer pay substantial income taxes.

Sales and Excise Taxes

A much more promising source of additional government revenue is indirect taxes on domestic transactions such as sales and excise taxes. **Sales taxes,** including **value-added taxes,** are broad-based consumption taxes imposed on all products except those specifically exempted, such as food, farm inputs, and medicine. **Excise taxes** are also taxes on consumption, but these levies are imposed only on specifically enumerated items—typically tobacco, alcoholic beverages, gambling, and motor fuel. On average, developing countries depend on domestic commodity taxes for nearly a third of total revenues (Table 13–4).

Virtually every developing country imposes some form of sales tax. In most the tax is not applied to retail sales because of the burdensome administrative requirements of collecting taxes from thousands of small retailers. In the past, as in Chile before 1970 and in some Indian states, the tax was imposed as a gross turnover tax collected at all levels of production and distribution, with harmful implications for efficiency, income distribution, and virtually every objective of tax policy. In developing countries, administrative problems are more tractable when the sales tax is confined to the manufacturing level: a much smaller number of firms is in-

12. Malcolm Gillis and Charles E. McLure, Jr., "Taxation and Income Distribution: The Colombia Tax Reform of 1974," *Journal of Development Economics,* 5, no. 3 (September 1978), 237.

volved and the output of manufacturers is far more homogenous than sales of retailers or wholesalers. For these reasons many low-income countries have utilized either the single-stage or the value-added form of manufacturers' tax, usually exempting very small producers. This kind of sales tax, however, involves more economic distortions than either a wholesale or a retail tax, and for that reason, as well as for revenue motives, more and more middle-income countries have turned to taxes at the retail level.[13]

Increasingly, these taxes have taken the form of one or another variant of the value-added tax (VAT), widely seen as the most effective method of taxing consumption yet developed. Nearly 60 countries, including all members of the European Community (EC), have adapted the VAT since it was first adopted in its comprehensive retail form in Brazil in 1967.[14] Nearly 40 developing countries had adopted the tax by 1989, either to replace older, outdated forms of sales taxes or to allow them to reduce reliance on harder-to-collect income and property taxes. Table 13–5 provides a chronology of adoption for the VAT in 25 selected developing countries, as well as the share of the VAT in GDP and in overall tax revenues.

Virtually all developing and industrial countries using the VAT have chosen to extend the tax through the retail level. A VAT extended through the retail level has a tax base that is virtually identical to a single stage of retail sales tax and, when imposed at the same rate as the latter tax, will generate almost identical revenues. Both are indirect taxes on consumption.[15]

Excise taxes might appear to represent an ideal source of additional tax revenue. They are typically imposed on sumptuary items having relatively inelastic demand. When the price elasticity of demand for such products is very low (as for tobacco products) or relatively low (as for alcoholic beverages), an increase in excise tax rates will induce little reduction in consumption of the taxed good. If price elasticity is as low as −0.2—not uncommon for cigarettes—then an additional 10 percent excise tax on this product would yield an 8 percent increase in tax revenues. Moreover, it is a hallowed theorem in optimal tax theory that taxes levied on items with inelastic demand and supply involve the smallest losses in economic efficiency, or what is the same thing, the least excess burden. **Excess burden** is defined as a loss in private welfare over and above the amount of government revenue collected from a tax.[16] Further, many agree, with much justification, that consumption of both tobacco and alcohol should be discouraged on health grounds.

All three considerations would seem to argue for heavy reliance on excise taxes in developing countries. However, it is unfortunately true that in addition to low price elasticity, items such as tobacco and alcoholic beverages have low income elasticity and thus tend to be more important in the budgets of low-income than

13. For a full discussion of the distortions involved in different forms of sales tax, see John Due and Raymond Mikesell, *Sales Taxation: State and Local Structure and Administration* (Baltimore: Johns Hopkins Press, 1983).

14. Carl Shoup, "Choosing Among Types of VAT," in Malcolm Gillis, Carl Shoup, and Gerry Sicat (eds.), *Value-Added Taxation in Developing Countries* (Washington, D.C.: World Bank, 1990).

15. As used in virtually all developing and in all industrial countries, the VAT is properly seen as an indirect tax on consumption: the base of the tax includes only consumption goods and services. A VAT can be structured so that the tax base is all income, but this tax is more difficult to administer and has been used in few countries (Argentina, Turkey). See Shoup, "Choosing Among Types of VAT."

16. For a further discussion of optimal taxation and excess burden, see Figure 13–1 and also Joseph Stiglitz, *Economics of the Public Sector* (New York: Norton, 1988).

Table 13–5 Value-Added Taxation

Country	Year VAT first introduced	VAT Revenues as % of GDP	VAT revenues as % of total tax revenue	Basic VAT rate (%)	Other VAT rates (%)
Low-income countries					
Malawi	1989	6	31	20	
Kenya	1990	8	31	18	
Lower-middle-income countries					
Pakistan	1990	2	10	15	
Nicaragua	1975	2	13	10	
El Salvador	1992	4	37	10	
Bolivia	1973	5	32	14.92	
Philippines	1988	2	10	10	
Romania	1993	7	19	18	
Sri Lanka	1995	6	30	25	
Indonesia	1985	4	22	10	
Peru	1976	3	32	18	
Morocco	1986	6	21	19	
Paraguay	1993	3	24	10	
Ecuador	1970	3	17	10	
Upper-middle-income countries					
Bulgaria	1994	3	7	18	
Tunisia	1988	3	10	17	6, 29
Turkey	1985	5	24	15	1, 8, 23
Brazil	1967	1	4	11	9
Panama	1977	2	6	5	10
Hungary	1988	8	14	25	10
Thailand	1992	3	19	7	
Uruguay	1968	7	22	22	12
Mexico	1980	3	19	10	
Greece	1987	14	39	18	4, 8
Chile	1975	9	37	18	
Venezuela	1993	1	3	10	
Korea, Rep.	1977	4	23	10	2, 3, 5
High-income countries					
Portugal	1986	7	17	16	5, 30
Ireland	1972	8	19	21	12.5
Spain	1986	4	14	15	3, 6
New Zealand	1986	6	18	12.5	
Israel	1976	12	31	17	6.5
Finland	1994	9	27	22	9,12
United Kingdom	1973	7	19	17.5	
Netherlands	1969	7	14	17.5	6
Sweden	1969	9	21	25	12, 21
Italy	1973	5	13	19	4, 9, 12
Norway	1970	9	18	22	
Belgium	1971	7	16	20.5	1, 6,12
Austria	1973	6	16	20	10, 32
Denmark	1967	10	25	25	
France	1968	8	19	18.6	2.1, 5.5
Japan	1989	1	8	3	4.5
Germany	1968	4	14	15	7

Sources: World Development Report 1994, Table 11; IMF, *Government Finance Statistics Yearbook 1994,* pp 42–43; and Glenn P. Jenkins, "Economic Reform and Institutional Innovation," April 11, 1995, unpublished paper.

high-income households. It follows that excise taxes on sumptuary items are decidedly regressive: poor people pay a higher proportion of their income in excise taxes than do rich people—a serious matter when the sumptuary items constitute a substantial portion of spending by poor people, as in most developing countries. In Indonesia, for example, the poorest 20 percent of Javanese households spent about 5 percent of total income on heavily taxed cigarettes in 1976, as opposed to 3.5 percent of income for persons with income more than five times as high.

New Sources of Tax Revenues

If higher rates on existing taxes are unlikely to raise revenues much, a second option for increasing public savings is to tap entirely new sources of tax revenues. In many developing countries, whether by accident, design, or simply inertia, many sources of tax revenue may have been overlooked entirely. Many countries have not collected taxes on motor vehicle registrations; some have not utilized urban property taxes as a significant source of revenue; many have not applied corporation income taxes to the income of state-owned enterprises. Kenya, for example, does not seriously tax farm land, and a few countries such as Indonesia until 1984 have not collected personal income taxes on salaries of civil servants.

The service sector furnishes other examples. Telephone service exists in all but the very poorest countries and is widespread in many, but is often untaxed. Some service establishments, such as restaurants and cabarets, are commonly taxed, but services of beauty shops, parking lots, tire-recap businesses, photofinishing firms, modern laundries, and foreign-travel agencies are among the more common items excluded from the tax base. Not only is taxation of this category of spending attractive from a revenue standpoint, but in developing countries such services typically face relatively income-elastic demand: because families with higher incomes purchase proportionately more of these items, they would tend to bear the greater burden of taxation, consistent with the equity objectives of fiscal policy. However, these services constitute a small fraction of consumption, even for upper-income groups, so their revenue potential is limited.

Changes in Tax Administration

A far more significant option for increasing tax revenues is to implement changes in tax administration that permit more taxes to be collected from existing tax sources, even at unchanged tax rates. The potential for increased revenues from such action is very large, and seldom realized, in virtually all developing countries. Shortages of well-trained tax administrators, excessively complex tax laws, light penalties for tax evasion, corruption, and outdated techniques of tax administration all combine to make tax evasion one of the most intractable problems of economic policy in developing countries.

Tax Administration in India and Bolivia in the 1980s

India during the 1980s provides one of the more egregious examples of poor tax administration. During the fiscal year 1981, for example, it was found that taxes were avoided on at least 40 and possibly 60 percent of potentially taxable income. Almost 70 percent of the taxpayers covered by a survey openly admitted bribing tax officials and three-quarters of the tax auditors admitted accepting bribes to reduce tax payments. The cost of a bribe was commonly known to be about 20 percent of the taxes avoided.[17]

In Bolivia during the same period the tax system was chaotic. More than 400 separate taxes were levied by the national, regional, and city governments. Taxpayer records were out of date and tax collections were recorded more than a year after they had been paid. Of 120,000 registered taxpayers, one-third paid no taxes at all, while 20,000 taxpayers who did pay were not on the register. The administration had virtually ceased its data processing. Administration had gotten so bad that government was helpless to collect taxes during the hyperinflation of the mid-1980s (see the box in Chapter 5). Tax collections fell to only 1 percent of GDP. Faced with this chaos, the Bolivian governrnent reformed its tax administration, simplifying it drastically. This, together with price stabilization (see Chapter 5), enabled the government to collect revenues equivalent to over 7 percent of GDP by 1990, a low ratio by world standards but a vast improvement for Bolovia.[18]

The boxed examples, which suggest the magnitude of the problem in India and Boliva, are typical of many, perhaps most, other developing countries. These examples suggest that efforts to collect a greater share of the taxes due under current law can increase revenues substantially. But the kinds of administrative reforms required are difficult to implement and especially difficult to sustain. Even Bolivia's successful reform raised its tax ratio to only 7 percent of GDP. Korea, a country noted for efficient and determined administration, failed in the 1960s to reach its goal of increasing collections by 40 percent through more effective enforcement, though it was able to reduce underreporting of nonagricultural personal income from 75 percent to slightly under 50 percent. Although administrative reform can help and can be important at any stage of development, better tax administration tends to improve with economic development. In a lower-middle-income country like Jamaica, more than a third of the potential tax base escapes taxation, compared to less than 15 percent in the United States or Canada.[19]

Fundamental Tax Reform

The final policy option available for increasing tax revenues is the most difficult to implement, but the most effective when it can be done. Fundamental tax reform requires junking old tax systems and replacing them with completely new tax laws and regulations. Implementing tax reform engenders enormous technical and informational, not to mention political, difficulties in all countries. In general,

17. Omkar Goswami, Amal Sanyal, and Ira N. Gang, "Taxes, Corruption and Bribes: A Model of Indian Public Finance," in Michael Roemer and Christine Jones (eds.), *Markets in Developing Countries: Parallel, Fragmented and Black* (San Francisco: ICS Press, 1991), pp. 201–13.

18. Carlos A. Silvani and Alberto H. J. Radano, "Tax Administration Reform in Bolivia and Uruguay," in Richard M. Bird and Milka Casanegra de Jantscher (eds.), *Improving Tax Administration in Developing Countries* (Washington, D.C.: International Monetary Fund, 1992), pp. 19–59.

19. James Alm, Roy Bahl, and Matthew Murray, "Tax Base Erosion in Developing Countries," *Economic Development and Cultural Change,* 39, no. 4. (July 1991), 849–72.

governments resist genuine efforts to reform the tax structure until fiscal crisis—in the form of massive budgetary deficits—threatens. Even during a fiscal crisis, it is difficult to mobilize a political consensus to allow unpopular tax measures to pass. Tax policies that protect favored groups and distort the allocation of resources did not just happen; more likely they were enacted at the behest of someone, ordinarily the privileged and the powerful.

It is probably true that tax reform is a topic about which more has been said, to less effect, than almost any topic in economic policy. This is no less true for the United States than for 50-odd developing countries where major tax reform efforts have been mounted since 1950. That the process is painful and slow is evident from the experience of several countries: in the United States the time lag between the birth of tax innovations (tax credit for child-care expenses, inflation proofing of the tax system) and their implementation is usually at least 15 years. If anything, the lag may be slightly shorter in developing countries.

In spite of the difficulties involved, some countries were able to carry through fundamental reforms in tax structure and administration before 1980. The classic example is Japan in the 1880s, when that society began its transformation to a modern industrial power. Korea implemented a major tax reform program in the early 1960s, as did Colombia (see the following boxed example) and Chile in the 1970s. But also during the 1970s major tax reform efforts went for naught in many more countries: Bolivia, Ghana, Liberia, and Peru, among others.

Lessons from Comprehensive Tax Reform: Colombia

In 1974 Colombia implemented one of the most ambitious tax reform programs undertaken. The Colombian experience illustrates both the potential payoffs and the difficulties involved in any serious tax reform effort.

In the last quarter of 1974 the new government of Alfonso Lopez Michelsen, in the midst of a national crisis, enacted a tax reform of very large magnitude. The reform, nearly a decade in the making, was engineered by an extraordinary group of officials as well versed in fiscal economics as any treasury department in the world. The reform package was comprehensive: it involved nearly all tax sources. It was geared to all four fiscal policy objectives: growth, equity, stability, and efficiency. The instruments employed were well suited to the objectives sought. The reform contained measures to increase progressivity that are still absent in tax systems of the United States and Canada. Numerous anomalies in the tax system that encouraged waste and inefficiency in the private sectors were introduced and were allowed to stand for a short time before they were struck down by the Colombian Supreme Court.

The reform's most striking initial achievements were its effects on tax-revenue growth and income distribution. In the first year following the reform, tax revenues grew by 45 percent, or more than twice the growth rate in revenues in the years prior to the reform. The early impact on income distribution was just as striking: in its first year the reform served to shift as much as 1.5 percent of GDP away from the top 20 percent of the income earners—a rare feat.

Many of the achievements of the reform effort proved short-lived, however. The reform initially caught most powerful economic interests with their defenses down. But by 1976 groups injured by the reform were able to have many key measures watered down or repealed, and taxpayers began to develop defense mechanisms against the new law and to exploit loopholes uncovered by the best legal minds in the country. Also, the reform effort paid far too little attention to the practical problems of implementation and to the strengthening of tax collection procedures. Nevertheless many of the innovations introduced in 1974 survived relatively intact through 1980, and many revenue-hungry and equity-oriented tax officials in other Latin American countries viewed much of the 1974 reform package as a model worth detailed study.

Since 1980, however, the pace of tax reform has quickened notably, in both developing and industrial countries, with many similarities in the various reform programs. Throughout much of the postwar period, tax systems were commonly fine-tuned in order to achieve a wide variety of nonrevenue objectives. In particular, governments in developed and developing nations alike commonly sought substantial income redistribution through the use of steeply progressive tax rates. Also, complex and largely inadministrable systems of tax incentives were widely used in attempts to redirect resources to priority economic sectors, to promote foreign investment, regional development, and even stock exchanges.

While fine-tuning tax systems may someday yield the desired results, this requires, at a minimum, strong machinery for tax administration and traditions of taxpayer compliance. Within developing countries, at least, there has been growing recognition that these conditions seldom prevail. Consequently, governments increasingly have turned away from reliance on steeply progressive tax rates and complicated, costly tax incentive programs.

The 1980s saw a worldwide movement toward an entirely different type of tax system, with a shift toward vastly simplified taxes imposed at much flatter rates and with much broader bases,[20] and with increasingly greater reliance on consumption rather than income taxation. Tax reform programs in Bolivia, Chile, Colombia, India, Indonesia, Jamaica, and Malawi exemplify most of these trends.[21]

Two aspects of this worldwide movement in tax reform are especially salient. First, top marginal income tax rates of 60 to 70 percent were not uncommon from 1945 to 1979. But since 1984, country after country has slashed the top marginal rate, often substantially. Table 13–6 shows that 31 developing countries have reduced the top marginal rate of income tax, many of them quite dramatically. During the same period, 20 industrial nations ranging from Australia and Austria through the United Kingdom and the United States also cut the top rate sharply.

In many of these cases, sharp cutbacks in the highest tax rates were accompanied by reforms involving a very substantial broadening of the income tax base,

20. Joseph A. Pechman (ed.), *World Tax Reform: A Progress Report* (Washington, D.C.: Brookings Institute, 1988), "Introduction," p. 13.

21. A number of these cases are discussed in Malcolm Gillis (ed.), *Tax Reform in Developing Countries* (Durham, N.C.: Duke University Press, 1989).

TABLE 13–6 Countries Reducing Highest Rates of Income Tax, 1984–1994

Country	1984	1994
Low-income countries		
Tanzania	75	30
Malawi	50	35
Uganda (1985)	70	30
India	62	40
Bangladesh	60	25
Kenya	65	45
Nigeria	70	35
Senegal (1985)	65	50
Ghana	65	35
Zimbabwe (1985)	61	50
Lower-middle-income countries		
Papua New Guinea	50	28
Pakistan (1985)	60	35
Bolivia	40	13
Philippines (1985)	60	35
Sri Lanka	55	35
Indonesia	45	25
Peru (1985)	50	37
Guatemala	42	25
Jamaica	58	25
Upper-middle-income countries		
Turkey (1985)	55	50
Botswana	75	40
Brazil (1985)	60	25
Costa Rica (1985)	50	25
Colombia	49	30
Thailand (1985)	65	37
Argentina (1985)	45	30
Mexico (1985)	55	35
Malaysia	55	34
Chile (1985)	56	50
Trinidad and Tobago	70	40
High-income country		
Singapore	45	30

Sources: George J. Yost, III (ed.), *1994 International Tax Summaries, Coopers & Lybrand International Tax Network* (New York: Wiley, 1994), and Glenn P. Jenkins, "Tax Reform: Lessons Learned," in Perkins and Roemer, *Reforming Economic Systems in Developing Countries.*

through the reduction of special tax incentives, abolition of tax shelters, and the like. This pattern was especially notable in Bolivia, Colombia, Indonesia, Jamaica, and Sri Lanka, so that even with a rate reduction, higher-income groups often ended up paying a higher proportion of total taxes than before.

Reasons for the worldwide shift toward lower tax rates on broader income tax bases are not difficult to find. First, income taxes imposed at high marginal rates have not been administrable, even in wealthy countries such as the United States. With high marginal tax rates, the incentive to evade taxes (through concealment of income) or avoid taxes (through hiring expensive legal talent to devise tax shelters) is very high. Second, the growing mobility of capital across international boundaries has meant that the risk of capital flight from a particular country increases when that country's top rates of income tax exceed those prevailing in industrial nations, where tax rates have been falling.[22] Third, the operation of the income tax systems of such developed nations as the United States and Japan has placed downward pressure on the tax rates everywhere. This is because of the *foreign income tax credit,* wherein a country like the United States allows foreign income taxes to be credited (subtracted) from U.S. taxes due on income repatriated from abroad, but only up to the amount of tax payable at U.S. rates, which was reduced from 50 to 28 percent in 1986. Finally, high marginal rates of income tax did not prove to be particularly efficacious in correcting severe inequalities in income distribution whether in rich or poor countries.

The second striking feature of recent tax reforms worldwide has been the steadily growing number of countries adopting the value-added tax. Several reasons account for the popularity of the VAT; the two most important are its reputation as a "money machine" and its administrative advantages, relative to other forms of sales taxes and to income taxes.[23]

The record of the VAT in generating large amounts of revenue quickly, and in a comparatively painless fashion, has given it a reputation as a money machine. Although this reputation stems largely from the experience in European countries, the record in developing countries does lend some support to the alleged revenue advantages of the VAT. In Indonesia, the 4 percent share of value-added tax in GDP in 1987 was nearly three times the share garnered in 1983 by the taxes it replaced. And for 15 of the 23 developing countries in Table 13–5, the share of VAT in GDP was higher than 3 percent; in all but three of these cases, the VAT constituted at least 20 percent of total tax revenue. Still, in five of the countries listed in Table 13–5, VAT revenues were less than 2 percent of GDP. Notwithstanding the marked revenue success of the VAT in nations such as Brazil, Chile, and Indonesia, its reputation as a money machine appears to have been at least slightly overstated.

Twenty years ago, it was common to hear the claim that the VAT was largely self-administering. This is not so, but it is true that the tax-credit type of VAT has three principal advantages over single-stage retail and nonretail sales taxes in limiting the scope for evasion. First, the VAT is self-policing to some extent because underpayment of the tax by a seller (except, of course, a retail firm) reduces the tax credits available to the buying firm. Even so, firms that are also subject to income taxes have incentives to suppress information on purchases and sales in order to avoid both the value-added and income taxes. Also, this possible advantage of the VAT is diminished when evasion at the final (retail) stage of distribution is endemic. Second, cross-checking of invoices enables the tax administration to match invoices received by purchasers against those retained by sellers. The cross-check feature is a valuable aid in audit activities, but is no substitute for a true, systematic audit. Third, the fact that a large share of the VAT is collected prior to the retail level is an advantage particularly because in most developing countries an abundance of small-scale retail firms do not keep adequate records.

22. For a cogent discussion of the implications for taxation of growing international mobility of financial and physical capital, see Dwight R. Lee and Richard B. McKenzie, "The International Political Economy of Declining Tax Rates," *National Tax Journal,* 42, no. 2 (March 1989), 79–87.

23. For a full statement of these reasons, see Alan A. Tait, *Value-Added Tax* (Washington, D.C.: International Monetary Fund, 1988), Chap. 1.

In sum, the administrative advantages of the VAT are very real, if sometimes exaggerated by enthusiastic proponents.[24]

TAXES AND PRIVATE INVESTMENT

Fiscal policy influences capital formation in the private sector by affecting both the capacity and the incentive to save and by affecting incentives to invest in private projects. Taxes impinge more directly, but not necessarily more importantly, on both sets of incentives than do government expenditures, and will be our prime focus here.

Taxes and Private Saving

An increase in taxes on households will come partly out of consumption and partly out of saving, but the effects of taxes in reducing consumption and saving, respectively, is a matter of some dispute. Some cross-country studies of saving behavior suggest that increases in taxes in developing countries merely reduce private-sector consumption with little or no effect on saving. Other studies cited in Chapter 12 conclude that there is a high degree of substitutability between private savings and taxes. The truth probably lies slightly closer to the latter observation.

Different taxes will have different impacts on the **capacity to save**. Although heavy sales taxes on highly price-elastic items of luxury consumption will curtail rates of growth of consumption for such items, heavy taxes on corporate income may come in large part at the expense of business savings that might have been plowed back into company investment. Where upper-income groups have a high propensity to consume, as has been often argued to hold for elites in many Latin American countries, increased taxes on them may have little impact on private savings. But where the same groups display strong saving propensities, as many argue is true for some ethnic minorities in Africa and Southeast Asia, higher taxes will have a relatively greater impact on saving. Further, heavier taxes on foreign natural-resource firms will ordinarily have minimal negative impact on the availability of private domestic savings unless such firms have local joint-venture partners and cut their dividends to them in response to reduced profitability.

There is less uncertainty concerning the effects of different forms of taxes on **incentives to save,** but even here offsetting considerations are present. Taxes on consumption probably impinge less severely on private savings than do taxes on income in most developing societies. Perhaps the only exception to this statement arises when households save primarily for the later purchase of items subject to heavy consumption taxes. Some observers have argued that this motivation for saving is common in many low-income countries, where the nature of extended-family relationships makes household saving difficult. In some societies households with incomes above subsistence share resources with poorer households within the family group to help them meet subsistence needs. This pattern is char-

24. For a succinct summary of some of these issues, see John F. Due, "Some Unresolved Issues in Design and Implementation of Value-Added Taxes," *National Tax Journal,* 42, no. 4 (December 1990), 383–98.

acteristic of many African countries and of many parts of rural Asia. Under such circumstances household saving is largely devoted to the purchase of prized durable goods, such as transistor radios, bicycles, and sewing machines. In high- and middle-income countries these are typically viewed as consumer goods that are strong candidates for taxation. But it may well be that in some poorer countries heavy taxation of such items also reduces incentives to save. It is even questionable whether products such as bicycles, sewing machines, and even small outboard motors should be viewed as consumer goods in many low-income societies. Purchasing a bicycle or a small outboard may allow a rural family to market garden produce and fish more easily, whereas sewing machines are ordinarily bought to generate extra income for the household.

On balance, consumption-based taxes are probably more favorable for growth in private saving than are income-based taxes. Virtually all developing countries tax consumption through such indirect means as sales and excise taxes. These levies, although not inherently regressive, are often perceived to be so. This perception has led many tax reformers to argue for direct taxes on consumption. Under a direct consumption tax, taxpayers would annually report total consumption as well as income. Consumption below the level thought minimally necessary for an adequate living standard would be exempt, and any consumption above that level would be taxed at rates that rise progressively with total consumption. If such a levy could be administered, it would stimulate savings, since a household could reduce its tax liability by not spending. Direct consumption taxes have been seriously proposed for the United States (1977), Britain (1978), Sweden (1976), and Australia (1976). Among developing countries they have been proposed for India, Guyana, and Sri Lanka and actually enacted in India in the 1950s. The Indian experiment was short-lived, however, as the tax involved required information beyond the capacities of the tax administration at the time; it proved impossible to administer. But in the 1990s the administrative problems, both real and imaginary, of direct consumption taxes are not so great as to preclude their consideration in many developing and industrial countries.

Taxes can affect incentives to save in other ways. To the extent that national savings rates are responsive to the after-tax rate of return on savings (a question examined in the next chapter), heavy taxes on income from capital (dividends and interest) reduce the volume of private savings available for investment. Likewise, to the extent that people save mainly to finance retirement, social security taxes can also reduce private and aggregate national saving if the social security system is financed on a pay-as-you-go basis (that is, from current revenues), as in the United States, Colombia, the Philippines, and India. Under a social security system financed in this manner, it is argued that individuals covered by the system will reduce their saving in anticipation of receiving future social security benefits. But there will be no corresponding increase in public saving because the social security taxes paid by those covered now are not set aside and invested, but rather are used to pay benefits to those already retired.

This is an important point, because many proposals have been made—and some enacted—for social security systems in Asia and Latin America intended to help increase the national saving rate. The argument that social security systems can foster domestic saving is correct only under two circumstances, both relatively uncommon in developing countries. First, social security systems that operate as true retirement funds can clearly help mobilize capital resources provided the funds are invested in projects with an adequate social marginal rate of return. Under such *provident funds,* the taxes collected from those covered are invested by the government in assets that earn returns; payments are made to retirees out of these returns rather than from taxes collected by those still working, as under the pay-as-you-go system. Under this approach, used in Chile and Singapore and for some workers in Malaysia and a few other countries, any decline in the private savings of those paying social security taxes is largely offset by a concomitant rise in public savings. But the use of provident funds is not widespread.

Even the pay-as-you-go system can increase national saving rates in its early years of operation if benefits are denied to those who retired before the system was implemented and if social security tax rates are set high enough to cover benefit payments for the first decade or so. In the early years the number of workers covered is large relative to the number of retirees, so that the disbursement of benefits is small compared to the inflow of revenues. Therefore a government seeking new temporary sources of public saving could enact a pay-as-you-go system for social security that would serve this purpose for a few years. Sooner or later, however, such a system would tend to reduce overall domestic savings, though not necessarily by as much as the social security taxes paid by covered workers.

Taxes and Capital Mobility

If a country's tax system operates to reduce private savings, it will tend to curtail private domestic investment. Beyond that effect, taxes can affect both the amount and allocation of private domestic investment undertaken out of any given volume of private capital available for investment.

We saw in Chapter 12 that in spite of exchange controls and similar restrictions, capital tends to be fairly mobile across international boundaries. If there are opportunities for earning returns abroad that promise higher after-tax returns than those available in a particular developing country, domestic capital will tend to flow to these opportunities. Of course, a critical factor determining after-tax returns in a given country is the nature of taxes on capital there. Suppose, for example, that capital owners in the Philippines can secure, on the average, before-tax returns equal to 15 percent of their investments and that capital income in that country is subject to a 50 percent tax. After-tax returns are then 7.5 percent. The same funds invested in well-developed capital markets in Hong Kong, where capital is less scarce, might obtain only a 12 percent return before taxes, but are taxed at only, say, 15 percent. The after-tax return in Hong Kong is therefore 10.2 percent. The difference of 2.7 percent in after-tax returns may be large enough to induce movement of Philippine savings to Hong Kong. In general, countries that attempt to impose substantially heavier taxes on capital income often experience outflows of domestic savings to countries employing lower tax rates on capital. This movement is quite distinct from the type of *capital flight* from developing to developed countries often observed in countries experiencing severe domestic political turmoil or exchange-rate uncertainties.

There is no shortage of low-tax foreign opportunities facing domestic savers in developing countries. *Tax havens* such as Panama and the Bahamas have been attractive to Latin American investors since the 1960s. Likewise, Hong Kong and Singapore financial markets draw substantial inflows of savings from other Asian countries. Increasingly, enterprises from countries such as India, with relatively high taxes on capital income, have become major investors in other developing countries where after-tax returns are higher than at home.

Most countries have recognized that capital is fairly mobile across national boundaries and have sought to keep taxes on capital income from reaching levels much above those prevailing worldwide. This is evident from an inspection of corporate income tax rates prevailing in most developing countries. In Latin America corporate tax rates are typically found in a band of from 25 to 40 percent, compared to 34 percent in the United States in 1990. In Southeast Asia corporate tax rates—other than those of Hong Kong—cluster in a narrow range of from 30 to 40 percent; the rate in Hong Kong is less than 20 percent.

Countries have sought to impede the outward mobility of capital through such devices as controls on movement of foreign exchange, imposition of domestic taxes on worldwide income of residents, and other devices. Flourishing business in tax-haven countries, coupled with very large investment holdings by citizens of developing countries in the United States, Switzerland, Hong Kong, and Singapore, are ample testament to the limited effectiveness of such controls.

Partly in order to stem capital outflow, and also to direct private investment into priority areas, such as basic industry, exports, or backward regions, many developing country governments selectively offer substantial tax incentives to domestic investors. The two main types of incentives are income tax holidays, wherein approved investments are exempted from income tax obligation for specified periods ranging from 3 to 10 years, and tax credits for investment, wherein a government allows an investor to subtract some portion of initial investment (usually 20 to 25 percent) from his income tax liabilities. On rare occasions these types of incentives for domestic investment have produced the desired results, but these devices suffer from a number of administrative and efficiency limitations. Because of these limitations, Indonesia in 1984 abolished all tax incentives and replaced them with the most effective tax incentive ever offered: lower tax rates for all firms.

INCOME DISTRIBUTION

As indicated in Chapter 4, a basic thrust of economic policy in many developing countries has been the mitigation of extreme income inequality. For decades developed and developing countries alike have sought to use the fiscal system, particularly taxation, to redress income inequalities generated by the operation of the private market. Social philosophers from John Stuart Mill and the eminent nineteenth-century Chilean historian Francisco Encina to John Rawls in the 1970s have sought to establish a philosophical basis for income redistribution, primarily through progressive taxes. Karl Marx also favored steeply progressive taxes in bourgeois societies, but for reasons other than income redistribution. Rather, in Marx's view, heavy taxes on capitalists were essential for speeding the decline of the capitalist state and its replacement by a socialist order.

There is no scientific basis for determining the optimal degree of income redistribution in any society. And across developing countries different views prevail as to the ideal distribution of income. But in virtually all countries the notion of *fiscal equity* permeates discussions of budgetary operations. In the overwhelming majority of countries fiscal equity is typically defined in terms of the impact of tax and expenditure policy on the distribution of economic well-being. Progressive taxes, those that bear more heavily on better-off citizens than on poor households, and expenditures whose benefits are concentrated on the least advantaged are viewed as more equitable than regressive taxes and expenditures.

Taxation and Equity

On the tax side of the budget, the materialistic conception of equity requires that most taxes be based on **ability to pay.** Ability to pay can be measured by income, consumption, wealth, or some combination of all three. Clearly, individuals with higher incomes over their life span have a greater ability to pay taxes, quite apart from the moral question of whether they should do so. Indeed the redistributive impact of taxation is almost always expressed in terms of its effects on income. However, philosophers from the time of Hobbes have argued that consumption furnishes a better index of ability to pay than income; in this view tax obligations are best geared to what people take out of society (consume) rather than what they put into society (as measured by income).

In practice developing countries have relied heavily on these two measures of ability in fashioning tax systems. Personal and corporate income taxes employ income as the indicator; sales taxes and customs duties are indirect assessments of taxes on consumption. But the ability to pay is not the exclusive guide to the assessment of taxes in all countries. Religious and cultural values often provide other bases for establishing tax liability. Nevertheless most societies do largely define equity in taxation as requiring taxation on the basis of ability to pay, and this is commonly interpreted to mean progressivity. At a minimum, equity is usually assumed to require the avoidance of regressive taxes whenever possible. There are a number of tax instruments that have been employed to secure greater progressivity in principle, if not in practice; all suffer from limitations to one degree or another.

Personal Income Taxes

The most widely used device for securing greater progressivity has been steeply progressive rates under the personal income tax. In some countries in some periods, nominal or legal marginal income tax rates have reached very high levels, even for relatively low incomes. Thus, for example, tax rates applicable to any income in excess of $1,000 in Indonesia in 1967 reached 75 percent, largely because tax rates were not indexed to rapid inflation; in Algeria in the 1960s all income in excess of $10,000 was subject to marginal tax rates of nearly 100 percent; Tanzania imposed top marginal rates of 95 percent as late as 1981.

Although in most developing countries marginal income tax rates are considerably lower than the examples above and, as is apparent from Table 13–6, have been falling, some countries still attempt to impose rates in excess of 50 percent.[25] Countries such as Brazil, Colombia, Costa Rica, Mexico, Singapore, and Sri Lanka generally hold maximum marginal rates to 40 percent or slightly less, and

25. Ten of the sixteen countries imposing income tax rates in excess of 50 percent in 1989 were in Africa, two were in Latin America, and the remainder were in Asia. Barlett, "The Worldwide Tax Revolution."

the maximum income tax rate in Indonesia has been 35 percent since that country implemented tax reform in 1984.

If the tax administration machinery functioned well and if capital were immobile among countries, the pattern of actual tax payments of high-income taxpayers would resemble the legal, or theoretical, patterns described above. In fact in most countries **effective taxes**—taxes actually collected as a percent of income—fall well short of theoretical liabilities. Faced with high income tax rates, taxpayers everywhere tend to react in three ways: (1) they evade taxes by concealing income, particularly capital income not subject to withholding arrangements; (2) they avoid taxes by altering economic behavior to reduce tax liability, whether by supplying fewer labor services, shipping capital to tax havens abroad, or hiring lawyers to find loopholes in the tax law; and (3) they bribe tax assessors to accept false returns.

For all these reasons, the achievement of substantial income redistribution through progressive income taxes has proven difficult in all countries, including the United States and also the three Scandinavian nations where tax rates were long among the world's most progressive. Tax avoidance is the favored avenue for reducing tax liability in the United States, where use of the other methods can result in imprisonment. But where tax enforcement is relatively weak, particularly where criminal penalties for evasion are absent and tax officials are deeply underpaid, tax evasion and bribery are more commonly utilized. The scope for substantial redistribution through the income tax is thus even more limited in developing countries than in the United States or Sweden.

Notwithstanding these problems, a significant share of the income of the wealthiest members of society is caught in the income tax net in many developing countries. Revenues from personal income tax collections in countries such as Colombia, South Korea, and Chile have been as high as 15 percent of total taxes and in a few others have run between 5 and 10 percent of the total. In virtually all developing countries the entirety of such taxes is collected from the top 20 percent of the income distribution. This means, of course, that the very presence of an income tax, even one imposed at proportional rather than progressive rates, tends to reduce income inequality. Income taxes, together with taxes on luxury consumption, constitute about the only feasible means of approaching income redistribution goals through the tax side of the budget.

Taxes on Luxury Consumption

In view of the difficulties of securing a significant redistribution through income taxes, many countries have sought to employ heavy indirect taxes on luxury consumption as a means of enhancing the progressivity of the tax system. Efforts to achieve this goal usually center on internal indirect taxes, such as sales taxes, and on customs duties on imports, but not excises on tobacco and alcohol.

Several developing countries have found that, provided tax rates are kept to enforceable levels, high rates of internal indirect taxes on luxury goods and services, coupled with lower taxes on less income-elastic items, can contribute to greater progressivity in the tax system. For revenue purposes countries typically impose basic rates of sales taxes on nonluxuries at between 4 and 8 percent of manufacturers' values. This is equivalent to retail taxes of between 2 and 4 percent because taxes imposed at this level exclude wholesale and retail margins. Food, except that consumed in restaurants, is almost always exempted from any sales tax intended to promote redistributive goals. In developing countries the exemption of food by itself renders most sales taxes at least faintly progressive, given the high proportion (up to 40 percent in many middle-income countries) of income of poor households spent on food. Sales taxes involving a limited number of luxury rates of between 20 and 30 percent at the manufacturers' level have been found to be workable in countries such as Colombia, Chile, Taiwan, and Korea.

The redistributive potential of sales tax rates differentiated in this way is, however, limited by the same administrative and compliance constraints standing in the way of the heavier use of income taxation in developing countries. While sales taxes are not as difficult to administer as income taxes, they do not collect themselves. A manufacturer's sales tax system employing three or even four rates may be administratively feasible in most countries, even when the highest rate approaches 40 percent. Rates much higher than that or reliance on a profusion of rates in an attempt to fine-tune the tax lead to substantial incentives and opportunities for tax evasion. Jamaica had over 15 rates prior to 1986, and Chile had over 20 from 1960 to 1970. In recognition of these problems, Indonesia adopted a flat-rate manufacturers' tax in 1985: the tax applies at a rate of 10 percent on *all* manufactured items and all imports. The tax is nevertheless slightly progressive since it does not apply to items that do not go through a manufacturing process, including most foodstuffs consumed by low-income families.

Although the use of internal indirect taxes, such as sales taxes, can contribute to income redistribution goals without causing serious misallocation of resources, the same cannot be said for the use of customs duties. Sales taxes are imposed on all taxable goods without regard to national origin, including goods produced domestically as well as abroad. Tariffs apply only to imported goods. Virtually all countries, developed and developing, utilize customs duties to protect existing domestic industry. Developing countries in particular employ customs duties as the principal means of encouraging domestic industry to produce goods that were formerly imported. This strategy, called **import substitution**, is examined at length in Chapter 19.

Deliberate policies to encourage import substitution through the use of high protective tariffs might, under certain conditions, lead to results sought by policy makers. But accidental import substitution arises when tariffs are used for purposes other than protection, and this is unlikely to have positive results. Many countries use high tariffs to achieve heavier taxation of luxury consumption. Often heavy tariffs are imposed on imported luxury items for which there is no intention of encouraging domestic production. Thus many Latin American and some Asian countries have levied customs tariffs of 100 to 150 percent of value on such appliances as electric knives, hair dryers, sporting goods, videocassette recorders, and mechanical toys. For most countries these items are clearly highly income elastic and are apt candidates for luxury taxation.

But efforts to tax luxuries through high customs duties leads to unintended—and almost irresistible—incentives for domestic production or assembly of such products. In virtually all countries save the very poorest, alert domestic and foreign entrepreneurs have been quick to seize upon such opportunities. By the time local assembly operations are established, they can usually make a politically convincing case that the duties should be retained to enable local production to continue, even when value added domestically is as low as 10 percent of the value of the product. Such operations, if subject to any local sales taxes, usually succeed in being taxed at the basic tax rate, usually 5 to 10 percent. By relying on tariffs for luxury taxation, the government ultimately forgoes the revenues it previously collected from duties on luxury goods, as well as severely undermining the very aims of luxury taxation.

If, instead, higher luxury rates on imports are imposed under a sales tax collected on both imports and any domestic production that may develop, unintended import substitution can be avoided. The use of import tariffs for luxury taxation—indeed for any purpose other than providing protection to domestic industry—is one illustration of the general problem of using one economic policy instrument (tariffs) to achieve more than one purpose (protection, luxury taxation, and revenues). Reliance on import duties for revenue purposes is subject to the same pitfalls just discussed: if it is desired to increase government revenues from imports, a 10 percent sales tax applied both to imports and any future domestic production will yield at least as much revenue as a 10 percent import duty, without leading to accidental protection.

Corporate Income and Property Taxes: The Incidence Problem

Income taxes on domestic corporations and property taxes are often mentioned as possible methods for securing income redistribution through the budget. It is true that corporate income is ultimately received, through dividends and capital gains, almost exclusively by the upper 5 to 10 percent of the income distribution. It is also true that ownership of wealth, which in many lower-income countries largely takes the form of land, tends to be even more concentrated than income. But to a greater extent in developing than in developed countries, efforts to secure significant fiscal redistribution through heavier taxes on domestic corporations and property are limited both by administrative and economic realities.

Administrative problems bedevil efforts to collect income taxes from domestic firms to at least as great an extent as for income taxes on individuals. Hence, in many countries such as China and Pakistan, where corporate taxes on local firms have been important, as much as two-thirds to three-fourths of nonoil corporate taxes flow from state-owned firms, not from private firms owned by high-income individuals. Taxes on land should be subject to less-severe administrative problems, since it is an asset that cannot be easily hidden. However, land valuation for tax purposes has proven difficult even in Canada and the United States; it is more difficult in developing countries. Other than Colombia, few developing countries have been able to assess property at anything approaching its true value.

Economic realities hinder efforts to achieve greater progressivity in the tax system through heavier use of corporate and land taxes, because of the tendency for taxation to unintentionally burden groups other than those directly taxed. This is the **incidence** problem. The incidence of a tax refers to its ultimate impact: it is not who actually pays the tax to the government, but those whose incomes are finally affected by the tax when all economic agents have adjusted in response to the tax. The point of incidence is not always the point of initial impact. Taxes on domestic corporations may reduce the incomes of capitalists, who in turn might shift their investment patterns to reduce taxation. The incomes of workers they employ and the prices charged to consumers may be affected as well. In the end taxes on land and improvement may not much reduce the incomes of landholders, but they may be reflected in higher prices charged to consumers. Ultimately, all taxes are paid by people, not by things such as corporations and property parcels.

The implications of incidence issues may be illuminated by a simple application of incidence analysis to the corporation income tax. Consider a profit-maximizing company that has no significant monopoly power in the domestic market. If taxes on the company's income are increased in 1996, then after-tax returns to its shareholders in 1996 will be reduced by the full amount of the tax. In the short term, incidence of the tax is clearly on shareholders. Since shareholders everywhere are concentrated in higher-income groups, the tax will be progressive in the short run. If capital were immobile, unable to leave the corporate sector, the long-term incidence of the tax would also rest on shareholders, and the tax would be progressive in the long run as well.

But in the long run capital can move out of the corporate sector. To the extent that capital is mobile domestically, but not internationally, the corporate tax will also be progressive in the long run. Returns on capital remaining in the corporate sector will be reduced by the tax. Untaxed capital owners employed outside the corporate sector will also suffer a reduction in returns, because movements of capital from the taxed corporate sector will drive down the rate of return in the non-taxed sector. Because the corporate tax reduces returns to capital throughout the economy, all capital owners suffer, including owners of housing assets, and, in a closed economy, the long-run incidence is again progressive.

However, few if any developing economies are completely closed; indeed, we saw in Chapter 12 that capital has in recent years become much more mobile internationally. To the extent that capital can move across national borders and to the extent that higher returns are available in other countries, domestic capital will migrate to escape higher corporate taxes. But as capital leaves an economy, both new and replacement investment and, ultimately, output will be curtailed and the marginal productivity of workers will fall. Prices of items produced with domestic capital will therefore rise. In this way an increase in corporate taxes may be borne by domestic consumers, who pay higher prices for the reduced supply of corporate-sector goods. Similarly, domestic workers, whose incomes are reduced when production is curtailed, may bear a part of the burden of the corporate tax.

Hence the corporate tax may be regressive (worsen the income distribution) in the long run. The degree of regressivity will depend on whether consumption by low-income groups is more or less capital-intensive and on the relative position in the income distribution of workers losing their jobs or suffering declining real wages. In the end capital owners may suffer no significant decline in their incomes. Although there are other plausible conditions under which an increase in the corporation income tax may not result in greater relative burdens on capitalists, the scenario outlined above is sufficient to illustrate that often the intentions of redistributive tax policy may be thwarted by all the workings of the economy. Thus policy makers cannot be sure that all taxes imposed on wealthy capital owners will ultimately be paid by them.

Limited Effects of Redistribution Policy

The foregoing discussion suggests that whereas some tax instruments may achieve income redistribution in developing countries, the opportunities for doing so are limited in most countries—a conclusion supported by a large number of empirical studies. With few exceptions these show that the inability to administer personal income taxes effectively, failure to utilize the limited opportunities for heavier taxes on luxury consumption, overreliance on revenue-productive but regressive excise taxes, and inclusion of food in sales taxes, all combine to reduce significantly the redistributive impact of tax systems. By and large, tax systems in developing countries tend to produce a burden that is roughly proportional across income groups, with some tendency for progressivity at the very top of the income scale. As a result the very wealthy do pay a somewhat greater proportion of their income in taxes than the poor, but the poor still pay substantial taxes: at least 10 percent of their income in many cases studied (Argentina, urban Brazil, Colombia, Jamaica, and six others).[26] This is the predominant pattern even in countries, such as Colombia, Jamaica, Tanzania, and Chile before 1970, that have placed strong policy emphasis on the use of tax tools to reduce income inequality. Of course, in the absence of such efforts, the after-tax distribution of income may have been even more unequal. This suggests that although difficult to implement and often disappointing in results, tax reforms intended to reduce income inequality are not futile exercises and they may serve the purpose of preventing taxes from making the poor worse off.

Expenditures and Equity

The limits of tax policy suggest that if the budget is to serve redistributive purposes, the primary emphasis must be on expenditure policy. Indeed where redistribution through expenditures has been a high priority of governments, the results have been generally encouraging. The effects of government expenditure on income distribution are even more difficult to measure than those of taxes. But both the qualitative and quantitative evidence available strongly indicate that in developing countries budget expenditures may transfer very substantial resources to lower-income households, in some cases as much as 50 percent of their income. And the pattern of benefits tends to be progressive: a much higher fraction of income goes to the poor households than to those in the upper reaches of the income distribution.

One study found that in Malaysia in the late 1960s the combined effect of taxes and recurrent government consumption expenditures was to transfer 5 percent of GNP from the two highest income classes to the two lowest income groups, with more than three-quarters of the transfer going to the poor. This figure understates the actual extent of the redistributive impact of expenditures since it does not include the effects of public investment, which was perhaps the most important tool of fiscal redistribution in Malaysia in 1968.[27] Another study found that in Indonesia in 1980 the tax system was only slightly progressive. But the expenditure side of the budget, with its emphasis on food subsidies and primary education, markedly helped the poor; benefits from government expenditure were slightly more than 50 percent of the income of the poorest income group.[28] Similarly, an exhaustive study of the net incidence of the Chilean budget for 1969 shows that although the tax system had virtually no effect on income distribution,

26. These Latin American studies have been summarized in Richard M. Bird and Luc Henry DeWulf, "Taxation and Income Distribution in Latin America: A Critical View of Empirical Studies," *International Monetary Fund Staff Papers* 20, November 1975, pp. 639–62. Results of studies on Indonesia and Jamaica may be found in Gillis, *Tax Reform,* Chaps. 4 and 5.

27. Donald R. Snodgrass, "The Fiscal System of Malaysia as an Income Redistributor in West Malaysia," *Public Finance,* 29, no. 1 (January 1972), 56–76.

28. Malcolm Gillis, "Micro and Macroeconomics of Tax Reform: Indonesia," *Journal of Development Economics,* 19, no. 2 (1986), 42–46.

government expenditures favored the poor: the lowest-income groups received only about 7.5 percent of national income, but about 15 to 18 percent of the benefits from government expenditure.[29]

Obviously not all government expenditures are effective in reducing income inequality. Some, like interest payments on government debt, have the opposite effect because interest income is concentrated in upper-income groups. But it is not difficult to identify those categories of budget outlays that tend to have the most marked effects on the incomes of the poor. Public expenditures on primary, but not university, education tend strongly to reduce income inequality (Chapter 10). Government spending for public health programs, particularly water supplies, sanitation, nutritional programs, and rural health clinics, also can have a clearly progressive impact (Chapter 11). Although many poor people live in huge cities such as Jakarta, Sao Paulo, Mexico City, Lagos, and Calcutta, in most developing countries most of the poorest people tend to live in rural areas and wealthy people tend to live in urban areas. Hence programs that reallocate government spending to rural areas (irrigation programs, secondary roads, erosion control) may tend to reduce income inequality overall, particularly in the case of irrigation.

Irrigation and Equity

Many economists have long believed that government investments in irrigation in developing countries were bound to result in significant benefits for poor rural households, primarily by the effects of increased irrigation on agricultural productivity. However, this view was widely questioned by many analysts in the 1970s. They claimed that irrigation tends to be adopted faster and more completely by large farmers at the expense of small farmers and landless laborers, because the large farmers are then more able to buy out the small ones and because the technology associated with irrigation is laborsaving.

Studies sponsored by the International Food Policy Research Institute (IFPRI) tend to confirm the older view: government investments in irrigation have not benefited the larger farmers more than small farmers and landless laborers. Rather, these studies find that the latter groups have made major increases in their incomes as a result of irrigation. This research was focused on ten project sites in Indonesia, Thailand, and the Philippines. It found that there was no tendency to merge farms after the introduction of irrigation and, particularly in Indonesia, that the gains to landowners accrued primarily to small farmers. Further, gains to landless labor were substantial, however these are measured, because irrigated areas use more workers per acre than nonirrigated farms.[30]

Subsidies for consumption of basic foodstuffs also can result in substantial redistribution, provided food subsidy programs are not accompanied by oppressive price controls on the production of food by poor farmers. Subsidies to subnational

29. Alejandro Foxley, Eduardo Aninat, and J. P. Arellano, *Redistributive Efforts of Government Programs* (Elmsford, N.Y.: Pergamon Press, 1980), Chap. 6.

30. IFPRI Report 8, no. 1, January 1986.

governments are often used to finance the provision of basic human needs, such as water, sewerage, education, and health services, all of which have benefits concentrated in lower-income classes. Housing subsidies favor the poor less frequently, since many programs for housing subsidies (Indonesia, Ghana, Pakistan) are in reality largely confined to government employees, a group that in most countries is relatively well-off.

Not all subsidy programs contribute to income redistribution even when redistribution is the announced goal. The most striking example has been that of subsidies for the consumption of petroleum products, particularly kerosene, in Bolivia, Colombia, Indonesia, Pakistan, and several other oil-producing countries. In all four cases mentioned, a principal justification offered for such subsidies was to assist low-income groups. In Bolivia through 1980 and in Colombia through 1974, this argument was extended to cover gasoline consumption, even though in both countries automobile ownership was largely confined to the upper 5 percent of the income distribution and in both, urban bus transport was already heavily subsidized. In Indonesia gasoline has been only lightly subsidized, but budget subsidies held prices of kerosene and diesel fuel at less than half the costs of production and distribution. Although it seems plausible that kerosene subsidies strongly favor the poor, this is not the case. The poorest 40 percent of families consume only 20 percent of the kerosene sold. Therefore for every 1 dollar of subsidy to the poor, relatively high-income families received 4 dollars of benefit. And since kerosene can be substituted for diesel fuel, the subsidy program included it as well to prevent diesel users from switching. The result was that subsidies to kerosene and diesel fuel averaged about 5 percent of total tax revenues in Indonesia from 1979 to 1981, a figure exceeding total capital expenditures for education during the same period.

Fiscal policy to redistribute income must be viewed in perspective. It is not the only, and not always the most effective, instrument for redistribution. Other chapters, especially Chapter 4, have drawn attention to the pivotal importance for income distribution of land tenure, the terms of trade between rural and urban areas, the growth of employment, the relative prices of labor and capital, the openness and market orientation of the economy, and other factors. Taxation and government expenditures can affect most of those factors to some extent, but other, more direct policy instruments may have greater impacts on income distribution. Each of these instruments, some of which force radical changes in the economy, has its economic and political dangers. But a government determined on a more equitable income distribution probably needs to employ all these measures—including progressive taxation and expenditure policies—to some degree.

Economic Efficiency and the Budget

Sources of Inefficiency

On the expenditure side of the budget, the tool we called *social cost-benefit analysis* (Chapter 6) can be deployed to enhance efficiency (reduce waste) in government spending. On the tax side, promotion of economic efficiency is more problematic.

All taxes, save lump-sum levies (poll taxes), lead to inefficiencies to one degree or another. Lump-sum taxes are not realistic options for raising government revenues given their high degree of regressivity. The objective is therefore one of minimizing tax-induced inefficiencies consistent with other goals of tax policy. In most developing societies this objective largely reduces to the necessity of identifying examples of waste engendered by taxes and purging them from the system. If a particular feature of a tax system involves large efficiency losses, called *excess burden* in fiscal economics, and at the same time contributes little or nothing to such other policy goals as income redistribution, then that feature is an obvious candidate for abolition. A full discussion of those elements of tax systems that qualify for such treatment is properly the subject of an extended public finance monograph. We can do little more here than indicate some of the principal examples.

A major source of inefficiency in taxation is excessive costs of tax administration. In some countries and for some taxes these costs have been so high that they call into question the desirability of using certain taxes for any purposes. This is true for certain kinds of narrow-based stamp taxes widely used in Latin America to collect government revenues on the documentation of transfer of assets, rental agreements, checks, and ordinary business transactions. Many stamp taxes cost more to administer than they collect in revenues.

In some countries even broad-based taxes have had inordinately high costs of collection. For example, sales taxes in Chile and Ecuador in the 1960s cost 1 dollar in administration for each 4 dollars collected, as opposed to about 1 dollar per 100 for most state sales taxes in the United States. And because taxes on capital gains are so difficult to administer everywhere—including North America—costs of collecting this component of income taxes often exceed revenues in developing countries.

Many developing countries, from Ghana to Colombia to Indonesia, have offered substantial tax incentives to encourage investment in particular activities and regions. Many of these, particularly income tax holidays for approved firms, have proven very difficult to administer, and few have led to the desired result.[31] Given persistently pressing revenue requirements in most countries, granting liberal tax incentives may have no other effect than requiring higher rates of tax on taxpayers who do not qualify for incentives. It is a dictum of fiscal theory that any economic wastes (inefficiencies) arising from taxation increase by the square of the tax rate employed, not proportionately. It is therefore not difficult to see that unsuccessful tax incentive programs involve inefficiencies for the economy as a whole that are not compensated by any significant benefits. Largely for this reason, Indonesia abolished all forms of tax incentives in a sweeping tax reform in 1984.

Finally, some features of major tax sources involve needless waste. From our earlier discussion of the use of import duties for luxury tax purposes, it is clear that this is often a major source of inefficiency. The use of progressive tax rates in a corporation income tax (as in Colombia until 1974, Venezuela, Mexico, Brazil, Ghana, and a score of other countries) is another example. Progressive rates of corporate tax, where they cannot be enforced, do little to contribute to income redistribution, and where they can be enforced, they lead to a variety of wastes. Two

31. See, for example, Arnold C. Harberger, "Principles of Taxation Applied to Developing Countries: What Have We Learned?" in Michael Boskin and Charles E. McLure, Jr. (eds.), *World Tax Reform: Case Studies of Developed and Developing Countries* (San Francisco: ICS Press, 1990).

of the most important are fragmentation of business firms and inefficiency in business operation. The incentive for fragmentation is evident: rather than be subjected to high marginal rates of taxes, firms tend to split up into smaller units and lose any cost advantages of size. Where high progressive rates are employed for company income, the tax will take a high proportion (say, 70 percent) of each additional dollar of earnings, so the incentive to control costs within the firm will be reduced. For example, for a firm facing a marginal tax rate of 70 percent, an additional outlay of $1,000 for materials will involve net costs to the firm of only $300, while taxes are reduced by $700.

Neutrality and Efficiency: Lessons from Experience

Experience around the world, both in developed and developing countries, seems to indicate that in societies where efficiency in taxation matters, that objective is best pursued by reliance on taxes that are as neutral as possible. A **neutral tax** is defined as one that does not lead to material change in the structure of private incentives that would prevail in the absence of the tax. A neutral tax system then, is one that relies, to the extent possible, on uniform rates: a tax on all income at a flat rate or a sales tax with the same rate applied to all food and services. A neutral tax system cannot be an efficient tax system.

An **efficient tax system** is one that involves a minimum amount of **excess burden** for raising a required amount of revenue, where excess burden of a tax is defined as the loss in total welfare, over and above the amount of tax revenues collected by the government. Figure 13–1 demonstrates how the excess burden of, say, a commodity tax is the greater the more elastic is the demand or the supply of the taxed item. The left-hand diagram depicts the inelastic case, good A, while the right-hand diagram shows the elastic case, good B. Constant marginal costs *(MC)* are assumed in both cases, and at the same level for both goods, in order to portray more starkly the contrasting results achieved in those cases. Before the tax is imposed on either good, equilibrium price and quantity are P_a

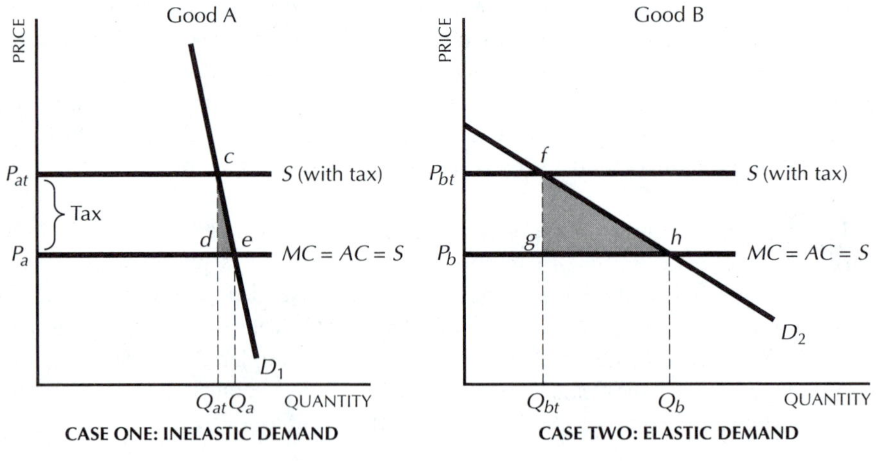

FIGURE 13–1 **Taxation and Efficiency: Excess Burden of Commodity Taxes with Constant Marginal and Average Costs, under Competition.** The shaded area in each case represents the excess burden of equal tax rates imposed on different goods. The greater the elasticity, the greater the excess burden.

and Q_a for good A and P_b and Q_b for good B. Now impose a tax rate (t) on both goods. The new equilibrium (posttax) magnitudes are P_{at} and Q_{at} for good A and P_{bt} and Q_{bt} for good B. For good A, the total amount of government revenue is the rectangle $P_aP_{at}cd$. The total loss in consumer surplus arising from the tax is the trapezoid $P_aP_{at}ce$. The excess of the loss in consumer surplus over the amount of government revenue is the conventional measure of efficiency loss from a tax, or excess burden. For good A, excess burden is the small triangle *cde*. By similar reasoning, excess burden in the case of good B is the larger triangle *fgh*. We may see that taxes of equivalent rates involve more excess burden when imposed on goods in elastic demand.

We can now see that efficient taxation requires neither uniformity nor neutrality, but many different tax rates on different goods, with tax rates lower for goods in elastic demand and higher for goods in inelastic demand. This is known as the **Ramsey rule** or the **inverse elasticity rule.** The problem is that a tax system on this rule would be decidedly regressive: the highest taxes would be required on foodstuffs, drinking water, and sumptuary items. Taxes would be lower on items such as clothing, services, and foreign travel, which tend to be both price- and income-elastic.

The principle of neutrality in taxation is not nearly as intellectually satisfying as a guide to tax policy as is efficient taxation. Nevertheless, neutral taxation is to be preferred as one of the underlying principles of taxation, along with equity, until such time as analysts are able to identify optimal departures from neutrality—and uniformity in tax rates—in real-world settings and until such time as administrative capacities are equal to the task of operating necessarily complicated structures of efficient or optimal taxes.

There is a paradox here. Neutral, uniform-rate taxes are less suited for efficiency goals than perfectly administered efficient taxes. Yet neutral tax systems are more likely to enhance efficiency in the economy than are efficient or optimal systems, since neutral systems with uniform rates can be administered most easily and are much less vulnerable to evasion. This is not to say that neutrality has ever been or should be the overriding goal of tax policy. Governments often undertake very deliberate departures from neutral tax treatment of certain sectors or groups of society in order to achieve other policy goals. But in real-world settings, these departures involve costs, not only in terms of tax administration, but often in both equity and efficiency terms as well. It is important that these costs be made as transparent as possible, so that policy makers may weigh them against expected gains from nonneutrality, including efficiency gains. Under present technology, major departures from neutrality in taxation are not likely to yield benefits commensurate with the costs. Neutrality in taxation may be the most advisable guide to efficiency in taxation for some time to come.

14

Financial Policy

A country's **financial system** consists of a variety of interconnected financial institutions, both formal and informal. Except in a handful of countries (including Liberia and several francophone African countries), a central bank lies at the core of the organized financial system and is responsible for the control of the money supply and the general supervision of organized financial activity. Virtually everywhere, and particularly in developing countries, the commercial banking system is the most visible and vital component of the formal financial system, as acceptor of deposits and grantor of shorter-term credit. Other elements of the formal financial system include savings banks, insurance companies, and in a growing number of middle-income countries, pension funds and investment banks specializing in long-term credit, as well as emerging stock exchanges. Coexisting with these modern financial institutions are the formal and largely unregulated systems of finance, including pawnshops, local moneylenders, trade credit, and other informal arrangements involving the borrowing and lending of money, such as intrafamily transfers and cooperative credit. In very low income countries, or even in some middle-income countries, the informal financial sector may rival the formal system in size.

Financial policy embraces all measures intended to affect the growth, utilization, efficiency, and diversification of the financial system. In North America and Western Europe the term "financial policy" is ordinarily used as a synonym for "monetary policy": the use of monetary instruments to reduce instability caused by fluctuations in either internal or external markets. In the United States these instruments include open-market operations, changes in legal reserve requirements of commercial banks and in shifts in central bank (Federal Reserve) lending (rediscount) rates to commercial banks; these terms are explained later in this chapter. In developing countries the term **financial policy** typically has a much broader meaning. Monetary policy is part of financial policy, but so are measures intended to encourage the growth of savings in the form of financial assets, to develop money and capital markets, and to allocate credit between different economic sectors.

THE FUNCTIONS OF A FINANCIAL SYSTEM

The financial system provides four basic services essential for the smooth functioning of an economy: First, it provides a medium of exchange and a store of value, called *money,* which also serves as a unit of account to measure the value of the transactions. Second, it provides channels for mobilizing savings from numerous sources and channeling them to investors, a process called *financial intermediation.* Third, it provides a means of transferring and distributing risk across the economy. Fourth, it provides a set of policy instruments for the stabilization of economic activity.

Money and the Money Supply

An economy without money as a **medium of exchange** is a primitive economy. Trade between individuals must take the form of high-cost, inefficient barter transactions. In a barter economy goods have prices, but they are expressed in relative prices of physical commodities: so many kilos of rice for so many liters of kerosene, so many meters of rope for so many pairs of sandals, and so on. Trading under such circumstances involves onerous information costs.

Few societies have ever relied heavily on barter because of the high costs implicit in this means of exchange. At some point prices of goods and services begin to be expressed in terms of one or more universally accepted and durable commodities, like gold and silver, or even beads and cowrie shells. The rise of commodity money diminishes the transaction and storage costs of trade, but still involves problems of making exchanges across space and time. Gold and silver prices do fluctuate, and the commodities are thus not fully reliable as **units of account.** As specialization within an economy increases, financial instruments backed by commodities appear. In the last century, with the rise of central banking all over the world, currency has evolved into *fiat* money: debt issued by central banks that is legal tender. It is backed not by commodities of equivalent value, but only by the full faith and credit of the central bank.

As markets widen and specialization proceeds apace, a need arises for still another financial instrument, **transferable deposits.** In the normal course of development, *checking* or *demand deposits*—deposits that may be transferred to any economic agent at the demand of the depositor—appear first and ordinarily bear little or no interest. Rising levels of economic activity, however, create increasing needs for transaction balances; individuals will always maintain some balances in demand deposits to meet these needs, but will tend to economize on the levels of such deposits if no interest is paid on them. With further monetization still another financial instrument begins to grow in importance: *time deposits,* which are also legally transferable on demand, but sometimes only after stated periods. Time deposits involve contractual interest payments; higher interest rates induce people to hold greater amounts of deposits in this form.

While checking (demand) and time deposits are **liabilities** (or debts) of commercial banks, they are **financial assets** for the persons who hold them. Both demand and time deposits are known as *liquid financial assets.* Unlike *nonfinancial assets* that can also be held by households and businesses (inventories, gold, land), demand and time deposits can be quickly and conveniently converted into their currency equivalents. *Currency* is, by definition, the most liquid of all assets. The concept of liquid financial assets is an important one in any discussion of financial policy in developing countries. For most developing countries, the movement of savers in and out of liquid financial assets may be the prime factor behind the success or failure of a financial policy. We will see that long-term shifts from tangible, or nonfinancial, physical assets to financial assets, particularly liquid assets, bodes well not only for economic growth but also for economic stability.

A country's **money supply** may be defined as the sum of all liquid assets in the financial system. While not all economists agree about what constitutes a liquid financial asset, most vastly prefer this money supply concept to those commonly employed in early postwar monetary analysis. Formerly the money supply was conventionally defined as the sum of only two liquid financial assets: currency in circulation outside banks (C) plus demand deposits (D), which together are known as M1 *(narrow money).* However, it later became clear that because depositors tend to view time and savings deposits (T) as almost as liquid as demand deposits, the former should also be included in any workable concept of money supply, called M2 *(broad money).* Finally, for high-income countries, specialized deposit-taking financial institutions have arisen and offer an array of options to savers other than those available in commercial and savings banks. The liabilities of these specialized institutions (O) are included in M3, *total liquid liabilities,* the broadest measure of money. Thus,

$$\mathrm{M1} = C + D \qquad [14\text{–}1]$$
$$\mathrm{M2} = \mathrm{M1} + T \qquad [14\text{–}2]$$
$$\mathrm{M3} = \mathrm{M2} + O. \qquad [14\text{–}3]$$

For most low-income countries and many middle-income countries, liquid financial assets constitute by far the greatest share of outstanding financial assets. But as income growth continues and the financial system matures, less-liquid financial assets assume progressively greater importance. These include primary securities such as stocks, bonds (issued both by government and firms), and other financial claims on tangible (physical) assets that are convertible into currency equivalents with only some risk of loss to the asset holder and are hence less liquid than demand or time deposits.

The evolution of financial activity follows no set pattern across countries. Differing economic conditions and policies may result in widely divergent patterns of financial growth. Nevertheless as per capita income rises, money increases as a ratio to GDP. Table 14–1 shows these patterns for broad money, M2. For all income classes shown in the table, the ratio of M2 to GDP rose substantially from 1970 to 1992. This reflects both economic growth and changing policies. Looking across countries, however, the pattern is not so clear-cut. On average, the advanced, high-income economies had much higher monetization ra-

TABLE 14–1 Broad Money (M2) as a Percentage of GDP, 1970 and 1992

	Percent of GDP			Percent of GDP	
	1970	1992		1970	1992
Low-income countries	23	41	*Upper-middle-income*		
Excluding India	23	32	*countries:*	27	39
Ethiopia	14	72	Colombia	19	21
Tanzania	25	35	Argentina	31	14
India	23	48	Mexico	16	30
Bangladesh	31	33	Malaysia	34	79
Kenya	30	37	Korea, Rep.	33	40
Nigeria	17	14			
Ghana	19	17	*High-income countries:*	59	75
Honduras	20	31	Saudi Arabia	18	47
			United Kingdom	35	97
Lower-middle-income			Japan	74	109
countries	25	45	Germany	51	66
Pakistan	43	43	United States	63	65
Bolivia	15	35			
Cameroon	15	21			
Philippines	29	36			
Sri Lanka	23	39			
Indonesia	10	46			
Peru	24	15			
Egypt	35	85			

Source: IMF, *International Financial Statistics Yearbook 1994,* country tables.

tios than the middle- and low-income countries. But there are no clear differences in the averages for lower-, lower-middle-, and upper-middle-income country groups. The variance among countries, even with similar incomes, is notable, as is the range among developing countries: from lows of 14 to 15 percent for low-income Nigeria and middle-income Peru and Argentina to highs of over 70 percent for Ethiopia, one of the poorest countries in the world, and middle-income Egypt and Malaysia. Even among industrial countries, Japan's ratio is two-thirds higher than those of Germany and the United States.

Liquid assets are not, however, the only source of financial growth. As financial markets widen with the spread of the money economy, they also tend to deepen as a greater variety of financial assets begins to appear. With rising incomes, a growing proportion of financial growth tends to come in the form of nonliquid financial assets, such as primary securities, suitable as a basis for the type of longer-term finance that commercial banking systems cannot easily provide. The **financial ratio** (the ratio of net financial assets to GNP) tends to rise steadily from less than 20 percent of GNP in very poor countries, such as Haiti or Chad, to between 60 and 80 percent in higher-income countries, such as Brazil, South Korea, and Venezuela, and as high as 200 percent in Malaysia by 1985. In very high income countries, including Canada and the United States, total financial assets are nearly twice as large as GNP, and three times GNP in Japan.[1] Here again there is no evidence of immutable laws of financial development. Many very high income industrial countries, including France and Holland, have financialization ratios a third of that of Japan. And many higher-income countries, particularly those with long inflationary histories (Uruguay, Brazil, Argentina), display a

1. *World Development Report 1989,* p. 39.

lower ratio of financial assets to GNP than poorer countries such as India and Thailand (89 and 65 percent, respectively).

Financial Intermediation

As financial structures become increasingly rich and diversified in terms of financial assets, institutions, and markets, the function of money as a medium of exchange, store of value, and unit of account tends to be taken for granted except in the context of situations of runaway inflation, discussed later in the chapter. As financial development proceeds, the ability of the financial system to perform its second major function—financial intermediation—grows as well. The process of financial intermediation involves gathering savings from multitudinous savers and channeling them to a much smaller but still sizable number of investors. With a few exceptions, households are the only net savers in developing countries. At early stages of economic development a preponderant share of intermediation activities tends to be concentrated in commercial banks. As development proceeds, new forms of financial intermediaries begin to appear and gradually assume a growing share of the intermediation function. These include investment banks, insurance companies, pension funds, and securities markets.

Financial intermediation activities are best measured through use of **flow-of-funds accounts,** which display the uses of finance by different economic sectors together with the sources of savings by sectors. These are akin to the flow matrix of input-output tables and social accounting matrices (see Chapter 6). Unfortunately, reliable flow-of-funds tables are available for only a few countries at present and cross-country generalization about intermediation based on such tables is not yet possible. In the absence of flow-of-funds accounts, we will employ the liquid asset-GDP ratio as an approximate measure of financial intermediation.

Financial intermediation is best seen as one of several alternative technologies for mobilizing and allocating savings. The fiscal system discussed in Chapter 13 furnishes another alternative, and we will see in the next chapter that reliance on foreign savings constitutes still another. Further, we will observe in this chapter that inflation has also been employed as a means of mobilizing resources for the public sector. Indeed a decision to rely more heavily on financial intermediation as a means of investment finance is tantamount to a decision to rely less heavily on the government budget, foreign aid and foreign investment, and inflation to achieve the same purpose.

Transformation and Distribution of Risk

Another major service provided by a well-functioning financial system is the transformation and distribution of risk. All economic activities involve risk taking, but some undertakings involve more risk than others. Individual savers and investors tend to be risk averse; the marginal loss of a dollar appears more important to them than the marginal gain of a dollar. But the degree of risk aversion differs among individuals. When risk cannot be diversified, or pooled, across a large number of individuals, savers and investors will demand greater returns, or premiums, for bearing risk, and activities involving high risk will tend not to be undertaken. But high-risk activities may well offer the greatest returns to the economy as a whole. A well-functioning financial system furnishes a means for diversifying, or pooling, risks among a large number of savers and investors. The system may offer assets with differing degrees of risk. Financial institutions that specialize in assessing and managing risks can assign them to individuals having different attitudes toward, and perceptions of, risk. Indeed a perfectly functioning financial system can reduce all risk premiums to zero, except for those *systematic risks* that can never be diversified away from the domestic economy, such as those arising from national disasters and recessions in the world economy.

Stabilization

Finally, the financial system provides instruments for the stabilization of economic activity in addition to those available under fiscal policy and direct controls. All economies experience cyclical changes in production, employment, and prices. Governments often attempt to compensate for these fluctuations through policies affecting the money supply. Because unemployment in developing countries is rarely of the type that can be cured by monetary expansion, the use of financial policy for stabilization purposes generally focuses on efforts to control inflation.

Inflation and Savings Mobilization

By the 1980s, **price inflation,** defined as a sustained increase in the overall price level, was generally regarded as a malady, which in its milder forms was annoying but tolerable, and in its moderate form corrosive but not fatal. Runaway inflation, also known as hyperinflation, however, has always been recognized as severely destructive of economic processes, with few offsetting benefits. Whereas a number of influential thinkers in the 1950s and 1960s advocated some degree of moderate inflation (for example, inflation rates between 8 and 12 percent) as a tool for promoting growth, few adherents of this view remain, for reasons discussed below. Many others did not actively advocate inflation, but tended to have a higher threshold of tolerance for a steadily rising general price level than is now common. They believed that development inevitably involved trade-offs between inflation and unemployment and that the wise course was to resolve the trade-off in favor of less unemployment and more inflation. Today few economists still believe in a fixed, long-term relation between inflation and unemployment, and there is a growing body of evidence, some of it presented in Chapter 5, that restraining inflation may enhance, rather than retard, prospects for long-run growth.

Inflation Episodes

Inflationary experiences vary widely among developing countries and generalizations are difficult to make. Nevertheless, postwar economic history offers some interesting national and regional contrasts in both susceptibilities to, and tolerances for, different levels of inflation. The period prior to the early 1970s was one of relative price stability in developing countries. In the southern cone of Latin America, however, particularly in Argentina, Brazil, and Chile, **chronic inflation**—prices rising 25 to 50 percent per year for three years or more—has been an enduring fact of economic life for much of the past four decades. The experience of these countries indicates that long periods of double-digit inflation does not necessarily lead to national economic calamity in all societies. In all, 15 countries experienced chronic inflation from 1950 to 1992, as shown in Table 14–2.

However, a tolerable rate of inflation in one country may constitute economic trauma in another. This may be seen more readily by considering the next phase of the often progressive inflationary disease called **acute inflation.** Acute inflation, defined here as inflation in excess of 50 percent for three or more consecutive years, was experienced by 15 countries over the postwar period, in some cases more than once per country. For Brazil, the progression from chronic to acute inflation did not result in any noticeable slowing of that country's relatively robust economic growth, whatever it may have meant for income distribution. In Ghana, on the other hand, a decade of acute inflation coincided with a decade of decline in GDP per capita. Although it may be tempting to attribute economic retrogression in Ghana to acute inflation, it is more likely that the same policies that

TABLE 14–2 Inflation Outliers: Episodes of Chronic,* Acute,† and Runaway‡ Inflation among Developing Countries, 1948–1992

	Average annual rates (%)					
	Chronic inflation (25–50%, 3 years)		Acute Inflation (50–100%, 3 years)		Runaway inflation (>200%, >1 year)	
	Years	Rate	Years	Rate	Years	Rate
Argentina	1950–74	27	1977–82	147	1976	443
			1986–87	111	1983–85	529
					1988–90	1400
Bolivia	1979–81	33	1952–59	117	1983–86	1132
Brazil	1957–78	36	1979–84	108	1985	227
			1986	145	1987–92	831
Chile	1952–71	29			1973–76	308
	1978–80	36				
	1983–85	26				
Colombia	1979–82	26				
	1988–92	28				
Dominican Republic			1988–92	51		
Ghana	1986–90	32	1976–83	73		
Indonesia					1965–68	306
Mexico			1982–88	70		
Nicaragua	1979–84	33			1985–91	2130
Paraguay			1951–53	81		
Peru	1975–77	32	1950–55	102	1988–91	1694
			1978–87	85		
Sierra Leone			1983–92	81		
South Korea			1950–55	95		
Tanzania	1980–89	27				
Turkey	1981–87	38	1978–80	69		
			1988–92	67		
Uganda	1990–92	37	1981–89	101		
Uruguay	1948–65	26	1965–68	83		
	1981–83	34	1972–80	68		
			1984–92	76		
Venezuela	1987–92	40				
Zaire	1981–82	36	1976–80	68	1991–92	2987
			1983–90	68		
Zambia	1985–87	44	1988–92	113		

*Annual average inflation rates between 25 and 50 percent for three or more consecutive years.
†Annual average inflation rates of greater than 50 percent for three or more consecutive years.
‡Annual inflation in excess of 200 percent for one or more years.
Source: IMF, *International Financial Statistics Yearbook 1994.*

led to sustained inflation were responsible for declines in living standards there.[2]

Although acute inflation has proven toxic to economic development in some settings and only bothersome in others, **runaway (hyper-) inflation** has almost always had devastating effects. Inflation rates in excess of 200 percent per year represent an inflationary process that is clearly out of control; eight countries have undergone this traumatic experience since 1950. The nadir of recent inflationary experience occurred in three Latin American countries: Bolivia and Argentina in 1985, Argentina again in 1988 to 1990, and Peru in 1988 to 1991. In Bolivia the annual rate of inflation over a period of several months in 1985 accelerated to a rate of nearly 4000 percent. In Argentina the monthly rate of price increases was 30.5 percent in June 1985 alone; on an annual basis that would have been an inflation rate of 2340 percent. In both Bolivia and Argentina for much of 1985, workers had little choice but to spend their paychecks within minutes of receipt, for fear that prices would double or triple over the next week. In Peru, hyperinflation in 1989 gave birth to publications devoted only to the tracking of inflation (see the box below).

Hyperinflation in Peru: 1988–1990

The economic and social havoc wrought by hyperinflation is difficult to comprehend for those who have not lived through the experience. The Peruvian hyperinflation which began in 1988 and continued until 1991 provides some rueful examples.

The inflationary process was triggered by large budgetary deficits and sustained by subsequent ongoing deficits, virtual economic collapse, and steadily rising inflationary expectations. Peru had already experienced two serious bouts with acute inflation since 1950 (see Table 14–2), but the pace of inflation in 1989 was the highest in the nation's history: 28 percent per *month,* or about 2000 percent per year. Moreover, inflation accelerated in the first six weeks of 1990, as prices rose by 6 percent per week, or about 1 percent per day. From January 1989 to December 1990, the value of the Peruvian currency (the intis) on the free market fell from 1,200 intis per dollar to 436,000 intis per dollar.

This hyperinflation may turn out to be one of the best documented in history: in 1988 Dr. Richard Webb, an internationally respected Peruvian economist, began to publish a magazine devoted essentially to helping producers and consumers cope with the chaos associated with runaway inflation. The magazine, called *Cuanto?* (How Much?) appeared monthly. It not only provided details on price developments for a large number of commodities and services, but it managed to extract what little humor there is in a situation where the price of a movie ticket rises while people are waiting in line to buy it or where a taxi driver must carry his fare money in a burlap bag because the domestic currency collected in fares each evening is too bulky to fit in his trousers.

But there is precious little that is funny about hyperinflation. In Peru, it

2. For a diagnosis of the causes of the Ghanian economic decline after 1962, see Michael Roemer, "Ghana, 1950 to 1980: Missed Opportunities," and Yaw Ansu, "Comments," both in Arnold C. Harberger (ed.), *World Economic Growth* (San Francisco: ICS Press, 1984), pp. 201–30.

was a story of government employees going without pay for weeks at a time, of indices of poverty nearly doubling from 1987 to 1989, further impoverishing the poorest 40 percent of the population. It was a story of precipitous decline in gross domestic product, and of the rise of pervasive black markets in everything from dollars to gasoline to cement. It was a time when, on each payday, laborers rushed to the market to buy their weekly food supplies before they were marked up overnight. It was a tale of wide variations in price rises, where prices for such items as pencils and chicken increased by more than 25 times from February 1989 to February 1990, but prices of light bulbs and telephone services increased by "only" tenfold.

Imagine life in Lima, the capital city, in the first few weeks of 1990, for a middle-income family trying to survive. For the first 40 days of the year, increases in the price of dying outpaced the price of living: the cost of funerals rose 79 percent, while house rent rose by 56 percent and the price of restaurant meals and haircuts increased by 44 percent.

By mid-1990, the economic paralysis of Peru was virtually complete. Peru's hyperinflation ended in 1992 (although inflation remained acute at 75 percent) as government reduced its budget deficit to 1 percent of GDP.

The 21 countries in Table 14–2 brought on inflation in three different ways. In one group—including Argentina, Chile, Ghana, Indonesia, Peru, and Zaire—large budget deficits relative to GDP were financed by borrowing from the central bank. In a second group—Paraguay in the early 1950s and Brazil and Uruguay before 1974—inflation was caused by a massive expansion of credit to the private sector. And in Nicaragua, Sierra Leone, Uganda, and Zaire, political strife or civil war exacerbated the fiscal and monetary causes of inflation. Whatever the initial impetus to inflation, as we shall see, once it begins to accelerate, the public begins to expect inflation to continue, and this leads to even higher, more-sustained price increases.

For developing countries as a group, Table 14–3 shows that, on average, inflation was only 13 percent a year until the oil crisis began in 1973, jumped to 21 percent a year during the period of rising oil prices until 1981, but then accelerated to more than 30 percent a year even as oil prices began falling, and exceeded 50 percent a year after oil prices collapsed in 1986. The industrial countries, in contrast, had much lower inflation throughout and the highest price increases coincided with the rise in oil prices.

These averages conceal more than they reveal, however. Asian countries, with moderate inflation before the oil crisis, were adept at stabilizing their economies and reducing inflation to single digits during and after the rise in energy prices. African countries went in the opposite direction; they accepted the "imported" inflation from higher oil prices (and their own commodity price boom) during the 1970s, and then in the 1980s chose to finance their deficits, using foreign aid and domestic borrowing, rather than to reduce them. Latin America stands out as the region of highest inflation. Not only did many Latin American countries borrow extensively during the 1970s to cover external deficits, they also refused to reduce their fiscal deficits when those loans had to be repaid, at higher interest rates, during the early 1980s. Inflationary deficit financing intensified throughout the 1980s

TABLE 14–3 Inflation by Regional Groupings, 1964–1992 (percent p.a.)

	1963–73	1973–81	1981–86	1986–92
World	6.3	13.8	14.1	21.1
Industrial countries	4.6	10.3	4.9	4.0
Developing countries	12.9	20.7	32.0	55.0
Africa	4.9	17.3	29.0	25.4
Asia	13.5	8.8	6.8	9.0
Middle East	4.2	16.6	18.8	14.0
Latin America	18.4	43.7	98.0	232.8

Source: IMF, *International Financial Statistics Yearbook 1994,* pp. 108–9.

in many countries. By the 1990s, however, there was a strong trend in both Africa and Latin America toward reduced deficits and lower inflation, as it became clear that economic growth was unlikely until inflation had been quenched.

Forced Mobilization of Savings

Chapter 13 identified a number of problems involved in the use of conventional taxes, such as income and sales taxes, for mobilizing public-sector savings. Another form of taxation is inflation. Governments from the time of the Roman Empire have recognized inflation as an alternative means of securing resources for the state. All that is required is that the stock of money be expanded at a sufficiently rapid rate to result in increases in the general price level and that people be willing to hold some money balances even as the values of these holdings decline. Inflation then acts as a tax on money holdings. At 15 percent inflation the annual tax on currency is 13 percent, and at 40 percent inflation the tax is 29 percent.[3] These are higher annual tax rates than any country has ever managed to impose successfully on any physical asset, such as housing, automobiles, or equipment. Under extremely high rates of inflation, as in the German hyperinflation of 1922 to 1923 or the Peruvian inflation of 1988 to 1990, households attempt to reduce holdings of money balances to virtually nothing. However, except during runaway inflation, because money is so convenient as a means of exchange and unit of accounts, people will always hold some money balances even if they must pay fairly heavy inflation taxes for the convenience.

Difficulties in collecting conventional taxes, the apparent ease of collecting inflation taxes, the convenience properties of money balances, and the view that in-

3. Say the nominal value of money balances at the beginning of a year is M_n, equal to the real value, M_r. Now if price inflation proceeds at a rate p per year, then after one year the real value of money balances M'_r would be

$$M'_r = M_r/(1 + p).$$

The tax on these balances is $T = M_r - M'_r$, and the tax rate is

$$t = \frac{M_r - M'_r}{M_r} = 1 - \frac{1}{1 + p} = \frac{p}{1 + p}.$$

If p = 40 percent, $t = p/(1 + p)$ = 29 percent.

flation taxes are progressive (richer people hold higher money balances) have led many policy makers and economists to view inflation as a desirable means of development finance. During the 1950s and 1960s the influential United Nations Economic Commission for Latin America saw moderate inflation as a means of "greasing the wheels" of development, forcing savings from holders of money balances and transferring such savings to governments that were strapped for investment resources. Accordingly, much effort was expended in the search for what was viewed as an "optimal" rate of inflation for developing societies: the rate that maximizes tax collections, including both conventional taxes and inflation rates.

Implementation of such a forced-savings strategy will tend to curtail private investment, since some of the inflation tax will come out of money balances that would have been used for investment in the private sector. However, proponents of tax maximization through inflation assumed that the government's marginal propensity to invest out of inflation taxes exceeded that of the private sector and that the government would invest in real assets as productive as the private investment it displaced. Therefore, it was thought, forced-savings strategies would never reduce total investment.

Two implicit assumptions lay behind the argument that the forced-savings strategy would improve economic welfare in developing countries. Collections of conventional taxes were believed to be highly responsive to inflationary growth; that is, the revenue elasticity of the conventional tax system with respect to nominal income growth is greater than 1.[4] And efficiency losses from inflation taxes were thought to be less than efficiency losses from the use of conventional taxes to increase government revenues. Indeed, it can be shown that under circumstances where (1) a government's marginal propensity to invest out of inflation taxes is unity or greater, (2) the revenue elasticity of the tax system is also unity or greater, and (3) the marginal efficiency costs of inflation taxes are less than those for explicit taxes, the growth-maximizing rate of inflation may be as high as 30 percent. However, these assumptions are so far divorced from economic realities in developing countries as to undermine severely, if not demolish, the case for forced savings through inflation.

First, there is little evidence that governments anywhere have a marginal propensity to invest out of inflation taxes that is near unity; recall Chapter 13's discussion of the Please effect. In order for tax maximization through inflation to stimulate growth, a government's marginal propensity to invest would have to rise with inflation. Research by George von Furstenberg of the IMF and others finds no support at all for even the weakest form of this hypothesis. Second, the net result of even moderate inflation on a government's total revenues (conventional

4. The revenue elasticity (E_R) measures the responsiveness of the tax system to growth in GDP. It is defined as the percent change in tax collections divided by the percent change in GDP, where Y = GDP, or

$$E_R = \frac{\Delta T/T}{\Delta Y/Y}.$$

If $E_R > 1$, then the tax system is revenue-elastic and taxes rise proportionally more than national income. For example, if $E_R = 1.2$, then for every 10 percent increase in GDP, tax collections rise by 12 percent. If $E_R < 1$, the tax system is revenue-inelastic; if $E_R = 0.8$, then with a 10 percent increase in GDP, tax collections rise by 8 percent.

taxes plus inflation taxes) may actually be to decrease the government's ability to expand total investment. This may easily occur if the revenue elasticity of the tax structure is less than unity, as is the case in many, but not all, developing countries. In such cases the growth in collections from conventional taxes lags well behind nominal GNP growth. Particularly in the early stages of an inflationary process, part of the higher inflation tax collections will be offset by a decline in the real value of conventional tax collections. Third, available evidence suggests that once inflation exceeds 2 percent per annum, the incremental efficiency losses from inflation taxes tend strongly to outweigh those from conventional taxes.[5] And it is well to note that since 1973, typical inflation rates in developing countries have been far above 2 percent (Table 14–3).

At best then, government mobilization of resources through inflation is a knife-edged strategy. Inflation rates must be kept high enough to yield substantial inflation taxes, but not so high as to cause holders of liquid assets to undertake wholesale shifts into real assets in order to escape the tax. Inflation rates must be kept low enough so that collections from conventional taxes do not lag far behind growth in nominal income and so that efficiency losses from inflation do not greatly exceed efficiency losses from higher conventional tax revenues. Paradoxically, then, the inflation tax device can work best where it is needed the least: in those countries having tax systems that are most responsive to growth in overall GDP and involve low efficiency costs. Countries with revenue-elastic tax systems do not need to resort to inflation in an attempt to finance expanded government investment. In this sense tax reform can be seen as a substitute for inflationary finance, but not the other way around.

Inflation as a Stimulus to Investment

The forced-savings doctrine was not the only argument employed in favor of purposeful inflation. For more than fifty years some economists argued that, even in industrial countries, rising prices can act as a stimulus to private business enterprise, as inflation was thought to be helpful in drawing labor and capital out of declining sectors of the economy and into dynamic ones. If true for industrial societies, then, it was reasoned, the argument might apply with special force in developing countries, where rigidities, bottlenecks, and immobilities were such that resources were particularly likely to be trapped in low-productivity uses. Inflation, it was argued, would help to speed up the reallocation of labor and capital out of traditional or subsistence sectors into the modern sectors with the greatest development potential. Thus moderate inflation was not only seen as inevitable, but desirable: a progressive government would actively seek some target rate of inflation, perhaps as high as 10 percent, in order to spur development.

Experience with development since 1950 strongly suggests that some inflation is indeed inevitable in developing societies seeking rapid growth in per capita income: factors of production are relatively immobile in the short run, and imbalances and bottlenecks in supply do develop in spite of the most careful planning. However, the deliberate use of sustained inflation to spur development is likely to achieve the desired results only under a limited set of circumstances.

5. George M. von Furstenberg, "Inflation, Taxes and Welfare in LDCs," *Public Finance,* 35, no. 2 (1980), 700–1.

First, if inflation is the result of deliberate policy or can otherwise be anticipated, then in a sustained inflationary process the approaching rise in prices will cause individuals and firms to adjust their expectations of inflation. To the extent that the inflation is anticipated, the supposed beneficial effects will never occur; people will have already taken them into account in their decision making.[6] For industrial societies, it would be difficult, at least for an economist, to accept the idea that behavior does not ultimately adjust to expectations of inflation. In developing countries, where all markets, including that for information, tend to be more imperfect than in developed countries, it might be argued that firms and individuals are less efficient in collecting and using information, including that pertinent to the formation of price expectations. Thus inflation may not be fully foreseen throughout the economy, and consequently rising prices may result in some stimulus to development in the short term. But it should be recognized that over the longer run a successful policy of deliberate inflation depends on people's not understanding the policy.

Second, the argument that deliberate inflation enhances private-sector performance overlooks the effects of inflation on risk taking. Inflation increases the riskiness of all investment decisions. Suppose that businesses can anticipate inflation with a margin of error of plus or minus 20 percent of the actual rate. (If the margin of error is wider, the effects about to be described will be more pronounced.) If inflation has been running at 5 percent per year, there may be a general expectation that it will settle within the range of 4 to 6 percent in the near future. But if inflation has been running at substantially higher rates, say, 30 percent, then expectations of future inflation may rationally be in the much broader range of 24 to 36 percent. The entrepreneur therefore faces far higher levels of uncertainty in planning investments and production. The more uncertain the future and future returns are, the more likely is the entrepreneur to reduce her risks. Investments with long lives (long gestation periods) tend to be more risky than those with short lives. Thus inflation tends to reduce private-sector investment in projects with a long-term horizon; the inhibiting effects rise with the rate of inflation. Unfortunately these are often precisely the types of investments most likely to involve high payoffs in terms of income growth for society as a whole.

Finally, inflation may severely curtail private-sector investment by constricting the flow of funds to the organized financial system if nominal interest rates are not allowed to rise as rapidly as the expected rate of inflation. As we shall see in the next sections, such situations are typical under strategies of shallow financial development.

In any case, many of the arguments developed in favor of deliberate inflation may have been little more than efforts to rationalize the failure of many governments (particularly in Latin America) to bring inflation under control. In most cases inflation in developed and developing countries has been more a consequence of policy miscalculation or economic dislocation (oil-price shocks, agricultural disasters, and so on) than a consciously chosen instrument of economic growth. Some reflective observers of inflationary dynamics, such as Albert Hirschman, have maintained that inflation is not usually the outcome of a system-

6. This observation dates at least as far back as the early 1930s, to the Swedish economist Knut Wicksell. It contains the germ of the idea behind the rational-expectations school of thought of the 1970s and 1980s.

atic set of choices designed to promote growth and other policy objectives. Rather, inflation usually represents the consequences of government temporizing, of postponing difficult decisions that might shatter a fragile consensus in governments with sharply divided constituencies.[7] Measures to increase collections from conventional taxes or to reduce government spending on programs enacted at the behest of powerful vested interests are examples of such difficult decisions. Avoiding such stabilizing changes is tantamount to choosing inflation, in the hopes that at some point in the future a more enduring coalition of constituencies can be assembled to directly confront difficult issues. Seen this way, inflation results not by design but by default.

Inflation and Interest Rates

The concept of real interest rates is central to the understanding of the implications of financial policy for growth and development. Interest rates may be viewed as prices of financial assets. The **nominal interest rate** on loans is the stated rate agreed between lender and borrower at the time of contracting a loan. The nominal rate of interest on deposits is the rate offered to savers at the time the deposit is made. The nominal rate is defined as an obligation to pay (on loans), or a right to receive (on deposits), interest at a fixed rate regardless of the rate of inflation. Currency, which is debt of the central bank but a financial asset for currency holders, bears a *nominal* interest rate of zero. In some countries, such as Indonesia, Turkey, and South Korea, interest is paid on demand deposits, but typically this asset also receives a nominal return of zero. Time deposits (including savings accounts) always bear positive nominal interest rates, ranging from as high as 30 percent in Indonesia in 1974 (for deposits committed for a two-year term) to as low as 4 percent in Ghana in the early 1970s. When an enterprise borrows from a commercial bank, the interest rate it agrees to pay is usually quoted in nominal terms, that is, independently of any changes in the general level of prices. Because costs are incurred in intermediating between savers and investors, the nominal lending rates must exceed nominal deposit rates or financial intermediaries will operate at a loss. However, in some countries, governments have, as a part of broader anti-inflationary programs, deliberately set lending rates below deposit rates and have subsidized banks to cover their losses, as in Korea (1960s) and Indonesia (1968 to 1980).

Nominal interest rates—those quoted by banks on loans and deposits—are often subjected to maximum ceilings imposed by governments. For example, usury laws and conventions throughout much of the history of the United States limited nominal interest rates that could be charged on loans both to private citizens and the government. Similar laws have operated in developing countries. Also, several organized religions support limitations on nominal rates to limit usury; this adds moral force to conventions limiting interest rates.

Nominal interest rates are significant for financial development because the nominal rate governs the *real* interest rate. The **real interest rate** is the nominal interest rate adjusted for inflation, or more precisely, the inflation rate expected by the public. Consider two depositors in different countries in otherwise identical

7. Albert O. Hirschman, *Journeys Toward Progress: Studies of Economic Policy-Making in Latin America* (New York: Twentieth Century Fund, 1963), pp. 208–9.

circumstances, except that in one country the inflation rate is expected to be 5 percent, and in the other 10 percent. If both receive nominal interest rates of 6 percent, then the real rate of interest in the first case is a positive 1 percent, and in the second case a negative 4 percent. The prospective value of the deposit will rise in the first and fall in the second.

Borrowers as well as depositors respond ultimately to real, not nominal, rates of interest. At sustained high rates of inflation, say, 30 percent per year, borrowers will be quite willing, indeed eager, to pay nominal interest rates of 30 percent per year, for loans then are costless: they can be repaid in money with purchasing power well below that at the time of borrowing. Where legal ceilings do not apply on nominal interest rates, they will tend to adjust as expected inflation rises and falls. However, in many countries, at least until recent financial market reforms, governments did place ceilings on nominal interest rates. Inflation often exceeded these ceilings, and this resulted in negative real rates

The relationship between real and nominal interest rates can be derived on the basis of a one-year deposit of one dollar that pays a nominal rate of interest i. At the end of the year, the deposit is nominally worth $1 + i$. If inflation is p per year, then the *real* value of the deposit at the end of the year is only $(1 + i)/(1 + p)$. The real rate of interest r is then this value minus the original deposit of one dollar, or

$$r = (1 + i)/(1 + p) - 1. \qquad [14\text{–}4]$$

Note that in this formula we must express rates in fractions, not percentages: 6 percent becomes .06.

For example, in Ecuador in 1992 the deposit rate was 34 percent and inflation was 45 percent. The real rate of interest on deposits was

$$r = (1 + .34)/(1 + .45) - 1 = -.076 = -7.6\%.$$

This means that a depositor would, at the end of a year, have lost 7.6 percent of the value of her funds, equivalent to a tax of 7.6 percent on her assets.

When inflation and interest rates are low, say below 10 percent, the real rate of interest can be approximated by a simple formula:

$$r = i - p. \qquad [14\text{–}5]$$

In Malaysia, where the deposit rate was 7 percent in 1992 and inflation was nearly 5 percent, the real rate of interest was $7 - 5 = 2$ percent a year.

In cases where conventional income taxes are collected on interest income, the tax (at rate t) must also be deducted from the nominal rate in order to arrive at the real deposit rate net of taxes r_n:

$$r_n = \frac{1 + i(1 - t)}{1 + p} - 1 = \frac{i(1 - t) - p}{1 + p}. \qquad [14\text{–}6]$$

Thus with only a 20 percent income tax on interest, Equation 13–6 shows that the real rate of deposit interest in Ecuador would have been minus 12 percent. Most countries do impose taxes on interest income.

The discussion of inflation and real interest rates brings us to the point where we may evaluate the role of financial policy in a systematic fashion. We shall see that the real interest rate is critical in determining the extent to which the financial system will be able to *mobilize and allocate* savings for development finance. It is important to note that this is not the same thing as saying that higher real interest rates will induce households to save higher proportions of their income than would be the case at lower real interest rates. This would imply that the interest elasticity of savings is greater than zero. But if savings and consumption decisions are responsive to the real rate of interest, the effects of financial policy on income growth will be magnified.

INTEREST RATES AND SAVING DECISIONS

In evaluating the impact of financial policy on economic growth, it is important to distinguish between the implications of real interest rates for consumption-saving decisions on the one hand and for decisions about the uses of savings—including the channels through which savings flow—on the other. Debate over the first question revolves around estimates of the interest elasticity of savings (ϵ_{sr}); debate over the second is couched in terms of the elasticity of demand for liquid assets with respect to the real interest rate (ϵ_{lr}).

Where both elasticities are zero, financial policy can only have a minimal role in the development process. Where both elasticities are high and positive, the scope for growth-oriented financial policy can be substantial. Where ϵ_{sr} is small or zero but ϵ_{lr} is positive and large, financial policy may still have significant impacts on savings mobilization through the financial system. Virtually all economists can agree that the real interest rate has a significant impact on the demand for liquid assets; that is, with higher real rates, a higher proportion of savings will be channeled through the financial system.

But the evidence is mixed on the extent to which higher real interest rates may stimulate savings and thus increase the ratio of national savings to gross national product.

In a summary of his own econometric tests on national savings rates, financial economist Maxwell Fry notes that in Asia, where real interest rates have generally been positive over the past two decades, the ration of gross national saving to GNP rises about 0.1 percentage point for each 1 percentage point rise in the real deposit rate. This response, though statistically significant, is too small to justify a rise in interest rates as the main approach to raising national savings. But Fry cites other studies that find higher elasticities of savings to real interest rates in much of the developing world except Latin America, where the elasticity is close to zero. There does appear to be a consensus that saving rates are determined more by income and by economic and demographic structure than by interest rates. In Asia, it appears that savings rates are strongly affected by the availability of banking services, as measured by the number of bank branches per 1000 people.[8]

Interest Rates and Liquid Assets

Whereas the role of the real interest rate in consumption-saving decisions is a matter of some dispute, the role of real interest rates in influencing the demand for liquid assets is rarely questioned, whether in developed or developing countries. Indeed, there is evidence that the real interest rate paid on deposits plays an even

8. Maxwell J. Fry, *Money, Interest and Banking in Economic Development,* 2d ed. (Baltimore: Johns Hopkins Press, 1995), pp. 162–69.

greater role in liquid asset demand in developing than in industrial countries. Furthermore, experience with marked adjustments in real interest rates in Korea (1965), Indonesia (1968 to 1969, 1974, and 1983), Taiwan (1962), and a host of Latin American countries, strongly indicates the significance of real interest rates for growth in money holdings and demand and time deposits (M2).

Liquid assets, or financial assets in general, represent one form in which savings out of past or current income can be held. The demand for liquid assets in economies where nominal interest rates are not allowed to adjust fully to expected rates of inflation, as has been true for many developing countries, is typically represented as a function of income, the real interest rate, and the real rate of return available on nonfinancial assets:

$$L/P = d + d_1Y + d_2g + d_3r, \qquad [14\text{–}7]$$

where L = liquid asset holdings; P = price level; Y = real income, that is, money income deflated by the price level; g = real return on nonfinancial assets; r = the real interest rate on deposits; and d = a constant; d_1 and d_3 are expected to be positive, and d_2 negative.

The values for the parameters in Equation 14–7 are readily understandable. As real income (Y) grows, the public will desire to hold more purchasing power in the form of cash and demand and time deposits, the principal forms of financial assets available in developing countries. In particular, d_1 is positive because at higher levels of real income there will be greater need for higher real levels of liquid balances to carry out transactions and meet contingencies. Clearly, liquid asset balances furnish a convenience service to asset holders. In industrial societies with highly developed financial systems and securities markets, it might be reasonable to expect something like a proportional relationship between growth in income and growth in demand for liquid assets. However, in developing countries the demand for liquid assets may, given relative price stability, rise at a faster rate than income because of the paucity of other financial assets in which to hold savings. That is, in developing countries the income elasticity of demand for liquid assets may be expected to exceed unity. Indeed, even for middle-income countries such as Malaysia, the demand for liquid assets grew twice as fast as real income did from 1970 to 1992. For many Latin American countries the long-run income elasticity of money demand is also often above unity. In such circumstances the rate of increase in the supply of liquid assets (M2) can exceed the rate of income growth by a substantial margin and price stability can still be maintained.

The sign for d_2, the coefficient of the return on nonfinancial assets, is negative since liquid assets are not the only repository for domestic savings. A range of assets, including nonfinancial assets and, in higher-income countries, nonliquid financial assets such as securities are available to savers. Higher returns on these nonliquid assets relative to liquid assets will induce a shift of savings out of the latter.

The coefficient d_3 of the real deposit rate has a positive sign, for at higher levels of real interest rates the public will be willing to hold larger liquid balances. Where r is negative, holders of all liquid assets pay hidden inflation taxes on their balances. Because higher rates of inflation tax are imposed on non-interest-bearing assets (cash and demand deposits) than on interest-bearing time deposits, savers will be less willing to hold liquid assets.

There have been numerous studies of the demand for liquid assets in a variety of developing countries over the past two decades. In these studies estimates of the elasticity of demand for liquid assets with respect to real interest rates vary according to differing economic conditions across countries. However, in country after country real interest rates have been a powerful factor affecting liquid asset demand. In Asia, where controls over interest rates have been most widely liberalized for the longest time, sharp increases in the real interest rate on time deposits (from negative to positive levels) have resulted in dramatic growth in the share of liquid assets in GNP. On the other hand, many Latin American and African countries have allowed real interest rates to remain negative over long periods. Consequently growth in the demand for liquid assets was minimal in these countries. In most, the share of liquid assets in GDP either declined or remained constant until after financial reforms were implemented in the 1980s or 1990s.

Table 14–4 shows real interest rates on deposits and bank loans for a number of developing countries. In 1980 there was a preponderance of negative real rates on

TABLE 14–4 Real Interest Rates, 1980 and 1992

	Real deposit rate		Real lending rate	
	1980	1992	1980	1992
Low-income countries				
Ethiopia	—	−6.2	—	−2.3
Mali	—	8.1	14.5	17.2
Tanzania	−20.2	—	−14.4	0.0
India	—	—	4.6	6.4
Bangladesh	−4.5	5.9	−1.9	10.3
Kenya	−7.1	−12.2	−2.9	−8.3
Nigeria	−4.3	−18.4	−1.5	−13.7
Senegal	−2.3	7.9	5.3	16.9
Ghana	−25.7	5.6	−20.7	—
Honduras	−9.4	3.2	0.3	11.9
Lower-middle-income countries				
Bolivia	−19.8	9.9	−13.0	29.8
Cameroon	−1.9	6.2	3.1	14.4
Philippines	−5.0	5.0	−3.6	9.7
Sri Lanka	−9.2	6.2	−5.6	1.4
Indonesia	−10.2	12.0	—	15.3
Peru	—	−8.0	—	57.8
Egypt	−10.3	−0.1	−6.1	6.2
Upper-middle-income countries				
Brazil	17.6	49.7	—	—
Hungary	−5.8	0.1	−0.3	5.8
Colombia	—	−0.2	—	8.1
Argentina	−10.6	−6.5	−6.9	−7.8
Mexico	−4.6	0.2	1.3	—
Malaysia	−0.5	2.3	1.0	3.1
Korea	−7.1	3.6	−8.3	3.6
High-income countries				
United Kingdom	−3.3	3.5	−1.5	5.5
Japan	−2.1	1.0	0.6	4.4
Germany	2.5	3.8	6.3	9.2
United States	—	—	1.6	3.2

Sources: World Development Report 1994, Table 12, and IMF, *International Financial Statistics Yearbook 1994,* pp. 106–9.

both deposits and loans. But by 1992, after financial market reforms and stabilization programs in many countries, most countries had positive real rates. Comparison with Table 14–1 shows many cases in which a marked rise in real interest rates or the maintenance of positive real rates over the period was accompanied by a jump in the ratio of broad money to GDP: India, Honduras, Bolivia, the Philippines, Sri Lanka, Indonesia, Egypt, Mexico, and Korea.

FINANCIAL DEVELOPMENT

Shallow Finance and Deep Finance

Policies for **financial deepening** seek to promote growth in the real size of the financial system: the growth of financial assets at a pace faster than income growth. In all but the highest-income developing countries, private-sector financial savings predominantly take the form of currency and deposits in commercial banks, savings and loan associations, postal savings accounts, and, in some countries, mortgage banks. Thus for most developing countries growth in the real size of the financial system is primarily reflected in growth in the share of liquid assets in GDP. In contrast, under **shallow finance** the ratio of liquid assets to GDP grows slowly or not at all over time and typically will fall: the real size of the financial system shrinks. Countries able to mobilize large volumes of government savings or foreign savings can sustain high growth rates even under shallow finance policies, although even these countries may find financial deepening attractive for reasons of employment and income distribution. But for countries where mobilization of government savings is difficult and foreign savings scarce or unwanted, deep finance may be essential for sustained income growth. This is because growth in the share of liquid assets in GDP provides an approximate indication of the banking system's ability to increase its lending for investment purposes. We will see that the hallmark of deep financial strategy is avoidance of negative real interest rates; shallow finance, on the other hand, typically involves sharply negative real interest rates.

Growth in the real size of the financial system enhances its capacity for intermediation: the gathering of savings from diverse private sources and the channeling of these savings into productive investment. The need for financial intermediation arises because savings endowments do not necessarily correspond to investment opportunity. Those individuals with the greatest capacity to save are not usually those with the entrepreneurial talents required for mounting new investment projects. Except in very simple, rudimentary economies, mechanisms are required to channel savings efficiently from savers to enterpreneurs. In rudimentary economies, production in farming, industry, and other activities is small scale and involves traditional technologies. Producers can ordinarily finance most of their modest investment requirements from their own current savings or those of their families (self-finance). Small-scale enterprises employing traditional technologies have an important role to play in development (see Chapter 18). Yet at some stage improvement in productivity (and therefore living standards) in any economy requires adoption of newer technologies. These typically involve lumpy investments that are ordinarily well beyond the financial capacity of all but the wealthiest families. Where enterprise finance is restricted to current family savings, only very wealthy groups can adopt such innovations. Thus a heavy reliance on self-finance tends to be associated with both low productivity and, usually, persistent income inequality.

Restriction to self-finance also guarantees that many productive opportunities involving high private and social payoffs will never be seized, because even the resources of the small number of very wealthy are not unlimited. Innovative, smaller-scale investors are not the only groups that fare poorly where financial intermediation is poorly developed; savers are penalized as well. Let us first examine the case where even the most basic financial intermediaries—commercial banks—are absent. Under these circumstances the domestic options open to savers are limited to forms of savings such as acquisition of gold and jewelry, purchase of land and consumer durable goods, or other relatively sterile forms of investment in physical assets. Alternatively, wealthier savers may ship their savings abroad. The common feature of all such investments is that the resources devoted to them are inaccessible to those domestic entrepreneurs who would adopt new technology, begin new firms, or expand production in existing enterprises. Savings in the form of physical assets like gold may be plentiful, as in France or India, but this type of savings is effectively locked away from investors or at a minimum may be trapped in declining sectors of the economy, unable to flow to sectors with the brightest investment prospects.

However, even where financial intermediation is poorly developed, individuals have the option of holding some of their savings in the form of currency. Additions to cash hoards are superior to investment in unproductive physical assets from an economywide point of view, since at least this serves to curtail the demand for physical assets, reduce upward pressures on their prices, and thus moderate domestic inflation. Nevertheless, savings held in this form are still relatively inaccessible to investors.

There are now virtually no societies where financial systems are as rudimentary as those sketched above. All developing countries have financial institutions, however embryonic, to serve as intermediaries between savers and investors, even where these intermediaries are limited to commercial banks that accept checking (demand) and time (savings) deposits from savers, for purposes of relending to prospective investors at short term. Intermediation flourishes under deep finance, but under strategies of shallow finance intermediation is constricted and the financial system can contribute little to further the goals of economic growth. Later we will see that shallow finance may have unintended effects on employment and income distribution as well.

Shallow Financial Strategy

Shallow financial policies have a number of earmarks: high legal reserve requirements on commercial banks, pervasive nonprice rationing of credit, and most of all, sharply negative real interest rates. Countries rarely, if ever, have consciously and deliberately adopted strategies of shallow finance. Rather, the repression of the financial system flows logically from certain policies intended to encourage, not hinder, investment.

In developed and developing countries alike, policy makers have often viewed low nominal rates of interest as essential for expansion of investment and have controlled interest rate levels tightly. Indeed, so long as the supply of investible funds is unlimited, low interest rates will foster all types of investment activities, as even projects with low returns will appear more attractive to investors. In accordance with that observation and in the belief that low interest rates are particularly essential to assist small enterprises and small farmers, governments have often placed low ceilings on nominal interest rates charged on all types of loans, quite apart from special credit programs involving subsidized credit for special classes of borrowers. Because financial institutions must ultimately cover costs (or else be subsidized by governments), low legal ceilings on nominal loan rates mean low nominal interest rates on deposits as well.

As long as inflation is held in check, low ceilings on nominal loan and deposit interest rates may not retard growth, even when these ceilings are set below the opportunity cost of capital. Indeed the United States over the period 1800 to 1979 managed rather respectable rates of income growth even in the presence of a set of archaic usury laws and other interest rate controls that (particularly before 1970) often involved artificially low, administered ceilings on interest rates. Even so, throughout most of the period before 1979 real interest rates in the United States remained positive; periods in which real interest rates were sharply negative were intermittent and confined to wartime (1812, 1861, 1917 to 1918, and 1940 to 1946).[9]

Usury laws and other forms of interest rate ceilings have been common in developing countries as well, for all the reasons given above plus one more: financial officials in many developing countries, observing gross imperfections in financial markets, have concluded that the market should not be permitted to determine interest rates. Monopoly (or oligopoly) power in financial markets—particularly in commercial banking—does in fact provide ample scope for the banks and other lenders to exercise market power in setting interest rates on loans at levels higher than the opportunity cost of capital.

There are ample observations of gross imperfections in financial systems in developing countries. Barriers to entry into banking and finance often allow a few large banks and other financial institutions to possess an inordinate degree of control over financial markets and thus to exercise monopoly power in setting interest rates. Often these barriers are a direct result of government policies, as governments may have prohibited new entrants into the field, adopted such stringent financial requirements for entry that only the very wealthy could amass the needed capital, or reserved permission for entry to political favorites who were attracted to banking and finance largely by the monopoly returns available when entry was restricted.

In this way one set of government policies—entry restrictions—helps give rise to the need for extensive controls on price charged by financial institutions. Typically these controls take the form of interest rate ceilings imposed to limit the scope of monopoly power in the financial system. Controls by themselves do not necessarily lead to shallow finance. It is the combination of rigid ceilings on nominal interest rates and inflation that impedes financial development and ultimately retards income growth.

Few economists believe that steeply positive real interest rates are essential for healthy growth in the real size of the financial system. In fact, the Chilean experience with very high real interest rates from 1981 to 1983 strongly suggests the op-

9. Steven C. Leuthold, "Interest Rates, Inflation and Deflation," *Financial Analysis Journal,* January–February 1981, pp. 28–51.

posite. Indeed there is no widely accepted answer to the question: What level of real interest rates is required for steady development of the financial system? Clearly the required real rate will differ across countries in different circumstances. In some, financial growth may continue even at zero or mildly negative real interest rates; for others, moderately high positive real rates of between 3 and 5 percent may be essential.

Apart from a few Latin American countries and Indonesia, most developing countries were able to keep rates of inflation at or below 5 to 6 percent prior to 1973. Inasmuch as nominal deposit rates were typically between 3 and 5 percent, real interest rates tended to be slightly positive or only mildly negative. When inflation accelerated in many developing countries after 1973, because few countries made more than marginal adjustments in nominal deposit rates, real interest rates turned significantly negative in many nations, as Table 14–4 shows for 1980. Negative interest rates endured in a few African and Latin American countries in the period 1983 to 1989.

When real interest rates turn significantly negative, then the maintenance of low nominal rates for the purposes of promoting investment and income growth becomes counterproductive. Inflation taxes on liquid financial assets bring real growth in the financial system to a halt. Sharply negative real rates lead to a shrinkage in the system, as the demand for liquid assets contracts. This tendency is evident from a comparison of Tables 14–1 and 14–4, which shows the tendency for negative real interest rates to be associated with decreases in the degree of monetization in countries such as Argentina, Ghana, Nigeria, and Peru.

Contraction in the financial system results in a reduction in the real supply of credit and thus constricts investment in productive assets. Under such circumstances nonprice rationing of investible resources must occur and can take many forms. In most developing countries only those borrowers with either the highest quality collateral or the "soundest" social and political connections, or those willing to make the largest side payments (bribes) to bank officers will be successful in securing finance from the organized financial system. These criteria do not yield allocations of credit to the most productive investment opportunities.

Negative real interest rates make marginal, low-yielding, traditional types of investment appear attractive to investors. Banks and financial institutions find such projects attractive as well, since they may be the safest and the simplest to finance and involve the most creditworthy borrowers. Satisfying the financial requirements of such investors constricts the pool of resources available to firms with riskier projects offering greater possibilities for high yields. Additionally, in the presence of substantial inflation, interest rate ceilings discourage risk taking by the financial institutions themselves, since under such circumstances they cannot charge higher interest rates (risk premia) on promising but risky projects. Also, negative real interest rates are inimical to employment growth, as they make projects with relatively high capital-output ratios appear more attractive than if real interest rates were positive. This implicit subsidy to capital-intensive methods of production reduces the jobs created for each dollar of investment, even as the ability of the financial system to finance investment is shrinking.

Negative real rates of interest tend to lower the marginal efficiency of investment in all the ways described. In terms of the Harrod-Domar model described in Chapter 3, shallow financial strategies cause higher capital-output ratios. Consequently growth in national income and, therefore, growth in savings tend to be lower than when real rates are positive. Therefore shallow finance retards income and employment growth even if the interest elasticity of savings is zero. And if savings decisions are responsive to real interest rates, then shallow finance will have even more serious implications for income growth, as the ratio of private savings to GDP will also contract.

Deep Financial Strategies

Deep finance as a strategy has several objectives: (1) mobilizing a larger volume of savings from the domestic economy, that is, increasing the ratio of national savings to GDP (where the interest elasticity of savings is thought to be positive and significant); (2) enhancing the accessibility of savings for all types of domestic investors; (3) securing a more efficient allocation of investment throughout the economy; and (4) permitting the financial process to mobilize and allocate savings to reduce reliance on the fiscal process, foreign aid, and inflation.

A permanent move toward policies involving positive real interest rates, or at a minimum avoidance of sharply negative real rates, is the essence of deep finance. In turn this requires either financial liberalization that allows higher nominal rates on deposits and loans, curbing the rate of inflation, or some combination of both.

Given the difficulties involved in securing quick results in reducing inflation to levels consistent with positive real rates of interest, the first step involved in a shift from shallow to deep financial strategies is ordinarily that of raising ceilings on nominal rates for both deposits and loans. In some cases this has required nominal interest rates as high as 30 percent on time deposits (Korea in 1966, Indonesia in 1968 and 1974).[10] In extreme cases of acute inflation the initial step has involved raising ceilings on nominal deposit rates to as much as 50 percent in Argentina and Uruguay in 1976 and to nearly 200 percent in Chile in 1974 (where real interest rates nevertheless remained negative until 1976). As the real rate moves toward positive levels, savers strongly tend to increase their holdings of liquid assets; this allows a real expansion in the supply of credit to investors. Marked increases in flows of savings to financial institutions have been observed when nominal rates were increased substantially, as in Uruguay in 1976, Indonesia in 1968 to 1969 and 1983, and Taiwan and South Korea in 1965. Notable responses have also occurred in countries where mildly negative real rates were moved closer to positive levels through increases in nominal rates: these include India and Sri Lanka after 1977 and Turkey after 1980.

Available evidence suggests that countries that attempt to maintain modestly positive real interest rates over long periods tend to be among those with the highest rates of financial growth, as we have already noted in comparing Tables 14–1 and 14–4. Nevertheless, one can have too much of a good thing. One factor contributing to sharply negative real GDP growth rates in Chile in 1982 and 1983 was the emergence of very high real interest rates in 1981 and 1982. The nominal interest rate on loans increased sharply, while at the same time there was a very

10. Ceilings need rarely be increased to the point where they match the *current* rate of inflation. For example, in Indonesia in 1974 the nominal ceiling on two-year time deposits was raised to only 30 percent, even though inflation over the previous 12 months was 42 percent. The increase in nominal rates, coupled with a battery of other measures, convinced depositors that real rates would soon be positive. All that is required is that the inflation expected by savers be reduced to levels closer to the nominal deposit rate.

large and unexpected drop in inflation: the real interest rate soared above 30 percent.[11]

Where finance is deep, inflation tends to be moderate; therefore savers are not subject to persistently high inflation taxes on liquid asset holdings. That being the case, they will be less inclined to shift their savings into much more lightly taxed domestic assets such as gold, land, or durable goods and foreign assets such as currencies or land and securities. Rather, financial resources that otherwise may have been utilized for these purposes flow to the financial system, where they are more accessible to prospective investors. Nonprice rationing of credit, inevitable under shallow finance, will diminish as well. As a result, the capacity of the financial system to identify and support socially profitable investment opportunities expands: higher-risk, higher-yielding investment projects stand a far better chance of securing finance under deep than shallow finance. Growth prospects are accordingly enhanced.

The preceding discussion represents but a sketch of policies designed to promote financial deepening. The focus has been on the real interest rate on deposits and loans when in fact a variety of other policies may be involved. These include central bank payment of interest on commercial bank reserves and avoidance of high legal reserve requirements to commercial banks. That positive real interest rates tend to lead to growth in the real size of banking systems is now rarely questioned. Such a development substantially enlarges the real flow of short-term credit, the stock-in-trade of commercial banks. However, investment finance problems do not end with provision of a growing real flow of short-term credit. As economies move to higher levels of per capita income, the pattern of investment shifts toward longer horizons. Longer-term investment requires longer- term finance. Commercial banks everywhere are ill suited for providing substantial amounts of long-term finance, given that their deposits are primarily of a short-term nature.

Therefore, as financial and economic development proceeds, the need for institutions specializing in longer-term finance rises accordingly: insurance companies, investment banks, and ultimately equity markets (stock exchanges) become important elements in financial intermediation. Nevertheless the type of well-functioning commercial bank system that tends to develop under deep finance is almost always a necessary condition for the successful emergence and long-term vitality of institutions specializing in longer-term investment finance. Where entry into financial activities is only lightly restricted, longer-term financial institutions may appear spontaneously.

But earlier we observed that entry into the financial field is rarely easy, and other factors also often lead to gross imperfections in financial markets. In such circumstances many developing country governments have found intervention essential in order to develop financial institutions specializing in longer-term finance. Intervention may take the form of establishment of government-owned development banks and other specialized institutions to act as distributors of government funds intended as a source of longer-term finance, as in Indonesia and

11. Chilean real GDP declined by 13.2 percent in 1982 and by 2.3 percent in 1983. For a comprehensive discussion of the Chilean economic debacle of 1982 to 1983, see Sebastian Edwards "Stabilization with Liberalization: An Evaluation of Chile's Experiment with Free-Market Policies 1973–1983," *Economic Development and Cultural Change,* 27 (September 1985), pp. 224–53.

Pakistan. In Mexico, Colombia, and Venezuela, governments have provided strong incentives for private-sector establishment of long-term financial institutions. Other governments have sought to create conditions favorable for the emergence of primary securities (stocks and bonds) markets, the source par excellence for long-term finance. In cases where these measures have been undertaken in the context of financial markets with strong commercial banking systems (South Korea, Thailand, Brazil, Mexico), efforts to encourage long-term finance have met with some success. In cases where commercial banking has been poorly developed as a consequence of shallow finance (Ghana, Uruguay before 1976), or where government has sought to "force-feed" embryonic securities markets through tax incentives and other subsidies (Indonesia before 1988, Kenya, Turkey), the promotional policies have been less effective.

Informal Credit Markets

The discussion of financial development has dealt with modern credit institutions, the formal market. But in many developing countries **informal credit markets** coexist with modern financial institutions. These markets arise in many forms. In rural India, village moneylenders make loans to local farmers who have no access to commercial banks. In Ghana and other West African countries, market women give credit to farmers by paying for crops in advance of harvest, and they assist their customers by selling finished goods on credit. In South Korea, established lenders literally make loans on the street outside modern banks; this justifies their designation as the "curb" market. In much of rural Africa, wealthy family members make loans to less fortunate kin, and all over the developing world there are cooperative arrangements to raise funds and share credit among members. Even in modern economies, pawnbrokers and others give credit outside the formal credit system.

Informal credit is generally financed by the savings of relatively wealthy individuals, such as local landowners, traders, family members who have moved into lucrative jobs or businesses, and the pooled efforts of cooperative societies. But informal lenders may also have access to the formal banking system and borrow there, to relend to customers with no access to banks. How can they do this if the banks cannot? First, because they know their borrowers so well and may have familial, social, or other ties to them, informal lenders face lower risks than distant, large banks that might loan to the same borrowers. Loan recovery rates are higher (usually much higher than found in large banks in developing countries) because those who borrow in informal markets know that the availability of loans in the future is dependent on repaying current loans. Second, they also face lower administrative costs in making loans. Of course, moneylenders do charge very high interest rates, and this is a third reason they coexist with banks, which are often prevented by law from charging rates high enough to cover the risks and costs of loans in small amounts to very small firms and low-income borrowers.

As modern credit institutions evolve, especially under deep financial policies, they draw customers and resources from the informal market. First, some of the largest and most creditworthy borrowers from informal lenders eventually qualify as borrowers in the formal market. Second, some moneylenders may themselves establish credit institutions within the informal system. Third, banks begin to attract savings from a wider group of households, some of which had previously directed their savings into informal channels. On all counts, the informal market is likely to shrink in size and coverage, though it is likely to exist in tandem for some time. The process may leave behind several kinds of borrowers, such as small farmers, traders, artisans, and manufacturers, who will still depend on the shrinking informal market for their credit. Competitive, efficient, and varied financial institutions—the kind encouraged by deep financial policies—will have incentives to integrate borrowers into the modern market, and thus reduce the adverse impacts of financial development on those who once depended upon informal credit markets.

Small-scale Savings and Credit Institutions: Bangladesh and Indonesia

In a number of countries, but most notably in Bangladesh and Indonesia, formal credit institutions have attempted to bridge the gap between small-scale borrowers in the informal sector and the formal financial system.

In Bangladesh, the Grameen Bank, founded by Muhammad Yunus more than two decades ago, provides credit to people in about a third of the country's 68,000 villages. The average loan is under $100 and the maximum is $200. Sixty-five percent of the borrowers are landless women and all loan recipients are poor. Loans are made to individual women, but only through local groups that provide social pressure for repayment. The loans are not heavily subsidized and the recovery rate exceeds 97 percent. Grameen Bank is more than a financial institution, however. Its loans require recipients to accept certain "social disciplines" such as cleanliness and family planning, and the bank provides such services as advice on home construction and access to education for some borrowers.[12]

In Indonesia, a government bank, the Bank Rakyat Indonesia, or BRI, provides full banking services, both loans and savings deposit facilities, to farmers, traders, and other small-scale borrowers through their branches in over 3000 villages. BRI charges market rates of interest, around 30 percent a year, on its loans and pays attractive rates, about 12 percent, on deposits. Though the lending rate appears high, it is considerably below the rates charged by informal money lenders. At these rates BRI has been able to attract sufficient savings deposits to more than finance its loan program, which has grown to over $1 billion of assets. Not only are 97 percent of the loans repaid on time, but the small credit and savings system is a major profit center for BRI.[13]

12. *World Development Report 1989,* p. 117, and A. Wahid, *The Grameen Bank: Poverty Relief* (Boulder, Colo.: Westview Press, 1993).

13. Richard H. Patten and Jay Rosengard, *Progress with Profits: The Development of Rural Banking in Indonesia* (San Francisco: ICS Press, 1991), and Marguerite Robinson, "Rural Financial Intermediation: Lessons from Indonesia," Cambridge, MA, Harvard Institute for International Development, Development Discussion Paper No. 434, October 1992.

We have seen from Table 14–3 that inflation was largely conquered in Asia during the 1970s, but accelerated in Latin America and Africa during and especially after the oil-price boom of the 1970s. By the mid-1990s, however, attempts to control inflation have been more serious and widespread. Monetary policy is the principal instrument used to achieve price stability.

Monetary Policy and Exchange-Rate Regimes

Appropriate use of monetary policy in controlling inflation depends critically on the type of exchange-rate regimes used by a country. Exchange-rate regimes form a continuum with **fixed (pegged) exchange rates** at one end and **floating (flexible) exchange rates** at the other. Under a fixed-exchange-rate system, a country attempts to maintain the value of its currency in a fixed relation to another currency, say the U.S. dollar: the value of the local currency is *pegged* to the dollar. This is done through intervention by the country's monetary authorities in the market for foreign exchange and requires the maintenance of substantial **international reserves** (reserves of foreign currencies), usually equivalent to the value of four or more months' worth of imports.

For example, consider a country such as Thailand. From 1987 to 1993, the Thai currency, the baht, was fixed at an exchange close to 25 baht to 1 U.S. dollar. Because the exchange rate, if left to its own devices, would change from day to day to reflect changes in both the demand for and supply of exports and imports and in capital flows, the government must be prepared to use the country's international reserves to buy or sell dollars at an exchange rate of 25 to 1 in order to keep the exchange rate from moving. If, for example, a poor domestic harvest caused the nation to increase its food imports, the baht-dollar exchange rate would tend to rise (the baht would depreciate, as its dollar value falls) in the absence of any net sales of dollars from Thailand's international reserves.

Under freely floating rates, the authorities simply allow the value of local currency vis-á-vis foreign ones to be determined by market forces. Between the two ends of this continuum (see Figure 14–1) lie a number of intermediate options.[14] Closest to the floating-exchange-rate option is the *wider band* system, wherein the exchange rate of a country is allowed to float or fluctuate within a predefined band of values, say between 23 and 27 baht to 1 U.S. dollar. But when conditions threaten to push the value of the currency beyond the band, the authorities intervene by buying or selling local currency as appropriate to stay within the band. Further along the continuum away from floating rates is the *managed float,* where there is no particular exchange rate that the authorities are committed to defend, but where they nevertheless intervene continuously at their discretion. A country with steadily shrinking international reserves might, for example, allow the value of its currency to depreciate against the value of other currencies, that is, allow the exchange rate to rise against other currencies.

Two other systems are closely related hybrids of fixed and floating rules. The *crawling peg,* used over a long period by Brazil, Colombia, and Indonesia, in-

14. For a full discussion of these and other types of exchange-rate regimes, see John Williamson, *The Open Economy and the World Economy* (New York: Basic Books, 1983), pp. 238–41, or Anne O. Krueger, *Exchange Rate Determination* (New York: Cambridge University Press, 1983), pp. 123–36.

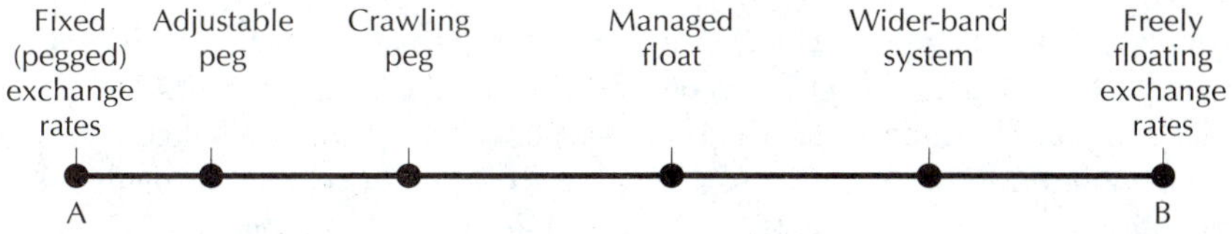

FIGURE 14–1 Continuum of Prototypes of Exchange-Rate Regimes. As one moves from point *A* on the left to point *B* on the right, both the frequency of intervention by domestic monetary authorities and the required level of international reserves tends to be lower. Under a pure fixed-exchange-rate regime (point *A*) authorities intervene so that the value of the currency vis-á-vis another, say the U.S. dollar, is maintained at a constant rate. Under a freely floating-exchange-rate regime, authorities do not intervene in the market for foreign exchange, and there is minimal need for international reserves; indeed, there can be no balance-of-payments deficit.

volves pegging the local currency against some other currency, but changing this in gradual, periodic steps to adjust for any differential between the country's inflation rate and the world inflation rate. Closest to a fixed-exchange-rate system is the *adjustable peg,* involving a commitment by the monetary authorities to defend the local exchange rate at a fixed parity (peg), while reserving the right to change that rate when circumstances require.

The currencies of the major industrial countries have all floated vis-á-vis one another since the early 1970s, with occasional intervention by national monetary authorities to prevent very sharp swings in rates. Most developing countries have adhered to either the adjustable-peg or the crawling-peg systems, although an increasing number, particularly in Africa, have been adopting floating-rate systems as part of stabilization programs. Since in practice both pegged systems are like fixed-rate regimes, for our analysis we will focus most of our attention on monetary policy issues arising under fixed exchange rates in small open economies.

Sources of Inflation

In open developing economies with fixed exchange rates, the rate of monetary expansion is no longer under the complete control of domestic monetary authorities. Rather, countries with fixed exchange rates may be viewed as sharing essentially the same money supply, because the money of each can be converted into that of the others at a fixed parity.[15] Under such circumstances, the stock of money *(M)* is by definition the sum of two components: the amount of domestic credit of the banking system that is outstanding *(DC)* and the stock of international reserves of that country *(IR),* measured in terms of domestic currency. There is therefore a domestic and an international component of the money supply. Thus we have

$$M = DC + IR. \qquad [14\text{–}8]$$

Changes in the domestic money stock can occur either through expansion of domestic credit or by monetary movements that lead to changes in international reserves. That is,

$$\Delta M = \Delta DC + \Delta IR. \qquad [14\text{–}9]$$

15. This section draws substantially on syntheses of monetary and international economics by Arnold C. Harberger. See his "A Primer on Inflation," and "The Inflation Syndrome," papers presented in the Political Economy Lecture Series, Harvard University, March 19, 1981.

Under fixed exchange rates a central bank of any small country can control *DC*, the domestic component, but it has only very limited control over *IR*, the international component. Under such circumstances developing countries that attempt to keep the rate of domestic inflation below the world inflation rate (through restrictive policies on domestic credit) will be unable to realize this goal. If, fueled by monetary expansion abroad (growth in the world money supply), world inflation initially is running in excess of domestic inflation, the prices of internationally traded goods will rise relative to those of domestic nontraded goods.[16] Imports will fall, exports will rise, and the balance of payments will move toward surplus and cause a rise in international reserves. Thus the foreign components of the money stock will rise. This is tantamount to an "importation of money" and will eventually undo the effort to prevent importation of world inflation. Again, a small country on fixed exchange rates can do little to maintain its inflation rate below that of the rest of the world. For very open countries with few restrictions on the movement of goods and capital into and out of the country, the adjustment to world inflation can be very rapid (less than a year). For less-open countries with substantial restrictions on international trade and payments, the process takes longer, but the outcome is inevitable under fixed exchange rates.

The fact that financial policy for stabilization in countries with fixed exchange rates is heavily constrained by international developments is sometimes taken to mean that changes in the domestic component of the money stock have no impact on prices in economies adhering to fixed exchange rates. On the contrary, excessive expansion in money and credit will surely result in domestically generated inflation that, depending on the rate of expansion, can for a time be well in excess of world inflation rates. However, such a situation cannot continue for long, as excess money creation will spill over into the balance of payments via increased imports and lead to a drain on international reserves and, ultimately, an inability to maintain the fixed exchange rate. As reserves dwindle, the country can no longer defend its exchange rate and devaluation becomes inevitable.[17] Inflation can therefore be transmitted to small, open economies through the working of the world economy or can be generated by domestic developments.

A small but growing number of developing countries have begun to employ floating exchange rates (point *B* on the continuum in Figure 14–1). A floating exchange-rate regime allows countries to insulate themselves from world inflation. Under such a system, the rise in world prices attendant on world inflation would initially favor exports from the country and discourage imports. As a consequence, the current account of the country's balance of payments would improve (see Chapter 15), international reserves would rise, and the exchange rate would soon appreciate (fewer baht would be required to buy dollars, for instance). The appreciation in the country's exchange rate would cancel out external price increases and prevent the importation of world inflation.

Under any exchange-rate regime, domestically generated inflation may result from excessive increases in domestic credit from the banking system to either the public or the private sector. Budgetary deficits of the central government must be

16. The above is but one of several mechanisms that led to changes in international reserves sufficient to thwart efforts by developing countries to insulate themselves from world inflation.

17. Import controls were frequently used to stem the drain of reserves and avoid devaluation for a time. But import controls engender another set of distortions and inefficiencies—explored in Chapter 19—that eventually require more drastic measures, including devaluation.

financed by borrowing. The embryonic nature of money and capital markets in most developing countries generally means that governments facing deficits must ordinarily resort to borrowing from the central bank, a process equivalent to direct money creation via the printing press. The result is a direct addition to the reserve base of the monetary system, an increase in so-called *high-powered money.* It is important, however, to recognize that not all budgetary deficits are necessarily inflationary. We have seen that a growing economy will be characterized by a growing demand for liquid assets, including money. Moderate budgetary deficits year after year, financed by the central bank, can help to satisfy this requirement without leading to inflation. In general the money stock may expand at least as fast as the growth in real income, with little or no inflationary consequences.

Earlier we saw that liquid assets are normally between 40 and 50 percent of GDP in developing countries (with wide variations), equivalent to roughly four to six months of income. Thus the public is generally willing to hold this much in money balances. A deficit of 2 percent of GDP financed by money creation would add only marginally to the money supply, and may easily be accepted by the public. But a deficit of 8 percent of GDP would increase the stock of money by an amount equal to one more month of income, an amount the public may be unwilling to hold (unless nominal interest rates on deposits are greatly increased). The excess would spill over into the higher prices.

Use of bank credit to finance government deficits has not been the only source of inflationary monetary expansion in developing countries. Sometimes excessive growth of credit to the private sector has played the most significant role in domestically generated inflationary processes. Nevertheless, as a general rule, inflation rates that are much in excess of world inflation have usually been traceable to budgetary deficits.

It is evident, then, that for countries attempting to maintain fixed exchange rates, efforts to avoid price increases in excess of world inflation must primarily be a matter of fiscal policy, not monetary policy. If budget deficits are not held to levels consistent with world inflation, even very deft deployment of monetary policy instruments will be unable to prevent rapid inflation, devaluation, or both. There is still a role for monetary policy in developing countries, but that role must be largely passive. Resourceful use of monetary policy can help by not making things worse, and also by moderating strong inflationary pressures until the budget can be brought under control, provided the latter is done fairly quickly.

We have seen that monetary factors are causes of inflation in both fixed- and floating-exchange-rate countries. In the case of fixed exchange rates, both world monetary expansion and domestic monetary expansion generate inflation; in flexible-exchange-rate countries, inflation arises from domestic monetary sources. But thus far, no mention has been made of so-called nonmonetary causes of inflation. It seems plausible that internal and external shocks, such as those arising from widespread crop failure in the domestic economy or a drastic increase in prices of imported energy, could have important effects on inflation in countries suffering such shocks. This is true, but the mechanism whereby nonmonetary factors may initiate or worsen inflation needs to be clearly portrayed.

Nonmonetary disturbances may indeed precipitate policy reactions that lead to domestic monetary expansion large enough to accommodate higher relative prices of food or oil, and large enough to cause inflation. In the absence of accommodating monetary expansion in the face of such shocks, inflation can be contained, but at some cost. In practice failure to allow the money supply to expand to accommodate higher relative prices of important goods leads to increases in unemployment that most governments find unacceptable. Therefore, as a matter of course, governments in such cases usually do attempt to allow monetary expansion sufficient to avoid unwanted consequences for employment. But it is important to remember that however advisable monetary accommodation may be on social and employment grounds, expansion in the money stock is required to fuel inflation, whatever the external or internal factors may be that precipitated the expansion. But this truth, known for centuries, is often incorrectly interpreted to mean that nonmonetary factors cannot "cause" inflation. They can, but only through an expansion of the national or international stock of money or both.

Controlling Inflation through Monetary Policy

The array of available instruments of anti-inflationary monetary policy in developed countries include: (1) open-market operations, wherein the central bank can directly contract bank reserves by sales of government securities;[18] (2) increases in legal reserve requirements of banks, so that a given volume of reserves will support a lower stock of money (and reduce the credit expansion multiplier as well); (3) increases in rediscount rates, so that commercial bank borrowing from the central bank becomes less attractive; and (4) moral suasion, wherein the exhortations of monetary authorities are expected to lead to restraint in bank lending policies.

For virtually all developing countries the first instrument—open market operations—is not available for inflation control. Securities markets are typically absent or not sufficiently well developed to allow the exercise of this powerful and flexible instrument, although some countries, including the Philippines and Brazil, have utilized this tool to a limited degree. The other three monetary policy instruments are employed, with varying degrees of success, in developing countries. In addition developing countries often resort to two other tools employed only infrequently in developed countries: (5) credit ceilings imposed by the central bank on the banking system and (6) adjustments in allowable nominal rates of interest on deposits and loans. Governments attempting to control inflation usually resort to all of these instruments, often together but sometimes separately, occasionally experiencing temporary success, as in Argentina in 1985, and occasionally enjoying transitory success, as in Indonesia in 1967 and 1968 and as in Bolivia in 1985 to 1986.

Reserve Requirements

All central banks require commercial banks to immobilize a portion of their deposits in the form of legal reserves that may not be lent to prospective customers. For example, legal reserve requirements for Indonesian and Malaysian banks in

18. Open-market operations are used as an instrument of monetary policy in countries with well-developed financial markets. When the Federal Reserve System in the United States or a central bank in Europe wants to curtail the growth of the money supply, it sells government securities (bonds, bills) in the open market. When a buyer pays for the securities, the effect is to reduce directly the reserves of the banking system, since the funds are transferred from commercial bank deposits or household cash holdings to the account of the Federal Reserve. When the Federal Reserve wants to expand the money supply, it buys securities on the open market and thus directly adds to bank reserves.

the late 1970s were expressed as 30 percent of deposits in domestic currency in the former and 20 percent of all deposits in the latter. Thus in Malaysia, for example, banks were required to add 20 units of currency to reserves for every 100 units of deposits. These figures are not too far out of line with legal reserve requirements in many industrial nations, where reserve ratios of 15 percent for demand deposits and 5 percent for time deposits are common.

Increases in reserve requirements can be used to help moderate inflation. An upward adjustment in reserve requirements works in two ways: it reduces the stock of money that can be supported by a given amount of reserves, and it reduces the money multiplier. The first effect induces banks to contract credit outstanding; the second reduces the growth in the money stock possible from any future increment to reserves.[19] Changes in legal reserve requirements are usually employed only as a last-ditch measure. Even small changes in the required ratio of reserves to deposits can have a very disruptive impact on commercial bank operations unless banks are given sufficient time to adjust.

Credit Ceilings

In some countries, such as Indonesia from 1947 to 1983 and at various times Malaysia, Sri Lanka, and Chile, credit ceilings have been used as supplementary instruments of inflation control. Indeed the International Monetary Fund often requires countries seeking balance-of-payments support to adopt credit ceilings as a prerequisite for IMF assistance. General ceilings of domestic credit expansion represent a useful method of controlling growth in domestic components of the money supply. Credit ceilings, however, do not allow full control of money supply growth in the overwhelming majority of developing countries operating under fixed-exchange-rate regimes, since the monetary authorities have no control over foreign components of the money supply. Nevertheless general credit ceilings can sometimes be usefully deployed in combating inflation in countries not experiencing major imbalances in external payments. Unfortunately, ceilings work best where they are needed the least, since countries attempting to deal with chronic inflation are usually the same countries that are experiencing the most destabilizing changes in their international reserve positions. Finally, general credit ceilings are unlikely to have much effect on inflation unless the government simultaneously takes steps to reduce the budgetary deficits that—except in major oil exporting countries—are typically the root causes of chronic, acute, and especially runaway inflation.

Countries often supplement general credit ceilings with specific ceilings on lending to particular sectors of the economy. Indonesia attempted to fine-tune credit controls in this way from 1974 to 1983, with poor results. The system of ceilings was so detailed and cumbersome that domestic banks were unable to come close to exhausting the ceilings. Excess reserves arose. The banks had little choice but to place their excess reserves in deposits overseas, primarily in banks in Singapore. As a result, many domestic firms in Jakarta were forced to seek

19. In its simplest form the money multiplier *(m)* can be expressed as:

$$m = (c + 1)/(c + k)$$

where c = the ratio of currency outside banks to deposits and k = the ratio of reserves to deposits. If k is raised, then m falls.

credit from Singapore banks, which held well over a billion dollars of deposits from Jakarta banks that might have lent to domestic firms at a lower rate in the absence of credit ceilings.

Interest Rate Regulation and Moral Suasion

In most industrial countries the central bank can influence interest rates by varying the *rediscount rate* charged on central bank loans to commercial banks that require additional liquidity. Because the rediscount rate is central to commercial banks' operations, it is important in determining the market rate of interest on both deposits and loans. As more developing countries adopt financial reforms that free interest rates from central bank control, they are better able to use the rediscount rate as a tool for influencing market interest rates.

In developing countries that have controlled rates on loans and deposits, the controlled rates have been instruments of anti-inflationary packages. Since 1973 the use of such interest rate adjustments has been common in Latin America, and increases in deposit rates and loan rates were major elements in stabilization programs in South Korea and Taiwan in the mid-1960s and in Indonesia in both 1968 and 1974. The objective in each case was twofold: to stimulate the demand for liquid assets and to discourage the loan demand for marginal investment projects on the part of private-sector borrowers. The extent to which such measures can be successful depends on the interest elasticity of the demand for liquid assets and the interest elasticity of the demand for loans. In most of the cases cited above, and particularly in the three Asian countries, both sets of elasticities were evidently sufficiently high, as the stabilization packages did succeed to a large degree.

Moral suasion by the monetary authorities, sometimes called "open-mouth operations" or "jawbone control," is practiced no less extensively in developing than in developed countries. Warnings and exhortations to commercial banks to restrict lending or to encourage them to focus lending on particular activities have been quite common in Ghana and were used at various times in Malaysia, Singapore, Brazil, and elsewhere, sometimes prior to the imposition of credit ceilings and often to reinforce pressures on banks to adhere to ceilings. In both developed and developing countries, however, moral suasion has proven credible only when accompanied by forceful use of more tangible instruments of monetary control.

15

Foreign Capital and Debt

Countries that are unable to generate sufficient domestic saving to finance economic growth have historically sought resources from other countries. The United States relied heavily on foreign saving, particularly during the antebellum period from 1835 to 1860. Likewise, Russia needed foreign saving to propel its development in the three decades before World War I and the communist revolution. Yet Japan became a modern nation even though it actively discouraged inflows of foreign saving and investment throughout its history. Foreign saving can help development but is not essential for it. Most developing countries still consider foreign saving to be an important ingredient in their development efforts. But controversy surrounds foreign aid, foreign investment, and the debt that has accrued from foreign borrowing. This chapter examines the roles of foreign saving in development and explores some of these controversies.

The concept of foreign saving can be approached from two different directions. Foreign saving can finance the amount by which investment exceeds domestic saving, $F = I - S$. Alternatively, foreigners can finance the trade deficit, which is the amount by which imports exceed exports, $F = M - E$. Because of the way gross domestic or gross national product is measured, foreign saving must be the same whichever definition we use.[1]

Table 15–1 places foreign saving in the context of the balance of payments, consistent with the second definition above. Receipts represent payments of foreign exchange to people or institutions inside the home country; expenditures are payments by the country to the outside world. By far the largest source of receipts for most countries is exports, while the largest expenditure is for imports. If we

1. This equivalence was discussed in Chapter 6; see Equations 6–5 and 6–7.

TABLE 15–1 Foreign Saving and the Balance of Payments for Developing Countries (approximate 1992 magnitudes in billion U.S. dollars)

	Receipts (+)	Expenditures (−)
1. Trade in goods and nonfactor services*	Exports = 1190	Imports = 1240
2. *Net resource transfer*	*Inflow = 50*	
3. Income payments†	Earned = 80	Paid = 140‡
4. Trade in goods and all services (1 + 3)	Exports = 1270	Imports = 1380
5. *Net resource flow (net foreign saving)*	*Inflow = 110*	
6. Repayment of principal on debt		Repaid = 100
7. Total payments (4 + 6)	Received = 1270	Paid = 1480
8. *Gross resource flow (gross foreign saving)*	*Inflow = 210*	

*Nonfactor services include freight, transportation, insurance, professional fees, and tourism.
†Factor services include dividends, interest, and wages.
‡Of which interest payments on foreign debt = $74 billion.
Sources: IMF, *Balance of Payments Statistics Yearbook 1993,* Vol. 44, Part 2, p. 26, and World Bank, *World Debt Tables 1994–1995,* Vol. 1, p. 170.

consider only trade in goods and services, excluding income payments (interest, dividends, and wages) to and from foreign sources, then the trade balance represents the **net resource transfer** (line 2 of the table). This is the contribution that foreign saving makes to development in goods and services that cannot be financed by exports. In Table 15–1, this is a net inflow of $50 billion to the developing countries in 1992.

If instead we include income receipts and payments as part of exports and imports, the trade balance is the **net resource flow** (line 5), an inflow of $110 billion in 1992. This concept of net foreign saving suggests that foreign resources finance goods and services for development (net transfers) as well as the payments of interest and dividends on earlier flows of foreign capital. Net resource flow can also be measured as the inflow of capital net of repayments of principal on loan obligations incurred by the home country. Adding debt principal repayments to the net flows would yield *gross resource transfer* (or gross foreign saving, line 8), $210 billion in 1992.

Foreign saving includes both official saving and private saving. Most **official saving** is on **concessional terms**, made available either as *grants* (outright gifts) or as *"soft" loans,* bearing lower interest rates and longer repayment periods than would be available in private international capital markets. Governments also make some loans on commercial terms, including export credits, equity investments, and *"hard" loans* from the World Bank and regional development banks.[2] Concessional flows are technically called **official development assistance** (ODA), but are popularly called **foreign aid**. Aid can be further divided into *bilateral aid,* given directly by one government to another, and *multilateral aid,* in

2. The regional development banks include the Asian, African, and Inter-American Development Banks and others. Most of these are patterned on the World Bank. International development banks are described below.

which the funds flow to international agencies like the United Nations, the World Bank, and the regional development banks, which in turn grant or lend the funds to recipient developing countries. Finally, aid can be in the form of *technical assistance,* the provision of skilled individuals to augment national expertise, or *capital assistance,* the provision of finance or commodities for a variety of purposes discussed later in this chapter.

Foreign private saving consists of four elements. *Foreign direct investment* is made by nonresidents, typically but not always by multinational corporations, in enterprises located in host countries; direct investment implies full or partial control of the enterprise and physical presence by foreign firms or individuals. *Portfolio investment* is the purchase of host country bonds or stocks by foreigners, without managerial control. This was a very important form of foreign investment in the nineteenth and early twentieth centuries, but fell into disuse after World War II. Portfolio investment has revived, however, as rich-country investors show interest in emerging stockmarkets, especially in Asia and increasingly in Latin America. *Commercial bank lending* to developing country governments and enterprises supplanted portfolio investment in importance for a time, but waned with the debt crisis of the 1980s, discussed later in this chapter. Finally, exporting firms, their commercial banks, and official banks offer *export credits* to importing countries as a way of promoting sales by permitting delayed payment for imports, often at commercial interest rates.

From 1970 to 1992, total net resource flows more than doubled in constant prices, a growth rate of 4.1 percent a year (Table 15–2). The net resource flow of

TABLE 15–2 Net Resource Flows to Developing Countries, 1970 to 1992 (billion U.S. dollars)

	1970*	1986	1992
Official development finance	12.1	44.0	54.6
Official grants	8.1†	16.0	34.5
Debt forgiveness	n.a.	0.3	2.0
Official loans	4.0‡	28.0	20.1
Bilateral	3.3	12.8	7.9
Multilateral	0.7	15.2	12.2
Private finance	7.0	19.9§	102.1§
Commercial bank loans	3.0	1.8	18.5
Portfolio investment	0.3	1.4	19.4
Foreign direct investment	3.7	10.1	47.3
Total net resource flow	19.1	63.9	156.6‖
Value of technical assistance	n.a.	8.7	16.3
Total with technical assistance	19.1	72.6	172.9
(In constant 1992 dollars)**	71.0	84.1	172.9

*Figures for 1970 are from a different source than the other years and may not be exactly comparable.
†Includes technical assistance and concessional loans.
‡Nonconcessional loans only.
§This sum is greater than the identified components because not all components are shown in the original source.
‖The total for net resource flow differs from that in Table 15–1, line 5, although the concept is the same. Table 15–1 is based on estimates from the recipient countries' balance-of-payments accounts, while Table 15–2 is based on reports from the donor countries. Reconciliation of such balance-of-payments data between countries is notoriously difficult and subject to large margins of error.
**Deflated using the import unit value index for developing countries from IMF, *International Financial Statistics Yearbook 1994.*
Sources: World Bank, *World Debt Tables 1994–1995,* pp. 10, 170 (1986 and 1992), and Development Assistance Committee, *Development Cooperation in the 1990s* (Paris: OECD, 1989), p. 150 (1970).

$157 billion in 1992 was equivalent to 3.3 percent of gross domestic product for the developing countries, a decline from almost 4 percent in 1970, and to roughly $34 per person. Official finance has grown very little in real terms since 1986, while private finance has recovered impressively from its depressed levels of the mid-1980s. Although official flows made up two-thirds of the total in 1986, their share had fallen to one-third by 1992. Direct investment accounted for over half of all private flows in 1992. However, during the intervening years commercial bank lending played a more important role: in the early 1980s it accounted for 70 percent of private resource flows, but then dried up as the debt crisis eroded international banks' confidence and profits.

Foreign Aid

Historical Role

Foreign aid as now conceived is a product of the post-World War II era. Its roots are in the Marshall Plan, under which the United States transferred $17 billion over four years, equivalent to about 1.5 percent of U.S. GNP, to help rebuild Europe after the war. Two elements of the Marshall Plan were believed at the time to have been crucial for its success: an influx of financial capital from the United States and coordinated plans to employ it productively to rebuild Europe's devastated physical capital stock.

The two decades after World War II saw the emergence of independent nations from Europe's colonies, especially in Asia and Africa. Encouraged by the success of Marshall Plan aid in rebuilding Europe, the United States took the lead in trying to help the newly emerging nations by providing that same element, capital, in the form of foreign aid, especially to countries that had development plans for investing the aid they received. Early aid programs also recognized that developing countries lacked certain kinds of skills and expertise, so donors also offered technical assistance programs, which supplied foreign experts in fields from economic planning to engineering to construction.

The motives behind the U.S. aid programs of the postwar years were complex and ranged from the selfish to the generous. The security of the United States was the center of Congress' concerns in approving both the Marshall Plan and the Point IV program, under which President Truman began to shift U.S. attention and resources toward the developing countries. This meant "containing communism" around the perimeter of the Soviet bloc as well as trying to ensure access to raw materials needed for U.S. industry. The prosperity of both the United States and its allies required expanding trade and investment, also promoted by aid. It was believed that development would serve both security and economic interests by reducing instability and giving the emerging nations a stake in the capitalist world order. The U.S. aid policy was also intended to encourage the new countries to maintain or adopt democratic political institutions and private-enterprise-based economies in the U.S. image. There was as well a core of humanitarian concern for the welfare of the world's poor. Indeed the strength of the early aid programs depended on this mixture of nationalistic and altruistic motives, which drew political support from a wide spectrum of opinion.

In the early postwar years of aid, the United States, the United Kingdom, and

France were the most important contributors; the latter two contributed mainly to their former colonies. As the other industrial countries began to recover and prosper, however, some of them became important donors. Table 15–3 shows net official development assistant from the countries of the Organization for Economic Cooperation and Development (OECD), including bilateral aid and contributions to multilateral organizations, from 1965 to 1992.[3] Although many OECD donors, including several not shown in the table, have increased their aid efforts substantially, on the whole the aid effort of the OECD countries declined substantially. The main culprits were the United Kingdom and especially the United States, whose aid effort shrank from 0.6 to 0.2 percent of GNP over these years. Rapid economic growth has helped Japan to become as large a donor as the United States. Over this period, also, the multilateral agencies, especially the World Bank, became important dispensers of capital. By 1992, the multilateral share of official loans had reached 61 percent, or 22 percent of all official development finance.

As the flow of aid expanded and more countries and multilateral agencies became important players, the economic development rationale for aid changed as well. During the 1950s the main economic goal was rapid growth of output and incomes, to be achieved by increasing the amount of domestic and foreign saving available for investment. By the 1960s the two-gap model, described in Chapter 6, augmented the Harrod–Domar perspective and foreign exchange became as important as capital. Human capital received emphasis beyond the recognized role of technical assistance, and aid programs spread into education, health, and other human services. During the late 1960s and the 1970s aid programs began to incorporate goals other than the promotion of economic growth: income redistribution, poverty alleviation, satisfaction of basic needs, and rural development became motivators for the aid programs of most donors. In the 1980s and early 1990s, the

TABLE 15–3 Net Official Development Assistance (Disbursements) from the OECD Countries to Developing Countries and Multilateral Agencies, 1965–1991

	Percent of GNP		Bn. U.S. $
Source	1965	1991	1991
Canada	0.19	0.45	2.6
France	0.76	0.62	7.5
Germany*	0.40	0.41	6.9
Italy	0.10	0.30	3.3
Japan	0.27	0.32	10.9
Netherlands	0.36	0.88	2.5
Sweden	0.19	0.92	2.1
United Kingdom	0.47	0.32	3.2
United States	0.58	0.20	11.2
OECD total	0.48	0.33	55.5†

*West Germany only in 1965; unified Germany in 1992.
†Table 15–3 counts disbursements as they are made by the donor countries to the developing countries and to multilateral agencies; Table 15–2 counts disbursements as they are received by the developing countries from both the bilateral and multilateral agencies. This difference in treatment helps to explain the slight difference in total ODA for 1988.
Source: World Development Report 1994, Table 18.

3. The OECD include the industrial countries of Western Europe, Canada, Japan, and the United States.

trends described in Chapter 5 led donors, particularly the World Bank, to focus more on macroeconomic stabilization and structural adjustment as goals of aid. More recently, environmental sustainability and democratization have become important aims of donors.

The 1992 total of official development finance, $55 billion from Table 15–2, is equivalent to 1.2 percent of GDP for the recipient low- and middle-income countries, or about $12 per capita. However, there are major and moderately systematic variations around this rather low average, as Table 15–4 reveals. First, there is a strong tendency for donors to use scarce concessional aid in favor of the poorest countries: aid represents a higher fraction of GNP for poorer countries in Table 15–4.

Some of the exceptions to this rule point to a second strong tendency. Among the 15 countries with lowest incomes, four of most populous have very low aid-GNP ratios: India, China, Pakistan, and Nigeria. Donors, faced with a choice of spreading their aid proportionally (to GNP or population) and thus having scant impact anywhere, or concentrating it where they can make a larger impact, choose the latter. Small countries thus get greater relative amounts of aid than do large countries.

Finally, Table 15–4 includes some examples of countries that are favored for political and strategic reasons. Mali and Senegal benefit disproportionately, as do

TABLE 15–4 Net Receipts of Official Development Assistance (ODA) by Selected Developing Countries, 1991

Country	GNP per capita ($)*	Net ODA: Mn. U.S. dollars	Net ODA: Percent of GNP*	Net ODA: Dollars per capita
Ethiopia	340	1091	17	21
Mali	500	455	19	52
Tanzania	630	1076	34	43
India	1210	2747	1	3
Bangladesh	1230	1636	7	15
Kenya	1360	873	11	35
Senegal	1750	577	10	76
Ghana	1890	724	10	47
China	1910	1954	0	2
Sri Lanka	1970	814	9	47
Pakistan	2130	1226	3	11
Nigeria	2160	262	1	3
Bolivia	2270	473	9	64
Philippines	2440	1051	2	17
Indonesia	2970	1854	2	10
Guatemala	3370	197	2	21
Egypt	3670	4988	15	93
Brazil	5260	182	0	1
Colombia	5760	123	0	4
Mexico	7490	1185	0	2
Malaysia	8050	289	1	16
South Korea	8950	54	0	1

*In this column, 0 means less than 0.5 percent.
Source: World Development Report 1994, Table 19.

all francophone African states, from France's generous aid program. Egypt, along with Israel, has been favored by the United States' involvement in the Middle East. Bolivia, both small and poor by Latin American standards, receives considerable U.S. aid to help suppress the cocaine trade. During the 1950s and 1960s, South Korea, Taiwan, Pakistan, Turkey, and other allied governments were favored recipients of U.S. aid. Although the manifestations of politically inspired aid are strongest in these cases, they are present to some extent in many other countries.

Aid Institutions and Instruments

Bilateral aid donors usually plan and dispense loans and grants through an aid agency, such as the United States Agency for International Development (USAID), Britain's Overseas Development Administration (ODA), the International Development Agencies of Canada (CIDA) and Sweden (SIDA), and others. The main **multilateral aid** agencies are the World Bank, the International Monetary Fund, the regional development banks, and the United Nations.

The largest and most influential of the multinationals is the **World Bank** (International Bank for Reconstruction and Development, or IBRD), together with its affiliates, the International Development Association (IDA) and the International Finance Corporation (IFC). Despite its leading role in the aid community, most of the capital supplied by the World Bank is not aid. The IBRD obtains its funds by borrowing on world capital markets at prevailing prime interest rates and relends to developing countries at slightly higher rates. It makes more capital available and at lower interest rates than could be obtained by the developing countries on their own. Its affiliate, the IFC, lends on commercial terms and takes minority equity positions in support of private foreign investments. Only the IDA, which channels contributions from the richer member countries to the poorer countries on very soft terms, dispenses aid in the strict sense. During the 1970s the World Bank became the world's leading center for research, information, and policy advice on economic development. In 1992 the World Bank group disbursed $15.6 billion in loans and concessional aid; when loan repayments to the Bank are included, however, the net resource flow was only $4.9 billion, 9 percent of total official development finance.[4]

The word "reconstruction" in the bank's title stems from its origin, at the Bretton Woods (New Hampshire) conference in 1944, when its first task was to help finance the reconstruction of war-torn European countries. The other institution founded at the conference was the **International Monetary Fund** (IMF), whose main charge was to reestablish an international system of national currencies in stable relation to each other, in support of a rejuvenated world trade system. The IMF played a significant role in the unprecedented expansion of world trade during the 1950s and 1960s. Although not primarily concerned with promoting development, IMF practices and resources have had a major effect on developing countries, and the Fund has increasingly turned its attention toward assisting them by offering balance-of-payments support in a variety of ways.

Each of the developing world's continents—Asia, Africa, and Latin America—has its own **regional development bank**. These each have separate "win-

4. World Bank, *World Debt Tables 1994–1995*, p. 171.

dows" that dispense hard and soft loans to member countries. Regional members and the major aid donors contribute to the capital of these banks, which also borrow on private capital markets to finance hard loans and receive contributions from aid donors for their soft loan windows. Other multilateral donors include the European Union (EU) and the Arab countries of the Organization of Petroleum Exporting Countries (OPEC). The EU originally concentrated its aid on the former French colonies in Africa, but now spreads its assistance more widely, especially in Africa. Arab OPEC, which was especially active during the late 1970s and early 1980s when oil prices were high, concentrates its assistance on Islamic states.

The United Nations has a concessional program, $1.5 billion of technical assistance in 1992.[5] This effort is coordinated by the United Nations Development Programme (UNDP), which makes grants to member countries. However, the specialized agencies of the United Nations, such as the U.N. Industrial Development Organization (UNIDO), International Labor Organization (ILO), and World Health Organization (WHO), among others, execute the technical assistance projects financed by UNDP.

Development assistance agencies deal with a wide range of aid instruments, both technical and capital assistance. Most of the capital aid is disbursed against specific projects, such as hydroelectric dams, roads, or rural development projects, and is called **project aid**. However, some bilateral agencies have made **program loans**, which finance general categories of imports and are conceived as broad support for the balance of payments. *Structural adjustment loans,* made especially by the World Bank to support economic reforms as described in Chapter 5, are program loans. *Food aid* is a kind of bilateral program loan since it provides commodities, mostly grains, that would otherwise have to be purchased with a country's own foreign exchange earnings.

Aid and Development

In a world of neoclassical growth, explained in Chapter 3, we can measure the contribution of aid and other foreign saving to development. In this model the role of foreign saving of all kinds is to augment domestic saving to increase investment and thus accelerate growth. If aid and other foreign saving added, say, 6 percent of GDP; if all of it went to additional investment; if the capital-output ratio were 3.0; and if the share of GNP earned by capital were 50 percent; then the growth rate would be increased by 1 percentage point.[6]

A glance at Table 15–4 shows that for some countries—Ethiopia, Mali, Tanzania, and Egypt—foreign saving is a large fraction of GDP and could be contributing 2.5 percent or more to the growth rate in this simple neoclassical

5. United Nations Development Programme, *1992 UNDP Annual Report* (New York: UNDP Division of Public Affairs, 1993), p. 24.

6. From Equation 3–6, $g_Y = a + w_K g_K + w_L g_L + w_T g_T$. An increase in the growth of the capital stock dg_K would cause an increase in the growth of GNP, $dg_Y = w_K dg_K$. How much does foreign aid contribute to the growth of the capital stock? If all of it were invested, then $dg_K = S_f/K = (S_f/Y)(Y/K)$. We know that the aid share in GNP, S_f/Y, is .06 and the capital-output ratio, K/Y, is 3, so $dg_K = .02$. If w_K, the share of capital income in GNP, is 50 percent, then this 2 percent increase in the annual growth of the capital stock adds $dg_Y = w_K dg_K = 0.5(.02) = .01$, or 1 percent, to the annual growth of income. In the Harrod-Domar model, where capital is the only input, its income share is 100 percent and foreign aid at 6 percent of GNP would add 2 percent a year to growth.

world. For countries like India, China, Indonesia, Mexico, and Brazil, foreign saving is a small fraction of GDP and could not have much impact on growth. In fact, there is no strong correlation across countries between aid receipts (as a share of GNP) and economic growth; this suggests the limitations of the neoclassical model. Developing countries may of course lack some important complementary inputs to development, such as human skills, administrative capacity, infrastructure, economic institutions, and political stability, without which even high saving rates may not stimulate growth. In addition, some economists have argued that foreign aid may not contribute much to additional savings or imports, but could be used instead to finance higher consumption or to reduce exports.

Figure 15–1 shows why these doubters are at least partly correct. A developing country, before it obtains aid, can produce consumption goods and capital goods along the production possibilities frontier *P*. To simplify, the diagram ignores international trade. Community tastes are defined by a set of indifference curves, of which two, labeled I and II, are shown. Without aid the country's welfare is maximized if it produces and consumes at point *A*, where the indifference curve I is tangent to the frontier *P*, with consumption at C_1 and investment at I_1. Now donor countries contribute an amount *AB* of aid. They intend that the full amount should be invested, and raise total investment to I_2. However, the offer of aid *AB* in effect moves the production frontier outward from *P* to *P′*.[7] With these

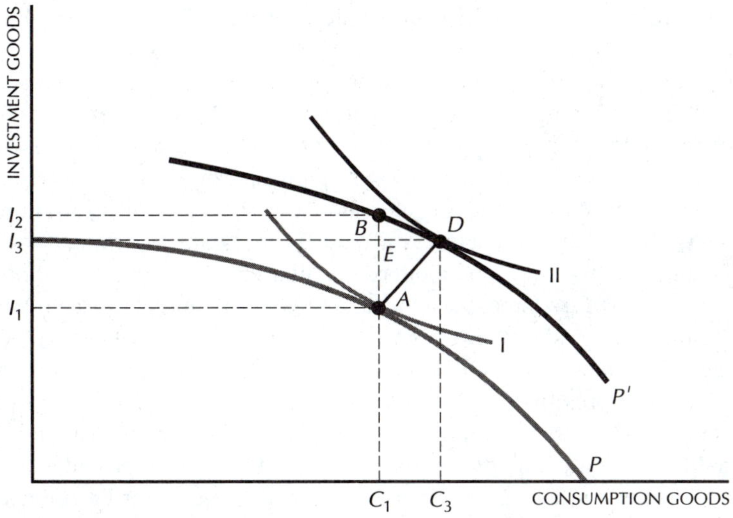

FIGURE 15–1 Impact of Aid on Investment and Consumption. Foreign aid totaling *AB* turns into actual new investment of only *AE*, because the country maximizes welfare on the new frontier, *P′*, at point *D*, not *B*. *P′* is not really a "production" frontier, but a "supply" frontier; see footnote 7.

Source: Adapted from Paul Mosley, "Aid, Savings and Growth Revisited," *Oxford Bulletin of Economics and Statistics* 42, (May 1980), 79–91.

7. The purist will worry about this shift in the production frontier. It is not production that has been increased, but the supply of goods through additional imports, financed by aid. Graphically this is equivalent to an outward shift in the frontier, in the same sense that additional income shifts the budget line outward for an individual consumer. Strictly speaking, however, the production frontier in Figure 15–1 remains *P*.

added resources the country maximizes its welfare by producing at point *D*, the tangency between *P*′ and indifference curve I_2. It consumes C_3 and invests I_3. Of the aid amount *AB*, *AE* (equal to $I_3 - I_1$) has been invested, as intended by the donors, but *BE* (equal to $I_2 - I_3$) has been consumed. If the country's tastes favored consumption over investment even more, then it would reach equilibrium at a point along *P*′ to the southeast of *D* and would convert even more of its aid into consumption.

The diagram demonstrates that the amount of aid actually used to increase investment rather than consumption will depend on production possibilities, community tastes, and other variables left out of the figure, such as trade. How can a country convert aid and other foreign savings, which are intended to be used for investment, into consumption? Some forms of foreign savings, such as program aid or commercial bank loans, are designed to provide finance for general purposes and thus deliberately give the recipient the kinds of choices demonstrated in Figure 15–1. Food aid, of course, is intended to increase or maintain consumption rather than investment. But even if all foreign savings were dispensed as project aid and targeted to specific investment projects, substitution would be possible. Project aid might, for example, be used for investments that the government or its private investors would have made even without aid. In that case resources are freed up for other purposes, including consumption. When aid finances projects that might not otherwise be implemented, a government may simply cut back on preferred projects because it wants to raise the share of consumption, for economic or political reasons. When substitutions of these kinds are possible, aid is called *fungible.*

Perhaps more important, a host of subtle influences of foreign saving on relative prices may also contribute to substitution. More capital in general could conceivably mean lower returns on investments and hence a greater tendency to consume in the recipient countries. More foreign exchange tends to lower its price (that is, to appreciate the exchange rate) and cause greater demand for imports, as intended by donors, but also creates a reduced incentive to produce for export, which is not intended. And food aid has a similar effect; it lowers food prices because it satisfies part of domestic demand, and hence reduces the incentive for domestic farmers to produce grains and other foods. These influences could be overcome by countervailing government policies, but governments may not undertake such measures for a variety of reasons. In sum, the contribution of aid and other foreign savings to development is not that they provide specific amounts of additional investment, imports, or food. Rather, foreign aid provides additional purchasing power and thus gives recipient governments and citizens more room to choose between consumption and investment, more imports and less exports, more food consumption or less food production, and so forth.

Additional macroeconomic resource flows are not the only mechanism by which donors try to enhance development, however. Aid can have four other kinds of influences on a country's development. First, most capital assistance goes to specific projects. Donors frequently use project aid to give special attention to particular sectors or kinds of activities, hoping to improve practices in those areas and to initiate developments that eventually become self-sustaining. Investment in wheat and rice production was a high priority for project aid during the late 1960s, for example, especially in Asia, while rural development projects were emphasized during the 1970s. It had become evident that neglect of rural investment had, in many countries, slowed economic growth and made it difficult to reduce poverty. Foreign assistance played a major role in spreading the Green Revolution, which delivered new seed varieties for wheat and rice, together with a "package" of inputs including fertilizers, pesticides, and water, and made countries such as India and Indonesia much less vulnerable to famine and better able to promote widespread economic development. The World Bank reports that, of 112 rural development projects surveyed in 1989, 63 earned at least 10 percent a year; the overall rate of return was 17 percent.[8] Although horror stories about failed aid projects are common enough, these and other examples suggest that project assistance can have a beneficial impact.

A second avenue to influence development is **technical assistance**. In 1992, technical assistance was valued at 30 percent of financial assistance (Table 15–2). Although the United Nations is perhaps the largest provider of technical assistance, all donors supply it to some extent. They provide experts in fields as diverse as agronomy, computer programming, economics, education, engineering, forestry, geology, law, management, medicine, and public health. Foreign experts are sent to perform jobs for which local professionals are not qualified or are in short supply. Technical assistance is not always effective. In the best cases, however, expatriate professionals become agents of change when they put new systems in place, influence local professionals to try new or improved ways of performing tasks, train local professionals, and help build new development institutions.

The third route for aid to influence development is through **conditionality**, the attempt by aid donors to use their assistance as a lever to influence policy in recipient countries. Some conditions tied to assistance do not advance development. Donors offer aid to reward political friends and military allies, and withhold it from those perceived as enemies. They tie aid funds to the purchase of goods and services in their own countries as a way of increasing their own markets for exports and of dampening the impact of aid on their own balance of payments. They channel it toward countries and institutions that adhere most closely to the donor's own views of economics and politics. These are perhaps the crassest uses of aid and they are generally confined to bilateral donors.

But donors, both bilateral and multilateral, also use aid to induce recipient governments to change their development policies in what donors believe to be the recipients' own best interests. Chapter 5 discussed donors' conditioning of aid on economic reforms such as currency devaluation, market liberalization, changes in tax systems, adoption of new wage and income policies, adjustments in food and other agricultural prices, and many other policy actions. To the extent that host governments acquiesce to such changes, policy leverage may be as important a contribution of aid programs to development as the resource flows they finance. It is an open question, however, whether donors can do more than push governments in directions they already wish to go. If host governments wish to resist conditions attached to aid, they have ways of appearing to accept conditions, but then not implementing them fully; and donors have reasons to continue offering their aid even if conditions are not met.

The fourth way that aid influences development is the most diffuse but perhaps

8. World Bank, "International Factors Reducing Poverty: Aid and Poverty," *World Development Report 1990,* p.131.

the most powerful. The international aid establishment directly and indirectly supports a large group of their own expert staff, university scholars, professional consultants, aid administrators, and others, from both the industrial and developing countries, who conceive and eventually popularize new ways of thinking about development issues. This diverse group has, over time, influenced the way developing-country scholars and policy makers think about many issues including economic reform, trade strategy, fiscal policy, rural development, and so on. Once this general and diffuse influence changes the minds of policy makers, foreign aid becomes far more effective in serving national development strategies because its basic premises are shared by recipients and donors.[9]

Foreign Investment and the Multinationals

Since the mid-1980s, developing countries have increasingly sought **foreign direct investment**; by 1992 it had grown sufficiently to account for 30 percent of the total net foreign resource flow (Table 15–1). Direct investment still generates much controversy, however. Its influence is magnified because foreign investment comes in a package that may include not only equity finance, but often much larger amounts of loan finance, management expertise, modern technologies, technical skills, and access to world markets. Indeed, it is often the nonfinancial elements of the investment package that are most desired by developing countries. Moreover, this package is controlled by multinational corporations, whose size and control over resources often match and sometimes outstrip that of the recipient country governments. Investment by a multinational corporation raises the specter of interference by, and dependence on, foreign economic powers beyond the control of the host country. This section examines the basis for these fears and the potential benefits and costs of foreign investment.

Multinationals' Investment Patterns

The overwhelming proportion of direct foreign investment in third-world countries is done by **multinational corporations** (MNCs); *transnational corporations* (TNCs) is an alternative term. A multinational is an enterprise that produces in more than one country and considers overseas operations to be central to its profitability. Multinational enterprises come in all sizes and from all regions of the world, including the developing countries, but a relatively small number are dominant. In 1980 roughly 10,000 MNCs were in existence, exercising control over nearly 90,000 foreign affiliates.[10] But only 500 of these firms accounted for 80 percent of the world's stock of direct foreign investment in that year.

Most multinationals are based in the industrial countries. By the end of the 1980s, over 95 percent of the yearly outward flow of foreign investment—almost $240 billion in 1990—was from rich-country investors. Most multinational investment is also directed toward other wealthy countries: in the late 1980s, at least 70 percent of the outflow of direct foreign investment was from one industrial

9. For a comprehensive review of the impact of foreign aid on development, see Robert Cassen et al., *Does Aid Work?* (London: Oxford University Press, 1986).

10. John Stopford, *The World Directory of Multinational Enterprises 1982–83* (Detroit: Gale Research Company, 1982), p. 2.

country to another. Of the $159 billion of private foreign assets located in developing countries in 1985, half was in Latin America and close to a third in Asia.[11] Direct investment in developing countries comes from three dominant countries. Over a five-year period during the 1980s, 30 percent of the flow of direct investment into developing countries came from the United States, 21 percent from Japan, and 19 percent from the United Kingdom.[12]

Contrary to popular belief, multinational investment in developing countries does not consist largely of manufacturing firms searching for "cheap" foreign labor. Indeed, among the major investing countries, only Germany had more than a third of its developing country assets in the manufacturing sector in the 1980s. Mining and modern services are the other main destinations for MNC investment, and both are capital-intensive sectors. Smaller multinationals from Korea, Taiwan, and Hong Kong and other middle-income countries do, however, invest overseas in export-oriented manufacturing in such labor-intensive industries as textiles, footwear, sporting equipment, and electronics assembly.

Characteristics of Multinationals

Not very long ago, the word "multinational" implied a giant, private, U.S. manufacturing company with lots of overseas operations. Today, multinationals are a much more diverse group. Only 161 of the world's largest 500 companies were American in 1994, according to *Fortune* magazine; 128 of them were Japanese. Multinationals are not even necessarily from the industrial countries. Fifteen developing countries had companies in the top 500, including Korea (12 entries), South Africa (4), India (3), and Turkey (3).[13] Nor are multinationals always private firms; the top 500 includes a number of giant, state-owned companies producing petroleum and steel, especially from the developing countries.

Nor are multinationals always large; small companies, especially in East and Southeast Asia, have been investing overseas for many years. The largest of the multinationals, however, are very large indeed, as Table 15–5 shows. Many multinationals have worldwide sales and assets that exceed the GDPs of some large developing countries. General Motors, the largest MNC, had sales in 1992 equivalent to more than half the GDP of India and larger than the Turkish GDP. The sales of Toshiba, the twenty-fifth largest multinational, exceeded the GDP of Egypt, the twenty-fifth largest economy.[14]

Benefits of Foreign Investment

Viewed as a **transfer of capital** from rich to poor countries, foreign direct investment, which includes investment by multinationals, is of growing importance. Recall from Table 15–2 that direct investment was only 15 percent of total net resource flows in 1986, but had grown to 27 percent by 1992. Table 15–6 shows the

11. United Nations Centre on Transnational Corporations (UNCTNC), *Transnational Corporations in World Development* (New York: United Nations, 1988), pp. 24–25.

12. Thomas L. Brewer, "Foreign Direct Investment in Developing Countries," World Bank Working Paper WPS 712, June 1991, p. 9.

13. *Fortune*, July 25, 1994.

14. Sales, a measure of gross output, is not comparable to GDP, a measure of value-added or net output; and assets are a stock while GDP is a flow. Nevertheless, the size comparisons of Table 15–5 are indicative.

TABLE 15–5 The Size of Multinationals and of Developing Country Economies, 1992 (billion U.S. dollars)

Rank*	Company (Country)	Sales	Assets	Employees (1000s)
1	General Motors (U.S.)	133	191	750
10	Hitachi (Japan)	61	77	332
25	Toshiba (Japan)	37	49	173
100	International Paper (U.S.)	14	16	73
500	Orkla (Norway)	3	2	15
Largest developing country MNCs†				
18	Samsung (Korea)	50	48	189
41	Daewoo (Korea)	28	39	79
56	Petroleos de Venezuela	21	33	55
57	Pemex (Mexico)	21	50	125
87	Ssangyong (Korea)	15	12	24
89	Petrobras (Brazil)	15	20	56
		GDP 1992		
1	China	506		
5	India	215		
10	Turkey	100		
25	Egypt	34		
50	Guatemala	10		
100	Niger	2		

*Ranked according to sales. †Rank in Fortune 500.
Sources: Fortune, July 26, 1994, and *World Development Report 1994,* Table 3.

flow of direct investment to the largest recipients among the developing countries. With the exception of Brazil, every one of these countries saw a major rise in foreign investment from 1980 to 1992. Nevertheless, for only two of them—Malaysia and Nigeria—was direct investment substantially more than 2 percent of gross domestic product in 1992. Among developing countries there is a tendency for direct investment to flow toward countries with rich natural resources and higher per capita incomes, just the opposite of the tendency with foreign aid.

The contribution of multinationals to **employment creation** in developing countries is not impressive. Of total employment in all sectors, multinationals ac-

TABLE 15–6 Foreign Direct Investment in Largest Recipient Developing Countries, 1980 and 1992

	Million U.S. dollars		
	1980	1992	Share GDP, 1992 (%)
China	0	11,156	2.2
Mexico	2,156	5,366	1.6
Argentina	678	4,179	1.8
Malaysia	934	4,118	7.1
Thailand	190	2,116	1.9
Indonesia	180	1,774	1.4
Brazil	1,911	1,454	0.4
Nigeria	−740	897	3.0
Turkey	18	844	0.8

Source: World Development Report 1994, Table 22.

count for less than 1 percent up to 6 percent in most developing countries. The contribution of MNCs to employment is more impressive in manufacturing alone, ranging from 10 to 23 percent in Argentina, Bolivia, Brazil, and Colombia and reaching over 50 percent in Singapore and Senegal.[15]

The issue is not gross employment, however, but net employment. How many jobs have been created by multinationals that would not otherwise have been created? The answer turns on a subsidiary question: Do multinational firms use more or less labor-intensive techniques than domestic firms? The spotty empirical evidence on this issue is hardly convincing one way or the other. To the extent that multinationals invest in sectors, such as petrochemicals and metals, that are inherently capital-intensive, they will employ relatively fewer workers per unit of investment than domestic firms that work in more labor-intensive industries. But the relevant comparison is between foreign and domestic firms in the same industries. Some studies find that foreign firms, wedded to capital-intensive techniques developed in their home markets where labor is expensive, tend to use these less appropriate techniques in developing countries as well. Yet there are also examples of multinationals using more labor-intensive techniques than comparable domestic firms. Much appears to depend on the extent of competition: when multinationals invest in domestic markets protected from domestic or foreign competition, they can afford to import capital-intensive production techniques. When they produce for export, however, or when they enter competitive domestic markets, competitive pressures force both multinationals and domestic firms to employ the lowest-cost techniques, and this frequently means more labor-intensive methods.[16] So job creation may depend as much on the host country's policies as on the multinationals' practices.

A third major benefit expected from foreign investment is the **transfer of technology**, skills, and know-how. Because much of the world's research and development activity has been undertaken within large firms in North America, Europe, and Japan, firms from these areas are a potentially rich source of valuable information about innovative products, manufacturing processes, marketing methods, and managerial approaches. Smaller multinationals, particularly those from other developing countries, offer other kinds of technological benefits: successful adaptation to local conditions of older technology from developed countries and new, cost-saving innovations in small-scale manufacture. If this information is transplanted to host countries, innovation and adaptation can eventually become consistent with less future dependence on multinational investors.

For some kinds of operation, such as logging, many manufacturing activities, and open-pit mining, acquisition of new information and methods by host-country workers and supervisors requires only a basic educational background and a willingness to work in a modern, structured enterprise with clear standards for work schedules and work pace. But in other activities, particularly in natural-resource-based industries such as steelmaking, copper smelting, and chemical manufacturing, absorptive capacity depends on a locally available stock of more highly trained technical personnel such as chemical engineers, metallurgists, geologists, biologists, industrial economists, and experienced managers.

15. UNCTNC, *Transnational Corporations in World Development,* p. 529.

16. Joseph M. Grieco, "Foreign Investment and Development: Theory and Evidence," in Moran et al., *Investing in Development: New Roles for Foreign Capital?*, pp. 47–48.

A few developing countries, such as India and Mexico, have trained relatively large numbers of technical industrial personnel and are able to absorb new technologies across a broad spectrum. Other countries have made strong efforts to train technical personnel specifically to take over important foreign-owned industries. Venezuela trained petroleum engineers and managers who now successfully run that sector; South Korea used its first chemical fertilizer plant, built and operated by a foreign firm, to train Koreans who soon were operating several other nationally owned fertilizer plants; and Malaysia became capable not only of operating its own rubber industry, but of conducting its own research on new species and methods of cultivation. Yet most developing countries do not have sufficient cadres of technically educated people to manage complex industries, and only a few have the educational establishments needed to begin rectifying this shortage.

Perspectives on technology transfer differ markedly between multinationals and developing countries. The firms view their investments in production of technology as a continuing process which should earn financial returns just as any investment would. Host countries, however, are concerned primarily with access to existing knowledge, and with some justification regard past multinational investments in technology as sunk costs not requiring reimbursement. Public goods theory, as well as casual observation, tells us that multinationals will withhold information on technologies when they would not otherwise be able to appropriate the returns.

A fourth benefit sought from multinational investment is **managerial capacity**, without which access to technology is largely ornamental. To be sure, many developing countries have gifted entrepreneurs and innovators, including the market women in West African countries such as Ghana and Nigeria; clusters of industrialists in such Latin American cities as Monterey, Medellin, and Sao Paulo; the Gujaratis of India; and communities of Chinese and Indians who have long resided in developing countries from East Africa to Southeast Asia. Nevertheless, only a few developing countries possess sufficient numbers of managers capable of organizing and operating large industrial projects such as those undertaken by multinational firms, and virtually all are short of people with advanced training and experience in management. The number of MBAs and experienced managers in a single company such as IBM can rival the entire population of MBAs and other managers in even some well-endowed developing countries. Still, managers are created all the time in the most dynamic of the developing countries, and the multinationals in particular employ and train them. The growth of MNCs from the developing countries themselves attests to their growing competence in management.

A fifth benefit is **access to world markets**. Developing countries capable of producing at competitive costs often find it difficult to penetrate foreign markets. Many multinationals, particularly in natural resources, chemicals, and other heavy industries, are vertically integrated, oligopolistic firms, for which many transactions take place within the firm. In the early 1980s, over 60 percent of all imports by multinational manufacturers in the United States were from affiliates overseas, while almost 40 percent of exports were also within firms.[17] Multinationals developed preferential access to customers by fashioning and adhering to long-term

17. UNCTNC, *Transnational Corporations in World Development,* p. 93. The ratios for Great Britian and Japan are lower, 27 percent, covering all industries.

contracts in standardized products, such as petroleum, or by acquiring a reputation for delivering a specialized product of satisfactory quality on a reliable schedule, as in construction and engineering. Developing country firms often require years to overcome such marketing advantages of the multinationals, although it is increasingly being done by firms in East Asia and elsewhere.

These benefits of multinational investment have for decades been made available to host countries only as an **investment "package"** incorporating equity capital (that is, ownership and control), management, technology, and marketing. During the early 1970s the Firestone Tire Company, for example, owned a rubber plantation and a tire factory in Ghana. It supplied the equipment (and thus the technology) for both facilities, along with financing and top management. Rubber was sold to its own tire plants, either in Ghana or the United States. Such investment packages have traditionally been offered "all or nothing," in the probably correct belief that the whole is more valuable than the sum of its parts, and also as a means of protecting the most crucial element, patented technology.

In recent years, developing countries have made some progress in "unbundling" the package to capture more of its benefits for themselves. Some multinationals have seen benefits in avoiding the risks of equity participation and maximizing the profits on sales of unbundled technology, management, or marketing access. Different contractual forms have been developed to transfer elements of the old package to host countries, including joint ventures in which the foreign firm takes less than a majority partnership; agreements in the petroleum industry to share production rather than ownership; licensing technology, as in the Korean automobile industry; management contracts in which a foreign firm runs the enterprise but may have little or no equity share; franchising products and brands, as done by MacDonalds in the United States and worldwide; and turnkey projects that are handed over to the host country firm after being started up by a multinational, a form used in building electric power plants, for example.

Another much-used route has been gradually to take over the management and ownership of existing foreign investments as the host country's capacities increase. Harvard economist Raymond Vernon has called this the "obsolescing bargain," in recognition of the shift in negotiating strength that occurs once the foreign investment is in place and the host country increases its ability to operate the facility.[18] Through these and other means, industrializing countries such as Brazil, Mexico, India, Korea, and Taiwan have not only developed their own petrochemical industries, for example, but have themselves become suppliers of technology and management to less-advanced countries.[19]

Unbundling is not suitable in every case, however. Some countries have begun to reconsider arrangements in which multinationals make their profits on the provision of technology, management, or market access, but have little or no profit incentive to manage the firm productively and leave all the risks to host-country firms. This reconsideration is one factor that, together with growing burdens of foreign debt, has led developing countries to view multinational investment more tolerantly in recent years.[20]

18. Raymond Vernon, *Storm over the Multinationals: The Real Issues,* (Cambridge, Mass.: Harvard University Press, 1977), p. 151.

19. Charles P. Oman, "New Forms of Investment in Developing Countries," in Moran et al., *Investing in Development: New Roles for Private Capital?*, 131–55.

20. UNCTNC, *Transnational Corporations in World Development*, p. 71.

Policies toward Foreign Investment

Host governments use a range of restrictions and incentives to capture as much as possible of the expected benefits from foreign investment, including performance requirements, local ownership requirements, restrictions on profit repatriation, monopoly privileges, and tax holidays. **Performance requirements** are generally tailored to fit each industry. Multinationals that assemble cars and other vehicles are often forced to increase annually the share of local content in each vehicle, for example, while those entering mining may commit themselves to future investments in domestic minerals processing. Policies that make foreign firms utilize local personnel are aimed not only at job creation but also at increasing absorptive capacity for the transfer of technology from multinationals. Developing countries have tried to promote technology transfer by imposing standards requiring multinationals to import only the most-advanced capital equipment rather than used machinery. But such measures work against other development goals because older equipment is likely to be more labor-intensive and less costly to operate. Ecuador has imposed special taxes on multinationals to finance government research and development, while India has required firms to invest in local research and development activities.[21]

Many host countries, particularly in Latin America and Southeast Asia, have made it mandatory for foreign investors to sell a specified share of equity, usually 51 percent, to local partners to form **joint ventures**. Through local ownership requirements, host governments hope to appropriate technology, limit the repatriation of profits, and maintain local control. Host countries assume that local joint-venture partners will become capable of matching technological and managerial capacities with foreign firms. However, many local joint-venture partnerships are *pro forma* arrangements involving local elites close to the centers of political power with little interest in business matters. And parent multinationals are often more reluctant to allow diffusion of technology to joint ventures than to wholly owned subsidiaries. Even when joint ventures do succeed in asserting greater national control over foreign investments, Raymond Vernon stresses that if local owners, in buying out their foreign partners, pay a price fully commensurate with the earnings they expect to receive, then the net effect is an export of scarce capital to the foreign multinational.[22]

Other common restrictions include ceilings on repatriation of profits to the parent corporation and stiff taxes on profit remittances. In Colombia profits remitted by a firm to a parent abroad were at one time limited to 15 percent of the firm's Colombian investments; Brazil has at times limited remittances to 10 percent of registered capital. Other countries, such as Argentina and Ghana, with no explicit ceilings on profit repatriation, still limit repatriation through the administration of foreign exchange controls.

Restrictions on multinationals can increase the benefits to host countries only if they do not deter foreign firms from investing. To accompany these policy sticks, most developing countries also offer policy carrots, especially protection from competition and tax incentives. **Protection** includes tariffs and quotas to reduce

21. Jack N. Behrman and William A. Fischer, *Overseas R&D Activities of Transnational Corporations* (Cambridge, Mass.: Oelgeschlager, Gunn and Hain, 1980), pp. 107–9.

22. Vernon, *Storm over the Multinationals: The Real Issues*, p. 168.

imports of competing goods, and the outright grant of monopoly control over local markets. Monopoly positions in local markets are frequently sought and sometimes granted, for example, by Kenya, Zambia, and for a time, Indonesia to foreign rubber tire manufacturers. Because import protection and monopoly control create higher domestic prices and profits, they often result in higher direct transfers from host country consumers to the multinationals' foreign stockholders.

The transfer from local consumers to foreign stockholders is even higher if **income tax incentives** are used to induce investment by foreign firms. While the variety of such incentives is almost limitless, the most common is *income tax holidays,* which exempt firms from paying taxes on corporate income, usually for three to six years. Most countries would otherwise tax profits at rates from 35 to 50 percent. For tax holidays to help the multinationals, they must be creditable against income taxes due to their home country governments. Otherwise, if home countries tax firms on worldwide income, as all industrial countries except France do, then taxes forgone by the developing country would simply be transferred to tax revenues of the multinational's home country. Most industrial countries now permit their firms to take credit for tax holidays granted abroad through tax treaties negotiated between host- and home-country governments.

Still, there remains substantial doubt that developing countries do receive benefits commensurate with the costs of the tax revenues they forgo. Tax holidays can only help the foreign investor if its project is profitable to begin with. Most studies conclude that income tax holidays have only marginal effects on multinational investment decisions; they reward the multinationals for doing what they would have done in any case. This is especially true for firms intending to produce in protected domestic markets of the host countries. Export-oriented, labor-intensive, "footloose" industries, however, may be more sensitive to tax holidays and other incentives.[23] A prominent example is the electronics industry, which utilizes large amounts of unskilled labor to manufacture semiconductor chips, make integrated circuits, and assemble parts of products such as electronic calculators and computers in countries such as Malaysia, Thailand, and Ecuador. But even in this case, inducements like tax holidays probably play a secondary role to more basic factors such as a stable source of low-cost, unorganized labor, decent living conditions for managers and engineers, reliable international transportation and communications facilities, and freedom from government regulation.

The combination of monopoly rights and tax holidays can result in large benefits to foreigners with little gain to host countries, as illustrated in Figure 15–2. Consider a multinational firm that has received monopoly rights to manufacture automobile tires for a developing country market and has also received a five-year tax holiday. For simplicity, assume the monopolist can produce at constant marginal cost MC and hence constant average cost AC. If the tire industry were a competitive industry consisting of many firms or if imports were allowed into the country, then the supply curve of that industry would be identical to $MC = AC$. The price of tires would then be P_c and the output of tires would be Q_c, the output that equates marginal cost with demand (average revenue).

A profit-maximizing monopolist, however, determines the level of output Q_m,

23. Louis T. Wells, Jr., "Investment Incentives: An Unnecessary Debate," *The CTC Reporter,* 22 (Autumn 1986), 58–60, and Steven Guisinger et al., *Investment Incentives and Performance Requirements* (New York: Praeger, 1985).

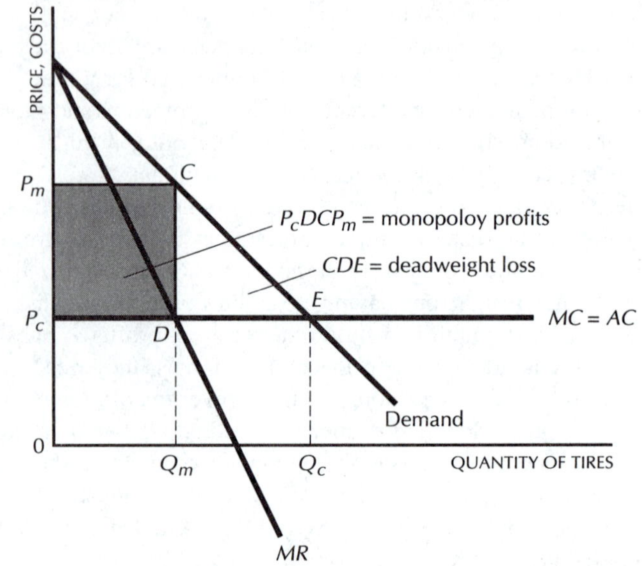

FIGURE 15–2 Interaction of Incentive Policies. A multinational subsidiary with monopoly rights and a tax holiday produces at Q_m instead of the competitive output Q_c. Consumers lose because they pay the monopoly price P_m rather than P_c. All monopoly profits P_cP_mCD are lost to the host country, until the tax holiday expires and the taxable portion of profits goes to the host country's treasury.

where marginal cost equals marginal revenue *MR*. Because Q_m is smaller than Q_c, it can be sold at a price of P_m, higher than the competitive price P_c. As a result, monopoly profits (rectangle P_cP_mCD) are generated, over and above "normal" (competitive) returns to capital. Consumers in the host country pay higher prices for fewer tires, and there is substantial economic waste (triangle *CDE,* the deadweight loss).[24] If the monopolist is a domestic firm, part of its profits will be taxed and there is a good chance that the after-tax portion will also remain available to the country. A foreign monopolist, however, is likely to repatriate its profits to the home country, and if it has a tax holiday, then all of area P_cP_mCD is lost to the country. After the tax holiday expires, tire consumers will continue to subsidize waste, but the host-country treasury will at least receive a share of the monopoly profits.

If strong incentives to attract multinational investors can cost the host country more than it gains, what are the alternatives? One approach, described in Chapter 5, would be to open up the economy to foreign trade as well as foreign investment, reduce government intervention in the domestic economy, and rely on market forces both to attract foreign investors and to regulate their behavior. Where market forces alone are deemed inadequate and some kind of protection is employed, then investment incentives should be reserved for potential export industries where clear performance targets can be established and where profits depend on efficient operation. A study by economists Dennis Encarnation and Louis Wells lends support to this strategy. They performed economic benefit-cost analyses on 50 foreign investment projects in a large Asian country, incorporating shadow prices and using the methods explained in Chapter 6. All of the export-

24. To interpret the meaning of triangle *CDE*, review Figure 13–1.

oriented projects had social rates of return above 10 percent, which they took to be the opportunity cost of capital. But in the four industries studied that were oriented to the protected domestic market, 30 to 70 percent of the projects were socially unprofitable, with rates of return below 10 percent. Moreover, the highest rates of failure were in most heavily protected industries.[25]

FOREIGN DEBT

The two forms of foreign saving discussed so far—foreign aid and foreign direct investment—both require repayment by the recipient country. Although technical assistance and some capital assistance come as grants, most foreign aid is in the form of loans on soft terms, on which interest payments are relatively low and repayment of principal is spread over many years. Direct investment carries the obligation to permit repatriation of dividends, but these are only earned on profitable investments. Except in severely distorted economies, profitable investments generate the resources needed to finance the repatriation of dividends. Three other forms of foreign saving have heavier burdens of repayment: export credits, portfolio loans, and commercial bank loans.

Commercial Borrowing

Of the three kinds of commercial borrowing, it was **commercial bank loans** that brought on the debt crisis of the 1980s. In the 1960s, commercial bank lending was a small if growing component of the resource transfer to developing countries. In 1970 it accounted for 16 percent of total net transfers (see Table 15–2). When OPEC raised prices in 1973–74 and again in 1979–80, the oil-producing states of the Middle East had large dollar surpluses to invest in world markets. One of their favorite investment outlets was bank deposits in the United States and Europe. The commercial banks, awash in "petrodollars," had to find profitable lending outlets and took renewed interest in lending to developing countries, especially those in South America and East Asia.

By 1983, annual commercial bank lending to developing countries had grown tenfold from its 1970 level, which represented at least a threefold expansion net of inflation. In 1983 the net value of commercial bank loans accounted for 37 percent of total net resource flows, and so exceeded foreign aid as a source of loan finance. The stock of accumulated debt owed by developing countries to commercial banks had expanded 17 times to $335 billion, more than half of all developing country debt (Table 15–7). In effect, the commercial banks channeled petrodollars from the wealthy oil exporters to the middle-income developing countries—a constructive form of intermediation for which they were applauded at the time.

The Repayment Crisis

In the early 1980s, borrowing countries, especially in Latin America, faced mounting debt and **debt service** (the payment of interest and principal). Latin

25. Dennis J. Encarnation and Louis T. Wells, Jr., "Evaluating Foreign Investment," in Moran et al., *Investing in Development: New Roles for Private Capital?*, pp. 61–85.

Table 15–7 Stocks of Long-Term Debt, All Developing Countries, 1970–1992 (billion U.S. dollars)

	1970	1983	1992
All sources	63	644	1308
Official creditors	32	221	666
Multilateral	7	80	239
(World Bank)	(2)	(37)	(98)
Bilateral	25	141	426
Commercial banks	20	335	248
Bonds	2	n.a.	141

Source: World Bank, *World Debt Tables 1994–1995,* Vol. 1, p. 171.

American countries' ratio of long-term debt to GNP rose from 18 percent in 1970 to 25 percent in 1980 and reached 60 percent during the mid-1980s (Table 15–8); the *debt service ratio,* which compares payments of principal and interest to earnings from the export of goods and services, was nearly 50 percent. In Argentina, debt service consumed 80 percent of export earnings; in Bolivia, Chile, and Mexico the ratio was between 50 and 60 percent.

These and other countries, not only in Latin America, began having difficulty generating sufficient government revenues and foreign exchange to service their debt. In the first half of 1982, eight countries had to reschedule their debt payments, compared to six reschedulings in all of 1981 and only three in 1978. In August 1982 Mexico declared a moratorium on the payment of interest on its foreign debt, and the debt crisis was in full cry. In 1985 there were 15 rescheduling packages and in 1987 more than 20 were concluded or negotiated. From 1983 to 1987, more than $300 billion of debt repayments had to be rescheduled.[26]

Table 15–8 Debt Ratios, Developing Countries, 1970–1988 (percent)

	1970	Maximum 1980–92	1992
All developing countries			
Long-term debt to GNP	14	43	29
Long-term debt to exports*	115	203	137
Total debt service to exports*	—	33	19
Latin America			
Long-term debt to GNP	18	60	32
Long-term debt to exports*	149	343	264
Total debt service to exports*	—	48	30
Debt service ratio† for:			
Argentina		80	65
Bolivia		60	39
Brazil		48	24
Chile		60	21
Mexico		54	44

*Exports of goods and services.
†Interest plus principal repayments as a percentage of exports of goods and services.
Source: World Bank, *World Debt Tables 1994–1995,* Vol. 1, p. 171, and First Supplement.

26. Rudiger Dornbusch, "Background Paper," in Twentieth Century Fund, Task Force on International Debt, *The Road to Economic Recovery* (New York: Priority Publications, 1989), pp. 29–30.

Once it became clear that many debtors would be unable to meet their obligations, the commercial banks stopped making voluntary loans to the debtors. The only commercial lending that took place after 1982 came as part of elaborate refinancing agreements involving the IMF, the World Bank, creditor governments, the commercial banks, and the debtor governments. Stabilization and structural adjustment packages were part of these agreements, providing official finance to underpin or substitute for commercial bank loans. The commercial banks would make additional loans to service payments on old loans, permit debtors to "capitalize" their interest payments by converting them into additional debt (on which interest was charged), reschedule payments of principal, or employ some combination of these mechanisms to **restructure** debt. By these means, it was hoped, the debtors could quickly become solvent and the overexposed U.S. banks would not become insolvent. By the late 1980s, however, few banks were interested in further lending. From 1980 to 1982, private creditors sent more than $50 million a year of net resources into developing countries (measured in 1986 prices); in 1987 the net resource flow was negligible.[27]

The impact on the most indebted countries was severe. For a country to turn from being a net borrower into a net repayer of loans, it must reverse the beneficial effects of foreign saving inflows. Instead of investing more than it saves, a country must generate a surplus of saving to be used for the repayment of debt. Instead of importing more than it exports, a repaying country must generate export surpluses because foreign lenders need to be repaid in dollars or other foreign currencies. Where net resource inflows once financed additional growth, net resource outflows from debtors reduce growth; in Table 15–1, line 2 changes from a net inward transfer (imports exceed exports) to a net outward transfer of resources. If debtor governments find it difficult to raise more taxes or reduce noninterest expenditures, as most did, they typically resort to inflationary financing that further destabilizes the economy. Capital flight exacerbates the crisis, as domestic savers try to move their assets to more stable financial markets.

Over 1978 to 1981, a group of 15 heavily indebted countries managed to attract sufficient foreign saving to pay the interest and principal due on their debt and still import about $9 billion more of goods and nonfactor services each year than they exported. But from 1983 to 1988, the 15 countries were forced into a reverse transfer—exports exceed imports—of almost $34 billion a year to service their debt.[28] From 1970 to 1981, these countries had enjoyed per capita income growth of 2.7 percent a year, invested 25 percent of their GDP, and tolerated inflation of 39 percent a year on average. During the debt crisis, however, from 1982 to 1988, the same 15 countries suffered declines in per capita income averaging 0.7 percent a year, were forced to reduce their investment to 18 percent of GDP, and inflated their economies by 149 percent a year.[29]

27. World Bank, *World Debt Tables 1989–1990,* Vol. 1, p. 10.

28. Annual average net outflows during the latter period were so much larger than the average net inflows of prior years because of the sharp decline in gross lending after 1982 noted above. Not only did countries have to repay their old debt, but they had to devote their own resources to purchase imports that had previously been financed by foreign borrowing.

29. Dornbusch, "Background Paper," p. 31.

Sustainable Debt

Why did the debt crisis occur? Foreign borrowing, as we have seen, is an accepted part of economic development. Access to foreign saving permits countries to invest more than they can save and to import more than their export earnings would otherwise allow. If the additional investment and imports are put to productive use, they should yield sufficient returns to pay the interest, dividends, and principal on the initial foreign inflows. Under these circumstances, continuing foreign borrowing and growing external debt can be sustainable and consistent with development.

We can determine the conditions for sustainable borrowing in terms of the **two-gap model** discussed in Chapter 6. Recall that foreign inflows can finance one of two possible gaps in an economy: (1) the foreign exchange gap, equal to imports (M) less exports (E) of goods and nonfactor services or (2) the gap between investment (I) and domestic saving (S_d). Foreign borrowing can also finance a third gap, the government budget deficit. If the foreign exchange gap is binding, then foreign inflows help growth by increasing the amount of imports. In any period, the increase in debt due to this inflow is

$$dD/dt = iD + M - X, \qquad [15\text{–}1]$$

where D is the stock of debt at any time, dD/dt is the change in the stock (the first derivative), and i is the average interest rate paid on all foreign inflows, including loans, equity, and grants. It is convenient to measure these flows in current dollars, the currency in which debt is conventionally measured. The simple differential equation can be solved under the following conditions: let E and M grow at the same exponential rate g_E, and find the long-run equilibrium conditions for sustainable foreign borrowing. In that case, the stock of debt will also grow exponentially at g_E, and in the long run the ratio of debt to exports will settle at

$$D/E = a/(g_E - i) \qquad [15\text{–}2]$$

where a is the ratio of the foreign exchange gap to exports, $(M - E)/E$, and is a constant under the assumption that imports and exports grow at the same rate.[30]

Equation 15–2 tells us that, for a given foreign exchange gap a, there is an equilibrium ratio of debt to exports that can be sustained. If g_E is greater than i, the gap can remain positive; this means that the country can continue to borrow and service its debt without a rise in its ratio of debt to exports. If the gap $(M - E)/E$ were 10 percent, the average interest rate were 7 percent (recall that grants and concessional loans have to be averaged in with commercial debt), and the growth of dollar earnings from exports g_E were 12 percent a year, then the ratio of debt to exports would settle at 2, which was about the average for the developing countries in the 1980s. If the growth of exports could be pushed above the growth of imports, the debt-export ratio would fall. If, on the other hand, the growth rate of exports were to fall below the interest rate, the only way to sustain debt would be to turn the foreign exchange gap into a surplus and begin repaying the debt, precisely what has happened in the high-debt countries of Latin

30. Equation 15–1 is solved to yield 15–2 by letting $D/D_0 = E/E_0 = M/M_0 = e^{gt}$ and substituting into Equation 15–1, noting that $d(e^{gt})/dt = ge^{gt}$. Then 15–1 becomes $g_E D = iD + M - E$, from which 15–2 can be readily derived. The result is given by Albert Fishlow, "External Borrowing and Debt Management," in Rudiger Dornbusch and F. Leslie C. H. Helmers, *The Open Economy: Tools for Policymakers in Developing Countries* (New York: Oxford University Press, 1988), pp. 220–21.

America. The key to sustaining debt under a foreign exchange constraint, then, is the ability of the debtor to put the additional resources to productive use in export industries, either directly or indirectly.

A similar calculation can be made for the investment-saving gap. The differential equation is

$$dD/dt = iD + I - S_d = iD + vY - sY = iD + (v - s)Y, \qquad [15\text{–}3]$$

where Y is GNP, v is the investment share of GNP, and s is the propensity to save out of GNP. As with the foreign exchange gap, assume that both debt and GNP grow at the same exponential rate g_Y. Then the long-run equilibrium ratio of debt to GNP is

$$D/Y = (v - s)/(g_Y - i). \qquad [15\text{–}4]$$

In this case, if $v - s$ were 3 percent of GNP, i averaged 7 percent on all foreign inflows, and the growth rate of GNP expressed in current dollars were 10 percent a year,[31] the debt-GNP ratio would settle at 1 and could be sustained at that level indefinitely. Although some countries reached debt-GNP ratios exceeding 1 during the 1980s, the Latin American debtors' ratios seldom exceeded 50 percent. From the saving-investment perspective, the requirement for sound debt management is to invest foreign saving in assets that are productive enough to boost the growth rate of GNP and to adopt policies that reduce the share of consumption in GNP.

At one level, the issue of managing foreign loans and grants to yield high growth rates is simple. If the country behaves as an enterprise, it will borrow only if it can invest in projects that have rates of return above the cost of borrowing. Then loans can be serviced out of the earnings from those investments. For the country there is a further condition, that the project must earn or save sufficient foreign exchange to transfer payments of interest and principal in foreign currency. Seen this way, foreign resources should only be sought if there are productive foreign-exchange-earning investment opportunities for them.

This approach is too restrictive, however. The question for both lenders and borrowers is whether the economy as a whole can generate sufficient income and export growth to service debt on schedule. Concern over specific projects is one aspect of this problem. But it is secondary to the larger issue of sound macroeconomic management. If an economy has been well managed and has proved itself able to use its resources productively and sustain growth over long periods, the role of foreign resources is to augment the entire investment menu. Precisely how these resources are invested is not important: additional loans are likely to be productively employed and serviced on schedule. Conversely, if an economy is poorly managed and unlikely to generate sufficient resources to service its debt, then precise targeting of loans toward specific projects, no matter how productive, is not much protection against default on those loans.

Causes of the Crisis

Although there is nothing inherent in foreign debt to cause a repayment crisis, defaults occurred frequently in many Latin American and European countries during the nineteenth century and the 1930s. The crisis of the 1980s was the first since

31. This is not as high as it seems. Remember we are measuring all quantities in current dollars, because that is the basis on which debt is serviced. If the real growth rate is 6 percent a year and the dollar rate of inflation is 4 percent a year, then the g_Y would be 10 percent a year.

World War II, however. In this instance, several things appear to have gone wrong at once.

First, several of the borrowing countries were profligate with their resources, ignoring principles of sound economic management. The oil shocks of 1973–74 and 1978–80 caused major disruptions in every economy in the world: oil importers had to adjust to lower standards of living and oil exporters had to learn to manage massive new revenues productively. Facing plunges in income that sometimes threatened political stability, many governments tried to compensate by increasing spending and thus increasing budget deficits. Having thereby stimulated inflation, some of these governments compensated further by maintaining their exchange rates at overvalued levels. This restrained price increases for imports and exportable goods, but also discouraged export growth and encouraged capital flight. When recycled petrodollars became available through the commercial banks, governments grabbed at the chance to boost investment and prevent declines in consumption. Unfortunately, in many cases investments were wasteful and there was too much consumption. Resources were not channeled into investments that would eventually pay off the debts with a surplus for the host country.

Why did the banks lend to profligate governments? The gush of petrodollars left the banks highly liquid, seeking profitable outlets for their deposits. Lending to developing countries seemed to provide an outlet that had not been fully utilized in recent years. Because the debt was **sovereign**, that is, guaranteed by governments, bankers apparently discounted the risk of default, even though history held many examples to the contrary. Once a few banks showed the way, others followed. And once the banks were heavily involved, further lending seemed a sensible way to keep debtor countries liquid enough to continue servicing earlier loans. Banks were encouraged by their own governments, especially the United States government, and the international agencies, all of whom hoped that the illiquidity of the early 1980s would disappear once the world economy recovered from its instability. Whatever the reasons for the banks' persistence in lending, it is clear that neither they nor their governments foresaw the generalized debt crisis.

Instability of the world economy precipitated the crisis. The unprecedented rises in oil prices have already been mentioned. During the latter 1970s, inflation in the United States reached double digits and the Federal Reserve Board tightened the money supply. The immediate consequence was that interest rates soared to a peak of 16 percent in 1981 before settling gradually into a range of 7 to 9 percent through the second half of the 1980s. Debtor countries were forced to pay the new rates if they had borrowed at flexible interest rates or if they had to refinance old loans now coming due, so their interest payments rose and became unpredictable. Tight money and fiscal stringency, especially in the United States, led to the world recession of 1981–82. Income in the industrial economies, having grown by more than 3 percent a year in the preceding years, slowed to 2 percent growth in 1980–81 and declined in 1982. The recession shrunk the markets for debtor country exports and caused a decline in commodity prices, which fell by one-third in the early 1980s relative to the prices of manufactures. These external shocks would seem compelling reasons for the debt crisis, except that not all debtors suffered equally. South Korea and Indonesia are among the world's largest debtors, yet sound economic policies have enabled them to service their debt while continuing to grow throughout the 1980s. It took a combination of the deteriorating world economy, poor domestic management, and the myopia of the commercial banks to bring on the crisis.[32]

Escape from the Crisis

The debt crisis of the 1980s was over by the mid-1990s. Although some countries remain deeply in debt, the largest Latin American debtors worked out of their insolvency and are now servicing their debt. Table 15–8 shows that, for Latin American countries, debt service ratios have receded from their high levels of the 1980s.

A group of low-income countries, mostly in Africa, also verge on bankruptcy, even though most of their foreign capital has been on very concessional terms. As an indicator of the difference between these groups, the African countries were paying only 2.9 percent average interest on new inflows and on average their loans were due to be repaid over 30 years. In contrast, the heavily indebted middle-income countries paid an average interest rate of 6.7 percent and their repayment period averaged 13 years.[33] For the latter group, debt relief involved a complex mix of action by the aid agencies and the commercial banks. For the African debtors the problem resolves into one of net aid flows, whether received as debt relief or as new concessional finance, from the multilateral and bilateral donors.

The Latin American debtors worked out of insolvency through complex debt relief agreements that involved the debtor governments; the international agencies, specifically the World Bank and IMF; the creditor governments, their treasuries, and aid agencies; and the commercial banks with loans to the debtor countries. Each agreement required a major negotiation among these parties, covering stabilization and structural adjustment programs, new aid and commercial credits, debt rescheduling, and a list of mechanisms for converting or retiring existing debt.

Stabilization and structural adjustment programs contribute to debt reduction by helping to reduce deficits in the government budget and the balance of payments, to contain inflation, to stimulate savings, and to generate more resources for investment and debt service. The cost of debt service is borne by citizens of the debtor country in the form of reduced incomes, higher taxes and fees, reduced services from government, and other adjustments that reduce levels of consumption. The funds provided by the IMF, the World Bank, and bilateral aid agencies are used to ease these burdens to some extent by financing imports and investment and, in some cases, by directly financing debt reduction. The cost of concessional finance from the multilateral and bilateral donors is borne ultimately by taxpayers in the industrial creditor countries.

The commercial banks at first entered these negotiations voluntarily, believing that relief in the form of new credits or rescheduled debt would stave off default until improvements in the world economy and better economic management enabled debtors to resume debt service. As this proved a false hope, banks became reluctant partners and increasingly pressed for official debt relief that would re-

32. On the causes of the crisis, see Dornbusch, "Background Paper," pp. 37–47, and John T. Cuddington, "The Extent and Causes of the Debt Crisis of the 1980s" in Ishrat Husain and Ishac Diwan (eds.), *Dealing with the Debt Crisis* (Washington, D.C.: World Bank, 1989), pp. 15–44.

33. *World Development Report 1994,* Table 24.

duce their exposure to losses from developing-country debt. By the late 1980s the creditor governments and international agencies were encouraging the banks to use a number of mechanisms from a menu of debt reduction devices. Banks have converted interest payments into additional principal, a way to decrease the debt service burden in the short run by increasing it in the long run. Interest is, of course, charged on the newly capitalized interest. They also **rescheduled debt principal**, which also puts off until tomorrow what debtors cannot service today. Rescheduling can be done through debt negotiations, or it can be done *de facto* when a debtor does not pay the principal due and the banks choose not to foreclose. Sometimes rescheduling agreements involve improved loan terms for the debtor.

The major money markets of the world have active secondary markets in all kinds of debt, public and private, where creditors can sell their claims against debtors at a discount that reflects market expectations about repayment. At the end of 1989, the commercial debt of the 17 most heavily indebted countries sold on the secondary market at only one-third of its par value. A buyer of such paper pays $33 to obtain a promise of repayment of $100 plus interest; this reflects the buyer's expectation that the chances of repayment are only slightly better than one in three. If the commercial banks believe the chances of repayment are less than one in three, they may forgo their claim of repayment and sell the loan on the secondary market, realizing a net loss of $67. Debtors, too, can purchase their own obligations on the secondary market, paying $33 to reduce the principal due by $100. Loan agreements normally prohibit borrowers from such **buybacks**, however, because they encourage debtors to default, driving down the price on the secondary market and making it more advantageous to buy back their debt.

Debt-equity swaps enable the debtor to pay the creditor in local currency, which can be used only for direct investment in the host country. A bank would accept cruzeiros in exchange for retirement of debt owed by Brazil, and then lend these funds to companies that could use them to finance equity investments. The debtor government does have to raise funds on the domestic market, however; this could be inflationary, could squeeze out domestic private investors, or could require tax increases and expenditure reductions. Debt-equity swaps thus solve the problem of the foreign exchange constraint, but do not solve the budgetary constraint. Furthermore, many swaps have financed investments that might have been financed in dollars in any case, representing no net gain to the country.[34]

When all forms of debt conversion are added up, the total of debt converted for the five years from 1988 to 1992 was $75 billion. Yet the total long-term debt of developing countries was about $1.3 trillion during those years; in heavily indebted Latin America, debt relief totaled $64 billion against debt of almost $400 billion.[35] Countries that escaped the debt crisis, especially those in Latin America, were helped by debt relief. But they may have been helped even more by the revival of the world economy in the early 1990s and by their own efforts to stabilize

34. On the subject of debt relief measures, see Dornbusch, "Background Paper," pp. 67-101; Husain and Diwan, *Dealing with the Debt Crisis,* "Introduction," pp. 1–11; Michel H. Bouchet and Jonathan Hay, "The Rise of the Market-Based 'Menu' Approach and its Limitations," in Husain and Diwan, *Dealing with the Debt Crisis,* pp. 147–58; and World Bank, *World Debt Tables 1989–1990,* Vol. 1, pp. 21–31.

35. World Bank, *World Debt Tables 1994–1995,* pp. 171, 173, 187, 189.

and reform their economies. Where the debt crisis hangs on, especially in Africa, continued aid is keeping economies afloat while economic reforms are being put in place.

The Mexican Debt Crisis[36]

By far the two largest debtors in the developing world in the 1980s were Brazil and Mexico, each with over $100 billion of outstanding debt in 1989. It is ironic that Mexico should have been so indebted, because in the latter 1970s it benefited from major increases in both oil production and rising oil prices. However, the Mexican government, like other oil-exporting governments, spent the country's windfall profligately and borrowed heavily against the prospect of a continued oil boom. Mexican debt rose from 12 percent of GNP in 1975 to 53 percent in 1982, the very years that oil exports were booming. By 1982, Mexico's debt-service ratio exceeded 50 percent. Despite the surge in resource flows from oil revenues and foreign borrowing, the Mexican economy actually grew faster, with less inflation, during the 17 years before the oil boom than it did during the boom, as Table 15–9 shows.

When the newly elected government of President Miguel de la Madrid took over in 1982, its finance minister, Silvio Herzog, told creditors that the country could not meet interest payments on its debt. This announcement alarmed the creditor banks, which held about 70 percent of Mexico's debt, and international institutions, not only because of the large Mexican debt, but because other countries were likely to follow Mexico's lead. At the time, it seemed quite possible that debtor insolvency could lead to failures of major U.S. banks and a worldwide financial panic.

To stave off this disaster and help Mexico work out of its debt problem, the commercial banks, their governments, and the international agencies put together packages of debt rescheduling, new lending by all institutions, and economic austerity for the Mexican economy. Mexico's trade balance, excluding interest payments, turned from a net inward resource transfer of 4.3 percent of GNP in 1981 to a net outward transfer of 2.4 percent of GNP in 1988; its investment share of GNP fell from 28 to 21

TABLE 15–9 Mexican Growth and Inflation, 1955–1992 (percent per year)

	1955–72	1973–81	1982–88	1988–92
Income per capita	3.3	2.6	−2.2	2.5
Real wages	3.7	3.1	−5.9	n.a.
Inflation	5	22	83	21

Sources: Rudiger Dornbusch, "Mexico's Economy at the Crossroads," *Journal of International Affairs,* 43, no. 2 (Winter 1990), 314, and World Bank, *World Tables 1994–1995,* pp. 456–57.

36. Based on accounts by Rudiger Dornbusch, "Mexico's Economy at the Crossroads," *Journal of International Affairs,* 43, no. 2 (Winter 1990), 313–26, and World Bank, *World Debt Tables 1989–1990,* Vol. 1, pp. 28, 52–53.

percent. The results of this austerity are evident in Table 15–9: incomes fell and inflation accelerated. It was starkly obvious that the price of debt repayment would be deep reductions in the welfare of the Mexican people.

After six years of debt-induced retrenchment that seemed to offer no real relief to Mexico or its creditors, a new debt reduction package was negotiated among all parties in 1989. The commercial banks were offered a menu of options. They could (1) exchange existing debt for new bonds at a 35 percent discount, (2) exchange old debt for new bonds at the same value but a reduced interest rate of 6.25 percent, or (3) make new loans of at least 25 percent of the amounts due them at market rates of interest over 15 years with a 7-year grace period when no principal would be due. In all cases, the new debt was to be considered "senior" to the old, with prior claims on payments, and the Mexican government pledged not to request rescheduling of the new debt. Mexico was also permitted to purchase its own debt at the substantial discounts offered on the secondary market as long as it was current on its interest payments. Principal and interest payments on the new bonds were guaranteed by a $7 billion fund established by the IMF, the World Bank, and the Japanese government.

By 1990, Mexico's economic situation had improved dramatically. In 1987, Mexico was transferring net resources (the surplus of imports over exports of goods and nonfactor services) outward by $8.6 billion a year; from 1989 to 1992, helped by the debt settlement and a resurgence of foreign investment, there was an inward net transfer of $4.8 billion a year. Over that period, income per capita grew by 2.5 a year, after seven years of decline. And inflation, which reached 83 percent a year during the debt crisis, was contained at 21 percent a year. The debt settlement was not the only force behind this improvement. The improving world economy and Mexico's own economic reforms (see Chapter 19) played major roles in the recovery.

PART 5

PRODUCTION AND TRADE

16

Agriculture

Understanding the nature of agriculture is fundamental to understanding development. The labor-surplus and neoclassical models presented in Chapter 3 dealt primarily with the nature of the relationship between the industrial and agricultural sectors. The problem of income distribution or extremes of poverty within developing nations discussed in Chapter 4 is substantially a question of how to do something about the rural poor. Nutrition, discussed in Chapter 11, is a question of food production and distribution. And the contribution of exports to development, as treated in Chapters 17 and 19, is for many countries a question of creating agricultural exports.

Much of this book has been about **rural development,** a term that refers to all those activities that affect the well-being of rural populations including the provision of basic needs, such as food, and the development of human capital in the countryside through education and nutrition programs. This chapter concentrates on problems that have a direct bearing on raising agricultural production and farmers' incomes. Indirect measures treated elsewhere in this book, even those as crucial as rural education, will be dealt with only in passing.

In a sense agriculture is simply one industry among many, but it is an industry with a difference. To begin with, the agricultural sector in a country at an early developmental stage employs far more people than all other industries and sectors put together—60 to 70 percent and more of the total work force are in agriculture in many of the poorer developing countries, including China and India. In contrast, agriculture in developed economies typically employs less than 10 percent of the workforce (3 percent in the United States). Second, agricultural activities have existed for thousands of years, ever since humankind gave up hunting and gathering as its main source of food. Because of this long history the rural economy is often referred to as **tradition bound.** Generating electric power or manufacturing automobiles can only be done by means based on modern science and engineering, but crops are often grown using techniques developed hundreds or even thousands of years before the advent of modern science. And the rural societies in which traditional techniques are used often develop customs and attitudes that reinforce older ways of doing things and thus make change difficult.

A third characteristic of agriculture that separates it from other sectors is the crucial importance of land as a factor of production. Other sectors use and require land, but in no other sector does land play such a central role. The availability of cultivable land, whether relatively plentiful in relation to population, as in the Americas, or scarce, as in much of Asia, fundamentally shapes the kind of farming techniques that can be used. Closely related to the central role of land is the influence of weather. No other sector is as subject to the vagaries of the weather as is agriculture. Land, like the weather, differs from place to place so that techniques suitable in one place are often of little use elsewhere. The manufacture of steel must also adjust to differences in the quality of iron ore from place to place, and similar problems occur in other industries; but the basic techniques in much of manufacturing are similar, at least within and often between countries. In agriculture differences in soil quality, climate, and the availability of water lead to the production of different crops and different ways of raising a particular crop, not only within countries, but even within provinces or counties of a single country.

Finally, agriculture is the only sector that produces food. Humankind can survive without steel or coal or electric power, but not without food. For most manufactured products, in fact, there are substitutes, but there is no substitute for food. Either food must be produced within a country or it must be imported.

Agriculture's Role in Economic Development

Agriculture's role in economic development is central because most of the people in poor countries make their living from the land. If leaders are seriously concerned with the welfare of their people, the only ways they can readily improve the welfare for the majority is by helping to raise first the farmers' productivity in growing food and cash crops and second the prices they receive for those crops. Not all increases in farm output benefit the majority of rural people, of course. The creation of mechanized, large-scale farms in place of small, peasant farms may actually make the majority of the population worse off. Although it is a necessary condition, raising agricultural output is not by itself sufficient to achieve an increase in rural welfare. We shall return to this problem later.

Most developing countries must rely on their own agricultural sectors to produce the food consumed by their people, although there are exceptions. Countries with large natural-resource-based exports, such as Malaysia or Saudi Arabia, have the foreign exchange necessary to import much of their food. But most developing countries cannot rely so heavily on foreign exchange earnings to feed their populations.

Farmers in developing countries must produce enough to feed themselves, as well as the urban population. Hence, as the proportion of the urban population rises, the productivity of farmers must also rise. If productivity does not rise (and in the absence of food imports), the models in Chapter 3 make it clear that the terms of trade will turn sharply against the industrial sector, cut into profits, and eventually bring growth to a halt.

The agricultural sector's size is the characteristic that gives agriculture such an important role in the provision of factor inputs, notably labor, to industry and to the other modern sectors. With 70 percent or more of the population in agriculture, the rural sector is virtually the only source of increased labor power for the urban sector. Importation of labor is possible, and there is usually population growth within the urban sector itself, but neither of these sources is likely to be sufficient for the long-term needs of economic growth. If there are restrictions on the movement of labor out of agriculture, economic development will be severely crippled. Serfs in Russia through the mid-nineteenth century, for example, were tied to their lord's land by law and hence were not free to move to the cities and into industry. Thus Russian industry did not begin to grow rapidly until after the serfs were freed. Today such feudal restrictions are increasingly rare, but heavy indebtedness by a farmer to a landlord-moneylender often has the same effect as tying an individual to the land and thus making the individual unavailable to modern industry.

The agricultural sector also can be a major source of capital for modern economic growth. Some writers have even suggested that agriculture is the main or even the sole source of capital in the early stages of development, but this overstates agriculture's role. Capital comes from invested savings and savings from income. However, even in the poorest countries the share of agricultural income in national product is typically less than half the gross domestic project. Over half the GNP is therefore provided by nonagricultural sectors (industry and services), and these sectors are often important contributors to saving and hence to investment. Furthermore, whereas imports of labor seldom provide a large portion of the domestic labor force, imports of capital, whether in the form of aid or private investment, sometimes do contribute a substantial share of domestic capital formation without drawing on the agricultural sector at all. South Korea is a case in point, where capital formation in the early years of rapid growth was provided mainly by foreign aid and in later years was increasingly paid for from the profits of the industrial sector.

If one treats foreign exchange as a separate factor of production, agriculture has an important role to play in the supply of this factor as well. As indicated in Chapter 17, developing countries' comparative advantage usually lies with natural resources or agricultural products. In only a few cases is the export of manufactures or of services the principal source of foreign exchange for a country in the early stages of modern economic growth. Thus, unless a country is rich in natural resources, such as petroleum or copper, the agricultural sector will play a key role in providing foreign exchange with which to import capital equipment and intermediate goods that cannot be produced at home.

Finally, the farming population of a developing country is, in some cases at least, an important market for the output of the modern urban sector. The qualification "in some cases" must be added because farm populations in some poor countries purchase very little from modern industry. This is particularly likely to be true where the distribution of income is extremely unequal, with most of the country's income, land, and other wealth in the hands of a small urban and rural upper class. In that situation the rural population may simply pay taxes and rents to wealthy urban residents and subsist on whatever is left over. Even cheap cloth from urban factories may be beyond the means of a very poor rural population. If income is less unequally distributed, however, the rural sector can be an important source of demand for industrial products. If a large rural market exists, industries can continue to grow after they have saturated urban demand for their product without turning to foreign markets until they are better able to compete.[1]

Self-Sufficiency and Dwindling World Food Supplies

One important aspect of agriculture's role in development typically gets a great deal of attention from economic planners: the degree to which a country wishes to achieve **food self-sufficiency.** Food self-sufficiency can take on several different meanings. At one extreme is the view that any dependence on foreign trade is dangerous to a country's economic health, and dependence on food imports is simply one part of this broader danger. More common is the view that food is a basic or strategic good, not unlike military weapons. If a country is dependent on others for food and hence for its very survival, the suppliers of that food will be in a position to bring the dependent country to its knees whenever it suits the supplier countries' purposes. Others argue that population growth is rapidly eating into the world's food surpluses, and countries relying on food imports will soon find themselves paying very high prices in order to get what they need from the world's dwindling surplus.

The national defense argument for food self-sufficiency may be valid under certain specific circumstances. Since a discussion of these circumstances would divert us into an analysis of complex international security issues, suffice it to say that the national defense argument is frequently used to justify policies that have little relationship to a country's real security.

The issue of a dwindling world food surplus cannot be dealt with so easily. History does not support the view that world supplies of exportable food are steadily diminishing. Data on world grain exports are presented in Table 16–1. What these and other data indicate is that although the world grain export surplus and the corresponding size of the deficit in importing countries fluctuates, the overall surplus is growing, not declining. In 1972, for example, bad weather struck a wide part of the globe, including the Soviet Union, China, India, and Indonesia. The resulting surge in demand for grain imports drove prices up sharply in 1973, but prices fell again when production in these deficit areas recovered. The 1972 to 1973 "crisis" was not significantly different in magnitude from other weather-induced fluctuations of the past. After 1973 grain exports rose substantially and prices fell.

Those who speak of an impending world food crisis are implicitly or explicitly forecasting the future. Continued population growth is rapidly pushing people out onto the world's diminishing supply of arable land. In places like Africa's Sahel agriculture may already have developed beyond the capacity of the land to sustain it. The real issue, however, is not whether the world is running out of surplus

1. There are a number of good studies that treat the role of agriculture in development, including C. Peter Timmer, *Agriculture and the State* (Ithaca, N.Y.: Cornell University Press, 1991); Thomas P. Tomich, Peter Kilby, and Bruce F. Johnston, *Transforming Agrarian Economies: Opportunities Seized, Opportunities Missed* (Ithaca, N.Y.: Cornell University Press, 1995); and Lloyd Reynolds, *Agriculture in Development Theory* (New Haven, Conn.: Yale University Press, 1976).

TABLE 16–1 World Cereal Exports (million metric tons)

Year	Exports
1962	85
1966	114
1970	113
1974	149
1978	191
1980	216
1985	224
1988	232
1991	234
1992	250
1993	231

Source: FAO, *Trade Yearbook 1972, 1976, 1978, 1987, 1989,* and *1993* (Rome: Food and Agricultural Organization, 1973, 1977, 1979, 1988, 1990, 1994).

land—it is—but whether yields on existing arable land can be raised fast enough to meet the needs of an increasing population with rising per capita incomes. The problem is not one of biology. Research in the plant sciences has shown that yields per acre could be higher than even those of such advanced agricultural systems as Japan's. And most of the world produces food at levels per acre nowhere near those of Japan. Although there is some biological limit to the capacity of the planet earth to produce food, the planet is not remotely close to that limit today.

The real danger of a long-term food crisis arises from a different source. From a scientific point of view, the countries that could expand food output dramatically may not do so because of internal social and economic barriers to technical progress in agriculture. At the same time, because of economic reasons, the world's few food-surplus countries may not be able to continue to expand those surpluses. Thus it is possible that the world could face growing food deficits in importing countries that are not matched by rising surpluses in exporting countries. Under such circumstances, food prices would rise sharply, and therefore only countries with large foreign exchange earnings could afford to continue to import sufficient food. Some of the poorest countries, including those where food imports make the difference between an adequate diet and severe malnutrition, may not have the foreign exchange earnings needed to maintain required imports. One must emphasize, however, that while the potential for a disaster of this kind is present, it is not today a reality; many economists believe it will never become a reality.[2] A possible future world food crisis is a weak basis for a country's economic planners to give a high priority to the development of agriculture.

LAND TENURE AND REFORM

Before we focus on agricultural production, it is best to explore the problem of land and the way it is owned and organized. Conditions of land tenure set the context within which all efforts to raise agricultural output must operate. Put differently, the property right that matters most in the agricultural sector is the right

2. Maldistribution within a country, however, can and does cause severe localized famines, sometimes accompanied by large-scale loss of life. See Jean Drèze and Amartya Sen, *Hunger and Public Action* (London: Oxford University Press [Clarendon], 1989).

over the use of land. If that right is well-defined as well as exclusive, secure, enforceable, and transferable, then farmers with those rights will have an incentive to invest and work the land efficiently.

Patterns of Land Tenure

Land tenure and **land-tenure relations** refer to the way people own land and how they rent it to others to use if they choose not to cultivate it themselves. In Europe during the Middle Ages, for example, a local lord owned a piece of land and allowed the local peasants to cultivate it. In exchange for cultivating that land, the peasant family had to deliver a part of the harvest to the lord, and members of the peasant family had to perform labor services in the lord's castle. In most cases the peasant could not freely leave the land to seek work in the city or with another lord. Peasants did flee, but the lord had the right to force them to return if they could be caught. Serfdom, as this system is sometimes called, was only a modest step up from slavery.

Serflike land-tenure relations prevail today in only a few remote and backward areas of the globe. The patterns that do exist, however, are diverse, as the following incomplete listing makes clear.

Large-scale modern farming or ranching usually refers to a large crop- or cattle-raising acreage which uses some hired labor but where many of the activities are highly mechanized. Many such farms are found in the United States, whereas much of Latin American agriculture is characterized by large modern farms that exist alongside small peasant plots.

Plantation agriculture is a system in which a piece of land is used to raise a cash crop such as tea or rubber, usually for export. Cultivation is by hired labor who are paid wages, and the plantation is run either by the owner or more frequently by a professional manager.

Latifundia is a term used in Latin America and Europe to refer to large estates or ranches on which the hired labor still have a servile (master-servant) relationship to the owner.

Family farms or independent peasant proprietors own plots of land (usually small) and operate them mainly or solely with their own family's labor. This type of tenure is dominant in Asia and Africa and is important in Latin America as well.

Tenancy usually refers to a situation where an individual family farms a piece of land owned by a landlord to whom the farmer pays rent. Much of Asian agriculture is made up of either individual peasant proprietors or tenants.

Sharecropping is a form of tenancy in which the farmer shares his crops with the landlord.

Absentee landlords, who are particularly important in Asia and Latin America, tend to live in cities or other places far away from the land they own. Landlords who do live near their land may have little to do with it except to collect rents. Some resident landlords provide seeds and certain kinds of capital to tenants.

Communal farming is practiced in parts of Africa, where inhabitants of villages may still own some of their land jointly. Individuals and families may farm plots on communal land, to which they gain access by custom or by allocation from the community's leaders. Europe in an earlier period also had such common lands, which were used, among other purposes, as pasture for the village cows.

Collectivized agriculture refers to the kinds of agricultural systems found for the most part in the states of the former Soviet Union, China prior to 1981, and Vietnam prior to 1989. Land, except for small family plots, is owned by a cooperative whose members are typically all or part of the residents of a single village. Management is by a committee elected by the villagers or appointed by government authorities, and members of the cooperative share in the output on the basis of the amount of labor they contribute to it.

There are numerous variations within and among these categories, but this list gives some idea of the great range of land-tenure systems that exist in the developing world. The kind of land-tenure system existing in any given country or region has an important bearing on economic development for several reasons. To begin with, prevailing land-tenure arrangements have a major influence on the welfare of the farm family. A family farming only one or two acres of land, that must turn over half its main crop to the landlord, will not have much left over to feed itself or to invest in improvements. Such a heavy rent burden may seem harsh, but half and more of the farmers in some major countries, such as China and South Korea before land reform and parts of Latin America and India today, labor under comparable conditions or worse.

A second important impact of the land-tenure system is on the prevailing degree of political stability. Families that own the land they cultivate tend to feel they have a stake in the existing political order, even if they themselves are quite poor. Because they possess land, they have something to lose from turmoil. Landless farm laborers and tenants who can be pushed off the land at the will of a landlord have no such stake in the existing order. The histories of many countries with large landless rural populations are often ones of periodic peasant rebellions. One such rebellion played a major role in bringing the Communists to power in China. Much of the history of modern Mexico has also been shaped by revolts of the landless.

Tenure and Incentive

Land-tenure systems also have a major impact on agricultural productivity. An individual proprietor who has well defined, exclusive, and secure rights to land knows that increased effort or skill that leads to a rise in output will also improve income. This result does not necessarily follow if the land is owned by someone else and property rights for the farmer are not well defined and secure. Under sharecropping, for example, the landlord gets a percentage share, typically a half of any increase in output. If a tenant's rent contract is only a year or two in length, a rise in output may cause the landlord to threaten eviction of the tenant so that all or much of the increase in production can be captured through a rise in the rent. In some countries landlords have had to draw up land-rental contracts of many years or even a lifetime's duration, precisely because tenants otherwise would have no incentive to invest in improvements or even to maintain existing irrigation and drainage systems.

Farms with large numbers of hired laborers have an even more difficult incentive problem, compounded by a management problem. Farm laborers are paid wages and typically do not benefit at all in any rise in production. One way around this difficulty is to pay on a **piece-rate basis,** that is, to pay workers on the basis of the number of bushels of cotton or tea leaves they pick. But although this system works at harvest time, it is virtually impossible to pay on a piece-work basis for the cultivation of crops. A laborer can be paid by the acre for planting wheat, but it will be many months before it will be possible to tell whether the planting job was done well or carelessly. In a factory, elaborate procedures can be set up by management to check on the pace and quality of work performed. But work in a factory is much easier to reduce to a routine that can be measured and supervised than is work on a farm. There are a thousand different tasks that must be performed on a typical farm; and supervision, even in the hands of a skilled manager, is seldom a good substitute for a farmer motivated by the knowledge that extra effort will lead directly to a rise in income.

Incentives under communal farming suffer in a different way. Property rights in this case are not exclusive because the land is owned in common, each individual family has an incentive to use the land to the maximum extent possible, but no one has much of an incentive to maintain or improve the land because the benefits of individual improvement efforts will go not mainly to the individual but to everyone who uses the land. Economists call this the **public goods** or **free-rider** problem. Everyone agrees that a fire department is necessary if a town is to avoid conflagration, but few people would voluntarily pay what the fire department is worth to them. Instead they would pay little or nothing in the hope that their neighbors would pay enough to maintain the department, but of course their neighbors would not pay enough either. The usual solution to this problem is to turn payment over to the town government and allow that government to assess taxes on everyone in town on an equitable basis. Similar solutions are found in communal agriculture. Certain dates can be set aside when everyone in the village is expected to show up and work on a particular land improvement, such as repair of a fence with a neighboring village. But the incentive to work hard in a common effort relies heavily on community social pressure plus the inner goodwill of each individual. If farmers were saints, goodwill would do the job, but for better or worse, farmers are like the rest of us.

Collectivized agriculture has some of the incentive and management problems of both plantation and communal agriculture, but with important differences. Because rights to the land are held in common, the free-rider problem is present, but its impact is modified by paying everyone "work points" on the basis of the amount of work they actually do. At the end of the year the total number of work points earned by collective members is added up and divided into the value of the collective's output to determine the value of each work point. The individual therefore has a dual incentive to work hard. More work means more work points, and indirectly it leads to higher collective output and hence a higher total income for that individual.

The incentive issue posed by collective agriculture is whether the work-point system is an adequate substitute for the motivation provided on a family farm where increased output benefits a farmer's own family and only that family. The main problem with the collective system is that an individual can sometimes earn work points by claiming to have worked hard, when in fact that person was off behind a tree sleeping or leaning on a hoe. The solution to the leaning-on-a-hoe problem is to have the leadership of the collective check up on how hard members are working, but that can introduce the supervision or management problem found in plantation labor, namely, that it is extremely difficult to supervise many agricultural activities. In general both the incentive and managerial problems worsen as the collective unit gets larger. In a unit of twenty or thirty families, the size of the Chinese production teams in the 1970s, families can supervise each other and penalize laggards. But in a unit of several thousand families, the size of the Chinese commune in the late 1950s, family members have little incentive to pressure laggards to work harder because no single individual's work, however poorly done, will have much impact on the value of a neighbor's work points. If everyone in the collective thinks this way, of course, the output of the collective will fall. By 1981 the Chinese leadership had decided that even the twenty- to thirty-family collective unit created incentive and managerial problems, and they introduced reforms that returned Chinese agriculture to a system of family farming.

From an incentive and management point of view, therefore, the family-owned farm would seem to be the ideal system. The analysis so far, however, has left out one very important consideration: economies of scale. In agriculture economies of scale may exist because certain kinds of machinery can be used efficiently only on large farms. On small farms tractors or combines may be badly underutilized. Such considerations help explain why many Latin Americans feel that large-scale farming is the most appropriate way to increase agricultural production and exports. Economies of scale may also exist because large collective units are better at mobilizing labor for rural construction activities than are individual family farms. We shall return to the question of scale economies later. Here all we can conclude is that the question of the ideal type of rural land-tenure system has not been completely resolved.

Land Reform

The reform of land-tenure systems can assume many different forms.[3] Here are some typical measures found in many reforms, starting with the least radical.

Reform of rent contracts ensures the tenure of a tenant farmer. Many tenants farm at the will of the landlord and can be easily removed at the end of a season. Laws requiring long-term contracts that restrict the landlord's right to remove a tenant can markedly improve the tenant's willingness to maintain and invest in the land, and also introduce a degree of stability into the family's life. In effect, these kinds of reforms strengthen the property rights of tenants at the expense of those of the landlord, but do not necessarily involve a transfer of income from owner to tenant.

Rent reduction typically involves a ceiling on the percentage share of the crop that a landlord can demand as rent. If the percentage share is substantially below what prevailed in the past, the impact both on tenant welfare and the tenant family's surplus available for investment can be substantial.

Land to the tiller (the former tenant) **with compensation** to the landlord for loss of land is a measure that can take many different forms. A government can pass a law setting a ceiling on the number of acres an individual can own and so force individuals to sell all land over that limit. Or the reform law can state that only those who actually till the land can own it, and all other land must be sold. A key issue in this kind of reform is whether the former landlord receives full or only partial compensation for the land that must be sold.

Land to the tiller without compensation involves the most radical transfor-

3. There are numerous studies of land reform. One of the best-known practitioners was Wolf Ladejinsky. See Louis J. Walinsky (ed.), *Agrarian Reform as Unfinished Business: The Selected Papers of Wolf Ladejinsky* (London: Oxford University Press, 1977).

mation of rural relations, except for the further step of collectivization. All land not cultivated by its owner is confiscated, and the former landlord receives nothing in return. Frequently in such reform the landlord may lose life as well as land.

The Politics of Land Reform

The main motive for undertaking land reform is usually political, not economic.[4] The politics that lead to reform are of two types. A society with a large tenant and landless laborer population that is controlled by other classes may find itself faced with increasing rural unrest. In the first type of land reform, to keep this unrest from blowing up into a revolution, bills are passed to reduce the burden on the peasantry and to give them a stake in continued stability. In the second type, land reform takes place after a revolution supported by the rural poor has occurred. The main purpose of reform in this case is to consolidate support for the revolution among the rural poor and to eliminate the economic base of one of the classes, the landlords, that was most opposed to the revolution.

The motive behind the Mexican land reforms of the twentieth century, for example, has been largely of the first type. Prior to the Mexican Revolution of 1911, land in Mexico had become increasingly concentrated in large haciendas ranging in size from 1,000 to over 400,000 acres. Although the revolution of 1911 was supported by those who had lost their land and other rural poor, those who took power after the revolution were largely from upper-income groups or the small middle class. This new leadership, however, had to deal with the continuing rural unrest that was often ably led by men such as Emiliano Zapata. To meet the challenge of Zapata and people like him, the Mexican government has periodically redistributed some arable land, most recently under the government of President Luis Echeverria in the 1970s. Mexican land-tenure relations, however, continue to be characterized by large estates existing alongside small peasant holdings. Reform eliminated some of the more extreme forms of pressure for more radical change, but Mexican agriculture still includes a large, poor, and not very productive rural peasant class.

The Chinese land reform of the 1940s and early 1950s under the leadership of the Communist party was a reform par excellence of the second type. The Communist revolution had been built primarily on the rural poor, and the landlord class was one of the main pillars of support of the existing Kuomintang government. Prior to the reform some 40 percent of the arable land had been farmed by tenants who typically paid half their main crop to the landlord as rent. The landlord, whether resident in the village or absentee, contributed little or nothing other than the land. After the reform, and prior to the collectivization of agriculture in 1955 to 1956, land was owned by the tiller and the landlord received no compensation whatsoever. In fact many landlords were tried publicly in the villages and either executed or sent off to perform hard labor under harsh conditions.[5]

The Japanese land reform that followed World War II was different in important respects from the Chinese experience. Land reform in Japan was carried out by the U.S. Occupation forces. The Occupation government believed that the

4. Elias Tuma, *Twenty-six Centuries of Agrarian Reform: A Comparative Analysis* (Berkeley: University of California Press, 1965).

5. Among the many descriptions of Chinese land reform is William Hinton, *Fanshen* (New York: Vintage Books, 1966).

landlord class had been an important supporter of the forces in Japanese society that brought about World War II. Small peasant proprietors, in contrast, were seen as a solid basis on which to build a future democratic and stable Japan. Since the Americans had won the war, Japanese landlords were not in a position to offer resistance to reform, and a thoroughgoing reform was carried out. Compensation of landlords was provided for in legislation, but inflation soon had the effect of sharply reducing the real value of the amounts offered. As a result Japanese land reform also amounted to confiscation of landlord land with little compensation.[6]

A second feature of land reform efforts is that land reform legislation is extremely difficult to enforce in the absence of a deep commitment from the government. Most developing countries have some kind of land reform legislation on the books, but relatively few have experienced real reform. In some cases no serious effort is made to enforce the legislation. In other cases the legislation is enforced but has little effect because of legal loopholes. India provides examples of both kinds of problems. In the Indian state of Bihar the government has awarded substantial tracts of land to the *harijan* (former untouchable) caste. But Bihar is a state where much of the real power rests in the hands of so-called higher castes that include many landlords, and these higher castes have forcibly prevented the *harijans* from taking over the land the government awarded to them. Elsewhere in India a law limiting the amount of land that can be owned by a single person has been enforced, but has had limited real effect. An individual with more land than allowed by law registers the extra land in the name of trusted relatives or associates. For truly enormous landholdings subterfuges of this kind may be impossible, but most landlords in India possess only several ten or a few hundred acres of land.

Land Reform and Productivity

The impact of land reform on agricultural productivity depends on what kind of system is being reformed as well as the content of the reform measures. Land reform has the greatest positive impact on productivity where the previous system was one of small peasant farms, with high rates of insecure tenancy (for example, one-year contracts) and absentee landlords. Under such conditions reform has little impact on cultivation practices since farms are small both before and after reform. Elimination of landlords also has little effect on productivity because they have nothing to do with farming. On the other hand, turning tenants into owners provides them with well-defined and secure property rights and hence with a greater incentive to invest in improvements. The Chinese, Japanese, and South Korean land reforms of the 1940s and 1950s were all essentially of this kind.

At the other extreme are reforms that break up large, highly efficient modern estates or farms and substitute small, inefficient producers. In many parts of the developing world, such as Mexico, Kenya, and Malaysia, large, highly mechanized estates using the most advanced techniques have grown up over time. The incentive problems inherent in the use of hired farm labor are at least partially overcome by the use of skilled professional estate managers. Often these estates are major suppliers of agricultural produce for export, and hence a crucial source

6. There are many studies of Japanese land reform, including R. P. Dore, *Land Reform in Japan* (London: Oxford University Press, 1959).

of the developing country's foreign exchange. If land reform breaks up these estates and turns them over to small peasant proprietors who know little about modern techniques and lack the capital to pay for them, the impact on agricultural productivity can be catastrophic. But there are also examples, as in the Kenyan highlands, where the breakup of large estates into small peasant holdings actually increased productivity, mainly because the small holdings were farmed much more intensively than the large estates. In between these two extremes are a myriad of variations with different impacts on productivity, both positive and negative.

Land Reform and Income Distribution

Land reform will have a major impact on the distribution of income in rural areas only if land is taken from landlords without compensation, or at least without anything close to full compensation. If former tenants are required to pay landlords the full market value of the land received, the society's distribution of wealth will be the same as before. The tenant will receive land together with a debt exactly equal to the value of the land, and hence the change in net wealth of the former tenants will be zero. The former landlord will surrender land but will acquire an asset of equal value in the form of a loan to the former tenant. Reform with full compensation may still be desirable on productivity grounds because of the advantages of strengthening property rights through owner rather than tenant cultivation, but initially at least the new owner will be just as poor and the new landlord just as rich as before. On the other hand, if the landlord is compensated with bonds paid for out of general tax revenues, the former tenant's income share may rise provided that the taxes to pay for this do not fall primarily on the tenant. The best-known successful land reforms have commonly involved little or no compensation for confiscated assets of landlords. Such was the case in Russia after 1917 and China after 1949, as well as in the Japanese and South Korean reforms after World War II. This discussion of land-tenure relations and their reform sets the scene for the discussion of agricultural production and how it can be raised. Much of the analysis that follows will deal with subjects like agricultural research or the uses of chemical fertilizer. But it must always be kept in mind that behind the use of better techniques and more inputs there must be a land-tenure system that provides farmers with well-defined, secure, and enforceable property rights and hence with the incentive to introduce those techniques and inputs, and then use them efficiently.

Technology of Agricultural Production

The popular view of traditional agricultural systems is that they are made up of peasants who have been farming the same way for centuries. The implication is that traditional farmers are bound by custom and incapable of making changes that raise the productivity and efficiency of their efforts. Custom in turn is reinforced by values and beliefs often closely tied to religion. Change thus becomes doubly difficult because to make a change may involve a rejection of deeply held religious beliefs. In this case only a revolution that completely overturns the traditional society and all it stands for holds out real hope for agricultural development.

Traditional Agriculture

Tradition-bound societies of this type do exist in the world, but the description does not fit the great majority of the world's peasant farmers. A great accumulation of evidence suggests that these farmers are efficient, that they have already made sensible—sometimes complex and subtle—adaptations to their environment, and that they are willing to make further changes to increase their welfare if it is clear that an improvement will result without an unacceptable risk of crop failure and hence starvation.[7]

When traditional agriculture is described as "efficient," the word is used in the same way as it has been used throughout this book. Given existing technology, traditional farmers get the most output they can from available inputs or they get a given level of output with the smallest possible use of inputs. Foreign advisors, regardless of their background, have often had to relearn this fact, sometimes at considerable cost. With a little reflection it is hardly surprising that traditional agriculture tends to be efficient within the limits of traditional techniques. The central characteristic of traditional technology is that it changes very slowly. Farmers thus are not in a position to constantly respond to changing agricultural methods; instead, they can experiment over long periods of time with alternative techniques until just the right method for the given technology is found. Long periods of time in this context may refer to decades or even to centuries. If a slightly deeper method of plowing or a closer planting of seeds will raise yields per acre, for example, one or two more venturesome farmers are eventually going to give such methods a try. At least they will do so if they have plows capable of deeper cultivation. If the techniques work, their neighbors will observe and eventually follow suit. Given several decades or a century all farmers in the region will be using similar methods.

This example brings out a closely related characteristic of traditional agriculture. In addition to being efficient, traditional agricultural techniques are not stagnant; they have evolved slowly over time. That peasant farmers in a traditional setting are willing to change if the benefits from a change are clearly perceived has been demonstrated over and over again. Some of the best evidence in support of this willingness to change is that provided by responses to changes in prices. Time and again as prices of cotton or tobacco or jute have risen relative to other farm prices, farmers—even in some of the poorest countries in the world—have rushed to increase the acreage of these crops. And the reverse has occurred when prices have fallen.

Change in traditional agriculture has involved much more than responses to fluctuations in relative prices. Long before the advent of modern science and its application to farming, there were fundamental advances in all aspects of agricultural technology.

Slash-and-Burn Cultivation

One of the most fundamental changes, of course, was the conversion of society from groups of hunters and gatherers of wild plants to groups of settled farmers who cleared and plowed the land. Initially settled farming often involved slash-and-burn methods of cultivation. In slash-and-burn agriculture, trees are slashed

7. One of the classic statements of this point has been made by Theodore W. Schultz, *Transforming Traditional Agriculture* (New Haven, Conn.: Yale University Press, 1964).

and fire is used to clear the land. The burnt tree stumps are left in the ground, and cultivation seldom involves much more than poking holes in the ground with a digging stick and dropping seeds into the holes. The original nutrients in the soil plus the nutrients from the burnt ashes make respectable yields possible for a year or two, after which most of the nutrients are used up, weed problems increase, and yields fall off drastically. Farmers then move on to slash and burn a new area, perhaps returning to the first area 20 or 30 years later when the land has regained a sufficient level of plant nutrients. Slash-and-burn agriculture is thus often referred to as a form of **shifting cultivation** or **forest-fallow cultivation.** This system requires a large amount of land to support a small number of people. Today the system exists mainly in remote, lightly populated areas, such as in the mountains of Laos and in parts of Africa and the Amazon.

The Shortening of Fallow

The evolution from slash-and-burn agriculture to permanent cultivation, in which a crop is grown on a piece of land once every year, can be thought of as a process of gradually shortening the period that land is left fallow. The term **fallow** refers to the time that land is left idle to allow the soil to reaccumulate the nutrients essential to successful cultivation. In Europe the shortening of fallow gradually took place during and after the Middle Ages, and annual cropping did not become common until the latter part of the eighteenth century. In China the evolution to annual cropping occurred at least a thousand years earlier. In both Europe and China the driving force behind this evolution was increased population pressure on the land.[8]

The elimination of fallow did not occur automatically or easily. Farmers had to discover ways to restore nutrients in the soil by rotating crops and by adding fertilizers such as compost and manure. Ploughs had to be developed to cultivate the land each year yet prevent it from being taken over by grasses. Each of these changes was at least as fundamental as many that have occurred in agriculture in the twentieth century. The difference is that these earlier changes took place over centuries rather than years.

Farming within a Fixed Technology

Once fallow was eliminated, increases in agricultural production could be obtained either by increasing yields on annually cropped land or by expanding onto previously uncultivated land. Where population pressure was particularly severe several centuries ago, grain yields reached levels per hectare higher than those found in many parts of the world even today. In China, for example, two crops a year of rice or of rice and wheat were common before the sixteenth century. By the mid-nineteenth century in both China and Japan average rice-paddy yields per acre over large areas had passed 2.5 to 3 tons per hectare, whereas in India and Thailand as late as the 1960s average rice yields were under 1.5 tons per hectare. Traditional agriculture was capable of achieving high levels of productivity per unit of land.

8. Ester Boserup, *The Conditions of Agricultural Growth: The Economies of Agrarian Change and Population Pressure* (Chicago: Aldine, 1965), and Dwight H. Perkins, *Agricultural Development in China, 1368–1968* (Chicago: Aldine, 1969).

What separates traditional from modern agricultural development, therefore, is not the existence of technological progress or the sophistication of the techniques used. Traditional agriculture experienced substantial technological progress, and the techniques used in highly populated areas at least were as sophisticated as many so-called modern techniques found today. The difference between traditional and modern agriculture is in the pace and source of change. In traditional agriculture, change is slow, whereas in modern agriculture, it is rapid. In modern agriculture, scientific research produces most of the new techniques used. In traditional agriculture, new techniques were sometimes the result of the tinkering of individual farmers, and at other times new inputs, such as improved seeds, were accidents of nature that led to a variety that produced higher yields or required a shorter growing season.

The principal problem of traditional agriculture, therefore, was that farmers worked most of their lives within a technology that changed very slowly. They could spend their energies raising the efficiency with which they used that technology, but the gains from higher levels of efficient use of a stagnant technique were limited. The improvements in technique that did occur happened over too long an interval of time to have anything but a marginal impact on rural standards of living.

Modernizing Agricultural Technology

Traditional agriculture can be modernized in two ways. The first is technological: specific inputs and techniques can be combined to produce higher agricultural production. Technological modernization deals with such issues as the role of chemical fertilizer and the relationship of fertilizer's impact to the availability of improved plant varieties and adequate supplies of water. These technological issues are the subject of this and the next section. The second approach to modernization concerns the mobilization of agricultural inputs and techniques in developing countries. How, for example, does a country mobilize labor for rural public works or create institutes that will develop new techniques suitable to local conditions? These issues of mobilization and organization are the subject of the following part of this chapter.

There is no universally best technology for agriculture. All agricultural techniques must be adjusted to local soil and climatic conditions and to local factor endowments. Even in industry, technology must be adapted to local conditions, but an automobile assembly plant in Ghana will look much like one of similar size in Indonesia. In agriculture, local conditions are fundamental, not secondary. Students from a developing country can be sent to advanced countries to learn how to develop improved plant varieties suitable to their country, but only occasionally will the plant varieties in the advanced country be directly transferable.

Still, generalizations can be made about the characteristics of modern agricultural technology. The technological development that occurs will differ markedly depending on whether a country has a large area of arable land and a small declining rural population or a large rural population on a very limited amount of arable land. The problem in the former is to get the most output possible out of its limited rural labor force. The latter country must also raise labor productivity. The key to success depends primarily on achieving rapid increases in the productivity of the land.[9] The fundamental difference between these two strategies can be illustrated with a simple diagram, Figure 16–1. As the figure makes clear, the United States and Japan have pursued fundamentally different agricultural strategies, and most other countries fall somewhere in between. In the United States, labor productivity is extremely high but yields per hectare are well below those of many countries, including more than a few of the less developed. In contrast, Japanese labor productivity in agriculture is only a fraction of that in the United States, but land productivity is several times that of the United States.

The difference between the two strategies involves basically different technologies. These different technologies are often called the mechanical package (of technologies) and the biological package. The **mechanical package** refers to the use of tractors, combines, and other forms of machinery primarily as substitutes for labor that has left the farm for the cities. The **biological package** refers to raising yields through the use of improved plant varieties such as hybrid corn or the new varieties of rice developed at the International Rice Research Institute in the Philippines. Because of the dramatic effect on yields of some of these new varieties, the phenomenon is often referred to as the **Green Revolution.** But these new varieties raise yields only if they are combined with adequate and timely

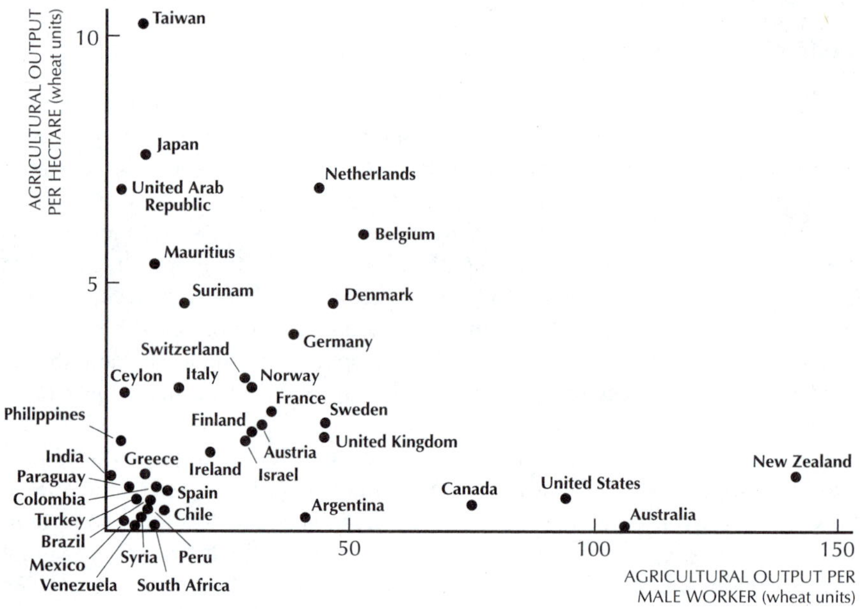

FIGURE 16–1 International Comparison per Male Worker and per Hectare of Agricultural Land. The dot for the United States indicates that U.S. grain output per farm worker was nearly 100 tons of wheat or its equivalent but U.S. yields per hectare were only about 1 ton. Mauritius, in contrast, had over 5 tons of output per hectare but little more than 10 tons per worker. Output data in the diagram are 1957 to 1962 averages; and labor and land data are for the year closest to 1960.
Source: Yujiro Hayami and Vernon W. Ruttan, *Agricultural Development: An International Perspective* (Baltimore: Johns Hopkins Press, 1971), p. 71.

9. The point is that innovation is induced by perceived needs. See Hans P. Binswanger and Vernon W. Ruttan, *Induced Innovation: Technology, Institutions and Development* (Baltimore: Johns Hopkins Press, 1977).

water supplies and increased amounts of chemical fertilizer. The basic production functions that describe these two packages therefore are fundamentally different. The isoquants of a production function representing the mechanical package indicate a high degree of substitutability (Figure 16–2), whereas the isoquants for the biological package are drawn in a way to indicate a high degree of complementarity (Figure 16–3). The L-shaped isoquants in Figure 16–3 indicate complementarity because only a limited number of fertilizer and water combinations will produce increases in grain output. Continual increases of only one input, such as fertilizer, will run into diminishing returns and then, where the curve flattens out, zero returns. Even with the biological package there is some substitutability but less than in the case of the mechanical package.

The Mechanical Package

To someone familiar with the cornfields of Iowa or the wheat fields of Nebraska and the Dakotas, mechanization means the use of large John Deere tractors and combines, metal silos with mechanical loading devices, and numerous other pieces of expensive equipment. Using such equipment, a single farmer with one assistant can farm hundreds of acres of land. But mechanization can also occur profitably on farms of only a few acres. As labor becomes more abundant and land less so, the mechanical package becomes less important in relation to the biological package, but mechanization still has a role to play even in poor, labor-intensive agricultural systems.

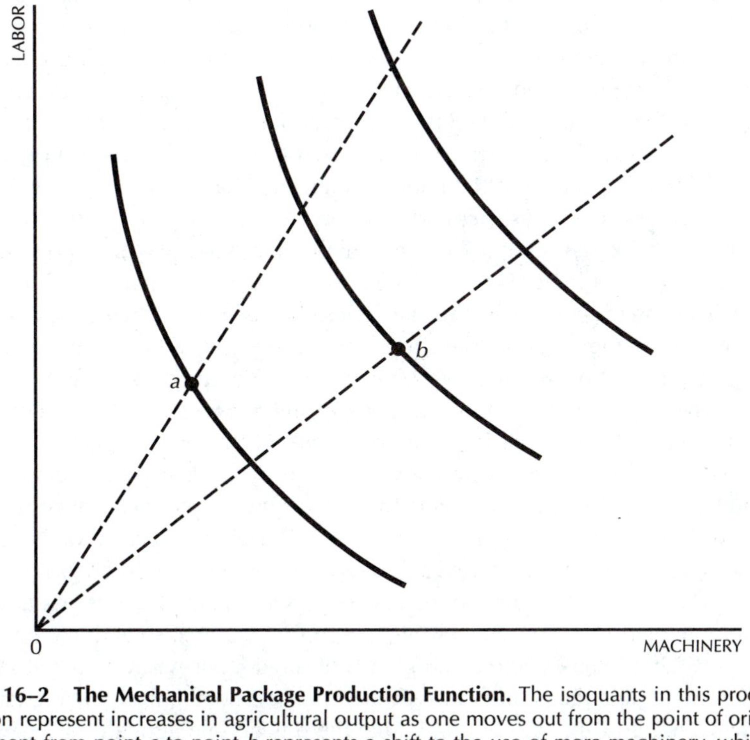

FIGURE 16–2 The Mechanical Package Production Function. The isoquants in this production function represent increases in agricultural output as one moves out from the point of origin (0). Movement from point *a* to point *b* represents a shift to the use of more machinery, which also involves a rise in agricultural output because machinery is a good substitute for labor.

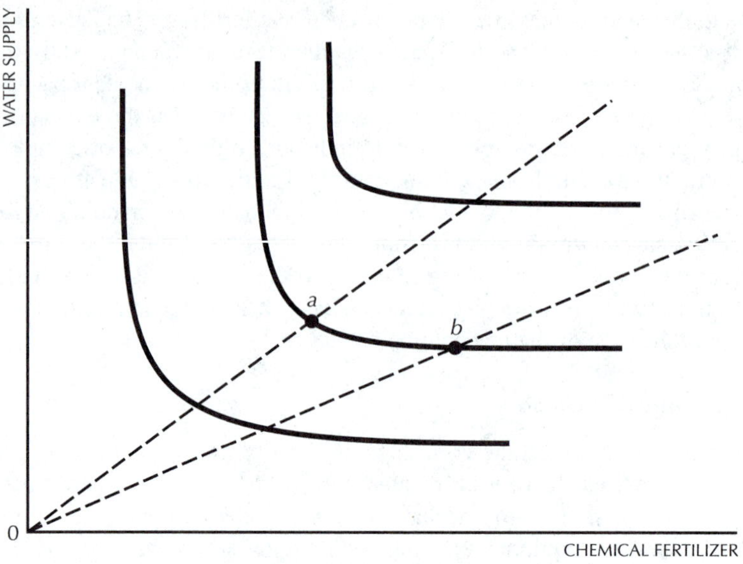

FIGURE 16–3 The Biological Package Production Function. The isoquants in this production function also represent increases in agricultural output as one moves out from the point of origin (0), but these isoquants, unlike those in Figure 16–2, indicate that there is little substitutability between inputs. An increase in fertilizer from point *a* to point *b*, for example, does not lead to a rise in agricultural output because the required increase in water supply to make the fertilizer effective has not occurred.

Mechanization of agriculture in labor-abundant developing countries is primarily a substitute for labor, just as in the labor-short U.S. Midwest. Even in countries such as China or India there are periods when the demand for labor exceeds its supply. When two rice crops are grown each year, for example, the first crop must be harvested, fields prepared, and the second crop transplanted—all within a matter of a few weeks. Transporting the harvest to market also takes an enormous amount of labor if goods must be brought in on carts hauled by men or animals, or as head loads by women, as is still the case in much of the developing world. One driver with a truck can do in a day what might otherwise take dozens of men and women several days to do. Nor can humans or animals working a hand pump or a water wheel move much water to the fields, however hard they work. A small diesel pump can move more water to higher levels than a large number of oxen turning wheels, and oxen cost more to feed than the pump costs to fuel.

Even when labor is extremely inexpensive, therefore, it can be economical to substitute machines for labor in some operations. Over the years manufacturers in Japan and elsewhere have developed whole lines of miniaturized machinery such as hand tractors and rice transplanters to meet this need, and these machines are in widespread use in the developing world. Not all mechanization in the developing world has been economic, however. Frequently tractors and other forms of farm machinery are allowed to enter a country duty free (when other imports have high tariffs) or are subsidized in other ways. Large farmers thus sometimes find it privately profitable to buy tractors and get rid of hired labor when, in the absence of subsidies, they (and the country) would be better off economically using laborers.

A major point of this discussion is that there is no one agricultural technology that is most efficient in all countries. The technology that produces a given level of output at the lowest possible cost in a country with a low per capita income is likely to be very different from the technology that produces the same product at the lowest cost in a country with a high per capita income. The reason is straightforward. Labor in a country with a low per capita income is typically paid much lower wages than in the richer country. Capital conversely is often less expensive in countries with a higher per capita income.

How this works can be illustrated by adding **isocost** lines to Figure 16–2. This is done in Figure 16–4. The isocost lines (*ac* and *bd*) illustrate the various combinations of labor and machinery that can be purchased for a given sum of money, say $1,000 at prices prevailing for machinery and labor in that country. The line *bd* represents the relative costs of these inputs in a high per capita income country where labor is expensive and capital relatively cheap. The line *ac* represents the situation in a poorer country where labor is inexpensive and capital is relatively costly. The objective for the efficient farmer is to produce the most output possible at a given cost (or to minimize the cost required to produce a given output). For the country with a low per capita income, that most efficient point is at *f* where its isocost line is tangent to the isoquant *efgh* of the production function. For the country with the higher per capita income and the relatively expensive labor, in contrast, tangency is achieved at point *g* on that same isoquant. At point *g* the richer country will use substantially more capital and less labor to produce the same level of output as will the poorer country producing at point *f*.

In some cases, however, the capital-intensive technology will be superior regardless of the relative prices of capital and labor. An example would be the use of tube wells with power pumps to replace wells dug by hand with water obtained with a bucket and rope. The latter uses much more labor but saves little or no capital. This situation is illustrated in Figure 16–5. The isocost lines of both the high and low per capita income countries, *ac* and *bd,* are tangent to the production isoquant at almost the same point (*e* is close to *f*). This situation where efficient sub-

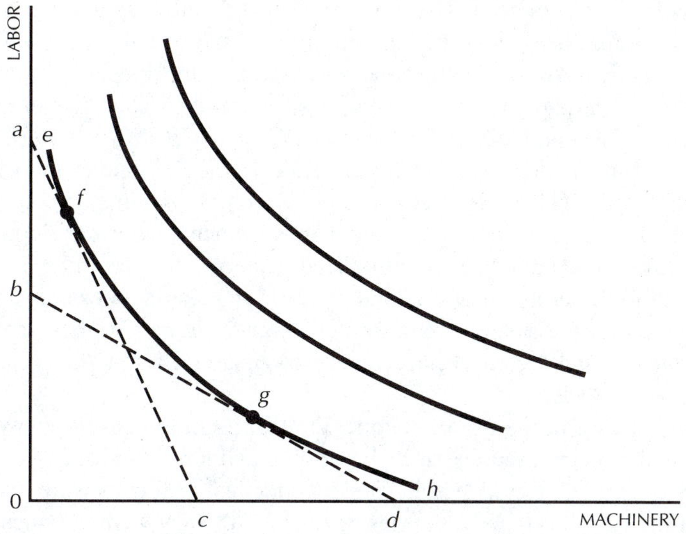

FIGURE 16–4 Choices of Technology with Differing Costs of Capital and Labor. The technology choices here are similar to those in Figure 16–2. Added are the isocost line for the high per capita income country *(bd)* and the low per capita income country *(ac)*.

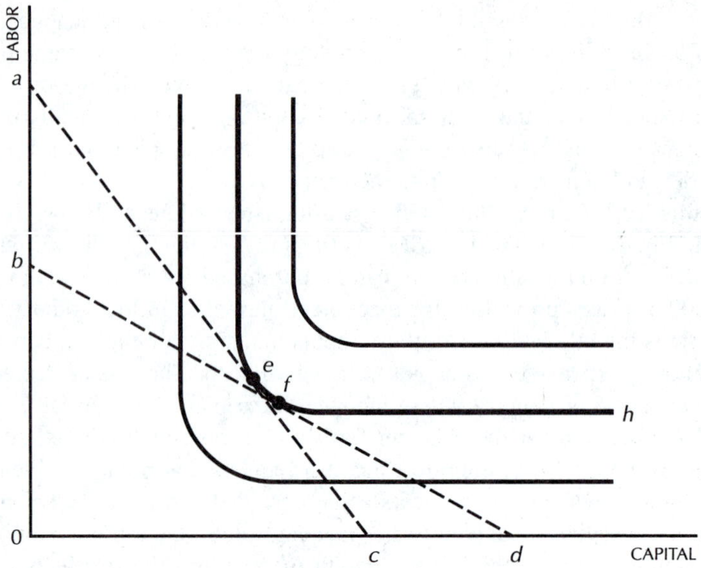

FIGURE 16–5 Choices of Technology with Differing Costs of Capital and Labor and Limited Substitutability between Capital and Labor. This figure is similar to Figure 16–4 except for the use of production function isoquants that indicate limited substitutability between capital and labor.

stitutability is limited is also commonly found with respect to some elements in the biological package, to which we now turn.

The Biological Package and the Green Revolution

The main impact of the biological package is to raise yields. There is nothing new about using improved plant varieties in combination with fertilizers and pesticides to raise yields of rice or corn. The use of modern scientific laboratories to develop the new varieties dates back half a century and more. Only in the 1960s and 1970s, however, have the methods so successful in the industrialized countries been applied throughout the developing countries. The founding of the International Maize and Wheat Improvement Center (CIMMYT[10]) in Mexico and the International Rice Research Institute (IRRI) in the Philippines marked the beginning of a truly international effort to develop high-yielding varieties of grain suitable to the tropical conditions found in so much of the developing world. National efforts preceded these international centers, and other international centers devoted to the problem of arid and semiarid developing areas have followed. The result has been a steady stream of new, high-yielding varieties of wheat and rice that have found increasing acceptance in Asia and Latin America, and to a lesser degree in Africa.

A rapid increase in the use of chemical fertilizers in the developing world had accompanied the increased use of high-yielding and other improved varieties (see Table 16–2). Prior to World War II, modern chemical fertilizers were virtually unknown in the less-developed countries. By the 1970s they were in widespread use

10. The acronym refers to the name in Spanish, *Centro Intenacional de Mejoramiento de Mais y Trijo.*

Table 16–2 Consumption of Chemical Fertilizer in Developing Countries (1000 metric tons of nutrient)

Year	Latin America	Far East*	Near East	Africa
1948–49—52–53 (annual average)	116.5	617.2	93.8	32.5
1961–62—65–66 (annual average)	609.7	1,839.3	379.3	192.2
1969–70	1,171.7	3,546.3	693.9	395.5
1979–80	6,720	9,473	2,831	1,142
1984	7,293	14,442	4,242	1,482
1988	8,807	19,237	5,019	1,694
1992–93	7,908	24,407	4,632	3,780

*Far East excludes Asian centrally planned economies.

Sources: FAO, *Production Yearbook 1970* (Rome: Food and Agricultural Organization, 1971); *Fertilizer Yearbook 1984* (Rome: Food and Agricultural Organization, 1985), p. 121; *Fertilizer Yearbook 1989,* pp. 88–89; *Fertilizer Yearbook 1993,* pp. 119–20.

from Brazil to India. Unlike machinery, chemical fertilizers can be purchased in almost any quantity and even very small amounts help yields. Thus, chemical fertilizers are within the reach of even quite poor peasants. The principal limitations on the greater use of chemical fertilizer have not been the conservatism of the peasants or their poverty, but the availability of supplies and the price at which these supplies have been sold. We will return to the price question later in this chapter.

A key component of the biological package is water. Improved plant varieties using more chemical fertilizer lead to dramatically higher yields only when there is an adequate and timely water supply. In much of the U.S. Midwest, rainfall provides all the water required and at the right time. In many parts of the developing world, rainfall is often inadequate or comes at the wrong time. In much of India, the difference between a good crop and a harvest failure still depends primarily on when the monsoon rains arrive and in what amount. As a result, efforts to raise yields in the developing world have often focused on measures to extend irrigation systems so that crops are less dependent on the vagaries of the weather.

Extending the irrigated acreage has often been seen as primarily a financial and engineering problem. If a country had enough money in the 1950s and 1960s (from aid or its own resources), it hired a group of engineers to build a dam to create a reservoir and canals to take water to the fields. As one dam project after another was completed, however, it became increasingly apparent that the irrigation potential of these systems was badly underutilized. Engineers could build the dams and the main canals, but they could not always get the farmer to build and maintain the feeder canals to the fields. Who should do the work and who would reap the benefits of these canals became entangled in the conflicting interests and local politics of rural society. Irrigation extension was as much a social as an engineering and ecological question.

More than anything else, the increased use of inputs from this biological package has made possible the steady, if unspectacular, expansion of agricultural output that has kept the food supply even with, or a bit ahead of, the rise in population (see Table 16–3). In the future, further development of improved varieties and expansion of irrigation systems, together with increased chemical fertilizer production, will remain the major contributors to higher yields. The main function of the mechanical package, in contrast, remains freeing labor from the

Table 16–3 Food Production per Capita in Developing Countries (indices 1979–1981 = 100)

Year	All developing countries	Latin America	Far East*	Near East	Africa
1980	99	99	99	100	100
1982	103	103	104	102	99
1984	107	101	112	96	93
1986	109	101	113	103	100
1988	111	105	117	102	99
1990	114	103	122	99	97
1991	113	102	123	96	98

* Does not include Asian centrally planned economies.
Source: FAO, *Production Yearbook 1971, 1980, 1981, 1984, 1989,* and *1991.*

burden of producing food so that it can do other, hopefully more productive, tasks. Whether those tasks will in fact be more productive depends on what is happening in the rest of the economy.

Mobilization of Agricultural Inputs

Although the technology of increasing agricultural output is well understood, the ways in which the relevant inputs can be mobilized are both complex and much less well understood. Some of the problems have already been touched on, both in the discussion of difficulties in expanding irrigation and in the earlier presentation of the relationship between land tenure systems, individual incentives, and management difficulties. Here we shall discuss some of these issues further in the context of the agricultural production function. In brief the question is: What are the alternative ways a rural society can supply itself with the necessary amounts of labor, capital, and improved techniques?

Rural Public Works Projects

Mobilizing labor to raise crops is primarily a question of individual and family incentives. The main determinants of these incentives are the nature of property rights over the use of land and the prices paid and received for agricultural inputs and outputs (treated later in this chapter). Mobilization of labor to create rural capital—roads, irrigation systems, and other parts of the rural infrastructure—is the topic of this section.

The creation of a rural infrastructure through the mobilization of rural labor has long been the dream of economic planners in the developing world. The idea is a simple one. In the off-season, labor in the rural sectors of developing countries is unemployed or underemployed. Therefore the opportunity cost of using that labor on rural public works projects is zero or near zero (although food consumption may go up for people doing heavy construction work).

To use this labor in factories, the factories must first be built, and that requires the use of scarce capital equipment. Furthermore, this equipment will lie idle when the rural workers return to the fields to plant and harvest their crops. No such problems exist, however, when off-season unemployed labor is used to build roads or irrigation canals. There is no need to buy bulldozers and other heavy equipment. If there is enough labor, shovels and baskets to carry dirt can accomplish much the same purpose, and farmers already have shovels and baskets or can easily make them. In the ideal situation, therefore, unemployed workers can first be put to work making crude construction tools, after which they can begin to create roads and canals. The end result is a major expansion in the rural capital stock at little or no cost to society other than the reduced leisure time of rural workers.

Effective implementation of rural public works programs using seasonally unemployed labor, however, has proved extremely difficult. The community development programs of India and elsewhere are widely perceived as failures. Time and again international aid agencies have started pilot public works projects, only to see the projects die quietly when aid money ran out. Of all the problems connected with the mobilization of unemployed rural labor, the most basic has been the lack of connection between those who did the work and those who reaped most of the benefits.

When an irrigation canal or a road is built, the main benefits that result take the form of higher yields on land near the canal or easier access to the market for crops grown on land near the road. Land or people living distant from the canal or road receives fewer benefits or none at all. If the people who own the nearby land are also those who did the work constructing a road or canal, then there is a direct relation between effort and reward. Unfortunately, more often than not the people who do the work reap few of the rewards. The extreme case is when the land serviced by the new canal or road is owned by absentee landlords. Absentee landlords are never mobilized for rural public works projects. It is landless laborers and tenants who do all the work, and the landlords who benefit in the form of increased rents. Workers on such projects must be paid wages, and these wages tend to be higher than is justified by their productivity. Rural construction with crude tools is, after all, very low productivity work. If the wages paid exceed the benefits of the project, it is hardly surprising that these projects come to an end when government or aid agency subsidies run out.

Labor Mobilization in Chinese Communes

Even when land is owned by those who cultivate it, there is a problem of matching effort and reward. A typical project may require the labor of an entire village or several villages, whereas the benefits go primarily to farmers in only one part of the village. The Chinese solution to this problem was to collectivize agriculture by forming people's communes.[11] An entire village owned its land in common. People who participated in public works projects received work points based on the amount of effort expended just as if they had spent their time cultivating crops. When the project was completed, the land in a part of the village would be more productive, but the higher productivity benefited the entire village. The gap between work and reward in effect had been closed.

The Chinese commune did make possible the more or less voluntary mobilization of large amounts of underemployed rural labor. Hills were

11. When China first collectivized agriculture (1955 to 1957), the Chinese called their rural collectives *producers' cooperatives,* but to simplify the discussion we refer to them as *communes.*

leveled to create new fields, new reservoirs dotted the countryside, and roads reached deep into the countryside where only footpaths had existed before. But the Chinese ran into the work-reward problem in a different form. As the rural works projects became larger and larger, it became necessary to mobilize labor from two-dozen villages, even though the benefits of the project went largely to only one or two of those villages.

The initial solution to this problem was to pool the land of all two-dozen into a single commune. Then increased productivity on the land around a single village would be shared by all 24 villages, and workers in those villages once again had an incentive to participate in the project. This larger commune, made up of two-dozen villages, however, immediately ran into all the incentive and managerial problems common to large collective units. The result was that despite all the construction activity, or even because of it, Chinese agricultural output fell; and small collective units called *production teams* replaced the large communes as the basic agricultural management unit, although the latter continued to exist and to perform some functions.

Clearly the problem of mobilizing unemployed labor to build rural infrastructure is more difficult than economists and others first thought. The complexity of successfully sharing the benefits is such that rural public works, though possible, are not the universal solution to the problem of rural development that some once thought them to be.

Rural Banks and Credit Cooperatives

A second approach to the problem of providing rural areas with sufficient capital for development is to establish rural banks or credit cooperatives that will lend to farmers. In traditional agriculture a farmer has only two sources of credit: members of the family and the local moneylender. Since the interest rates charged by moneylenders typically range from 30 or 40 percent to over 100 percent a year, a farmer goes to a moneylender only when desperate. Peasants do not borrow from moneylenders to buy more fertilizer or a new pump. Only rarely will such investments be productive enough to make it possible to pay off loans with exceedingly high interest charges.

There are numerous reasons why urban commercial banks do not move in and take over from the moneylenders. Because of their location, urban banks lack the knowledge and skills necessary to operate efficiently in rural areas. On the other hand, local moneylenders know the reliability of the people to whom they are lending and the quality of land put up as collateral. Individuals without land, of course, have difficulty getting money even from local moneylenders. Women in particular may have difficulty when they farm land registered in the name of an absent husband—a frequent occurrence in Africa and elsewhere.

Credit cooperatives set up by the small farmers are one potential solution to this problem. The idea is that each farmer is capable of saving a small sum, and if these sums are pooled, one or two farmers can borrow a substantial sum to buy a new thresher or pump. The next year it will be another farmer's turn, and so on. In the meantime those who put their money in the cooperative will draw interest, and thus be encouraged to save more. But this approach has flaws. Farmers' savings tend to be small, and hence the cooperatives tend to be financially weak. More seriously, farmers in developing countries have little experience relevant to the effective operation and management of the cooperatives. In addition, economic, social, and political conflicts within the village may make it impossible to decide something as simple as who will get the next loan.

Because of these and other problems, the establishment of rural credit institutions usually requires significant injections of both money and personnel from outside the village, usually from the government. The entry of the government, however, does not necessarily or even usually, solve the underlying difficulties. A common occurrence is for a rural credit institution to be set up with funds from the central government's budget. These funds are then lent to local farmers not only at rates far below those charged by private credit sources but at rates so low that each loan requires a subsidy from the government. Since the rates are low and the credit institutions are run by government personnel, local farmers with political clout have both the incentive and the means to grab the lion's share of the financing available. Corrupt bank officials may also skim off some of the funds, and corrupt officials are seldom among the poorer elements in the village. Equally or more serious is the fact that these loans are often never paid back, so that the new credit institution must be constantly resupplied from the central budget or go out of business. Too frequently the government personnel running the local bank or cooperative lack the will or the authority to make their clients live up to their contracts.

The problems involved in setting up effective rural credit operations can be overcome. States with well-trained banking personnel and a strong government administration capable of drawing up sensible procedures and enforcing them are certainly able to make rural credit institutions work.

Well-trained personnel and effective government administrators are in short supply in a great many developing countries, but this need not be an insurmountable barrier. The Indonesian state-owned Bank Rakyat Indonesia (BRI), for example, has revamped the incentive systems for its rural lending and savings mobilization personnel. The result has been a manyfold rise in rural lending and an even larger increase in rural savings deposits—all happening at the same time that government subsidies to the BRI rural credit program were eliminated.

Extension Services

If one key to rapid progress in rural areas depends on the introduction of new inputs and new techniques, it follows that some of the most important rural institutions are those responsible for speeding the transfer of these new techniques to the farmers. **Extension services,** as these institutions are usually called, provide the key link between the research laboratories or experimental farms and the rural population that must ultimately adopt what the laboratories develop.

The key to the effectiveness of the extension worker is contact and trust. Rural education helps to increase the channels of contact, because if farmers can read, contact can be made through the written as well as the spoken word. Trust is necessary, because even if there is contact, the farmer may not believe what is read or heard. Trust, of course, depends not only on the extension worker's honesty or personality, but fundamentally, on the competence of the extension worker and of the research system. Giving a farmer bad advice that leads to crop failure is likely to close the channels of communication for some time. Making contact and establishing trust is further complicated because extension workers are usually men whereas those doing the farming, particularly in parts of Africa, are women.

These remarks are common sense, but they get at the heart of the failure of extension services in many developing countries. Frequently, training for the extension service is seen not as a way of learning how to help farmers but as a way of entering the government bureaucracy and escaping from the rural areas. Some extension workers are government clerks living in town and just as averse to getting their hands dirty as their colleagues in the tax collection bureau or the post office. Even when they do visit the farmers they are supposed to be helping, they know so little about how farmers really operate that they are incapable of pointing out genuinely useful new methods. Too often the extension worker visits the village, tells the farmers what is good for them, and departs; the farmers are left to guess as best they can whether the gain from using the new idea is worth the risk of failure.

At the other end of the spectrum are extension workers who are well-trained and who live in the villages and work closely with the farmers when new techniques are being introduced. Chinese communes in the 1960s and 1970s, for example, sent one of their members off for training on the condition that the individual would return to work for the commune. The same can happen in villages where family farms predominate, although the absence of the authoritarian controls found in China makes it more difficult in many places to guarantee that the individual sent will return. Another variation on this theme, tried by CIMMYT among others, is for the basic research to be carried out on farmers' fields rather than in separate experimental stations.

There is much that we do not yet know about the spread of advanced technology in agriculture, but an effective extension service is only a part of the picture. To a large degree, farmers learn from their neighbors. However, if one local farmer owns 30 acres and farms it with a large tractor and the neighboring farmers have only 5 acres and no tractors, the farmers with 5 acres may feel they have little to learn from the experience of their neighbor. More evidence is required, but technology appears to travel more rapidly when neighboring farms in a country or region are much alike. Extremes of inequality thus may impede technological progress as well as being undesirable on equity grounds.

As this discussion of mobilizing rural labor and capital and of accelerating the rate of technical advance makes clear, agricultural development in the developing countries is not solely a scientific or an engineering problem. It also depends on the quality of government administration at both central and local levels.

The Development of Rural Markets

One common theme in the preceding chapters has been the importance of avoiding major distortions in the structure of prices. Nowhere is an appropriate price structure more important than in the agricultural sector. But in agriculture as in other sectors there must first be a market before prices can have widespread effects. And in the rural areas of developing countries the existence of an effectively operating market cannot be taken for granted.

There are virtually no areas of the world today where subsistence farming in its purest form still exists. All farmers specialize to some degree and trade their surplus output on some kind of market. Economic development is usually accompanied by the increasing size and sophistication of this rural marketing network, and in turn that improved network has an important impact on productivity in agriculture. The key to an increasing role for the market is specialization, and specialization depends on economies of scale, low-cost transport, and acceptable risk.

Economies of scale are at the heart of specialization. If everyone could produce everything they needed at the lowest possible cost, there would be no need to turn over certain tasks to others. In fact economies of scale are pervasive. In the most advanced agricultural sectors such as the U.S. Midwest, farmers grow only one or two crops and rely on the market for all their other needs. In developing countries, the single greatest barrier to taking advantage of these economies of scale is transport costs. The absence of good roads or of trucks to run on them can mean that it can cost as much to move a bulky commodity 50 miles as to produce it in the first place. In the United States, wheat is turned into flour in large mills, and farmers buy bread in the local supermarket as everyone else. In developing countries, only wheat destined for urban consumption is processed in large mills. In rural areas, wheat is processed at home or in village mills, because to take the wheat to a large, distant mill would be prohibitively expensive. In large parts of southern Sudan, to take an extreme but not uncommon example, there are no all-weather roads at all, and large regions are completely cut off from the outside world during the rainy season. Regions such as this cannot readily specialize in crops for sale in the cities or for export abroad.

In large parts of the developing world, therefore, improvements in the transport system and hence in marketing can have a major impact on agricultural productivity. Construction of an all-weather road system in South Korea in the 1970s, for example, made it possible for millions of Korean farmers to increase dramatically their emphasis on vegetables and cash crops destined for urban and export markets. Even the simple device of building paved bicycle paths connecting to the main road made it possible for Hong Kong farmers to expand their vegetable acreage. In the absence of refrigerated transport, many vegetables spoil quickly, and hence it does not pay to raise them if too much time elapses between the harvest and their sale on the market. Furthermore, enormous amounts of labor are required if the vegetables must be carried every day on human backs across muddy fields. The ability to move the vegetables along a paved path on the back of a bicycle can make the difference between growing vegetables or concentrating on rice, which has to be moved to market only once a year.

Even when the transport system is adequate, farmers in developing countries may limit their dependence on the market because of the risk it entails. While cash crops can fail due to bad weather or pests, the principal risk from market dependence is that the price of the crop being raised will fall sharply by the time the farmer is ready to sell. For large farmers in advanced economies, a fall in price of their main crop leads to a reduction in their income. If the fall is large enough, that farmer may be forced to borrow from a local bank to tide him over until prices rise again. Or he may merely have to draw from the family's savings account. In developing countries a fall in the price of a cash crop, particularly if food prices are rising simultaneously, may lead to a drop in a farm family's income to a level below that necessary to survive. Credit may tide the family over, but interest rates will be so high that once in debt, the farmer may never be able to pay off creditors and will lose the land put up as collateral. Most farmers in developing countries avoid becoming dependent on a single cash crop and instead devote part of their land to meeting their family's food requirements. Their average income over the long run might be higher if they planted all their land in cotton or tobacco, but they might not live to see the long run if one or two years of depressed prices wipe them out.

Governments can take measures to reduce both transport costs (by building roads) and risks (by guaranteeing prices and other similar measures), and thereby develop more efficient markets. But governments also can, and often do, take measures that inhibit the development of rural marketing. Governments around the world have seldom had a real understanding of the role of rural traders, of the numerous middle traders who make a marketing system work. Middle traders are seen as exploiters who get between the producer and consumer; they drive the price paid to the producer down and that charged to the consumer up and reap huge monopoly profits. In response to political pressures from farmers, governments have often moved to take over the rural marketing system in order to improve its operation and eliminate the monopoly profits.[12] The temptation for governments to take this step is particularly strong where the middle traders are of a different race from the majority of the population, as is the case in much of Southeast Asia, where Chinese play a major role in marketing, and in East Africa, where descendants of nineteenth- and early-twentieth-century Indian immigrants now control the wholesale and retail trade.

Although occasionally government involvement improves rural marketing, more often such involvement is based on a wrong diagnosis of the problem. The price at which a farm product is sold in the cities is markedly higher than the price paid to the farmer, but the difference has little to do with monopoly profits. The real cause is the high cost of transport and a generally rudimentary system of distribution and marketing. It is not that rural traders get paid so much, it is just that it takes so many of them to get the goods to market. When the government takes over, it does not change this basic situation. For a high-cost, private rural trading network the government often substitutes an even higher cost bureaucratic control of the movement of goods.

Agricultural Price Policy

This discussion of agricultural development has stressed the central role of institutional change such as land reform and the creation of effective rural credit, marketing, and extension systems. It has also emphasized the importance of government investment in infrastructure, notably in agricultural research. But the creation of new rural institutions can take a long time. Needed changes in the land tenure system, in particular, can be blocked by powerful interests for decades and even longer. Nor can an agricultural research system be created in a few years' time. New plant varieties suitable to local conditions may take a decade to develop. If the plant scientists needed to carry out the research have not yet been trained, the process can take longer.

12. The problems created by too much government interference in agricultural marketing in Africa are discussed in Elliot Berg et al., *Accelerated Development in Sub-Saharan Africa* (Washington, D.C.: World Bank, 1981).

The Multiple Role of Prices

There is one area, however, where government intervention has an immediate and often profound positive or negative impact. Most governments in both industrialized and developing countries intervene in agricultural markets to set prices both for the rural producer and the urban consumer. How they intervene can have a profound effect both on agricultural production and on consumption. Specifically, the prices at which grain and other agricultural produce are bought and sold play three, and sometimes four, vital roles:

1. The prices paid to farmers, and the relation of those prices to the prices farmers pay for key inputs, such as fertilizer, have a major impact on what and how much those farmers can produce.

2. The prices paid to farmers, together with the quantity of produce sold, are the primary determinants of farmers' cash income.

3. The prices at which agricultural products are sold in the cities are major determinants of the cost of living of urban residents in developing countries.

4. The prices of agricultural products, particularly in many African countries, are often controlled by government marketing boards that manipulate them to earn profits for the government, a slightly disguised form of taxation.[13]

Prices have a profound impact on agricultural production because most farmers, even in very poor countries, are interested in raising their income. While some hold that peasants grow particular crops or use particular inputs because that is the way their grandfathers did it, study after study has shown that when prices change, peasant farmers respond much like any profit-maximizing businessperson operating in a world fraught with uncertainty. If the price of cotton rises relative to, say corn, farmers will grow more cotton even in very traditional societies.

The most important price relationship from the standpoint of agricultural production is that between farm outputs and purchased inputs, notably chemical fertilizer. From the farmer's point of view it makes sense to use more chemical fertilizer so long as it increases the value of farm output by more than its cost. (This is simply a manifestation of the profit-maximizing rule that the use of a factor of production should be increased as long as the factor's marginal revenue product exceeds its marginal cost.) The simplest and most-effective ways of increasing rice yields are to raise the price of rice or to lower the price of chemical fertilizer or to do both. As studies of rice production in Asia have shown, there is a clear relationship between the rice yield per acre in a country and the rice-fertilizer price ratio. Other elements are also at work, but the role of prices is a primary influence. This basic point is illustrated with the diagrams in Figure 16–6.

Part A is a simple one-input–one-output production function. The production function is drawn to reflect diminishing returns. If we know the prices of both fertilizer and rice, we can easily derive the marginal cost and marginal revenue curves facing the individual farmer, as is done in Part B.

If the price of fertilizer is lowered, the marginal cost curve will fall from MC_1

13. For a full discussion of the multiple role of prices, see C. Peter Timmer, Walter P. Falcon, and Scott R. Pearson, *Food Policy Analysis* (Baltimore: Johns Hopkins Press, 1983), and Isabelle Tsakok, *Agricultural Price Policy: A Practitioner's Guide to Partial-Equilibrium Analysis* (Ithaca, N.Y.: Cornell University Press, 1990).

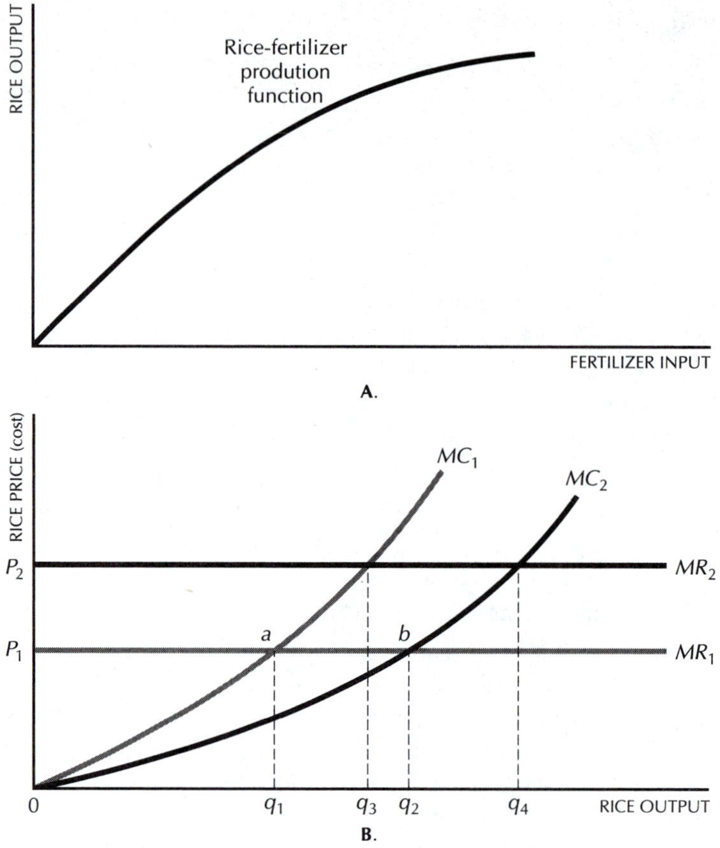

FIGURE 16–6 **Rice Production and the Rice-Fertilizer Price Ratio.**

to MC_2 and rice production will rise from q_1 to q_2 as farmers maximize their profits at point *b* instead of point *a* by increasing the use of fertilizer. Similarly, a rise in the price from P_1 to P_2 while holding fertilizer prices constant will increase rice output from q_1 to q_3.

The Impact of Subsidies

One of the most persistent problems facing planners and politicians in the developing world is the conflict between urban consumers and rural producers over appropriate agricultural prices. Since food purchases account for at least half the budget of urban consumers in most developing countries, a substantial increase in the price of food will cut sharply into the income of all but the richest urban people. Even governments indifferent to the welfare of their poorer urban residents cannot ignore the political impact of major increases in food prices. From Japan in the 1920s to Zambia in the 1990s, food price rises have triggered massive rioting that has threatened the very existence of particular regimes. (This phenomenon is closely akin to—and often part of—the politically dangerous transition from controlled to liberalized economies discussed in Chapter 5.) Because political leaders themselves live in urban areas, and because urban residents are in a better position than rural villagers to threaten governments, many states attempt to hold food prices down even during periods of general inflationary pressure. The result is depressed prices for farmers that reduce both farm income and farm output.

Especially (but not exclusively) in some developed countries the political power of the farmers is such that governments raise farm purchase prices in order to gain rural support. Democracies that still have large or politically powerful rural populations are particularly likely to respond to these pressures. The United States and Japan in the 1950s and 1960s, Japan and the European Community from the 1960s into the 1990s, and South Korea in the late 1960s and early 1970s are examples. The result is that prices are favorable to higher yields, but the income and production benefits of the higher prices may not be equitably distributed. In some countries it is richer farmers who market a high percentage of their output and hence gain most from high prices. Small subsistence farmers market little and hence gain little. In other countries, however, all farmers market a high percentage of their crop and hence all gain from higher prices.

Where both urban and rural residents have considerable political influence, governments have sometimes tried to maintain both low urban food prices and high farm purchase prices. Japan since World War II and South Korea and Mexico in the 1970s all pursued this dual goal. Since the government must pick up the deficit resulting from selling food at prices below what it cost to purchase, only governments with large resources or those willing to forgo other high-priority goals can afford this policy. Thus there is no single right answer to how high prices to farmers should be. Ultimately the decision turns on political as well as economic judgments.

One common way to subsidize grain marketing is for the government to absorb the often substantial costs of moving grain from the farm to the urban retail market. Who benefits from this process depends on how the subsidy is handled. Several of the possibilities are illustrated in Figure 16–7, in which marketing costs are represented by the vertical distance between the farmer's grain supply curve and the retail supply curve facing urban residents. These costs are assumed to be a constant amount per unit of grain marketed. On a free market without subsidy, the retail price of grain on the urban retail market would be p_1 and the price received by farmers would be p_2. As this diagram indicates, if the subsidy goes to farmers, the result can be either a rise in grain storage or exports. If the subsidy goes to urban consumers, on the other hand, the excess demand will lead to a rise in imports.

It is not just foreign trade in grain that is affected by these subsidies. The cost of marketing must be borne by someone, and in these cases it will most likely be an expenditure item in the government's budget. Or the grain marketing authority may borrow from the central bank to cover its costs, but without the ability of ever paying the loan back. The macroeconomic effects of these subsidies can be substantial, particularly in countries where a large portion of marketed agricultural produce is subsidized.

Overvalued Exchange Rates

Because the high cost of large subsidies to government marketing boards becomes increasingly obvious to policy makers over time, steps are usually taken to eventually bring these costs under control even though the political cost can be high. There is another way of subsidizing urban consumers or rural producers, however,

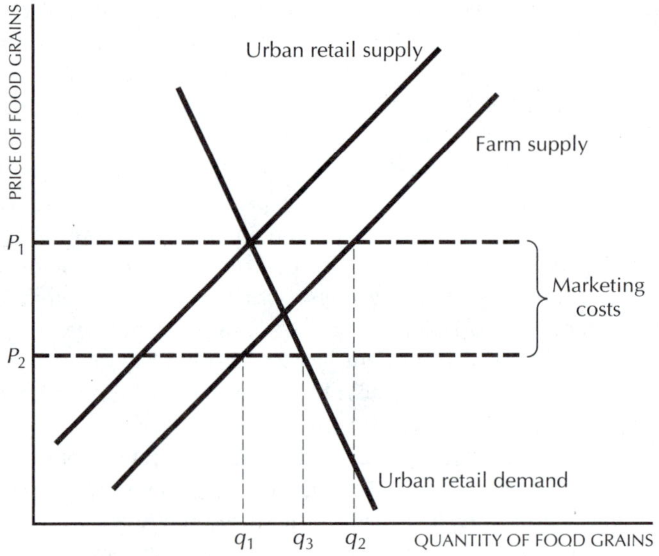

FIGURE 16–7. **Effect of a Marketing Subsidy on Supply and Demand for Food Grains.** If farmers receive the marketing cost subsidy P_1 P_2, then the farmers' price rises to P_1 and farm output rises from q_1 to q_2. Since food-grain supply now exceeds demand, the excess must either be stored or exported. On the other hand, if urban consumers are given the entire P_1P_2 subsidy, then the price paid by these consumers will fall to P_2 and their demand will rise from q_1 to q_3. The excess in demand will then have to be supplied from imports, or the government will have to ration the allocation of food grains to urban consumers.
Source: This diagram is a modified version of that in Timmer, Falcon, and Pearson, *Food Policy Analysis,* p. 198.

that has a less obvious effect on the government budget but a profound effect on the economy: the use of an *overvalued exchange rate* (see Chapter 19). The impact of an overvalued exchange rate on the grain market is illustrated in Figure 16–8. If, at an equilibrium exchange rate, the world price of grain is P_2, then domestic demand, represented by the curve *DD*, will be $0q_4$, and the domestic supply of grain will exceed demand by the amount q_4q_2. This excess could be either stored or exported. But if this nation's currency becomes overvalued, the world price of grain expressed in terms of domestic currency will fall from P_2 to P_1. Domestic food-grain supply, in this case, will fall to q_3, and the excess of demand at this price q_3q_1 will be made up with imports or by restricting urban demand through rationing. Thus, although this method of subsidizing urban consumers does not show up as an expenditure item in the government budget or a loss for the grain marketing board, it has a large negative impact on domestic agricultural production. Domestic agricultural production would fall from q_2 to q_3.[14]

An undervalued exchange rate, of course, will have a positive impact on farm output, but poor urban and rural purchasers of food grain may be forced by high prices to reduce substantially their intake of food, and this may lead to malnutrition and worse. In developing countries the poor spend a high proportion—over 50 percent—of their budget on food. A price increase for food thus represents a

14. For a study of how trade and macroeconomic policies affect agriculture, see Romeo Bautista and Alberto Valdés, *The Bias Against Agriculture: Trade and Macroeconomic Policies in Developing Countries* (San Francisco: ICS Press, 1993).

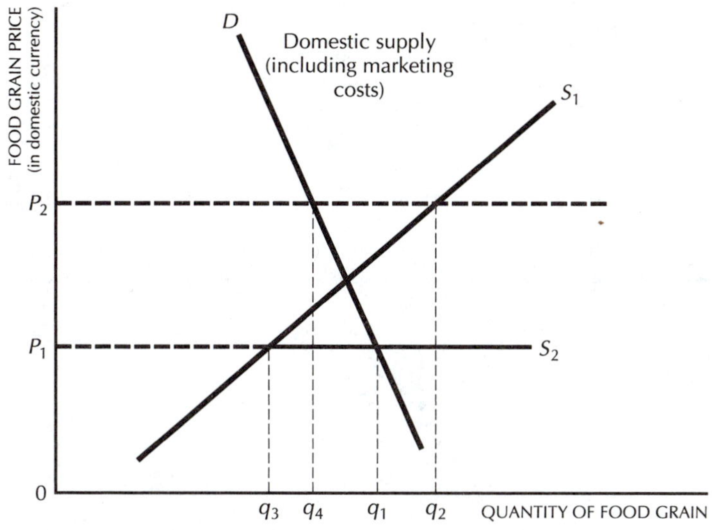

FIGURE 16–8. The Grain Market with an Overvalued Exchange Rate. If the world price of grain is P_2, then domestic demand (*DD*) will be q_4, and domestic supply (s_1s_2) will be q_2 and result in excess stocks for storage or export. With an overvalued exchange rate represented by P_1, however, domestic demand (q_1) exceeds domestic supply (q_3) and requires imports or rationing.

sharp drop in income for these people. They can try to maintain food consumption by cutting back on other items in their budget, but these are usually necessities as well.

Agricultural price policies, therefore, have a profound effect on both agricultural production and on the standard of living and even the basic health of the poorer segments of a country's people. Since agricultural prices and the exchange rate are usually set by the government in developing countries, it is technically a simple matter to change these prices to reflect the objectives of the government. Price changes involve few of the institution-building or implementation problems connected with developing an effective extension system or mobilizing labor for public works projects. Price changes, however, do involve readily apparent costs to those on the receiving end of higher prices. If these people are in a position of influence, the political barriers to effective price policy can be formidable.

17

Primary Exports

Every country trades with the outside world. The nature of that trade—the menu of goods that a country exports to other countries and imports from them—plays a central role in determining the character of development. Countries export commodities in which they enjoy a **comparative advantage**, as defined in the next section. This chapter discusses countries whose comparative advantages lie in primary commodities: food, agricultural raw materials, timber, metal ores, petroleum, and natural gas. Chapter 19 describes development strategies that attempt to change comparative advantage from primary products to manufactures.

Comparative Advantage

Trade theorists have tried to explain why nations trade and how they benefit from it largely under assumptions of *static conditions* that hold all domestic factors of production (land, other natural resources, labor, and capital) in fixed supply. The resulting **theory of comparative advantage** is rich in its implications about the gains from trade, the following among them: (1) Any country can increase its income by trading, because the world market provides an opportunity to buy some goods at relative prices that are lower than those which would prevail at home in the absence of trade. (2) The smaller the country, the greater this potential gain from trade, but all countries benefit to some extent. (3) A country will gain most by exporting commodities that it produces using its abundant factors of production most intensively, while importing those goods whose production would require relatively more of the scarcer factors of production.

The first implication is a subtle one that requires elaboration. To simplify greatly, assume that two countries, which can be called Mexico and the United States, both produce only two products, vegetables and computers, and use only one factor of production, labor. Table 17–1 shows the labor-days required to produce these products in each country.

Notice that in this example it takes more labor days to produce either product in Mexico. Despite this, it is to the advantage of the United States to buy vegetables in Mexico, even though they can be produced at home with less labor, and to sell computers to Mexico in return. In the United States labor costs dictate that a computer sell for the equivalent of 5 tons of vegetables.[1] But if the United States sells 1 computer in Mexico, it can buy 6 tons of vegetables for consumption. So if labor is shifted from farming to manufacturing computers, U.S. consumers can eat more vegetables than if there is no trade with Mexico, while buying the same number of computers. Mexico, which has to produce 6 tons of vegetables to buy 1 computer in the home market without trade, is better-off to switch its labor into producing more vegetables and selling them to the United States, where it only needs to trade 5 tons of vegetables for a computer and can save the other ton for its own consumption.

The important point of this example, and the core of comparative advantage, is that both countries can gain from trade whenever the **relative prices** of commodities in each country differ in the absence of trade. If the two countries do trade, then the relative price of vegetables in terms of computers would settle between five and six, the two relative prices prevailing before trade. The final trade price, which can be called the **world price,** will settle closer to the initial price in the market of the country whose economy is larger. Thus small countries benefit more from trade because the gains are greater the more the pretrade relative price differs from the posttrade world price. To see this, consider an extreme case in which the U.S. economy is so large that the posttrade price settles at the U.S. price before trade. Then the United States cannot gain from trade (nor can it lose), while Mexico would gain to the full extent of the price difference.

The theory of comparative advantage is posed here in the very simple form developed by David Ricardo during the nineteenth century: two countries, two goods, and only one factor of production, labor. Some of the complexities of the real world can be incorporated into the theory, however. A trading world of many countries can be handled by taking the home country, say, Kenya, and treating the

Table 17–1 Production Costs and Comparative Advantage

	Mexico	United States
Labor-days to produce:		
Vegetables (1 ton)	5	4
Computers (1)	30	20
Relative price (tons of vegetables per computer)	6	5

1. If each ton of vegetables requires 4 labor-days to produce, then it takes 5 tons of vegetables to absorb the same labor as 1 computer, which uses 20 labor-days. This formula for calculating relative prices works in this oversimplified example because labor is the only input into production.

rest of the world as its trading partner. The complexities of many goods will be addressed in Chapter 19. The theory was expanded to deal with two factors, such as labor and capital, by the Swedish economists, Eli Heckscher and Bertil Ohlin, during the first half of the twentieth century. Under certain conditions the Heckscher-Ohlin theory can be extended to include more factors of production and to yield another implication, that a country exports products that use its abundant factors of production more intensively and imports products that require relatively more of its scarce factors.

The implications of this more general approach to comparative advantage are encapsulated in Figure 17–1. In Chapter 6, where the production frontier was introduced, we divided the economy into production of X goods and Y goods, without being specific about the nature of those goods. In Figure 17–1, the economy of our **home country** is divided instead into **exportable goods**, such as vegetables, that are produced using relatively land- and labor-intensive methods, and **importable goods**, such as computers, produced using relatively capital-intensive methods. As shown in the diagram, the home country is relatively well endowed with land and labor, so the production frontier is skewed to the right, depicting the country's greater capacity to produce vegetables than computers. The country's collective utility in consuming these goods is represented by the community indifference curves, also introduced in Chapter 6.

Without trade, the home country achieves its greatest utility by producing and consuming at point *A*, the tangency of the indifference curve I and the production frontier. The slope at *A* determines the domestic relative price of vegetables in terms of computers. Assume that the rest of the world is better endowed with capital than with labor and land relative to the endowments of the home country and that world consumers have tastes broadly similar to those of the home country. Then on world markets the relatively higher production of computers compared to

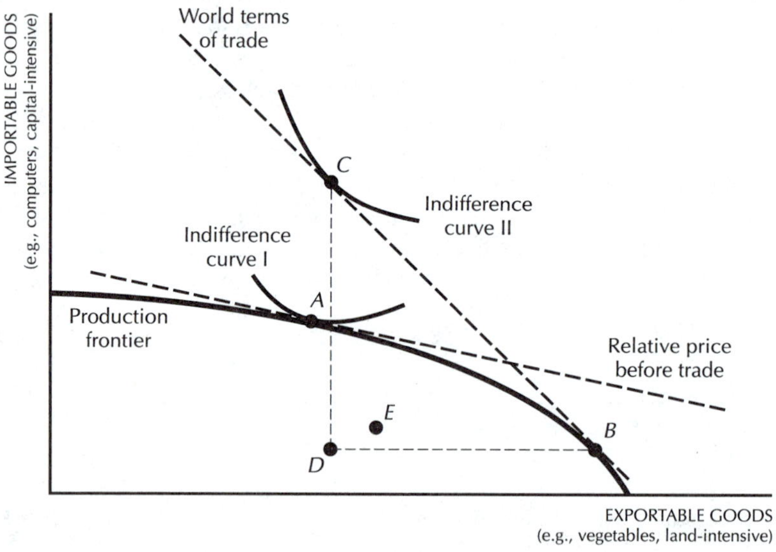

FIGURE 17–1 Gains from Trade. Before trade, a country both produces and consumes at a point like *A*. With trade, a country produces at a point like *B* and can increase its consumption of both goods and move to a higher indifference curve at *C*.

the demand for computers will drive its price lower than in the home country; and the relatively lower production of vegetables compared to the demand for vegetables will drive their price higher than in the home country. Since only relative prices matter, these two statements mean the same thing: in world markets the price of vegetables in terms of computers will be higher than in the home country.

This difference in relative prices between the home country and the rest of the world presents an opportunity for the home country to improve its welfare through trade. **With trade** the country, taking advantage of its factor endowment, can produce more vegetables and fewer computers and sell vegetables on the world market at the higher relative price, labeled the *world terms of trade* in Figure 17–1. In producing more vegetables, the home country moves along the production frontier from *A* to *B*, where the terms-of-trade line is tangent to the production frontier. With vegetables to export, the country can then import computers and consume more of *both* goods. The consumption point *C* is determined by the tangency of the terms of trade line with indifference curve II. The country now exports *BD* of vegetables and imports *DC* of computers, given by the *trade triangle BCD*. As indifference curve II is above and to the right (northeast) of curve I, the country is better-off with trade than without it.

This is a general result: Any country, whatever its size and stage of development, can benefit from trade in the way shown in Figure 17–1, from small countries like Ghana or Belgium to large ones like China, India, and the United States. Large countries and others whose exports command a large share of world markets, such as Saudi Arabia in oil, Zambia in copper, or Sri Lanka in tea, may, in the process of expanding their trade, reduce the relative world price received for their exports. But even they still gain from trade if only their relative domestic prices would, in the absence of trade, differ from relative world prices.

Although every country can gain from trade, not all individuals or groups within each country share such gains. In the vegetables-computers example of Figure 17–1, the producers of vegetables enjoy gains when trade is initiated because they sell more vegetables at a higher price. The consumers of computers also gain from trade, because they can consume more at a lower price. But once trade begins, computer manufacturers face competition from imports, and hence sell fewer computers at a lower price than before, while consumers of vegetables must pay higher prices. Comparative advantage theory tells us that the gains outweigh the losses for the country as a whole, but that may be cold comfort to producers of computers and consumers of vegetables. The losers from trade may share in the gains if suppliers of capital and labor to the computer industry find it easy to shift into the production of vegetables or if mechanisms exist to transfer income from the gainers to the losers. In most countries, neither condition holds to a sufficient degree, especially in the short to medium term. Therein lies the seed of political opposition to policies that promote freer trade, even though all countries gain from it.

Export Characteristics of Developing Countries

In their statistical analysis of cross-country patterns of development, economists Moises Syrquin and Hollis Chenery found that as incomes per capita rose from the neighborhood of $300 to $4,000 (in 1980 prices), the average export share of gross domestic product rose from 15 to 21 percent.[2] Size makes a considerable difference, however: for an average small country with a population of less than 25 million and income per capita of $700, exports of goods and services constituted about 25 percent of GDP, compared with only 15 percent for a typical large country with the same income. Large countries tend to export a smaller share of their total output because their larger markets can accommodate more industries economically; and they tend to have a greater diversity of resources that makes it possible to produce a wider range of goods.

Some sense of the wide variety of individual country characteristics can be had from column 3 of Table 17–2. Large countries like China, India, Brazil, Bangladesh, and Pakistan export a low share of gross domestic product, ranging from 10 to 17 percent in 1992. But countries of any size that are well endowed with petroleum and other natural resources export much more: from 25 percent of GDP for Venezuela; around 30 percent for Chile, Indonesia, and Zambia; to 39 percent for Nigeria. Smaller countries without rich resource endowments show a wide range of export ratios, from 7 percent for war-torn Ethiopia, around 20 percent for Colombia and Tanzania, to around 35 percent for Thailand and Ivory Coast. Most of these countries depend heavily on agricultural exports. Malaysia, rich in natural resources but also successful in the transition to manufactured exports, exports an astounding 78 percent of its GDP. Some of these ratios are undoubtedly understated. Because the data only cover goods exported through official channels, they omit goods exported through parallel markets in countries like Ethiopia, were civil war prevailed until the early 1990s; Tanzania, where inflation and a controlled exchange rate made exports unprofitable through the 1980s; and Colombia and Bolivia, where illegal drugs are important exports.

Knowing the factor endowments of developing countries helps explain the kinds of goods they export and import. Natural resources dictate the exports of the oil-rich countries of the Persian Gulf, Southeast Asia, and Latin America; copper exporters such as Zambia, Zaire, Chile, and Peru; and timber exporters such as Malaysia and Ghana. Tropical climate may be considered a factor of production that helps to explain the exports of foods such as coffee, cocoa, bananas, and vegetable oils and raw materials such as rubber and cotton. Abundant labor suggests the export crops that can be produced efficiently with labor-intensive methods, such as coffee, tea, rice, and tobacco, and of labor-intensive manufactures such as textiles, clothing, and electronic components. The relative lack of both made and human capital in developing countries indicates that they would gain by importing goods that use these factors intensively; such goods include most capital equipment and many intermediate products from the chemical, petroleum, and metals industries.

A standard description of a developing country would state that only one or a few primary commodities are responsible for most export earnings; many countries in Table 17–2 exhibit that characteristic. The extreme cases of export concentration include many of the major petroleum exporters, Ghana in cocoa, the Ivory Coast in cocoa and coffee, Colombia in coffee and cocaine (not a part of the official estimates!), Chile and Zambia in copper, and Jamaica in bauxite and alu-

2. Moises Syrquin and Hollis Chenery, *Patterns of Development, 1950–1983,* World Bank Discussion Paper No. 41, Washington, D.C., 1989, p. 20. Figures are for merchandise exports, excluding the export of services such as tourism, construction, etc.

TABLE 17–2 Export Characteristics of Selected Developing Countries

Country	Population (millions)	GNP per capita (Int'l $s)	Export* share of GDP (%)	Major primary exports†	Share of primary goods in merchandise exports (%)
China	1,162	1,910	n.a.	Petroleum	21
India	884	1,210	10	None	29
Indonesia	184	2,970	29	Petroleum	53
Brazil	154	5,250	10	Coffee, iron ore	42
Nigeria	102	1,440	39	Petroleum	99
Pakistan	119	2,130	17	Cotton, rice	21
Bangladesh	114	1,230	10	Jute goods, raw jute	18
Mexico	85	7,490	13	Petroleum	47
Philippines	64	2,480	29	Coconut products	27
Thailand	58	5,890	36	Rice, rubber, tapioca	34
Egypt	55	3,670	27	Petroleum, cotton	65
Ethiopia	55	340	7	Coffee, hides	97
South Korea	44	8,950	n.a.	None	7
Colombia	33	5,760	19	Coffee, fuel oil	68
Tanzania	26	630	21	Coffee, cotton	85
Kenya	26	1,360	27	Petroleum, tea, coffee	71
Peru	22	3,080	10	Copper, zinc, petroleum, lead	80
Venezuela	20	8,790	25	Petroleum	89
Malaysia	19	8,050	78	Rubber, palm oil, wood, petroleum	39
Sri Lanka	17	2,810	32	Tea, rubber, coconut	28
Ghana	16	1,890	16	Cocoa, wood	99
Saudi Arabia	17	11,170	n.a.	Petroleum	99
Chile	14	8,090	31	Copper	85
Ivory Coast	13	1,640	34	Coffee, cocoa	90
Guatemala	10	3,370	18	Coffee, sugar	70
Bolivia	8	270	15	Tin, gas, zinc, silver	88
Senegal	8	1,750	23	Petroleum products, fish, groundnuts & oil, phosphates	78
Jamaica	2	3,770	n.a.	Alumina, bauxite, sugar	45
Zambia	8	n.a.	29	Copper	99

*Exports of goods and nonfactor services.
†Commodities accounting for at least 5 percent of merchandise export revenues in 1988.
Sources: World Development Report 1994, Tables 1, 9, 15, and 30, and IMF, *International Financial Statistics Yearbook 1989* (major commodities).

mina. Not surprisingly the very large countries show a much more diversified pattern. What may be surprising is that many of the primary-product exporters are highly diversified. In three of the cases shown—Bolivia, Malaysia, and Peru—no one product dominates, and at least four commodities each account for 5 percent or more of total earnings.

However suggestive the theory of comparative advantage may be for developing countries, it is only the beginning of an explanation of development through international trade. The theory fails to explain growth and structural change because it excludes growth in the stocks of productive factors, as well as improvements in the quality or productivity of those factors. The theory thus provides no mechanism to explain how economies evolve over time and change the composition of their output, their consumption, and their trade.

In order to understand how trade and development interact, one affecting the other, it is necessary to adopt an eclectic approach, using trade theory where it is useful but reverting frequently to other kinds of analysis. The unifying theme is trade strategies: how different approaches to trade, favoring different types of exports and imports, lead to different kinds of economic development. The first such strategy, **primary-export-led growth** is examined in the balance of this chapter.

Primary Exports as an Engine of Growth

Before the 1950s, it was conventional wisdom that the road to development could be traversed most rapidly by following comparative advantage, exporting foods and raw materials, raising per capita income, and permitting structural change to take place as a consequence. The United States, Canada, Australia, and Denmark had become developed countries at least partly by following this path, and Argentina had gone quite far in that direction. Many countries in the third world, such as Colombia, Mexico, Ghana, Nigeria, Malaysia, and the Philippines, have undergone significant structural change as a consequence of primary exports, although these changes have propelled them only part of the way to development. Students of development, observing such cases, have noted three kinds of benefits to primary-export-led growth: improved utilization of existing factors of production, expanded factor endowments, and linkage effects.

Improved Factor Utilization

Static models of the gains from trade start with a country that is not trading and show what happens when it is opened to trade. An isolated country, shut off from world markets, might have substantial amounts of land that is either idle or used in relatively unproductive ways. Recall the land-abundant, capital-short country of Figure 17–1. In that case all factors of production are fully employed without trade. However, by reallocating resources—producing and exporting more land-intensive goods, such as vegetables, rice, or cocoa, and importing more manufactures, such as computers, cloth, or chemicals—the country can consume more of both kinds of commodities and increase its welfare. The country moves along its production frontier, from *A* to *B* in Figure 17–1. Land, the abundant factor of production, is utilized more intensively with trade in the sense that its productivity (the yield per hectare) has risen as labor shifts from manufacturing to agriculture.

If, instead, the country has idle resources before trade begins, it can gain even more substantially from trade. This case is represented in Figure 17–1 by points *D* and *E*, within the production frontier. Trade may stimulate the economy so that all factors of production are fully utilized and the country, able to produce more of both goods, moves toward its frontier.

This static model of the gains from trade can, with imagination and some judicious simplification, be applied to the development of several countries. In the nineteenth century the United States and Canada had abundant land in relation to their endowments of labor and capital. Much of this land was idle, so both countries produced at points within their production frontiers. British demand for cotton and wheat enabled North America to bring this land into production and move toward the production frontier by growing cotton and wheat for export, while importing the manufactured goods it could not produce as efficiently as Britain.

Burmese economist Hla Myint has observed that when parts of Africa and Asia came under European colonization, the consequent expansion of their international trade enabled those areas to utilize their land or labor more intensively to produce tropical foodstuffs such as rice, coca, and oil palm for export. Myint applies Adam Smith's term **vent for surplus** to these cases (as well as the cases of surplus land in the Americas and Australia).[3] The concept implies that some land or labor is idle before trade and that trade enables these economies to employ either land or labor more fully.

However, when underutilized land or labor was vented as a result of colonization, as was typical during the nineteenth century, the gains from trade were often purchased at high cost to the indigenous population. Land which may have been idle or utilized at low productivity was frequently alienated from its occupiers, whether these were American Indians, the Kikuyu and other peoples of East Africa, or Javanese farmers. Colonizers also used taxation and coercion to keep plantations and mines supplied with low-cost labor in many parts of Africa and Asia. And especially in British India, the movement along a production frontier toward greater production for export often resulted in cheap imports to compete with traditional handicraft industries and the displacement of artisans and workers. The questions about colonization—which cannot be answered in this text—are whether the distribution of gains from trade favored native populations enough to compensate them for the losses they bore and whether colonial economies propelled indigenous people toward development or retarded their eventual progress.

Expanded Factor Endowments

Once the profitable opportunities in tropical agriculture or natural resources become apparent, foreign investment is likely to be attracted to the country, first to exploit the country's comparative advantage and, perhaps eventually, to invest in other sectors. The influx of foreign investors has been the familiar story in all mineral-exporting industries and in many tropical-product industries in which plantation agriculture was the rule: Standard Oil in Venezuela, British Petroleum in Iran, Anaconda in Chile, Alcoa in Jamaica, Lever Brothers and Firestone in West Africa, and United Fruit in Central America are only some of the more vis-

3. Hla Myint, "The 'Classical Theory' of International Trade and the Underdeveloped Countries," *Economic Journal,* 68 (1959), 317–37.

ible of scores of examples. Capital has frequently brought migrant labor to the mines and plantations, as occurred in Southern and West Africa, Malaysia, Sri Lanka, and many other places. Both foreign investment and migrant labor were of course prominent features in the development in the "new lands" of the Americas and Australia in the nineteenth century. The emergence of new lines of export production is also likely to open up many new profitable outlets for investment that foreign capital will not completely satisfy, whether in the export sector itself or in related industries. These opportunities represent an outward shift of the demand for domestic savings and should induce some supply response and further increase investment in the economy.

Thus the expansion of potential markets for primary products can lead to expanded supplies of foreign investment, domestic savings, labor, and skilled manpower to complement the fixed factors of production, land and natural resources. Not only does trade help an economy move toward its production frontier and then along it, but trade can also expand the frontier outward and enable the economy to produce more of all goods than before.

Linkage Effects

The notion of export-led growth implies some stimulus to other industries that would not otherwise expand. When the growth of one industry, such as textiles, creates sufficient demand for some input, such as cotton or dyestuffs, it may stimulate domestic production of that input. Hirschman coined the phrase **backward linkage** for this stimulus.[4] Backward linkages, which were described in Chapter 3, are particularly effective when the using industry becomes so large that supplying industries can achieve economies of scale of their own, lower their production costs, and become more competitive in domestic or even export markets. The wheat industry worked this way in North America in the nineteenth century; it created sufficient demand for transportation equipment (especially railway rolling stock) and farm machinery that these industries became established in the United States. In Peru the rapid expansion of the fishmeal industry during the 1950s and 1960s led directly to the production of fishing boats and processing equipment. The boat-building industry became efficient enough to export fishing craft to neighboring countries, and the processing-equipment industry gave Peru a start on one kind of capital-goods production that can supply a wide range of food-processing industries.[5]

The linkage between food processing for export (rice, vegetable oils, tea) and a processing-equipment industry might well be repeated in other developing countries over time. Three conditions would contribute to such linkages. Production should initially take place in small units that use simple technology to give the fledgling equipment industry a chance to master production techniques and learn its trade by repetitive production. The export industry should grow steadily over time and thus promise a continuing market for its suppliers. And the export sector

4. Albert O. Hirschman, *The Strategy of Economic Development* (New Haven, Conn.: Yale University Press, 1958), Chap. 6.

5. Michael Roemer, *Fishing for Growth: Export-Led Development in Peru, 1950–1967* (Cambridge, Mass.: Harvard University Press, 1970).

should be large enough to enable equipment manufacturers eventually to achieve scale economies. These conditions were met in fishmeal and can be met in several agricultural fields. But they are generally not satisfied in mining, which typically requires complex equipment for large-scale investments that must be implemented in the shortest time possible, conditions under which domestic infant industries are unlikely to thrive.

Linkages may also develop indirectly through the demand by income recipients for consumption goods. The **consumption linkage** is most likely to operate if a large labor force is paid wages above previous levels, and a demand created for mass-produced consumer goods like processed foods, clothing, footwear, furniture, radios, televisions, packaging materials, and so forth. The North American wheat industry, with its extensive endowment of land, high labor productivity, and egalitarian income distribution based on family farms, successfully stimulated local consumer goods industries. Neither plantation agriculture in Africa, with its large labor force but low wages, nor mining industries, which pay high wages but employ relatively few workers, are able to generate adequate demand to stimulate local consumer goods industries.

The provision of overhead capital—roads, railroads, power, water, telecommunications—for the export industry can lower costs and otherwise open opportunities for other industries. The classic example is the railroad in the nineteenth-century United States. Built to connect the East Coast with the grain-producing states of the Midwest, it lowered the costs of transporting both inputs and outputs for the manufacturing industry in the wheat-exporting region.[6] Harbors and rail and road networks built to facilitate the export of copper in southern Africa, cocoa and timber in Ghana, tea in India, and beef in Argentina have had similar effects on domestic manufacturing industries. Power projects that are made economically feasible by export industries, such as the Akosombo Dam in Ghana and the Guri Dam in Venezuela, provide cheap power that may encourage the domestic manufacturing industry.

Primary export sectors may also encourage the development of local entrepreneurs and skilled laborers. The growth of the Peruvian fishmeal industry, with its many small plants, encouraged scores of new entrepreneurs and trained many skilled workers to operate and maintain equipment. These resources then became available for subsequent development. Rubber, palm oil, and tin production for export have encouraged entrepreneurs in Malaysia, and small-scale farming for export has proved to be an outlet for entrepreneurial talent in several African countries.

The best case for petroleum, mining, and some traditional agricultural crops is the **fiscal linkage.** Governments can capture large shares of the rents from these exports as taxes or dividends and use the revenue to finance development in other sectors. Although a government is obviously better-off with than without such revenues, its effectiveness in stimulating self-sustaining development in the rest of

6. Albert Fishlow, *American Railroads and the Transformation of the Antebellum Economy* (Cambridge, Mass.: Harvard University Press, 1965), and Robert W. Fogel, "Railroads as an Analogy of the Space Effort: Some Economic Aspects," in Bruce Mazlish (ed.), *Space Program: An Exploration in Historical Analogy* (Cambridge, Mass.: MIT Press, 1965).

the economy depends critically on the kinds of programs and interventions that it undertakes.[7]

Barriers to Primary-Export-Led Growth

Since the late 1950s some economists and many third-world leaders have argued that primary exports other than petroleum cannot effectively lead the way to economic development: markets for primary products grow too slowly to fuel growth, the prices received for these commodities have been declining, earnings are too unstable, and linkages do not work. We examine each of these arguments in turn.

Sluggish Demand Growth

In a world of balanced growth, exporters of primary products could expect their exports to expand at the same pace as national incomes of the countries that import primary products, and they could also expect their own incomes to grow at that rate. Faster income growth for primary exporters would require structural changes such as import substitution. The world is not balanced in this way, however, and economists skeptical of primary-export potential have cited structural shifts in the industrial world that seem to condemn third-world primary exports to slower growth than industrial world incomes.[8]

It is a common observation, known as **Engel's law**, that the demand for staple foods and beverages grows more slowly than income (see Chapter 3). For the industrial world the income elasticity of demand for foods is probably below one-half. Thus even if the growth in production of foodstuffs in the industrial world fell short of income growth, there is a *prima facie* case that its imports of foods would lag behind income growth. Technological change in manufacturing also works against the consumption of raw materials, as producers attempt to reduce costs by raising the yield of finished products from a given input of raw material and substituting synthetics for natural materials. Metal cans contain less tin, modern looms waste less cotton yarn and use more synthetic fibers, sawmills turn wood shavings into boards, automobiles use less steel, vehicle tires use synthetic rubber, plastic pipe replaces iron or copper pipe, and so forth. From 1963 to 1986, while world industrial production grew by 3.9 percent a year, the consumption of

7. The impact of export industries on economic development through various forms of linkages is the focus of a body of literature called **staple theory,** which tries to explain differing impacts by differing characteristics of production technologies. For examples of the genre, see Robert E. Baldwin, *Economic Development and Export Growth: A Study of Northern Rhodesia, 1920–1960* (Los Angeles: University of California Press, 1966); Douglass C. North, "Location Theory and Regional Economic Growth," *Journal of Political Economy,* 63 (1955), 243–85; Roemer, *Fishing for Growth;* and Melville H. Watkins, "A Staple Theory of Economic Growth," *Canadian Journal of Economics and Political Science,* 29 (1963), 141–58. Perhaps the ultimate expression of production characteristics and linkages as determinants of development patterns is the essay by Albert O. Hirschman, "A Generalized Linkage Approach to Development, with Special Reference to Staples," in Manning Nash (ed.), *Essays on Economic Development and Cultural Change* (Chicago: University of Chicago Press, 1977), pp. 67–98.

8. An early and articulate proponent of this view is Ragnar Nurske, *Equilibrium Growth in the World Economy* (Cambridge, Mass.: Harvard University Press, 1961), Chaps. 10 and 11.

natural raw materials grew by only 1.5 percent a year.[9] Concurrently, in affluent societies expenditures shift away from goods and toward services, and so further reduce the expected growth of material imports relative to income.

World Bank data confirm this gloomy picture. The share of nonfuel raw materials and food imports in total industrial-country imports has fallen substantially, from 38 percent in 1965 to about 16 percent in 1992. With imports in the industrial world growing at 5.0 percent a year, imports of nonfuel raw materials and foodstuffs, valued in constant prices, appear to have grown by only 1.7 percent a year over more than a quarter century, too slow to fuel economic development in primary exporting countries.[10]

Despite the broad trend, there are likely to be encouraging prospects for some primary commodities and some primary-exporting countries. Many of the raw materials now prominent in world trade were hardly on the scene at the turn of this century and thus have undergone substantial growth. The demands for petroleum, rubber, copper, aluminum, newsprint, plywood, and vegetable oils received substantial boosts from technological innovation or from high income elasticities of demand, the very factors cited against raw material exports. Several commodities have experienced substantial export growth rates since 1960: exports of sorghum, wheat, fish, soybeans, vegetable oils, oilseed cake and meal, fertilizers, timber, alumina and aluminum, and nickel all grew by at least 5 percent a year for at least 20 years since 1960, valued at constant prices.[11] Over the past 30 years, several small countries that are mainly exporters of primary products have sustained some periods of moderately rapid growth, including Botswana, Cameroon, Costa Rica, the Dominican Republic, Guatemala, Indonesia, Ivory Coast, Kenya, Malawi, Malaysia, the Philippines, and Thailand.

With slower growth in the industrial countries, the impact of Engel's law, and materials-saving innovations, it seems unlikely that the developed countries will import enough tropical foods and raw materials to fuel an era of rapid development for the third world as a whole over the next few decades. Nevertheless, some commodities will face brisk demand growth and some countries will benefit substantially from producing such exports.

Primary-Export-Led Growth in Malaysia

When Malaysia achieved independence in 1957, it was close to the archetypical single-crop economy: rubber accounted for well over half of its export earnings and about a quarter of Malaysia's gross domestic product. The second largest export, tin, earned between 10 and 20 percent of total export revenues. Neither commodity faced a bright future: demand for rubber was constrained by the availability of cheap synthetic substi-

9. World Bank, *Global Economic Prospects and the Developing Countries* (Washington, D.C.: World Bank, 1994), pp. 39–40.

10. *World Development Report 1990,* Tables 14 and 15, and *World Development Report 1994,* Tables 13 and 14.

11. World Bank, *Commodity Trade and Price Trends,* 1987–1988 ed. (Washington, D.C.: World Bank, 1988), and World Bank, *Price Prospects for Primary Commodities, 1990–2005* (Washington, D.C.: World Bank, 1993).

tutes and the tin market was plagued by production exceeding likely demand. It would have been natural for the new country's planners to fall prey to the dominant export pessimism of the day and build a development strategy around import substitution.

But Malaysia enjoys a rich resource base with a relatively small population and its development strategy was based on its comparative advantage. The country invested in research to reduce the costs of growing rubber and maintained its competitiveness with synthetic rubber. Measured relative to import prices, rubber export revenues fell by only 4 percent from 1960 to 1987. At the same time, Malaysia invested in planting oil palm and this new export grew in volume by 15 percent a year from 1960 to 1987. Petroleum exports grew by a steady 8 percent a year and exports of logs and timber expanded by a total of 82 percent from 1960 to 1987. During this period, Malaysia also invested in manufacturing for export. Although primary products earned over 90 percent of export revenues in 1965, by 1992 manufactures had grown sufficiently to account for 61 percent of export revenues. Thanks to investments in both primary and manufactured exports, Malaysia's total export earnings, deflated by import prices (that is, its income terms of trade; see next section) grew by 7 percent a year for three decades.

As a consequence of its investments in primary and manufactured exports, Malaysia has sustained rapid economic growth, over 6 percent a year from 1965 to 1992. Its per capita income of $8000 in purchasing power parity terms puts Malaysia on a par with Mexico and Greece, even though in the mid-1960s its average income was close to that of Zambia and El Salvador. Although still dependent on exports for over 75 percent of its GDP, Malaysia's diversified export base, efficient production, and high income provide the resources for continued rapid development.[12]

Declining Terms of Trade

An influential school of thought, led by Argentine economist Raul Prebisch and Hans Singer of the University of Sussex, has argued that not only will primary exports face sluggish growth of demand, but that, over the long run, prices received for these commodities will fall on world markets relative to the prices of developing countries' imports of manufactures from developed countries.[13] The most commonly used measure of these relative prices is the commodity or **net barter terms of trade**, T_n. T_n is a ratio of two indexes: (1) the average price of a country's exports (P_e), which can be approximated by dividing an index of export volume into an index of export revenue, and (2) the average price of its imports (P_m), determined for imports by the same method as P_e. The commodity terms of trade rise if export prices rise relative to import prices.

12. Data are from the *World Development Report 1990;* World Bank, *World Tables 1994;* and IMF, *International Financial Statistics Yearbook 1990.*

13. United Nations (Raul Prebsich), *The Economic Development of Latin America and its Principal Problems* (Lake Success, N.Y.: 1950): Hans W. Singer, "The Distribution of Trade between Investing and Borrowing Countries," *American Economic Review,* 40 (May 1950), 473–85.

Empirical tests of the Prebisch-Singer hypothesis reach ambiguous conclusions at best. In his 1950 monograph, Prebisch used data on the terms of trade for Great Britain from the 1870s to the 1930s that seemed to support his contention. Prebisch's data were imperfect, however, and inadvertently biased in favor of his hypothesis. In subsequent years, other economists have tried to replicate Prebisch's results using different data sets and various periods of time, with conflicting results.[14] Georgetown University economist John Cuddington and associates have used improved data to measure the terms of trade for 24 primary commodities, excluding oil, for the period from 1900 to 1988.[15] Figure 17–2 shows the results. The net barter terms of trade for primary commodities fluctuated widely and suffered a precipitate drop in the early 1920s.

One interpretation of these data is that, except for the sharp fall of prices in 1920–21, there has been no statistically significant downward trend in the net barter terms of trade, so the Prebisch-Singer hypothesis cannot be sustained.[16] If

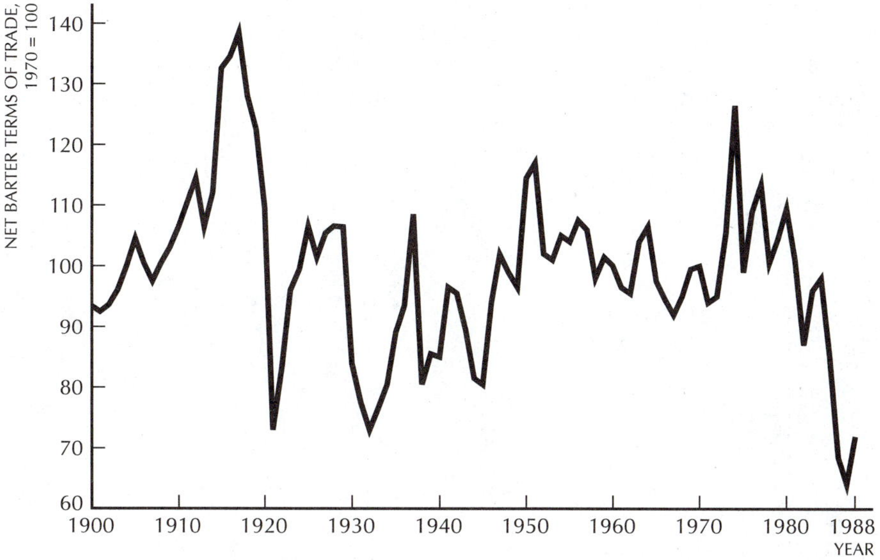

FIGURE 17–2 Net Barter Terms of Trade, Primary Commodities, 1900–1988. A geometric index for 24 commodities, excluding fuels, shows no trend over 88 years, despite wide fluctuations and a sharp drop in 1921.

Source: John Cuddington and Hong Wei, "An Empirical Analysis of the Prebisch-Singer Hypothesis: Aggregation, Model Selection and Implications," Working Paper No. 90-12, Economics Department, Georgetown University.

14. For a summary of these results, see Bela Balassa, "Outward Orientation," in Hollis Chenery and T. N. Srinivasan, *Handbook of Development Economics,* Vol. 2 (Amsterdam: North-Holland, 1989), pp. 1653–59.

15. The numerator of T_n, P_e, is a geometric average of the price indexes for 24 nonfuel commodities; the denominator P_m is an index of unit values for manufactured goods. See John T. Cuddington and Carlos M. Urzua, "Trends and Cycles in the Net Barter Terms of Trade: A New Approach," *Economic Journal,* 99 (June 1989), 426–42.

16. This is the conclusion reached by Cuddington and Urzua.

oil and other fuel prices were included in the index, and there is no reason why they should not he, they would reinforce this conclusion. Some econometricians disagree, however, and, using similar data but different techniques, find significant declines in the net barter terms of trade of at least 0.7 percent per annum.[17]

Although the Prebisch-Singer hypothesis is properly addressed by looking at commodity data, it is the terms of trade for a country that really matters in its development. Figure 17–3 shows two different measures of the net barter terms of trade since 1954. When oil exporters are included, the terms of trade of developing countries rose dramatically after 1972 and remained high, despite the fall of oil prices during the 1980s. But the terms of trade for non-oil-exporting developing countries declined over the period.

However, the net barter terms of trade tell us little about income or welfare, which ought to be the basis for judging changes in world trade conditions. A better measure of the income effect of price changes would be the **income terms of trade**, T_i, which measures the purchasing power of exports by comparing an index of export revenues to an index of import prices. This is equivalent to the net barter terms of trade multiplied by the volume of exports (Q_e), or $T_i = P_eQ_e/P_m = T_nQ_e$. If, for example, Zambia increases its copper exports and causes the world price to fall, but less than proportionately to the volume increase (that is, the absolute value of the demand elasticity for Zambian copper is greater than 1), then

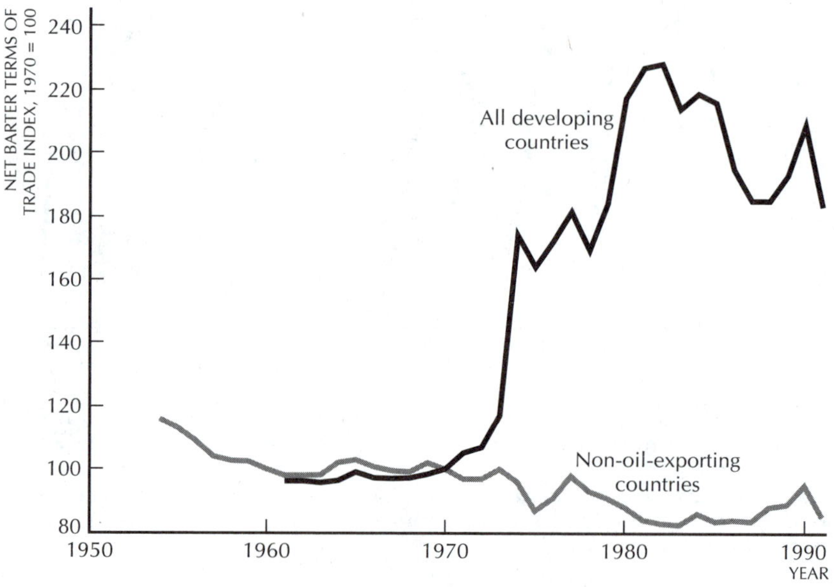

FIGURE 17–3. Net Barter Terms of Trade, Developing Countries, 1954–1988. For non-oil-exporting countries, the terms of trade show a decline of about 1 percent a year over the whole period. When all developing countries are included, there has been a dramatic rise in the terms of trade since 1972.

Source: IMF, *International Financial Statistics Yearbook 1993.*

17. These studies are summarized by David Sapsford and V. N. Balasubramanyam. "The Long-run Behavior of the Relative Price of Primary Commodities: Statistical Evidence and Policy Implications," *World Development,* 22, no. 11 (November 1994), 1737–45.

copper revenue will increase and, in the absence of import price changes, the income terms of trade will rise.[18] Assuming the resources shifted into copper production could not have produced goods or services of equal value in other sectors, Zambia would be unambiguously better-off than before. For non-oil developing countries as a group, the income terms of trade rose almost 6 percent a year from 1954 to 1991.

Similarly, an increase in Zambia's copper production due to higher productivity may cause world copper prices to fall. But if the price decline is less than the percentage rise in the productivity (Z_e) of all factors engaged in production for export, the factors engaged in copper mining would be better-off than before. The **single factoral terms of trade,** T_s measures factor income relative to factor inputs and import prices, or $T_s = (P_e/P_m)Z_e = T_nZ_e$. Note that a rise in either the income or single factoral terms of trade implies an improvement in income or welfare relative to that country's previous situation. But if, as is often the case, either index rises less than export volume, this also implies that exporting countries are sharing part of the potential gains with importing countries, as Prebisch and Singer suggest.

Should we have any theoretical expectations about future trends in the terms of trade? Pessimists can point to the sluggish growth in demand for primary products to argue that the terms of trade for these commodities will decline over time. More fundamentally, to the extent that developing countries increase their output of primary exports as a means of growing faster than the industrial countries, prices of their exports may be expected to fall relative to those of industrial country exports, simply because the supply of developing-country primary exports will be increasing faster than the demand for them.

Theoretical considerations can also lead to the opposite conclusion, however. Primary products are produced by factors in limited supply, particularly land, mineral deposits, and other natural resources. Although technological innovations can be expected to increase the productivity of these resources, they are not inexhaustible, as discussed in Chapter 7. If world income continues to grow, even slowly, it seems likely that eventually demand will grow faster than supply for many primary commodities. The prices of those commodities should then rise relative to the prices of manufactures, which are produced with labor and capital, the supply of which is expanding. Wood prices have been growing steadily, for example, although the demand for energy resources has not yet begun to outstrip the discovery and development of new supplies (see Chapter 7).

Ghana—A Case of Arrested Development

At independence in 1957, Ghana was probably the richest country in black Africa, with a per capita income close to $500 (in 1983 prices). By 1983, its per capita income had fallen to $340, below that of Kenya, Sudan, and Pakistan. Many things went wrong for Ghana in that quarter

18. The price elasticity of demand for the exports of any one country is $e_i = e_w/s_i$, where e_w is the worldwide price elasticity of demand for the commodity and s_i is the market share of the country. Even if e_w is quite low, say -0.3, if the country's market share is below 30 percent, which would be quite large, the price elasticity facing that country would be more negative than -1.

century, but the failure of export policy was crucial.[19] Like Malaysia, Ghana was a one-export country in the late 1950s: cocoa earned almost 60 percent of export revenues and represented almost a fifth of GDP. But in contrast to Malaysia, Ghana under its charismatic leader, Kwame Nkrumah, turned sharply away from its export base to invest in import-substituting industries. In this it failed. Had export agriculture, forestry, and mining been maintained, Ghana might have earned sufficient revenues to make a gradual transition into import substitution. But so abrupt was the disinvestment in primary exports that cocoa exports halved in volume from the early 1960s to the middle 1980s, and other exports did not make up that deficit.

Ghana's failure to utilize its generous export base is made more vivid by the performance of its next-door neighbor, the Ivory Coast. With virtually the same resource base, the Ivory Coast invested enough to maintain its coffee exports and then diversified into cocoa (just as Ghana was disinvesting), wood, and other primary products. Over two decades, export volume more than doubled, and per capita GDP grew to nearly twice that of Ghana, despite substantial immigration from less prosperous neighboring countries.[20]

Fluctuating Export Earnings

Not only do the net barter terms of trade show a secular decline, but they also fluctuate considerably, as is evident from Figures 17–2 and 17–3. Conventional wisdom has generally held that the instability in export earnings would be transmitted to the domestic economy and make domestic demand unstable and investment more risky. Fluctuating domestic demand, coupled with uncertain access to imported materials, would then discourage investors and reduce economic growth. Export instability may also confuse the signals conveyed by relative prices, so that investors are unable to select the most productive investments. This **signaling effect** raises the capital-output ratio and reduces the growth rate for any given level of investment.

One theory of consumption, the **permanent-income hypothesis**, suggests the opposite result, however. Income earners count on some level of relatively certain annual income and try to maintain consumption patterns based largely on that *permanent* income. The more income fluctuates around this permanent level, the more will be saved in order to maintain the permanent level of consumption through good times and bad.[21] If fluctuating export earnings transmit income instability to households, they will save more, so the country will be able to finance more investment and grow faster. Which effect is likely to dominate?

Harvard economist David Dawe tested these propositions econometrically. He proposed a measure of export instability that compares deviations in earnings

19. On Ghana's development policies, see Michael Roemer, "Ghana 1950–1980: Missed Opportunities," in Arnold Harberger (ed.), *World Economic Growth* (San Francisco: ICS Press, 1984), pp. 201–26.

20. *World Development Report 1990* and World Bank, *World Tables 1989–1990.*

21. Odin Knudsen and Andrew Parnes, *Trade Instability and Economic Development,* (Lexington, Mass.: Heath Lexington Books, 1975), pp. 81–128.

around a five-year trend to gross domestic product. Thus countries with larger export fluctuations and larger export-GDP ratios are the most affected. Among a sample of 85 countries over 15 years (1970 to 1985), Dawe finds that export instability does raise the ratio of investment to GDP, consistent with the permanent income hypothesis. Nevertheless, instability reduces the rate of GDP growth.[22] The reason, he suggests, may be that the signaling effect is especially strong and so reduces the productivity of all investment even as the permanent income effect increases the quantity of investment.

This finding poses a dilemma for development strategy. If its comparative advantage lies in primary exports with fluctuating prices in world markets, will a country's growth be enhanced by following comparative advantage more than it is hurt by accepting export fluctuations? Case histories of experience in both Asia and Africa suggest that countries following their comparative advantages, even if they lie in primary exports, grow faster than those that turn away from this path.[23] However, the successful primary exporters also diversified their export base, both within primary products and by shifting gradually to manufactured exports, to reduce the instability of total export earnings. They did this by first investing in primary exports, as Malaysia, rather than by turning away from them, as Ghana (see boxed examples).

Commodity Agreements

Developing countries made several attempts in the 1970s and 1980s to **raise the prices** of specific export commodities. In order to raise export prices, it is necessary either to restrict output (that is, to shift the supply curve to the left) or to impose a common export tax. If world demand for the commodity is inelastic (that is, the price elasticity is between -1 and 0) as is true for most tropical food exports, then restricting supply causes a more than proportional increase in price and an increase in total revenues to exporters. If, however, world demand is elastic, as may be true for meat, fish, dairy products, and many manufactured goods, then supply restrictions raise prices less than proportionally and revenues fall.

Output restriction works best when large majorities of both producing and consuming countries participate. The International Coffee Agreement, first negotiated in 1960, worked this way for a time. Export quotas were allocated to all producers, while most Western consuming countries agreed to buy only from producing members of the agreement. Exporters could sell to nonquota markets, such as Eastern Europe and most developing countries, but at market prices that could be substantially lower than in participating countries.

Under certain conditions producers may be able to restrict demand and raise prices without the agreement of consumers. Among many unsuccessful attempts to accomplish this looms the one dramatic success, the Organization of Petroleum Exporting Countries (OPEC). From 1972 to 1982, OPEC raised oil prices from under \$4 a barrel to over \$30, a real increase (allowing for international inflation) of 240 percent. The slippage of OPEC prices after 1982 and the collapse in 1986

22. David C. Dawe, "Essays on Price Stablization and the Macroeconomy in Low Income Countries," Harvard University Ph.D. Dissertation, May 1993, pp. 50–107.

23. See David L. Lindauer and Michael Roemer (eds.), *Asia and Africa: Legacies and Opportunities* (San Francisco: ICS Press, 1994), especially Chaps. 1 and 4.

suggest the limitations of producer agreements, but does not detract from its dramatic accomplishments of the 1970s. This example has stimulated exporters of other commodities, especially minerals, to form their own **cartels**, as price-raising agreements among commodity producers may be called.

Attempts to raise world prices for primary exports are akin to a *zero-sum game* in which the gains of one group of countries (the producers) are offset by the losses of another group (the consumers and the foreign owners of capital). Even when developing-country exports are the object of price-raising agreements, potential losers include other developing countries that import these commodities. Developing-country importers of petroleum were among the hardest hit by OPEC's price-fixing cartel.

Consumer countries have been more willing to help **stabilize commodity prices**. Stabilization requires some central authority—a large company, a private cartel, a single government, a cartel of producing countries, or an international agency—to intervene in the market, buying the commodity when prices are falling and selling from their stocks when prices are rising. To do this, the authority must control a *buffer stock* and must have access to funds that can be used to increase that stock when necessary. The principle of stabilization is easy, but the application is fraught with difficulty. First, if predictions of future prices turn out to be higher than the actual average price, the authority will on balance buy more for the buffer stock than it sells and eventually may be unable to finance further purchases. Conversely a low prediction results in excessive sales, depleting and possibly exhausting the buffer stock.

Second, even if price forecasts are accurate, the authority must set floor and ceiling prices that it can maintain. Should speculators sense that the authority's resources are too limited they can bid the price up or down, depending on whether stocks or finance are in short supply, to break through the ceiling or floor and make a certain profit. Finally, if buffer stocks lead to higher inventories of a commodity than would otherwise be held, this represents a real resource cost to someone. Thus the eventual success of price-stabilizing agreements depends not only on whether the technical problems can be overcome, but also on the assessment of consuming countries about the costs to them of continued price fluctuations.

Stabilizing world commodity prices is not necessarily the same thing as stabilizing a particular country's export earnings. If one country's production is unstable because of variable weather, strikes, or other disruptions, then a stable world price can increase the variability of earnings.[24] An alternative with considerable appeal is to compensate directly for earnings fluctuations rather than to stabilize prices. Two such schemes are in existence: the Compensatory Financing Facility of the International Monetary Fund and the Stabex scheme operated by the European Community. Under the IMF facility countries can borrow to finance balance-of-payments deficits that are partially caused by a drop in export revenues below a five-year moving average. The EC scheme permits borrowing if a country's particular commodity export revenues, earned from the Community, fall below a four-year average.

24. Jere R. Behrman, *Development, the International Economic Order and Commodity Agreements* (Reading, Mass.: Addison-Wesley, 1978). Chapter 3 provides an analytical treatment of commodity agreements and summarizes the conditions under which stable prices will stablize or destablize revenues.

Ineffective Linkages

It is a paradox of development that many economies have failed to develop despite booming primary export industries. One of the reasons for this is implicit in the previous discussion of **linkages:** backward, forward, and consumption linkages often fail to work. The petroleum industry and, with a few exceptions, the mining industry, generally remain *enclaves,* remote from other centers of production and ill adapted to link with them economically. Neither backward linkages to suppliers of production materials and equipment nor consumption linkages are likely to work. In some instances railroads and ports built for the mines do aid other industries by lowering costs and stimulating investment, but examples of remote or specialized overhead capital can also be found. Liberia's rail and harbor link with its iron mines is poorly placed to stimulate agriculture or other industry, and the pipelines and tanker ports of the petroleum industry have no uses outside that sector. Some agricultural export sectors, particularly plantations in colonial Africa, also had few effective linkages, because they use few inputs and pay low wages. However, small-farm, labor-intensive agriculture typically does have effective linkages through transport and marketing services and consumer demand by farm families.

If petroleum and mining industries create few backward or consumption linkages, they can generate **forward linkages** to industries whose principal input is the export sector's output. Thus Venezuela is using its iron ore, natural gas, and hydroelectric power to produce steel, partly for export and partly for domestic use. If, and only if, the domestic steel is cheaper than imported steel, it may stimulate further forward linkages to steel-using industries like construction, transport equipment, processing equipment, and oil derricks. Other mineral and timber exporters are trying to exploit forward linkages, and they either substitute processed exports for raw materials or divert part of their raw materials into inputs for domestic industry.

Forward-linked industries are often encouraged through taxes or outright bans on the exports of primary products. Indonesia, for example, has banned the exports of logs and heavily taxed the exports of sawn wood to encourage the plywood and furniture industries. Because the price of the primary export is determined in world markets, export taxes and bans reduce the price of the primary commodity in the domestic market. Downstream industries then have a higher margin between the purchase price of the raw material and the export (or domestic) price of the processed good. Farmers, loggers, and miners are taxed to provide greater incentives for processors and manufacturing firms. This is one form of *protection* and is similar in its effects to protection against imports, the subject of the next chapter.

These **resource-based industrialization strategies** may succeed in expanding the industrial base and increasing the economic benefits derived from a natural resource. However, resource processing is no panacea for development. Most of the mineral-processing industries share with mining the characteristics of large scale, capital intensity, sophisticated technology, and high wages, so they tend to be extensions of the export enclave, and generate little employment and realize few linkages to the rest of the economy. Nor is there much diversification of risk in moving from crude to refined petroleum exports or from bauxite to aluminum.

Dutch Disease

Booming primary exports may fail to stimulate development for another, more pervasive reason, which has been labeled **Dutch disease**. This syndrome derives its name from the experience of the Netherlands after 1960, when major reserves of natural gas were discovered. The ensuing export boom and the balance-of-payments surplus promised new prosperity. Instead, during the 1970s the Dutch economy suffered from rising inflation, declining exports of manufactures, lower rates of income growth, and rising unemployment. The oil boom of the 1970s and early 1980s produced similar paradoxes in a number of countries, including Saudi Arabia, Nigeria, and Mexico. Economists began to realize that Dutch disease might be a very general phenomenon, applicable to all countries that "enjoy" export booms of primary commodities.[25] Because, as we shall see, it is the influx of foreign exchange that causes Dutch disease, the syndrome can also result from large inflows of foreign capital in any form. The import of gold and silver from the Americas, for example, may have helped to retard Spain's industrialization in the sixteenth century and a surge of investment to the United States probably helped to make its industries less competitive in the 1980s. How can this happen?

The key to this paradox is to understand (1) how export booms affect a country's **real exchange rate** and (2) how the real exchange rate, in turn, affects other industries. The *official* or *nominal exchange rate* is simply the price at which anyone holding foreign exchange, such as dollars, can convert it into local currency, say pesos in Mexico, naira in Nigeria, or rupiah in Indonesia. It is generally convenient to speak of this price or rate in local currency per unit of foreign currency, say pesos per dollar. The real exchange rate corrects the nominal rate for inflation. It is an index of prices, like the terms of trade, not a price itself. One formula for the real exchange rate is

$$\text{RER} = E_o(P_w/P_d), \qquad [17\text{–}1]$$

where RER is an index of the real exchange rate, the value in the current period, say 1990, divided by the value in a base period, say 1985; E_o is an index of the official (nominal) exchange rate; P_w is an index of prices in world trade; and P_d is an index of domestic prices, either a wholesale or consumer price index. When the real exchange rate rises—that is, there are more pesos or naira or rupiah per dollar—there is *real depreciation* of the peso or naira or rupiah, because it takes fewer dollars to buy the same amount of pesos than before. When the RER falls, there is *real appreciation* of the currency, because pesos are worth more in dollars than before. Official devaluations, which raise the peso price of dollars, cause the real rate to depreciate, at least initially. If domestic prices then increase more rapidly than world prices, however, the local currency appreciates in real terms.

To understand how the real exchange rate becomes the key to the Dutch disease paradox, begin with the impact of the real exchange rate on export industries other than the booming primary export industry. Table 17–3 demonstrates that, with a fixed nominal exchange rate, domestic inflation in excess of world inflation causes

25. Dutch disease has been analyzed from a theoretical standpoint by W. Max Corden and S. Peter Neary, "Booming Sector and Deindustrialization in a Small Open Economy," *Economic Journal,* 92 (December 1982), 825–48. The application of this theory to developing countries is explored by Michael Roemer, "Dutch Disease in Developing Countries: Swallowing Bitter Medicine," in Matts Lundahl (ed.), *The Primary Sector in Economic Development* (London: Croom-Helms, 1985), pp. 234–52.

TABLE 17–3 Effects of Inflation and Devaluation on Exporters' Profits

Today: Exchange rate = 12 pesos per dollar; Real exchange rate = 100.	
1. Exporter sells goods worth	$ 100,000
2. For which exporter receives local currency of	P 1,200,000
3. If exporter's costs—all domestic—are	P 900,000
4. Then exporter's profits are	P 300,000
Three years later, after primary export boom: Cumulative domestic inflation has been 33% more than world prices; Real exchange rate appreciated to 75.	
1. Exporter sells goods worth	$ 100,000
2. For which exporter receives local currency of	P 1,200,000
3. If exporter's costs—all domestic—are	P 1,200,000
4. Then exporter's profits are	P 0
Three years later, but with currency devalued by 33% to 16 pesos per dollar; Real exchange rate restored to 100.	
1. Exporter sells goods worth	$ 100,000
2. For which exporter receives local currency of	P 1,600,000
3. If exporter's costs—all domestic—are	P 1,200,000
4. Then exporter's profits are	P 400,000
5. Which, deflated by 33% to Year 1 prices, are again	P 300,000

exporters' profits to decline: wages and the prices of domestic inputs rise faster than the price of exported output. This is, of course, the same thing as a real rate appreciation, since RER would fall in Equation 17–1. (The same reduction in profitability would follow from an appreciation of the nominal exchange rate, that is, from lowering the peso price of a dollar.) If exporters' profits fall, they are likely to produce less for export, and so reduce incomes and employment in export industries. Exporters' profitability could be restored by a nominal devaluation that offsets domestic inflation, as shown in the last section of Table 17–3.

Booming raw material exports cause just such appreciations of the real exchange rate as are illustrated in Table 17–3. This can occur in two ways. First, the influx of foreign exchange from higher export earnings creates a surplus of foreign currency which tends to drive down its price in the domestic currency, as would occur for any commodity. Unless the central bank tries to maintain the official exchange rate at its former level, this shift in supply causes the currency to appreciate in value.

Second, higher income from booming primary exports also spurs faster domestic inflation. It does this because the additional income creates greater demand for all goods and services in the economy. To the extent that this demand spills over into more imports, there is an outflow of foreign exchange but no inflation, because the price of imports is not much affected by demand in a single country. Economists call any good that is or could be imported or exported a **tradable.** Some of the new demand from the export boom will, however, go into goods that are produced domestically and not imported or exported, which economists call **nontradables.** Examples of nontradables include transportation, construction, electricity and other utilities, household and other personal services, and manufactures or farm products that are heavily protected and not subject to competition from imports.[26] Because there is a limited supply of nontradables, especially in the first months or years of the boom, the greater demand results in higher prices

26. The definitions of tradables and nontradables are made more precise in Chapter 20.

of nontradables, that is, in domestic inflation. From Equation 17–1 and Table 17–3 we know that if domestic inflation exceeds world inflation, the real exchange rate appreciates (RER falls).

Now the paradox can be explained: Booming primary exports, by stimulating more rapid domestic inflation and thus causing the real exchange rate to appreciate, also render other exports less competitive and hence less profitable. Producers of tradables, both exporters and import competitors, face rising prices for their purchases of nontradable goods and services, including the wages of their workers. But they cannot charge higher prices because they compete with foreign producers, either as exporters or as import competitors. These farmers and manufacturers face a profit squeeze that will cause some of them to reduce production and employment. The boom in primary exports and nontradables is partly offset by a depression in other tradable industries.

Because mineral and other primary sectors typically pay high taxes, one of the symptoms of Dutch disease is the swelling of government revenues. This **fiscal linkage** can be used to stimulate development, especially if the additional revenues are invested in public services such as infrastructure, education, and health, or to promote efficient investment in tradable sectors, notably agriculture and manufacturing, that have been rendered less competitive by the primary export boom. Although some governments used their fiscal resources effectively during the 1970s oil boom, the record was generally dismal. It is precisely when fiscal resources are generously available that finance ministers have the most difficult time resisting political and social pressures for higher expenditures.

The depredations of Dutch disease are often fatal to development aspirations, as the boxed example of Nigeria illustrates. But this is not necessarily so. Some countries have turned their resource windfalls into sustained development, as demonstrated by the case of Indonesia.[27] Determined governments can take several steps to allay the symptoms of Dutch disease.

The cure for Dutch disease depends on preventing or reversing real appreciation of the currency. In most cases this requires a devaluation of the currency, accompanied by government budget surpluses and by strong restraints over money creation by the central bank, both aimed at curbing inflation. The government needs to resist demands for expansion and save its new-found revenues until there is time to plan sensible, well-targeted projects with high returns. Such an investment policy accomplishes two things. First, it harnesses export windfalls to finance sound, long-term development. Second, by delaying the new expenditures, government acts *countercyclically,* and so helps to stabilize the economy by spending less during the most inflationary period of the export boom and more after the boom has faded.[28] These *stabilization measures* are explored in depth in Chapter 20.

For reasons already discussed in Chapter 5, policies of restraint, essential to stabilization, are seldom popular and are often vigorously opposed by political pressure groups. Although the medicine for Dutch disease is easy to prescribe and

27. World Bank economist Alan Gelb and associates have documented six cases of Dutch disease in *Oil Windfalls: Blessing or Curse?* (New York: Oxford University Press for the World Bank, 1988).

28. If, however, the permanent income hypothesis is valid, the households will save much of the windfall and the burden on government is less. David Bevan, Paul Collier, and Jan Gunning, *Controlled Open Economies: A Neoclassical Approach to Structuralism* (London: Oxford University Press [Clarendon], 1990) argue that this was the case in Kenya during the commodity boom of the late 1970s.

essential for the patient's health, it is not often taken in sufficient doses to affect a cure.

Nigeria: A Bad Case of Dutch Disease [29]

In 1973–74, the oil embargo imposed by Arab countries, followed by the activation of OPEC as an effective cartel, quadrupled the price of petroleum on world markets. In 1979–80, the price doubled again, so that by the end of 1980 the terms of trade for oil exports, relative to the price of imports, was nearly seven times the level in 1972. In Nigeria, higher export prices generated an "oil windfall" that added 23 percent to nonmining gross domestic product in the middle 1970s and again in the early 1980s.

Nigeria's political history has been marked by intense competition among ethnic groups—culminating in the Biafran war of the late 1960s—and one of the major battlegrounds of this strife has been the incidence of taxation and government expenditure. Under this kind of pressure, the Nigerian government spent all its oil windfall. Public investment rose from 4 to 30 percent of nonmining GDP and the average pay for civil servants was doubled in 1975. Much of the new-found revenue was squandered on wasteful projects. The second oil windfall only whetted fiscal appetites even more: from 1981 to 1984, the budget deficit averaged 12 percent of nonmining GDP.

Fiscal excesses exacerbated the tendency of export windfalls to create inflation. Prices rose while the central bank kept the nominal exchange rate fixed, so that by 1984 the real exchange rate had appreciated to nearly three times its level in 1970 to 1972. Over the decade ending in 1984, Nigeria's nonoil exports fell almost 90 percent in nominal terms—a classic if extreme symptom of Dutch disease.

Agriculture suffered worst. Because rural constituencies were politically weak, little of the oil windfall was invested in agriculture, while vast amounts were spent, and wasted, on infrastructure and industry. From 1973 to 1984, the quantity of agricultural exports fell by more than two-thirds, while agriculture output per capita and total calorie consumption per capita both declined. From 1972 to 1981, growth in nonmining GDP was a respectable 5.3 percent, but this was only 60 percent of the growth rate during the five years before the oil price boom. It can be argued that Nigeria might have been better off without its oil boom.

Indonesia: Finding a Cure [30]

Indonesia was both the poorest and the largest country in the world to receive substantial oil windfalls. At first, the oil boom affected Indonesia much as it did Nigeria. The 1973–74 boom added 16 percent to nonmin-

29. This account is based on Henry Bienen, "Nigeria: From Windfall Gains to Welfare Losses?" in Gelb, *Oil Windfalls: Blessing or Curse?* pp. 227–60.

30. This account is based on Bruce Glassburner, "Indonesia: Windfalls in a Poor Rural Economy," in Gelb, *Oil Windfalls: Blessing or Curse?* pp. 197–226.

ing GDP and the 1979–80 price surge raised the windfall to 23 percent. Of the first windfall, the government itself spent more than 60 percent. From 1974 to 1978, the real exchange rate appreciated an average 33 percent over its preboom level, a bit more than in Nigeria at that time.

Yet the outcome was very different in Indonesia. Throughout the boom period, government was required to balance its budget each year and, because all controls had been removed from foreign exchange transfers, stringent management of the money supply was necessary to protect foreign exchange reserves. These self-imposed restraints limited the impact of windfalls on inflation.

The Indonesian government adopted two policies that took advantage of oil windfalls for national development goals. First, investment in agriculture had a high priority, especially the goal of achieving self-sufficiency in rice production. The government financed irrigation systems, encouraged the adoption of new rice varieties, subsidized fertilizer and pesticide sales, provided credit to farmers, invested in rural health and education facilities, and built roads and other infrastructure in rural areas. By the mid-1980s, Indonesia was self-sufficient in rice and by 1982–83 its total food output per capita was a third above its 1970 level—a performance far above average for all developing and industrial countries over the period.

The second policy was to devalue the exchange rate enough to avoid real appreciation. Major devaluations were imposed in 1978, 1983, and 1986, after which the rate was managed flexibly to maintain its real value. At the end of the oil boom period in 1984, the Indonesian real exchange rate had been *de*preciated 8 percent from its 1970 to 1972 average. Consequently, over the period from 1971 to 1984, the quantity of nonoil exports grew by over 7 percent a year and, from 1972 to 1981, nonmining GDP expanded by over 8 percent a year.

Thus shrewd policy played a major role in affecting an early cure for incipient Dutch disease. The government's decisive action was made possible by its stability and longevity: the Suharto government came to power in 1966 and many of its key economics ministers remained in place for two decades. It and the previous government placed great stress on integrating the multitude of ethnic groups of this diverse country, and so avoided the conflicts over fiscal resources that paralyzed Nigeria. Moreover, the country had an important advantage over other oil exporters: its large labor force, nearly two-thirds of it working in rural areas in 1970, dampened any tendencies for surges in wages and thus in domestic prices throughout the oil boom.

18

Industry

The concept of development and the process of industrialization have often been treated as synonymous, ever since the Industrial Revolution enabled Britain to raise its industrial production by 400 percent over the first half of the nineteenth century.[1] From then until the present the dominant criterion for development has been the rise in per capita income brought about largely by industrialization.

INDUSTRY AS A LEADING SECTOR

From Chapter 3's discussion of cross-country patterns, we know that higher shares of gross domestic product generated by industry are closely associated with rising income per capita. Figure 18–1 shows this pattern for manufacturing value-added in 1992 for 17 large countries (with populations over 25 million) and 20 small ones. In making such cross-country comparisons, economists conventionally segregate large from small countries. Nations with larger markets are able to develop a wider range of industries sooner in their development because they can take advantage of *scale economies* within the domestic market.[2] Hence we expect large countries to industrialize faster than small ones.

Both tendencies are evident in Figure 18–1. At any level of income per person, the average for large countries, determined by the regression line, is higher than

1. E. J. Hobswbawm, *The Pelican Economic History of Britain,* Vol. 3, *Industry and Empire* (Baltimore: Johns Hopkins Press, 1969).
2. The concept of *scale economies* is explained later in this chapter.

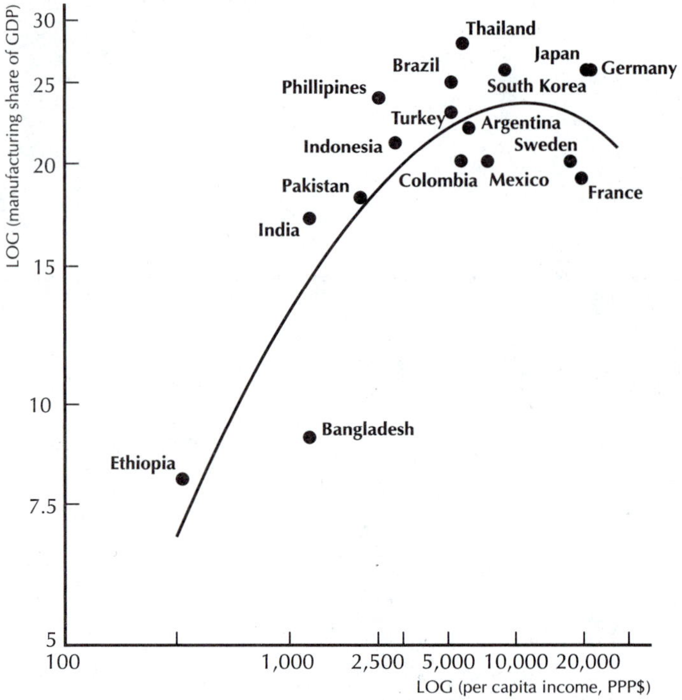

A. MANUFACTURING SHARE OF GDP FOR LARGE COUNTRIES, 1992

FIGURE 18–1 **Manufacturing Share of GDP, Large and Small Countries, 1992.** Large countries same incomes. In both cases, there is a tendency for manufacturing value-added to rise as a *Source: World Development Report 1994,* pp. 166–67, 220–21.

for small countries. Yet for both sets of countries, there is a strong correlation between industrialization and average income. On average for large countries, as income quintuples from $1,000 to $5,000 per person (in purchasing power parity), manufacturing value-added rises from 13 to 22 percent of GDP. In an average small country undergoing the same change in income, the manufacturing share rises more sharply, from about 7 percent to about 17 percent of GNP. A country with per capita income growing at 3 percent a year would take 54 years to make this transition.

Manufacturing share does not grow indefinitely. Somewhere between $10,000 and $20,000 per capita, the ratio of manufacturing value-added to GDP begins to decline, as advanced economies move out of manufacturing into modern service industries. This is indicated in Figure 18–1 by the regression line, which peaks after $10,000 and begins to decline.[3]

But wide variations are evident. Among large countries with similar incomes, Bangladesh has a manufacturing share of only 8 percent, whereas India's is 21 percent; Colombia and Mexico have shares of 20 percent, whereas Thailand's is 28 percent. Among small countries, Uganda's share is only 4 percent in contrast

3. The regression equations were of the form $\log MS = a + b \log y + c (\log y)^2$, where MS is the manufacturing share and y is PPP income per capita. The coefficient c was negative and significant in both cases, and so gave the curved shape of the regression line.

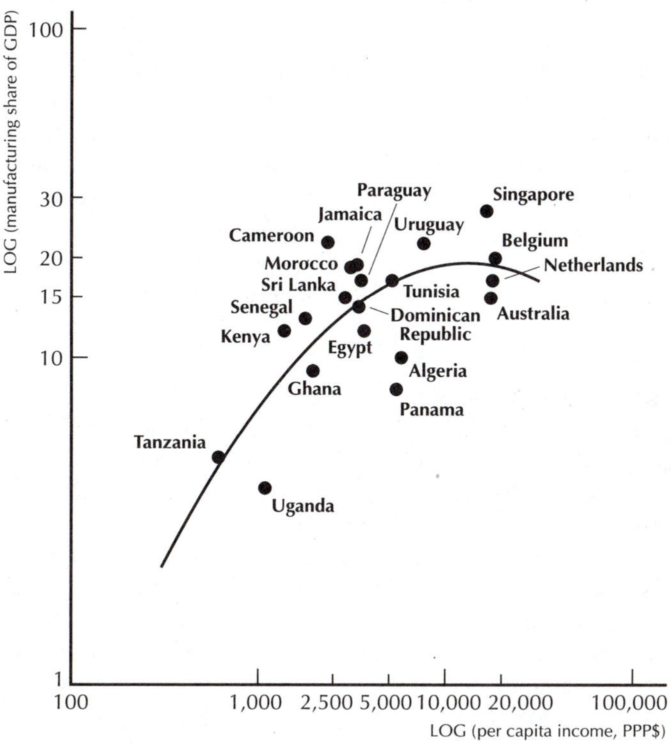

B. MANUFACTURING SHARE OF GDP FOR SMALL COUNTRIES, 1992

(with populations over 25 million) are, on average, more industrialized than small ones at the share of GDP as average income rises, up to a level of about $10,000.

to Kenya at 12 percent, and Panama at 8 percent contrasts with Uruguay at 22 percent. The differences may be due to differing endowments: Colombia's productive agriculture and Mexico's oil deposits give those countries the opportunity to grow with less investment in industry than poorly endowed countries such as South Korea. They may be due to strategy: Thailand and India adopted policies, though very different ones, to speed industrialization. Or differences may be due to location and historical circumstance: Uganda is landlocked and suffered prolonged civil war while Kenya is centrally placed to serve a regional market and has enjoyed relative stability.

Cross-country patterns imply that value-added in manufacturing ought to grow more rapidly than GDP in the typical developing country. This prediction is partially borne out by World Bank data. For the low- and middle-income countries as a whole, over the period from 1965 to 1990, manufacturing grew by 7.2 percent a year, compared to 4.8 percent a year for GDP. But this average pattern is not observed in most of the individual countries: of 42 developing countries for which data are available from 1965 through 1990, manufacturing grew at least 1 percent a year faster than GDP in only 19 of them; in most of the others, the differences in growth rates were less than 1 percent a year.[4]

4. *World Development Report 1992,* pp. 220–21.

Linkages

If manufacturing generally and early developing branches of manufacturing in particular are to lead economic development, they ought to have more **backward linkages** than other sectors, in the sense described by Albert Hirschman and introduced in Chapter 3. There have been several attempts to measure linkages. Those used by Pan Yotopoulos and Jeffrey Nugent seem as easy to understand and useful for our purposes as any.[5] Not surprisingly, linkage formulas depend on input-output tables, which are constructed to display linkages within an economy. A **direct backward linkage** for any industry *j*, is measured as

$$L_{bj} = \sum_i a_{ij}, \qquad [18\text{–}1]$$

where L_{bj} is the index of backward linkage, and a_{ij} is the Leontief (input-output) coefficient defined in Chapter 6. Thus a measure of backward linkage for any industry is simply the sum of its domestic input coefficients. If, for example, the textile industry adds value equal to 30 percent of its output, and imports inputs equivalent to another 15 percent of output, its backward linkage index L_b will be 55 percent, the share of domestically purchased inputs (100 − 30 −15 = 55).

Those who recall Chapter 6 will immediately recognize that this index captures only the direct links. But if textile production stimulates cotton growing, might not cotton in turn stimulate fertilizer production? It is easy to incorporate these indirect effects by summing the direct and indirect coefficients of the Leontief inverse, designated r_{ij}, to get

$$L_{tj} = \Sigma r_{ij}, \qquad [18\text{–}2]$$

where L_{tj} is an index of direct plus indirect or **total backward linkages** from the *j*th industry.[6]

There is an analogous simple measure of **direct forward linkages:**

$$L_{fi} = \sum_j X_{ij}/Z_i, \qquad [18\text{–}3]$$

where L_{fi} is the forward linkage index for the *i*th industry, X_{ij} is the output of the *i*th industry that is purchased by each *j*th user industry (the row of the input-output table), and Z_i is the production of good *i* for both intermediate and final use.

Yotopoulos and Nugent have used input-output tables for five developing countries (Chile, Greece, Mexico, Spain, and South Korea) to measure the linkage indices for 18 industries. The results are shown in Table 18–1. For leather, the next-to-last column tells us, for example, that for each additional dollar of leather goods produced, production of all inputs must rise by $2.39. A high index indicates that expansion of the industry will stimulate production in other sectors of the economy. Manufacturing industries dominate the upper ranks of Table 18–1 on the basis of both direct and total backward linkages. The early-developing sectors—leather, clothing, textiles, and food and beverages—represent four of the first five branches ranked by total backward linkages. Primary industries, utilities, and services are low on both lists. Hence an unbalanced-growth strategy should, to stimulate investment in other sectors, begin with the early-developing indus-

5. Pan A. Yotopoulos and Jeffrey B. Nugent, "A Balanced-Growth Version of the Linkage Hypothesis: A Test," *Quarterly Journal of Economics,* 87 (May 1973), 157-71; reprinted in their text, *Economics of Development: Empirical Investigations* (New York: Harper & Row, 1976), pp. 299–306.

6. The Leontief inverse matrix is explained in footnote 3 of Chapter 6.

TABLE 18–1 Sectoral Linkage Indices and Rankings in Five Less-Developed Countries*

	Direct forward linkage index (L_f)	Rank	Direct backward linkage index (L_b)	Rank	Total backward linkage index (L_t)	Rank
Leather	0.645	4	0.683	2	2.39	1
Basic metals	0.980	1	0.632	5	2.36	2
Clothing	0.025	18	0.621	6	2.32	3
Textiles	0.590	8	0.621	7	2.24	4
Food and beverage manufactures	0.272	16	0.718	1	2.22	5
Paper	0.788	3	0.648	3	2.17	6
Chemicals and petroleum refining	0.599	7	0.637	4	2.13	7
Metal products and machinery	0.430	13	0.558	9	2.12	8
Wood, furniture	0.582	9	0.620	8	2.07	9
Construction	0.093	17	0.543	10	2.04	10
Printing	0.508	10	0.509	12	1.98	11
Other manufactures	0.362	15	0.505	13	1.94	12
Rubber	0.453	12	0.481	14	1.93	13
Minerals (nonmetallic)	0.870	2	0.517	11	1.83	14
Agriculture	0.502	11	0.368	15	1.59	15
Utilities	0.614	6	0.296	16	1.49	16
Mining	0.638	5	0.288	17	1.47	17
Service	0.378	14	0.255	18	1.41	18

*Chile, Greece, South Korea, Mexico, and Spain.
Source: Yotopoulos and Nugent, "A Balanced-Growth Version of the Linkage Hypothesis," Table 2, p. 163.

tries and then move to chemicals and metal products. Advocates of import substitution strategies find sustenance in these findings.

But what do these indices really mean? Should a country base its development strategy on them, even if rapid growth is the principal goal? These particular measurement formulas have been attacked for several reasons, many of them sound ones. But alternative and more-complicated formulations give similar rankings anyway. The real issue is whether a mechanical summing up of input-output coefficients for one country really tells us anything about the dynamic processes of growth in another country. The textile industry, which ranks high in Table 18–1 according to its total backward linkage coefficient, may well require inputs of cotton and synthetic fibers. But whether this additional demand will lead to new investment in farming and chemicals depends on many conditions, none of them reflected in the index. Can cotton be grown in the country at all and if so, at what cost? It might remain cheaper, and to the country's advantage, to import cotton and use the land to grow more profitable crops. If cotton is already being grown and exported, can output expand to accommodate the textile plant or would it simply divert exports? Reduced exports would of course cancel the backward linkage effect.

The potential linkage back to synthetic fibers raises additional issues. Petrochemical industries are subject to substantial economies of scale, and it would take a considerable expansion of the textile industry to justify the very large investment in petrochemicals. If protection is used to keep out imports of synthetic fibers, the textile industry itself would suffer higher costs and perhaps lose its impetus to expand. However, it is also possible that some infant supplier industries may have the potential to reduce costs over time—learning by doing—if they are given a chance.

The requirements for effective forward linkages from manufacturing are even more stringent. To continue the example, textiles have a large forward linkage index, primarily to the clothing industry. But does domestic cloth stimulate the clothing industry? It can if textiles can be produced at costs below the world price of imported cloth. Otherwise the user industry is better-off importing its input. If clothing manufacturers are forced, through tariffs or import controls, to take more expensive domestic cloth, this would discourage, rather than stimulate, the forward linkage.

The static linkage indices can help direct attention to potential linkages, but detailed studies are required to consider all the relevant conditions and to pinpoint the ways in which investment in one industry will lead to investment in others. These studies may well show that some manufacturing sectors can lead growth in certain countries. But some of the references cited in Chapter 17 demonstrated that certain primary sectors also generate effective linkages, and there is no overwhelming case favoring manufacturing on this ground.

Urbanization

Since the Industrial Revolution, urbanization and industrialization have moved in tandem. England started the nineteenth century with 30 percent of its people living in cities and ended the century with an urban population share over 70 percent.[7] The trend toward urbanization with industrial development is evident today in cross-country comparisons, depicted in Figure18–2. As average incomes grow from about $750 per capita (in PPP) to $7,500, both the manufacturing workforce

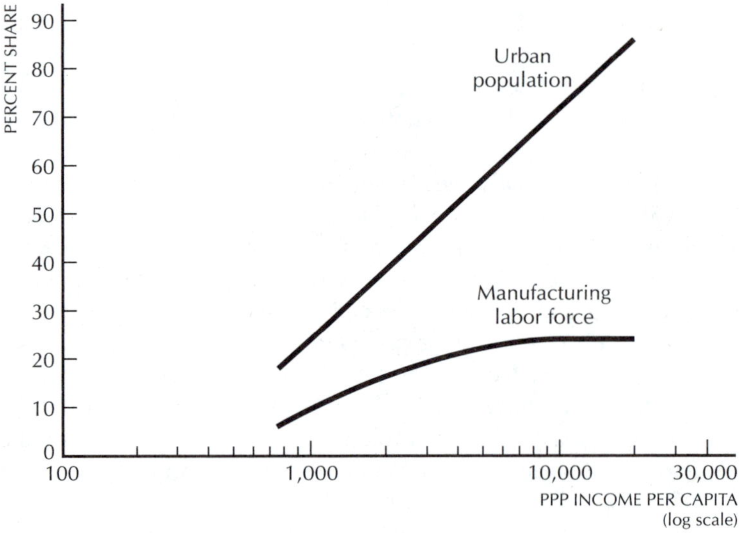

FIGURE 18–2 Industrialization and Urbanization Cross-country regressions indicate that as GNP per capita rises up to about $7,500, the manufacturing work force grows from an average 6 percent of the labor force to 24 percent, while the urban share of the population grows from 18 to 66 percent. But urban growth continues even though manufacturing's share of the workforce levels off.

7. Hobsbawm, *Industry and Empire,* Fig. 13.

and the urban population grow as shares of the total workforce and population. Beyond $7,500, however, the urban share continues to rise even though manufacturing no longer employs an increasing share of the workers.

What causes rapid urbanization as industrialization proceeds? Several **external economies** (see Chapter 5) benefit manufacturing firms in urban settings. Large populations reduce the firms' costs of recruiting labor of all kinds, but especially skilled workers and technicians. Moreover, in cities workers usually find their own housing, so firms do not have to provide it, as they might in rural areas or small towns. **Infrastructure,** including industrial sites, electricity, water, sewage, roads, railroads, and in many cases ports, is provided by the government in the cities at costs that reflect substantial scale economies. Health and education facilities are also more highly developed in the cities.

Each firm also benefits from the **economies of agglomeration** that result from the presence of many other firms, because a wide range of necessary inputs and services becomes available. Manufacturers can reduce transport costs and shipping delays if they locate near their suppliers. They also benefit from the proximity of repair and other industrial services. Financial markets cluster in cities where domestic and international communication facilities are available and cheap. Manufacturers need access to banks and other financial institutions. They also need the city's communications to stay in touch with distant suppliers and markets, especially export markets. When the city in question is a national capital, manufacturers may locate there to gain ready access to government officials who control investment licenses and incentives, import allocations, and a myriad of other policy and administrative devices that affect the profitability of the firm. Finally, the strong preferences of capitalists, managers, and technicians for the amenities of large cities can be a significant reason for locating there.

Once a city is established, its large market creates reinforcing attractions. Distribution costs are minimized when the firm locates near its largest market. If the costs of shipping output weigh heavily in firms' costs, and especially if they are more important than the costs of transporting inputs, firms will be pulled toward cities. This attraction is particularly strong in developing countries, where intercity and rural-urban transport networks are sparse or costly. In developed countries, where transport networks are dense and efficient, manufacturing tends to be more footloose and seeks out advantages like cheap labor with less regard for transport costs.

But urbanization has its costs, as the residents of every large city in the world observe daily: overcrowding, unsanitary conditions, displacement of rural migrants, crime. These too have been features of industrialization for two centuries. During the first half of the nineteenth century, London and the other growing cities of Britain were dismal places:

> Smoke hung over them and filth impregnated them . . . the elementary public services—water supply, sanitation, street-cleaning, open spaces, and so on—could not keep pace with the mass migration of men into the cities, thus producing, especially after 1830, epidemics of cholera, typhoid and an appalling constant toll of the two great groups of nineteenth-century urban killers—air pollution and water pollution, or respiratory and intestinal disease. . . . New city populations . . . pressed into overcrowded and bleak slums, whose very sight froze the heart of the observer.[8]

8. Hobsbawm, *Industry and Empire,* p. 86

Migrants to the large cities of the third world probably do not have to put up with conditions as bad as those of early nineteenth-century London, but cities like Calcutta, Lagos, and São Paulo contain large slums with many of the same kinds of problems.

Industrializing cities become magnets for rural workers seeking jobs at higher wages, a pervasive third-world phenomenon explored in Chapter 9. Despite the risks of unemployment and congested living conditions, urban life may still be attractive to many rural dwellers, relative to the opportunities available at home. The costs of congestion are external diseconomies like the costs of exploiting common resources discussed in Chapter 7: each new migrant will benefit on average, but in so doing, will reduce the well-being of all others, even if only slightly. The social costs are high, however, because this marginal reduction in well-being must be added up for all residents of the city.

No government feels comfortable with crowded cities, and many have attempted to stem the flow of migration. Over the long run this can best be done by encouraging rural development as actively as industrialization, using the wide range of land tenure, investment, price incentive, and other policies described in Chapter 16. A complementary approach is to encourage the dispersal of new industries to smaller cities through the provision of infrastructure, incentives, and controls over location. Spreading investment reduces congestion and may also reduce the cost of migration. Migrants will have shorter average distances to travel, so more of them can search for jobs without a commitment to permanent residence in cities remote from their homes. The decentralization of industry also has complementary benefits for agriculture; it distributes urban markets and manufactured supplies more widely among the farming population.

Industrial dispersion does have costs, however. Infrastructure costs may be greater in small towns, which have not provided as much of the basic facilities as large cities. To this must be added the higher costs of transport and other infrastructure required to connect dispersed industrial locations. Even with this wider network of transport and communications in place, private firms—and society—incur higher costs of hauling freight (both their material inputs and their final outputs) if they do not locate in the most efficient place; of communicating with suppliers, customers, and financial institutions, not to mention government officials; and of waiting with idle facilities while parts and repair specialists from distant places arrive to fix broken equipment. Whether the benefits of dispersal justify the costs will depend on the circumstances. Costs will be lower if the population is already dispersed, if several urban centers and connecting infrastructure already exist, and if the new sites have obvious advantages, such as nearby raw materials or abundant water.

Investment Choices in Industry

Chapter 3 introduced the proposition that, because factors of production can be substituted for one another in many production processes, economies were able to conserve capital and get more growth out of a given amount of saving. Chapter 9 used the same analytical device—the neoclassical production function—to demonstrate that policies to make labor less expensive and capital more expensive could move producers toward investments that employ more labor and less capital for a given level of output. But is there enough variance in production techniques to make such policies effective in conserving capital and creating more employment for a given amount of production? For industry, the answer is yes.

Choice of Technique

Table 18–2 illustrates the choice of technology for a single industry, textile weaving. Three alternative technologies are included: an older, semiautomatic loom (T1); a more modern, fully automatic, high-speed loom (T3); and an intermediate technology (T2). More alternatives could have been shown, including handloom weaving, which is still used in some Asian countries. As expected, the three technologies show increasing capital intensity, in the sense that the ratio of capital to output rises, and decreasing labor intensity. The treatment of Chapter 9 has been augmented by the consideration of other operating costs, including rental space, power, and differential wastage of the main input, yarn. In many cases modern equipment conserves both energy and material inputs and lowers production costs.

Analysis of the choice of technology is conveniently done using project analysis as described in Chapter 6. Revenues and costs, including the cost of investment, can be discounted over the life of each technology and the technology with

TABLE 18–2 Choice of Technology in Textile Weaving

	Alternative technology*		
A. *Inputs* (per million yards of shirting)	T1	T2	T3
1. Equipment cost ($1,000)	80.0	200.0	400.0
2. Labor (person-years)	22.0	11.0	5.0
3. Other costs ($1,000/ year)†	11.4	9.3	6.7
B. *Factor costs*	Rich Country		Poor Country
1. Real interest rate (% p.a.)	5.0		10.0
2. Present-value factor (20 years)‡	12.46		8.51
3. Wages ($1,000/year)	15.0		1.5
	Alternative technology		
C *Present value of costs* ($1,000)§	T1	T2	T3
Rich country			
1. Capital charges	80	200	400
2. Wages	4112	2056	935
3. Other costs	142	116	83
4. Total	4334	2372	1418
Poor country			
1. Capital charges	80	200	400
2. Wages	280	140	64
3. Other costs	97	79	57
4. Total	457	419	521

*Technologies are: T1—semiautomatic loom, T2—intermediate technology, and T3—fully automatic, high-speed loom.
†Includes cost of space, power, and wastage of yarn, all of which vary depending on the technology. Excludes the common cost of yarn in the finished product.
‡Present value of $1 per year for 20 years at the interest rate shown in B1.
§Wages and other costs discounted at appropriate interest rate over 20 years using present value factor in B2.
Source: Adapted from data in Howard Pack, "The Choice of Technique and Employment in the Textile Industry," in A. S. Bhalla (ed.), *Technology and Employment in Industry* (Geneva: International Labour Office, 1975), pp. 153-74.

the highest net present value chosen as the most economic. In Table 18–2, it is assumed for simplicity that all techniques produce cloth of equal quality and value, so revenues are not brought into consideration. Instead, the present value of costs is minimized.

Part B of the table presents indicative factor costs for a rich country and a poor one: workers in the rich country are paid ten times the wage of workers in the poor one, whereas the real interest rate in the poor country is twice that of the rich one. Under those conditions, investors in the rich country would minimize costs by choosing the most modern looms, largely because these require so much less labor. Investors in the poor country should select the intermediate technology. However, should the annual wage in the poor country be $1,000 a year instead of $1,500, which is a realistic possibility, the oldest and most labor-intensive technology would minimize costs. Figure 18–3 represents these technological choices as a production isoquant similar to those of Figures 3–2 and 9–3, only in a form more realistic for alternative technologies in single industries.

The range of technologies represented in Figure18–3 is realistic for the weaving industry in a developing country. The scope for technological choice in this industry can be indicated by the range of capital-labor ratios from the most to the least capital-intensive technology. The capital-labor ratio of technology T3 is 22 times that of technology T1. The study from which these figures are taken gives a

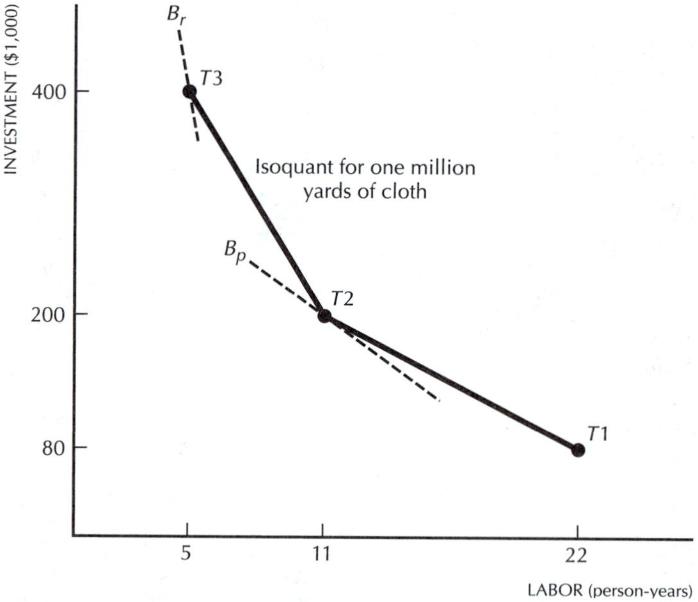

FIGURE 18–3 Technological Choice in the Weaving Industry. Three alternative weaving technologies T1, T2, and T3 are taken from Table 18–2. Each represents a different ratio of capital to labor. Because the industry, or even a single firm, is able to use any combination of technologies, production could take place at all combinations of labor and capital along *T1T2* and *T2T3*. Thus an isoquant can be traced from *T1* to *T2* to *T3*. The slopes of the budget lines B_rB_r and B_pB_p represent the ratio of wages to capital charges for the rich and poor countries, respectively. They indicate costs will be minimized for the rich country by using the most capital-intensive technology T3, whereas the poor country should use intermediate technology T2. Were wages in the poor country only slightly lower relative to capital costs, the most labor-intensive technology T1 might well be optimal.

similar range for cotton spinning, whereas cement-block-making in Kenya alone exhibits a ratio of 11:1.[9]

Even if the scope is narrowed to a choice between the appropriate technology (T2 for the poor country in Figure 18–3) and the most capital-intensive alternative (T3), there is a wide range of technologies available in several industries; for shoe manufacturing, the most capital-intensive technology has a capital-labor ratio 2.8 times that of the appropriate technology; for cotton weaving, the ratio is 4.3; for cotton spinning, 7.3; for brickmaking, 13.8; for maize milling, 3.3; for sugar processing, 7.8; for beer brewing, 1.5; for leather processing, 2.3; and for fertilizer manufacturing, 1.1.[10]

The cumulative impact of the choice of more labor-intensive technologies can be considerable. In one indicative experiment, Howard Pack, an American economist who specializes in the choice of technology, assumes that each of the nine industries listed in the previous paragraph receives $100 million of investment. If all of this were spent on the most capital-intensive technology, it would generate employment of 58,000 and value-added of $364 million a year. But if invested in the appropriate technology instead, the same investment would create over four times the employment (239,000) and 71 percent more value-added ($624 million).[11]

Despite the advantages to be gained in both output and employment from using appropriate, more-labor-intensive methods in developing countries, we observe many industrial plants using processes that are too capital-intensive. Several possible explanations for this were given in the discussion of the employment problem of Chapter 9 and elsewhere in this text: market prices of productive factors typically do not reflect true factor scarcities (opportunity costs or shadow prices) and so distort technology choice; more labor-intensive methods are usually embodied in older models of equipment, frequently available only in used machinery, which may be difficult to learn about, obtain, and maintain; newer equipment may manufacture products of higher quality and value; or managers may not be skilled in handling large labor forces. These factors are often exaggerated. In any case, most of them can be incorporated in present value calculations that reveal least-cost technologies.

These factors probably do not explain the wide range of technologies, many of them apparently inappropriate, that can be observed in a single country or in similar countries. There may be two further explanations for this. First, different firms can face different factor prices. Foreign firms usually have access to cheaper capital than domestic companies can obtain, so their optimal choice of technology is more capital intensive. (However, this may be countered by the multinational firm's greater knowledge of and easier access to machinery using older techniques, some of which may be in use in older plants of the same company.) Among domestic companies, small firms, with limited access to formal capital markets, may have to pay more for their capital than large firms. Similarly, small firms may escape both unionization and minimum-wage laws, and so are able to

9. Howard Pack, "The Choice of Technique and Employment in the Textile Industry," p. 169, and Frances Stewart, "Manufacture of Cement Blocks in Kenya," in Bhalla, *Technology and Employment in Industry*, p. 221.

10. Howard Pack, "Aggregate Implications of Factor Substitution in Industry Processes," *Journal of Development Economics,* 11, no. 1 (August 1982), 7.

11. Ibid., p. 10.

employ workers at lower costs. In Indonesia, economist Hal Hill observed four textile-weaving technologies in operation, with a capital-output ratio for the most modern looms over 200 times that for traditional handlooms. Two of these technologies represented least-cost choices for their firms. Surprisingly, these were the two most capital-intensive. But when shadow prices were used, only the more labor-intensive of the two techniques remained appropriate.[12]

Second, investors may purchase inappropriate equipment because they and their managers have a strong bias toward the most modern machinery and the highest possible quality of output, with less emphasis on profitability and other economic considerations. Harvard management expert Louis Wells has called this the behavior of "engineering man."[13] If the characteristics of management constrain the choice of technology, the selection may be technique T3 in Figure 18–3, even though the budget line indicates the choice of technique T2. Such noneconomic behavior is more likely to prevail in highly protected, monopolistic situations, where a decision to produce at less than minimum cost will not threaten the firm's existence. State-owned enterprises are particularly prone to inefficiencies of this type.

Economies of Scale

In decisions about alternative technologies, **economies of scale** may be a crucial consideration. It has been observed by economists at least since Adam Smith that for many kinds of production, larger facilities may be able to produce at lower unit costs than small ones. For example, steel produced in a mill designed for two million tons a year might cost 15 percent less than steel produced in a mill designed for only one million tons. As the scale of output rises, the potential average cost falls. (However, if the larger mill produces only one million tons, its average cost is likely to be higher than the small mill, because the small one was designed for lower output and the large one was not.) Readers familiar with the theory of the firm will recognize the concept of **long-run average cost**, the potential unit cost of output when plant size is variable. If the long-run cost curve declines over a range of output relevant to the plant in question, as depicted in Figure18–4, there are economies of scale.

Scale economies arise for a number of reasons. (1) Some costs, such as research and design efforts or start-up costs, may be fixed over a wide range of output. (2) The amount and cost of materials used in capital equipment will rise with output, but not always in proportion. For example, the capacity of a boiler is related to its volume, which for a sphere varies as the cube of its radius, whereas the material used to build it is related to its area, proportional to the square of the radius. (3) The amount of inventories and other working capital does not rise proportionally to output. (4) Greater scale permits greater specialization of both workers and equipment (the point emphasized by Adam Smith), which in turn permits higher productivity. (5) Larger production runs reduce the number of times equipment must be set up or readjusted for each run. For example, a plant

12. Hal Hill, "Choice of Technique in the Indonesian Weaving Industry," *Economic Development and Cultural Change,* 31, no. 2 (January 1983), 337–54.

13. Louis T. Wells, Jr., Economic Man and Engineering Man: Choice of Technique in a Low-wage Country," in C. P. Timmer et al. (eds.), *The Choice of Technology in Developing Countries* (Cambridge, Mass.: Center for International Affairs, Harvard University, 1975), pp. 69–94.

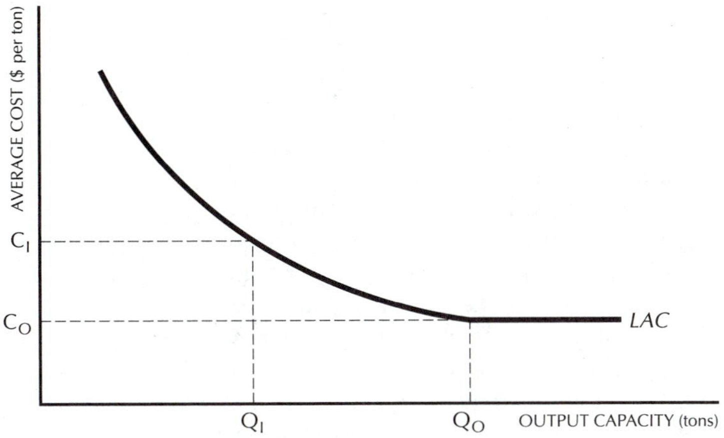

FIGURE 18–4 Economies of Scale. The long-run average cost curve *LAC* shows the average cost for plants designed to produce at any capacity. Average cost falls as capacity rises up to Q_0, sometimes called the *minimum efficient scale* (MES). Q_1 is half Q_0. The percentage by which C_1 exceeds C_0 is a measure of the economies to be gained by building plants to a larger scale.

that produces two or more products with one machine, such as metal cans of different sizes, could be run more efficiently once it has enough volume to produce each on a separate machine and reduce setup costs. (6) Larger producers may be able to obtain quantity discounts when they procure inputs. These economies all apply to individual plants. At the level of the firm, further economies may arise in management, transport, marketing, and finance as more plants are added.

These cost savings can be quite important in manufacturing certain products. Table 18–3 presents data on scale economies for several industries in Europe in the early 1980s. The **minimum efficient scale** (MES) is defined as a plant large

TABLE 18–3 Economies of Scale in Manufacturing*

Product	% increase in average cost	At plant capacity = this % of MES†	MES* as % of U.K. market
Refrigerators	7	33	85
Electric motors	15	50	60
Steel	11	33	27
Synthetic rubber	15	50	24
Petrochemicals	19	33	23
Tires	5	50	17
Oil refineries	4	33	14
Beer	5	33	12
Kraft paper	13	50	11
Cement	26	33	10
Glass bottles	11	33	5
Dairy products	2	67	1
Flour	21	67	1

*Estimates come from studies of European industries conducted from the late 1960s through the early 1980s.

†Minimum efficient scale is defined as the output beyond which average costs cease to decline (Q_0 in Figure 18–4) or beyond which no larger plants have been built.

Source: Cliff Pratten, "A Survey of the Economies of Scale," in Commission of the European Communites, *Research on the "Cost of Non-Europe,"* Vol. 2, *Studies on the Economics of Integration* (Luxembourg: Commission of the European Communities, 1988).

enough so that no further economies can be gained by building a larger facility, Q_0 in Figure 18–4. The first column of the table gives the percentage by which average cost would be greater if a plant were built to a smaller capacity; the second column shows that capacity (either 1/3, 1/2, or 2/3 of the MES). In practice, if the largest plant in existence does not exhaust the potential scale economies, investigators often take that output as the MES until a larger plant is built.

Some of the cost increases in column 1 are significant: from 11 to 26 percent for electric motors, steel, synthetic rubber, petrochemicals, Kraft paper, cement, glass bottles, and flour. However, this is not very meaningful unless we know how large the MES is relative to the national market. The last column shows how large the MES is compared to the market in the United Kingdom. For all except glass, dairy products, and flour, these efficient plants would fill from 10 to 85 percent of British demand for those products. For refrigerators and electric motors, the minimum-efficient-size plant could supply well over half of demand.

The market in the United Kingdom is comparable to that in the largest developing countries if gross domestic product is measured in terms of purchasing power parity. Over a billion people in China, with PPP average income only an eighth of Britain's, have a GDP 2.5 times that in the United Kingdom; India's GDP is about the same as Britain's; Brazil, Mexico and Indonesia have economies 60 to 80 percent that of the United Kingdom. But in Nigeria, the largest economy in Africa, the Philippines, and Pakistan GDP is only a fifth that of Britain. Moreover, in developing countries it is likely that the effective demand for modern manufactures is considerably smaller than indicated by the comparison of GDPs, because in Britain a much larger share of the population has reached middle-class standards of income. Where markets are much smaller than the minimum efficient scale, unit costs may be much higher than those indicated in the table. Such an industry would remain viable only if protected from imports and given a monopoly.

The characteristics of these large-scale industries shed light on the industrialization process. Those with largest cost savings and the largest potential market shares are all, with the exception of beer, either producer goods (electric motors, steel, synthetic rubber, for example) or consumer durables (refrigerators and others not shown, such as automobiles). Thus the nondurable consumer goods industries such as processed foods, textiles, clothing, and footwear, develop early at least in part because economies of scale are not a barrier, except in the smallest economies. The barriers to backward integration are also suggested by scale economies in producer goods.

Despite the existence of scale economies it may be efficient to build small plants in developing countries. A steel plant, for example, should be built when it can produce at a cost below the price of imported steel. This may happen long before the market grows to accommodate a steel mill of minimum efficient scale. Economic size is only one of the factors that bears on efficiency. All the others mentioned earlier in this text—productivity, opportunity costs of capital and labor, availability of raw materials and complementary inputs, managerial skills, market organization—also affect the outcome and may outweigh the effects of scale economies. Techniques such as project appraisal (Chapter 6) can be employed to analyze the impact of all these elements on profitability.

Moreover, the domestic market is not the only possibility. The "virtuous circle," through which export markets make it possible to attain scale economies, which in turn increase export competitiveness, was one of the forces behind Britain's Industrial Revolution. Indeed if a domestic industry in a small developing country were efficient enough to compete with foreign plants at any given output, then scale economies would not matter: the home industry could export enough to achieve any scale desired. Developing countries like South Korea and Brazil have achieved scale economies, even in industries like steel and automobiles, with the help of export markets. Economic integration among developing countries may help other countries to do the same.

Small-Scale Industry

Although economies of scale require large plants in some branches of production, there are many other industries in which small- and medium-scale firms can compete effectively with large ones (see Table 18–4). This is especially true in developing countries, where many widely used manufactured items—including most food and tobacco products, textiles, clothing, footwear, furniture and other wood products, cement blocks, bricks, tiles, and various simple metal products—are commonly made by smaller firms.

It has often been argued that developing-country governments should promote small-scale industry as either a complement or an alternative to large-scale modern manufacturing. India, probably the postindependence leader in planning for large-scale industrialization, has also pursued small-industry development with vigor, a legacy of Ghandi's famous advocacy of small units using traditional technologies. China's use of small-scale rural industry in support of local self-reliance is equally well-known. E. F. Schumacher, author of *Small is Beautiful,* founded a movement of small-industry enthusiasts.[14] Over the years, very few development plans have failed to pay homage to the goal of small-industry development.

Advocates of small-industry promotion promise a wide range of benefits, including accelerated employment creation, income generation for the poor, dispersal of economic activity to small towns and rural areas, and mobilization of latent entrepreneurial talent. They have also argued that support for small enterprise and the **informal sector** (see Chapter 9) will create a wider base of political support for capitalism and free-market policies.[15]

Shortly we will assess the potential of small industry to realize these hopes, but first we need to consider what "small industry" really means. There are several different ways to classify manufacturing plants by scale, none perfect. Classifying by the number of workers employed has the advantage that data are widely available. Units with one to four workers (usually a proprietor and family members) can be classified as **cottage shops,** whereas larger plants can be divided into small enterprises (sometimes 5 to 19 workers), medium enterprises (20 to 99), and large enterprises (100 or more), respectively. Such distinctions are arbitrary. In a large country, or a small industrial one, a plant employing 200 workers would be considered small. Moreover, when plants are classified by other criteria, such as capital invested or technology used, they may shift into different categories.

14. E. F. Schumacher, *Small is Beautiful* (London: Sphere Books, 1974).

15. See Hernando de Soto, *The Other Path* (New York: Harper & Row, 1989) and P. N. Dhar and H. F. Lydall, *The Role of Small Enterprises in Indian Economic Development* (Bombay: Asia Publishing House, 1961).

Cottage shops and small enterprises employ one-half to three-quarters of all manufacturing-sector workers in many low-income countries. Their share in manufacturing value-added is likely to be much lower, however, usually about one-fourth of the total. This marked discrepancy between the employment share and the value-added share shows that value-added per worker is much lower on average in small plants than in large ones. In part, this reflects the greater labor intensity of small plants.

Since low-income countries typically have abundant labor but little capital, most economists would expect labor-intensive technologies to be efficient in these settings. By this line of reasoning, the fact that small firms are usually more labor-intensive is sometimes taken to mean that they are more efficient than large firms. As part of the informal sector, small firms may be exempted from, or escape the enforcement of, taxes, minimum-wage laws, employment codes, and other regulations that raise the costs of larger firms. They may also lack access to subsidized loans, foreign exchange at overvalued (cheap) rates, and controlled imports, which artificially lower the costs of larger firms. It has been theorized that this freedom from many sources of factor-price distortion may induce small firms to use resources more efficiently than large firms. Alternatively, however, they might simply use all resources less efficiently—capital, labor, and material inputs. Attempts to measure the relative efficiency of different-size plants in industries where large and small firms coexist have generally been unable to reach firm conclusions.[16] Such comparisons face many difficulties in any case, not least the fact that product quality may differ greatly between large and small firms. Although cottage shops make cheap plastic sandals, for example, large plants may produce shoes of higher quality.

As a country develops, the average size of its industrial plants tends to rise as implied by Table 18–4. This rise is associated with the expansion of markets, which permits a few firms in some industries to expand and realize economies of scale and thereby beat out their smaller competitors. A related factor is declining transportation and communication costs, which facilitate the integration of na-

TABLE 18–4 Share of Small Establishments in Total Manufacturing Employment, 1980s (percent)

GNP per capita ($)	Distribution of employment by size class (%)			
	1–4 workers	5–19	20–99	100+
$100–$500	64	7	4	25
$500–$1,000	41	12	10	37
$1,000–$2,000	11	13	14	61
$2,000–$5,000	8	11	17	64
Over $5,000	4	6	20	70

Source: Donald R. Snodgrass and Tyler S. Biggs, *Industrialization and the Small Firm: Patterns and Policies* (San Francisco: ICS Press, forthcoming).

16. Ian M. D. Little, Dipak Mazumdar, and John M. Page, Jr., *Small Manufacturing Enterprises* (New York: Oxford University Press for the World Bank, 1988). They also claim to detect a tendency for medium-size firms to be most efficient.

tional markets and permit goods to be manufactured in least-cost locations and then shipped to their final markets. Thus the "natural monopoly" conferred on smaller local firms by high transportation costs and poor communication begins to break down. Industrialization also tends to narrow productivity and wage differentials among units of different sizes, a condition for the efficient allocation of resources.

The presence of many small firms in most poor countries—and the many people who depend on them for a living—does not necessarily mean that government should promote or subsidize small-scale industry. Most of the cottage shops and small enterprises in low-income countries probably have little capacity for enterprise growth. They typically provide a living for the proprietor and a few family members at a standard above that of peasant farmers but below that provided by efficient modern firms. Like small family farms, most of these "livelihood enterprises" survive as long as no better economic opportunities present themselves, then gradually disappear as the modern sector of the economy develops and workers move on to higher-productivity employment. Only a few small- and medium-scale enterprises have the potential to modernize themselves, upgrade their technologies, and compete successfully with larger firms. To do so, they must usually define some niche of excellence. The small firms that do survive in industrial countries tend to be just as capital-intensive and high-tech as larger firms in the same economy and to differ from them only in degree of specialization.

Can the promotion of small-scale industry deliver the benefits promised by its advocates? Let us examine the evidence on each of the claims noted earlier.

Small plants are generally more labor-intensive than large ones, although there are many labor-intensive large firms as well. Labor intensity contributes to equity in countries where income is very unequally distributed and people often have difficulty finding remunerative employment. The amount a worker earns is more important than merely having a job, however, and the level of pay is ultimately linked to productivity. In small industries in the poorest countries, labor productivity is low and most jobs in small firms provide little more than a chance to share in the general poverty. Government policy should aim not just at raising employment but at helping firms of all scales to develop new markets, adopt new technologies, and raise labor productivity. This is more likely to occur in medium-scale firms than in very small ones.

The claim that small-scale industry promotes regional decentralization also needs considerable qualification. Although it is true that many small firms are located in rural areas and small towns, these tend to be traditional "livelihood enterprises" that are likely to lose out in the process of industrialization. Keeping them alive through subsidization might increase equity, but at a high cost to efficiency and long-term growth. Modern small firms, in contrast, cluster in large cities, perhaps even more densely then large firms. Large firms are more self-sufficient and rely on economies of scale to lower production costs. Small firms, however, depend more on **economies of agglomeration** generated by proximity to firms engaged in similar or complementary activities. Most small producers need access to intermediate material inputs and thus prefer to be close to ports and other transport facilities. They are less likely than large firms to train their own workers, so they benefit from being near urban growth centers where skilled workers are located.

Small-scale industry does indeed serve as a breeding ground for potential entrepreneurs. Most societies have actual or potential entrepreneurs in farming, retail trading, transportation, and other small-scale activities. Small-scale industry represents a feasible step for these entrepreneurs, who would be blocked from entering manufacturing if large amounts of credit and the ability to manage large-scale enterprises were essential. Small enterprises can sometimes be developed in imitation of earlier entrants and so require less-innovative entrepreneurs. Some small firms have the potential to grow to medium or even large enterprises. It is important, however, not to yield to romanticism. Statistically, very few small firms even survive over long periods of time, let alone grow up to be medium or large enterprises. The rate of business failure is high among small firms in all countries.

Government can assist by providing a legal system, supporting financial and other institutions, and pursuing market-based policies that permit successful enterprises to flourish and require unsuccessful ones to meet market pressures or give way to more efficient alternatives. Most governments can begin by eliminating the many facets of policy that discriminate against small firms. Controlled imports and subsidized credit seldom reach small firms, whereas licensing requirements, health regulations, zoning restrictions, and other measures are often used actively to discourage small enterprises, especially those operating in the informal sector. In the kind of market-based, outward-looking regime described in Chapter 19, small firms should thrive if they have the economic advantages claimed for them by the advocates of small-scale industrialization.

Even in a deregulated, market-oriented economy, however, many feel that small industry needs special help from government to overcome some of its initial handicaps. A fairly standard package of services is used to provide this assistance.[17] It includes credit, usually provided through a small-industry development bank or similar institution; technical advice, organized along the lines of an agricultural extension service; training programs for managers and skilled workers; help in setting up procurement and marketing channels; and industrial estates that provide sites with infrastructure and a focal point for the assistance package. The idea behind this kind of package is to help inexperienced entrepreneurs over their early hurdles, introduce them to regular marketing channels, and eventually make them self-reliant.

However, the package is expensive and often ineffective. It requires government agencies to make contact with numerous and varied individual entrepreneurs and to offer assistance tailored to their specific needs, and thus draws heavily on the government's limited managerial and technical resources. Firms served by these programs often find the advice they receive unhelpful and the places in industrial estates that they are offered poorly located or too expensive. Many have failed to repay their loans, and this has sometimes resulted in the bankruptcy of the specialized lending institution. At best, the expense and complexity of small-industry assistance programs limits their outreach to a small fraction of target firms. Nor is it clear that government agencies have the skills and nimbleness required to help small entrepreneurs deal with market situations. Thus this approach is no substitute for general economic policies that permit small operators to do what they do best.

17. See Eugene Staley and Richard Morse, *Modern Small Industry for Developing Countries* (New York: McGraw-Hill, 1965).

Township and Village Enterprises in China

The Chinese have done what appears to be difficult in market economies: they have established modern small- and medium-sized factories in the Chinese countryside. In the first phase of successful development, the emphasis was on the supply of farm inputs, equipment, and consumer goods to communes and other rural customers. Several conditions made possible this early development. China's rural transport and marketing system was poorly developed, so that rural communities were isolated from urban centers of production. Centralized planning and control of industrial goods intensified this isolation, because communes wanting fertilizer or trucks had to apply to authorities located in urban centers—a process that entailed long delays and often was not successful. It was in the communes' interests for their regions to become self-reliant in agricultural inputs to avoid these delays, and it was also in the planners' interests if local materials, capital, and labor could be used, so that other industrial priorities were not sacrificed. Local industry had the additional advantages of bringing modern technology directly to the countryside and of helping to narrow the economic and social gap between farm and city.

It was this knowledge of technology and of how to organize a factory that proved to be so valuable to China's industrial development effort after market-oriented reforms were introduced in the early 1980s. With the abolition of central planning and the communes, part of the original rationale for these rural industries disappeared, but now these enterprises could buy whatever inputs they wanted and could afford on the open market. Renamed "township and village enterprises," these factories began producing a wider and wider range of products not only for the countryside, but for the urban areas and for export as well. Because these enterprises were small and remote from Beijing, they were able to avoid the constant interference of the government bureaucracy that plagued the large state-owned enterprises. Also, because they were small, it was acceptable politically to let loss-making township and village enterprise fail. Because no one was available to subsidize their losses, these industries had to work extra hard to make sure they stayed profitable.

The result of these developments was that the share of state-owned enterprises in gross industrial output fell from 77 percent of the total at the beginning of the reform period (1978) to around 40 percent in 1994, with township and village enterprises' making up most of the remainder. The average growth rate of these township and village enterprises during the past decade has been over 20 percent per year. Employment in township and village enterprises rose from 28 million in 1978 to 123 million in 1993, accounting for most of the rise in nonfarm employment in China.

Industry and Development Goals

Industrialization is not a panacea for underdevelopment. But two of its strengths are essential for any development program. As suggested by the Lewis-Fei-Ranis two-sector model (Chapter 3), greater productivity in industry is a key to increased per capita income. And manufacturing provides a much larger menu of possibilities for efficient import substitution and increasing exports than is possible with primary industries alone.

Industrialization and rural development must proceed in tandem. Industry can supply agriculture with inputs, especially fertilizer and simple farm equipment, that raise farm productivity. If manufacturing is efficient, these inputs may be supplied more cheaply than imports. The relationship is reciprocal, because agriculture supplies raw materials for manufacturing, such as cotton and other fibers, rubber, or tobacco. Agriculture and industry also provide reciprocal consumer goods markets. If agricultural incomes grow in egalitarian fashion—which may require land reform and broad-based rural development—then manufacturing will enjoy a wide and growing market for its consumer goods, one that may enable it to achieve scale economies in both production and marketing. Similarly, the growth of urban incomes, stimulated by industrial expansion, should provide a continuing stimulus to agricultural output and productivity through increasing demand for food. The key to growing food demand is expanding employment and improved urban income distribution.

Industry cannot by itself generate sufficient jobs to absorb the growing number of workers or to equalize income distribution, especially in the poorest countries. Liberalized economies, with reduced controls and market prices closer to scarcity values, can help to arrest the tendency toward capital intensity and inappropriate, modern technologies in manufacturing and thus to raise job creation in industry. A renewed emphasis on small industry may also help. Moreover, to the extent that intermediate or innovative technologies are needed to save capital and create more jobs relative to output, an innovative, efficient capital goods industry is an essential part of a development strategy. But in the final analysis much of the burden for employment creation and income equalization will lie outside industry, in agriculture and the services.

Industry has been seen as a key to another goal of many developing countries: reduced dependence. If a country wants the capability of doing without imports of essential commodities, it must develop both integrated industrial structure and a productive agriculture. If it wishes to exclude foreign political and cultural influence, it must learn to operate its manufacturing plants without foreign help. Much of the discussion about reduced dependence really is about increasing autarky or self-sufficiency; this implies that a country must produce everything it needs. But an alternative goal suggests the capability of producing a wide variety of goods efficiently enough to trade them on world markets and obtaining some goods overseas when it is advantageous to do so. This leads to the outward-looking strategy discussed in the next chapter.

Behind these considerations lurks a hidden development goal: industrialization for its own sake. Despite advice from many quarters to temper their protective and other industrial policies and instead to promote greater efficiency, employment, and equity, many governments continue to establish the most modern, capital-intensive industries available. This cannot be attributed entirely to misguided policy. The desire to have modern industry may be as great for a country as the desire for a radio or car can be for an individual. To the extent that modern manufacturing is a goal in itself, the best that development economists can do is to point out how much could be accomplished with alternative policies and measure the costs of industrialization in terms of other goals that remain to be achieved.

19

Trade and Industrialization

The previous two chapters, on primary exports and industry, may appear to suggest a certain determinism in development. Factor endowments, working through comparative advantage, dictate an important role for primary exports, at least in the early stages of development. Meanwhile, industrialization proceeds as income grows, guided by factor endowments, structural considerations, and the nature of industrial technology. But this overstates the case. Within the limits of factor endowments, structure, and technology there is considerable scope for policies to accelerate (or retard) the pace of industrialization, to alter the mix of industries, and to influence the technologies employed.

The relative factor endowments that dictate the export of primary products change with population growth, degradation of natural resources, capital accumulation, education of the labor force, and the acquisition and adaptation of newer technologies. Most, though not all, countries' comparative advantages move with development away from land- and resource-intensive products toward manufactures: to labor-intensive products first, then to capital-intensive and skill-intensive industries, and eventually to products embodying newer technologies. Virtually all governments attempt to hasten this gradual shift to a more industrial economy. And, depending on the strategy a government adopts, there is some choice about which patterns are followed and even the possibility of marked deviations from the "norms" established by industrialization elsewhere.

The choice of industrial strategy depends on a country's approach to trade. Two different trade strategies have been employed by governments to force the pace of changing comparative advantage and to alter the pattern of industrialization: import substitution and outward-looking development.

Two Industrial Strategies

Import Substitution

Import substitution, the replacement of imports by products from domestic industry, was the principal path to industrialization for almost two centuries following England's emergence as the first industrial power in the Industrial Revolution of the eighteenth century. In the newly independent United States, Alexander Hamilton's 1791 *Report on Manufactures* argued for tariffs to protect U.S. manufacturers from cheap British imports, and President Jefferson unintentionally boosted U.S. manufacturing by the politically inspired Embargo of 1807. Friedrich Lizst, the German economist, espoused protective tariffs as an instrument to industrialize Germany in the mid-nineteenth century. All the major European powers, including Russia both before and after the Communist revolution, and Japan protected their manufacturing as it became apparent that military strength depended on industrial strength.

In the developing world, import substitution was first explored in Latin America when their primary export markets were severely disrupted, first by the Great Depression of the 1930s and subsequently by the scarcity of commercial shipping during World War II. Emerging from the war with fledgling industries, countries like Argentina, Brazil, Colombia, and Mexico began systematically to erect barriers against competing imports from the United States. The export pessimism chronicled by Argentine economist Raul Prebisch, Hans Singer, and others (see Chapter 17) reinforced protectionist sentiment, and Latin America developed import substitution regimes with a multitude of protective techniques that were later emulated by other developing countries. In Asia and Africa, independence following World War II was the stimulus to embark on import substitution. By the 1960s import substitution had become the dominant strategy of economic development.

The underlying concept of import substitution is simple. First, identify large domestic markets, as indicated by substantial imports over the years. Then ensure that the technologies of production can be mastered by local manufacturers or that foreign investors are willing to supply technology, management, and capital. Finally, erect **protective barriers,** either tariffs or quotas on imports, to overcome the high initial cost of local production and make it profitable for potential investors in the target industries. This approach has generally meant that consumer goods industries, especially processed foods, beverages, textiles, clothing, and footwear, became the first targets for investment. These products are manufactured with relatively standardized technologies easily accessible to developing-country producers, and it was believed that consumers could bear the higher costs of local production without disrupting development. The other major category of manufactured imports before industrialization began was capital goods. Increased investment was essential to development, however, and it was believed that the higher costs of capital equipment would discourage investors.

Infant Industries

Economists find much to criticize in the protective structures of both developing and industrial countries, as this chapter will make clear. But there are valid arguments in favor of protective tariffs as a tool of industrialization, centering on the concept of an **infant industry.** Domestic capitalists, private or public, and their managers need to acquire a technology new to the country, whether this be the means to manufacture a product not previously made at home, such as the plastic material polyvinyl chloride, or a new process to produce familiar products at higher quality or lower cost per unit, such as a computer-controlled steel rolling mill. The products and technologies acquired by countries industrializing today have been manufactured and used by the more industrial countries for some time. So newly industrializing countries need only purchase technologies "off the shelf."

The managers and workers of the infant industry must then learn to use these technologies efficiently by the standards of the industrial countries. In some cases, this may require some engineering adaptation of the technology to suit local conditions. This process of **learning by doing** can take several years. Until these infant industries gain the necessary experience, however, they cannot manufacture profitably and sell at the price of competing imports. Private investors might finance these near-term losses if the prospects are good for long-term profits. In developing countries, however, domestic capitalists often appear to shun projects with long-delayed returns and capital markets are usually not sufficiently developed to assemble the funds of many savers into large, long-term loans for industry. The alternative, almost universally employed, is for government to protect infant industries from competing imports by imposing tariffs or import quotas.[1]

To justify protection or a subsidy, an infant industry must eventually become capable of competing against imports in the home market or, a stronger condition, in export markets. This suggests a temporary tariff, one that declines toward zero as productivity increases and costs fall. Even a temporary tariff may not be justified if the eventual benefits to society of establishing the new industry, suitably discounted as explained in Chapter 6, do not exceed the costs of protection.[2] All too often these conditions are not met. The industrial landscape is littered with infants that never grew up and require protection indefinitely, from the petrochemical industry of Colombia to the textile industry of Kenya.

For reasons that will become apparent, import substitution is a limited strategy. After an initial burst of industrial growth, the strategy typically bogs down. Once new industries saturate the domestic market, their growth is constrained by the average growth of the economy. Often this happens at levels of production that do not achieve economies of scale. Lack of competition dulls the incentive to increase productivity, especially as profits depend as much on levels of protection as on cost-saving improvements. The contradictory incentives of protection, described later in this chapter, discourage backward integration into intermediate

1. Most economists consider subsidies to be a superior alternative because they require a budget outlay that makes clear the cost of protection. Virtually all governments have preferred to use tariffs or quotas and make consumers pay instead.

2. For a complete specification of the infant industry argument, see Harry G. Johnson, "Optimal Trade Interventions in the Presence of Domestic Distortions" in R. E. Caves et al., *Trade, Growth and the Balance of Payments*, (Amsterdam: North-Holland, 1965), pp. 3–34.

goods industries. And the high costs embedded in protected manufacturing make it difficult for firms to compete in markets abroad.

Outward-Looking Industrialization

To sustain industrialization, it may be necessary to pursue an alternative and **outward-looking strategy,** one that shifts the focus from import substitution for the domestic market toward manufacturing for export to foreign markets. What is it about export-led growth that conveys advantages over import substitution? The answer dates back to Adam Smith who, in *The Wealth of Nations,* recognized that export markets would permit factories to produce more of any single item and thus to specialize more than if they produced only for the home market. Longer production runs reduce the setup costs of switching from one product to another and specialization permits each firm to learn more about manufacturing its products efficiently. International market competition provides the stimulus to do both.

In the two centuries since *The Wealth of Nations*, innovations in both products and technologies led to plants that had to be large to be efficient (see Chapter 18). In the production of chemicals, metals, automobiles, and other products, large plants in small home markets needed export markets to achieve economies of scale. If, as economists hypothesize, industrial productivity improves with practice, then learning by doing can be accelerated by more rapid growth of production through exports. And greater exposure to world markets enhances the opportunities to observe and adopt new technologies. University of Pennsylvania economist Howard Pack places these advantages in the context of dynamic allocative efficiency: When export markets exist, labor, capital, and even land can be moved rapidly from low- to high-productivity uses without encountering diminishing returns.[3]

A government pursuing an outward-looking strategy has to turn the entire incentive system inside out, and make it more profitable for firms to sell overseas while diminishing the profits from sales at home. Neoclassical economists prescribe, not a bias toward exports, but rather a regime that is neutral in its treatment of exports, import substitutes, and nontraded goods. With minimal government interventions and taxes, the market determines most prices and allocations, and leaves government to determine the rules of the game and to correct for the market failures described in Chapter 5. Hence private firms, governed by markets, determine what is produced for the home market and for export. This prescription has dominated the literature on development for the past two decades and formed the basis for most programs of structural adjustment toward a more outward orientation.[4] But in practice things are not so simple.

3. These and other observations on the advantages of exports can be found in Howard Pack, "Industrialization and Trade," in H. Chenery and T. N. Srinivasan (eds.), *Handbook of Development Economics,* Vol. II (Amsterdam: North-Holland, 1989), pp. 333–80.

4. Four prominent economists who strongly influenced thinking about inward versus outward strategies are Gustav Ranis, "Industrial Sector Labor Absorption," *Economic Development and Cultural Change,* 21 (1973), 387–408; Anne O. Krueger, *Foreign Trade Regimes and Economic Development: Liberalization Attempts and Consequences* (Cambridge, Mass: Ballinger, 1978); Jagdish N. Bhagwati, *Foreign Trade Regimes and Economic Development: Anatomy and Consequences of Exchange Control Regimes* (Cambridge, Mass: Ballinger, 1978); and Bela Balassa, "The Process of Industrial Development and Alternative Development Strategies," *Essays in International Finance*, 141 (1980).

The Asian Tigers

Seven countries in Asia—South Korea, Taiwan, Hong Kong, and Singapore, the "four tigers," along with Indonesia, Malaysia, and Thailand, the three "little tigers" of Southeast Asia—have set the pace for the rest of the developing world in using outward-looking strategies to stimulate rapid growth and industrialization. Table 19–1 shows that rapid export growth, especially in Korea and Taiwan, fueled the growth in per capita income that was two to three times the rate for the average middle-income country over 27 years. The four tigers, or **newly industrializing countries,** were primarily exporters of manufactures, while the three Southeast Asian countries were still moving from their primary export bases toward greater reliance on manufactured exports.

Because their export-led performance has been outstanding, these Asian economies, especially the four tigers, have become models for less-dynamic economies to emulate. As models, however, these countries pose a problem for the neoclassical approach to outward-looking growth. Not only did this group of countries use trade strategies that differed from one another in important respects, but some of the strategies were highly interventionist. The extreme cases have been Korea and its own model, Japan. Both countries have had stiff protective barriers against imports and have controlled interest rates at below-market levels, directing cheap credit to favored industries and firms. What has made this approach outward-looking is that access to protected domestic markets and provision of subsidized credit have been used by government officials as an incentive to induce, and sometimes to force, firms to meet ambitious export targets. In essence, the tools of protection were used to help fledgling exporters who were learning by doing: adopting new technologies, learning how to master them, reducing costs of production, finding and entering markets overseas, and eventually competing on equal terms with foreign firms.[5]

At the other extreme among the Asian tigers has been Hong Kong, which

Table 19–1 Exports and Economic Growth in Asia, 1965–1992

Country	Growth of merchandise exports (% p.a.)	Share of manufactured exports in total exports (%)	Growth of GNP per capita (% p.a.)
South Korea	20.2	93	6.7
Taiwan	15.2*†	93‡	6.9*
Hong Kong	7.5	95	5.8
Singapore	7.0	78	6.9
Malaysia	7.4	61	4.4
Thailand	11.2	67	4.5
Indonesia	7.8	48	4.4
Middle-income countries	3.0	49	2.2*

*To 1990. †Includes nonfactor services. ‡1988.
Sources: World Development Report 1990 and *1994*, and World Bank, *World Tables 1994*.

5. The revisionist school on Korea, questioning the neoclassical approach, was led by Alice Amsden, *Asia's New Giant: South Korea and Late Industrialization* (New York: Oxford University Press, 1989).

comes as close to the neoclassical, free-trade model as any country in the world. Singapore, also a very open economy with low protection, nevertheless diverges from the neoclassical norm in that many of its largest export industries are government-owned service firms in telecommunications, port services, an international airport, and air transport. Taiwan and the three Southeast Asian countries have used a mixed approach. Although protectionist and interventionist, they all employed devices, such as export-processing zones (EPZs, industrial estates where duties are not paid) and exemptions from import duties and licensing, that insulated their export industries from the distortions of the home market and permitted them to buy inputs and sell their outputs at close to world market prices, as the neoclassical strategy dictates.[6]

What, then, is the essence of the outward-looking strategy as defined in practice by the Asian tigers? Four elements were common to all seven countries. *First,* these seven governments gave high priority to rapid economic development. Corruption and rent-seeking, though present, were kept within limits and ultimately subordinated to economic growth. Economic technocrats were given substantial influence over policy and insulated from political forces. And, in Southeast Asia, ethnic minority Chinese citizens, as well as foreign investors, were encouraged to invest and expand their firms. *Second,* economies were managed soundly, with small budget deficits, moderate inflation, and exchange rates that did not stray far from market-determined levels. *Third,* factor markets were highly flexible. Labor markets were not encumbered with controls. Though credit markets were repressed in most countries, nonfavored borrowers could seek loans either in active parallel credit or *curb* markets, as in Korea and Taiwan, or in overseas markets, as in the other five countries. *Fourth,* as already noted, exporters were able to import and sell at close to world market prices.[7]

Trade Policies

The core idea behind an outward-looking trade strategy is that producers of import substitutes and especially of exports should become competitive through market incentives; they should buy their inputs and sell their outputs in the home market at or close to world market prices. In contrast, the core idea behind import substitution is that infant industries cannot survive at first without higher prices in the home market than they could charge in competition with imports. Three instruments of government trade policy are used to provide higher prices or lower costs at home: tariffs on imports, quotas that restrict import quantities, and subsidies and other government favors that benefit some firms or industries over others within the economy. In this section we show how it is possible to combine all three policy instruments into measures of the extent to which domestic prices are distorted from world prices. A fourth policy instrument, the exchange rate, treats

6. Taiwan's interventionist strategy is documented by Robert Wade, *Governing the Market: Economic Theory and the Role of Government in East Asian Industrialization* (Princeton, N.J.: Princeton University Press, 1990).

7. The common features of Asian growth are explored in David L. Lindauer and Michael Roemer (eds.), *Asia and Africa: Legacies and Opportunities in Development* (San Francisco: ICS Press, 1994), especially Chap. 1. The World Bank, which has been an important bastion of the neoclassical approach, has attempted to reconcile neoclassical and revisionist thinking in its much-discussed book, *The East Asian Miracle: Economic Growth and Public Policy* (Washington, D.C.: World Bank, 1993).

all traded goods uniformly, but changes the relationship between traded and non-traded goods.

Protective Tariffs

In the early stages of import substitution, when a protective tariff is placed on competing consumer goods imports, not one but two significant aids are provided simultaneously to the potential manufacturer. First and obviously, the domestic price of the good, say cloth, will be raised above the world price. For the importing country, the world price of imported cloth is the cost of the cloth landed at the port of entry, the *c.i.f.* (including costs, insurance, and freight) or *border price.* With no tariff, the domestic price of cloth would settle at the world price. When a tariff is imposed, the domestic price must rise above the world price. If the home country's demand for imports does not affect world prices (that is, the world supply is perfectly elastic) and if the tariff does not preclude imports altogether, then the domestic price will rise by the full extent of the tariff. Any potential manufacturer can charge anything up to the tariff-supported domestic price and still compete with imports, assuming its quality is comparable and domestic consumers do not prefer imports simply because they are foreign.

This effect of an increased domestic price is called **nominal protection** and is depicted in Figure 19–1. At a world price P_w (equal to the border price, c.i.f.) consumers demand Q_1 of cloth and local producers find it profitable to produce Q_2;

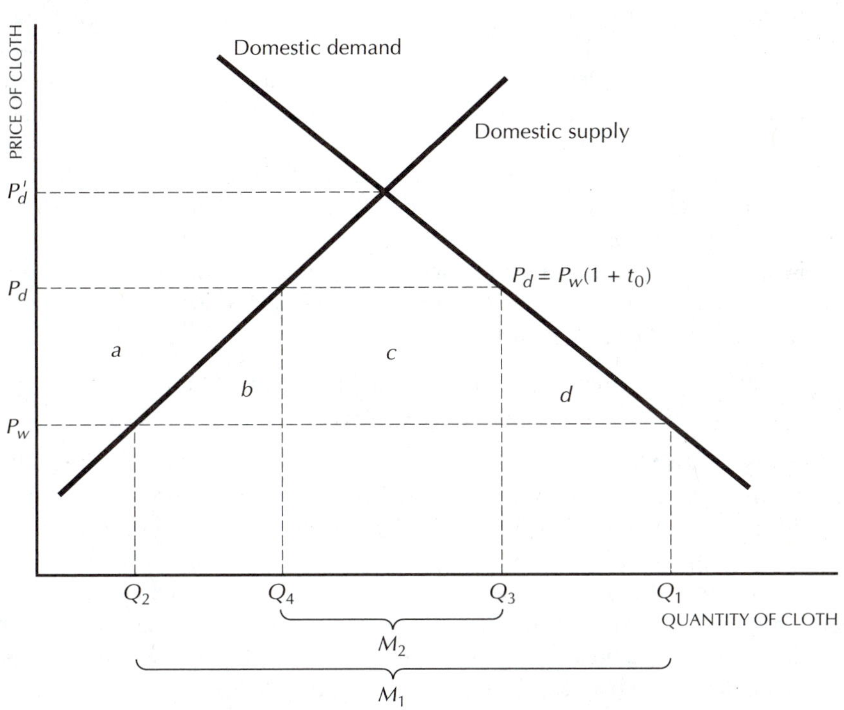

FIGURE 19–1 Nominal Tariff Protection. The imposition of a protective tariff t_0 causes the domestic price P_d to rise above the world price P_w. Domestic production therefore increases. The resulting loss in consumers' surplus ($a + b + c + d$) is offset by the gain in producers' surplus (a) and in tariff revenue for the government (c). The remaining areas b and d represent deadweight losses.

the balance, $M_1 = Q_1 - Q_2$, is imported. If an ad valorem (that is, a percentage) tariff t_0 is imposed on imports competing with domestic cloth and if world supply is perfectly elastic, then the domestic price rises to P_d; this reduces the quantity demanded to Q_3 and increases domestic production to Q_4. Imports are thus reduced to $M_2 = Q_3 - Q_4$. The *protective effect,* given by the increase in domestic output from Q_2 to Q_4, entails a rent or *producers' surplus,* given by trapezoid a; and a *resource cost,* given by triangle b, because factors of production are diverted from more productive uses into import substitution for imported cloth. The government's tariff revenue is represented by rectangle $c = t_0 P_w M_2$. Consumers pay for protection by the loss of *consumer surplus,* equal to area $a + b + c + d$, generated by both the higher price and reduced consumption. Area $b + d$, two triangles representing welfare losses that are not compensated by gains to anyone, is called the *deadweight loss.* A prohibitive tariff would raise the domestic price to P'_d, at which point domestic demand equals domestic supply and no cloth is imported.

The second aid to domestic manufacture is that tariffs are typically not as high on the imported inputs required for production. If the textile manufacturer is to import cotton to spin into yarn and weave into cloth, then the manufacturer's concern is not only with the price of the cloth but with the margin between the cost of imported cotton (and other imported inputs, such as chemicals and dyes) and the sale price of finished cloth. It is within this margin that the manufacturer must pay wages, rents, and interest on borrowed capital and extract profit. The greater that margin, the more room there is to accommodate higher factor costs and the higher is the potential profit. This margin is the *value-added* measured *in domestic prices.* It can be increased by raising tariffs on competing imports of finished products, lowering tariffs on imported inputs, or both. This dual effect of the tariff structure is called *effective protection.*

To measure the concept of effective protection, it is necessary to compare two margins: first, the margin between the domestic, tariff-determined prices of inputs and outputs, or *value-added measured at domestic prices,* and, second, the same margin measured at world or c.i.f. prices, which is called *value-added at world prices.* The fraction by which the first margin exceeds the second is called the **effective rate of protection,** abbreviated ERP:

$$\text{ERP} = \frac{\text{value-added (domestic prices)} - \text{value-added (world prices)}}{\text{value-added (world prices)}} \quad [19\text{–}1]$$

To refine this further, note that value added at domestic prices (V_d) is the difference between the potential domestic price (P_d) and the potential domestic cost of material inputs per unit of output (C_d). Further, the potential domestic price is equivalent to the world price (P_w) plus the increase permitted by the ad valorem tariff on competing imports (t_0), whereas potential domestic cost equals the cost at world prices (C_w) plus any increase permitted by the ad valorem tariff on imported inputs (t_i). The denominator of Equation 19–1, value-added at world prices (V_w), is the difference between P_w and C_w.[8] Given this, then,

8. A complication is the cost of inputs, such as electricity and water, that are not traded and therefore do not have a world price. These can either be treated as a cost of production at zero tariff, in which case they cancel out of the numerator and appear only in the denominator, or be broken down into their local and imported components, with the imported components, such as fuel to generate electricity, treated as traded inputs and the local costs, such as wages, treated as part of value-added.

$$\text{ERP} = \frac{(P_d - C_d) - (P_w - C_w)}{P_w - C_w} \quad [19\text{–}2]$$

$$= \frac{P_w(1 + t_0) - C_w(1 + t_i) - (P_w - C_w)}{P_w - C_w}.$$

$$= \frac{P_w t_0 - C_w t_i}{P_w - C_w}. \quad [19\text{–}3]$$

As a last refinement, Equation 19–3 can be put in terms of a dollar of output by dividing the fraction through by P_w. The cost of an input for a dollar's worth of output, C_w/P_w, can be designated a, an input coefficient. If we then allow for several inputs, each with its own input coefficient a_i and its own tariff t_i, then the formula can be written

$$\text{ERP} = \frac{(t_0 - \Sigma a_i t_i)}{(1 - \Sigma a_i)}.\text{[9]} \quad [19\text{–}4]$$

To illustrate the workings of effective protection, assume, using Equation 19–3, that \$100 of cloth, valued at world prices, would require \$60 of material inputs, such as cotton and chemicals, also valued at world prices. Value-added is \$40 at world prices. If the government has imposed a uniform duty of 10 percent on both competing imports and imported inputs, then

$$\text{ERP} = 100(.10) - 60(.10)/(100 - 60) = 0.10.$$

A uniform tariff, 10 percent in this case, yields an effective rate of protection of the same amount. If, however, in order to encourage investment in the textile industry, the government were to permit textile firms to import cotton and chemicals duty-free, then $t_i = 0$ and

$$\text{ERP} = 100(.10)/40 = 0.25.$$

Effective protection is now 25 percent. If instead, the input duty stayed at 10 percent but competing cloth imports were taxed at 20 percent, the ERP would rise to 35 percent. This latter case is illustrated graphically in Figure 19–2.

The implication of the third example is that, even though only modest nominal protection is provided, the domestic manufacturer enjoys a large margin of 35 percent over value-added at world prices. If the local manufacturer takes advantage of the effective protection afforded by the tariff structure, it can earn high profits, pay high wages, or simply accommodate inefficiencies and costs substantially above those of foreign competitors. The higher is effective protection, the greater the incentive to establish the industry in the country and the greater the economic costs of doing so.

Tariff structures in most countries, including most industrial countries, are like those in the latter two textile examples: duties tend to escalate from low rates on imported industrial inputs to higher rates on imports of finished goods that compete with domestic manufactures. In fact the levels of protection in this hypothetical example are modest by world standards. It is common to observe effective protection of 100 percent or more in several industries in countries strongly pursu-

9. For a complete, although advanced, treatment of effective protection, see W. M. Corden, *The Theory of Protection* (London: Oxford University Press, 1971), especially Chaps. 2 and 3.

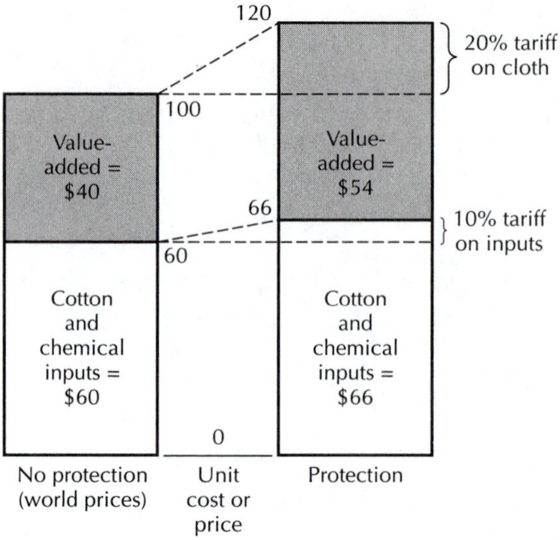

FIGURE 19–2 Effective Protection. With no tariffs, cloth is produced using inputs costing $60 and is sold in the domestic market at $100, the world price; value-added is $40. If cloth is protected with a 20 percent tariff but there is also a 10 percent tariff on cotton and chemical imports, the domestic sales price can rise to $120, inputs now cost $66, and value-added by domestic producers can rise to $54, which is 35 percent above value-added at free trade.

ing import substitution. Not only is the level high, but there is a wide range of protective rates that result in severe discrimination against particular kinds of investment. The fairly typical pattern of protection is illustrated by the data in Table 19–2 for Bangladesh in 1984 and Brazil and the Philippines in the mid-1960s.

The average level of effective protection for manufacturing as a whole ranges from moderate (the Philippines) to high (Brazil). However, the structure within manufacturing is widely skewed. Consumer goods are highly protected and intermediate goods are comfortably protected, though at lower rates. The capital goods industries receive less protection, however, because taxes on capital goods discourage investors; rates are especially low in Bangladesh for machinery and in Brazil and the Philippines for transport equipment (which does not include automobiles, a consumer durable). As a consequence, the incentive to invest in capital goods production is less than in other manufacturing and the development of this

TABLE 19–2 Effective Rates of Protection

Sector	Bangladesh (1984)	Brazil (1966)	Philippines (1965)	Norway (1954)
Agriculture	13	46	33	34
Mining	n.a.	−16	−9	−7
Manufacturing	114	127	53	9
Consumer goods*	n.a.	198	72	29
Intermediate goods*	n.a.	151	45	9
Machinery	10	93	24	18
Transport equipment	n.a.	−26	−3	−6

*Aggregates for consumer goods and intermediate goods are simple, unweighted averages of constituent industry data.

Sources: For Bangladesh, Thomas L. Hutcheson and Joseph J. Stern, "The Methodology of Assistance Policy Analysis," Harvard Institute for International Development, Development Discussion Paper No. 226, April 1986, and for other countries, Bela Balassa et al., *The Structure of Protection in the Developing Countries* (Baltimore: John Hopkins Press, 1971), p. 55.

sector typically lags behind the others. More damaging in terms of many development objectives, manufacturing as a whole enjoys a substantial advantage over agriculture, which faces effective rates of protection ranging downward from 46 percent to only 13 percent in these examples. In many countries, agriculture has negative effective protection.[10] These biases against investment in agriculture and in capital-goods industries are characteristic of import substitution to stimulate self-sustaining development. Though industrial countries, like Norway in the table, have also used biased protective structures, they were not as extreme as developing countries like Bangladesh (and have been considerably neutralized by the multilateral tariff reforms of the past 30 years).

Import Quotas

The protective effects of tariffs can also be achieved through restrictions on imports, known as **quantitative restrictions** (QRs), *quotas,* or *import licensing.* For both the government and domestic manufacturers, import quotas have the advantage of permitting a known quantity of imports. With tariffs the quantity of imports depends on the elasticities of supply and demand, which are only approximately known in advance. A quota that limits imports to the same quantity as a tariff would have most of the same effects. To see this, refer back to Figure 19–1. Instead of the tariff t_0, assume the government limits imports of cloth to the quantity $M_2 = Q_3 - Q_4$. As with the tariff the domestic price would still rise to P_d, domestic production would rise form Q_2 to Q_4 and cause a resource cost measured by triangle b, and consumption would fall from Q_1 to Q_3 and add the area of triangle d to the deadweight loss. But in two important respects import quotas have different effects than tariffs.

The first difference is that the government no longer collects tariff revenues. Instead the government issues licenses to a limited number of importers, giving them the right to purchase imports of cloth up to a total of M_2 in Figure 19–1. If the government were to sell these import licenses at auction, potential importers would be willing to buy licenses for as much as $P_d - P_w$ per unit of imports. They could then purchase each unit of imported cloth for P_w, the world price, and break even by selling it at the domestic price P_d. In that case the auction price for import licenses would just equal the tariff t_0 that would have led to the same quantity of imports. The government would collect the same revenue as under a tariff, rectangle c in Figure 19–1, though in the form of fees for import licenses.

Most governments do not auction import licenses, however, but give them free to a limited number of those importers who apply for them. Then although the importers pay only P_w for their imports, they can sell them at the domestic price P_d in Figure 19–1 and keep for themselves a windfall profit of $P_d - P_w = t_0$. This rent—often called a **quota rent** or *premium*—can be substantial, so import licenses are valuable to their recipients. Much effort is expended and large bribes are offered to obtain import licenses, with consequences discussed later in this chapter.

10. A negative effective rate of protection can have two meanings. If the rate is small, it means that the industry faces high taxes on either its inputs or its own outputs, as is likely to be true for many primary exporting industries. Alternatively, a very high negative ERP usually indicates that the industry is so inefficient that its inputs cost more in foreign exchange than its outputs are worth at c.i.f. prices; that is, value-added is negative if measured at world prices! Then the denominator of Equation 19–3 or 19–4 becomes a small negative number.

The second difference between quotas and tariffs is that quotas can convert a single domestic manufacturer into a monopolist that can charge whatever price maximizes profits. So long as imports can continue to enter the country, even at a high tariff, domestic producers are forced to compete with imports at a domestic price determined by the world price plus the tariff (P_d in Figure 19–1). But if the tariff is converted to a quota, even though the same quantity of imports is allowed in, then domestic producers no longer have to compete with imports. Once the quota has been filled, there is no alternative source of supply to compete with domestic monopolists. Local suppliers can then use their market power to restrict domestic output and charge a monopolist's price above the world price plus tariff, with a consequent loss to consumers and a net loss to the economy. It is because of these two consequences of quotas—the revenue loss and the monopoly effect—that trade reforms and international trade agreements often start with the conversion of quotas to equivalent tariffs, which bears the inelegant name *tariffication.*

Subsidies and Export Protection

Exports and even nontraded goods can be "protected" if we broaden the term to include, not only tariffs, but subsidies and other preferential treatment, which can provide the same relative profitability as tariffs. If textile production receives a 20 percent protective tariff while steel production receives a 20 percent subsidy on output, there is no change in their relative profitability. The only difference is that textile consumers pay for that industry's protection while taxpayers, through government, pay for the steel industry's protection. Figure 19–3 shows the equivalence of tariffs and subsidies.

Economists generally prefer the use of subsidies instead of protective tariffs because, as shown in Figure 19–3, consumers purchase more of a good under a subsidy while society pays no more for production than under an equivalent tariff. Thus welfare losses under a subsidy, triangle *b*, are smaller than those under an equivalent tariff, triangles *b* plus *d*.[11] Also, because subsidies usually appear in the government's budget and must be financed through taxation, there is an annual accounting for the costs of protection offered in this way. Government is, therefore, more restrained in conferring this kind of protection and is correspondingly more likely to adhere to infant industry rules, and keep protection moderate and short-lived.[12] In addition, subsidies can be more precisely targeted than protective tariffs. Whatever the source of high costs—expensive capital, high wage rates, or lack of trained workers—subsidies can be paid to offset those costs. Protective tariffs, in contrast, can only compensate by raising the domestic price of output.

This broader view of protection, incorporating both tariffs and subsidies, is measured by the **effective rate of subsidy** (ERS), a concept derived from the effective rate of protection (ERP). The formula for ERS is similar to that for ERP (Equation 19–4), and its implications are the same. However, the ERS incorpo-

11. This ignores the additional distortions and welfare losses introduced when government tries to finance the subsidy by raising additional tax revenue or cutting expenditures. If consumers are taxed to pay the subsidy, the outcome and welfare loss is identical to that with a tarriff, as in Figure 19–1.

12. But not necessarily. The United States and especially the European Community have subsidized their farmers for decades at rates that rival the effective rates protection provided for industry by import-substitution regimes.

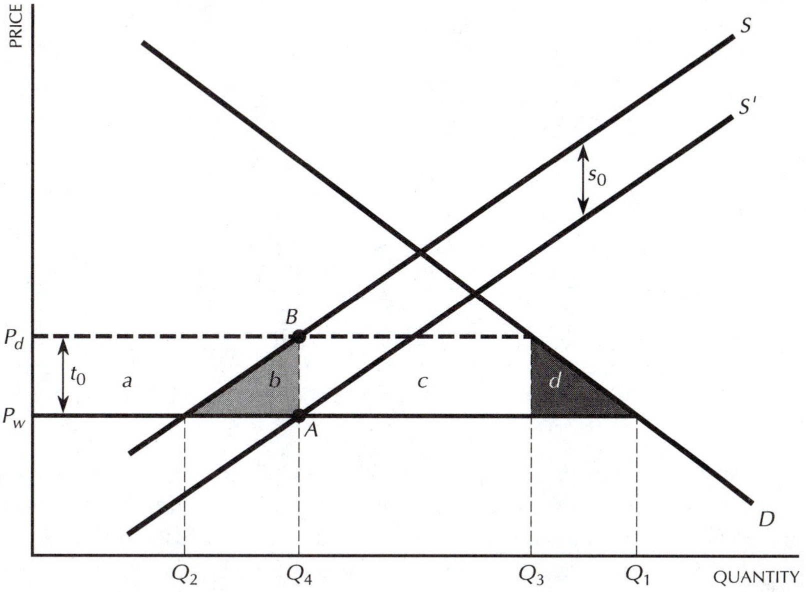

FIGURE 19–3 Comparison of Tariffs and Subsidies. If, instead of a tariff t_0 (see Figure 19–1), the industry were given an equal subsidy, $s_0 = t_0$, the effective supply curve shifts from *S* to *S′*. As with the tariff, domestic production is at Q_4 and producers receive the same price $P_d = P_w(1+ s_0)$. However, consumers now purchase Q_1 instead of Q_3 and pay the world price P_w instead of P_d. The subsidy is area *a* + *b*, paid by taxpayers instead of consumers. The deadweight loss is only triangle *b*, less than *b* + *d* under a tariff. But if purchasers of the good were taxed at the rate t_0 to pay for the subsidy, the outcome would be identical to that in Figure 19–1.

rates five elements, two of which are not in the ERP: (1) tariffs on imports competing with domestic output and on inputs, t_0 and t_i, as under ERP; (2) subsidies on outputs and inputs paid directly to the industry, s_0 and s_i, which could have been included in Equation 19–4 as part of the ERP; (3) the premiums due to quota restrictions on imports, q_0 and q_i, which could also have been included in the ERP of Equation 19–4; (4) relative subsidies in the form of preferential corporate income taxes that are lower than the average paid by other industries, s_t; and (5) relative subsidies in the form of below-average interest rates on loans, s_b. Because the last two elements are calculated as deviations from average rates of tax or interest, they can be either positive or negative for any industry, though for the entire economy they each must sum to zero. The formula for ERS, derived from Equation 19–4, is

$$\text{ERS} = \frac{(t_0 + s_0 + q_0) - \Sigma a_i(t_i - s_i + q_i) + s_t + s_b}{1 - \Sigma a_i}. \qquad [19\text{–}5]$$

The ERS is a comprehensive indicator of the extent to which protection affects the relative profitability of various industries. Under import substitution regimes, the ERS is expected to be highest for firms that compete with imports in the domestic market, as is true for the ERP. Under an outward-looking policy regime, however, import-substituting industries should not be favored over export industries; the ERS should be more uniform, with less variance among industries. Table 19–3 shows the ERS for six economies in the late 1960s. Argentina and Israel

Table 19–3 Effective Rates of Subsidy, 1969 (percent)

	All industries		Manufacturing	
	Exports	Dom. sales	Exports	Dom. sales
Inward looking				
Argentina	−17	55	−29	116
Colombia	−12	−1	10	32
Israel	19	79	38	82
Outward looking				
Korea	9	10	14	7
Singapore	1	8	−1	4
Taiwan	16	2	21	17

Source: Bela Balassa et al., *Industrial Strategies in Semi-Industrialized Countries* (Baltimore: Johns Hopkins Press, 1982).

display the pattern typical of import-substituting countries: the ERS for export-oriented industries is much lower than that for industries selling primarily in the domestic market. In contrast, considering all industries, Korea's regime is nearly neutral between exports and domestic sales, while Taiwan's is biased in favor of exports. Within manufacturing, Singapore and Taiwan have nearly neutral regimes, while Korea shows a proexport bias, the opposite of Argentina.[13]

Neoclassical economists prefer that incentives be neutral and determined as much as possible by market mechanisms. But neutral or proexport incentives can be achieved through market interventions and subsidies, as in Korea, where government took a number of steps to favor firms that exported. Government-controlled banks loaned to large export firms at preferential interest rates. During the 1960s, when import controls were tight, export firms were given licenses for imported inputs in excess of their needs for export production; the balance would be used to produce for the protected domestic market. Income taxes were lower for export firms, either through lower tax rates or informally, as tax authorities winked at tax evasion by firms meeting their export targets. And the Korean government invested heavily in ports, roads, communications, and other infrastructure required by exporters. In Korea, in contrast to an inward-looking regime, a firm could not take advantage of protection or other market distortions unless it met stringent export targets.

Exchange-Rate Management

Trade or commercial policies—tariffs, quotas, subsidies, below-market interest rates, and other interventions—are intended to differentiate among different kinds of tradable goods: industrial import substitutes versus primary exports, capital goods imports versus consumer imports, manufacturing exports versus agricultural exports, and so on. The exchange rate, however, treats all tradable goods uniformly but alters the price between tradables and nontradables (such as local

13. British political economist Robert Wade calculates, based on the data used to compile Table 19–3, that although Korea's incentive structure appears to be evenhanded between aggregate exports and aggregate domestic sales, the variance within these categories is not very different from those of Argentina, Colombia, and Israel, which were on average more protectionist. See Robert Wade, *Governing the Market: Economic Theory and the Role of Government in East Asian Industrialization* (Princeton, N.J.: Princeton University Press, 1990), p. 56.

transportation, power and water supplies, personal and household services, and government services). To fully understand the import substitution and outward-oriented strategies, it is necessary to bring exchange rate policy into play and analyze its interaction with trade policies. Figure 19–4 helps to do this.

The schedules in Figure 19–4 are *total revenue curves,* giving exporters' supply of and importers' demand for foreign exchange. The vertical axis is the exchange rate measured in local currency, for example, pesos per dollar. If the exchange rate is allowed to float, then in the absence of tariffs or quotas an exchange rate of e_e would just clear the market and be an equilibrium. If tariffs are imposed on imports, the demand curve shifts downward because importers are then unwilling to offer as many pesos per dollar of imports. This lowers the equilibrium peso-per-dollar rate to e_t. Note that at e_t, not only is import demand reduced, but so is the supply of exports. A tariff of any kind, whether to promote industrialization or to raise revenue, thus discriminates against both imports and exports.

When countries do not leave their exchange rates to market forces, but operate **fixed exchange rates,** two other outcomes are possible. Often the official exchange rate e_o is held below e_t. Because the peso price of the dollar is so low, import demand is high (M_d) and export supply is low (E_s); this creates a potential deficit in the current account of the balance of payments. To reduce this deficit, governments typically resort to import quotas and controls over all foreign exchange transactions. The rate e_o is considered **overvalued** in the sense that the dollar price of pesos (the reciprocal of that shown in the diagram) is too high to maintain equilibrium without controls and high tariffs; the peso-per-dollar rate e_o is therefore too low.

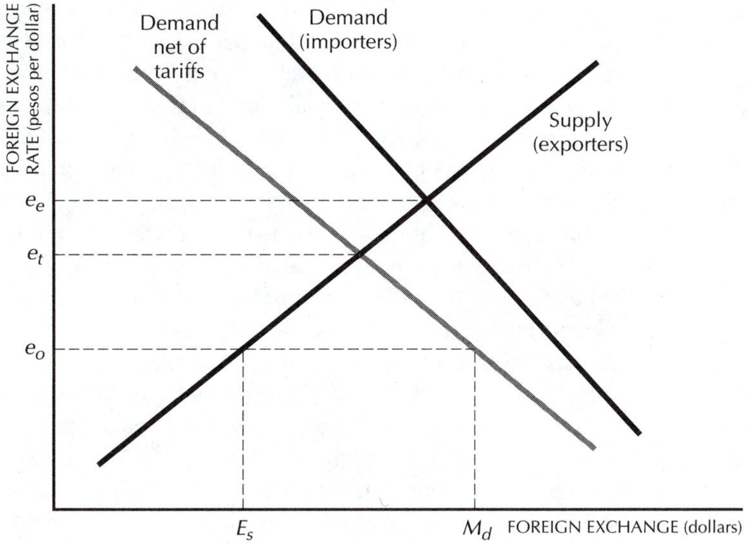

FIGURE 19–4 Overvalued and Undervalued Exchange Rates. The official exchange rate e_o is overvalued: it is too high in dollars per peso or too low in pesos per dollar to balance the demand for foreign exchange with the supply of foreign exchange without high protective tariffs, import quotas, and restrictions on other foreign exchange transactions. Rate e_u, in contrast, is undervalued: it favors exports over imports and generates a trade surplus.

Exchange rates become overvalued for a variety of reasons. The genesis of the problem is sometimes a boom in primary exports, which causes appreciation of the real exchange rate, as explained in the discussion of Dutch disease in Chapter 17. Also, as incomes rise with development and import demand increases, devaluation may be required to help stimulate the production of import substitutes and nontraditional exports, and thus to maintain equilibrium in the balance of payments. Domestic inflation, if it causes domestic prices and costs to rise faster than the world average, also requires devaluation to maintain the real exchange rate.

For much of the period after World War II most governments maintained fixed exchange rates and were reluctant to risk the destabilizing political effects of devaluation. The exchange rate is one of the most pervasive prices in the economy, perhaps affecting more transactions than any other single price. To change it, especially by the large amounts sometimes required, means changing the relative wealth of influential segments of the population. Not only are the relative prices of imports raised, but in order to prevent domestic prices from rising as much as the currency is devalued, wages and other incomes must be restrained by government policy. Frequently it is the politically powerful who would lose by these measures, especially urban workers, middle-class professionals, the military, civil servants, the upper classes, and others whose consumption depends substantially on imports. For these reasons governments have resisted devaluation, and when they have undertaken it, have often devalued by too little in the face of growing demand and continuing inflation. Hence there was, until the 1990s, a tendency for exchange rates to remain overvalued in the developing world.[14] This tendency has been alleviated by the greater flexibility in exchange rates since 1971 and the wave of economic reforms during the 1980s and 1990s, discussed in Chapter 5.

An overvalued exchange rate not only discourages exports, it also encourages imports, as can be seen in Figure 19–4. Yet overvalued rates were a hallmark of protectionist regimes that tried to exclude imports that competed with domestic production. This paradox is explained by the interactions among the exchange rate, tariffs, and quotas. When an overvalued rate exposes import-competing industries to greater price competition from abroad, these industries depend more on high effective protection from tarriffs and quotas to shield them from cheap imports. Industries without such protection are unlikely to find it profitable to produce for either the home or foreign market. Recall, then, the highly skewed protective structure presented in Table 19–2: consumer goods and intermediate goods manufacturing can overcome the overvalued exchange rate with their high effective rates of protection from tariffs and import quotas. But agricultural and capital goods manufacturing are more exposed to import competition at the low local currency prices engendered by the overvalued exchange rate.

The second possibility for a fixed rate in Figure 19–4 is an **undervalued** exchange rate e_u. At this rate, with more pesos per dollar (less dollars per peso) than in equilibrium, exports are favored over imports and there will be a balance-of-trade surplus. Undervalued rates, though not as common as overvalued rates, have been used by proexport regimes such as that in Taiwan during the 1980s. Despite the success of export-oriented regimes in achieving rapid economic growth, economists like undervalued rates only slightly better than overvalued ones. Export

14. The economic and political difficulties of devaluation make selective tariffs and quota restrictions even more appealing to governments, despite the allocative inefficiencies such measures entail.

surpluses require either an outflow of capital or a rise in foreign reserves to balance international accounts. Either can be useful in a developing country, as when it is necessary to repay debt or to counter a temporary fall in the terms of trade. Otherwise, foreign investment is made abroad and excess reserves are accumulated at the expense of domestic investment, which is essential to sustain economic development.

To this point we have been concerned about the *level* of the exchange rate. Investors, however, earn returns over several years and are equally concerned with *expected changes* in the exchange rate over time. If investors perceive that the exchange rate may become overvalued in the foreseeable future, they will be discouraged from starting or expanding export industries. To reassure investors, government has to establish a history of maintaining the *real value* of the exchange rate over time, that is, the extent to which the nominal exchange rate has kept pace with inflation at home and abroad. To measure this, we employ the **real exchange rate,** introduced in Equation 18–1 as

$$\text{RER} = R_o P_w / P_d. \qquad [19\text{–}6]$$

R_o is an index of the official or nominal exchange rate (e_o); P_w is an index of world prices in foreign currency; and P_d is an index of domestic prices. A rise in RER is a real devaluation (because R_o is measured in pesos per dollar); a fall is a real appreciation.

We have seen in Table 17–3 how the appreciation of the real exchange rate will reduce the profitability of any firm producing exports or import-competing goods. And volatility of the real rate makes profits less certain, reducing expected profitability of investments in exports. Thus an important indicator of an outward-looking policy regime is, first, that the exchange rate be set at a level that makes it profitable to invest in exports and, second, that the real exchange rate be maintained at a steady level over long periods.

The central bank, which usually manages the exchange rate, has two instruments to do this. It can change the official exchange rate, and if the budget deficit is under control, it can restrict the rate of money creation to restrain domestic price inflation (see Chapter 20). If domestic inflation can be kept no higher than the rate of world price inflation, the official exchange rate can be kept fixed. It is not always within the central bank's power to keep domestic inflation that low, however. To compensate for domestic prices that rise more rapidly than world prices, it is necessary to devalue the official exchange rate periodically to maintain exporters' incentives. In recent years many governments have depoliticized exchange rate management by resorting to more frequent and much smaller devaluations if price inflation required it. This technique of flexible exchange rate management, called a **crawling peg,** is characteristic of an outward-looking policy regime.

Figure 19–5 shows how Thailand, one of the fastest-growing economies in the world, managed its real exchange rate from 1970 to 1991. The official and parallel market exchange rates were nearly identical throughout two decades; this indicates that currency traders had confidence in the rate set by the central bank. The real rate was managed within about 5 percent above and below the mean from 1970 until 1983. In the mid-1980s, the government decided that a faster shift from agriculture to manufacturing was needed to sustain rapid growth and devalued the

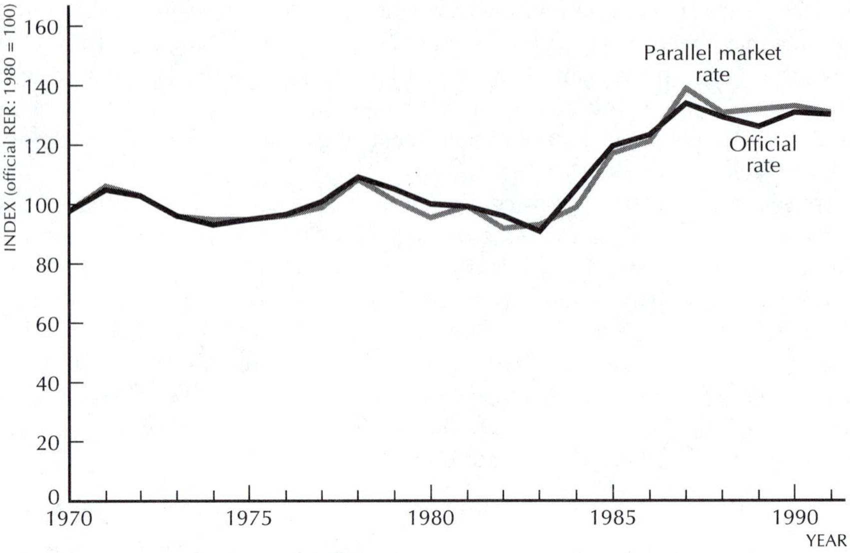

FIGURE 19–5 Real Exchange Rate, Thailand, 1970–1990. The parallel and official exchange rates were very close throughout two decades. The real rate was kept within a narrow band from 1970 to 1983, then devalued by about 45 percent, and maintained on a higher plateau after 1987.

exchange rate to spur the growth of manufactured exports.[15] After a real devaluation that reached 45 percent by 1987, the rate was maintained on a new, higher plateau.

Although the real exchange rate is widely used, a more comprehensive indicator is the **real effective exchange rate,** or REER. It incorporates both the real exchange rate and an index of nominal protection N:

$$\text{REER} = R_o N P_w / P_d. \qquad [19\text{–}7]$$

N and hence REER must be defined separately for exportables and importables. In the case of importables,

$$N_m = (1 + t_m + q_m)^t / (1 + t_m + q_m)^0, \qquad [19\text{–}8]$$

where t, s, and q are the average tariff, subsidy, and quota premium rates, respectively, on imports; the subscript m refers to imports; and the superscripts t and 0 refer to the current and base years. For exportables,

$$N_e = (1 - t_e + s_e)^t / (1 - t_e + s_e)^0, \qquad [19\text{–}9]$$

where t and s are the tax and subsidy rates on exports, with subscript e.

In reforming trade regimes to become more outward-looking, t_m and q_m are reduced via tariff reform and deregulation, while t_e is reduced and s_e may be increased to increase profits for exporters. Thus a reform would cause REER_e to rise and REER_m to decline. After an outward-looking reform, the policy goal is to ensure both that REER_e not appreciate and that REER_e stay in line with REER_m. Because the index N changes very little except during trade reforms, the real ex-

15. Narongchai Akrasanee, David Dapice, and Frank Flatters, *Thailand's Export Growth: Retrospect and Prospects* (Bangkok: Thailand Development Research Institute, 1990).

change rate RER is generally used instead of the more complex and harder-to-measure REER.

OUTCOMES

Import Substitution in General Equilibrium

The process of import substitution is represented in Figures 19–6 through 19–8. Figure 19–6 depicts the imposition of uniform protective tariffs, say in 1965, when the country produces at point *A* and consumes at *C* under world terms of trade favorable to its export. Imposition of the tariff, presumed here to be uniform on all imports, swings domestic relative prices in favor of importable goods. Production moves towards point *B* where more of the importable and less of the exportable are produced. If the country is relatively small and does not affect world prices, trade can take place at the same terms of trade as before, so that consumption settles somewhere, such as point *E*, along line *BD*, drawn parallel to the terms-of-trade line. Consumption of both goods is lower than before the tariff, so consumers' well-being has been reduced. Both imports and exports have also fallen, as indicated by the line segment *BE* (the hypotenuse of the trade triangle, see Figure 17–1), which is shorter than *AC*. Initially, this shift from free trade necessarily reduces both trade and consumers' welfare.

If protection successfully stimulates investment in infant industries and subsequent growth is substantial, the production frontier will be pushed outward, as in Figure 19–7, and after several years consumer welfare will have increased. Over time, as more import substitutes become available, their relative domestic price is likely to fall, even if the protective tariff is maintained. So the 1990 domestic price line is drawn with a steeper slope than the 1965 line in Figure 19–6. In 1990, then, production takes place at a point like *F*, where the domestic price line

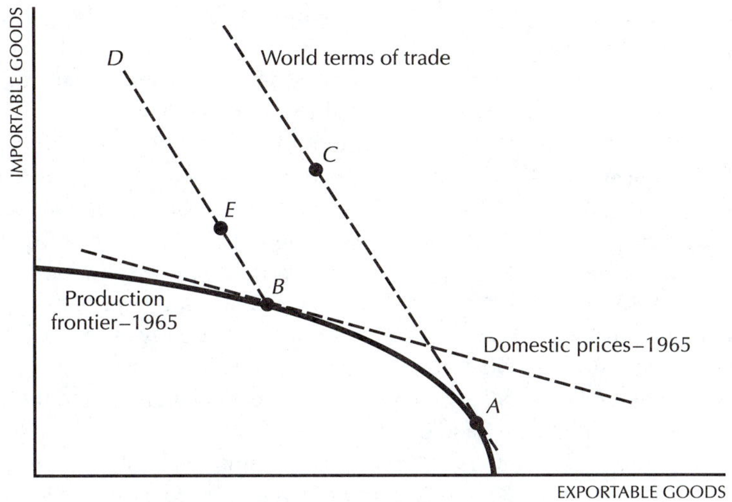

FIGURE 19–6 Imposition of Protective Tariff (situation in 1965). A protective tariff increases the relative domestic price of importables and induces a rise in their production from point *A* to point *B*. At first, consumption of both goods falls from points *C* to *E*.

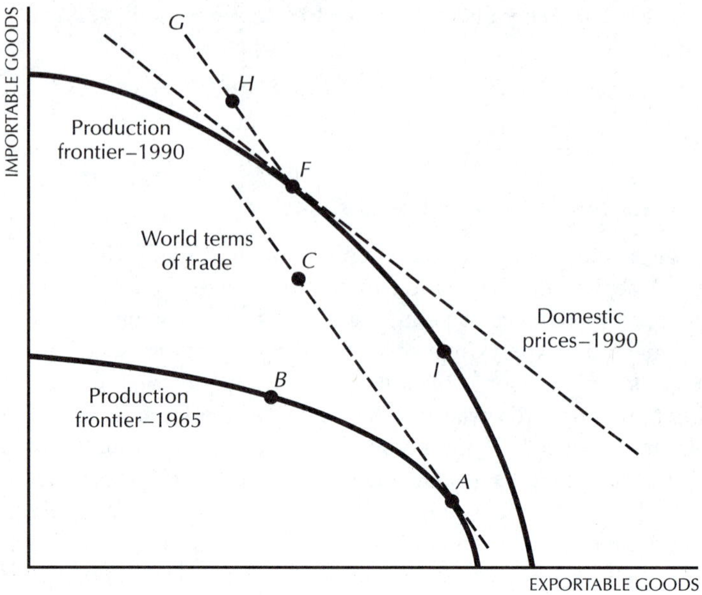

FIGURE 19–7 Import Substitution after 25 Years of Rapid Growth, 1990. After 25 years of successful import substitution, the production frontier has been shifted outward sufficiently to enable the country to produce at point *F* and to consume at point *H*, on a higher indifference curve than at a point *C* before the imposition of a tariff.

is tangent to the new frontier, and consumption can take place at a point like *H*, somewhere along line *FG*, drawn parallel to the original world terms of trade (which are presumed not to have changed since 1965). In 1990 consumers are better off at *H* than they had been in 1965 at *C*, since they are on a higher indifference curve (not shown). There is also less trade than in 1965 (*FH* is shorter than *AC*). However, once the production frontier has been expanded, consumers' welfare could be improved still more by removing tariffs and reverting to the world terms of trade. Producers would then move along the 1990 frontier to point *I*, permitting consumption at a point to the northeast of *H*, on a still higher indifference curve. Trade would be increased compared to the situation at point *F*. This is the desirable result that attracts advocates of import substitution.

Too often, however, slow or arrested growth is the outcome of protective policies. In that case, shown in Figure 19–8, trade and consumer welfare may never reach their former levels. With slow growth, producers reach point *J* on the 1990 frontier, but consumption, at a point like *L*, remains below the original point *C*. Trade is reduced from its 1965 level. Here again consumption of both goods could be increased if the country reverted to world prices and moved production from *J* to *M* on the new frontier. Note that once import substitution has taken place, a return toward free trade can always improve welfare compared to both the protected position and the initial free-trade position.

In both Figures 19–7 and 19–8, imports fell while total output rose (measured in constant prices), so the *ratio of imports to national product* must have declined. Countries that have managed to use import substitution as a spur to economic growth, as depicted in Figure 19–7, should have a falling import ratio and sustained increases in GDP over a long period. In fact, very few countries ever

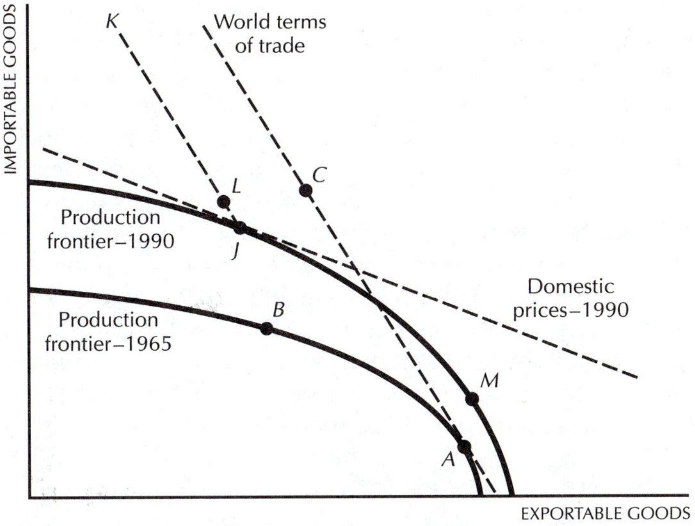

FIGURE 19–8 Import Substitution after 25 Years of Slow Growth, 1990. If, instead, import substitution does not move the production frontier outward as substantially as in Figure 19–7, production will take place at a point like *J* and consumption, at *L*, will remain on an indifference curve lower than at the starting point *C*.

reduce the ratio of import to national income while also growing rapidly, even if import substitution does occur. (The experience of Kenya, one of the few exceptions, is described in the box.)

Import Substitution in Kenya

Kenya is one of the few countries whose GDP grew by 5 percent a year or more from 1970 to 1992 while its import-GDP ratio fell. This small, open economy provides an example of both the potential power and the structural difficulties of import substitution. Kenya's population of 26 million generated a GDP of $310 per capita in 1992 ($1360 in purchasing power parity prices of the United States), giving Kenya a total domestic market about 3 percent the size of India's and 14 percent the size of Colombia's domestic markets. Kenya exports goods and nonfactor services equal to 27 percent of its GDP, down from 30 percent in 1970. In 1992 27 percent of its GDP and 55 percent of its exports came from agriculture, which has been relatively favored by policy compared to other African countries and to most import-substituting regimes.

Yet Kenya pursued import substitution as a means of industrializing both before and especially after independence in 1963, utilizing high protective tariffs, quotas, and outright bans on competing imports to attract investors. Effective rates of protection ranged from slightly negative, especially on agricultural processing industries, to levels of 100 to 500 percent for chemical industries based on simple last-stage mixing and for the assembly of vehicles and consumer durables. After substantial liberalization in the early 1980s, about a third of imported items, many of them potential competitors with local industry, remained under highly restrictive import licensing. In 1960, Kenya imported over a third of its GDP. By 1992, imports were down to 25 percent of GDP. From 1970 to 1980, manufacturing grew by 10 percent a year, but from 1980 to 1992 the rate had slowed to only 5 percent a year. During the peak of import susbstitution, from 1972 to 1983, the leading industries, with annual growth exceeding 10 percent, were vegetables, clothing, footwear, paper, printing, petroleum refining, rubber products, plastic products and vehicle assembly; all but the first are typical first-stage import substitution leaders. Also typical of import susbstitution, the import share of machinery and equipment more than doubled from 11 percent in 1965 to 24 percent in 1983, while the share for nonfood consumer goods fell from 18 to 7 percent.

By the end of the 1970s, it became generally recognized in Kenya that import substitution had run its course. The domestic market was too small to attract many more industries, manufacturing costs were generally too high to permit rapid growth of manufactured exports, and further backward integration into intermediate goods would mean even higher costs for user industries. During the 1980s, economic growth slowed to just over 4 percent a year after its spurt of almost 8 percent a year from 1965 to 1973. Since 1980, Kenya has been shifting, somewhat hesitantly, toward a more outward-looking policy for industry.[16]

Probably the most important single determinant of imports is the level of exports, which is, for all countries, the largest source of foreign exchange to pay for imports. For some countries, especially the Asian exporters, import substitution and export expansion took place simultaneously, so import ratios rose. Conversely, when import ratios fall, it is often caused more by export contraction than by import substitution. Even where import substitution is taking place, part of the fall in import ratios is usually canceled by the new industries' own demands for imported inputs and by increased consumer demand for imports with rising incomes.

Rents and Other Adverse Incentives

Underlying the protective regime is a set of incentives that reward political astuteness and **rent-seeking** (described in Chapter 5) more than economic competitiveness. Protective duties and access to low-cost inputs make the import-substituting firm profitable. Should the competitive positions of domestic firms be eroded by higher domestic costs, reduced import prices, or better quality foreign goods, the natural reaction of protected firms is to return to government for enhanced protection. This blunts the competitive instincts of entrepreneurs who, in the absence of government support, would have had to cut costs, improve quality, and thus raise productivity.

In this environment of government intervention the most successful managers are those who have political skills: who can bargain effectively with, or simply bribe, officials who administer import quotas and determine tariff rates or who

16. Data are from *World Development Report 1994;* Central Bureau of Statistics, *Economic Survey 1990* (Nairobi: Government of Kenya Printer, 1990) and earlier issues; and unpublished reports.

have close ties with the political and bureaucratic elite. These tendencies exist in most political-economic regimes, but seem to be accentuated by import substitution strategies.

Because import-substituting industry typically produces at high cost, it has little potential to penetrate export markets without large subsidies. Export subsidies have been part of several import substitution regimes: in Pakistan exporters of nontraditional goods got access to licensed imports that carried large quota premiums, in Colombia exporters were granted certificates entitling them to income tax reductions, and in Ghana cash subsidy payments were offered. These schemes worked for a time in Pakistan and Colombia, but in most countries such subsidies were weak antidotes to the much stronger incentives to produce for the protected domestic market. And, with the notable exception of the Asian tigers, government officials often made it difficult for exporters to actually collect export incentives, sometimes attempting to collect rents by threatening to withhold payments otherwise.

Import substitution incentives also lead to potentially severe misallocations of national resources. The overvalued exchange rate and low duties on capital and imported inputs encourage producers to use more of these imports than is warranted by scarcities in the economy. Investment is encouraged to be more capital-intensive than is desirable, and the growth realizable from a given amount of saving and limiting employment creation is reduced.

Exports, Growth, and Productivity

The performance of economies following outward-looking strategies stands in marked contrast to most other middle-income countries, which followed import substitution, as shown in Table 19–1. The World Bank, in a study of the high-performing Asian economies, attempts to relate export performance and openness of the economy to the growth in income per capita and the growth in total factor productivity.[17] Multiple regressions over 1960 to 1985 covering more than fifty countries show that both income growth and factor productivity growth correlate significantly with the average share (over the entire period) of manufactured exports (in either total exports or gross domestic product). The share of manufactured exports is expected to be higher for countries that successfully pursued outward-looking industrialization. The impact of manufactured export shares on income growth is small, however. Other determinants of growth have a much greater impact: a country's income relative to the United States in 1960,[18] the rate of primary enrollment in 1960 (as a proxy for educational endowment), and the average share of investment in GDP. When productivity growth is being explained, manufactured export shares appear to be more important.

In any case, these correlations do not prove that outward orientation causes more rapid economic growth. At best they indicate a close association between the two. It is entirely plausible that causation runs the other way: rapid income

17. World Bank, *The East Asian Miracle: Economic Growth and Public Policy* (Washington, D. C.: World Bank, 1993). The authors use the term *high-performing Asian economies,* or HPAE, to cover the seven Asian tigers.

18. The lower a country's starting income is, the easier it is to grow fast by "catching up," that is, importing equipment and techniques using existing technologies that are nevertheless advanced for the poor country.

and productivity growth, by increasing productive capacity and reducing costs, can make a country more competitive in world markets, and lead to faster growth of manufactured exports. If relative income levels, educational attainments, and investment ratios explain a significant share of income and productivity growth, then these factors may also be responsible for rapid growth of manufactured exports. Economists are not yet sure.

Despite this uncertainty, it is clear that, while the outward-looking regimes in Asia enjoyed unprecedented rapid growth in exports and income over two to three decades, the more inward-looking regimes of Latin America and Africa lagged well behind. Many factors, cultural, political, and economic, undoubtedly contributed to this performance. Investment in human and made capital are central to rapid development and may well be more essential than outward orientation. But it remains a good bet that a focus on export growth plays a role in making educated labor and capital more productive than it can be within a protected, inward-looking economic regime, plagued by price distortions, quantitative restrictions, and rent-seeking.

Factor Markets and Government Intervention

In the neoclassical version of the outward-looking strategy, relative scarcities of productive factors—land, natural resources, labor, and capital—are the guiding forces behind industrialization, as predicted by the Heckscher-Ohlin theory of comparative advantage (Chapter 17). As export and income growth lead to higher savings and as education spreads and workers become more skilled, industrializing countries shift from labor-intensive export industries, such as textiles, footwear, and plywood, to exports of steel, ships, machinery, automobiles, electronics, and others that embody more capital and more skills. Korea and Taiwan have moved quite far along that path. Japan, of course, has gone beyond these products into goods embodying advanced technology.

Well-functioning labor and capital markets ought to reflect changing factor endowments in changing relative prices and generate such export transitions automatically. Even if government tries to push industrialization faster than justified by market conditions, fluid factor markets are needed to reallocate labor and investment toward the newly favored industries. The countries of East and Southeast Asia have, by and large, had labor markets in which wages reflected labor abundance and thus encouraged the first stages of labor-intensive, export-oriented industrialization. Government action to discourage strong labor unions played a hand in keeping wages low. Once the rapidly growing demand for workers absorbed the labor surplus, market wages began to rise. In Korea this occurred in the late 1960s, and in Malaysia during the 1980s; Indonesia, with its larger rural labor force, has not yet reached that point.

Except in Hong Kong and Singapore, however, the Asian tigers intervened in credit markets to keep interest rates suppressed and credit allocations under government influence. In Korea the government used its control of the major banks to channel credit at below-market interest rates to the large conglomerates, or *chaebol,* that it favored as vehicles to promote later-stage exports. Other, mostly smaller, firms were forced to borrow in the informal credit (*curb*) market, where interest rates reflected capital scarcity. Real interest rates on loans from banks were negative for several years during the 1970s, while curb market rates were 15 to 20 points above bank rates from 1965 to 1985.[19] This two-tiered credit market encouraged the transition into capital-intensive exports, such as steel, ships, and cars, more rapidly than the unrestrained market would have done.

The tendency was reinforced by the Korean government's policies on technology and firm size. The initial spurt of labor-intensive exports such as textiles, clothing, footwear, and plywood took place in a large number of medium-size firms. By the 1970s, however, the government was encouraging the *chaebol* to move into steel, ships, automobiles, electronics, chemicals, and other heavy export industries. All the weapons of state economic power were employed, including subsidized credit, preferential taxes, personal favors, and political sanctions. State firms were also employed as vehicles to obtain new technology, notably in the fertilizer, petrochemical, and steel industries, to train Korean managers and engineers, and in some cases to spawn new firms once the technology had been mastered. Foreign firms were discouraged from entering these markets, where they would have had a competitive advantage. And, key to the entire strategy, the government made it clear that the ability to export was the ultimate measure of success.[20] The push into heavy industries in the 1970s failed in many instances and was very costly to the economy, but did result in a range of new export industries and provided a base for reform and expansion in the 1980s. It also accelerated a tendency toward industrial concentration. In 1974 the five largest *chaebol* had combined sales of less than 12 percent of gross national product; by 1984 their sales exceeded 50 percent of GNP.[21]

Taiwan employed a similar mix of policies but stayed closer to the market-based strategy than Korea—a result of politics more than of economics. The Kuomintang government, exiles from China's mainland, did not wish to share political or economic power with native Taiwanese, yet wished to encourage rapid development. A strategy that promoted the growth of small firms reconciled these two goals, and this in turn dictated greater dependence on market mechanisms. From 1966 to 1981, the share of manufacturing workers employed by firms of less than 500 workers actually rose, from 65 to 72 percent; in Korea, in contrast, the share employed in smaller firms fell from 74 to 59 percent. Government did use protection, subsidized bank lending, and other interventions to promote the establishment of large-scale, heavy industries that produced intermediate goods. Many such firms were controlled by the government or Kuomintang party. But the curb market was efficient in channeling credit to small firms, which were the principal exporters, and for this sector market allocations were more important than government intervention.[22]

The governments of Indonesia, Malaysia, and Thailand intervened extensively

19. Vittorio Corbo and Sang Woo Nam, "The Recent Macroeconomic Evolution of the Republic of Korea: An Overview," World Bank, Economic Research Department, Discussion Paper DRD 208, 1986.

20. These policies are described by Amsden, *Asia's New Giant,* and Pack and Westphal, "Industrial Strategy and Technological Change."

21. Amsden, *Asia's Next Giant,* p. 116. The same caveat applies here as in the discussion of multinational firms in Chapter 15: sales and GNP are not comparable measures. But the large rise in this ratio is indicative.

22. Tyler Biggs and Brian Levy, "Strategic Interventions and the Political Economy of Industrial Policy in Developing Countries," in D. H. Perkins and M. Roemer (eds.), *Systems Reform in Developing Countries* (Cambridge: Harvard University Press, 1991), pp. 365–401. Robert Wade, *Governing the Market,* puts greater stress on government's role in promoting industrialization.

in credit markets, and trade-based incentive systems were as distorted as elsewhere. All three countries maintained convertible currencies and permitted relatively easy access to foreign capital markets, however, so that the larger firms, owned mostly by ethnic Chinese businessmen, could find capital abroad at international interest rates if necessary. All three countries encouraged foreign investment as well. And each of them found a device to insulate their fledgling export industries from the controls and price distortions of the protected domestic market. Malaysia used duty-free zones that allowed electronics and other firms to import and export without being taxed, Indonesia established an agency in the Ministry of Finance that granted exemptions from import licensing restrictions and drawbacks of duties on imported inputs, and Thailand gave similar privileges to investors who qualified for them.[23]

Reconciling Import Substitution and Export Growth

We have seen how import substitution is ridden with internal contradictions that sap its energy, lead to industrial stagnation, and close the economy out of potential export markets. Yet if domestic entrepreneurs, managers, and workers are to learn how to manufacture new products using new technologies, even if they aim eventually for export markets, they require some form of protection from outside competition.[24] How can the failure of protection be reconciled with the need for it, even as a first step toward outward-looking industrialization?

An outward-looking strategy that accommodates import substitution could have three components. *First,* the infant industry concept, strictly interpreted, should guide trade policy. Tariff protection should be granted only to those industries that have some prospect of competing as exporters or as import substituters without protection, and then only if the initial costs of protection are expected to be fully compensated by the eventual benefits of domestic production. Tariffs, or preferably subsidies, should be moderate and temporary, with predetermined rates of decline; quotas should never be used.

Second, if the government is capable of doing so, it could follow in the footsteps of Japan and Korea by extending protection and subsidized credit only to firms that achieve agreed-on, ambitious export targets. The likely losses suffered by firms in the early years of exporting would be compensated for by higher profits at home, but firms would also be learning how to compete abroad. This approach is not for all countries, however. Targeted interventions require disciplined officials who grant privileged access or other favors on the basis of excellent export performance or other transparent criteria, rather than use their power principally for personal gain. Where governments are less determined or less disciplined in their implementation of growth policies, a strategy that depends more on markets and broadly based incentives, minimizing government intervention in detail, is probably advisable.

Third, industries that are competitive in world markets should not be protected, but encouraged to export instead. This may require special measures to ensure ready access to imports at world market prices, as in Southeast Asia, though the

23. See Lindauer and Roemer, *Asian and Africa,* especially Chaps. 1 and 11.

24. Henry Bruton provides a compelling statement of this necessity in his article "Import Substitution" in Chenery and Srinivasan, *Handbook of Development Economics,* pp. 1601–44.

need for intervention diminishes the less protectionist is the trade regime. Domestic firms may at first be incapable of moving directly into export industries. But foreign investors will be able to do so if a liberal investment climate attracts them, as discussed in Chapter 15. This has been the pattern in Southeast Asia, where firms from the industrial countries and, increasingly, from East Asia have played major roles in the manufactured export boom since the mid-1980s.

Trade Reform in Mexico, 1985–1989[25]

Leaders in Mexico, among the most protectionist of nations, recognized by the mid-1980s that shielding the economy from foreign competition had created noncompetitive industries that could not sustain rapid economic growth. In July 1985, as part of a strategy to overcome its debt crisis, the government of President Miguel de la Madrid launched a daring trade reform.

Restrictive licensing of imports was ended for most categories; whereas 92 percent of domestic production had been protected by licensing before the reform, by the end of 1989 import restrictions covered only 20 percent of production. To compensate, the authorities devalued the peso, so that the real official rate depreciated by over 40 percent through the end of 1986, and raised tariffs from an average 23.5 percent in June 1985 (based on production weights) to 28.5 percent six months later. The additional protection from devaluation and tariff increases helped to keep imports from rising and shielded domestic producers.

In 1986, however, a bold program of tariff reduction was announced and implemented over the following two years. By the end of 1989 the production-weighted average tariff had fallen to 12.5 percent, less than half its level in December 1985. And after 1986, the real exchange rate began to appreciate, and so further exposed domestic industry to import competition. The result was an import boom: dollar expenditures on merchandise imports doubled from 1987 to 1989 after seven years of decline and stagnation. Under such intense foreign competition, domestic restructuring began to take place.

Mexico's stabilization and structural adjustment have had moderate success. Direct investment from abroad, which had virtually disappeared by the mid-1980s, revived to record levels. Indeed, strong capital inflows of all kinds contributed to the exchange rate appreciation. Merchandise exports, which had been stagnant throughout the 1980s, began growing by more than 9 percent a year from 1988 through 1991. And gross national product, also stagnant throughout the 1980s, began a modest recovery to 4.4 percent a year from 1988 to 1991.

Mexico's reforms have been entrenched. In 1986, Mexico joined the General Agreement on Tariffs and Trade (GATT; see next section), in effect subjecting its trade reforms to international agreement. During the latter

25. Based on Adriaan Ten Kate, "Liberalization and Economic Stabilization in Mexico: Lessons of Experience," *World Development,* 20, no. 5 (May 1992), 659–72.

half of the 1980s, it used macroeconomic policies to overcome imbalances, rather than reversing the trade reforms. In 1993, Mexico joined the United States and Canada in the North American Free Trade Agreement, and so further opened its economy.

World Trading Arrangements

As a group, the developing countries have become significant suppliers of manufactured goods. From 1965 to 1991, while the volume of all exports from developing countries tripled, the volume of manufactured exports to the industrial countries multiplied 75-fold, an annual growth rate of 18 percent (see Table 19–4). Export products range from textiles, clothing, and footwear to wood paneling, machinery, electronics, chemicals, and automobiles. Developing-country exports of manufactures more than doubled their share of total imports into developed countries from 1970 to 1991, but still accounted for only 16 percent. In clothing, however, developing-country exports accounted for more than half of total industrial-country imports, and in textiles the share was one-quarter.

Protection in the North

The success of the newly industrializing countries of Asia and Latin America in penetrating northern markets for labor-intensive manufactures is a signal that comparative advantage has shifted toward the developing countries for a range of labor-intensive and resource-based manufactures once produced more efficiently in the industrial countries. Lower wages in the newly industrializing countries are no longer offset by proportionately lower productivity, the effect of workers' learning by doing; local managers, too, have learned how to operate industrial units more productively; in the case of steel and other resource-based products,

Table 19–4 Exports of Manufactures from Developing Countries to Industrialized Countries, 1965–1991*

	1965	1991
Value in billion U.S. dollars		
All Manufactures (5–8)†	3.8	282.4
Chemicals (5)	0.2	13.4
Machinery‡ (7)	0.1	96.3
Other (6 + 8)	3.5	172.7
Textiles (65)	0.7	16.3
Clothing (84)	0.3	53.6
Share (percent) of industrial country imports		
All Manufactures (5–8)	6.6	15.5
Chemicals (5)	2.8	6.5
Machinery‡ (7)	1.3	10.9
Other (6 + 8)	12.0	23.6
Textiles (65)	10.7	24.7
Clothing (84)	22.9	55.2

*Market economies only, excluding formerly socialist Asian and Eastern European countries and Cuba. (Socialist Asian countries are: China, North Korea, Vietnam, Mongolia, Cambodia, and Laos.)
†Figures in parentheses give the standard industrial trade classification (SITC) for each group of commodities.
‡Includes vehicles.
Source: United Nations, *Yearbook of International Trade Statistics 1992,* Vol.1, Special Tables B and C.

some developing countries have ready access to raw materials and fuels that were exhausted long ago in the industrial countries; and greater openness to foreign investment has made new technologies and international marketing skills more easily available to developing-country exporters.

This shift, together with Japan's export dynamism, has engendered a protectionist reaction in the industrial countries. But the nature of protection has changed. Before and during the Great Depression of the 1930s, industrial countries erected high tariff barriers that were intended to protect domestic jobs but actually deepened the depression by reducing trade. A series of negotiating rounds after World War II reduced the tariffs on most trade to very low levels, although tariffs on goods traded among industrial countries were cut more than goods exported principally by developing countries. In the United States, average tariffs, about 50 percent of import value in the 1930s, had been reduced to only 5 percent by 1985, about the same level as in Europe and Japan.

The **General Agreement on Tariffs and Trade** (GATT) was established as a mechanism to negotiate and then to monitor multilateral tariff reductions. Tariffs under GATT are based on the **most favored nation** (MFN) principle: all trading partners enjoy the lowest duty rate an importing country accords to any of its trading partners. Note that the most favored nation principle is not an exceptional favor granted by one country to another, as often alleged in the United States during debates about trade with China and Russia. It is, rather, the norm in world trade and must by international law be given to all members of GATT.

With low tariffs and GATT rules, it became difficult to protect declining industries. Instead, starting in the 1960s, the United States and the EEC began to negotiate **voluntary export restrictions** (VERs) with trading partners, especially Japan and the newly industrializing countries, to restrict the export of sensitive goods such as textiles, clothing, and steel, in which the industrial countries were losing comparative advantage. This new mechanism was added to more traditional **nontariff barriers** (NTBs) that are practiced by all countries. These include unilateral restrictions on the quantities of imports, as well as regulations affecting quality standards, packaging, labeling, health inspection, environmental protection, and so forth, established ostensibly to protect consumers but frequently utilized to protect competing domestic manufacturers.

All countries would gain, in the manner described in Chapter 17, if production of labor- and resource-intensive products moved to the south, while the north concentrated on temperate-zone farm products, more technologically sophisticated and more capital-intensive exports, and financial, communications, and professional services. Although all countries would gain in the long run, the readjustments require disinvestment from declining industries in the short run, which in turn means temporary unemployment for workers in those industries. The potential gains are widely spread across large populations of consumers, who may not always be aware that such gains exist. The smaller losses, in contrast, accrue to concentrated groups of workers, managers, and owners in protected industries such as textiles, clothing, footwear, steel, and automobiles, who are fully aware of these potential losses and fight vigorously to avoid them. In these circumstances, it becomes politically difficult to capture the gains from freer trade.[26]

26. A general statement of this problem is contained in Mancur Olsen, *The Rise and Decline of Nations* (New Yale University Press, 1982).

Attempts have been made to estimate the cost to the United States and Canada of protecting jobs in declining industries.[27] In the United States, where displaced workers remained unemployed on average for one year, the deadweight loss in protecting textiles and clothing (triangles *b* plus *d* in Figure 19–1) was estimated to be $14 for every $1 of benefit to the workers whose jobs were saved. In Canada, where the estimate incorporated the higher costs of nontariff barriers, the ratio was $70 of costs to society for every $1 of net income saved by workers who held their jobs.[28] And in the United States auto and steel industries in 1983, the cost of protecting one job was estimated to equal the wages of six workers. But even these costs do not capture all the losses to importing countries from their own protection. Tariffs or NTBs reduce the volume of imports and keep the exchange rate at higher (overvalued) levels, and thus make export industries less competitive in world markets. Reduced exports mean fewer jobs in those industries, and some economists believe the net gain in jobs may be negligible. If so, the costs per job saved may, literally, approach infinity.

The costs to developing countries are also high. Protection limits their gains from trade, makes it harder to repay debt, discourages investment, and thus reduces potential growth. During the 1990s, political leaders north and south have begun to realize that, with the potential losses so high on both sides, ways must be found to reduce protection and liberalize trade. Three different approaches have been proceeding simultaneously, often pushed by the same leaders: multilateral trade reform, integration among southern countries, and trading blocks that include countries in the north and south.

Multilateral Trade Reform

The various postwar negotiations to reduce tariffs were tedious and difficult, but successful. Negotiations to eliminate quantitative restrictions have been much more difficult, but have finally begun to yield results. The most recent GATT agreement, the so-called Uruguay round, was completed at the end of 1993. It further reduced tariffs on manufactured goods by about a third and attacked some trade barriers that had escaped earlier rounds. Agricultural protection, formerly excluded from negotiations, was incorporated for the first time by requiring countries to shift from quantitative restrictions to tariffs (*tariffication*) and by reducing subsidies that enable industrial countries to cut into the markets of tropical countries. The Multi-Fiber Agreement, which has restricted textile and clothing imports in the industrial countries, will be phased out over a ten-year period. Trade in services was brought under the GATT for the first time, albeit in a very partial way. Industrial countries, especially the United States, won stricter adherence to *intellectual property rights* that prevent the use of written, recorded, or filmed material and computer programs without permission. And the organization that oversees the GATT has been superceded by the World Trade Organization (WTO), which governs the agreements reached during the Uruguay round.

27. *World Development Report 1984*, p. 40, and *World Development Report 1987*, p. 152.

28. With voluntary export restraints, the tariff revenue lost to the home government, area *c* in Figure 19–1, may be captured by the exporting country as they charge higher prices.

Integration in the South

The developing countries, frustrated by their inability to gain wider access to industrial-country markets or to improve their terms of trade with these markets, have exhorted each other to form larger and more meaningful regional trade groups. Groups of countries would try to stimulate development by granting preferential access to each other's exports, placing relatively less emphasis on access to industrial-country markets. Table 19–5 shows that the value of trade among developing countries multiplied 18 times from 1970 to 1990; allowing for inflation, intrasouth trade grew more than fivefold in real terms. For manufactured exports the quantity of intrasouth trade expanded ninefold over those two decades. In 1990, manufactured exports were about a third of total developing-country exports. Proponents of regional trade groups hope that greater economic integration among developing countries would increase the importance of intra-developing-country trade to the benefit of all participants.

Three systems of trade arrangements can be defined, in increasing degree of economic integration. **Free-trade areas** eliminate tariffs among member countries, though each member is permitted to set its own tariffs on imports from the outside world. The North American Free Trade Agreement among Canada, Mexico, and the United States is the most recent example. Because members are typically free to set their own external tariffs, free-trade associations represent minimal cooperation and integration. **Customs unions** also eliminate tariffs among members, but go beyond free-trade areas by erecting a common external tariff against imports from the rest of the world. The Preferential Trade Area of eastern and southern African countries, which began in 1984 to reduce internal tariffs for selected commodities, is intended to become a full-fledged customs union.

Common markets move several steps closer to full integration. In addition to free trade among members and a common external tariff, common markets either eliminate or substantially reduce restrictions on the movements of labor and capital among member states. They may go further to promote coordinated fiscal, monetary, and exchange-rate policies and may cooperate in many other ways. Both the Central American Common Market and the East African Community had achieved important elements of economic integration until political differences among members destroyed each grouping. The European Union (EU) is the

TABLE 19–5 Trade among Developing Market Countries

	1970	1990
Value of intra-South exports in billion U.S. dollars		
All exports (0–9)	11.9	219.3
Manufactures (5–8)	4.6	143.4
*Share (%) of intra-developing-country trade in total developing-country exports**		
All exports (0–9)	20.1	28.6
Manufactures (5–8)	27.2	33.5

*By current market value.
Source: World Resources Institute, *World Resources 1994–95* (New York: Oxford University Press, 1994), p. 263.

most integrated group in the world today. It has largely eliminated tariffs and customs procedures among its member states and harmonized taxes, fees, regulations, and procedures affecting trade.

Static Gains from Integration

Customs unions (which we use here as a shorthand for all regional preferential trading arrangements) may benefit their members by conveying **static gains,** in the form of one-time improvements in resource allocations, and by offering **dynamic gains,** stimulating investment in production for export and linked industries. The traditional analysis of the static gains from customs unions makes the distinction between *trade creation* and *trade diversion.*

Trade is **created** when a new customs union, which lowers the duty on imports from all member countries, permits some member, say country A, to export more to another, say country B, by displacing the production of country B's own industries. The import-competing industry in country B was presumably able to sell in the home market because the protective duty shielded it from the exports of more-efficient, lower-cost industries in other countries. When the customs union lowers the duty on exports from other member countries, more-efficient industries in those countries can then compete with country B's firms in their own markets. More is traded than before, hence the term **trade creation.** Although some producers in country B are disadvantaged by the change, presumably there are others that benefit from the lower duties in other member countries' markets, and of course consumers benefit from lower prices and wider selection. Gains from trade creation are analogous to gains from the opening of trade (see Chapter 17), except that they take place in the limited world of the customs union.

Because customs unions also discriminate against outside countries, they may cause **trade diversion** by permitting member country A to export more to country B, and so displace imports previously bought from a nonmember country. If before the union, country B had a most-favored-nation tariff, that is, all other countries were treated equally, then the outside country's exports must have been cheaper than those of country A, or else country B would have imported from country A in the first place. Once the union is formed, consumers in country B will buy from producers in country A at a lower cost to the consumers, because of the preferential tariff, but at a higher cost in foreign exchange to the country as a whole. Part of the revenue previously earned on imports from nonmember countries is now paid to exporters in country A, who are less-efficient producers than their outside competitors.

From each member country's standpoint the customs union is beneficial if trade creation outweighs trade diversion. This is more likely to be the case if customs union partners have different relative resource endowments or if their consumers have different tastes, so that the members have comparative advantages in the export of different commodities. For example, if Mexico, with comparative advantages in vegetables and petroleum, were to join in a customs union with Colombia, with comparative advantages in coffee and textiles (to oversimplify greatly), trade is likely to be created and both countries would benefit. But on the whole neighboring developing countries tend to export similar goods and there is a presumption that trade diversion would be large. In the old East African Community, for example, much of the trade in manufactured goods came from industries, such as tire manufacturing in Kenya, that could not compete with the outside world. Tanzania and Uganda had to pay higher prices for these manufactures than if they had purchased from outside the market. Note that even if, on balance, trade creation within the union exceeds trade diversion, so long as there is some diversion nonmember countries are losers.

Dynamic Gains and Risks of Integration

Most advocates of customs unions among developing countries argue that the major gains are not static, but dynamic. Customs unions widen the market for industries in all member countries, with the attendant benefits noted earlier in this chapter. Economies of scale may be realized by some industries whose outputs would be too small if confined to the home market. One potentially important, if largely unimplemented, feature of the Andean Pact and the Association of Southeast Asian Nations (ASEAN) is the *complementation agreement,* under which large-scale infant industries are allocated to member countries. Then each member can benefit from starting industries such as petrochemicals, fertilizer, pulp and paper, vehicle manufacture, and basic metals, while each shares the costs.

Customs unions also increase competition among producers in the member countries. This can be especially important for large-scale industries that would otherwise monopolize home markets at efficient levels of output. But it can have a much more pervasive effect; it can sharpen entrepreneurial and managerial performance in all industries. Intensified competition is thought to have played a major role in stimulating European growth after the formation of the European Common Market and may have contributed to the temporary success of the Central American Common Market as well. One manifestation of increased competition is a characteristic pattern of trade in customs unions: much of the new trade is in similar or even identical products. To some extent this represents specialization in fine detail; one textile firm narrows its products to concentrate on the few things it does especially well. To some extent it may represent more-efficient subregional patterns of trade, a realignment to reduce transport costs once borders no longer serve as barriers. But a lot of the trade in similar goods may reflect greater competition and a wider range of choice for consumers. Trade in similar goods belies the trade creation approach, which predicts that countries will gain only if they export dissimilar goods.

These dynamic effects act over the long run to induce greater investment and hence accelerate growth within the customs union and to restructure the economy toward exports of all kinds. Given these advantages, why are there so few examples of successful customs unions in the developing world? One major problem has been the distribution of the gains, whether static or dynamic. When the East African Community was functioning, Kenya, which had moved faster to industrialize, exported more to its neighbors than it imported. Investment flowed into Kenya to take advantage of the industrial infrastructure and the central location of Nairobi. This concentration of gains in Kenya contributed to the demise of the East African experiment and helped to dampen the ardor of countries like Bolivia and Ecuador for the Andean Pact in South America.

The concentration of gains—real or perceived—in the more-advanced member countries leads to political tensions. Conversely, political disagreements among neighbors become much more dangerous when those neighbors are tied together in economic arrangements. Each partner, but especially the economically less advanced ones, can use participation as a whip to threaten other partners if decisions are not taken in its favor. Political tensions among Uganda, Tanzania, and Kenya eventually destroyed the East African Community. Chile withdrew from the Andean Pact over political disagreements with Peru and other countries. The potential for such schisms always exists and substantially increases the risk a country takes when it enters an integration scheme. To achieve the gains of customs unions, each country must develop its economy in ways that may not make much sense in the absence of a union. Malaysia might invest in a fertilizer plant intended to serve the ASEAN countries. But if the free-trade area does not develop or if political arguments make it ineffective, Malaysia has considerably more fertilizer capacity than it can use if it remains a high-cost producer.

Will the developing countries move toward greater trade with each other? The potential advantages are great, but so are the risks. To be successful, any integration plan must bring the promise of substantial additional investment in the foreseeable future and must provide for a broad and equitable distribution of the benefits of union. Member countries will have to be governed by leaders who recognize common interests and are prepared to cooperate with their neighbors. The political risks are reduced, the wider is membership in the union, so that no single country can destroy the arrangement by withdrawing. Thus the newly emerging Preferential Trade Area of eastern and southern Africa has a better chance of avoiding crippling political conflicts than did the East African Community.

Trading Blocs

Trading arrangements are changing rapidly in the 1990s. While the EU has become more integrated and is expanding, the Eastern European trading bloc, COMECON, and the Soviet Union itself have disappeared. Canada, Mexico, and the United States are now joined in NAFTA, which other Latin American countries are hoping to join. Japanese trade, investment, and aid dominate economic relations among the countries of East and Southeast Asia; this creates a *de facto* economic sphere of influence, though decidedly not a formal trade arrangement. And the Asia Pacific Economic Cooperation group (APEC), which includes many countries of Asia and the Americas bordering the Pacific Ocean, plans to become a free-trade area in the first twenty years of the next century. These newly emerging trading blocs may begin to supplant the global, multilateral trading arrangements, governed by the GATT and now the WTO, that have guided international trade for almost five decades since World War II. How will the changes affect developing countries?

The answer, of course, depends. The EU has always granted preferential access to exports from its members' former colonies in Africa and the Caribbean and has not been markedly more protectionist toward other developing countries than the United States and Japan. Mexico will be the prime beneficiary under NAFTA, because its much smaller economy now has access to the large U.S. market. Other Latin American countries are likely to benefit eventually, while those left out, and the aggressive exporters of East and Southeast Asia, which have depended heavily on the U.S. market, are likely losers. It is doubtful whether Japan could fully replace the United States as an export destination for the latter countries. If, however, the ambitious plans for APEC eventually incorporate Pacific Basin countries in a free-trade area, most of the developing countries of eastern Asia and the Americas will become part of a large and rapidly growing bloc. But the populous countries of South Asia, notably Bangladesh, India, and Pakistan, have not been prominently mentioned as candidates for inclusion in any of the emerging blocs. African countries, though tied to Europe, might be squeezed out of the dynamic markets of Asia and the Americas.

The possible emergence of large regional trading blocs creates uncertainty for many developing countries. The potential exists for substantial trade diversion and an unequal distribution of dynamic gains away from excluded countries, toward those within the new trading agreements. The threat of losses among many developing countries may be a spur to new arrangements to stimulate trade among southern countries, as is already occurring within southern Africa and within Southeast Asia. The emerging APEC, however, is an example of interregional cooperation among so large a group that trade creation and dynamic gains are likely to exceed the loses. Moreover, if regional arrangements go far enough, the habit of more open borders may well give a boost to reforms in worldwide, multilateral trade under the World Trade Organization. The advantages of outward orientation for both developing and industrial countries argue in favor of multilateral trade reforms in preference to a strengthening of regional trading blocs, however organized.

20

Managing an Open Economy

Economic development takes place in the long term. Most of the processes discussed in the previous chapters, whether improving human welfare or increasing saving or shifting toward manufactured exports, take years and even decades to bear significant results. If policy makers in developing countries gaze only at the far horizon, however, they are unlikely ever to reach it. Much happens in the short term, within a few months or a couple of years, to throw an economy off balance and make it difficult and sometimes impossible to pursue long-term strategies. Policy makers need to emulate the ship's captain who, always steering toward his port of destination, nevertheless must deal decisively with any storms at sea.

Among the most dangerous and likely of these storms are changes in world prices that throw the balance of payments into deficit, excessive spending that fuels inflation, and droughts or other natural disasters that disrupt production. Unless a government counteracts these economic shocks, they create greater uncertainty and higher risk for private producers and investors, who take evasive actions that reduce future investment, worsen the crisis, and cause development efforts to founder.

During the 1970s and 1980s, many economies became unbalanced because of unstable world market conditions: Sharp rises in oil prices during the 1970s were followed by equally precipitate declines in the mid-1980s. A cycle began with rising world inflation during the 1970s, followed by corrective policies, especially in the United States, that included monetary restraint and rising interest rates and led to a world recession in the early 1980s. Wide swings in the major exchange rates characterized both decades.

Some governments, especially those in East and Southeast Asia, managed their economies shrewdly enough to overcome, and even to benefit from, these changing conditions. But a larger number of developing countries was unable to cope. Several governments, particularly in Latin America and Africa, made the situation worse. These governments allowed their exchange rates to become overvalued; this contributed to growing deficits in the balance of payments. These deficits were financed by borrowing abroad, so countries accumulated debt that could not be serviced. These governments also ran budget deficits that had to be financed through the banking system, which expanded the money supply and fed inflation. Many governments then intervened in markets to counter the effects of profligate macroeconomic management.

In Chapter 5 we discussed the consequences of such **macroeconomic instability.** Countries with overvalued exchange rates and rapid inflation have been unable to grow rapidly, in contrast to those, especially in East and Southeast Asia, with well-managed economies (recall Figures 5–1 and 5–2). *Stabilization programs,* many funded by the IMF, are intended to correct these macroeconomic imbalances.

In this chapter we develop a mechanism for analyzing the macroeconomic policies that a developing country should pursue to stabilize its economy and create a climate for faster economic growth. The model developed here incorporates the two main policy approaches for correcting macroeconomic imbalances: *reductions in expenditure* such as lower government budget deficits and slower creation of money, and *adjustments in relative prices,* particularly exchange-rate devaluation.

Equilibrium in a Small, Open Economy[1]

Developing economies have two features that are central to understanding how macroeconomic imbalances occur and can be corrected. First, they are **open economies,** in that trade and capital flow across their borders in sufficient quantities to influence the domestic economy, particularly prices and the money supply. Most economies are open in this sense, especially since economic reforms in China beginning in the late 1970s and the collapse of the Soviet economies in the late 1980s. Today only a few economies, such as Cuba and Burma, are so heavily protected and regulated that they might not qualify as open to trade and finance.

Second, these are **small economies,** meaning that neither their supplies of exports nor their demand for imports has a noticeable impact on the world prices of these commodities and services. Economists call these countries *price takers* in world markets. A number of developing countries can exert some influence over the price of one or two primary exports in world markets: Brazil in coffee, Saudi Arabia in oil, Zambia in copper, South Africa in diamonds, for example. But they

1. In developing this and the next two sections, we acknowledge an intellectual debt to Shantayanan Devarajan and Dani Rodrik, who wrote an excellent set of notes for their class on macroeconomics for developing countries at Harvard's John F. Kennedy School of Government in the late 1980s, and to Richard E. Caves, Jeffrey A. Frankel, and Ronald W. Jones, who develop the open economy model in Chapter 19 of *World Trade and Payments: An Introduction* (Glenview, Ill.: Scott, Foresman, Little, Brown: 1990).

almost never affect the price of goods they import, and for macroeconomic purposes it is usually adequate to model even these countries as price takers.[2]

These two qualities—smallness and openness—are the basis for the **Australian model** of a developing economy.[3] Chapters 17 and 19 used simple general equilibrium models to describe comparative advantage (Figure 17–1) and economic growth through import substitution (Figures 19–5 to 19–7). In those models the two goods were importables and exportables. The Australian model lumps importables and exportables together as *tradables* and distinguishes these from all other goods and services, called *nontradables*. We used this specification in Chapter 17's discussion of Dutch disease.

Tradable goods and services are those whose prices within the country are determined by supply and demand on world markets. Under the small-economy assumption, these world market prices cannot be influenced by anything that happens within the country and so are *exogenous* to the model (determined outside the model). The domestic price of a tradable good is given by $P_t = eP_t^*$, where e is the nominal exchange rate in local currency per dollar (pesos per dollar for Mexico or rupees per dollar for Pakistan) and P_t^* is the world price of the tradable in dollars. Even if the supply of and demand for tradables changes within an economy, the local price will not change because domestic supply and demand have a negligible influence on the world price. Adjustment of the exchange rate does change the domestic price, however. Because this model simplifies all tradables into one composite good, the price of tradables P_t is best thought of as an index, a weighted average of the prices of all tradables, much like a consumer price index.

Tradables include exportables, such as coffee in Kenya and Colombia, rice in Thailand, beef in Argentina, cattle in West Africa, palm oil in Malaysia and Indonesia, copper from Peru and Zambia, oil from the Middle East, and textiles and electronics from East Asia, and importables, such as rice in West Africa, oil in Brazil or Korea, and intermediate chemicals and machinery in many developing countries.

Nontradables are goods and services, such as transportation, construction, retail trade, and household services, that are not easily or conventionally bought or sold outside the country, usually because the costs of transporting them from one country to another are prohibitive or because local custom inhibits trade. Prices of nontradables, designated P_n, are therefore determined by market forces within the economy; any shift in supply or demand will change the price of nontradables. Nontradable prices are thus *endogenous* to the model (determined within the model). P_n is, like P_t, a composite or weighted average price incorporating all prices of nontradable goods and services.

Internal and External Balance

Figure 20–1 depicts equilibrium under the Australian model. The vertical axis represents nontradables (N); the horizontal axis takes both the exportables and the

2. Among developing countries, China and India are large enough that they could become exceptions to the small country rule, given continued growth in China and both greater growth and openness in India.

3. So called because it was developed by Australian economists including W. E. G. Salter, "Internal Balance and External Balance: The Role of Price and Expenditure Effects," *Economic Record,* August 1959, pp. 226–38; Trevor W. Swan, "Economic Control in a Dependent Economy," *Economic Record,* November 1956, pp. 339–56; and W. Max Corden, *Inflation, Exchange Rates and the World Economy* (Chicago: University of Chicago Press, 1977). Australia is also a small, open economy.

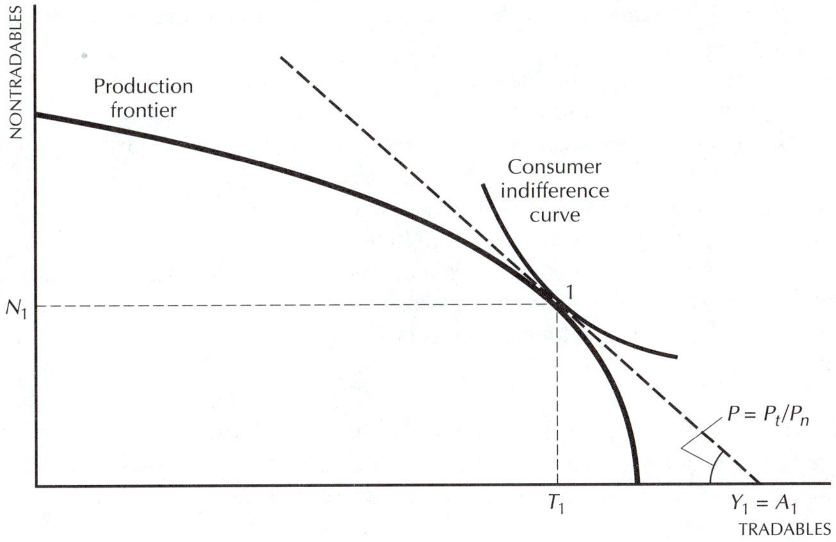

FIGURE 20–1 Equilibrium in the Australian model. With equilibrium at point 1, the tangency of the production frontier and a community indifference curve, the country produces and consumes T_1 of tradables and N_1 of nontradables. The relative price P is a measure of the real exchange rate (see text). National income measured in tradable prices is Y_1.

importables of previous diagrams (Figures 17–1 and 19–5 to 19–7) and treats them together as tradables (T). The production frontier shows the menu of possible outputs of the two kinds of goods, N and T. The community indifference curves show consumer preferences between consumption of tradables and nontradables.

Equilibrium is at point 1, the tangency of a consumer indifference curve and the production possibilities frontier. At this point, the production of tradables, determined by the production frontier at point 1, is T_1, equal to the demand for tradables, determined by the indifference curve at 1; and similarly, for nontradables, supply equals demand at N_1. This is a defining characteristic of equilibrium in the Australian model: at point 1, the markets for both goods are in balance. Put another way, there is **external balance,** because the supply of tradables equals demand, and **internal balance,** because the supply of nontradables equals demand.

The tangency of the indifference curve and production frontier also determines the relative price of tradables in terms of nontradables, $P = P_t/P_n$. The slope of the relative price line P_1 gives this price in Figure 20–1. The relative price P is an alternative measure of the **real exchange rate** and is one of the important innovations of the Australian model.[4] This formulation separates out prices that are under the influence of monetary and fiscal policy and domestic market forces, P_n, from prices that can be changed only by adjustments of the nominal exchange

4. Chapters 17 and 19 defined the real exchange-rate index as RER $= R_0P_w/P_d$. R_0 is an index of the nominal exchange rate, whereas in this chapter we use e, the nominal exchange rate itself. P_w is an index of world prices, often the U.S. consumer or wholesale price index, and is similar or identical to P^* as measured in practice. But P_d is a domestic consumer or wholesale price index that includes both tradable and nontradable prices, while P_n is an index of nontradable prices only. Thus the Australian formulation of the real exchange rate is a more precise definition than those given in the earlier chapters.

rate, $P_t = eP_t^*$. Note that P_1 is the only real exchange rate consistent with equilibrium in the model.

If P rises (the price line becomes steeper in the diagram), tradables become more expensive relative to nontradables. Producers then attempt to switch along the production frontier away from N goods, toward T goods. Consumers attempt to switch in the opposite direction, up along the indifference curve to consume less T goods and more N goods. Thus a rise in P should work to increase the surplus of T-good production over consumption.

If the production of T goods exceeds consumption of T goods, there is an external surplus, which is identical to a surplus in the balance of trade. To see this, start with the definition of the trade balance as

$$B_t = E - M, \qquad [20\text{–}1]$$

where E and M are exports and imports. Because exports are the surplus of supply over demand for exportable goods, while imports are the opposite, a surplus of demand over supply, we can write the balance of trade as

$$\begin{aligned} B_t &= \text{value of E-goods supply} - \text{value of E-goods demand} \\ &\quad - (\text{value of M-goods demand} - \text{value of M-goods supply}) \\ &= \text{value of E-goods supply} + \text{value of M-goods supply} \\ &\quad - (\text{value of E-goods demand} + \text{value of M-goods demand}) \\ &= \text{value of tradables supply} - \text{value of tradables demand}, \end{aligned}$$

or, if we let the supply of tradables be X_t and demand be D_t,

$$B_t = P_t X_t - P_t D_t = P_t(X_t - D_t). \qquad [20\text{–}2]$$

In Figure 20–1, with the economy in equilibrium, consumption of tradables is equal to production, so the balance of trade is zero.

The value of income (GNP) can also be found in Figure 20–1. It is the sum of the value of output of N goods (N_1) and T goods (T_1). This value is given by Y_1, the intersection of price line P_1 from point 1 to the T axis.[5] In national income accounting, we distinguish two concepts. Gross national *product,* a measure of the value of output, is given by

$$Y = C + I + E - M, \qquad [20\text{–}3]$$

where C and I are consumption and investment by both government and the private sector. Gross national *expenditure,* often called **absorption,** is

$$A = C + I = Y + M - E. \qquad [20\text{–}4]$$

When, as in Figure 20–1, the economy is in equilibrium, $E = M$ and income equals absorption. Indeed, this is a condition of equilibrium.

This exploration of the Australian model has yielded three results. *First,* macroeconomic equilibrium is defined as a balance between supply and demand in two markets: nontradable goods (internal balance) and tradable goods (external balance). *Second,* to achieve equilibrium in both markets, two conditions must be satisfied: expenditure (absorption) must equal income, and the relative price of

5. Along the T axis, Y_1 is measured in prices of the T good, so $P_tY_1 = P_tT_1 + P_nN_1$ or $Y_1 = T_1 + (P_n/P_t)N_1$. But $P_n/P_t = \Delta T/\Delta N$, with $\Delta N = N_1$ and $\Delta T = Y_1 - T_1$, the distance along the T axis from T_1 to Y_1. Thus the value of both goods in T prices is $T_1 + Y_1 - T_1 = Y_1$.

tradables (the real exchange rate) must be at a level that equates demand and supply in both markets (P_1 in Figure 20–1). *Third,* this also suggests two remedies for an economy that is out of balance: a government can achieve equilibrium—stabilize the economy—by adjusting absorption, the nominal exchange rate, or both. Generally both instruments must be used to achieve internal and external balance.

The Phase Diagram

Using the perspective of trade theory, we have tied the small, open economy model of macroeconomic management to the tools of analysis already used in this text. But the principles of stabilization can be explored from a more useful perspective, the **phase diagram.** To develop this approach, consider the markets for tradables and nontradables from the perspective of conventional supply and demand diagrams, as in Figure 20–2.

In these diagrams, we use the real exchange rate, which is the relative price of T goods in terms of N goods (P_t/P_n), as the price in both markets. For tradable goods that gives a conventional supply and demand diagram: as the price rises, supply increases and demand decreases. But in the nontradables market, a rise in P means a fall in the relative price of N goods, so supply decreases and demand increases. Note that in both markets, any increase in expenditure, or absorption A, causes an outward shift of the demand curve: at any price, consumers will buy more of both goods.

To use these diagrams as a basis for macroeconomic analysis, we need to change the interpretation of the supply curve for tradables. Until now, we have assumed that all tradables are produced within the home country. But foreign investment and foreign aid can add to the supply of tradables by financing additional imports. Thus the supply curve should not be X_t, but $X_t + F$, where F is the inflow of long-term foreign capital in the form of aid, commercial loans, and investment.

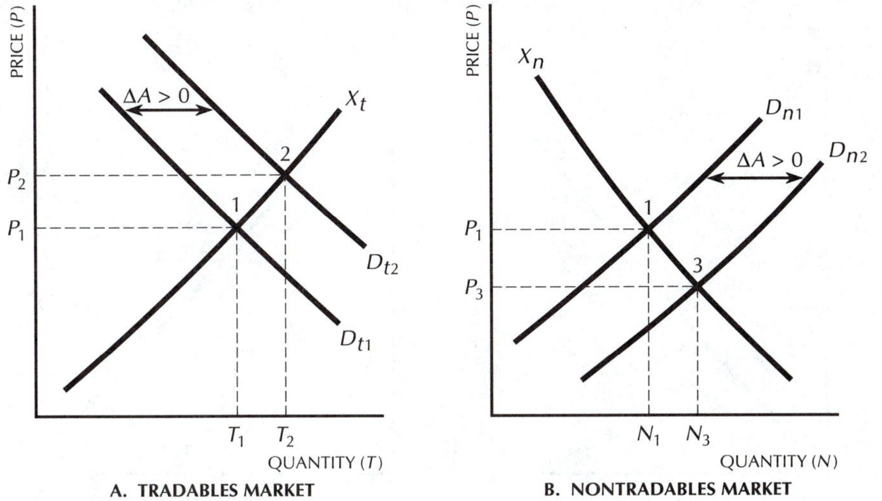

FIGURE 20–2 **Tradables and Nontradables Markets.** Supply is denoted by X and demand by D. The price P in both diagrams is P_t/P_n. In Part A, the demand and supply curves for tradables X_t and D_t have the conventional slopes. But in Part B the slopes are reversed: X_n falls as P rises (because the relative price of N is falling) and D_n rises as P rises. In both markets, demand increases when absorption (expenditure) increases, shown by an outward shift of D_t and D_n.

Figure 20–2 constitutes a simple model of the small, open economy that is based on two variables: the real exchange rate P on the vertical axis, and absorption A, which determines the position of the demand curves. These are, of course, the conventional variables of microeconomics, price and income. But in this model they are also the two main macroeconomic policy tools of government: the exchange rate and the level of expenditure. Because these two variables are central to macroeconomic management, it would be helpful to develop a diagram that uses them explicitly on the axes.

Figure 20–3 does this. It puts the real exchange rate $P = eP^*_t/P_n$, on the vertical axis, and real absorption A on the horizontal axis. The diagram also contains two curves, each representing equilibrium in one of the markets. Along the *EB*, or *external balance,* curve, the T-goods market is in balance ($X_t = D_t$). Along the *IB*, or *internal balance,* curve, the N-goods market is in balance ($X_n = D_n$).

The slopes of the two curves *EB* and *IB* can be derived from Figure 20–2. In the tradables market, when absorption is A_1, there is equilibrium at P_1, where T_1 is produced and consumed. This equilibrium point 1 is also shown in Part A of Figure 20–3. If absorption increases to A_2 in Figure 20–2, the demand curve moves outward, and shifts equilibrium to point 2. Note that with higher absorption A_2, the real exchange rate P_2 must be higher to restore equilibrium in the T-goods market. Increased absorption raises the demand for T goods. To meet this demand, it is necessary to raise output, which can only be achieved through a higher relative price of T goods, P_2. This higher price also helps to regain balance by reducing the demand for T goods along the new demand curve. Point 2 is transferred to Figure 20–3 at (P_2, A_2).

In the nontradables market, when absorption is A_1, there is equilibrium at P_1, where N_1 is produced and consumed. This equilibrium point 1 is also shown in Part B of Figure 20–3. If absorption increases to A_2 in Figure 20–2, the demand curve moves outward, and shifts equilibrium to point 3. In the N-goods market, higher absorption A_2 requires a lower, or appreciated, real exchange rate to restore

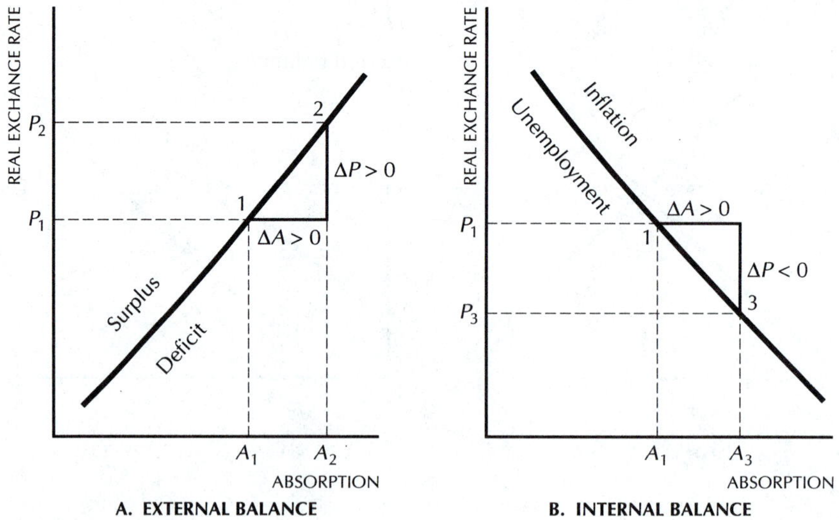

FIGURE 20–3 The Phase Diagram. The axes are the main policy variables, the real exchange rate P and real absorption A. The curves show equilibrium in the T-goods market (external balance *EB*) and N-goods market (internal balance *IB*).

equilibrium. Increased absorption raises demand for N goods, which can be met by raising output, which can only be achieved through a lower relative price of T goods, P_3. This lower real exchange rate, or higher price of N goods, also helps to regain balance by reducing the demand for N goods along the new demand curve. Point 3 is transferred to Figure 20–3 at (P_3, A_2).

Figure 20–3 also shows the **zones of imbalance.** In the T-goods market, Part A, for any given level of absorption, say A_1, any real exchange rate greater than P_1 would cause external surplus: the production of tradables would exceed the demand for tradables because the relative price P would be at a more depreciated level than required for equilibrium. Any real exchange rate below (more appreciated than) P_1 would cause an external deficit, and the demand would exceed the supply of tradables. Thus the zone of surplus is to the northwest of *EB* and the zone of deficit is to the southeast.

In the N-goods market, Part B, there is inflation to the right of the *IB* curve, where the demand for N goods exceeds the supply. In that region, for any given real exchange rate, such as P_1, absorption is too high, say A_3. To the left is the zone of unemployment, where there is an excess supply of N goods. In that region, for any given real exchange rate, say P_3, absorption is too low, say A_1.

The meaning of inflation and unemployment is precise in our model, but not in the real world. It is best to think of inflation as being an increase in prices faster than is customary in the country in question. That rate would be quite low in Germany, Japan, or China, probably less than 5 percent a year, but quite high in Brazil or Argentina. Unemployment implies not only jobless workers, but also idle capital and other factors of production. In other words, there is unemployment when an economy is inside the production frontier in Figure 20–1. A country may have high levels of labor unemployment but be unable to increase output because it is fully utilizing its capital or land.

Equilibrium and Disequilibrium

The two balance curves are put together in Figure 20–4. All along the external balance curve the demand for T goods equals the supply produced at home plus any net foreign capital inflow. All along the internal balance curve the demand for N goods equals the supply of N goods. The only point where there is both internal and external balance—equilibrium in both the T- and N-goods markets—is the intersection of the two curves, at point 1. This is sometimes called the *bliss point.* It is the same as the tangency of the indifference curve to the production frontier in Figure 20–1 at point 1. The objective of macroeconomic policy is to adjust the exchange rate and absorption to keep an economy stable, in both external and internal balance at point 1.

Economies spend considerable time in one of the four zones of imbalance shown in Figure 20–4. Zone *A* to the north of point 1 is a region of external surplus and inflation, where the exchange rate is *undervalued.* In Zone *B* to the east of equilibrium, the economy faces inflation and a foreign deficit, due principally to excessive expenditure (absorption is greater than income). To the south of point 1 is Zone *C*, where the exchange rate is *overvalued* (too appreciated) and there is both unemployment and an external deficit. And west of the bliss point the economy is in Zone *D* where, because of insufficient absorption, there is unemployment of all resources but a foreign surplus.

Once in disequilibrium, economies have built-in tendencies to escape back into

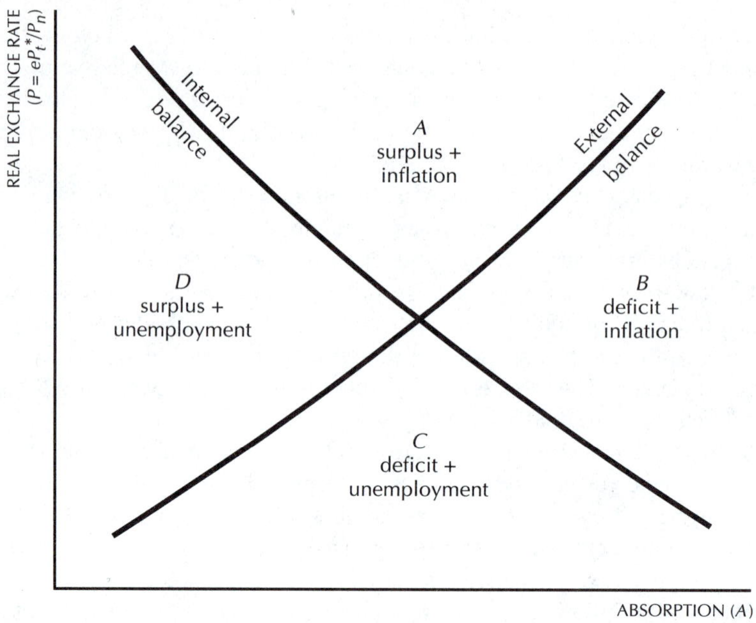

FIGURE 20–4 Zones of Imbalance. The economy is in equilibrium only at point 1, the intersection of the *EB* and *IB* curves. Zones of imbalance are labeled. For example, in Zone *A* to the north, supply of T goods exceeds demand, so there is a surplus, and demand for N goods exceeds supply, so there is inflation.

balance. Figure 20–5 describes them separately for external balance (Part A) and internal balance (Part B). Start with an external surplus, point 1 in Part A. The excess supply of tradables generates two self-correcting tendencies. First, the net inflow of foreign exchange adds to international reserves. If the central bank takes no countermeasures, the money supply will increase and interest rates will fall and induce both consumers and investors to spend more. The increase in absorption moves the economy rightward, back toward external balance. Second, the inflow of foreign exchange will create more demand for the local currency and, if the exchange rate is free to float, will force an appreciation. This is a move downward in the diagram, also toward the *EB* line. The net result of these two tendencies is the resultant, shown as a solid line in the diagram, heading toward external balance. If instead the economy starts in external deficit at point 2, the tendencies are the opposite but the result is the same: a tendency to regain external balance.

The tendency to regain internal balance is shown in Part B. When there is inflation (point 3), it affects both the real exchange rate and real absorption. If the nominal exchange rate remains fixed (or is not allowed to depreciate as fast as inflation), the rise in P_n causes a real appreciation. At the same time, the rise in prices can cause a fall in the real value of absorption, assuming that the central bank does not take steps to increase the money supply to compensate for inflation. Under these assumptions, the economy would move from inflation at point 3 back toward internal balance. Unemployment (point 4) would be self-correcting, also, if prices are able to fall as easily as they rise, but this is seldom the case.

Though these self-correcting tendencies exist, in practice they often fail to work smoothly or quickly enough because of *structural rigidities* in the economy. For

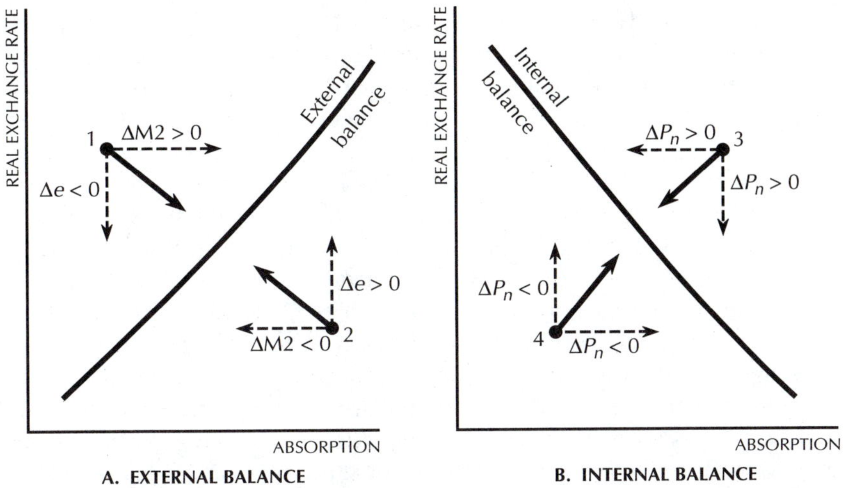

FIGURE 20–5 **Tendencies toward Equilibrium.** If the economy faces an external surplus (point 1 in Part A), reserves and the money supply tend to rise while the exchange rate tends to appreciate; this drives the economy toward external balance. Conversely for a deficit. If the economy faces inflation (point 3 in Part B), the rise in prices leads to real appreciation of the exchange rate and a reduction in the real value of absorption; this moves conditions toward internal balance. Conversely for unemployment at point 4 but only if prices can fall flexibly.

instance, exchange-rate changes may take time to affect actual imports and exports, perhaps as long as two years to have a full impact. In economies like Ghana and Zambia, dominated by one or two export products such as cocoa and copper, with long gestation periods for new investment, supply elasticities for tradables may be especially low and foreign deficits can persist for a time despite real devaluations.

Nontradables prices probably do rise very quickly when demand exceeds supply, as in Part B of Figure 20–5. But in many developing economies inflation, once started, may resist corrective policies and prices do not fall so easily when there is unemployment: unions strike wage bargains that try to maintain real wages by continually raising nominal wages, banks use their market power to keep interest rates high, producers are dependent on imports whose prices are responsive only to exchange rate adjustments, and large firms with monopoly or oligopoly power keep prices up to cover costs that resist downward pressures. Such rigidities have been cited frequently to explain chronic trade deficits and inflation in Latin America, especially in Argentina and Brazil.

However, arguments about structural rigidities can be overstated. There is some flexibility in production for most export industries, even in the short term. And many producer prices are quite flexible, including those of most farm products, those in the large informal sector, and even those of some modern manufacturing firms. Nevertheless, the automatic tendencies toward external and internal balance that are depicted in Figure 20–5 are likely to be too slow and politically painful to satisfy most governments.

Not all the barriers to adjustment are structural. Sometimes policies work against adjustment. When foreign reserves fall, for example, the money supply would also fall automatically unless the central bank's policy is to *sterilize* these shifts by expanding domestic credit to compensate for the fall in reserves and keep the money supply from falling. Sterilization prevents the move from points 1 or 2 of Figure 20–5 toward external balance. And nominal exchange rates respond to changing market conditions, as shown in Panel A, only if the exchange rate is allowed to float or if the government makes frequent adjustments in the nominal exchange rate to match changing economic conditions.

However, the opposite policy—a fixed nominal exchange rate—is needed if inflation in nontradables prices is to cause a real exchange-rate appreciation, as depicted at point 3 of Figure 20–5. This fixed nominal rate is called an exchange rate *anchor,* because the fixed rate alone can halt the upward drift of prices, as the economy moves due south from point 3 in Part B. Chile used such an anchor to slow inflation during the late 1970s (see the box). If government devalues the rate to keep up with inflation—Brazil's practice for many years—then real appreciation is thwarted and there is no anchor. Similarly, real absorption falls with inflation only if the government fixes its expenditure and its deficit in nominal terms and allows inflation to erode the real value of expenditure and if the central bank restrains the money supply to grow more slowly than inflation. More typically, the fiscal authorities adjust expenditure, while the monetary authorities adjust both the money supply and the nominal exchange rate, to fully compensate for inflation. In that case, rising prices have no impact on the real exchange rate or real absorption and an inflationary economy remains at point 3 in Figure 20–5.

Stabilization Policies

Whether the barriers to rapid automatic adjustment are inherent in economic structure or are created by policy contradictions, in most cases governments need to take an active role to stabilize their economies. They have three basic instruments for doing so: exchange-rate management, fiscal policy, and monetary policy.

Alternative **exchange-rate regimes** were introduced in Chapter 14. Governments can vary the exchange rate by having the central bank offer to buy and sell foreign currency at a predetermined or *fixed* official exchange rate (e in our nomenclature) that can nevertheless by changed from time to time or by allowing the rate to *float* in the currency market, though the central bank may sometimes intervene to influence the price. An intermediate case is the *crawling peg* under which the central bank determines the rate but changes it frequently, as often as daily, to ensure that the official rate stays in line with domestic and world inflation; this results in a constant or slowly adjusting real exchange rate (P).

Governments have two policies that can influence the level of absorption. **Fiscal policy**—adjusting levels of government expenditure and taxation—directly affects the government's components of consumption and investment. It also influences private expenditure, especially consumption, which depends on *disposable income,* or income net of taxes. **Monetary policy** also affects private expenditure. If the central bank acts to increase the money supply, as described in Chapter 14, it increases the liquidity of households and firms, lowers interest rates, and stimulates private consumption and investment.

The power of the phase diagram is that it indicates the necessary directions for these policies, depending on the state of the economy. Figure 20–6 provides such a policy map. It shows the same external and internal balance lines as in the previous diagrams, but adds a new element: four policy quadrants, I to IV, within which the policy prescription is always the same.

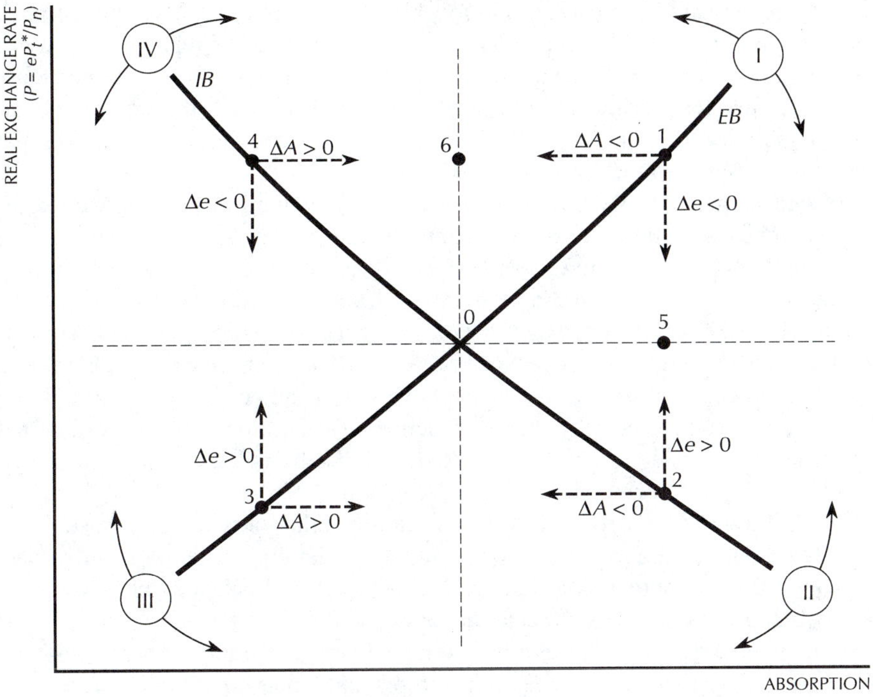

FIGURE 20–6 Policy Zones. From any position of disequilibrium, two policy adjustments are generally needed to restore internal and external balance. In each of Quadrants I to IV, a particular combination of exchange rate and absorption policy is prescribed.

Take, for example, point 1, which has been placed on the external balance line but in the inflationary zone. For many years Brazil was in a this situation, with buoyant exports and balance in foreign payments, but chronic inflation running from 40 to well over 100 percent a year. Because the demand for nontradables exceeds supply, we know that one necessary correction is a reduction in real absorption—monetary and fiscal *austerity*—that would reduce demand and move the economy due west from point 1. But if that is the only policy taken, the economy would not reach internal balance until point 4, in the zone of external surplus. One imbalance would have been exchanged for another. To avoid generating a surplus, reduced absorption needs to be accompanied by an appreciation of the exchange rate, a move due south from point 1. The result would be a move approximately toward the equilibrium or bliss point, 0.

Note three things about this result. *First,* this combination of policies, austerity and appreciation, would work from any point within Quadrant I to return the economy to equilibrium. That is, the same combination would be needed whether the economy had inflation with a moderate external surplus or inflation with a moderate deficit, either just above or just below the *EB* line. If the economy starts just below external balance, with a moderate deficit, it may seem strange (*counterintuitive*) to recommend an appreciation that would, on its own, worsen the deficit. But the reduction in absorption, needed to reduce inflation, would also reduce the deficit because it also lowers the demand for tradables. Indeed, it would reduce the demand for tradables too much and throw the economy into surplus; this is the reason that an appreciation is needed. Of course, the relative intensity of each policy would be different, depending where in Quadrant I the economy starts. But the basic principle holds: anywhere in Quadrant I, the right combination of policies is austerity and appreciation, the combination that moves the economy toward point 0.

Second, in general, two policy adjustments are required to move toward equilibrium. This is a simple example of the general rule enunciated by the Dutch economist Jan Tinbergen: in order to achieve a number of policy goals, it is generally necessary to employ the same number of policy instruments. Here we have two goals—internal and external balance—and need adjustments in both appreciation (austerity) and the real exchange rate (appreciation) to reach them both. It is not always necessary to use two goals, however. If the economy lies just to the east of equilibrium at point 5, then a reduction in absorption will achieve internal and external balance simultaneously. And if the initial situation is point 6, due north of 0, then appreciation alone will do the job.

Third, we could view the policy prescription in either of two ways. Austerity is needed to reduce inflation (move west) and appreciation is used to avoid surplus (move south). Or appreciation can be targeted on internal balance (move south toward point 2), but alone would cause a deficit, so that austerity is then required to restore external balance. Thus there is no logic in macroeconomics suggesting that one particular policy should be assigned to one particular goal. Economic institutions often do this anyway. In practice the central bank might use the exchange rate to achieve external balance while the finance ministry uses the budget for internal balance. But if these two approaches are not coordinated, they may well fail to reach equilibrium.

With these principles established for Quadrant I, it is fairly routine to go around the map in Figure 20–6 and see what policy responses are required.

- In Quadrant II at a point like 2, with an external deficit but internal balance, exchange-rate devaluation is needed to restore foreign balance, but taken alone would push the economy into inflation. Fiscal and monetary austerity are also needed to avoid inflation and reach equilibrium. We could have reversed this assignment of policies and used austerity to achieve external balance and devaluation to stimulate the economy. Many African countries were in this situation during the 1970s and early 1980s, with low inflation but an insufficiency of export earnings and foreign investment to pay for the imports required for economic development.

- In Quadrant III at point 3, an expansionary fiscal-monetary policy would eliminate unemployment, but at the cost of a foreign deficit, so devaluation is needed to reach equilibrium. Or devaluation could stimulate employment, and so require expansion to eliminate the resulting surplus. This is the situation of a mature industrialized economy during a recession, with unemployed labor and capital, but it is not so common in developing countries.

- In Quadrant IV at point 4, exchange-rate appreciation can eliminate the external surplus while fiscal expansion prevents unemployment. Or fiscal expansion can end the surplus while appreciation prevents the resulting inflation. A few countries in Asia, such as Taiwan (see the box) and Malaysia in the 1980s, have been in this situation.

So the principles of macroeconomic stabilization are simple: if policy makers know where to place their economy on this map, they know how to move toward equilibrium. But how do policy makers know where they are? The answer lies partly in measurement, partly in art. Regularly available data on the balance of payments and changes in reserves and on inflation can help locate an economy with respect to the external and internal balance lines. Data on the nominal and real exchange rates, on the budget deficit, and on the money supply can indicate movements from one policy quadrant to another. In principle, econometric models can locate the economy and indicate the policies needed to balance it. In practice, especially but not only for developing economies, such models can be too imprecise and too unstable to be wholly dependable. The art of stabilization policy comes in knowing just how hard to push on each component of policy and how long to keep pushing. In this, experience in managing a particular economy is as important a guide as the models estimated by economists.

TALES OF STABILIZATION

Throughout this book we have referred to different kinds of economic problems that are associated with developing countries, including Dutch disease, debt crises, terms-of-trade shocks, foreign exchange shortages, destructive inflation, and droughts or other natural catastrophes. The Australian model and its phase diagram can be used to show how these and other shocks affect macroeconomic balance and how they should be handled.

Dutch Disease

Chapter 17 described the strange phenomenon of Dutch disease, in which a country that receives higher export prices or a larger inflow of foreign capital may end up worse off than without the windfall. Dutch disease was first analyzed by Australian economists Max Corden and Peter Neary using a version of the open economy model.[6] Figure 20–7 traces the impacts of a windfall gain using the phase diagram.

An economy in equilibrium at point 1 suddenly begins to receive higher prices for its major export or is favored by foreign aid donors or foreign investors. All the oil producers, from Saudi Arabia to Indonesia to Mexico, were in this position in the 1970s, as were coffee (and many other commodity) exporters during the boom of the mid-1970s. Egypt and Israel were rewarded with large aid programs by the United States after the Camp David accord of 1978, as was Ghana by the World Bank and others during its stabilization of the 1980s. Both Chile in the late 1970s and Mexico after its stabilization in the late 1980s received large inflows of private capital, much of it a return of previous flight capital. Foreign exchange windfalls are more frequent than is sometimes supposed.

When the windfall occurs, the supply of tradable goods rises at any given price. This can be shown as a rightward shift in the supply curve in Figure 20–2A. In the phase diagram of Figure 20–7, there is a rightward shift in the *EB* curve. At

6. W. Max Corden and J. Peter Neary, "Booming Sector and Deindustrialisation in a Small Open Economy," *Economic Journal*, 92 (1982).

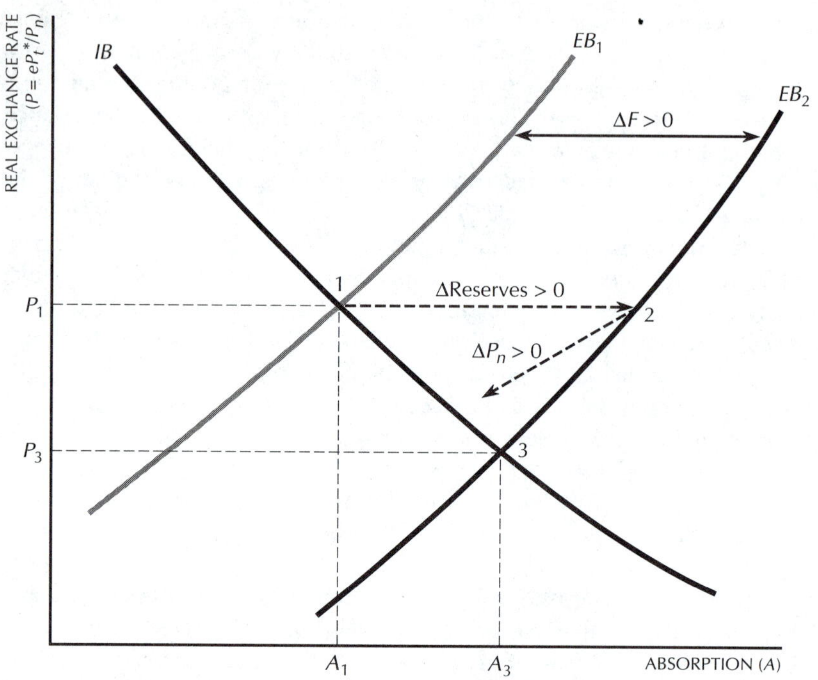

FIGURE 20–7 Dutch Disease. An export boom or capital inflow shifts the *EB* curve rightward and leaves the economy at point 1 in surplus. As reserves accumulate and the money supply rises (or as the government and consumers spend the windfall), absorption rises and the economy moves eastward, into inflation. As nontradable prices rise, the real exchange rate appreciates. At the new equilibrium, point 3, because *P* is lower, the supply and demand is balanced with less production of T goods, and more output of N goods, than before. The loss of tradable output is what makes this a "disease."

point 1, for example, which had been in external equilibrium along EB_1, the economy is now in surplus, so the new *EB* curve must be to the right, for example at EB_2. The economy cannot remain at point 1 because the inflow of reserves increases the money supply; this adds to demand, and because the windfall will increase private income and government revenue, leads to greater expenditure. So absorption rises—a move from point 1 toward point 2. This moves the economy off its internal balance, into inflation.[7]

The resulting rise in P_n has two effects: a reduction in real absorption that partially corrects the initial rise in *A* and, assuming the official rate is fixed, a real appreciation of the exchange rate. (The real rate would also appreciate if the nominal rate were floating, because the greater supply of foreign currency would drive the price of foreign currency down.) Thus the economy would first move from point 1 toward 2 in Figure 20–7, and then begin to head in the general direction of the new equilibrium, point 3. In this case, market forces are likely to be sufficient to reach the new equilibrium unless the authorities act to prevent appre-

7. If the windfall is an inflow of capital, this treatment is precise. In the case of a rise in export prices, however, the move from point 1 to 2 is an approximation. Strictly speaking, a rise in export prices should raise P_t^*, a depreciation of the real exchange rate that moves the economy upward from point 1, after which the economy moves east toward EB_2.

ciation and maintain real absorption, and thus keep the economy in an inflationary posture like point 2.

What, then, is the problem? The economy is at a new equilibrium; its terms of trade have improved; its currency has appreciated, and so citizens have more command over foreign resources; people are spending and consuming more without having to work any harder. There are two flaws in this otherwise idyllic picture. First, such windfalls are generally temporary. When export prices fall or the capital inflow dries up, the *EB* curve will shift back and a costly adjustment will be necessary. We analyze that process in the next section.

The second problem is that, in shifting from the old to the new equilibrium, there have to be adjustments in the economy. The real exchange rate P is lower, so X_t has fallen, while X_n has risen. Because the booming export sector will not retrench, nonboom tradables bear the brunt of the adjustment. Frictions in the labor market are likely to mean at least temporary unemployment as workers switch from tradable to nontradable production. If the tradable sector includes modern manufacturing, then long-term development may be set back because manufacturing is the sector likely to yield the most rapid productivity growth in the future. And if tradable industries close, it will be more difficult to make the inevitable adjustment back toward point 1 when the windfall is over. It is this decline in nonboom-tradable production that turns a foreign exchange windfall into a "disease."

What can be done to cure the disease? Government could try to move the economy back toward the old (and probably future) equilibrium at point 1. Its tools are the official exchange rate, which would have to be devalued against the tendencies of market forces, and expenditure, which would have to be reduced through restrictive fiscal and monetary policies that also reduce inflation (lower P_n or at least its growth). The resulting buildup of reserves and bank balances would have to be sterilized through monetary policy so they would be held as assets and not spent. It is a neat political trick to manage an austere macroeconomic policy in the face of a boom, because all the popular pressures are for more spending. Not too many countries have managed it. Indonesia is among the few that have; we discussed Indonesia's therapy for Dutch disease in a box in Chapter 17.

Debt Repayment Crisis

When Mexico announced in 1982 that it could no longer service the debt it acquired during the oil boom of the 1970s, many other developing countries followed Mexico's lead and the financial world entered a decade of debt crisis (Chapter 15). Most Latin American countries have largely overcome their debt problems, but many African countries continue to struggle to repay the money they have mostly borrowed from aid agencies. Although debt service insolvency encroaches gradually on an economy and can be foreseen, it often appears as a national crisis because economic management has been inept.

The formal analysis of a debt crisis is similar to that of a another common phenomenon, a **decline in the terms of trade** that leads to a foreign exchange shortage, which in turn is simply the reverse of Dutch disease. Thus the oil exporters, such as Indonesia, Nigeria, and Venezuela, faced a similar kind of crisis once oil prices began falling in the 1980s.

Figure 20–8 captures this process. An economy in balance at point 1 needs to find additional resources to repay its foreign debt or needs to adjust to falling

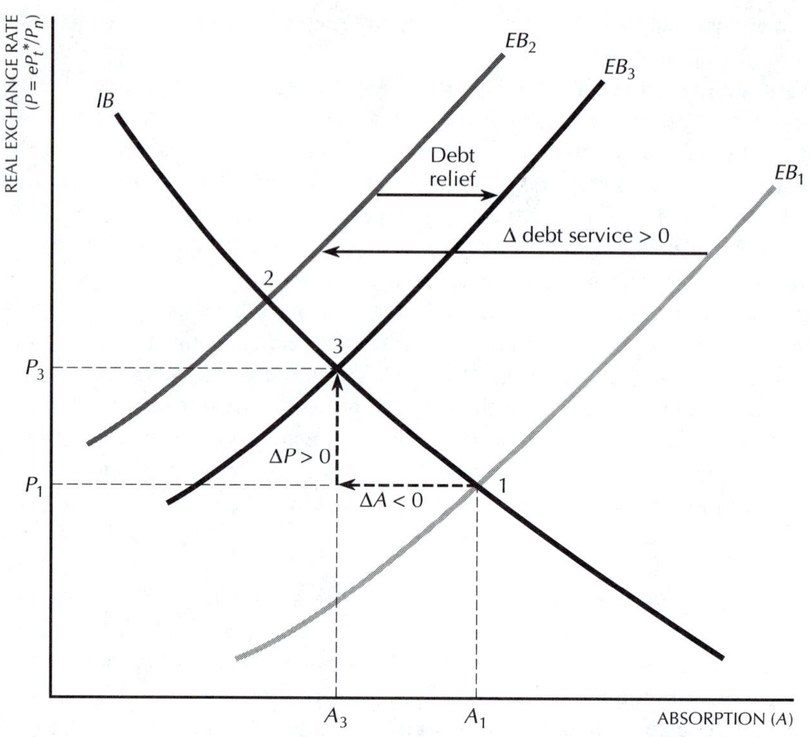

FIGURE 20–8 Debt Crisis or Declining Terms of Trade. An economy in equilibrium at point 1 suddenly needs to repay its debt (or faces falling export prices). External balance shifts from EB_1 to EB_2, though debt relief or increased foreign assistance might reshift the balance line back to EB_3. If policies accommodate the fall in reserves and income, absorption will decline. A devaluing exchange rate, via central bank action or market forces, will help the economy move to its new equilibrium at point 3. With more tradables produced and less consumed, the surpluses can be used to repay debt.

terms of trade. The supply of tradables therefore shifts to the left in Figure 20–2A; in the phase diagram, the *EB* curve also shifts leftward to EB_2.[8] If the crisis leads to debt relief or additional foreign aid, the curve would not move so far, but might settle at EB_3.

Now in foreign deficit, the economy will begin losing reserves. If the government has to repay some of the debt or if falling export prices cut into its revenues, the government needs to reduce its expenditures as well. Both cause a reduction in absorption. These actions move the economy toward external balance but also into unemployment. To gain the new equilibrium at point 3, it is also necessary to devalue the currency. This could be done by the central bank under a fixed rate or by the foreign exchange market under a floating rate. At the new equilibrium, the country is producing more and consuming less tradables, because *P* has risen. This is, of course, a loss of welfare for the populace. The surplus of X_t over D_t is used to repay the debt or simply compensates for reduced export prices.

Debt crises, and the hardships they cause, are not an inevitable consequence of borrowing to finance development. If the borrowed resources are invested produc-

8. Strictly speaking, we cannot analyze the fall in export prices this way, but it is a reasonable approximation for many situations. See footnote 7.

tively, they will increase the potential output of both tradables and nontradables. Added production will increase incomes and generate the capacity to repay the debt out of additional income, without a crisis and an austerity program. Countries such as Korea and Indonesia have been large international borrowers, but have escaped debt crises.

Pioneering Stabilization: Chile, 1973–1984[9]

In the last year of the Salavatore Allende regime in Chile, when the public sector deficit soared to 30 percent of GNP and was financed mostly by printing money, inflation exceeded 500 percent a year. In 1973, General Augusto Pinochet overthrew Allende and established an autocratic regime. An early goal of his government was to stabilize the economy. It proved to be a difficult task of many years, with important lessons for later stabilizations in Latin America.

Faced by rapid inflation and unsustainable external deficits, the government imposed a fiscal and monetary shock on the economy. The budget deficit was cut to 10.6 percent of GNP in 1974 and again to 2.7 percent in 1975. Monetary policy was tight: from the second quarter of 1975 through the middle of 1976, it has since been estimated, households and firms were willing to hold more money than was in circulation. But inflation persisted; consumer prices nearly doubled in 1977.

Despite draconian measures, prices continued to rise for two reasons. First, the peso was aggressively devalued to improve the foreign balance, the more so because of the 40 percent fall in copper prices in 1975. In 1977 the peso was worth about one-eightieth of its 1973 value against the dollar. Second, wages in the formal sector were determined by rules that permitted adjustments based on the previous year's rate of inflation—a rule that helped to perpetuate the higher rates of earlier years. It was also argued by some that monetary policy was not stringent enough.

In 1978 the government switched gears and began using the exchange rate as its main anti-inflation weapon. At first a crawling peg was adopted with preannounced rates, the *tablita,* that did not fully adjust to domestic inflation. In 1979 the rate was fixed at 39 to the dollar for three years. The appreciating real exchange rate, or *anchor,* did help to control inflation, which was down to 10 percent by 1982. But it also discouraged export growth and contributed to a growing current-account deficit. At the same time, Chile liberalized its controls over foreign capital flows and attracted large inflows of loans: net long-term capital rose from negligible amounts before 1978 to average over $2 billion a year in the next five years, equivalent to 8 percent of GNP in 1980. This inflow not only financed the growing current deficit, but itself contributed to the real appreciation of the exchange rate.

It was not until after 1984 that Chile finally achieved a semblance of both internal and external balance. It did so through a large real devalua-

9. Based on the account by Vittoria Corbo and Andrés Solimano, "Chile's Experience with Stabilization Revisited," in Michael Bruno et al., *Lessons of Economic Stabilization and its Aftermath* (Cambridge, Mass.: MIT Press, 1991).

tion, approaching 50 percent, supported by tighter fiscal and monetary policies. After a decade and a half of falling income per capita, Chilean incomes grew by 5.8 percent a year from 1985 to 1991.

Stabilization Package: Inflation and a Deficit

External shock is not the only way an economy gets into trouble. Reckless or misguided government policies are often to blame. Impatient with sluggish development or intent on benefiting its constituencies, a government expands its spending and incurs a budget deficit. Unable to finance the deficit by borrowing from the public, the ministry of finance sells short-term bills to the central bank; this adds to the money supply. The economy drifts into inflation and a foreign deficit, at a point like point 1 in Figure 20–9, far from equilibrium at point 2 on the economy's original external balance curve EB_1. When economies become unstable in this way, private investors get skittish and try to invest in nonproductive assets like land or, more often, to invest abroad; this deepens the external deficit. The government, recognizing the error of its ways, or just hoping for some outside help to avoid painful adjustment, calls in the IMF.

The core IMF stabilization program consists of a reduction in the government's budget deficit and programmed targets for domestic credit that in effect cap the growth of the money supply. Together these measures reduce absorption in the

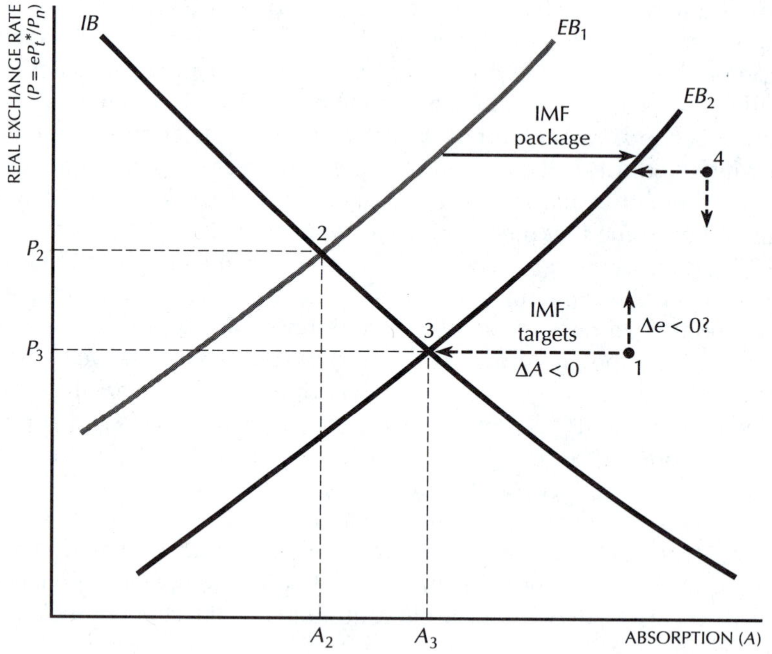

FIGURE 20–9 Stabilization from Inflation and a Deficit. An economy at point 1, far from equilibrium at point 2, needs above all to reduce absorption through austerity: reduced budgetary deficits and slower growth of the money supply. An IMF and donor package of aid might bring equilibrium closer by shifting the external balance to EB_2, but the aid package will be conditional on the austerity program. Whether any exchange rate action is required depends on the precise initial position, point 1.

economy and move it westward from point 1, closer to external and internal balance. IMF packages frequently include an exchange rate devaluation as well. Whether this is needed or not depends on the precise location of the economy (point 1) relative to equilibrium (point 2). In some cases the reduction in absorption will be sufficient to reach both internal and external balance. As pictured in Figure 20–9, a small devaluation would be needed to reach point 2 and avoid unemployment.

However, IMF programs usually come with substantial aid attached, not only from the Fund, but from the World Bank and bilateral donors. The aid package, by adding to the economy's capacity to buy tradables, would shift the *EB* curve to the right, to EB_2 in the diagram, and move equilibrium to point 3. Notice two things about this aid package. First, it reduces the need for austerity for some extent, as A_3 is greater than A_2. Second, it reduces the need for devaluation of the exchange rate. Indeed, as shown, there is little or no need to devalue to move from 1 to 3. Donors and the IMF nevertheless frequently insist on devaluation. Sometimes that may be a requirement just to reach a point like 3. In other cases they may have in mind a self-sustaining stabilization that will be valid even after aid is reduced and the external balance curve moves back toward EB_1. Whatever their motive, it is important to realize that aid itself is a partial substitute for both devaluation and for austerity. In essence, the aid does what higher production of tradables would otherwise have to do and it finances expenditures that would otherwise have to be cut. Ghana's experience, which fits this description, is discussed in the boxed example.

Another kind of stabilization can also be illustrated with Figure 20–9, **rapid** (or **hyper-) inflation.** In Bolivia's hyperinflation of the mid-1980s (see Chapter 5) or the chronic inflations in Brazil and Argentina, external balance is a secondary consideration or not a major problem. Point 4 in the diagram depicts this situation. Austerity is still required to move toward equilibrium at point 2 or 3 (if there is an aid package). But devaluation would only intensify inflation. Instead, there needs to be an appreciation of the currency, which also dampens inflation. One way to achieve this would be to fix the nominal rate and let the continuing (if decreasing) inflation in nontradable prices (P_n) work to appreciate the real rate *P*. This is the *exchange rate anchor,* a device used often in Latin America, especially in Chile during the late 1970s, in Bolivia during the mid-1980s, and in Argentina during the 1990s. It has the disadvantage that a lower real rate discourages export growth. Yet investment in new exports may be part of a strategy to open the economy, diversify exports, and move the external balance curve to the right.

Recovering from Mismanagement: Ghana, 1983–1991[10]

In 1983, after a decade of economic mismanagement, Ghana's gross national product was 20 percent below its 1974 peak, investment was only 4 percent of GNP, exports had sunk to 6 percent of GNP, and inflation rocketed to 120 percent for the year. After a decade of economic decline, Ghana's military government, headed by Flight Lieutenant Jerry Rawlings,

10. This account is based on Ishan Kapur, et al., *Ghana: Adjustment and Growth, 1983–91* (Washington, D.C.: International Monetary Fund, 1991).

was ready to undertake drastic measures to stabilize the economy and restart economic development.

Working closely with the International Monetary Fund, Ghana focused on three deep-seated problems: exchange-rate reform, fiscal adjustment, and monetary policy. At first, the government maintained its fixed exchange rate, but drastically devalued the cedi from 2.75 to the dollar in 1983 to 90 by 1986. In 1986 Ghana adopted a restricted floating currency, using periodic auctions to determine the rate. The official exchange market was broadened in 1988 when many foreign exchange bureaus were authorized to trade currencies, and virtually absorbed the parallel market in currency; by 1990 the banks were empowered to trade in an interbank currency market. This completed the move to a floating rate regime. By the end of 1992, the cedi traded at 520 per dollar.

In 1983, with fiscal revenues less than 6 percent of GNP, the urgent need was to restore revenues and control expenditures. The deficit was cut from 6.2 to 2.7 percent of GNP in the first year of austerity, and by 1985 the government had begun a major public investment program to stimulate growth. By 1988, the government had restored total expenditures to 15 percent of GNP, 20 percent of which was investment, and was running a surplus of nearly 4 percent of GNP.

Throughout the period the money supply was constrained, but inflation remained stubbornly above 20 percent a year until 1991, when it was reduced to 16 percent and real interest rates finally became positive. Because food prices play a large role in the consumer price index, investment in food production was seen as an important component of any long-run attack on inflation.

The aid donors responded handsomely to Ghana's stabilization and the accompanying economic reforms: the sum of net official transfers and net long-term capital rose from just over $100 million in 1983 to $585 million in 1991.

Stabilization did help to restore economic growth. From the depression of 1983 to 1991, GNP grew by 5.1 percent a year and investment rose to 17 percent of GNP. The improvement, though dramatic in relation to the early 1980s, still left Ghana with a lot to be done: in 1991 income per capita remained 25 percent below its 1973 level.

Drought

The human tragedy of drought or other natural disasters in places such as Ethiopia, the West African Sahel, and India before the Green Revolution dwarfs issues of macroeconomic management. But the adept management of an economy racked by natural disaster is essential to reduce the misery of starving or displaced people. Drought, for example, reduces a country's capacity to produce food, export crops, and, in some countries, generate electricity from hydropower. At the same time, incomes are lower because farmers and others have less product to sell. Government then needs to provide social safety nets; this means spending more on the provision of food, transport, health services, and sometimes shelter. Foreign governments often provide financial, food, and technical aid in these situations.

The macroeconomic reflection of a drought is depicted in Figure 20–10. The economy begins in equilibrium at point 1. Drought reduces the economy's capacity to produce both nontradables (some foods, hydroelectricity, water supplies) and tradables (export crops, importable foods, some manufactures). We show this as a leftward shift in both the *IB* and *EB* lines: reduced output of X_n at any given price means a larger zone in which D_n exceeds X_n; this is inflationary. Similarly for X_t; and this enlarges the area of deficit. The new external balance curve EB_2 may be augmented (shifted back to the right) by foreign aid to EB_3, in which case the new equilibrium is point 3.

The economy, still at point 1, is inflationary. The fall in incomes creates a tendency for absorption to shrink on its own and move the economy leftward toward the new equilibrium. But at the same time government tries to spend more to relieve hunger, disease, and other problems. The outcome depends on the relative force of these tendencies. The impacts of most natural disasters are temporary, typically lasting a year, though some African droughts have been much longer. It is appropriate to try to ride out such shocks with minimal adjustment, especially if foreign aid can bear much of the burden. Thus, for example, even if exchange-rate

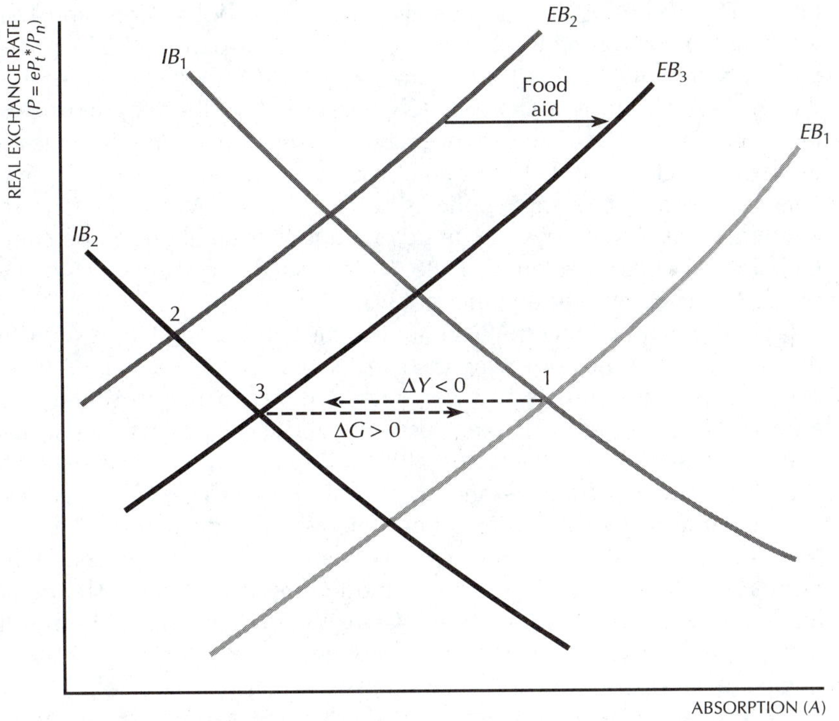

FIGURE 20–10 Drought. Drought or another natural disaster reduces the capacity to produce both nontradables and tradables, so the curves shift to the west. Disaster relief from abroad augments the external balance curve, and shifts it to EB_3, with equilibrium at point 3. Remaining temporarily at point 1, the economy becomes inflationary. The reduction in output and thus in incomes reduces absorption, but government's need to spend more on relief tends to offset this move toward equilibrium. The outcome could be continued inflation.

adjustment is called for to reach equilibrium, it is unlikely to work very well during a drought and should probably be resisted. This could also be said for fiscal austerity, except that the rise in prices can itself deepen the suffering of those already hurt by the drought. If government is able to shift its expenditures so that a greater portion goes into alleviating the impacts of the drought, it may be able to relieve the worst suffering while restricting the rise of total expenditures and containing inflation.

Accumulating Reserves: Taiwan, 1980–1987[11]

By 1980, Taiwan had established an economic growth record that was being cited as a model for other developing countries. The government's macroeconomic policy had always been conservative. When the second oil crisis hit in 1979–80, and as Taiwan began to lose diplomatic standing while China regained its place in the official world order, macroeconomic policy was tightened further.

The central bank began to undervalue its exchange rate and became more restrictive in its monetary policy. The Taiwan dollar was depreciated from 36 per U.S. dollar in 1980 to 40 in 1983, while the real rate depreciated 15 percent against an average of the U.S. dollar, yen, and Hong Kong dollar, representing Taiwan's major trading partners. (Hong Kong trade was mainly destined for China.) From 1980 to 1984, increases in the money supply as a share of GNP were below the long-term trend. Fiscal policy was neutral, however: both expenditures and revenues fell as shares of GNP and left the deficit roughly constant. The results of exchange rate and monetary policies were dramatic. While exports rose moderately as a share of GNP, imports plunged from about 45 percent of GNP in 1980 to 35 percent in 1986. Reserves rose from under 15 percent of GNP in 1980 to over 60 percent by 1987.

From the national income accounts, a current-account surplus must be matched by a surplus of saving over investment, or $S - I = E - M$. The necessary savings surplus was generated by both a rise in saving, from around 30 to almost 40 percent of GNP, and a fall in investment, from over 30 to under 20 percent of GNP. The savings surplus was generated in part by structural factors and in part by the rise in real interest rates caused by monetary stringency. Real interest rates on loans, which had been slightly negative in 1980, rose to a range of 8 to 10 percent a year from 1982 to 1986. Furthermore, domestic credit was tight. The central bank sterilized the rise in foreign reserves by forcing a sharp drop in the increments to private domestic credit: net new loans fell to only 5 percent of GNP by 1986.

There was a price to be paid for accumulating reserves. The unemployment rate, which had been 1.2 percent in 1980, rose to 2.9 percent in 1985. The growth rate of GNP, which was nearly 10 percent a year from

11. The data for this case comes from Republic of China, *Taiwan Statistical Data Book 1993* (Taipei: Republic of China, 1993).

1970 to 1980, was a little below 7 percent from 1980 to 1985, after which it recovered to about 8 percent a year. Still, measured against most other countries' performances, this was an enviable record. By the mid-1980s, informed opinion in Taiwan turned against mercantilist policies while the U.S. government exerted pressure on Taiwan to reverse its policies. The real exchange rate was appreciated 25 percent, fiscal and monetary policies became more expansionary, and the days of large surpluses and unrestrained reserve accumulation were over.

Bibliography and Additional Readings

Chapter 1. Introduction

Fatimah Daud. *Minah Karan: The Truth about Malaysian Factory Girls.* Kuala Lumpur: Berita Publishing, 1985.

Kamal Salih and Mei Ling Young. "Changing Conditions of Labour in the Semiconductor Industry in Malaysia," *Labour and Society,* 14 (1989), 59–80.

World Bank. *World Development Report.* New York: Oxford University Press, annual.

Chapter 2. Starting Modern Economic Growth

Obstacles to Development

Alexander Gerschenkron. *Economic Backwardness in Historical Perspective.* Cambridge, Mass.: Harvard University Press, 1962.

W. W. Rostow. *Stages of Economic Growth.* 2d ed.; New York: Cambridge University Press, 1971; 1st ed., 1960.

Imperialism

Paul Baran. *The Political Economy of Growth.* New York: Monthly Review Press, 1957.

Celso Furtado. "The Brazilian 'Model' of Development," in Charles K. Wilber (ed.), *The Political Economy of Development and Underdevelopment.* New York: Random House, 1979, pp. 324–33.

Keith Griffin and John Gurley. "Radical Analyses of Imperialism, the Third World, and the Transition to Socialism," *Journal of Economic Literature,* 23, no. 3 (September 1985).

Merilee Grindle and John Thomas. "Policy Makers, Policy Choices, and Policy Outcomes: The Political Economy of Reform in Developing Countries," in Dwight Perkins and Michael Roemer (eds.), *Reforming Economic Systems in Developing Countries.* Cambridge, Mass.: distributed by Harvard University Press, 1991, pp. 81–114.

Dwight H. Perkins and Michael Roemer (eds.). *Reforming Economic Systems in Developing Countries.* Cambridge, Mass.: distributed by Harvard University Press, 1991.

Alan Hodgart. *The Economics of European Imperialism.* New York: Norton, 1977.

Karl Marx. *Das Kapital.* 1867.

Joan Nelson. "Comparative Perspectives: The Politics of Economic Adjustment in Developing Nations," Washington, D.C., Overseas Development Council, 1988.

Robert I. Rhodes (ed.). *Imperialism and Underdevelopment: A Reader.* New York: Monthly Review Press, 1970.

Historical Heritage and Economic Development

Keith Hart. *The Political Economy of West African Agriculture.* New York: Cambridge University Press, 1982.

Albert O. Hirschman. "Ideologies of Economic Development in Latin America," in *A Bias for Hope.* New Haven, Conn.: Yale University Press, 1971.

Anthony G. Hopkins. *An Economic History of West Africa.* New York: Columbia University Press, 1973.

E. S. Mason, Mahn Je Kim, Dwight H. Perkins, Kwang Suk Kim, and David C. Cole. *The Economic and Social Modernization of the Republic of Korea.* Cambridge, Mass.: Harvard University Press, 1980.

D. H. Perkins (ed.). *China's Modern Economy in Historical Perspective.* Stanford, Calif.: Stanford University Press, 1975.

Chapter 3. Growth and Structural Change

Production Functions

World Bank. *World Tables 1983,* Vol. 1, Economic Data. Washington, D.C.: World Bank, 1983.

World Bank. *World Tables 1994.*

The Harrod-Domar Model

Evsey Domar. "Capital Expansion, Rate of Growth and Employment," *Econometrica,* 1946, pp. 137–47.

———. "Expansion and Employment," *American Economic Review,* 37 (1947), 34–55.

Roy F. Harrod. "An Essay in Dynamic Theory." *Economic Journal,* 1939, pp. 14–33.

The Changing Structure of Output

Hollis B. Chenery, Sherman Robinson, and Moshe Syrquin. *Industrialization and Growth: A Comparative Study.* London: Oxford University Press, 1986.

——— and Moises Syrquin. *Patterns of Development, 1950–1970.* London: Oxford University Press, 1975.

——— and Lance J. Taylor. "Development Patterns: Among Countries and Over Time," *Review of Economics and Statistics,* 50 (November 1968), 391–416.

Edward F. Denison. *Accounting for United States Economic Growth, 1929–1969.* Washington, D.C.: Brookings Institution, 1974.

Irving Kravis, Alan Heston, and Robert Summers. *International Comparisons of Real Product and Purchasing Power.* Baltimore: Johns Hopkins Press, 1978.

Dale Jorgenson, Frank Gallop, and Barbara Fraumeni. *Productivity and U.S. Economic Growth.* Cambridge, Mass.: Harvard University Press, 1987.

Simon Kuznets. *Economic Growth and Structure.* New York: Norton, 1965.

———. *Modern Economic Growth.* New Haven, Conn.: Yale University Press, 1966.

Dwight H. Perkins and Moshe Syrquin. "Large Countries: The Influence of Size," in Hollis B. Chenery and T. N. Srinivasan (eds.), *Handbook of Development Economics* Vol. 2. Amsterdam: North-Holland, 1989.

W. W. Rostow. *Theorists of Economic Growth from David Hume to the Present.* London: Oxford University Press, 1990, Part III.

Moshe Syrquin. "Patterns of Structural Change," in Hollis B. Chenery and T. N. Srinivasan (eds.), *Handbook of Development Economics* Vol. 1. Amsterdam: North-Holland, 1988.

Two-Sector Models

J. C. Fei and Gustav Ranis. *Development of Labor Surplus Economy.* Homewood, Ill.: Irwin, 1964.

Dale W. Jorgenson. "Testing Alternative Theories of the Development of a Dual Economy," in I. Adelman and E. Thorbecke (eds.), *The Theory and Design of Development.* Baltimore: Johns Hopkins Press, 1966.

W. Arthur Lewis. "Economic Development with Unlimited Supplies of Labor," *The Manchester School,* 22 (May 1954), 139–91.

———. *The Theory of Economic Growth.* Homewood, Ill.: Irwin, 1955.

Balanced versus Unbalanced Growth

Albert O. Hirschman. *The Strategy of Economic Development.* New Haven, Conn.: Yale University Press, 1958.

Ragnar Nurkse. *Problems of Capital Development in Underdeveloped Countries.* New York: Oxford University Press, 1953.

Paul N. Rosenstein-Rodan. "Problems of Industrialization of Eastern and South-eastern Europe," *Economic Journal,* June–September 1943; reprinted in A. N. Agarwala and S. P. Singh (eds.), *The Economics of Underdevelopment.* New York: Oxford University Press, 1963.

Chapter 4. Development and Human Welfare

Concepts and Measures

Gary S. Fields. *Poverty, Inequality and Development.* London: Cambridge University Press, 1960.

Charles R. Frank, Jr., and Richard C. Webb (eds.). *Income Distribution and Growth in the Less-Developed Countries.* Washington, D.C.: Brookings Institution, 1977.

Allen C. Kelley. "The Human Development Index: Handle with Care," *Population and Development Review,* 17, no. 2 (1991), 315–24.

Morris David Morris. *Measuring the Condition of the World's Poor. The Physical Quality of Life Index.* Elmsford, N.Y.: Pergamon Press for the Overseas Development Council, 1979.

Dudley Sears. "The Meaning of Development," in Charles K. Wilber (ed.), *The Political Economy of Development and Underdevelopment.* New York: Random House, 1973.

Amartya K. Sen. *On Economic Inequality.* New York: Norton, 1973.

Richard Szal and Sherman Robinson. "Measuring Economic Inequality," in *Income Distribution and Growth in the Less-Developed Countries.* Washington, D.C.: Brookings Institution, 1977, pp. 491–533.

United Nations Development Program. *Human Development Report.* New York: Oxford University Press, annual 1990–1994.

Wouter van Ginneken and Jong-goo Park (eds.). *Generating Internationally Comparable Income Distribution Measures.* Geneva: International Labor Office, 1984.

Patterns of Inequality and Poverty

Irma Adelman and Cynthia Taft Morris. *Economic Growth and Social Equity in Developing Countries.* Stanford, Calif.: Stanford University Press, 1973.

——— and Sherman Robinson. *Income Distribution Policy in Developing Countries. A Case Study of Korea.* Stanford, Calif.: Stanford University Press, 1978.

Montek S. Ahluwalia. "Income Inequality: Some Dimensions of the Problem," in Hollis Chenery et al. (eds.), *Redistribution with Growth.* New York: Oxford University Press, 1974, pp. 3–37.

———. "Inequality, Poverty and Development," *Journal of Development Economics,* 3 (1976).

Gary S. Fields. "Changes in Poverty and Inequality in Developing Countries," *The World Bank Research Observer,* 4, no. 2 (July 1989), 167–85.

Frida Johansen. "Poverty Reduction in East Asia. The Silent Revolution," World Bank Discussion Paper No. 203, 1993.

Simon Kuznets. "Economic Growth and Income Inequality," *American Economic Review,* 45, no. 1 (March 1955).

Gustav F. Papanek and Oldrich Kyn. "The Effect on Income Distribution of Development, the Growth Rate and Economic Strategy," *Journal of Development Economics,* 23 (1986), 55–65.

Susan M. Randolph and William F. Lott. "Can the Kuznets Effect Be Relied on to Induce Equalizing Growth?" *World Development,* 21, no. 5 (May 1993), 829–40.

World Bank. *World Development Report 1990* [special issue on poverty]. New York: Oxford University Press, 1990.

Theories of Inequality and Poverty

William R. Cline. "Distribution and Development: A Survey of the Literature," *Journal of Development Economics,* 1975, pp. 359–400.

W. Arthur Lewis. "Economic Development with Unlimited Supplies of Labor," *Manchester School,* 22 (1954).

Strategies for Growth with Equity

Entisham Ahmad and Yan Wang, "Inequality and Poverty in China: Institutional Change and Public Policy, 1978–1988," *World Bank Economic Review,* 5, no. 2 (1991), 231–58.

Hollis Chenery et al. (eds.). *Redistribution with Growth.* London: Oxford University Press, 1974.

Giovanni Andrea Cornia, Richard Jolly, and Frances Stewart (eds.). *Adjustment with a Human Face,* 2 vol. London: Oxford University Press (Clarendon), 1987.

International Labor Office. *Employment, Growth and Basic Needs: A One-World Problem.* New York: Praeger, 1977.

John Mellor. *The New Economics of Growth: A Strategy for India and the Developing World.* Ithaca, N.Y.: Cornell University Press, 1976.

Rati Ram. "The Role of Real Income Level and Income Distribution in Fulfillment of Basic Needs," *World Development,* 13, no. 5 (May 1985), 589–94.

T. N. Srinivasan, "Development, Poverty and Basic Human Needs: Some Issues," *Food Research Institute Studies,* 16, no. 2 (1977), 11–28.

CHAPTER 5. GUIDING DEVELOPMENT: MARKETS VERSUS CONTROLS

The March toward Markets

Bela Balassa. "Exports and Economic Growth: Further Evidence," *Journal of Development Economics,* 5, no. 2 (1978), 181–89.

Jagdish Bhagwati. *Foreign Exchange Regimes and Economic Development: Anatomy and Consequences of Exchange Control Regimes.* Cambridge, Mass.: Ballinger Press, 1978.

Henry J. Bruton. "The Import Substitution Strategy of Economic Development." *The Pakistan Development Review,* 10 (1970), 123–46.

Anne O. Krueger. *Foreign Exchange Regimes and Economic Development: Liberalization Attempts and Consequences.* Cambridge, Mass.: Ballinger Press, 1978.

———. "The Political Economy of Rent-Seeking," *American Economic Review,* 64, no. 3 (1974), 291–303.

Ian M. D. Little. *Economic Theory, Policy, and International Relations.* New York: Basic Books, 1982.

———, Tibor Scitovsky, and Maurice Scott. *Industry and Trade in Some Developing Countries.* London: Oxford University Press, 1970.

Ragnar Nurkse. *Equilibrium Growth and the World Economy.* Cambridge, Mass.: Harvard University Press, 1961.

Jeffrey Sachs and Andrew Warner. "Economic Convergence and Economic Policies," Harvard Institute for International Development, Development Discussion Paper No. 502, March 1995.

Theodore W. Schultz. *Transforming Traditional Agriculture.* New Haven, Conn.: Yale University Press, 1964.

Hans W. Singer. "The Distribution of Trade between Investing and Borrowing Countries," *American Economic Review,* 40 (1950), 470–85.

Moshe Syrquin and Hollis Chenery. "Three Decades of Industrialization," *World Bank Economic Review,* 3, no. 2 (1989), 145–81.

United Nations (by Raul Prebisch). *The Economic Development of Latin America and its Principal Problems.* Lake Success, N.Y.: 1950.

World Bank. *The East Asian Miracle: Economic Growth and Public Policy.* London: Oxford University Press, 1993.

Implementing Market Reforms

Maxim Boyco, Andrei Shleifer, and Robert Vishny. *Privatizing Russia.* Cambridge, Mass.: MIT Press, 1995.

Armeane M. Choksi and Demetrius Papageorgiou (eds.). *Economic Liberalization in Developing Countries.* New York: Blackwell, 1986.

Sebastian Edwards and Sweder van Wijnbergen. "Disequilibrium and Structural Adjustment," in Hollis Chenery and T. N. Srinivasan (eds.), *Handbook of Development Economics,* Vol. 2. Amsterdam: North-Holland, 1989, pp. 1481–533.

Stanley Fischer. "The Role of Macroeconomic Factors in Growth," *Journal of Monetary Economics,* 32 (1993), 485–512.

Tony Killick (ed.). *The Quest for Economic Stabilization: The IMF and the Third World.* London: Heinemann, 1984.

Janos Kornai. *The Road to a Free Economy.* New York: Norton, 1990.

David Lindauer and Michael Roemer. *Asia and Africa: Legacies and Opportunities in Development.* San Francisco: ICS Press, 1994.

Juan Antonio Morales and Jeffrey D. Sachs. "Bolivia's Economic Crisis," in J. D. Sachs (ed.), *Developing Country Debt and the World Economy.* Chicago: University of Chicago Press, 1989, pp. 57–79.

Joan M. Nelson. "The Political Economy of Stabilization: Commitment, Capacity and Public Response," *World Development,* 12, no. 10 (1984), 983–1006.

——— et al. *Fragile Coalitions: the Politics of Economic Adjustment.* Washington, D.C.: Overseas Development Council, 1989.

——— (ed.). *Economic Crisis and Policy Choice: The Politics of Adjustment in the Third World.* Princeton, N. J.: Princeton University Press, 1990.

Mancur Olsen. *The Rise and Decline of Nations.* New Haven, Conn.: Yale University Press, 1982.

Theodore Panayotou. *Green Markets: The Economics of Sustainable Development.* San Francisco: ICS Press, 1993.

Dwight H. Perkins. "Reforming China's Economic System," *Journal of Economic Literature,* 26, no. 2 (June 1988), 601–45.

———. "Completing China's Move to the Market," *Journal of Economic Perspectives,* 8, no. 2 (Spring 1994), 23–46.

——— and Michael Roemer. *Reforming Economic Systems in Developing Countries.* Cambridge, Mass.: Harvard University Press, 1991.

Jeffrey D. Sachs. "The Bolivian Hyperinflation and Stabilization," *American Economic Review,* 77, no. 2 (May 1987), 279–83.

Paul Streeten. "Structural Adjustment: A Survey of the Issues and Options," *World Development,* 15, no. 12 (December 1987), 1469–82.

Lance J. Taylor. *Varieties of Stabilization Experience: Toward Sensible Macroeconomics in the Third World.* London: Oxford University Press (Clarendon), 1988.

Raymond Vernon (ed.). *The Promise of Privitization: A Challenge for American Foreign Policy.* New York: Council on Foreign Relations, 1988.

John Williamson (ed.). *IMF Conditionality.* Washington, D.C.: Institute for International Economics, 1983.

World Bank. *Accelerated Development in Sub-Saharan Africa.* Washington, D.C.: World Bank, 1981.

———. *World Development Report 1989* (on financial systems reform). New York: Oxford University Press, 1989.
———. *World Development Report 1991*. London: Oxford University Press, 1991.

Chapter 6. Planning Models

Keynesian Models

Jere Behrman and James Hanson. *Short-Term Macroeconomic Policy in Latin America*. Cambridge, Mass.: National Bureau of Economic Research, 1979.
Hollis Chenery and Alan Strout. "Foreign Assistance and Economic Development," *American Economic Review*, 56 (1966), 679–733.
Ronald McKinnon. "Foreign Exchange Constraints and Economic Development," *Economic Journal*, 74 (1964), 388–409.
Lance J. Taylor. "Theoretical Foundations and Technical Implications," in C. R. Blitzer et al. (eds.), *Economy-wide Models and Development Planning*. London: Oxford University Press, 1975, pp. 33–109.
———. *Macro Models for Developing Countries*. New York: McGraw-Hill, 1979.
Jan Tinbergen. *Economic Policy: Principles and Design*. Amsterdam: North-Holland, 1956.
———. *Central Planning*. New Haven, Conn.: Yale University Press, 1976.

Interindustry and General Equilibrium Models

Hollis Chenery and Paul Clark. *Interindustry Economics*. New York: Wiley, 1959.
Kemal Dervis, Jaime de Melo, and Sherman Robinson. *General Equilibrium Models for Developing Countries*. London: Cambridge University Press, 1982.
Robert Dorfman, Paul Samuelson, and Robert Solow. *Linear Programming and Economic Analysis*. New York: McGraw-Hill, 1958.
Graham Pyatt and Erik Thorbecke. *Planning Techniques for a Better Future*. Geneva: International Labor Office, 1976.
Sherman Robinson. "Multisectoral Models," in Hollis B. Chenery and T. N. Srinivasan (eds.), *Handbook of Development Economics*, Vol. 2. Amsterdam: North-Holland, 1989, pp. 885–947.

Project Appraisal

Arnold Harberger. *Project Evaluation: Collected Papers*. Chicago: Markham, 1974.
I. M. D. Little and James A. Mirrlees. *Project Appraisal and Planning for Developing Countries*. New York: Basic Books, 1974.
Michael Roemer and Joseph J. Stern. *Cases in Economic Development*. London: Butterworths, 1981.
——— and ———. *The Appraisal of Development Projects*. New York: Praeger, 1975.
United Nations Industrial Development Organization by P. Dasgupta, S. Margolin, and A. Sen. *Guidelines for Project Evaluation*. New York: United Nations, 1982.

Jeffrey Sachs and Andrew Warner. "Natural Resources and Economic Growth," Harvard Institute for International Development, February 1995.

Market Failures

Edward B. Barbier. *Economics, Natural Resource Scarcity and Development.* London: Earthscan Publications Limited, 1989.

John M. Hartwick and Nancy D. Olewiler. *The Economics of Natural Resource Use.* New York: Harper & Row, 1986.

Harold Hotelling. "The Economics of Exhaustable Resources," *Journal of Political Economy,* 39 (1931), 137–75.

Tom Tietenberg. *Environmental and Natural Resource Economics.* Glenview, Ill: Scott Foresman, 1988.

Policy Solutions and Policy Failures

Robert Coase. "The Problem of Social Cost," *Journal of Law and Economics,* 3 (October 1960), 1–44.

John A. Dixon and Maynard M. Hufschmidt (eds.). *Valuation Techniques for the Environment.* Baltimore: Johns Hopkins Press, 1986, pp. 121–40.

Bjorn Larsen and Anwar Shah. "World Fossil Fuel Subsidies and Global Carbon Emissions," World Bank, Working Paper WPS 1002, October 1992.

Theodore Panayotou. *Green Markets: The Economics of Sustainable Development.* San Francisco: ICS Press, 1993.

———. "Conservation of Biodiversity and Economic Development: The Concept of Transferable Development Rights," *Environmental and Resource Economics,* 4 (1994), 91–110.

David W. Pearce and R. Kerry Turner. *Economics of Natural Resources and the Environment.* Baltimore: Johns Hopkins Press, 1990.

Paul R. Portney. "The Contingent Valuation Debate: Why Economists Should Care," *Journal of Economic Perspectives,* 8, no. 4 (1994), 3–17.

Robert Repetto and Malcolm Gillis (eds.). *Public Policies and the Misuse of Forest Resources.* London: Cambridge University Press, 1988.

Jeffrey R. Vincent. "Reducing Effluent While Raising Affluence: Water Pollution Abatement in Malaysia," Harvard Institute for International Development, March 1993.

Jeffrey Vincent. "The Tropical Timber Trade and Sustainable Development," *Science,* 256 (1992), 1651–55.

Measuring Sustainability

Yusuf J. Ahmad, Salah El Serafy, and Ernst Lutz (eds.). *Environmental Accounting for Sustainable Development.* Washington, D.C.: World Bank, 1990.

Ernst Lutz (ed.). *Toward Improved Accounting for the Environment.* Washington, D.C.: World Bank, 1993.

Jeffrey Vincent and Rozali bin Mohamed Ali. *Natural Resources, Environment, and Development in Malaysia: An Economic Perspective,* unpublished manuscript, 1994.

Global Sustainability

Robin Broad. "The Poor and the Environment: Friends or Foes?" *World Development,* 22, no. 6 (June 1994), 811–22.

Irving M. Mintzer (ed.). *Confronting Climate Change.* London: Cambridge University Press, 1992.

Theodore Panayotou. "Financing Mechanisms for Agenda 21," Harvard Institute for International Development, March 1994.

Mary Tiffen and Michael Mortimore. "Malthus Controverted: The Role of Capital and Technology in Growth and Environment Recovery in Kenya," *World Development,* 22, no. 7 (July 1994), 997–1010.

World Bank. *World Development Report 1992.* Washington, D.C.: World Bank, 1992.

World Commission on Environment and Development (The Brundtland Commission). *Our Common Future.* New York: Oxford University Press, 1987.

World Resources Institute. *World Resources 1992–1993.* New York: Oxford University Press, 1992.

CHAPTER 8. POPULATION

A Brief History of Human Population

Lester R. Brown. *In the Human Interest.* New York: Norton, 1974.

Carlo Cipolla. *The Economic History of World Population.* 7th ed.; New York: Barnes & Noble, 1978.

The Demographic Future

Thomas W. Merrick. "World Population in Transition," *Population Bulletin,* 41, no. 2 (January 1988), 8–16.

The Causes of Population Growth

Gary Becker. *A Treatise on the Family.* Cambridge, Mass.: Harvard University Press, 1981.

John C. Caldwell. "The Soft Underbelly of Development: Demographic Transition in Conditions of Limited Economic Change," *Proceedings of the World Bank Annual Conference on Development Economics 1990,* pp. 207–69.

———. "Toward a Restatement of Demographic Transition Theory," *Population and Development Review,* 2, nos. 3–4 (September–December 1976), 225–55.

Richard Easterlin. "Modernization and Fertility: A Critical Essay," in R. Bulatao and R. Lee (eds.), *Determinants of Fertility in Developing Countries,* Vol. 2. New York: Academic Press, 1983, pp. 562–86.

Michael S. Teitelbaum. "Relevance of Demographic Transition Theory for Developing Countries," *Science,* 188 (May 2, 1977), 420–25.

Analyzing the Effects of Rapid Population Growth

Nancy Birdsall. "Economic Approaches to Population," in Hollis B. Chenery and

T. N. Srinivasan (eds.), *Handbook of Development Economics,* Vol. 1. Amsterdam: North-Holland, 1988, pp. 477–542.

Ester Boserup. *Economic and Demographic Relationships in Development.* Baltimore: Johns Hopkins Press, 1990.

Colin Clark. "The 'Population Explosion' Myth," *Bulletin of the Institute of Development Studies* (Sussex, England), May 1969.

———. "The Economics of Population Growth and Control: A Comment," *Review of Social Economy,* 28, no. 1 (March 1970).

Ansley J. Coale and Edgar M. Hoover. *Population Growth and Economic Development in Low-Income Countries: A Case Study of India's Prospects.* Princeton, N.J.: Princeton University Press, 1958.

Rati Ram and Theodore W. Schultz. "Life Span, Savings, and Productivity," *Economic Development and Cultural Change,* 27, no. 3 (April 1979), 394–421.

Julian Simon. *Theory of Population and Economic Growth.* Oxford: Blackwell, 1986.

———. *The Ultimate Resource.* Princeton, N.J.: Princeton University Press, 1981.

Population Policy

Nick Eberstadt. "Recent Declines in Fertility in Less-Developed Countries and What 'Population Planners' May Learn from Them," *World Development,* 11, no. 3 (March 1985), 113–38.

"Fertility and Family Planning Surveys: An Update," *Population Reports* ser. M, no. 8, Baltimore, Johns Hopkins Press, September–October 1985.

Marshall Green. "The Evolution of US International Population Policy, 1965–92: A Chronological Account," *Population and Development Review,* 19, no. 2 (June 1993), 303–21.

W. Parker Mauldin and Bernard Berelson. "Conditions of Fertility Decline in Developing Countries, 1965–75," *Studies in Family Planning,* 9, no. 5 (1978).

National Academy of Sciences. *Population Growth and Economic Development: Policy Questions.* Washington, D.C.: National Academy Press, 1986.

John A. Ross, W. Parker Mauldin, S. R. Green, and E. Romana Cooke. *Family Planning and Child Survival Programs as Assessed in 1991.* New York: Population Council, 1992.

World Bank. *World Development Report 1984.* New York: Oxford University Press, 1984, pp. 51–206.

Chapter 9. Labor's Role

Analyzing Employment Issues

George A. Akerlof and Janet L. Yellen (eds.). *Efficiency Wage Models of the Labor Force.* London: Cambridge University Press, 1986, "Introduction," pp. 1–21.

Albert Berry. "The Labor Market and Human Capital in LDCs," in Norman Gemmell (ed.), *Surveys in Development Economics.* Oxford: Blackwell, 1987, pp. 205–35.

Albert Berry and R. H. Sabot. "Unemployment and Economic Development," *Economic Development and Cultural Change,* 33, no. 1 (October 1984), 99–116.

Peter Gregory. "An Assessment of Changes in Employment Conditions in Less Developed Countries," *Economic Development and Cultural Change,* 28, no. 4 (July 1980), 673–700.

International Labor Office. *Towards Full Employment.* Geneva: International Labor Organization, 1970.

Lawrence F. Katz. "Efficiency Wage Theories: A Partial Evaluation," *NBER Macroeconomics Annual 1986.* Cambridge, Mass.: National Bureau of Economic Research, 1986, pp. 235–76.

Dipak Mazumdar. "The Urban Informal Sector," *World Development,* 4, no. 8 (August 1976), 655–79.

Mark Rosenzweig. "Labor Markets in Low-Income Countries," in Hollis B. Chenery and T. N. Srinivasan (eds.), *Handbook of Development Economics,* Vol. 1. Amsterdam: North-Holland, 1989, pp. 713–62.

Joseph E. Stiglitz. "Economic Organization, Information and Development," in Chenery and Srinivasan, *Handbook of Development Economics,* Vol. 1, pp. 93–160.

Labor Reallocation

Jagdish Bhagwati and Martin Partington. *Taxing the Brain Drain: A Proposal.* Amsterdam: North-Holland, 1976.

John R. Harris and Michael P. Todaro. "Migration, Unemployment and Development: A Two-Sector Analysis," *American Economic Review,* 60 (March 1970), 126–42.

Ragnar Nurkse. *Problems of Capital Formation in Underdeveloped Countries.* Oxford: Blackwell, 1957; first published in 1953.

Jeffrey G. Williamson. "Migration and Urbanization," in Chenery and Srinivasan, *Handbook of Development Economics,* Vol. 1, pp. 425–65.

Employment Policy

Henry Bruton, "Technology Choice and Factor Proportions Problems in JDCs," in Norman Gemmell (ed.), *Surveys in Development Economics.* Oxford: Blackwell, 1987, pp. 236–65.

S. J. Burki et al. "Public Works Programs in Developing Countries: A Comparative Analysis," World Bank Staff Working Paper No. 224, February 1976.

Edgar O. Edwards (ed.). *Employment in Developing Nations.* New York: Columbia University Press, 1974.

Richard B. Freeman. "Labor Market Institutions and Policies: Help or Hindrance to Economic Development?" in *Proceedings of the World Bank Annual Conference on Development Economics 1992,* pp. 117–44.

Howard Pack and Larry E. Westphal. "Industrial Strategy and Technological Change: Theory versus Reality," *Journal of Development Economics,* 22 (1986), 87–128.

Lyn Squire. *Employment Policy in Developing Countries: A Survey of Issues and Evidence.* New York: Oxford University Press for the World Bank, 1981.

Frances Stewart. "Technology and Employment in LDCs," in Edwards, *Employment in Developing Nations,* pp. 83–132.

Susumu Watanabe. "Exports and Employment: The Case of the Republic of Korea," *International Labour Review,* 106, no. 6 (December 1972), 495–526.

Louis T. Wells. "Economic Man and Engineering Man: Choice of Technology in a Low-Wage Country," in C. Peter Timmer et al. (eds.), *The Choice of Technology in Developing Countries: Some Cautionary Tales.* Cambridge,

Mass.: Harvard University Center for International Affairs, 1975, pp. 69–93.

Larry E. Westphal. "Fostering Technological Mastery by Means of Selective Infant-Industry Protection," in Simon Teitel (ed.), *Trade, Stability, Technology and Equity in Latin America.* New York: Academic Press, 1982, pp. 255–79.

Larry E. Westphal, Linsu Kim, and Carl J. Dahlman. "Reflections on the Republic of Korea's Acquisition of Technological Capability," in Nathan Rosenberg and Claudio Frischtak (eds.), *International Technology Transfer: Concepts, Measures, and Comparisons.* New York: Praeger, 1985, pp. 167–221.

Lawrence White. *Industrial Concentration and Economic Power in Pakistan.* Princeton, N.J.: Princeton University Press, 1974.

CHAPTER 10. EDUCATION

Importance of Education

George Psacharopoulos and Maureen Woodhall. *Education for Development: An Analysis of Investment Choices.* New York: Oxford University Press, 1985.

Theodore W. Schultz. "Investment in Human Capital," *American Economic Review,* 51 (January 1961), 1–17.

World Bank. *World Development Report 1980.* New York: Oxford University Press, 1980.

Trends and Patterns

M. Blaug, R. Layard, and M. Woodhall. *Causes of Graduate Unemployment in India.* Harmondsworth, England: Penguin, 1969.

Martin Carnoy. "Rate of Return to Schooling in Latin America," *Journal of Human Resources,* Summer 1967, pp. 359–74.

Russell Davis. "Planning Education for Development," Harvard Institute for International Development, Development Discussion Paper No. 60, June 1979.

World Bank. *Primary Education. A World Bank Policy Paper.* Washington, D.C.: World Bank, 1990.

Education's Role in Development

Mark Blaug. "The Empirical Status of Human Capital Theory: A Slightly Jaundiced Survey," *Journal of Economic Literature,* 14, no. 3 (September 1976), 827–55.

M. Boissiere, J. B. Knight, and R. H. Sabot. "Earnings, Schooling, Ability, and Cognitive Skills," *American Economic Review,* 75, no. 5 (December 1985), 1016–30.

Philip H. Coombs with Manzoor Ahmed. *Attacking Rural Poverty: How Nonformal Education Can Help.* Baltimore: Johns Hopkins Press, 1974.

Ronald Dore. *The Diploma Disease. Education, Qualification and Development.* Berkeley: University of California Press, 1976.

Philip J. Foster. "The Vocational School Fallacy in Development Planning," in C. A. Anderson and M. J. Bowman (eds.), *Education and Economic Development.* Chicago: Aldine, 1966, pp. 142–63.

Paolo Freire. *Pedagogy of the Oppressed,* translated from the Portuguese by Myra Bergman Ramos. New York: Seabury Press, 1970.

Robert H. Haveman and Barbara L. Wolfe. "Schooling and Economic Well-Being: The Role of Non-Market Effects," *Journal of Human Resources,* 19, no. 3 (1984), 377–407.

Arthur Hazlewood et al. *Education, Work, and Pay in East Africa.* London: Oxford University Press (Clarendon), 1990.

Ivan Ilich. *Deschooling Society.* New York: Harper & Row, 1970.

Emmanuel Jiminez. "The Public Subsidization of Education and Health in Developing Countries. A Review of Equity and Efficiency," *World Bank Research Observer,* 1, no. 1 (January 1986), 111–29.

John B. Knight and Richard H. Sabot. *Education, Productivity, and Inequality. The East African Experience.* New York: Oxford University Press for the World Bank, 1990.

Herbert S. Parnes. *Forecasting Educational Needs for Economic Development,* Mediterranean Regional Project. Paris: Organisation for Economic Cooperation and Development, 1962.

George Psacharopoulos. "Education and Development: A Further International Update and Implications," *Journal of Human Resources,* 20, no. 4 (1985), 583–604.

———. "Education and Development: A Review," *World Bank Research Observer,* 3, no. 1 (January 1988.).

———. "Returns to Investment in Education: A Global Update," *World Development,* 22, no. 9 (September, 1994); 1325–43.

T. Paul Schultz. "Education Investments and Returns," in Hollis B. Chenery and T. N. Srinivasan (eds.), *Handbook of Development Economics,* Vol. 1. Amsterdam: North-Holland, 1989, pp. 543–630.

Theodore W. Schultz. "The Value of the Ability to Deal with Disequilibrium," *Journal of Economic Literature,* 13, no. 3 (September 1975), 837–46.

Jan Tinbergen and H. C. Bos. "A Planning Model for the Educational Requirements of Economic Development," in *Econometric Models for Education.* Paris: Organisation for Economic Cooperation and Development, 1965.

UNESCO. *Statistical Yearbook 1993.* Paris: UNESCO, 1994.

United Nations Programme. *Human Development Report 1993.* New York: Oxford University Press, 1994. "Overview," pp. 1–8, and "Assessing Human Development," pp. 10–20.

World Bank. *Financing Education in Developing Countries. An Exploration of Policy Options.* Washington, D.C.: World Bank, 1986.

———. *World Development Report 1991.* New York: Oxford University Press for the World Bank, 1991, pp. 42–51, 52–69.

Chapter 11. Health and Nutrition

Health in Developing Countries

Samuel H. Preston. "The Changing Relationship between Mortality and Level of Development," *Population Studies,* 29, no. 2 (January 1975), 231–48.

———. *Mortality Patterns in National Population, with Special Reference to Recorded Causes of Death.* New York: Academic Press, 1976.

Amartya Sen. "More than 100 Million Women are Missing," *New York Review of Books,* December 20, 1990, pp. 61–66.

United Nations Children's Fund (UNICEF). *The State of the World's Children.* New York: Oxford University Press, annual.

World Bank. *Health Sector Policy Paper.* 2d ed.; Washington, D.C.: World Bank, 1980.

Effects of Health on Development

Jere R. Behrman and Anil B. Deolalikar. "Health and Nutrition," in Hollis B. Chenery and T. N. Srinivasan (eds.), *Handbook of Development Economics,* Vol. 1. Amsterdam: North-Holland, pp. 631–711.

Jere R. Behrman. "Health and Economic Growth: Theory, Evidence, and Policy," in *Macroeconomic Environment and Health.* Geneva: World Health Organization, 1993, pp. 21–61.

Richard Feuchem et al. *Water, Health and Development: An Interdisciplinary Evaluation.* London: Tri-Med Books, 1974, Chap. 9.

Selma Mushkin. "Health as an Investment," *Journal of Political Economy,* 70, no. 5, part 2 (Supplement, October 1962), 129–57.

C. Peter Timmer. "Food Policy, Food Consumption, and Nutrition," Harvard Institute for International Development, Development Discussion Paper No. 124, October 1981.

Malnutrition

Jere R. Behrman, Anil B. Deolalikar, and Barbara L. Wolfe. "Nutrients: Impacts and Determinants," *World Bank Economic Review,* 2, no. 3 (September 1988), 299–320.

Alan Berg. *The Nutrition Factor: Its Role in National Development.* Washington, D.C.: Brookings Institution, 1973.

———. *Malnutrition. What Can Be Done? Lessons from World Bank Experience.* Baltimore: Johns Hopkins Press for the World Bank, 1987.

——— and James Austin. "Nutritional Policies and Programs: A Decade of Redirection," *Food Policy,* 9, no. 4 (November 1984), 304–12.

Thomas T. Poleman. "Quantifying the Nutritional Situation in Developing Countries," *Food Research Institute Studies,* 18, no. 1 (1981), 1–58.

Shlomo Reutlinger. "Malnutrition: A Poverty Problem or a Food Problem?" *World Development,* 5, no. 8 (August 1977), 715–24.

——— and Marcelo Selowsky. *Malnutrition and Poverty: Magnitude and Policy Options.* World Bank Occasional Papers No. 23, Baltimore, Johns Hopkins Press, 1976.

Amartya Sen. "Ingredients of Famine Analysis: Availability and Entitlements," *Quarterly Journal of Economics,* 96, no. 3 (August 1981), 433–64.

C. Peter Timmer, Walter P. Falcon, and Scott R. Pearson. *Food Policy Analysis.* Baltimore: Johns Hopkins Press, 1983.

Medical Services

Frederick Golladay and Bernhard Liese. "Health Problems and Policies in Developing Countries," World Bank Staff Working Paper No. 412, August 1980.

James Kocher and Richard Cash. "Achieving Health and Nutritional Objectives within a Basic Needs Framework," Harvard Institute for International Development, Development Discussion Paper No. 55, March 1979.

Michael Lipton. *Why Poor People Stay Poor: Urban Bias in World Development.* Cambridge, Mass.: Harvard University Press, 1977.

Sources of Savings

International Monetary Fund. *Government Financial Statistics Yearbook 1989.* Washington D.C.: International Monetary Fund, 1990.

Raymond F. Mikesell and James E. Zinser. "The Nature of the Savings Function in Developing Countries: A Survey of the Theoretical and Empirical Literature," *Journal of Economic Literature,* 11, no. 1 (March 1973), 1–26.

Stanley Please. "Savings Through Taxation: Reality or Mirage?" *Finance and Development,* 4, no. 1 (March 1967), pp. 24–32.

Alan Tait, Wilfred Gratz, and Barry Eichengreen. "International Comparisons of Taxation for Selected Developing Countries," *International Monetary Fund Staff Papers* 26, no. 1, March 1979, pp. 123–56.

Vito Tanzi. "Quantitative Characteristics of Tax Systems in Developing Countries," in David Newbery and Nicholas Stern (eds.), *Modern Tax Theory for Developing Countries.* Forthcoming.

Determinants of Private Savings

Ranadev Banerji. "Small-Scale Production Units in Manufacturing: An International Cross-Section Overview," *Weltwirtschaftliches Archiv,* 114, no. 1 (1978).

Angus Deaton. "Saving in Developing Countries: Theory and Review," *Proceedings of the World Bank Annual Conference on Development Economics,* 1989.

Robert H. Frank. "The Demand for Unobservable and other Non-Positional Goods," *American Economic Review,* 75 (March 1985).

Fortune Magazine. Various issues 1980–1995.

Nicholas Kaldor. "Problems Economicas de Chile," *El Trimestre Economico,* 26, no. 102 (April–June 1959), 193, 211–12.

Philip Musgrove. "Income Distribution and Aggregate Consumption Function." *Journal of Political Economy,* 2, no. 88 (June 1980), 504–25.

Constantino Lluch, Alan Powell, and Ross Williams. *Patterns in Household Demand and Savings.* New York: Oxford University Press, 1977.

F. Modigliani, R. Brumberg, and A. Ando. "Life Cycle Hypothesis of Savings: Aggregate Implication and Tests," *American Economic Review,* 52, no. 3 (1963).

Roger S. Smith. "Factors Affecting Saving, Policy Tools and Tax Reform: A Review," *International Monetary Fund Working Paper* No. 89/47, May 23, 1989, Table 2.

Donald Snodgrass and Tyler Biggs. *Industrialization and the Small Firm: Patterns and Policies.* San Francisco: ICS Press, forthcoming.

International Mobility of Capital and Domestic Saving Mobilization

Ranadev Banerji. "Small-Scale Production Units in Manufacturing: an International Cross Section Overview," *Weltwirtschafliches Archiv,* 114, no. 1 (1978).

Jeremy Greenwood and Kent Kimbrough. "Capital Controls and the World Economy," *Canadian Journal of Economics,* 19, no. 2 (1986), 111–16.

Arnold Harberger. "Vignettes on the World Capital Market," *American Economic Review,* 70, no. 2 (May 1980), 331–37.

Larry Summers. "Issues in National Savings Policy," *National Bureau of Economic Research Working Paper* No. 1710, Cambridge, Mass., September 1985.

CHAPTER 13. FISCAL POLICY

Expenditure Policies and Public Saving

Anita Bhatia. "Military Expenditures and Economic Growth," Washington, D.C., World Bank, 1987.
Malcolm Gillis. "Tacit Taxes and Sub-Rosa Subsidies," in Richard Bird (ed.), *More Taxing Than Taxes.* San Francisco: ICS Press, 1991.
Peter Heller. "Underfinancing of Recurrent Development Costs," *Finance and Development,* 16, no. 1 (March 1979), 38–41.
Norman Hicks. "Expenditure Reductions in Developing Countries," Washington, D.C., World Bank, 1988.
International Monetary Fund. *Government Finance Statistics Yearbook 1994.* Washington D.C.; 1994, pp. 46–47.
R. P. Short. "The Role of the Public Enterprises: An International Statistical Comparison," IMF, Dept. Memo 83/34, Washington, D.C., 1983.

Tax Policy and Public Saving

James Alm, Roy Bahl, and Matthew Murray. "Tax Base Erosion in Developing Countries," *Economic Development and Cultural Change,* 39, no. 4 (July 1991), 849–72.
Richard Bird and Oliver Oldman (eds.). *Readings on Taxation in Developing Countries.* 3d ed.; Baltimore: Johns Hopkins Press, 1975.
John F. Due. "Some Unresolved Issues in Design and Implementation of Value-Added Taxes," *National Tax Journal,* 42, no. 4 (December 1990), 383–98.
——— and Raymond Mikesell. *Sales Taxation: State and Local Structure and Administration.* Baltimore: Johns Hopkins Press, 1983.
Dwight R. Lee and Richard B. McKenzie. "The International Political Economy of Declining Tax Rates," *National Tax Journal,* 42, no. 2 (March 1989), 79-87.
Malcolm Gillis. "Tacit Taxes and Sub-Rosa Subsidies," in Richard Bird (ed.), *More Taxing Than Taxes.* San Francisco: ICS Press, 1991.
——— (ed.). *Tax Reform in Developing Countries.* Durham, N.C.: Duke University Press, 1989.
———. "Federal Sales Taxation: Six Decades of Experience," *Canadian Tax Journal,* January–February 1985.
——— and Charles E. McLure, Jr. "Taxation and Income Distribution: The Colombian Tax Reform of 1974," *Journal of Development Economics,* 5, no. 3 (September 1978), 237, 249.
Omkar Goswami, Amal Sanyal, and Ira N. Gang. "Taxes, Corruption and Bribes: A Model of Indian Public Finance," in Michael Roemer and Christine Jones (eds.), *Markets in Developing Countries: Parallel, Fragmented and Black.* San Francisco: ICS Press, 1991, pp. 201–13.
Arnold C. Harberger. "Principles of Taxation Applied to Developing Countries:

What Have We Learned?" in Michael Boskin and Charles E. McLure, Jr., *World Tax Reform: Case Studies of Developed and Developing Countries.* San Francisco: ICS Press, 1990.

IFPRI Report 8, no. 1, January 1986.

International Monetary Fund. *Government Finance Statistics Yearbook.* Washington, D.C.: International Monetary Fund, various years, country tables.

Glenn P. Jenkins. "Tax Reform: Lessons Learned," in Dwight H. Perkins and Michael Roemer (eds.). *Reforming Economic Systems in Developing Countries.* Cambridge, Mass.: Harvard Institute for International Development, 1991.

———. "Economic Reform and Institutional Innovation," April 11, 1995, unpublished paper.

Richard A. Musgrave et al. *Fiscal Reform in Bolivia: Final Report and Staff Papers of the Bolivian Mission on Tax Reform.* Cambridge, Mass.: Harvard Law School, International Tax Program, 1981.

Joseph A. Pechman (ed.). *World Tax Reform: A Progress Report.* Washington, D.C.: Brookings Institute, 1988, "Introduction," p. 13.

Robert Repetto and Malcolm Gillis (eds.). *Public Policies and the Misuse of Forest Resources.* New York: Cambridge University Press, 1988, "Conclusions," Chap. 10.

Carl Shoup. "Choosing Among Types of VAT," in M. Gillis, C. Shoup, and Gerry Sicat (eds.), *Value-Added Taxation in Developing Countries.* Washington, D.C.: World Bank, 1990.

Carlos A. Silvani and Alberto H. J. Radano. "Tax Administration Reform in Bolivia and Uruguay," in Richard M. Bird and Milka Casanegra de Jantscher (eds.). *Improving Tax Administration in Developing Countries.* Washington, D.C.: International Monetary Fund, 1992, pp. 19–59.

Joseph Stiglitz. *Economics of the Public Sector.* New York: Norton, 1988.

Harvey Rosen. *Public Finance.* Homewood, Ill.: Irwin, 1985.

Alan A. Tait. *Value-Added Tax.* Washington, D.C.: International Monetary Fund, 1988, Chap. 1.

Vito Tanzi. "Quantitative Aspects of Tax Systems in Developing Countries," in David Newberry and Nicholas Stern (eds.), *The Theory of Taxation for Developing Countries.* London: Oxford University Press, 1987.

World Bank. *World Development Report 1988.* New York: Oxford University Press for the World Bank, 1988, pp. 43–185.

George J. Yost III (ed.). *1994 International Tax Summaries, Coopers & Lybrand International Tax Network.* New York: Wiley, 1994.

Income Distribution

Richard M. Bird and Luc Henry DeWulf. "Taxation and Income Distribution in Latin America: A Critical View of Empirical Studies," *International Monetary Fund Staff Papers,* 20, November 1975, pp. 639–82.

Alejandro Foxley, Eduardo Aninat, and J. P. Arellano. *Redistributive Effects of Government Programs.* Elmsford N.Y.: Pergamon Press, 1980, Chap. 6.

Malcolm Gillis. "Micro and Macroeconomics of Tax Reform: Indonesia," *Journal of Development Economics,* 19, no. 2 (1986), 42–46.

Donald R. Snodgrass. "The Fiscal System as an Income Redistributor in West Malaysia," *Public Finance,* 29, no. 1 (January 1974), 56–76.

Introduction

Maxwell J. Fry. *Money, Interest and Banking in Economic Development.* 2d ed.; Baltimore: Johns Hopkins University Press, 1995, pp. 162–69.

International Monetary Fund. *International Financial Statistic,* various issues, 1970–1994.

Ronald I. McKinnon. *Money and Capital in Economic Development.* Washington, D.C.: Brookings Institution, 1973.

Inflation and Savings Mobilization

Yaw Ansu. "Comments," in Arnold C. Harberger (ed.), *World Economic Growth.* San Francisco: ICS Press, 1984.

Arnold C. Harberger. "A Primer on Inflation," *Journal of Money, Credit and Banking,* 10, no. 4 (November 1978), 505–21.

Albert O. Hirschman. *Journeys Toward Progress: Studies of Economic Policy-making in Latin America.* New York: Twentieth Century Fund, 1963, pp. 208–9.

Michael Roemer. "Ghana, 1950 to 1980: Missed Opportunities," in Arnold C. Harberger (ed.), *World Economic Growth.* San Francisco: ICS Press, 1984, pp. 201–30.

George M. von Furstenberg. "Inflation, Taxes, and Welfare in LDCs," *Public Finance,* 35, no. 2 (1980), 700–10.

Interest Rates and Saving Decisions

Michael J. Boskin. "Taxation, Savings and the Rate of Interest," *Journal of Political Economy,* 8b, no. 2, part 2 (April 1978), 3–27.

Alberto Giovanni. "The Interest Elasticity of Savings in Developing Countries," *World Development,* 11 (July 1983), 601–8.

Larry Summers. "Capital Taxation and Capital Accumulation in a Life-Cycle Growth Model," *American Economic Review,* 71 (September 1981), 533–44.

Colin Wright. "Savings and the Rate of Interest," in Arnold C. Harberger and Martin Bailey (eds.), *The Taxation of Income from Capital.* Washington, D.C.: Brookings Institution, 1969.

Financial Development

Sebastian Edwards. "Stabilization with Liberalization: An Evaluation of Chile's Experiment with Free-Market Policies 1973–1983," *Economic Development and Cultural Change,* 27 (September 1985), 224–53.

Sergio Pereira Leite. "Interest-Rate Policies in West Africa," *International Monetary Fund Staff Papers* 29, no. 1 (March 1982), 48–76.

Steven C. Leuthold. "Interest Rates, Inflation and Deflation," *Financial Analysis Journal,* January–February 1981, pp. 28–51.

Richard H. Patten and Jay Rosengard. *Progress with Profits: The Development of Rural Banking in Indonesia.* San Francisco: ICS Press, 1991.

Marguerite Robinson. "Rural Financial Intermediation: Lessons from Indonesia," Cambridge, Mass., Harvard Institute for International Development, Development Discussion Paper No. 434, October 1992.

A. Wahid. *The Grameen Bank: Poverty Relief.* Boulder, Colo.: Westview Press, 1993.

World Bank, *World Development Report 1989.*

Monetary Policy and Price Stability

Arnold Harberger. "A Primer on Inflation," *Journal of Money, Credit and Banking,* 10, no. 4 (November 1978), 505–21.
Anne O. Krueger. *Exchange Rate Determination.* New York: Cambridge University Press, 1983, pp. 123-36.
John Williamson. *The Open Economy and the World Economy.* New York: Basic Books, 1983, pp. 238–41.

Chapter 15. Foreign Capital and Debt

Development Assistance Committee on the OECD. *Development Cooperation in the 1990s.* Paris: OECD, 1989.
International Monetary Fund. *Balance of Payments Yearbook 1990,* Vol. 44, Part 2. Washington, D.C.: International Monetary Fund, 1993.
———. *International Financial Statistics Yearbook.* Washington, D.C.: International Monetary Fund, annual.
United States Agency for International Development. *Congressional Presentation.* Washington, D.C.: annual.
World Bank. "International Factors Reducing Poverty: Aid and Poverty," *World Development Report 1990.* Washington, D.C.: World Bank, 1990, p. 131.
———. *World Debt Tables.* Washington, D.C.: World Bank, annual.

Foreign Aid

Robert L. Ayres. *Banking on the Poor.* Cambridge, Mass.: MIT Press, 1984.
Robert Cassen et al. *Does Aid Work?* London: Oxford University Press, 1986.
Jonathan Eaton. "Foreign Public Capital Flows," in Hollis B. Chenery and T. N. Srinivasan (eds.), *Handbook of Development Economics,* Vol. 2. Amsterdam: North-Holland, 1989, pp. 1305–86.
Joint Ministerial Committee of the Boards of Governors of the World Bank and the International Monetary Fund. *Aid for Development: The Key Issues.* Washington, D.C.: 1986.
Paul Mosley. "Aid, Savings and Growth Revisited," *Oxford Bulletin of Economics and Statistics,* 42 (May 1980), 79–91.

Multinationals' Investment Patterns

Jack N. Behrman and William A. Fischer. *Overseas R & D Activities of Transnational Corporations.* Cambridge, Mass.: Oelgeschlager, Gunn and Hair, 1980.
Fred C. Bergsten, Thomas P. Horst, and Theodore H. Moran. *American Multinationals and American Interests.* Washington, D.C.: Brookings Institution, 1978.
Thomas L. Brewer. "Foreign Direct Investment in Developing Countries," World Bank Working Paper WPS 712, June 1991, p. 9.
Eliana Cardoso and Rudiger Dornbusch. "Foreign Private Capital Flows," in Hollis B. Chenery and T. N. Srinivasan (eds.), *Handbook of Development Economics,* Vol. 2. Amsterdam: North-Holland, 1989, pp. 1387–439.
Dennis J. Encarnation and Louis T. Wells, Jr. "Evaluating Foreign Investment," in

Moran, *Investing in Development: New Roles for Foreign Capital?* pp. 61–85.

Fortune, July 25, 1994.

David Goldsborough. "Foreign Direct Investment in Developing Countries," *Finance and Development,* March 1985.

Joseph M. Grieco. "Foreign Investment and Development: Theory and Evidence," in Moran, *Investing in Development: New Roles for Foreign Capital?* pp. 47–48.

Steven Guisinger et al. *Investment Incentives and Performance Requirements.* New York: Praeger, 1985.

G. K. Helleiner. "Transnational Corporations and Direct Foreign Investment," in Chenery and Srinivasan, *Handbook of Development Economics,* Vol. 2, pp. 1441–80.

Theodore H. Moran (ed.). *Multinational Corporations.* Lexington, Mass.: Lexington Books, 1985.

——— et al., *Investment in Development: New Roles for Foreign Capital?* Washington, D.C.: Overseas Development Council, 1986.

Charles P. Oman. "New Forms of Investment in Developing Countries," in Moran, *Investing in Development: New Roles for Foreign Capital?* pp. 131–55.

John Stopford. *The World Directory of Multinational Enterprises 1982–1983.* Detroit: Gale Research Company, 1982.

United Nations Centre for Transnational Corporations (UNCTNC). *Transnational Corporations in World Development.* New York: United Nations, 1988.

Raymond Vernon, *Storm over the Multinationals: The Real Issues.* Cambridge, Mass.: Harvard University Press, 1977.

Louis T. Wells, Jr. "Investment Incentives: An Unnecessary Debate," *The CTC Reporter,* 22 (Autumn 1986), 58–60.

The Debt Crisis

Rudiger Dornbusch. "Background Paper," in Twentieth Century Fund, Task Force on International Debt, *The Road to Economic Recovery.* New York: Priority Publications, 1989.

———. "Mexico's Economy at the Crossroads," *Journal of International Affairs,* 43, no. 2 (Winter 1990), 313–26.

Albert Fishlow. "External Borrowing and Debt Management," in Rudiger Dornbusch, F. Leslie C. H. Helmers, *The Open Economy: Tools for Policymakers in Developing Countries.* New York: Oxford University Press, 1988, pp. 187–222.

Ishrat Husain and Ishac Diwan (eds.). *Dealing with the Debt Crisis.* Washington, D.C.: World Bank, 1989.

Carol Lancaster and John Williamson (eds.). *African Debt and Financing.* Washington, D.C.: Institute for International Economics, 1986.

Jeffrey Sachs. "The LDC Debt Crisis," *NBER Reporter,* Winter 1986, pp. 15–16.

Chapter 16. Agriculture

Agriculture's Role in Economic Development

Carl Eicher and John Staatz. *Agricultural Development in the Third World.* 2d ed.; Baltimore: Johns Hopkins Press, 1990.

Bruce F. Johnston and Peter Kilby. *Agriculture and Structural Transformation.* London: Oxford University Press, 1975.
J. W. Mellor and B. F. Johnston. "The World Food Equation: Interrelations among Development, Employment, and Food Consumption," *Journal of Economic Literature,* no. 22 (1984).
J. Mohan Rao. "Agriculture in Recent Development Theory," *Journal of Development Economics,* no. 22 (1986).
Lloyd Reynolds. *Agriculture in Development Theory.* New Haven, Conn.: Yale University Press, 1976.
T. W. Schultz. *Transforming Traditional Agriculture.* New Haven, Conn.: Yale University Press, 1964.
Erik Thorbecke (ed.). *The Role of Agriculture in Economic Development.* New York: Columbia University Press, 1969.
C. Peter Timmer. "The Agricultural Transformation," in Hollis B. Chenery and T. N. Srinivasan (eds.), *Handbook of Development Economics,* Vol. 1. Amsterdam: North-Holland, 1988.
——— (ed.). *Agriculture and the State.* Ithaca, N.Y.: Cornell University Press, 1991.
World Bank. *World Development Report 1982.* New York: Oxford University Press, 1982.

Self-Sufficiency in Food

R. Barker, E. Bennagen, and Y. Hayami. "New Rice Technology and Policy Alternatives for Food Self-Sufficiency," in International Rice Research Institute, *Economic Consequences of the New Rice Technology.* Los Banos, Philippines: International Rice Research Institute 1978, pp. 337–61.
Lester Brown. *By Bread Alone.* New York: Praeger, 1974.
Jean Drèze and Amartya Sen. *Hunger and Public Action.* London: Oxford University Press (Clarendon), 1989.
Richard Goldman. "Staple Food Self-Sufficiency and the Distributive Impact of Malaysian Rice Policy," *Food Research Institute Studies,* 14, no. 3 (1975), 251–93.

Land Reform

Ronald P. Dore. *Land Reform in Japan.* London: Oxford University Press, 1959.
William Hinton. *Fanshen.* New York: Vintage Books, 1966.
Elias Tuma. *Twenty-six Centuries of Agrarian Reform: A Comparative Analysis.* Berkeley: University of California Press, 1965.
Louis J. Walinsky (ed.). *Agrarian Reform as Unfinished Business: The Selected Papers of Wolf Ladejinsky.* London: Oxford University Press, 1977.

Technology of Agricultural Production

Hans B. Binswanger. "Agricultural Mechanization: A Comparative Historical Perspective," *World Bank Research Observer,* 1, no. 1 (January 1986).
——— and Prabhu Pingali. "Technological Priorities for Farming in Sub-Saharan Africa," *World Bank Research Observer,* 3, no. 1 (January 1988).
——— and Vernon W. Ruttan. *Induced Innovation: Technology, Institutions and Development.* Baltimore: Johns Hopkins Press, 1978.
Ester Boserup. *The Conditions of Agricultural Growth.* Chicago: Aldine, 1965.
Dana G. Dalrymple. *Development and Spread of High Yielding Wheat Varieties in*

Developing Countries. Washington, D.C.: Agency for International Development, 1986.

Yujiro Hayami and Vernon W. Ruttan. *Agricultural Development: An International Perspective.* Baltimore: Johns Hopkins Press, 1971.

Dwight H. Perkins. *Agricultural Development in China, 1368–1968.* Chicago: Aldine, 1969.

Theodore W. Schultz. *Transforming Traditional Agriculture.* New Haven, Conn.: Yale University Press, 1964.

Mobilization of Agricultural Inputs

S. J. Burki, D. G. Davies, R. H. Hook, and J. W. Thomas. *Public Works Programs in Developing Countries: A Comparative Analysis,* World Bank Staff Working Paper No. 224, February 1976.

Uma Lele. *The Design of Rural Development: Lessons from Africa.* Baltimore: Johns Hopkins Press, 1975.

Dwight H. Perkins and Shahid Yusuf. *Rural Development in China.* Baltimore: Johns Hopkins Press, 1984.

Agricultural Price Policy

Hussein Askari and John Cummings. *Agricultural Supply Response: A Survey of the Econometric Evidence.* New York: Praeger, 1976.

Romeo Bautista and Alberto Valdés. *The Bias against Agriculture: Trade and Macroeconomic Policies in Developing Countries.* San Francisco: ICS Press, 1993.

Elliot Berg et al. *Accelerated Development in Sub-Saharan Africa.* Washington, D.C.: World Bank, 1981.

Walter P. Falcon and C. Peter Timmer. "The Political Economy of Rice Production and Trade in Asia," in L. Reynolds (ed.), *Agriculture in Development Theory.* New Haven, Conn.: Yale University Press, 1975.

Raj Krishna. "Agricultural Price Policy and Economic Development," in H. M. Southworth and B. F. Johnston (eds.), *Agricultural Development and Economic Growth.* Ithaca, N.Y.: Cornell University Press, 1967.

C. Peter Timmer, Walter P. Falcon, and Scott R. Pearson. *Food Policy Analysis.* Baltimore: Johns Hopkins Press, 1983.

Isabell Tsakok. *Agricultural Price Policy: A Practitioner's Guide to Partial Equilibrium Analysis.* Ithaca: Cornell University Press, 1990.

Rod Tyers and Kym Anderson. *Disarray in World Food Markets: Quantitative Assessment.* London: Cambridge University Press, 1992.

Chapter 17. Primary Exports

Comparative Advantage

Richard E. Caves, Jeffrey A. Frankel, and Ronald W. Jones. *World Trade and Payments: An Introduction.* 5th ed.; Boston: Little Brown, 1990.

Moises Syrquin and Hollis B. Chenery. *Patterns of Development, 1950–1983.* Washington, D.C.: World Bank, 1989.

United Nations. *Yearbook of International Trade Statistics.* New York: United Nations, annual.

John Williamson. *The Open Economy and The World Economy.* New York: Basic Books, 1983.

Primary Exports as an Engine of Growth

Robert E. Baldwin. *Economic Development and Export Growth: A Study of Northern Rhodesia, 1920–1960.* Los Angeles: University of California Press, 1966.

David Bevan, Paul Collier, and Jan Gunning. *Controlled Open Economies: A Neoclassical Approach to Structuralism.* London: Oxford University Press (Clarendon), 1990.

John Cuddington and Hong Wei. "An Empirical Analysis of the Prebisch-Singer Hypothesis: Aggregation, Model Selection and Implications," Working Paper No. 90–12, Economics Department, Georgetown University.

David C. Dawe. "Essays on Price Stabilization and the Macroeconomy in Low Income Countries," Harvard University Ph.D. dissertation, May 1993.

Albert Fishlow. *American Railroads and the Transformation of the Antebellum Economy.* Cambridge, Mass.: Harvard University Press, 1965.

Robert W. Fogel. "Railroads as an Analogy to the Space Effort: Some Economic Aspects," in Bruce Mazlish (ed.), *Space Programs: An Exploration in Historical Analogy.* Cambridge, Mass.: MIT Press, 1966.

Arnold Harberger (ed.). *World Economic Growth.* San Francisco: ICS Press, 1984.

Albert O. Hirschman. *The Strategy of Economic Development.* New Haven, Conn.: Yale University Press, 1958, Chap. 6.

———. "A Generalized Linkage Approach to Economic Development, with Special Reference to Staples," in Manning Nash (ed.), *Essays on Economic Development and Cultural Change.* Chicago: University of Chicago Press, 1977, pp. 67–98.

Stephen R. Lewis, "Primary Exporting Countries," in Hollis B. Chenery and T. N. Srinivasan (eds.), *Handbook of Development Economics,* Vol. 2. Amsterdam: North-Holland 1989, pp. 1541–600.

David Lindauer and Michael Roemer (eds.). *Asia and Africa: Legacies and Opportunities for Development.* San Francisco: ICS Press, 1994.

Hla Myint. "The 'Classical Theory' of International Trade and the Underdeveloped Countries," *Economic Journal,* 68 (1959), 317–37.

Douglass C. North. "Location Theory and Regional Economic Growth," *Journal of Political Economy,* 63 (1955), 243–285.

Michael Roemer. *Fishing for Growth: Export-Led Development in Peru, 1950-1967.* Cambridge, Mass.: Harvard University Press, 1970.

David Sapsford and V. N. Balasubramanyam. "The Long-Run Behavior of the Relative Price of Primary Commodities: Statistical Evidence and Policy Implications," *World Development,* 22, no. 11 (November 1994), 1737–45.

Melville H. Watkins. "A Staple Theory of Economic Growth," *Canadian Journal of Economics and Political Science,* 29 (1963), 141–58.

World Bank. *Price Prospects for Primary Commodities, 1990–2005.* Washington, D.C.: World Bank, 1993.

———. *Global Economic Prospects and the Developing Countries.* Washington, D.C.: World Bank, 1994, pp. 39–40.

Barriers to Primary-Export-Led Growth

Bela Balassa. "Outward Orientation," in Hollis B. Chenery and T. N. Srinivasan (eds.), *Handbook of Development Economics,* Vol. 2. Amsterdam: North-Holland 1989; pp. 1645–89.

Jere R. Behrman. "Commodity Price Instability and Economic Goal Attainment in Developing Countries," *World Development,* 15, no. 5 (May 1987), 559–73.

———. *Development, The International Economic Order and Commodity Agreements.* Reading, Mass.: Addison-Wesley, 1978.

John T. Cuddington and Carlos M. Urzua. "Trends and Cycles in the Net Barter Terms of Trade: A New Approach," *Economic Journal,* 99 (June 1989), 426–42.

W. Max Corden and S. Peter Neary. "Booming Sector and Deindustrialization in a Small Open Economy," *Economic Journal,* 92 (December 1982), 825–48.

Alan Gelb et al. *Oil Windfalls: Blessing or Curse?* New York: Oxford University Press for the World Bank, 1988.

Odin Knudsen and Andrew Parnes. *Trade Instability and Economic Development.* Lexington, Mass.: Heath Lexington Books, 1975.

Ragnar Nurkse. *Equilibrium Growth in the World Economy.* Cambridge, Mass.: Harvard University Press, 1961.

Michael Roemer. "Dutch Disease in Developing Countries: Swallowing Bitter Medicine," in Matts Lundahl (ed.), *The Primary Sector in Economic Development.* London: Croom-Helms, 1985.

———. "Ghana 1950–1980: Missed Opportunities," in Arnold Harberger (ed.), *World Economic Growth.* San Francisco: ICS Press, 1984, pp. 201–26.

———. "Resource-based Industrialization: A Survey," *Journal of Development Economics,* 6, no. 6 (June 1979), 163–202.

Hans W. Singer. "The Distribution of Trade Between Investing and Borrowing Countries," *American Economic Review,* 40 (May 1950), 470–85.

United Nations (Paul Prebisch). *The Economic Development of Latin America and its Principal Problems.* Lake Success, N.Y.: United Nations, 1950.

World Bank. *Commodity Trade and Price Trends.* Washington, D.C.: World Bank, annual.

CHAPTER 18. INDUSTRY

Industry as a Leading Sector

E. J. Hobsbawm. *The Pelican History of Britain,* Vol. 3, *Industry and Empire.* Baltimore: Penguin, 1969.

David S. Landes. *The Unbound Prometheus: Technological Change and Industrial Development in Western Europe from 1750 to the Present.* London: Cambridge University Press, 1969.

Stanford Research Institute et al. *Costs of Urban Infrastructure for Industry as Related to City Size in Developing Countries: India Case Study.* Menlo Park, Calif.: Stanford Research Institute, 1968.

Moises Syrquin and Hollis Chenery. "Three Decades of Industrialization," *The World Bank Economic Review,* 3, no. 2 (1989), 141–81.

Pan A. Yotopoulos and Jeffrey B. Nugent. "A Balanced-Growth Version of the Linkage Hypotheses: A Test," *Quarterly Journal of Economics,* 87 (1973), 157–71.

Investment Choices in Industry

American Rural Small-Scale Industry Delegation. *Rural Small-Scale Industry in the People's Republic of China.* Berkeley: University of California Press, 1977.

Ranadev Banerji. "Average Size of Plants in Manufacturing and Capital Intensity," *Journal of Development Economics,* 5 (1978).

P. N. Dhar and H. F. Lydall. *The Role of Small Enterprises in Indian Economic Development.* New York: Asia Publishing House, 1961.

Hal Hill. "Choice of Technique in the Indonesian Weaving Industry," *Economic Development and Cultural Change,* 31, no. 2 (January 1983), 337–54.

International Labor Office. *Employment, Income and Equality: A Strategy for Increasing Productive Employment in Kenya.* Geneva: International Labor Office, 1972.

Ian M. D. Little, Dipak Mazumdar, and John M. Page, Jr. *Small Manufacturing Enterprises.* New York: Oxford University Press for the World Bank, 1988.

Alan S. Manne (ed.). *Investments for Capacity Expansion: Size, Location and Time Phasing.* Cambridge, Mass.: MIT Press, 1967.

Howard Pack. "Aggregate Implications of Factor Substitution in Industry Processes," *Journal of Development Economics,* 11, no. 1 (August 1982).

———. "The Choice of Technique and Employment in the Textile Industry," in A. S. Bhalla (ed.), *Technology and Employment in Industry.* Geneva: International Labor Office, 1975.

C. F. Pratten. *Economies of Scale in Manufacturing Industry.* London: Cambridge, University Press, 1971.

E. F. Schumacher. *Small is Beautiful.* London: Sphere Books, 1974.

Donald R. Snodgrass and Tyler Biggs. *Industrialization and the Small Firm: Patterns and Policies.* San Francisco: ICS Press, forthcoming.

Eugene Staley and Richard Morse. *Modern Small Industry for Developing Countries.* New York: McGraw-Hill, 1965.

Hernando de Soto. *The Other Path.* New York: Harper & Row, 1989.

William F. Steel. *Small-Scale Employment and Production in Developing Countries: Evidence from Ghana.* New York: Praeger, 1977.

Frances Stewart. "Manufacture of Cement Blocks in Kenya," in A. S. Bhalla (ed.), *Technology and Employment in Industry.* Geneva: International Labor Office, 1975.

Louis T. Wells, Jr. "Economic Man and Engineering Man: Choice of Technique in a Low-wage Country," in C. P. Timmer et al. (eds.), *The Choice of Technology in Developing Countries.* Cambridge, Mass.: Center for International Affairs, Harvard University, 1975, pp. 69–74.

Jeffrey Williamson. "Regional Inequality and the Process of National Development: A Description of Patterns," *Economic Development and Cultural Change,* 13 (1965), 3–45.

CHAPTER 19. TRADE AND INDUSTRIALIZATION

Two Industrial Strategies

Alice Amsden. *Asia's New Giant: South Korea and Late Industrialization.* New York: Oxford University Press, 1989.

Bela Balassa. "The Process of Industrial Development and Alternative Development Strategies," *Essays in International Finance,* 141 (1980).

———, "Outward Orientation," in Hollis B. Chenery and T. N. Srinivasan (eds.), *Handbook of Development Economics,* Vol. 2, Amsterdam: North-Holland, 1989, pp. 1645–89.

Jagdish N. Bhagwati. *Foreign Trade Regimes and Economic Development: Anatomy and Consequences of Exchange Control Regimes.* Cambridge, Mass.: Ballinger 1978.

Henry J. Bruton, "Import Substitution," in Hollis B. Chenery and T. N. Srinivasan (eds.), *Handbook of Development Economics,* Vol. 2. Amsterdam: Elsevier, Science Publishers, 1989, 1601–44.

Harry G. Johnson. "Optimal Trade Interventions in the Presence of Domestic Distortions," in R. E. Caves et al., *Trade, Growth, and the Balance of Payments.* Amsterdam: North-Holland, 1965, pp. 3–34.

Anne O. Krueger. *Foreign Trade Regimes and Economic Development: Liberalization Attempts and Consequences.* Cambridge, Mass.: Ballinger, 1978.

David L. Lindauer and Michael Roemer (eds.). *Asia and Africa: Legacies and Opportunities in Development.* San Francisco: ICS Press, 1994.

Howard Pack. "Industrialization and Trade," in Hollis B. Chenery and T. N. Srinivasan (eds.), *Handbook of Development Economics.* Vol. 2, Amsterdam: North-Holland, 1989, pp. 333–80.

Gustav Ranis. "Industrial Sector Labor Absorption," *Economic Development and Cultural Change,* 21 (1973), 387–408.

Robert Wade. *Governing the Market: Economic Theory and the Role of Government in East Asian Industrialization.* Princeton, N.J.: Princeton University Press, 1990.

World Bank. *The East Asian Miracle: Economic Growth and Public Policy.* Washington, D.C.: World Bank, 1993.

Trade Policies

Narongchai Akrasanee, David Dapice, and Frank Flatters. *Thailand's Export Growth: Retrospect and Prospects.* Bangkok: Thailand Development Research Institute, 1990.

Bela Balassa et al. *The Structure of Protection in the Developing Countries.* Baltimore: Johns Hopkins Press, 1971, p. 55.

———. *Industrial Strategies in Semi-Industrialized Countries.* Baltimore: Johns Hopkins Press, 1982.

W. M. Corden. *The Theory of Protection.* London: Oxford University Press, 1971.

Outcomes

Tyler Biggs and Brian Levy. "Strategic Interventions and the Political Economy of Industrial Policy in Developing Countries," in D. H. Perkins and M. Roemer (eds.), *Systems Reform in Developing Countries,* Cambridge, Mass.: Harvard University Press, 1991, pp. 365–401.

Henry J. Bruton. "The Import Substitution Strategy of Economic Development," *Pakistan Development Review,* 10 (1970), 123–46.

Tun-jen Cheng. "Political Regimes and Development Strategies: South Korea and Taiwan," in Gary Gireffid and Donald Wyman (eds.), *Manufacturing Miracles,* Princeton, N.J.: Princeton University Press, 1991.

Vittorio Corbo and Sang Woo Nam. "The Recent Macroeconomic Evolution of the Republic of Korea: An Overview," World Bank, Economic Research Department, Discussion Paper DRD 208, 1986.

Albert O. Hirschman. "The Political Economy of Import Substitution," *Quarterly Journal of Economics,* 82 (1968), 1–32.

Helen Hughes (ed.). *Achieving Industrialization in East Asia.* Cambridge, U.K.: 1988.

Adriaan Ten Kate. "Liberalization and Economic Stabilization in Mexico: Lessons of Experience," *World Development,* 20, no. 5 (May 1992), 659–72.

Lawrence J. Lau (ed.). *Models of Development: A Comparative Study of Economic Growth in South Korea and Taiwan.* San Francisco: ICS Press, 1990.

I. M. D. Little, Tibor Scitovsky, and Maurice Scott. *Industry and Trade in Some Developing Countries.* London: Oxford University Press, 1970.

Howard Pack and Larry E. Westphal. "Industrial Strategy and Technological Change," *Journal of Development Economics,* 22, no. 1 (June 1986), 87–128.

World Trading Arrangements

Jagdish Bhagwati. *Protectionism.* Cambridge, Mass.: MIT Press, 1988.

Harry G. Johnson. *Money, Trade, and Economic Growth.* London: Allen & Unwin, 1962, Chap. 3.

Mancur Olson. *The Rise and Decline of Nations.* New Haven, Conn.: Yale University Press, 1982.

United Nations. *Yearbook of International Trade Statistics.* New York: United Nations, annual.

Jacob Viner. *The Customs Union Issue.* New York: Carnegie Endowment for International Peace, 1950.

Chapter 20. Managing an Open Economy

Equilibrium in a Small, Open Economy

Richard E. Caves, Jeffrey A. Frankel, and Ronald W. Jones. *World Trade and Payments.* Glenview, Ill.: Scott, Foresman, Little, Brown, 1990, Chap. 19.

Rudiger Dornbusch. *Open Economy Macroeconomics.* New York: Basic Books, 1980.

W. Max Corden. *Inflation, Exchange Rates and the World Economy.* Chicago: University of Chicago Press, 1977.

W. E. G. Salter. "International Balance and External Balance: The Role of Price and Expenditure Effects," *Economic Record,* August 1959, pp. 226–38.

Trevor W. Swan. "Economic Control in a Dependent Economy," *Economic Record,* November 1956, pp. 339–56.

Tales of Stabilization

Michael Bruno et al. *Lessons of Economic Stabilization and Its Aftermath.* Cambridge, Mass.: MIT Press, 1991.

W. Max Corden and J. Peter Neary. "Booming Sector and Deindustrialization in a Small, Open Economy," *Economic Journal,* 92 (1982).

Ishan Kapur, et al. *Ghana: Adjustment and Growth, 1983–91.* Washington, D.C.: International Monetary Fund, 1991.

Mark Lindenberg and Noel Ramirez. *Managing Adjustment in Developing Countries.* San Francisco: ICS Press, 1989.

I. M. D. Little et al. *Boom, Crisis and Adjustment: The Macroeconomic Experience of Developing Countries.* Washington, D.C.: World Bank, 1993.

David E. Sahn (ed.). *Adjusting to Policy Failure in African Economies.* Ithaca, N.Y.: Cornell University Press, 1994.

World Bank. *Adjustment in Africa: Reforms, Results and the Road Ahead.* London: Oxford University Press, 1993.

Index

Abdullah, Rachmina, 3–5
absentee landlords, 428, 433, 445
absolute poverty, 84
absorption, 540–41, 543–46
Adelman, Irma, 82, 84, 563, 564
adjustable peg, 385
adjusted net domestic product (ANDP), 181–82
adjusted net national product (ANNP), 180–81
advantages of backwardness, 29
Africa:
  debt crisis in, 417, 419
  labor surplus in, 60
  tax ratios in, 330
African sleeping sickness (trypanosomiasis), 281
Agarwala, A. N., 62*n*, 563
Agency for International Development (AID), 209
age structures, 193
aggregate production functions, 41
agricultural sector:
  biological package in, 438, 442–44
  demographic influence of, 194
  developmental role of, 424–27
  diminishing returns in, 51
  environmental degradation and, 157–58, 159
  GNP estimation for, 37
  industrial sector vs., 47–60
  labor force in, 222, 227–28, 423–24
  land use in, 424, 427–34
  mechanization in, 438, 439–42
  mobilization of inputs in, 444–50
  pollution and, 157–58, 159
  price policy and, 448, 450–55
  production functions in, 439
  productivity of, 424–25, 433–34, 436–37
  sustainable harvests and, 159
  technology and production in, 434–44
  traditional farming in, 424, 435, 436–37
Ahluwalia, Montek S., 82*n*, 83*n*, 564
Ahmad, Entisham, 565
Ahmad, Yusuf J., 568
Ahmed, Manzoor, 270*n*, 572
Akerlof, George A., 226*n*, 570
Akrasanee, Narongchai, 518*n*, 586
Allende Gossens, Salvador, 553
Alm, J., 338*n*, 576
A–matrix, 139
Amsden, Alice, 505*n*, 525*n*, 585
Andean Pact, 533, 534
Anderson, C. A., 270*n*, 572
Anderson, Kym, 582
Ando, A., 575
Aninat, Eduardo, 353*n*, 577
Ansu, Yaw, 365*n*, 578
Arellano, J. P., 353*n*, 577
Argentina, political instability of, 26
Arnold, Fred, 235*n*
Asian tigers, 505–6
Asia Pacific Economic Cooperation group (APEC), 534–35
Askari, Hussein, 582
assets:
  financial, 360, 361–62
  liquid financial, 360–61, 373–76
  nonfinancial, 360
Association of Southeast Asian Nations (ASEAN), 533, 534
Austin, James, 574
Australian model, 538–41
Ayres, Robert L., 579

backward economies, 6
backward linkages, 63–64, 464
Bahl, Roy W., 338*n*, 576
Bailey, Martin, 578

balanced growth, 62–65, 101, 466
balance equations, 146
balance of payments, 29
Balassa, Bela, 109, 469*n*, 504*n*, 510, 565, 583, 585, 586
Balasubramanyam, V. N., 470*n*, 583
Baldwin, Robert E., 466*n*, 583
Banerji, Randev, 316*n*, 575, 584
Bangladesh:
  establishment of, 26
  life expectancy for males in, 275
  savings and credit institutions in, 383
banking systems:
  anti–inflationary monetary policy and, 388–89
  central, 358–59, 387, 517, 545–46
  commercial, 358, 359, 360, 361, 371, 377, 378, 381
  reserve requirements in, 388–89
  rural, 446–47
  size of, 381–82
Baran, Paul, 32, 561
Barbier, Edward B., 159*n*, 184*n*, 568
Barker, R., 581
Barro, Robert, 36
barter economies, 359
Bartlett, Bruce, 347*n*
basic human needs, 93–94
  in health care strategy, 293
  overall indicators and, 77–80
  public programs for, 93–94
  social indicators and, 76–77
Bautista, Romeo, 454*n*, 582
Becker, Gary, 206–7, 569
behavioral relationships, 146
Behrman, Jack N., 408*n*, 579
Behrman, Jere R., 280*n*, 286*n*, 474*n*, 567, 574, 583
benefit–cost ratio (BCR), 148, 289*n*
Bennagen, E., 581
Berelson, Bernard, 219*n*, 570
Berg, Alan, 285*n*, 289*n*, 574
Berg, Elliot, 450*n*, 582
Bergsten, Fred C., 579
Berry, Albert, 570
Bevan, David, 478*n*, 583
Bhagwati, Jagdish N., 109, 236, 504*n*, 565, 571, 585, 587
Bhalla, A. S., 489*n*, 491*n*, 585
Bhatia, Anita, 326*n*, 576
Bienen, Henry, 479*n*
big–bang approach, 27–28, 126–27
Biggs, Tyler, 316*n*, 496, 525*n*, 575, 585, 586
big push, 63
binding constraint, 136
Binswanger, Hans P., 438*n*, 581
biological package, 438–39, 442–44
Bird, Richard M., 329*n*, 338*n*, 352*n*, 576, 577
Birdsall, Nancy, 569
birth control:
  Malthus on, 202–3
  see also family planning
birth rate:
  defined, 192
  demographic changes linked to, 203–4, 197–99
  see also fertility rate
Black Death (bubonic plague), 194
black market, 113
Blaug, Mark, 253, 572
bliss point, 543
Blitzer, C. R., 567
Boissiere, M., 267*n*, 572
Bolivia:
  stabilization programs in, 117–18, 126, 128
  tax administration in, 338
  tax evasion in, 338
border price, 507
Bos, H. C., 573
Boserup, Ester, 211, 436*n*, 570, 581
Boskin, Michael J., 319*n*, 355*n*, 577, 578
Bouchet, Michel H., 418*n*
Bowman, M. J., 270*n*, 572
Boyco, Maxim, 566
brain drain, 235–36, 260
Brazil:
  deforestation in, 174
  development pattern of, 85–86
Brewer, Thomas L., 403*n*, 579
Britain, *see* England; United Kingdom
Broad, Robin, 186*n*, 569
Brown, Lester R., 194*n*, 569, 581
Brumberg, R., 575
Bruno, Michael, 553*n*, 587
Bruton, Henry J., 108*n*, 244*n*, 245*n*, 526*n*, 565, 571, 585, 586
bubonic plague (Black Death), 194
budgetary savings, 304–5, 307
budget policy, *see* fiscal policy
budgets:
  deficit financing and, 327, 554–55
  government, 321–22
buffer stocks of commodities, 474
Bulatao, R., 207*n*, 569
Burki, S. J., 571, 582
buybacks, 418

Caldwell, John C., 207, 569
Camp David accord, 549
Canada, protectionist policy of, 530
capital:
  from agricultural sector, 425
  effective use of, 301
  factor–price distortions of, 239
  human, 250–51, 279–81, 300
  international mobility of, 317–19, 345–46, 351
capital assistance, 393
capital deepening, 209–10
capital fundamentalism, 299–300
capital–output ratio, 42
capital widening, 209–10
Cardoso, Eliana, 579
Carnoy, Martin, 253, 572
cartels, 474
Carter, Jimmy, 107
Casanegra de Jantscher, Milka, 338*n*, 577
Cash, Richard A., 574
cash crops, 449–50
Cassen, Robert, 402*n*, 579
Castro, Fidel, 290
Caves, Richard E., 503*n*, 537*n*, 582, 586, 587
Central American Common Market, 531, 533
centrally planned economies, 103–6, 112
  limitations of, 104–5
Centro Internacional de Mejoramiento de Mai y Trio (CIMMYT), 442, 448
Ceylon, *see* Sri Lanka
Chenery, Hollis B., 110, 111, 143, 146*n*, 226*n*, 280*n*, 469*n*, 504*n*, 526*n*, 563, 564, 565, 566, 567, 571, 574, 579, 581, 582, 583, 584, 585, 586
  on input–output analysis, 141*n*
  on patterns of development, 35, 36, 49–51, 61, 459–60
  two–gap model of, 136–37, 414
Cheng, Tun–jen, 586
childbearing, motivations for, 205
children, nutritional problems of, 287

Chile:
consumption propensities of rich in, 313
provident–fund approach to social security in, 345
savings patterns in, 315
stabilization in, 553–54
tax policy and redistribution expenditures in, 352–53
China, People's Republic of
agricultural systems in, 123, 430–31, 445–46
Cultural Revolution in, 269
development pattern of, 90
distrust of market forces in, 104
economic liberalization in, 91
educational policy in, 269
employment policies in, 246
as exception to low–income norms, 11, 12
family planning in, 213–14
health care system in, 293
industrial vs. agricultural investment in, 49
labor in, 59–60, 445–46
land reform in, 432
price reform in, 121
privatization in, 124, 127
Soviet planned economy and, 30, 103–5
township and village enterprises in, 499
Choksi, Armeane M., 566
Cipolla, Carlo, 194*n*, 569
civil rights, deprivation of, 111
Clark, Colin, 211, 570
Clark, Paul, 141*n*, 567
class savings hypothesis, 314
Cline, William R., 564
Coale, Ansley J., 209, 570
Coase, Robert, 172, 568
Cole, David, 562
collectivized agriculture, 428–29, 430–31, 445–46
Collier, Paul, 478*n*, 583
Colombia:
cigarette smuggling in, 332, 333
ILO employment mission to, 230
personal income taxes in, 334
tax reform in, 339–40
colonialism:
factor utilization and, 463
local economic growth suppressed by, 20–21, 25
Marxist theory applied to, 30–31
COMECON, 105, 534
command economy, 99, 109, 121
commercial borrowing, 411–13
commercial project appraisal, defined, 153
commodity agreements, 473–74
commodity terms of trade, 468–70
common markets, 531–32
common property, 166, 200
common resources, 101, 157–58, 159
government regulation of, 165, 167–77
management difficulties of, 167
property rights and, 165–67
restricting access to, 169
communal farming, 428, 430–31
Communist countries:
educational policies in, 269
socialism in, 103
see also specific countries
community indifference curves, 133–34
comparative advantage, theory of, 28, 456–59, 462
competition:
customs unions and, 532–33
market reform and, 112
property rights and, 165
complementation agreements, 533
compound interest, 147
compradores, 32
computable general equilibrium (CGE) model, 131, 145–46
for South Korea, 84
conditionality, of IMF loans, 116
consistency planning models, 132, 134–35, 140, 142
constant prices, 149
consumer surplus, 508
consumption:
linkage, 465
standards, 185
Cooke, E. Romana, 570
Coombs, Philip H., 270*n*, 572
Corbo, Vittorio, 525*n*, 553*n*, 586
Corden, W. Max, 476*n*, 509*n*, 538*n*, 549, 584, 586, 587
Cornia, Giovanni Andrea, 94*n*, 565
corporate dividends, 315
corporations:
income taxes and, 337, 350–51
savings behavior of, 315–16
see also multinational corporations
cost–benefit analysis:
in development planning, 131, 146–54
of education, 262
foreign exchange and, 150
investment plan analysis as model for, 131, 146–48
and natural resource depletion, 156–57, 158–59, 176–77, 178–79
shadow pricing in, 150–54
over time, 162–64
cost–effectiveness, benefit–cost ratio compared with, 289*n*
costs of urbanization, 232
cottage shops, 495–96
crawling peg, 384–85, 517, 546
credit ceilings, 389–90
credit cooperatives, 446–47
critical minimum effort, 63
cross–section data, 61, 81, 83, 275
Cuba:
command economy in, 105
health in, 290–91
Cuddington, John T., 417*n*, 469, 583, 584
Cummings, John, 582
currency, devaluation of, 27, 118
customs unions, 531, 532

Dahlman, Carl J., 245*n*, 572
Dalrymple, Dana G., 581
Dapice, David, 518*n*, 586
Dasgupta, P., 567
Daud, Fatimah, 3*n*, 561
Davies, D. G., 582
Davis, Russell, 258*n*, 572
Dawe, David C., 472–73, 583
deadweight loss, 508
death, leading causes of, 279, 285, 293
death rate:
age–specific, 193
defined, 192
demographic changes linked to, 197–99, 203–4
development and, 275–76
infant, 14, 193, 199, 276
Deaton, Angus, 311*n*, 314, 575
debt crisis, *see* foreign debt
debt–equity swaps, 418
debt–for–nature swaps, 172*n*, 186
debt relief mechanisms, 417–19
debt service ratio, 412
deep financial policies, 376–77, 380–82

degree of development, 6
de Melo, Jaime, 146*n*, 567
demographic momentum, 202
demographic projections, 201–2
demographic transition of industrial countries, 195–96
demography, vocabulary of, 192–93
Denison, Edward F., 45, 47, 67, 563
Deolalikar, Anil B., 248*n*, 286*n*, 574
dependency ratio, 200
dependent economy model, *see* Australian model
deregulation, 107, 119
Dervis, Kemal, 146*n*, 567
de Soto, Hernando, 495*n*, 585
devaluation of currency, 27; *see also* exchange rates
Devarajan, Shantayanan, 537*n*
developing countries:
  advantages of, 29
  categories of, 6–7
  classification of, 21–22
  deficit financing and, 366–67
  diverse historical backgrounds of, 19–21
  educational trends in, 255–59
  export characteristics of, 459–62
  export of manufactured goods and, 528–29, 531
  foreign debt of, 411–20
  foreign investment in, 33
  government expenditures and, 322
  health in, 273–79
  inflation in, 363–67
  investment ratios in, 303–4
  labor supply in, 221–24
  long–term vs. short–term economic policy in, 536–37
  policies toward multinationals by, 408–11
  trading blocs and, 535
  unemployment and, 228–30
  see also less developed countries
development, economic:
  agricultural sector and, 424–27
  approaches to, 15–17
  capital fundamentalism and, 299–300
  Chenery's normal pattern of, 49–51
  continuum in, 9–15
  cross–section data on, 61, 83, 275
  defined, 7–8, 26, 68
  education and, 259–71
  finance and, 376–83
  foreign savings and, 398–402
  health programs and, 272–73, 279–81
  human welfare and, 68–95
  industrialization and, 481, 499–500
  inflation and, 113–14
  international obstacles to, 28–34
  long–term vs. short–term policy in, 536–37
  management of, 99–106
  open economy management and, 536–49
  policy failures and, 173–77, 536–37
  policy solutions and, 165–73
  political obstacles to, 24–28
  politics of, 25–28
  prerequisites for, 19, 22–24
  radical model of, 90–91
  science and, 23–24
  as socio–political phenomenon, 19
  structural change and, 35–36
  sustainable development and, 186–87
  terminology of, 6–7
  unsustainable, 157
  see also sustainable development
development assistance agencies, 397–98
DeWulf, Luc Henry, 352*n*, 577
Dhar, P. N., 495*n*, 584
diarrhea, 293
Dickens, Charles, 69
diminishing returns, 51
"diploma disease," 258
discounting, 147
discount rate, 148, 151, 161*n*, 162–65
disease:
  deaths caused by, 279
  nutrition deficiencies and, 284–85
  sanitation improvements and, 281–82
Diwan, Ishac, 417*n*, 418*n*, 580
Dixon, John A., 177*n*, 568
Domar, Evsey, 35, 41, 562; *see also* Harrod–Domar production function model
Dore, Ronald P., 258, 269*n*, 433*n*, 572, 581
Dorfman, Robert, 145*n*, 567
Dornbusch, Rudiger N., 412*n*, 413*n*, 414*n*, 417*n*, 418*n*, 419, 579, 580, 587
Drèze, Jean, 427*n*, 581
dropouts, 257
drought, 556–58
Due, John F., 335*n*, 343*n*, 576
Duesenberry, James, 312
Duesenberry relative income hypothesis, 312–13
Dutch disease, 476–80, 549–51
dynamic gains, 532

early industries, 61
earnings, education and, 265–68
East African Community, 531, 532–33, 534
Easterlin, Richard, 206–7, 569
Eastern Europe, market mechanisms for, 105, 116, 121, 126, 127
Eaton, Jonathan, 579
Eberstadt, Nick, 570
Echeverría Alvarez, Luis, 432
economic behavior, changes in, 184–85
economic efficiency, 354–57
economic equilibrium, 537–49
  achieving, 549
  disequilibrium and, 543–46
  Dutch disease and, 549–51
economic project appraisal, defined, 153
economic stability, 353–54, 359, 363, 478, 546–59
economic theory, development and, 15–16
economies of agglomeration, 487, 497
economies of scale:
  in agriculture, 430–31, 449
  in industrial sector, 48, 492–95
  in market economies, 100
Ecuador, inflation and savings in, 372
education:
  cost–benefit analysis of, 262–69
  defined, 251, 254–55
  developmental role of, 259–71
  formal modeling and, 269
  importance of, 251–54
  in LDCs, 253–54, 255–59
  nonformal, 255, 259, 270–71
  rural, 448
  types of, 254–55
educational deepening, 229, 266
educational vouchers, 270
Edwards, Edgar O., 244*n*, 571
Edwards, Sebastian, 381*n*, 566, 578
effective rate of production (ERP), 508–11, 512–13
effective rate of subsidy (ERS), 512–14
effective tax rates, 348
efficient taxes, 356–57
Egypt, subsidy programs in, 27, 289
Eichengreen, Barry, 308*n*, 575
Eicher, Carl, 580

elasticity:
defined, 54
of substitution, 241
electronics industry, in Malaysia, 3–5
emigration, 235–36
employment:
foreign investment and, 404–5, 408
future patterns of, 260–61
government policies on, 236–48
patterns of, 222–24
see also labor; unemployment
employment creation:
cost–benefit analysis and, 152
equitable growth and, 94–95
factor prices and, 240–43
income distribution and, 246
industrialization and, 237
investments, labor and, 246–47
by multinationals, 404–5
rural–urban migration and, 231–35
small-scale industry and, 247–48
strategies for, 248–49
two approaches to, 238–39
Encarnation, Dennis J., 411*n*, 579
Encina, Francisco, 346
enclaves, 475
energy consumption, 11
energy pricing, 174–76
Engel, Ernst, 48
Engel's law, 48, 62, 285, 466, 467
England:
demographic experience of, 195
modern economic growth in, 18, 19
see also United Kingdom
entrepreneurship, 498
environmental degradation, 155–59, 162, 165
costs of, 179
as global phenomenon, 156, 157–58
government regulation and, 165, 167–77, 184–85
poverty and, 185–86
sustainable development and, 155–56, 186–87
environmental health, 281–82
Essay on the Principle of Population (Malthus), 203
Ethiopia, 34
Europe, economies of scale in, 493–94
European Community (EC), 335, 512*n*
European Economic Community:
stabilization program of, 474
value–added tax (VAT) used by, 335
European Union (EU), 398, 534
economic integration of, 531–32
excess burden in tax systems, 355, 356–57
exchange rates:
agricultural sector and, 453–55
anchor, 546, 555
changes in, 517, 545
conversion problems and, 37–38
fixed, 515, 546
floating, 546
foreign, 150
inflation and, 385–88
management of, 514–19
nominal, 476
overvalued, 113, 115, 453–55, 515–16, 543
real, 476–77, 478, 517, 539–40, 541–46
real effective, 518–19
types of, 384–85, 546
undervalued, 516–17, 543
excise taxes, 334, 335, 337
explicit costs, 263
exportable goods, 458
export concentration, 460, 462
export credits, 393
export instability, 472–73
export–led growth:
advantages of, 504
Asian tigers and, 505–6
import substitution and, 526–27
export pessimism, 107
export processing zones (EPZs), 4, 506
export taxes, 333
extension services, 447–48
external balance, 539–41, 542, 543–46, 548–49
external diseconomies, 101, 158
external economies, 100–101, 487
externalities, 47, 156–57, 158–59, 165, 176–77

factor cost, 37
factor markets, 524–26
factor price distortions, 239–43
factor productivity, 109–10
Falcon, Walter P., 451*n*, 454, 574, 582
fallow, shortening of, 436
family farming, 428, 430–31
family planning, 204–5
in China, 213–14
government policies on, 212–19
in Indonesia, 216–17
in Kenya, 212–13
famine, 286
farming, *see* agricultural sector
Federal Reserve Board, 416
Fei, John C. H., 36, 52, 55, 88–89, 563
fertility, replacement level of, 202
fertility rate:
current, 196–99
defined, 193
income distribution and, 218
marital, 204, 218–19
modern theories of, 204–7
see also birth rate
fertilizers, 442–43, 451
Feuchem, Richard, 281*n*, 574
feudalism, 20, 21, 425
fiat money, 359
Fields, Gary S., 76, 81*n*, 563, 564
financial intermediation, 359, 362, 376–77
financial policy:
deep, 376–77, 380–82
defined, 320, 359
developmental role of, 376–83
shallow, 376–80
in U.S. vs. developing countries, 358–59
financial ratio, 361–62
financial systems:
components of, 358
functions of, 359–63
monopoly power in, 378
fiscal linkage, 465, 478
fiscal policy, 546
defined, 320
income redistribution and, 353–54
private capital formation and, 343
Fischer, Stanley, 113–14, 566
Fischer, William A., 408*n*, 579
fisheries, 159–61
Fishlow, Albert, 414*n*, 465*n*, 580, 583
fixed proportions production function, 145
Flatters, Frank, 518*n*, 586
flow matrix, 138
flow-of-funds accounts, 362
Fogel, Robert W., 465*n*, 583
food:
aid, 398, 400
consumption, 285–87
entitlements, 286

food (*continued*)
national balance sheets, 282–83
security, 286
supplementation programs for, 288
work programs for, 248
food supply:
population growth linked to, 203
world, 426–27
forced–savings strategies, 367–69
foreign aid:
capital fundamentalism and, 299–300
historical role of, 394–97
institutions for, 397–98
types of, 392–93
foreign debt, 411–20
causes of crisis in, 415–17
commercial borrowing and, 411
repayment crisis in, 411–13, 415–16, 551–54
resolution of crisis in, 417–20
sustainable debt and, 414–15
foreign direct investment, *see* investment, foreign direct
foreign exchange:
control of, 240
in cost–benefit analysis, 150
export taxes and, 333
import duties in, 332–33
multinational investment and, 402–11
see also trade
foreign exchange rates, *see* exchange rates
foreign income tax credits, 342
foreign savings, 391
categories of, 305, 392–93
developmental role of, 398–402
domestic vs., 317
historical examples of, 391–93
recent trends in, 393–94
forest–fallow cultivation, 436
forests, 163–64, 166, 173–74
Fortune, 316, 403, 404, 575
forward linkages, 64, 475
Foster, Philip J., 270*n*, 572
Foxley, Alejandro, 353*n*, 577
Frank, Charles R., Jr., 76*n*, 564
Frank, Robert H., 313*n*, 575
Frankel, Jeffrey A., 537*n*, 582, 587
Fraumeni, Barbara, 563
Freeman, Richard B., 571
free markets, 15–16
free–rider problem, 430
free–trade areas, 531–34
Freire, Paolo, 269*n*, 572
Friedman, Milton, 313
Frischtak, Claudio, 245*n*, 572
Fry, Maxwell J., 373, 578
fuel crisis of the 1970s, 140
functional distribution of income, 70–71
Furtado, Celso, 32, 561

Gallop, Frank, 563
Gandhi, Indira, 214–15
Gandhi, Mohandas K., 495
Gang, Ira N., 338*n*, 576
Gelb, Alan, 478*n*, 584
Gemmell, Norman, 244*n*, 570, 571
General Agreement on Tariffs and Trade (GATT), 527, 529, 530, 534
Uruguay round of, 530
General Theory of Employment, Interest and Money, The (Keynes), 317
Germany, modern economic growth in, 22
Gerschenkron, Alexander, 22, 29, 561
Ghana:
export policy of, 471–72
mismanagement in, 555–56
Gillis, Malcolm, 174*n*, 176*n*, 329*n*, 333*n*, 334*n*, 335*n*, 340*n*, 352*n*, 568, 576, 577
Gini concentration ratio, 72–74
Giovanni, Alberto, 578
Gireffid, Gary, 586
Glassburner, Bruce, 479*n*
global sustainability, 182–87
global warming, 156, 179, 186
goals, national:
project appraisal and, 151–53
shadow prices and, 153–54
Goldman, Richard, 581
Goldsborough, David, 580
Golladay, Frederick, 289*n*, 574
goods and services:
exportable, 458
importable, 458
luxury, 32–34
nontraded, 38, 477–78, 538, 539–40, 541–43
recurrent government expenditures on, 323–26
tradable, 477–78, 538, 539–40, 541–43
Gorbachev, Mikhail, 91, 105
Goswami, Omkar, 338*n*, 576
government expenditures:
consumption vs. capital, 321
countercyclical, 478
defined, 320
on education, 253–54
growth trends and, 322–23
on health programs, 280–81, 289–90
income distribution and, 352–54
in mixed economies, 99–103
recurrent, 323–26, 352
government regulation, 165, 167–77, 184–85, 546
government revenues, defined, 320
gradualism, 126, 127–28
grain, high–yield varieties of, 436–37, 442
Gratz, Wilfred, 308*n*, 575
Green, Marshall, 570
Green, S. R., 570
Green Revolution, 86, 109, 438–39, 442–44, 556
Greenwood, Jeremy, 318*n*, 575
Gregory, Peter, 230*n*, 571
Grieco, Joseph M., 405*n*, 580
Griffin, Keith, 31*n*, 562
Grindle, Merilee, 562
gross domestic product (GDP), 36, 175, 180, 366, 387, 403, 473, 520
fertility and, 197–98
gross national product (GNP):
defined, 36, 180
development patterns and, 35
estimation of, 36–41
industry vs. agricultural share in, 47–51
natural resources and, 155*n*, 180–82
overall indicators and, 77–80
social indicators and, 76–77
gross resource transfer, 392
growth, economic:
balanced, 62–65, 101, 466
defined, 7–8
empirical analyses of, 61–62
equality and, 76
equitable strategies for, 90–95
equity and, 76
human resource development and, 251
inequality as cause of, 89
investment requirements for, 300–304
models for, 41–47, 178
outward–looking strategies vs. import substitution and, 523–24

politics of, 25–28
poverty reduction and, 82–84
primary–export–led, 462–80
sluggish, 466–68
sources of, 45–47, 65–67
growth accounting, 46
Guisinger, Steven, 409*n*, 580
Gunning, Jan, 478*n*, 583
Gurley, John, 31*n*, 562

Hadi, Yusuf, 181*n*
Haile Selassie, 34
Hamilton, Alexander, 502
Hanson, James, 567
Harberger, Arnold, 319*n*, 355*n*, 365*n*, 385*n*, 472*n*, 567, 575, 576, 578, 579, 583
Harris, John R., 231, 233–34, 571
Harrod, Roy, 35, 41, 562
Harrod–Domar production function model, 41–42, 379–80
capital fundamentalism and, 299
for consistency planning, 134–35
neoclassical production function vs., 140
Hart, J. Keith, 562
Hartwick, John M., 568
Haveman, Robert H., 264*n*, 573
Hay, Jonathan, 418*n*
Hayami, Yujiro, 438, 581, 582
Hazlewood, Arthur, 268*n*, 573
health, defined, 273
health conditions:
in developing countries, 273–79
developmental role of, 272–73
improvements in, 14–15
health programs:
developmental role of, 281–82
for nutritional improvement, 272–73, 279–81
underfinancing of, 293–95
Heckscher, Eli, 458, 524
Helleiner, Gerald K., 580
Heller, Peter, 325*n*, 576
Helmers, F. L. C. H., 414*n*, 580
Herzog, Silvio, 419
Heston, Alan, 81*n*, 563
Hicks, Norman L., 330*n*, 576
high–income economies, 7, 186–87, 322
high–powered money, 387
high tax effort nations, 330–32
Hill, Hal, 492, 585
Hinton, William, 432*n*, 581
Hirschman, Albert O., 63, 107, 370–71, 464, 466*n*, 484, 562, 563, 578, 583, 586
Hobbes, Thomas, 347
Hobsbawm, E. J., 481*n*, 486*n*, 487*n*, 584
Hodgart, Alan, 562
Hong Kong, capital migration from, 318
Hong Wei, 583
Hook, R. H., 582
Hoover, Edgar M., 209, 570
Hopkins, Anthony G., 562
Horst, Thomas P., 579
Hotelling, Harold, 568
Hufschmidt, Maynard M., 177*n*, 568
Hughes, Helen, 586
human capital, 178, 179*n*, 250–51, 272, 279–81, 300
defined, 178*n*
human development index (HDI), 78–79
human resource development, 251
Husain, Ishrat, 417*n*, 418*n*, 580
Hutcheson, Thomas L., 510
hyperinflation, 363, 365, 367, 555
in Peru, 365–66

Illich, Ivan, 269*n*, 573
imperialism, theories on, 30–34
implicit costs, 263
importable goods, 458
import duties, 332–33, 348, 349–50
imports:
licensing systems for, 112, 118, 240, 511–12
over–invoicing of, 319*n*
import substitution, 107, 502, 506
consequences of, 519–23
defined, 15, 63, 349
export growth and, 526–27
in Ghana, 471–72
in Kenya, 521–22
measuring of, 520–21, 522
vs. outward–looking strategies, 523–24, 526–27
overvalued exchange rates and, 515–16
protective tariffs and, 507–11
quotas and, 511–12
rents and, 522–23
undervalued exchange rates and, 516–17
see also protective tariffs
inadequate information, 102
income:
education and, 251–53
food consumption and, 285–87
inequality of, 19, 32–34
life expectancy and, 12, 275–79
natural capital and, 155
permanent vs. transitory, 313
private savings habits and, 311–16
unequal distribution of, 33
income, per capita:
agricultural sector and, 48–49
defined, 7*n*
growth in low–income countries, 13
inequality patterns and, 80–82
population shift and, 48
population size and, 208
shortcomings of, 9
income distribution:
budgetary subsidies and, 327–28
determinants of, 84
employment creation accelerated by, 246
equality vs. equity in, 76
evaluation of, 70–74, 79–80
fertility and, 218
government confiscation and, 90–91
land reform and, 434
poverty and, 74–76
project appraisal and, 152–53
taxation policy and, 346–54
theories of, 87–90
income tax holidays, 409
income terms of trade, 470–71
incremental capital–output ratio (ICOR), 42
economic growth and, 44–45
fixed vs. variable (neoclassical), 43
indexing, of wages to inflation, 116, 117
index–number problems, 38–41
India:
colonialism and, 20–21, 106
development pattern of, 86
forest management in, 166
income inequality in, 70, 86
labor policy in, 238–39
land reform in, 433
population policy in, 214–15
small–scale industry in, 248
socialism and, 105–6
tax administration in, 337–38
tax evasion in, 337–38
indifference curves, 132–34

indirect taxes, 93
Indonesia:
  credit controls in, 389–90
  currency devaluation in, 129–30, 318
  Dutch disease in, 479–80, 551
  education in, 251–52
  environmental degradation in, 162
  excise taxes in, 337
  family planning in, 216–17
  fuel subsidy program in, 354
  government intervention in, 525–26
  independence of, 20–21
  kerosene subsidy in, 176
  low-wage employment in, 226–27
  savings and credit institutions in, 383
  stabilization programs in, 129–30
  urban informal sector in, 226–27
induced migration, 231–32
industrial countries:
  government expenditures and, 322
  World Bank classification of, 6–7
industrialization:
  development goals and, 481, 499–500
  growth patterns in, 61–65
  labor absorption by, 236–38
  linkage studies on, 484–86
  outward-looking, 504, 505–6, 526
  per capita income growth and, 481–83
  resource-based strategies for, 475
  trade and, 501–2
  urbanization and, 486–88
  Western initiation of, 18–19
Industrial Revolution:
  demographic changes of, 194, 203
  export markets in, 63
  modern economic growth and, 18, 481
industrial sector:
  agricultural sector vs., 47–51, 52
  decentralization of, 488, 497
  economies of scale in, 48, 492–95, 497
  government-owned, 506
  informal vs. formal sectors in, 247, 495
  investment choices in, 488–500
  pollution and, 157–58
  small-scale manufacturing in, 495–99
inequality, 68, 70
  of education, 257–58
  national case histories of, 84–86
  patterns of, 80–86
  of rich and poor nations, 186–87
  theories of, 87–90
infant industries:
  complementation agreements and, 533
  protective tariffs for, 101–2, 503–4
  subsidies for, 101, 503–4
infants:
  death rates of, 14, 193, 199, 276
  nutritional problems of, 288
inflation:
  acute, 364
  chronic, 363–64
  critical view of, 363–67
  defined, 40, 363
  in developing countries, 363–67
  development and, 113–14
  effect of deficit on, 387
  interest rates and, 371–73
  as investment stimulus, 369–71
  monetary policy and, 388–89
  runaway, 363, 364, 365, 555
  sources of, 385–88
  stabilization programs for, 113–16, 554–55
  as taxation, 368–69
informal credit markets, 382–83
infrastructure, 155, 175–77, 487–88
initial subsidies, 101
input–output analysis for interindustry models, 137–41
input–output coefficients, 139
interest on government debts, 327, 418
interest rates:
  controlled ceilings on, 240, 377–78, 380, 505
  inflation and, 371–73
  negative, 377–80
  real, 113, 149
  real vs. nominal, 371–73
  regulation of, 390
  savings decisions and, 373–76
intergovernmental transfers, 329–30
interindustry models, 131, 137–46
intermediate goods, 36
internal balance, 539–41, 542, 543–45, 548–49
internal rate of return (IRR), 148
internal rate of return on education, 263
International Bank for Reconstruction and Development (IBRD), *see* World Bank
International Coffee Agreement (1960), 473
International Development Association (IDA), 6*n*, 397
International Finance Corporation (IFC), 397
International Labor Organization (ILO), 248*n*
International Maize and Wheat Improvement Center (CIMMYT), 442, 448
International Monetary Fund (IMF), 575, 579
  Compensatory Financing Facility of, 474
  credit ceilings prerequisite and, 389
  loan policy of, 397
  refinancing agreements with, 413
  stabilization packages of, 114–16, 118, 126, 417, 537, 554–55, 556
  standby credits by, 116
  structural adjustments by, 94, 397, 417
international reserves, 384, 385–86
International Rice Research Institute (IRRI), 442
inverse elasticity rule of taxation, 357
investment:
  capital–intensive vs. labor–intensive, 301–3
  in human capital, 250–51, 272, 279–81, 300
  inflation and, 369–71
  in infrastructure, 175–77
  portfolio, 393, 411
investment, foreign direct:
  benefits of, 403–7
  defined, 402
  developing countries' policies on, 408–11
  impact of, 402
  multinational package of, 403–4
  multinationals' patterns of, 402–3
Iran, political instability of, 26–27
irrigation programs, 353, 443
isoquants, 43
Ivory Coast, export policy of, 472

Japan:
  export policy of, 529
  land reform in, 432–33
  per capita income in, 19
Java, soil erosion in, 159
Jefferson, Thomas, 502
Jenkins, Glenn P., 577
Jimenez, Emmanuel, 293*n*, 294, 573
Johansen, Frida, 564
Johnson, Harry G., 503*n*, 586, 587
Johnson, Lyndon B., 106
Johnston, Bruce F., 426*n*, 581, 582
joint ventures, 407, 408

Jolly, Richard, 94*n*, 565
Jones, Christine, 338*n*, 576
Jones, Ronald W., 537*n*, 582, 587
Jorgenson, Dale W., 36, 563

Kaldor, Nicholas, 313, 314, 575
Kantorovich, Leonid, 137
Kapital, Das (Marx), 30*n*
Kapur, Ishan, 555*n*, 587
Karachi Plan, 259
Katz, Lawrence F., 226*n*, 571
Kelley, Allen C., 564
Kenya:
  East African Community and, 534
  educational policy in, 268–69
  family planning in, 212–13
  import substitution in, 521–22
  labor surplus in, 60
Kenyatta, Jomo, 213
Keynes, John Maynard, 106, 311, 317
Keynesian absolute income hypothesis, 311
Keynesian growth models, 131, 134–37
Khomeini, Ayatollah Ruhollah, 26–27
Kilby, Peter, 426*n*, 581
Killick, Tony, 117*n*, 566
Kimbrough, Kent, 318*n*, 575
Kim Kwang Suk, 562
Kim Linsu, 245*n*, 572
Kim Mahn Je, 562
Knight, J. B., 267*n*, 268*n*, 572, 573
Knudsen, Odin, 472*n*, 584
Kocher, James, 574
Korea, *see* South Korea
Kornai, Janos, 566
Kravis, Irving, 563
Krishna, Raj, 582
Krueger, Anne O., 108*n*, 109, 384*n*, 504*n*, 565, 579, 586
Kuznets, Simon, 8, 35, 36, 88, 102, 563, 564
  on income distribution, 80–81, 88
kwashiorkor, 284
Kyn, Oldrich, 81*n*, 564

labor:
  marginal product of, 52, 231
  reallocation of, 230–36
  rural mobilization of, 444–46
  utilization of, 228–30, 237–38
  see also employment; unemployment
labor force:
  defined, 228
  growth of, 221–22
  industrial expansion and, 236–38
  three–tiered structure of, 224–28
  women in, 228
labor productivity, 220–21
labor surplus:
  in Africa, 60
  in China, 59–60
  defined, 51
  Marx on, 87
labor–surplus model, LDCs and, 88–90
Ladejinsky, Wolf, 431*n*
Lancaster, Carol, 580
land, productivity of, 427
Landes, David S., 584
land reform:
  income distribution and, 434
  politics of, 431–32
  productivity and, 433–34
  types of, 430–31
land tenure:
  categories of, 428–29
  political stability and, 429
  productivity incentive and, 429–31
Lange, Oscar, 122
Larsen, Bjorn, 175*n*, 568
late industries, 61
latifundia, 428
Latin America:
  colonialism in, 21
  debt crisis in, 411–12, 417, 418–19
  import substitution in, 502
  school systems in, 255–56
Lau, Lawrence J., 586
Layard, R., 253, 572
Lee, Dwight R., 342*n*, 576
Lee, R., 207*n*, 569
Leite, Sergio Pereira, 578
Lele, Uma, 582
Lenin, V. I., 30
Leontief production functions, 139, 141, 145, 484
Leontief, Wassily, 137
Lesotho, health effects of safe water supplies in, 281
less developed countries (LDCs):
  defined, 6
  employment structure in, 224–28
  government population control in, 212–19
  income distribution in, 70–72
  labor force in, 221–24
  population growth in, 209–12
  reform incentives for, 95
  social services in, 93
  sustainable development and, 186–87
  tax revenues of, 93
  underutilized capital equipment in, 247
  see also developing countries
Leuthold, Steven C., 378*n*, 578
Levy, Brian, 525*n*, 586
Lewis, Stephen, 583
Lewis, W. Arthur, 35–36, 52, 88–89, 107, 230–31, 563, 564
liberalization, 119, 120, 127–28
Libya, petroleum development in, 8
Liese, Bernhard, 574
life expectancy:
  defined, 193, 273
  human development index for, 78
  income and, 12, 275–79
  male vs. female, 275
lifetime earnings curves, 262
Lindauer, David, 128*n*, 473*n*, 506*n*, 526*n*, 583, 566, 586
Lindenberg, Mark, 587
linear programming, 131, 142, 144–45
linkages, 63–65, 484–86
  benefits of, 464–66
  ineffective, 475
  planning models and, 137
Lipton, Michael, 292*n*, 574
liquid financial assets, 360, 373–78
literacy, 11, 12, 257
Little, I.M.D., 108*n*, 565, 567, 585, 587
"livelihood enterprises," 497
Lizst, Friedrich, 502
Lluch, Constantino, 575
long run, defined, 317
long–run average cost, 492
Lopez Michelsen, Alfonso, 339
Lorenz curves, 71–75
Lott, William F., 564
lower–middle–income economies, 7
low–income countries:
  defined, 6

low–income countries (*continued*)
recent GNP growth in, 13
sustainable development and, 186–87
low tax effort countries, 330–32
Lucas, Robert, 36
lump–sum taxes, 354–55
Lundahl, Matts, 476*n*, 584
Lutz, Ernst, 181*n*, 568
luxury consumption, taxes on, 348–50
luxury goods, demand for, 32–34
Lydall, H. F., 495*n*, 584

McKenzie, Richard B., 342*n*, 576
McKinnon, Ronald, 136–37, 567, 578
McLure, Charles E., Jr., 319*n*, 334*n*, 355*n*, 576, 577
macroeconomic imbalances, 102, 113–14, 537
macroeconomic management, 102, 537, 541, 542, 556
made capital, 178–79
natural capital and, 179–80, 182
Madrid, Miguel de la, 419, 527
Malaysia:
export processing zones (EPZs) in, 4
foreign investment in, 4–5
government intervention in, 525–26
primary export–led–growth in, 467–68
sustainable development in, 181–82
tax policy and redistributive expenditures in, 352
water pollution in, 170–71
malnutrition, 273, 279, 282–89
types of, 284–85
Malthus, Thomas, 57, 87, 202–3, 205, 206, 208
global sustainability and, 182–84, 185
Manne, Alan S., 585
manpower planning, 260–62, 269
manpower requirements, 140
manufacturing–oriented countries, 110
Mao Zedong, 108, 213
marasmus, 284
Marcos, Ferdinand, 318
marginal abatement costs, 167–69, 171–73
marginal external costs, 167–69, 171–73
marginal net benefit, 163
marginal product of labor, 52
marginal propensity to consume (MPC), 308–9
Margolin, S., 567
market economy, 99, 105, 109
national goals and, 102
market failures, 100–103, 112, 154, 259, 321
sustainable development and, 156–65
market mechanisms, 105, 106, 112
market prices:
defined, 37
shadow prices as ideal for, 153–54
market reforms, 270
benefits of, 126–28
competition and, 119–20
controls for, 106–7
credibility of, 125
dismantling controls for, 118–19
implementations of, 111–30
locking in, 125
market signals for, 112, 122–25
natural resources and, 186–87
progress towards, 106–30
resurgence of, 107–11
scarcity prices and, 120–22
shock treatment and, 105, 126–27
structural adjustment, 118–19, 120–22
system for, 125–30
markets:
free, 15–16
parallel, 113
rural, 448–50
market signals, 112, 122–25
market system, government controls vs., 99–130, 177
markup pricing, 117
Marshall Plan, 106, 394
Marx, Karl, 562
capitalist development theory of, 22, 30, 87, 88
on economic inequality, 69
on taxation, 346
Mason, E. S., 562
materials balances, Soviet method of, 140
maternal and child health (MCH) programs, 288
Mauldin, W. Parker, 219*n*, 570
Mazlish, Bruce, 465*n*, 583
Mazumdar, Dipak, 496*n*, 571, 585
mechanical package, 438, 439–42, 443–44
medical services, 289–93
Mellor, John W., 92*n*, 565, 581
Merrick, Thomas W., 202*n*, 212*n*, 569
Mexico:
debt crisis in, 419–20, 551
Dutch disease in, 476
as example of comparative advantage, 457
land reforms in, 432
market reforms in, 125, 128
trade reform in, 527–28
middle–income economies, defined, 6–7
middle industries, 61
migration:
international, 235–36
rural–rural, 234–35
rural–urban, 200–201, 231–35, 487, 488
urban–rural, 234
Mikesell, Raymond F., 309*n*, 335*n*, 575, 576
military spending, 32, 326
Mill, John Stuart, 346
mineral resources, nonfuel, 470–71
minimum efficient scale (MES), 493–94
minimum–wage laws, 239–40
Mintzer, Irving M., 569
Mirrlees, James A., 567
mixed economies, 99–103
computable general equilibrium models for, 145
modern economic growth:
defined, 8
fundamental structural changes of, 18
history of, 18–19
see also growth, economic
modernization, 8
Modigliani, Franco, 575
Moi, Daniel Arap, 213
monetary policy, 546
financial policy vs., 358–59
inflation controls and, 388–89
price stability and, 384–90
money, 359–62
money supply:
components of, 385–86
defined, 360
monopoly power:
competition vs., 112, 165*n*
defined, 100
monopoly rights, 409–10
Morales, Juan Antonio, 117*n*, 566
Moran, Theodore H., 407*n*, 579, 580
morbidity, defined, 273
Morris, Cynthia Taft, 82, 564
Morris, Morris David, 77*n*, 564
Morse, Richard, 498*n*, 585
mortality:
defined, 273

income level and, 273–76
reduction in, 275–76
Mortimore, Michael, 186*n*, 569
Mosely, Paul, 399, 579
most favored nation (MFN) principle, 529
Multifiber Arrangement, 530
multinational corporations (MNCs):
access to world markets by, 406–7
characteristics of, 403
investment packages of, 407
investment patterns of, 402–3
local joint ventures with, 407, 408
managerial capacity of, 406
taxation of, 409–10
Murray, M., 338*n*, 576
Musgrave, Richard A., 577
Musgrove, Philip, 313*n*, 575
Mushkin, Selma, 279*n*, 574
Myint, Hla, 463, 583

Nash, Manning, 466*n*, 583
National Academy of Sciences, 211
national income accounts:
accounting systems, 155
calculation of, 71*n*, 180–82
faults of, 181*n*
natural capital, 155, 178–79
defined, 178
made capital and, 179–80, 182
measuring, 178–79, 180
natural resources:
as capital, 155, 178–79
depletion of, 157, 158, 180, 183–85
drought, 556–58
efficient use of, 180, 187
as energy reserves, 174–75
governmental regulation and, 165, 167–77
industrialization strategies based on, 475
national income and, 180–82
natural vs. made capital and, 179–80, 182
nonrenewability of, 37, 155–56, 162–63, 168, 184
overexploitation of, 165, 173–77, 185–86
population and, 183–84
poverty and, 185–86
property rights and, 165–67
renewable, 159–62, 163–64, 178
rents on, 165–66, 169, 170, 179–80
rich vs. poor nations and, 186–87
species extinction and, 161–62
taxation and, 169–71, 334
time and, 162–64
Neary, S. Peter, 476*n*, 549, 584, 587
Nelson, Joan, 125*n*, 126, 562, 566
neoclassical production function, 43, 145
neoclassical school of development, 109
Asian tigers and, 505–6
sustainability and, 184–85
neoclassical (marginal productivity) theory of income distribution, 88
net barter terms of trade, 468–70, 472
net cash flow, 146–48
net national product, 180–81
net present value (NPV), 148, 161
net resource flow, 392
net revenue, 160–61, 163
net source transfers, 392
neutral taxation, 356–57
Newberry, David, 330*n*, 575, 577
New Deal, 106
new growth economics, 47
newly industrializing countries (NICs), 5, 7, 108, 109, 505
Nigeria, Dutch disease in, 479
Nkrumah, Kwame, 472
nominal interest rate, 371
nominal protection, 507–8
nonexcludability of public goods, 321
nonrenewable resources, 37
nonrival consumption of public goods, 321
non–tariff barriers (NTBs), 529, 530
North, Douglass C., 466*n*, 583
North America, wheat industry in, 463, 464
North American Free Trade Agreement (NAFTA), 125, 128, 528, 531, 534
North Korea, 105
Nugent, Jeffrey B., 484, 485, 584
Nurkse, Ragnar, 62, 107*n*, 230–31, 466*n*, 563, 565, 571, 584
nutrition:
food consumption and, 285–87
improvement programs and, 287–89
standards of, 282–83, 286–87

objective functions of planning models, 133–34, 142, 144
obsolescing bargain, 407
official development assistance (ODA), 392, 395, 396
Ohlin, Bertil, 458, 524
oil prices, 26, 108, 174–76, 473–74, 558
Oldman, Oliver, 576
Olewiler, Nancy D., 568
oligopoly power, 100
Olson, Mancur, 529*n*, 566, 587
Oman, Charles P., 407*n*, 580
open access, 157
open economies, 537–38
equilibrium in, 537–49
model of, 549
open market operations, 388
opportunity costs, 148–50, 231
optimality planning, 132–34, 142
optimal taxation, 357
optimum population theory, 207–8
oral rehydration therapy (ORT), 293
Organization for Economic Cooperation and Development (OECD), 7, 300, 308, 395, 579
Organization of Petroleum Exporting Countries (OPEC), 398, 411, 473–74
outward–looking strategy, 504
exchange rate management for, 517–19
export protection and, 512–14
government intervention for, 524–26
vs. import substitution, 523–24, 526–27
industrialization and, 504, 505–6, 526
limitations of, 504
outcome of, 504
trade and, 506–7
overhead investment, 101
Overseas Development Council (ODC), 77
overvalued exchange rates, 453–55, 515–16

Pack, Howard, 245*n*, 489*n*, 491, 504, 525*n*, 571, 585, 586, 587
Page, John M., Jr., 496*n*, 585
Pakistan:
civil war in, 26
import licensing in, 240
Panayotou, Theodore, 124*n*, 166*n*, 174*n*, 185*n*, 187*n*, 566, 568, 569
Papageorgiou, Demetrius, 566
Papanek, Gustav F., 81*n*, 564
parallel markets, 113
parasitic conditions, 279
Park Chung Hee, 27

Park Jong–goo, 564
Parnes, Andrew, 472*n*, 584
Parnes, Herbert S., 260, 573
Partington, Martin, 236*n*, 571
Patten, Richard H., 383*n*, 578
Pearce, David W., 167*n*, 171*n*, 568
Pearson, Scott R., 451*n*, 454, 574, 582
Pechman, Joseph A., 340*n*, 577
perestroika, 91
performance requirements, 408
Perkins, Dwight H., 436*n*, 525*n*, 562, 563, 566, 577, 582, 586
permanent–income hypothesis, of savings behavior, 313–15, 472
permits for pollution, 171–73, 185
Peron, Juan, 26, 27, 106
Peru:
  fishmeal industry in, 464
  hyperinflation in, 365–66
  income distribution in, 90
phase diagram, 541–43
Philippines, capital mobility and, 318
physical quality of life index (PQLI), 77–79
piece–rate basis of agricultural wages, 429–30
Pingali, Prabhu, 581
Pinochet Ugarte, Augusto, 553
planning models, 131–54
  computable general equilibrium (CGE), 84, 131, 145–46
  consistency vs. optimality in, 132
  cost–benefit analysis and, 131, 146–54
  input–output tables and, 131, 138–39
  linear programming, 131, 142, 144–45
  overdetermined, 135
  redundancy in, 136
  social accounting matrix (SAM), 131, 141–43, 146
plantation agriculture, 428
Please, Stanley, 309, 575
Please effect, 309, 368
"Point IV" program, 394
Poland:
  big–bang approach in, 27–28, 126–27
  market economy established in, 105
Poleman, Thomas T., 574
political independence, 25
political rights, deprivation of, 111
political stability, 24–25
politics:
  food prices and, 452–53
  land reform and, 432–33
poll taxes, 354
pollution, environmental, 101, 156, 157–58, 162, 165, 167, 179, 183–84
  costs of, 184–85
  license for, 170–73
  regulation of, 165, 167–77
population:
  as economic resource, 192
  government policies on, 212–19
  optimum, 207–8
  per capita income and, 48
  private savings habits and, 315
  redistribution of, 217
population growth, 191–92
  arguments on, 211
  causes of, 202–7
  conclusions on, 211–12
  developmentalist approach to, 218–19
  development and, 209–10
  doubling time of, 192–93
  dynamic models of, 208–9
  effects of, 207–12
  ethical values and, 281
  Fei–Ranis two–sector model and, 55–57
  natural resources and, 183–84
  neoclassical model and, 57
  Ricardo on, 57
  see also family planning
population trends:
  current, 196–201
  future, 201–2
  historical, 193–96
  before Industrial Revolution, 194
  post–World War II, 195–96
  in preagricultural era, 190
  pre–World War II, 194–95
portfolio investment, 393, 411
Portney, Paul R., 168*n*, 568
poverty, 68, 70
  case histories of, 84–86
  environmental degradation and, 185–86
  low national income per capita and, 82–83
  patterns of, 80–86
  standards of, 75
  theories of, 87–90
  world, 83–84
Powell, Alan, 575
Pratten, C. F., 493*n*, 585
Prebisch, Raul, 107, 468–69, 470, 471, 502, 565, 584
Preferential Trade Agreement, 531, 534
present value, 146–48
Preston, Samuel H., 277, 573
prices:
  in agricultural sector, 448, 450–55
  basic macro, 301
  commodity agreements and, 473–74
  energy, 174–76
  equitable growth and, 94–95
  factor, 239–43
  flexible vs. fixed, 117
  of food, 286, 287, 452–53
  monetary policy and, 384–90
  relative, 120
  scarcity, 120–22
  shadow, 150–54
  in socialist economies, 103, 121
  subsidies vs., 512
  world, 457, 507
price stabilization, 28, 112–19
price takers, 537
primary–export–led growth:
  barriers to, 466–80
  benefits of, 462–66
  in Malaysia, 467–68
  see also growth, economic
primary–oriented countries, 110
Principles of Political Economy and Taxation, The (Ricardo), 51
priority weights in linear programming, 144
private rate of return on education, 262–65
privatization, 123–25, 165–67
process industries, 241
production costs, 169–71
production functions:
  agricultural, 44, 52
  defined, 41
  fixed vs. variable ICOR in, 43–44
  growth sources and, 45
  Harrod–Domar model of, 41–42, 45
  neoclassical, 43–44
production possibility frontier, 132, 134
productivity:
  growth, 523–24
  of labor, 178, 220–21, 279–80

land reform and, 433–34
profit maximization, 112, 120, 122, 124
program loans, 398, 400
progressive taxes, 93, 346–47, 348–49
project aid, 398, 400
project appraisal, 146–54
national goals and, 151–53, 176–77
terminology of, 153
property rights, 111, 123–24, 165–67, 185
property taxes, 350–51
protectionism:
costs of, 529–30
"new," 110
in the North, 528–30
protective barriers, 502, 505
protective tariffs, 349–50, 408–9
Asian tigers and, 505–6
benefits of, 507–11
infant industry and, 101–2, 503–4
quotas vs., 511–12
protein–calorie malnutrition (PCM), 285
provident fund approach, 345
Psacharopoulos, George, 251*n*, 264, 572, 573
public enterprises, *see* state–owned enterprises
public goods problem, 430
public services:
BHN programs of, 93–94
for health, 289–93
public works, rural projects in, 444–46
purchasing power parity, 10–11, 38, 39
Pyatt, Graham, 142*n*, 567

quantitative restrictions, 511
quota premiums, 511
quotas, on imports, 511–12

racial minorities, 102
Radano, Alberto H. J., 338*n*, 577
Ram, Rati, 211, 565, 570
Ramirez, Noel, 587
Ramos, Myra Bergman, 269*n*, 572
Ramsey rule, 357
Randolph, Susan M., 564
Ranis, Gustav, 36, 52, 55, 88–89, 504*n*, 563, 586
Rao, J. Mohan, 581
rate of depletion, 159
rate of natural increase, 192
rates of return on education investment, 262–65
ratio of imports to national product, 520–21, 522
Rawlings, Jerry, 555–56
Rawls, John, 346
raw materials, export taxes on, 333
Reagan, Ronald, 107
real effective exchange rate (REER), 518–19
real exchange rate (RER), 476–77, 478, 517–19, 539–40, 541–46
real interest rate, 371–72
real world considerations, 543, 549
recession, 4, 416
recreation, value of, 177, 179
recurrent government expenditures, 323–26, 352
rediscount rate, 390
redistribution with growth (RWG), 90–94
regional development banks, 397–98
regressive taxes, 93
relative income hypothesis, 311–13, 315
relative poverty, 84
relative prices, 120, 457
rents:
defined, 108
import substitution and, 522–23
on natural resources, 165–66, 169, 170, 179–80
rent–seeking, 108, 522
repeaters, 257
Repetto, Robert, 174*n*, 176*n*, 333*n*, 568, 577
Report on Manufactures (Hamilton), 502
rescheduling of payments, for debt crisis, 417
research and development programs, 405, 408
reserve requirements, 388–89
reserves, accumulating, 558–59
resource–based industrialization strategies, 475
resource rents, 161
restructured debt, 413
Reutlinger, Shlomo, 574
revolution, 429, 432
Reynolds, Lloyd, 426*n*, 581, 582
Rhodes, Robert I., 562
Ricardo, David, 208
theory of comparative advantage by, 457
two–sector development model of, 35, 51, 52, 87
on wages, 57, 88
risks, 102
transformation and distribution of, 362–63
Robinson, Marguerite S., 226, 383*n*, 578
Robinson, Sherman, 76*n*, 84, 143, 146*n*, 563, 564, 567
Rodrik, Dani, 537*n*
Roemer, Michael, 128*n*, 338*n*, 365*n*, 464*n*, 466*n*, 472*n*, 473*n*, 476*n*, 506*n*, 525*n*, 526*n*, 562, 566, 567, 576, 577, 578, 583, 584, 586
Romer, Paul, 36
Roosevelt, Franklin D., 106
Rosen, Harvey, 577
Rosenberg, Nathan, 245*n*, 572
Rosengard, Jay, 383*n*, 578
Rosenstein–Rodan, Paul, 62, 107, 563
Rosenzweig, Mark, 571
Ross, John A., 570
Rostow, Walt W., 26, 561, 563
Rozali bin Mohamed Ali, 181*n*, 568
rural development, 92, 423
rural labor market, 227–28
rural prices, 95
rural–urban migration, 200–201, 231–35, 487, 488
Russia:
capital accumulation in, 22–23
feudalism in, 20, 425
market economy, establishment of, 105, 116, 121, 126, 127
privatization in, 124
see also Soviet Union
Ruttan, Vernon W., 438, 581, 582

Sabot, R. H., 267*n*, 268*n*, 570, 572, 573
Sachs, Jeffrey D., 111, 117*n*, 155*n*, 565, 566, 568, 580
Sahn, David E., 587
sales taxes, 334–37, 348–50, 355
Salih, Kamal, 3*n*, 561
Salter, W.E.G., 538*n*, 587
Samuelson, Paul, 145*n*, 567
Sang Woo Nam, 525*n*, 586
sanitation, 281–82
Sanyal, Amal, 338*n*, 576
Sapsford, David, 470*n*, 583
savings:
classifications of, 304–5
corporate, 305, 315–16
domestic, 304–7, 310–11, 317
economic growth, and, 24, 89–90
forced mobilization of, 367–69
foreign, 304, 305, 317
government, 304–5, 307–10
household, 305, 311–15
interest rates and, 373–76
mobilization of and inflation, 363–73

savings (*continued*)
  private domestic, 304, 305, 310–11, 343–45
  sources of, 304–11
  taxes and, 343–45
schistosomiasis, 281
Schultz, Theodore W., 109, 122, 211*n*, 250–51, 435*n*, 565, 570, 572, 573, 581, 582
Schultz, T. Paul, 573
Schumacher, E. F., 495, 585
Scitovsky, Tibor, 108*n*, 565, 587
Scott, Maurice, 108*n*, 565, 587
Sears, Dudley, 564
secondary job creation, 237
self–government, 20
Selowsky, Marcelo, 574
Sen, Amartya K., 76*n*, 275*n*, 286, 427*n*, 567, 581, 564, 573, 574
Serafy, Alah El, 568
serfdom, 425, 428
shadow prices, 150–54
Shah, Anwar, 175*n*, 568
shallow financial policies, 376–80
sharecropping, 428, 429
shifting cultivation, 436
Shleifer, Andrei, 566
shock therapy, 105
Short, R. P., 328*n*, 576
short run, defined, 317
Shoup, Carl, 335*n*, 577
Sicat, Gerry, 335*n*, 577
signaling effect, 472
Silvani, Carlos A., 338*n*, 577
Simon, Julian, 211, 570
Singapore, population policy in, 217–18
Singer, Hans W., 107, 468–69, 470, 471, 502, 565, 584
Singh, S. P., 62*n*, 563
single factoral terms of trade, 471
size distribution of income, 70–71
slash–and–burn cultivation, 435–36
Slemrod, Joel, 319*n*
small economies, 537–38
Small is Beautiful (Schumacher), 495
small–scale industry, 247–48, 495–99
Smith, Adam, 35, 463, 492, 504
Smith, Roger S., 315*n*, 575
smuggling, 332, 333
Snodgrass, Donald R., 316*n*, 352*n*, 496, 575, 577, 585
social accounting matrix (SAM), 131, 141–43, 146
social costs, 158–59, 169–71
social indicators, 76–77
socialist countries, 90–91, 99
socialist economies, 99, 103–6
social opportunity costs, 148–50
social project appraisal, defined, 153
social rate of return on education, 263–64
social security systems, 344–45
social well–being, progress in, 14–15
Solimano, Andrés, 553*n*
Solow, Robert, 35, 45, 47, 145*n*, 567
South Korea:
  CGE model for, 84
  chaebol in, 524–25
  development pattern of, 85
  export of, 514, 525
  government intervention in, 524–25
  labor–intensive manufacturing in, 238, 403, 524
  tax administration in, 338
  technology acquisition by, 245
Southworth, H. M., 582
sovereign debt, 416
Soviet Union:
  basic–industry development strategy in, 91
  central planning in, 29–30, 103–5
  collapse of, 105
  distrust of market forces in, 104, 105
  economic plans of, 103–5
  method of materials balance in, 140
  perestroika in, 91
  state capitalism in, 90
  see also Russia
Squire, Lyn, 571
Sri Lanka (Ceylon), 126
  demographic experience of, 196
  development pattern of, 86
  education policy in, 255, 258
  food–subsidy programs in, 289
  health in, 278–79
Srinivasan, T. N., 143, 146*n*, 226*n*, 280*n*, 469*n*, 504*n*, 526*n*, 563, 565, 566, 567, 570, 571, 574, 579, 581, 583, 585, 586
Staatz, John, 580
Stabex, 474
stability, economic, 353–54, 359, 363, 537
stabilization policies, 546–49
  austerity vs. appreciation in, 547–49
  in Chile, 553–54
  examples of, 549–59
Staley, Eugene, 498*n*, 585
stamp taxes, 355
standard deviations, defined, 77*n*
standby credits (IMF loans), 116
state–owned enterprises (SOEs), 110, 123–25, 328–29
  growth of, 328
  privatization of, 28
static efficiency, 120
static gains, 532
Steel, William F., 585
sterilization, 214, 215, 217, 545–46
Stern, Joseph J., 510, 567
Stern, Nicholas, 330*n*, 575, 577
Stewart, Frances, 94*n*, 244*n*, 245–46, 491*n*, 565, 571, 585
Stigler, George, 74*n*
Stiglitz, Joseph, 226*n*, 335*n*, 571, 577
Stopford, John, 402*n*, 580
Streeten, Paul, 566
Strout, Alan, 136*n*, 567
structural rigidities, 544–45
subsidy programs:
  in agricultural sector, 452–53
  Asian tigers and, 505
  in education, 270
  export protection and, 512–14
  of food prices, 288–89
  government expenditures on, 327–28
  income redistribution and, 353–54
  for infant industries, 101, 503–4
  for wages, 241
substitutes, concept of, 22–24
substitution effects, food consumption and, 286
Suharto, 129, 216, 480
Sukarno, 216
Summers, Larry, 319*n*, 576, 578
Summers, Robert, 81*n*, 563
supply and demand elasticities, 128
sustainable debt, 414–15
sustainable development, 155–56
  concept of, 179–80
  economic reform and, 177
  global, 182–87
  market failures and, 156–65
  measuring, 177–82
  national policy for, 156, 165, 167–77, 181–82

natural capital and, 155, 178–79
nonrenewable resources and, 155–56
policy failures and, 173–77
policy solutions and, 165–73
time and, 162–65
Swann, Trevor W., 538*n*, 587
Syrquin, Moises, 49*n*, 110, 111, 459–60, 563, 565, 582, 584
Szal, Richard, 76*n*, 564

Tait, Alan A., 308*n*, 342*n*, 575, 577
Taiwan:
accumulating reserves in, 558–59
international economic system and, 33
takeoff, 26
Tanzania:
educational policy in, 268–69
socialist economy of, 105, 246, 269
Tanzi, Vito, 330*n*, 575, 577
tariffication, 512, 530
tariffs, *see* protective tariffs
taxes, taxation:
administration of, 337–38, 350, 355
capacity of, 330
direct consumption, 343–44
domestic investment incentives and, 346
efficiency in, 354–57
equity in, 347
evasion of, 331, 332–33, 334, 337–38, 348
on foreign trade, 332–33
incidence of, 350–51
income, 333–34, 340–42, 347–48, 409–10
increases in, 331
indirect, 93
inflation and, 367–69
on interest income, 372
international capital mobility and, 345–46, 351
inverse elasticity rule of, 357
for market reform, 125
neutrality in, 356–57
new sources for, 337
private investment and, 343–46
progressive, 93, 340–41, 346–47, 348–49
property, 350–51
regressive, 93, 351, 352
sales, 334–37, 348–50, 355
structural reform of, 338–43
sustainable development and, 169–71, 185
value–added, 334–37, 342–43
tax havens, 345–46
tax holidays, 409
tax ratios, 308–9
Taylor, Lance J., 49*n*, 61, 116, 117*n*, 122*n*, 563, 566, 567
teacher shortages, 256
technical assistance, 393
technological innovations, 140–41
technology:
in agriculture, 434–44
appropriateness of, 244–46
choice of, 489–92
foreign investment and, 407, 408
in medical services, 292
multinationals' transfer of, 405–6
price incentive school of, 245
radical reform school of, 246
sustainable development and, 156, 179, 183–85, 187
technologist school of, 245–46
Teitel, Simon, 245*n*, 572
Teitelbaum, Michael S., 204*n*, 569
tenant farming, 428, 431
Ten Kate, Adriaan, 527*n*, 586
terms of trade, 55, 468–71
decline in, 551
single factor, 471
world, 458–59
textile weaving, 489
Thailand:
exchange rate management in, 517–18
government intervention in, 525–26
recreational facility in, 177
third world, defined, 7
Thomas, J. W., 248*n*, 562, 582
Thorbecke, Erik, 142*n*, 563, 567, 581
Tietenberg, Tom, 160*n*, 162, 169*n*, 568
Tiffen, Mary, 186*n*, 569
time, value of, 162–65
time deposits, 359–60, 371, 377
time profile, 147–48
time–series data, 81
Timmer, C. Peter, 243*n*, 426*n*, 451*n*, 454, 492*n*, 571, 574, 581, 582, 585
Tinbergen, Jan, 260, 547, 567, 573
Todaro, Michael P., 231, 233–34, 571
Tomich, Thomas P., 426*n*
total revenue curves, 515
trade:
benefits of, 29, 462–66
colonialism and, 20
comparative advantage and, 456–59
creation vs. diversion of, 532
free, 531–34
industrialization and, 501–2
integration in the South, 531–32
outward–looking policy strategy, 506–7
reform in Mexico, 527–28
reforms and, 530
terms of, 468–71
world arrangements for, 528–35
see also foreign exchange
trading blocs, 534–35
tragedy of the commons, 101
transferable deposits, 359
transfer of capital, 403–4
transnational corporations, *see* multinational corporations
transport systems, 449, 487
Truman, Harry S., 394
trypanosomiasis (Africa sleeping sickness), 281
Tsakok, Isabelle, 451*n*, 582
Tuma, Elias, 432*n*, 581
Turner, R. Kerry, 167*n*, 171*n*, 568
two–sector models:
labor–surplus, 52–57
neoclassical, 57–60
Tyers, Rod, 582

underdeveloped institutions, 102
underemployment, 52
undervalued exchange rates, 516–17
unemployment:
defined, 228
disguised, 51–52, 107, 229–30
educated, 258, 259
rates of, 228
United Kingdom:
economies of scale in, 494
see also England; Wales, demographic experience of
United Nations, 181
foreign aid agencies of, 398
World Health Organization of (WHO), 273, 398
United Nations Centre on Transnational Corporations (UNCTNC), 403*n*, 405*n*, 406*n*, 407*n*, 580

United Nations Children's Fund (UNICEF), 94, 293, 573
United Nations Development Program (UNDP), 78–79, 398
United Nations World Conference on Education for All, 260
United Nations World Population Conference (1974), 218
United States:
  agricultural strategy in, 438
  foreign aid programs of, 394–95, 397
  income taxes in, 334
  inflation in, 416
  multinationals based in, 403
  protectionist policy of, 529, 530
  shallow financial policies in, 378
  wheat industry in, 464
units of account, 359
upper–middle–income economies, 7
urban bias, health services and, 291–92
urbanization, 200–201, 486–88
urban sectors of labor market, 224–27
Urzua, Carlos M., 469*n*, 584
usury laws, 371, 378

Valdés, Alberto, 454*n*, 582
value–added, 36, 37, 508
value–added tax (VAT), 334–37, 342–43
van Ginneken, Wouter, 564
variable proportions production function, *see* neoclassical production function
vent for surplus, 29, 463
Vernon, Raymond, 407, 408, 566, 580
Vietnam, 105, 116, 123, 126, 127
Vincent, Jeffrey R., 170*n*, 174*n*, 181, 568
Viner, Jacob, 587
Vishny, Robert, 566
vocational schools, 270
voluntary export restrictions (VERs), 529
von Furstenberg, George, 368–69, 578

Wade, Robert, 506*n*, 514*n*, 525*n*, 586
wage–rental ratio, 241
wages:
  indexing of, 116, 117
  institutionally fixed (minimum), 53–54, 239–40
  piece–rate basis for, 429–30
  population growth and, 55–56
  salaries and, 323–325
  subsidized, 241
Wahid, A., 383*n*, 578
Wales, demographic experience of, 195
Walinsky, Louis J., 431*n*, 581
Warner, Andrew, 111, 155*n*, 565, 568
Watanabe, Susumu, 238*n*, 571
water supplies, 281–82, 443
Watkins, Melville H., 466*n*, 583

Wealth of Nations, The (Smith), 504
Webb, Richard C., 76*n*, 365, 564
welfare, human, 68–95
  basic human needs approach to, 77, 93–94
  evaluation of,@S1:70–80
  see also inequality; poverty
welfare functions, 144
welfare weights, 144, 153
Wells, Louis T., Jr., 243, 409*n*, 411*n*, 492, 571, 579, 580, 585
Westphal, Larry E., 245, 525*n*, 571, 572, 587
wheat industry, 463, 464
White, Lawrence J., 240, 572
Wicksell, Knut, 370*n*
Wijnbergen, Sweder van, 566
Wilber, Charles K., 561, 564
Williams, Ross, 575
Williamson, Jeffrey, 585
Williamson, John, 117*n*, 384*n*, 566, 571, 579, 580, 582
Wolfe, Barbara L., 264*n*, 573, 574
Woodhall, Maureen, 251*n*, 253, 572
World Bank, 83, 94, 176, 181, 276, 577
  affiliates of, 397
  economic classifications by, 6–7, 9
  economic growth study of, 523
  educational achievement tests by, 257
  food subsidies by, 289
  foreign aid programs of, 126, 395, 397, 398
  on health services, 293
  population policy and, 209–10
  stabilization programs of, 549, 555
  structural adjustment by, 118–19, 398, 417
World Health Organization (WHO), 273, 398
world price, 457, 507
World Trade Organization (WTO), 530, 534, 535
Wright, Colin, 578
Wyman, Donald, 586

Yan Wang, 565
Yellen, Janet L., 226*n*, 570
Yeltsin, Boris, 105
Yost, George J., III, 577
Yotopoulos, Pan A., 484, 485, 584
Young, Mei Ling, 3*n*, 561
Yunus, Muhammad, 383
Yusuf, Shahid, 582

Zaire, colonialism and, 20–21
Zambia, copper production, 163
Zapata, Emiliano, 432
zero population growth (ZPG), 197
zero–sum game, 476
Zhou Enlai, 213
Zinser, James E., 309*n*, 575
zones of imbalance, 543

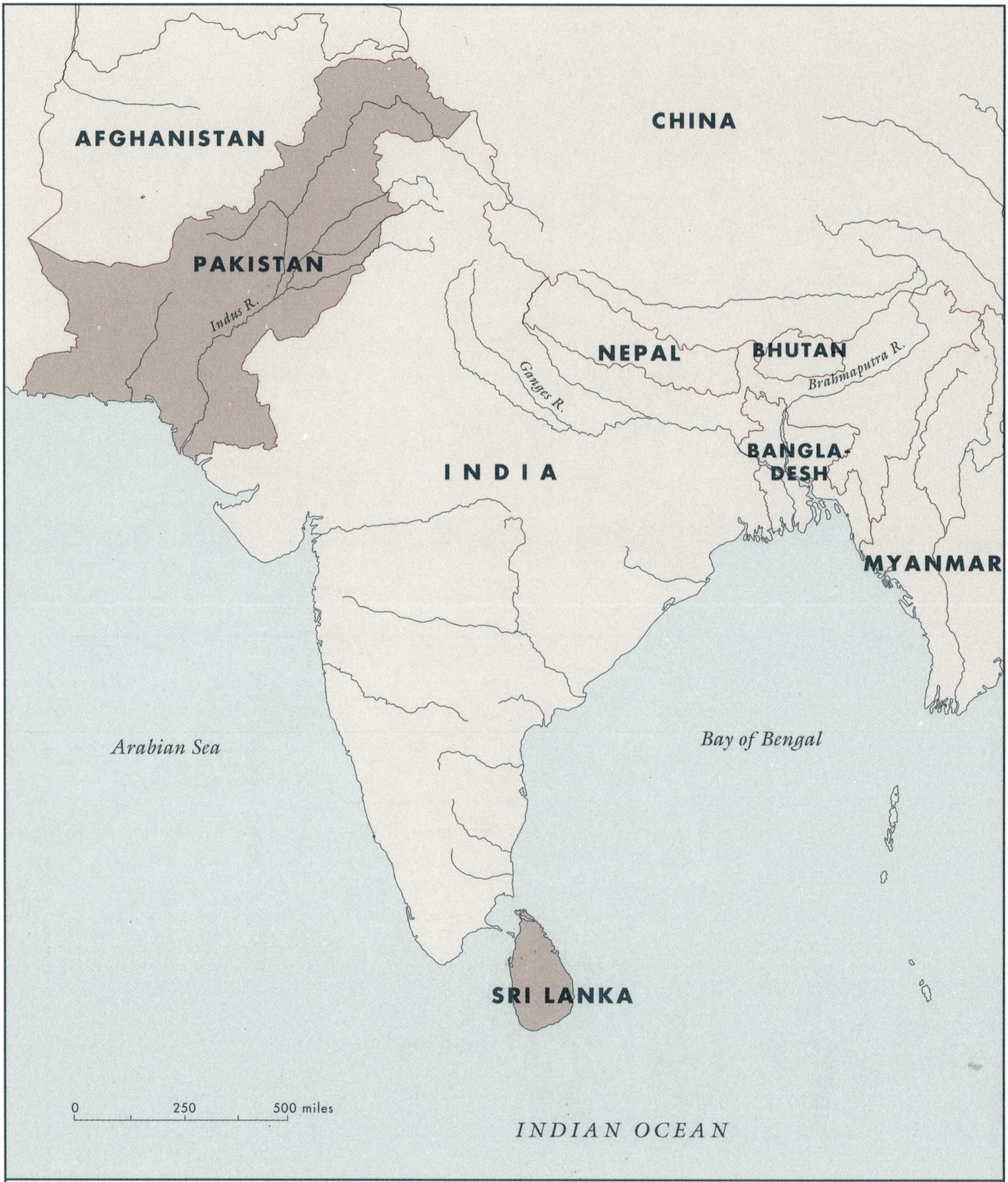

Gross domestic product per capita, 1992

$2,000 and less

$2,001 to $5,000

$5,001 to $10,000

More than $10,000

Sources: World Development Report 1994 and Human Development Report 1994.

SOUTH ASIA

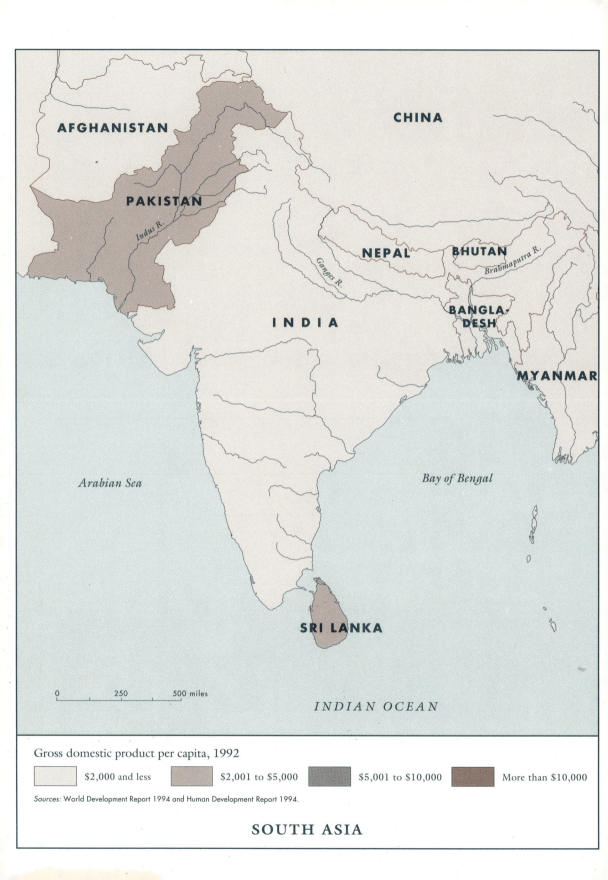